10th EAI International Conference on Performance Evaluation Methodologies and Tools (VALUETOOLS 2016)

Taormina, Italy
25 - 28 October 2016

ISBN: 978-1-5108-4011-9

Printed from e-media with permission by:

Curran Associates, Inc.
57 Morehouse Lane
Red Hook, NY 12571

Some format issues inherent in the e-media version may also appear in this print version.

Printed by Curran Associates, Inc. (2017)

For permission requests, please contact European Alliance for Innovation (EAI)
at the address below.

European Alliance for Innovation (EAI)
c/o Volha Shaparava , Dr
Publications
Via alla Cascata 56/D - 38123 Povo,
Trento - Italy

publications@eai.eu

Additional copies of this publication are available from:

Curran Associates, Inc.
57 Morehouse Lane
Red Hook, NY 12571 USA
Phone: 845-758-0400
Fax: 845-758-2633
Email: curran@proceedings.com
Web: www.proceedings.com

TABLE OF CONTENTS

Generalizing Window Flow Control in Bivariate Network Calculus to Enable Leftover Service in the Loop

Michael Beck
University of Kaiserslautern
Distributed Computer Systems Lab (DISCO)
Germany
beck@cs.uni-kl.de

Jens Schmitt
University of Kaiserslautern
Distributed Computer Systems Lab (DISCO)
Germany
jschmitt@cs.uni-kl.de

ABSTRACT

With the works of Cruz [8, 9, 7] the theory of network calculus emerged. As methodology it has grown to capture more complex queueing systems, including a wide variety of scheduling disciplines and topologies (see [6]); furthermore, this theory has been extended into stochastic versions that effectively capture random effects like the statistical multiplexing gain [10] or arrivals and service as stochastic processes (e.g. [1]). Many of the original, deterministic results of network calculus have been carried over to these extensions – known today as Stochastic Network Calculus (SNC).

The results for window flow controlled systems (WFC systems), however, eluded a corresponding stochastic analysis ever since. This has been marked as an open and challenging problem for over a decade [5]. Only recently, progress towards a stochastic analysis of WFC systems has been made [5, 2, 11, 3].

We briefly sketch the mechanics of the stochastic extension of network calculus: The event one is interested in (e.g., a delay bound) is first analyzed for sample paths satisfying certain conditions on the arrival and service processes. This first step is a logical implication, which takes place inside the space of possible sample paths. The probability of the event happening is then bounded by the probability of the conditions being fulfilled – the second step. That second step usually invokes bounds on the processes' tails or moment-generating functions. This two step procedure is characteristic for SNC [6].

The main contribution of the recent results towards window flow controlled systems [11, 3] are related to the second step. Regarding the first step, results of (deterministic) bivariate network calculus [4] are re-used. This paper shows that the existing available results for the first step are not sufficient to analyze window flow controlled systems in the presence of crossflows, i.e., in the highly relevant case of multiple flows sharing the network. Indeed, the first step of SNC, using deterministic arguments, must be developed further to cover such scenarios. We address this by formulating a general result about WFC systems within the notation of σ-additive operators. With this theorem we achieve two goals: First, we have a single formulation for WFC systems and are able to recover previous results as special cases. Second, and more importantly, we cover a wide variety of systems, including those with crossflows. As such this paper provides a missing piece for the further research towards the stochastic analysis of window flow controlled systems.

VALUETOOLS 2016, October 25-28, Taormina, Italy

1. REFERENCES

[1] H. Al-Zubaidy, J. Liebeherr, and A. Burchard. A (min, x) network calculus for multi-hop fading channels. In *INFOCOM, Proc. IEEE*, pages 1833–1841, April 2013.

[2] M. Beck and J. Schmitt. Window flow control in stochastic network calculus. Technical Report 391/15, University of Kaiserslautern, September 2015.

[3] M. Beck and J. Schmitt. Window flow control in stochastic network calculus – the general service case. In *Proc. Valuetools*, January 2016.

[4] C.-S. Chang. *Performance Guarantees in Communication Networks*. Telecommunication Networks and Computer Systems. Springer-Verlag, 2000.

[5] F. Ciucu, M. Fidler, J. Liebeherr, and J. Schmitt. Network calculus. *Dagstuhl Reports*, 5(3):63–83, March 2015.

[6] F. Ciucu and J. B. Schmitt. Perspectives on network calculus: no free lunch, but still good value. *Proc. of ACM SIGCOMM*, pages 311–322, August 2012.

[7] R. Cruz. Guaranteed throughput for window flow control in a multi-tasking environment. In *Proc. IEEE CISS*, March 1991.

[8] R. L. Cruz. A calculus for network delay, Part I: Network elements in isolation. *IEEE Transactions on Information Theory*, 37(1):114–131, January 1991.

[9] R. L. Cruz. A calculus for network delay, Part II: Network analysis. *IEEE Transactions on Information Theory*, 37(1):132–141, January 1991.

[10] C. Li, A. Burchard, and J. Liebeherr. A network calculus with effective bandwidth. *IEEE/ACM Transactions on Networking*, 15(6):1442–1453, December 2007.

[11] A. Shekaramiz, J. Liebeherr, and A. Burchard. Window flow control systems with random service. 2015. URL: `http://arxiv.org/abs/1507.04631`.

Generalizing Network Calculus Analysis to Derive Performance Guarantees for Multicast Flows

Steffen Bondorf
Distributed Computer Systems (DISCO) Lab
University of Kaiserslautern
D-67653 Kaiserslautern, Germany
bondorf@cs.uni-kl.de

Fabien Geyer
Airbus Group Innovations
Dept. TX2P
D-81663 Munich, Germany
fabien.geyer@airbus.com

ABSTRACT

Guaranteeing performance bounds of data flows is an essential part of network engineering and certification of networks with real-time constraints. A prevalent analytical method to derive guarantees for end-to-end delay and buffer size is Deterministic Network Calculus (DNC). Due to the DNC system model, one decisive restriction is that only unicast flows can be analyzed. Previous attempts to analyze networks with multicast flows circumvented this restriction instead of overcoming it. E.g., they replaced the system model with an overly-pessimistic one that consists of unicast flows only. Such approaches impair modeling accuracy and thus inevitably result in inaccurate performance bounds.

In this paper, we approach the problem of multicast flows differently. We start from existing DNC analyses and generalize them to handle multicast flows. We contribute a novel analysis procedure that leaves the network model unaltered, preserves its accuracy, allows for DNC principles such as pay multiplexing only once, and therefore derives more accurate performance bounds than existing approaches.

CCS Concepts

•**Networks → Network performance evaluation;** *Network performance analysis;* Network performance modeling; •**Computing methodologies → Symbolic and algebraic algorithms;** *Symbolic calculus algorithms;*

Keywords

Delay bounds, deterministic network calculus, feed-forward networks, multicast flows

1. INTRODUCTION

Distributed embedded electronic applications communicating via packet networks have become the norm in various industries such as automotive, avionic or automation. In such industrial applications, real-time constraints on packet delay and jitter are usuallyrequired in order to ensure the specified processes behavior. Due to certification of systems as well as reliability demands, formal methods are applied to validate these timing constraints. They allow for hard guarantees via upper bounds. While different analytical methods have been proposed in the literature, Deterministic Network Calculus (DNC) established itself as common tool to analyze asynchronous communications in packet networks. A concrete example of this is Avionic Full-Duplex Ethernet (AFDX), a communication technology based on Ethernet and already deployed in avionic systems. Network calculus has proven a key tool for the certification of the deterministic property of the networks used for fly-by-wire [10].

An important property of those industrial networks is that communications are usually based on the multicast paradigm, where packets being sent by one sender are duplicated by switching elements in the network and received by multiple receivers. Using DNC on such multicast protocols requires some adaptations, since this method is restricted to the analysis of unicast communications. As detailed later, in Section 3, previous attempts for using DNC to analyze multicast communications only circumvented its current restriction. They do not provide a solution to overcome this limitation. Those approaches cannot benefit from all DNC capabilities to provide accurate end-to-end guarantees and networks designed based on them will be over-dimensioned.

We address the open issue of multicast flow analysis with DNC. We contribute two approaches that turn out to be steps generalizing existing analyses. The first one, Explicit Intermediate Bounds (EIB), is an approach where multicast flows are cut into sequences of unicast sub-flows. End-to-end performance bounds are then derived from sub-flow results. It does not require a transformation of the network, however, it amends a step to the analysis. Our second generalization finally leads to a DNC multicast feed-forward analysis. Neither transforming the network nor cutting any flows is required. Therefore, more accurate bounds are obtained since existing DNC principles can be applied in order to reduce effects such as flow multiplexing or burstiness. We numerically evaluate our proposed methods on two AFDX networks given in the literature and show that our DNC results are on par with other analytical methods or outperform them.

This paper is organized as follows: Section 2 gives a brief background on deterministic network calculus and we derive the foundation for our generalizations. In Section 3, we present related work on multicast flow analysis. Sections 4 and 5 contribute generalizations of DNC analyses for the study of multicast flow guarantees. We evaluate our approaches in Section 6 and Section 7 concludes the paper.

VALUETOOLS 2016, October 25-28, Taormina, Italy

2. NETWORK CALCULUS BACKGROUND

We present in this section a brief overview of deterministic network calculus. For a more in-depth description, we refer the reader to [9] and [14].

2.1 Flow and Server Modeling

In network calculus, flows correspond to unidirectional and unicast communications between two servers. They are modeled as functions of their cumulative arrival of data. More formally, those functions belong to the following set $\mathcal{F}_0$ of non-negative, wide-sens increasing functions:

$$\mathcal{F}_0 = \{f : \mathbb{R} \to \mathbb{R}^+ \mid f(0) = 0, \forall 0 \leq s < t : f(s) < f(t)\}$$

In order to compute bounds on the flows, we are interested in the functions $A(t)$ corresponding to the data arriving in a given server s at time t, and $A'(t)$ the amount of data processed by the server at time t. Using this formalism, the following delay definition can then be derived:

Definition 1 (Flow delay). *Assume a flow with input A and crosses a server s and results in the output A'. The (virtual) delay for a data unit arriving at time t is*

$$D(t) = \inf\{\tau \geq 0 \mid A(t) \leq A'(t + \tau)\}$$

Instead of directly working with A, network calculus makes use of the concept of arrival curves, which is a function bounding the maximal arrivals of a flow:

Definition 2 (Arrival curve). *Given a flow with input A, a function $\alpha \in \mathcal{F}_0$ is an arrival curve for A iff*

$$A(t) - A(s) \leq \alpha(t - s), \forall t, s, 0 \leq s \leq t$$

Definition 3 (Service curve). *If the service provided by a server s for a given input A results in an output A', then s offers a service curve $\beta \in \mathcal{F}_0$ iff*

$$A'(t) \geq \inf_{0 \leq s \leq t}\{A(t - s) + \beta(s)\}, \forall t$$

2.2 (min, +) Algebra

Network calculus was formalized as a (min, +)-algebraic framework in [9, 14], enabling an easier description of operations on flow and server descriptions.

Definition 4 ((min, +) operations). *The (min, +) convolution and deconvolution of two functions $f, g \in \mathcal{F}_0$ are defined as:*

$$\textit{Convolution: } (f \otimes g)(t) = \inf_{0 \leq s \leq t}\{f(t - s) + g(s)\}$$

$$\textit{Deconvolution: } (f \oslash g)(t) = \sup_{s \geq 0}\{f(t + s) - g(s)\}$$

Using those (min, +) operations, one can rewrite the previous definitions as $A' \geq A \otimes \beta$ and $A \otimes \alpha \geq A$.

Moreover, (min, +) convolution allows DNC to concatenate the service of consecutive servers $\langle 1, \ldots, n\rangle$, so-called tandems, into a single service curve:

Theorem 1 (Concatenation of servers). *Consider a single flow f crossing a tandem of servers $s_1, \ldots, s_n$ where each server s_i offers a service curve β_i. The overall service curve for f is their concatenation by convolution:*

$$\beta_i \otimes \cdots \otimes \beta_n = \bigotimes_{i=1}^{n} \beta_i$$

Given a strict service curve that guarantees a minimum output of β if data is present at a server, we lower bound the service left-over for a specific flow:

Theorem 2 (Left-over service curve). *Consider a server s that offers a strict service curve β. Let s be crossed by flows f_0 and f_1, with arrival curves α_0, respectively α_1. Then the worst-case residual resource share under arbitrary multiplexing of f_1 at s is:*

$$\beta^{\text{l.o.}f_1} = \beta \ominus \alpha_0$$

with $(\beta \ominus \alpha)(d) = \sup\{(\beta - \alpha)(u) \mid 0 \leq u \leq d\}$ denoting the non-decreasing upper closure of $(\beta - \alpha)(d)$.

Last, we use these curves to derive performance bounds.

Theorem 3 (Performance bounds [14]). *Consider a flow f with arrival curve α traversing a server s with a service curve β. The following bounds can be derived:*

$$\textit{Backlog: } Q(t) \leq \sup_{s \geq 0}\{\alpha(s) - \beta(s)\} = (\alpha \oslash \beta)(0)$$

$$\textit{Delay: } D(t) \leq \inf\{d \geq 0 \mid (\alpha \oslash \beta)(-d) \leq 0\}$$

$$\textit{Output: } \alpha'(d) = (\alpha \oslash \beta)(d)$$

with α' being an output arrival curve for A'.

2.3 Network Analysis

Using the definitions and theorems presented above, the end-to-end performances of flows interacting on a network of servers can be computed. We call the analyzed flow *flow of interest*, abbreviated foi.

2.3.1 *Tandems of Servers*

The foi's path defines the sequence (tandem) of servers that defines its end-to-end delay. For bounding this delay, different methods have been proposed in the literature.

Total Flow Analysis (TFA) [14].

The TFA first computes per-server delay bounds. Each one holds for the sum of all the traffic arriving to a server, i.e., these bounds are independent of the foi. The flow's end-to-end delay bound is derived by summing up the individual server delay bounds on its path. The TFA's server-isolating approach constitutes a direct application of Theorem 3; it is known to be inferior to the following analyses [14, 18].

Separated Flow Analysis (SFA) [14].

The SFA is a direct application of other theorems: first compute the left-over service of each server on the foi's path using Theorem 2, then concatenate them using Theorem 1 and finally derive the end-to-end delay bound using Theorem 3. Deriving the end-to-end delay bound using only one service curve will consider the burst term of the foi only once, a property called Pay Burst Only Once (PBOO).

Pay Multiplexing Only Once (PMOO) [18].

The PMOO analysis first convolves the tandem of servers before subtracting the cross-traffic. Using this order, the bursts of the cross-traffic appear only a single time compared to the SFA analysis where the bursts are included at each server. Therefore, multiplexing with cross-traffic is only paid for once. However, [17] showed that the PMOO method does not necessarily outperform the SFA.

2.3.2 *Feed-forward Networks*

For more involved feed-forward networks, a procedure to combine tandem analyses to a network analysis exists. In order to integrate the analysis of multicast flows into DNC, we derive this procedure in great detail. Here, we contribute the following result: a precise structure of the steps taken by any DNC network analysis. The well-elaborated structure we establish in this section, also serves us to judge and compare different approaches to aiming for performance bounds in feed-forward networks with multicast flows.

In previous work, two basic steps of the analysis have already been identified [5]: *1)* cross-traffic arrival bounding and *2)* flow of interest performance bounding. They are tailored to a compositional unicast flow analysis. We call it the *unicastFFA* and derive its steps in unprecedented detail:

unicastFFA Step 1: Cross-traffic Arrival Bounding. The first unicastFFA step abstracts from the feed-forward network to the foi's path – a tandem of servers that can be analyzed with one of the existing procedures. In detail, this step proceeds as follows:

(i) Starting at the locations of interference with the foi, cross-flows are backtracked to their sources. This procedure derives the dependencies between the foi, its cross-flows, their cross-flows, etc., in a recursive fashion. A new instance of this sub-step is started for any cross-flow of the current cross-flow under consideration. Due to the network's feed-forward property, the recursion is guaranteed to terminate.

(ii) Next, the dependencies are converted into equations, i.e., a sequence of algebraic operations for each location of interference with the foi. They capture the worst-case transformation of flow arrivals towards foi.

(iii) Finally, the equations are solved to obtain the bounds on cross-traffic arrivals.

After these substeps, all cross-flows' arrivals are bounded with arrival curves (arrival bounds).

unicastFFA Step 2: foi Performance Bounding. Given the cross-traffic arrival bounds from step 1, step 2 does not need to consider the part of the network traversed by these flows nor the potentially complex interference patterns they are subject to. The foi's end-to-end delay bound in the feed-forward network is derived with a tandem analysis.

Note, that this step provides information required in the previous one. It defines the flow of interest and thus its cross-flows as well as their locations of interference used in step 1(i). This step is strongly based on the tandem analysis that, in turn, is derived from the aim to analyze a unicast flow from end to end. It is not directly applicable to the analysis of multicast flows and thus needs generalization.

2.4 Multicast Flows

As defined at the beginning of this section, flows and network analysis in network calculus have been mostly focused on the modeling of unidirectional and unicast communications. Such a model is not directly applicable to multicast network protocols, where packets are duplicated at certain points of the network in order to provide one-to-many communications as illustrated in Figure 1.

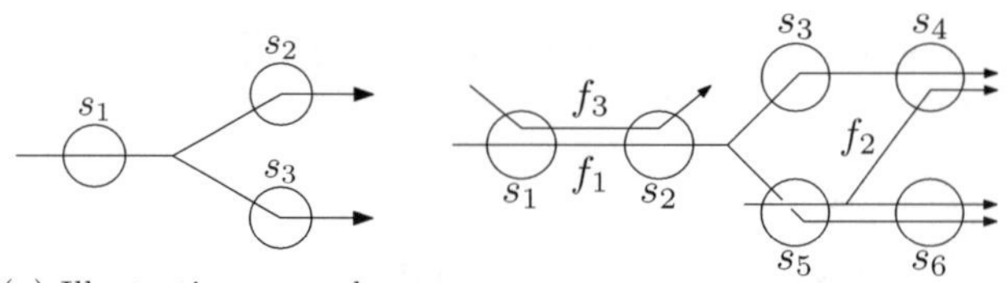

(a) Illustrative example.

(b) Running example.

Figure 1: Multicast networks.

We define the following terms for describing parts of a multicast flow:

Definition 5 (Trajectory and fork). *A trajectory of a given source-sink pair corresponds to the equivalent unicast flow going from the source to the sink. A fork corresponds to a server where packets are duplicated.*

In the following, we will provide an illustration as well as a running example. They are meant to serve two distinct purposes: On the one hand, we depict the basic idea behind the approaches to handle multicast flows with the minimal network of Figure 1a. Additionally, we will analyze the network of Figure 1b with the given approach. Analyzing flow f_2 makes this network minimal w.r.t. covering all effects relevant to DNC and multicast flows: There one multicast flow in each step of the analysis, cross-traffic arrival bounding (f_1) as well as flow of interest analysis (f_2). Moreover, a unicast flow is present and this network allows us to observe the impact of different flow analyses described earlier in Section 2.3.1 (TFA, SFA with the PBOO effect, PMOO).

3. RELATED WORK

In this related work section, we provide two DNC approaches to the analysis of multicast flows. For both, we focus on how these approaches enable the unicastFFA of the previous section to analyze networks with multicast flows.

unicastFFA Transformation: A Set of Unicast Flows

A first approach to circumvent this issue is to transform a multicast flow to a set of unicast flows. It was mentioned as a possibility to cope with multicast flows in [6]. Each trajectory will become one independent unicast flow, as illustrated in our two sample networks (Figures 2a and 2b).

From a procedural point of view, the unicast transformation does not integrate into the unicastFFA. It only enables for using it by a preceding step that transforms the network. This step is static, i.e., it does not consider the unicastFFA's information like the flow(s) that are under analysis.

The foremost problem of this approach is its overly pessimistic assumption about resource demand of multicast flows. On common sub-paths of a multicast flows' trajectories, i.e., the servers before a fork, multiple unicast flows compete for resources. The unicastFFA thus models the worst case with mutual interference between these flows that are not present in the original network model.

On the other hand, this approach allows for the PBOO and the PMOO principle in the unicastFFA.

Multicast TFA

Grieu [11] proposes a procedure to apply the TFA presented in Section 2.3.1 in the analysis of multicast flows. It is tailored to the TFA and shares its inherent isolation of servers.

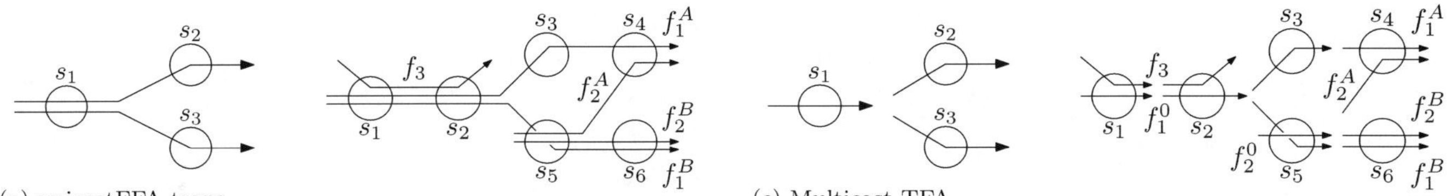

(a) unicastFFA transformation illustration.

(b) unicastFFA transformation applied to the running example.

(c) Multicast TFA illustration.

(d) Multicast TFA applied to the running example.

Figure 2: Existing DNC approaches to the multicast analysis applied to the networks presented in Figure 1.

Thus, it does not integrate into the unicastFFA for deriving delay bounds. Figures 2c and 2d depict this procedure on the illustration and the running example, respectively. Flows are cut between all servers, the arrivals are aggregated and a server-local delay bound is computed. In a second step, the server delay bounds on the trajectory of interest are summed up. As this last step is similar to the unicastFFA step 1, it inherits its decisive TFA shortcomings. I.e., neither the PMOO nor the PBOO principle are implemented and the delay bounds are known to be inaccurate.

Related Approaches

The existing DNC approaches both have significant drawbacks. Therefore, the literature created novel multicast analyses based on the DNC system description.

The *Trajectory Approach* (TA) is an adaptation to the study of network delays of the holistic approach [19]. It was originally developed to give bounds on the scheduling of tasks on a processor. The approach was initially proposed in [16] and later extended to FIFO systems in [15]. [1] applied TA to the study of avionic networks with multicast flows and showed, via numerical evaluations, that it outperforms the multicast TFA.

The *Forward End-To-End Delay Approach* (FA) has been proposed more recently in [13]. It addresses the shortcomings of the TA. Similarly to the TA, FA is also an adaptation of the holistic approach to the case of FIFO networks. [13] and [12] applied the FA to the performance evaluation of avionic networks with multicast flows and showed that this approach outperforms the multicast TFA as well.

Although FA sets its focus on the end-to-end analysis – similar to the DNC tandem analyses – neither FA nor TA have been benchmarked against a modern DNC that implements PBOO or PMOO. This can be attributed to the lack of such an analysis for multicast flows. In this paper, we will generalize multicast TFA as well as the unicastFFA in order to provide such DNC solutions and benchmarking results.

4. EXPLICIT INTERMEDIATE BOUNDS

Explicit Intermediate Bounds (EIB) analysis is the generalization of the multicast TFA analysis. We do not create an entirely new analysis (unlike TA and FA) but adapt the model such that we can analyze it with our NC tools. EIB combines the strengths of the two related approaches from above. Like the TFA, it follows the foi's trajectory of interest without additional cross-traffic assumptions. Moreover, it proceeds in tandems like the set of unicast flows. Therefore, it can benefit from both the PBOO and the PMOO principle on these tandems – unlike the server-local approach responsible for TFA's general inferiority w.r.t. delay bounds.

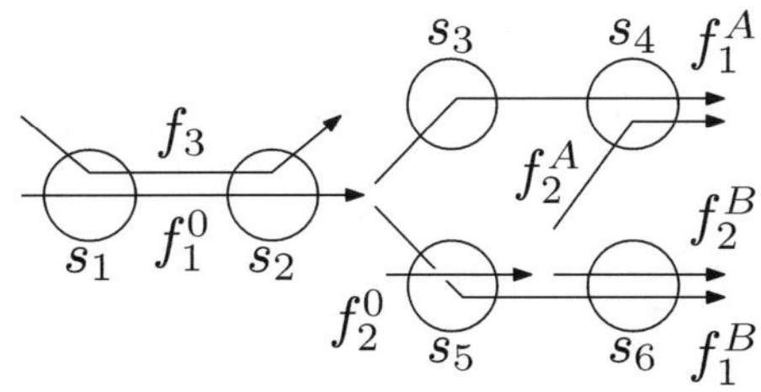

Figure 3: Application of the EIB analysis to the studied scenario: multicast flows are cut into unicast sub-flows.

We achieve this by an approach consisting of two parts:

1. A static, preceding step takes the network description and transforms it for analysis. In contrast to the multicast TFA, we cut multicast flows after forking locations only; not after every server. These are the locations of explicit intermediate bounds. In our illustrative example, the result is equal to the multicast TFA (Figure 2c). However, we transform the network into tandems that are crossed by parts of the multicast flows. This is revealed by our running example. For instance, compare the tandems $\langle 1, 2\rangle$ and $\langle 3, 4\rangle$ of multicast TFA (Figure 2d) with EIB (Figure 3).

2. The locations of cuts is static, i.e., only defined by the network, not the foi. The EIB analysis can be viewed to create a global worst case for all flows, independent of the foi. Afterwards it runs a unicastFFA in its second part.

These two steps are, however, not as separated as in the literature's multicast TFA. We integrate the EIB idea into the unicastFFA is as follows:

- Step 1: An adaptation of the cross-traffic arrival bounding is required at the locations of explicit intermediate bounds. Previously, tandems for analysis were defined by the common path of flow aggregates [6]. Using EIB, we have an additional restriction for the tandem lengths as we derive the output bound at the server a multicast flow forks. I.e., when the backtracking reaches such a server, the search for a tandem to operate on terminates. A new instance of unicastFFA step 1 is started with this server being the last one for the next tandem in the analysis.

- Step 2: The flow of interest analysis actually becomes a "trajectory of interest" analysis. Yet, for multicast flows it is not able to analyze the trajectory in an end-to-end fashion with a single left-over service curve.

A multicast flow's entire trajectory will consist of at least two tandems as it has at least one fork location to cut at. Thus, the PMOO principle cannot be implemented entirely; similar to the FIFO multiplexing tandem analysis LUDB [2].

We call this integrated procedure EIB unicastFFA; the name emphasizes the application of this specific way to obtain results with the EIB idea. Regarding the results themselves, EIB unicastFFA and EIB are synonymous as both of the above procedures yield the same performance bounds.

Analysis of the Running Example

As mentioned above, the difference between multicast TFA and EIB unicastFFA becomes apparent in more involved networks. We derive the left-over service curves for multicast flow f_2 of our running example (Figure 3) to depict the new analysis. We follow the EIB unicastFFA procedure that does not reveal a preceding EIB step.

EIB unicastFFA step 1. Bounding the delay of f_2 requires to bound the interference of multicast cross-flow f_1. The first location of interference with f_2 is at s_5 where we need to backtrack f_1^B. EIB enforces a cut after f_1's fork at server s_2 that we need to consider. We get $\alpha_5^{f_1^B} = \alpha_5^{f_1^0}$, i.e., the backtracking is stopped there. In a second instance of EIB unicastFFA step 1, f_1^0 is backtracked in order to derive its explicit intermediate bound at the output of s_2 / at the input of server s_5:

$$\alpha_5^{f_1^B} = \alpha^{f_1^0} \oslash \beta_{\langle 1,2\rangle}^{\text{l.o.}f_1^0}$$

In contrast to the multicast TFA, we can benefit from either SFA/PBOO or PMOO in the derivation of $\beta_{\langle 1,2\rangle}^{\text{l.o.}f_1^0}$. The according derivation that applies both alternatives is called aggregate arrival bounding, aggrAB, [6]:

$$\begin{aligned}\alpha^{f_1^0} \oslash \beta_{\langle 1,2\rangle}^{\text{l.o.}f_1^0} &= \left(\alpha^{f_1^0} \oslash \left(\left(\beta_1 \ominus \alpha^{f_3}\right) \otimes \left(\beta_2 \ominus \alpha_2^{f_3}\right)\right)\right) \\ &\quad \wedge \left(\alpha^{f_1^0} \oslash \left(\left(\beta_1 \otimes \beta_2\right) \ominus \alpha^{f_3}\right)\right)\end{aligned}$$

where $\alpha_2^{f_3}$ corresponds to the arrival bound of f_3 at s_2.

At the second location of interference between f_1 and f_2, server s_4, we need to backtrack trajectory f_1^A. This yields

$$\begin{aligned}\alpha_4^{f_1^A} &= \alpha_5^{f_1^B} \oslash \beta_3 \\ &= \left(\alpha^{f_1^0} \oslash \beta_{\langle 1,2\rangle}^{\text{l.o.}f_1^0}\right) \oslash \beta_3 = \alpha^{f_1^0} \oslash \left(\beta_{\langle 1,2\rangle}^{\text{l.o.}f_1^0} \otimes \beta_3\right)\end{aligned}$$

Note, that we cannot derive a left-over service curve $\beta_{\langle 1,2,3\rangle}^{\text{l.o.}f_1^A}$ due to the cut enforced by EIB. In general, this prevents the implementing of the PMOO principle.

EIB unicastFFA step 2. Next, we bound the delay of trajectory f_2^A. Again, it cannot be done with a single, PMOO left-over service curve due to EIB's cut between s_5 and s_6. In this case, the cut means SFA is the only analysis option:

$$\begin{aligned}\beta^{\text{l.o.}f_2^A} &= \beta_{\langle 5,4\rangle}^{\text{l.o.}f_2^A} \\ &\text{(cut enforced by EIB, no single-tandem analysis)} \\ &= \beta_5^{\text{l.o.}f_2^A} \otimes \beta_4^{\text{l.o.}f_2^A} \\ &= \left(\beta_5 \ominus \alpha_5^{f_1^B}\right) \otimes \left(\beta_4 \ominus \alpha_4^{f_1^A}\right)\end{aligned}$$

where $\alpha_5^{f_1^B}$ and $\alpha_4^{f_1^A}$ have been derived in EIB unicastFFA step 1, the cross-traffic arrival bounding.

In the analysis of f_2, the delay bound for trajectory f_2^B remains to be bounded. Again, we need to derive the according left-over service curve that illustrates the proceedings of EIB unicastFFA:

$$\begin{aligned}\beta^{\text{l.o.}f_2^B} &= \beta_{\langle 5,6\rangle}^{\text{l.o.}f_2^B} \\ &\text{(cut enforced by EIB, no single-tandem analysis)} \\ &= \beta_5^{\text{l.o.}f_2^B} \otimes \beta_6^{\text{l.o.}f_2^B} \\ &= \left(\beta_5 \ominus \alpha_5^{f_1^B}\right) \otimes \left(\beta_6 \ominus \alpha_6^{f_1^B}\right)\end{aligned}$$

Most notably, f_2^B sees multi-hop interference by f_1^B but the left-over service curve derivation cannot make use of the PMOO principle. EIB inhibits an end-to-end analysis in this unicastFFA step 2, only SFA/PBOO can be applied

Theoretical Evaluation

We conclude this section by a theoretical evaluation of the EIB approach against the previous DNC approaches:

- *Relation to multicast TFA:*
  The integration into the unicastFFA constitutes a generalization of the multicast TFA. On every tandem to analyze in either of the two unicastFFA steps, we can apply the TFA depicted in Section 2.3. Then, an additional intermediate step that separates the individual servers is executed and the per-server results are composed to the respective tandem result. The multicast TFA delay bounds cannot outperform those of EIB with either SFA or PMOO analysis on all tandems.
- *Relation to unicastFFA transformation:*
  In contrast to this section's EIB, the unicastFFA transformation allows for a single end-to-end left-over service curve for every trajectory of interest. I.e., it can fully benefit from the PMOO principle. However, the cuts enforced by EIB can also have a positive effect. They break the $\otimes$'s commutativity, allowing to better exploit service rates on the tandem. This is a variant of the problem shown in [17], but with a handicapped PMOO. None of the alternatives is strictly superior.

5. A MULTICAST FEED-FORWARD ANALYSIS PROCEDURE

In this section, we generalize the unicastFFA presented in Section 2.3.2 to networks with multicast flows. We call this generalized method *multicast Feed-Forward Analysis*, or mcastFFA. This allows us to make use of the knowledge only available in the unicastFFA itself. In contrast to the existing DNC approaches and the EIB analysis, no network transformation is amended to the analysis. We do not create a network-wide worst-cast setting for all flows before executing the unicastFFA. Instead, our generalization solely constructs a single flow of interest's worst case during analysis – a less pessimistic setting than the network-wide one for all flows at once. With this approach, the mcastFFA analysis obtains best results by exploiting the PMOO and PBOO principles to a larger extent than the EIB.

Figure 4a illustrates the basic idea behind our solution: If we analyze this multicast flow's trajectory crossing s_2,

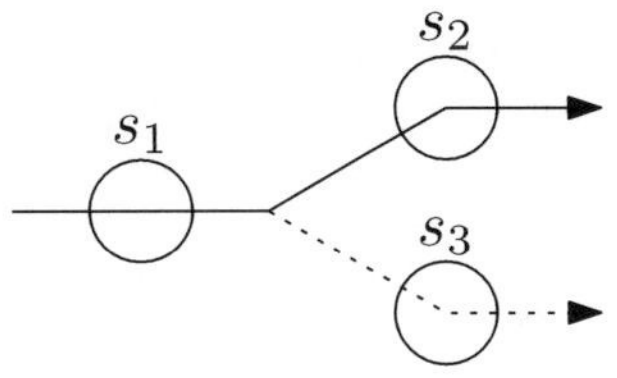

(a) mcastFFA illustration.

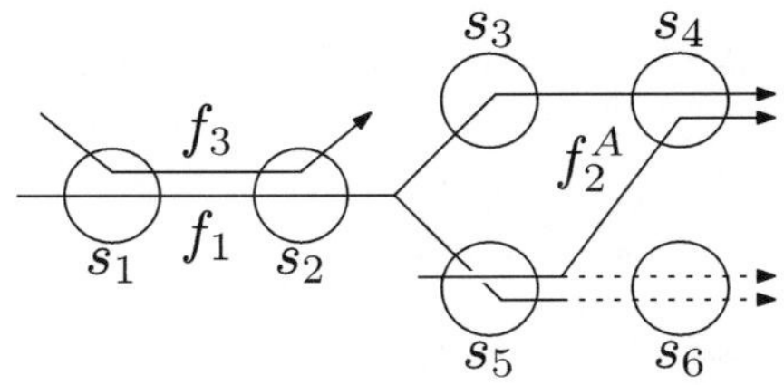

(b) Running example, trajectory f_2^A.

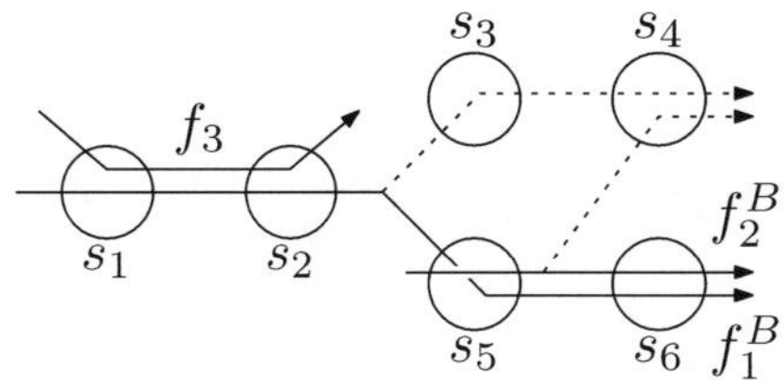

(c) Running example, trajectory f_2^B.

Figure 4: Application of mcastFFA. The dashed lines depict parts of flows that are not considered in the current analysis.

the other trajectory crossing s_3 becomes irrelevant for the delay bound computation. We neither need to add an entire cross-flow for it nor do we require the output bound from s_1. Thus, mcastFFA can treat the multicast trajectory (or unicast flow) of interest in an end-to-end fashion and apply, for instance, the PMOO principle.

The main challenge of this approach is to reduce the network to relevant servers as well as (partial) flows and multicast flow trajectories. This may constitute considerable effort in large networks. Therefore, we present a solution that generalizes the unicastFFA analysis in order to gain from its efficiency [3]. I.e., deriving the sub-network relevant to a specific foi is part of the analysis proceedings, not covered by a separate step. Our mcastFFA solution is mainly based on the newly derived sub-step 1(i) of the unicastFFA: backtracking of dependencies.

In this step, dependencies of a flow on others are derived by traversing the network in the opposite direction of links [5]. The entire unicastFFA starts this procedure with the flow of interest. Our mcastFFA will iterate over all n trajectory of interest and execute separate analyses. In case of a unicast flow, we get $n = 1$; for multicast flows n equals the amount of trajectories (source/sink-pairs). Multicast cross-flows are traversed backwards, too, such that their fork locations do not enforce to cut the tandem to analyze; the relevant trajectory of the cross-flow is known and can be treated similar to a unicast cross-flow. Namely, the mcastFFA is a generalization of the known unicastFFA and thus it operates on longer tandems than EIB.

Whereas the EIB required to explicitly consider each location a multicast flow forks, the mcastFFA implicitly restricts the analysis to the trajectory relevant for the analysis. After the backtracking, we know the entire sub-network whose servers and (partial) flows appear in the analysis equation of unicastFFA step 1(ii). I.e., we rely on the detailed understanding of unicastFFA that we derived in Section 2.3.2.

Analysis of the Running Example

We will derive the left-over service curves for f_2's trajectories in order to compare them against the EIB unicastFFA. For brevity, we restrict the depiction to f_2^A's cross-traffic arrival bounding (mcastFFA step 1, Figure 4b) and f_2^B's delay bounding (mcastFFA step 2, Figure 4c). These derivations depict the crucial improvement of mcastFFA's proceedings in both of the analysis steps. They point out the reduction of the network and the increased tandem lengths.

mcastFFA step 1. We consider f_2^A's cross-traffic arrival bounding. Backtracking will be "local" to a single trajectory of a multicast cross-flow. In our example, we finally have established the possibility to apply the PMOO-principle when computing f_1^A's aggregate arrival bound aggrAB at server s_4 [6]. See $\alpha_4^{f_1^A}$ in the follwoing left-over service curve derivation we require to bound cross-traffic arrivals:

$$\beta^{\text{l.o.}f_2^A} = \beta_{\langle 5,4\rangle}^{\text{l.o.}f_2^A}$$

(only single-hop interference so cutting is fine)

$$\begin{aligned} &= \beta_5^{\text{l.o.}f_2^A} \otimes \beta_4^{\text{l.o.}f_2^A} \\ &= \left(\beta_5 \ominus \alpha_5^{f_1^B}\right) \otimes \left(\beta_4 \ominus \alpha_4^{f_1^A}\right) \\ &= \left(\beta_5 \ominus \left(\alpha^{f_1} \oslash \beta_{\langle 1,2\rangle}^{\text{l.o.}f_1}\right)\right) \otimes \left(\beta_4 \ominus \left(\alpha^{f_1} \oslash \beta_{\langle 1,2,3\rangle}^{\text{l.o.}f_1^A}\right)\right) \end{aligned}$$

A cut of $\beta_{\langle 1,2,3\rangle}^{\text{l.o.}f_1^A}$ into $\beta_{\langle 1,2\rangle}^{\text{l.o.}f_1} \otimes \beta_3^{\text{l.o.}f_1^A}$ was needed in the EIB analysis, meaning that PMOO could not be implemented.

This advantage is also depicted in Figure 4b where f_1 retains its multicast shape in the mcastFFA's point of view.

mcastFFA step 2. For the second trajectory of f_2, f_2^B, our mcastFFA derives $\beta^{\text{l.o.}f_2^B} = \beta_{\langle 5,6\rangle}^{\text{l.o.}f_2^B}$. Again, we are not enforced to cut this trajectory's path (see Figure 4c) and in contrast to EIB we can apply alternative tandem analyses:

- SFA/PBOO:

  $$\beta^{\text{l.o.}f_2^B} = \beta_{\langle 5,6\rangle}^{\text{l.o.}f_2^B}$$

  (cut enforced by SFA, no single-tandem analysis)

  $$\begin{aligned} &= \beta_5^{\text{l.o.}f_2^B} \otimes \beta_6^{\text{l.o.}f_2^B} \\ &= \left(\beta_5 \ominus \alpha_5^{f_1^B}\right) \otimes \left(\beta_6 \ominus \alpha_6^{f_1^B}\right) \\ &= \left(\beta_5 \ominus \left(\alpha^{f_1} \oslash \beta_{\langle 1,2\rangle}^{\text{l.o.}f_1}\right)\right) \otimes \left(\beta_6 \ominus \left(\alpha^{f_1} \oslash \beta_{\langle 1,2,5\rangle}^{\text{l.o.}f_1^B}\right)\right) \end{aligned}$$

  Note, that the actual trajectory of the cross-flow, f_1 or f_1^B, was automatically chosen correctly by the backtracking. Moreover, note the contrast to EIB: We can derive f_1^B's arrivals at s_6 with an end-to-end left-over service curve that, in turn, can make use of aggrAB.

- PMOO:

  $$\beta^{\text{l.o.}f_2^B} = \beta_{\langle 5,6\rangle}^{\text{l.o.}f_2^B}$$

  (there is no enforced cut)

  $$\begin{aligned} &= (\beta_5 \otimes \beta_6) \ominus \alpha_5^{f_1} \\ &= (\beta_5 \otimes \beta_6) \ominus \left(\alpha^{f_1} \oslash \beta_{\langle 1,2\rangle}^{\text{l.o.}f_1}\right) \end{aligned}$$

  where $\beta_{\langle 1,2\rangle}^{\text{l.o.}f_1}$ can be computed either applying the left-over service curve derivation of SFA/PBOO or PMOO.

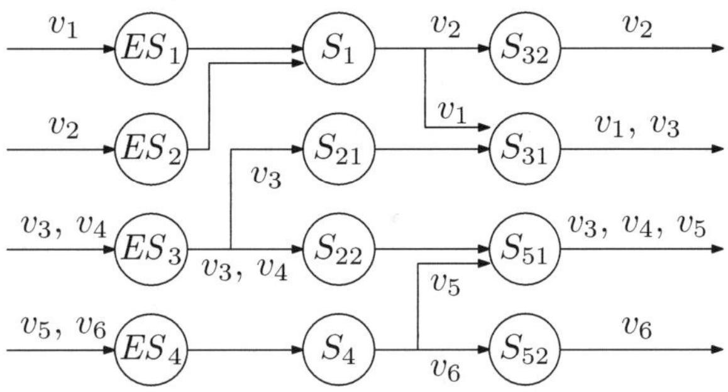

(a) AFDX network.

Flow	From [13] TA	From [13] FA	u. trans. PMOO[1]	EIB TFA[2]	EIB SFA	EIB PMOO	mcastFFA SFA	mcastFFA PMOO
v_1	**82**	**82**	**82**	**82**	**82**	**82**	**82**	**82**
v_2	**72**	**72**	**72**	**72**	**72**	**72**	**72**	**72**
$v_{3(S_{31})}$	**82**	**82**	92	**82**	**82**	**82**	**82**	**82**
$v_{3(S_{51})}$	**82**	112	92	102	102	92	102	**82**
v_4	**82**	112	92	102	102	92	102	**82**
v_5	-	112	92	102	102	92	102	**92**
v_6	**72**	82	**72**	82	82	72	82	**72**

(b) Delay bounds (values given in μs, least bounds in bold).

Figure 5: Simple AFDX network evaluation of [13], extended with DNC's EIB and mcastFFA delay bounds.

This derivation is illustrated in Figure 4c. Compared to Figure 3, we indeed notice the longer tandem for the second trajectory of f_2.

Theoretical Evaluation

We conclude this section by a theoretical evaluation of mcastFFA against the related DNC approaches:

- *Relation to unicastFFA (Section 2.3.2):* The mcastFFA is a generalization of the unicastFFA. Analysis of unicast flows in either of the two steps remains unaffected (see f_3 in the running example).
- *Relation to unicastFFA transformation (Section 3):* Like the unicastFFA transformation, the mcastFFA is able to derive a PMOO end-to-end left-over service curve. However, it does so without the additional cross-traffic assumptions introduced by the unicastFFA transformation. I.e., there are less cross-flows to consider in the analysis, left-over service curves will be larger and delay bounds will be smaller. Thus, mcastFFA outperforms unicastFFA transformation.
- *Relation to EIB unicastFFA:* In comparison to EIB, we gained the ability to operate on end-to-end tandems. This constitutes increased flexibility to cut this tandem during the analysis: Our mcastFFA is compatible with SFA/PBOO, PMOO, aggrAB, or [3] for best attainable left-over service curves. This best solution to cut a tandem and combine subtandem results might coincide with EIB's enforced alternative, i.e., mcastFFA is indeed a generalization of EIB unicastFFA.

Before evaluating our contributions, let us briefly clarify their impact on the server backlog bound Q presented in Theorem 3. Deriving these bounds requires the arrival bounds of all flows at a server. I.e., in the DNC analysis procedures, (EIB) unicastFFA and mcastFFA, step 1 is crucial for the result accuracy; step 2 is not required. As shown with the running example, we improved of cross-traffic arrival bounding in case there are multicast flows present. Thus, backlog bounds are also improved by our contribution.

6. NUMERICAL EVALUATION

We have shown in Sections 4 and 5 that our proposed approaches are superior to the previous network calculus ones, presented as related work in Section 3. We investigate now in this section the gains in terms of accuracy of end-to-end delay bounds via a numerical evaluation. We study the two AFDX networks presented in [13] and [12]. This allows us to benchmark our proposed approaches with the TA and FA since numerical results are given in the literature. Note, that [12] extends the TA and FA by a grouping property that accounts for serialization of packetized flows when crossing links. We leave its implementation in the generalized DNC solutions, based on [8], to future work and restrict our comparison to the non-serialized results. This also allows us to use the range of established SFA/PBOO and PMOO $\beta^{\mathrm{l.o.}}$ derivations implemented in the DiscoDNC tool [4] as well as the aggrAB arrival bounding. I.e., we inherit the DiscoDNC assumptions of a fluid model and curves that can be decomposed into a set of either token buckets or rate latencies.

The first network, illustrated in Figure 5a, is a simple AFDX scenario with only one multicast flow (v_3) and a simple flow interference pattern. The second network, illustrated in Figure 6a, is a more complex AFDX scenario with two multicast flows (v_2 and v_9). Numerical results on the end-to-end delay bounds of the different flows are shown in Figures 5b and 6b, respectively. Key observations w.r.t. the performance of DNC analyses confirm our conjectures:

- mcastFFA with PMOO produces gains of 8.74% and 13.08% respectively compared to the multicast TFA.
- mcastFFA produces more accurate bounds than the EIB analysis, since it can operate on longer tandems.
- For some flows, all results are equal. These are simplistic cases that become less in the larger network.

Next, we compare mcastFFA to TA and FA. We observe that mcastFFA results are never inferior to these contenders. Moreover, cases of equal results often coincide with the simplistic ones where even mutlicast TFA is competitive. This is especially visible in the second scenario with less competitive TA and FA bounds. A maximum gain of 5.86% compared to TA and 18.58% compared to FA is achieved in this small AFDX scenario. AFDX networks as deployed in existing Airbus aircraft are already far bigger and more involved than the ones of Figures 5a and 6a. They consist of ~1000 multicast flows (virtual links, VLs) that have an average of ~6.5 trajectories per VL. Therefore, the improvements we achieve with DNC's PMOO in conjunction with mcastFFA is expected to be considerably larger in practice.

[1]unicastFFA transformation approach with the stated PMOO end-to-end left-over service curve derivation.
[2]Remember, that EIB with TFA corresponds to the multicast TFA analysis presented as related work in Section 3.

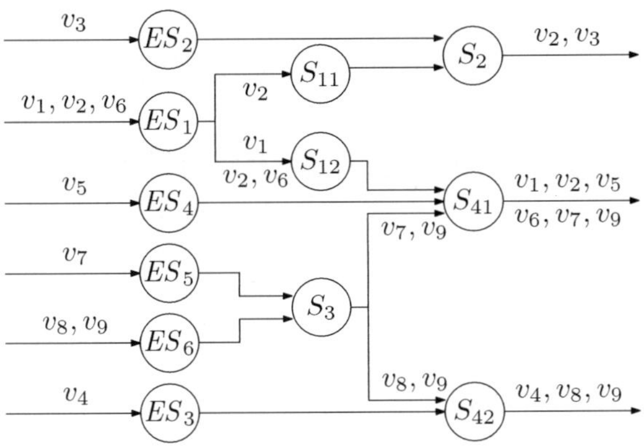

(a) AFDX Network.

Flow	From [12]		u. trans.	EIB			mcastFFA	
	TA	FA	PMOO[1]	TFA[2]	SFA	PMOO	SFA	PMOO
v_1	142	192	142	182	182	142	182	**122**
$v_{2(S_2)}$	**122**	**122**	142	**122**	**122**	**122**	**122**	**122**
$v_{2(S_{41})}$	**142**	192	**142**	182	182	162	182	**142**
v_3	66	**56**	**56**	**56**	**56**	**56**	**56**	**56**
v_4	**56**	66	**56**	**56**	**56**	**56**	**56**	**56**
v_5	106	106	**96**	**96**	**96**	**96**	**96**	**96**
v_6	142	192	142	182	182	142	182	**122**
v_7	-	152	142	142	142	142	142	**132**
v_8	**92**	122	102	112	112	102	112	**92**
$v_{9(S_{41})}$	-	162	142	152	152	142	152	**132**
$v_{9(S_{42})}$	**92**	122	102	112	112	102	112	**92**

(b) Delay bounds (values given in μs, least bounds in bold).

Figure 6: More complex AFDX network evaluation of [12], extended with DNC's EIB and mcastFFA delay bounds.

7. CONCLUSION

In this paper, we tackled the problem of analyzing multicast flows with deterministic network calculus. DNC was tailored to the analysis of unicast flows – a property that was assumed to invariantly hold. Therefore, previous approaches for the DNC analysis of multicast flows tried to adjust to this restriction by, e.g., pessimistic re-modeling of the network. This lead to inaccurate performance bounds and the development of alternative, non-DNC analyses to derive multicast flow guarantees. In contrast, we generalized DNC unicast feed-forward analysis to a multicast one.

We took two crucial steps to achieve this, both constituting an analysis approach of their own: the EIB analysis and the mcastFFA. In theoretical and numerical evaluations we showed that this paper contributes a single best DNC analysis for multicast flows, the mcastFFA. Not only does it outperform any other DNC approach, the evaluation of AFDX scenarios from the literature also shows that DNC achieves at least the results of competing analyses (Trajectory Approach and Forward Analysis). Moreover, the presented mcastFFA has the flexibility to be combined with any DNC tandem analysis and improvement thereof. For instance, [7], [3], FIFO multiplexing service analysis [2] or packetization [8] can tighten guarantees in AFDX networks.

8. REFERENCES

[1] H. Bauer, J. Scharbarg, and C. Fraboul. Applying and Optimizing Trajectory approach for performance evaluation of AFDX avionics network. In *Proc. IEEE ETFA*, 2009.

[2] L. Bisti, L. Lenzini, E. Mingozzi, and G. Stea. Numerical Analysis of Worst-Case End-to-End Delay Bounds in FIFO Tandem Networks. *Springer Real-Time Systems Journal*, 2012.

[3] S. Bondorf, P. Nikolaus, and J. B. Schmitt. Delay bounds in feed-forward networks – a fast and accurate network calculus solution. *arXiv:1603.02094*, 2016.

[4] S. Bondorf and J. B. Schmitt. The DiscoDNC v2 – A Comprehensive Tool for Deterministic Network Calculus. In *Proc. EAI ValueTools*, 2014.

[5] S. Bondorf and J. B. Schmitt. Boosting Sensor Network Calculus by Thoroughly Bounding Cross-Traffic. In *Proc. IEEE INFOCOM*, 2015.

[6] S. Bondorf and J. B. Schmitt. Calculating Accurate End-to-End Delay Bounds – You Better Know Your Cross-Traffic. In *Proc. EAI ValueTools*, 2015.

[7] S. Bondorf and J. B. Schmitt. Improving Cross-Traffic Bounds in Feed-Forward Networks – There is a Job for Everyone. In *Proc. GI/ITG MMB & DFT*, 2016.

[8] M. Boyer and P. Roux. A common framework embedding network calculus and event stream theory. *hal-01311502*, 2016. Working paper or preprint.

[9] C.-S. Chang. *Performance Guarantees in Communication Networks*. Springer, 2000.

[10] F. Geyer and G. Carle. Network engineering for real-time networks: comparison of automotive and aeronautic industries approaches. *IEEE Communications Magazine*, 2016.

[11] J. Grieu. *Analyse et évaluation de techniques de commutation Ethernet pour l'interconnexion des systèmes avioniques*. PhD thesis, INPT, 2004.

[12] G. Kemayo, N. Benammar, F. Ridouard, H. Bauer, and P. Richard. Improving AFDX End-to-End delays analysis. In *Proc. of IEEE ETFA*, 2015.

[13] G. Kemayo, F. Ridouard, H. Bauer, and P. Richard. A Forward end-to-end delays Analysis for packet switched networks. In *Proc. of RTNS*, 2014.

[14] J.-Y. Le Boudec and P. Thiran. *Network Calculus: A Theory of Deterministic Queuing Systems for the Internet*. Springer, 2001.

[15] S. Martin and P. Minet. Schedulability analysis of flows scheduled with FIFO: application to the expedited forwarding class. In *Proc. of IPDPS*, 2006.

[16] J. Migge. *L'ordonnancement sous contraintes temps-réel un modèle à base de trajectoires*. PhD thesis, INRIA Sophia Antipolis, 1999.

[17] J. B. Schmitt, F. A. Zdarsky, and M. Fidler. Delay Bounds under Arbitrary Multiplexing: When Network Calculus Leaves You in the Lurch ... In *Proc. IEEE INFOCOM*, 2008.

[18] J. B. Schmitt, F. A. Zdarsky, and I. Martinovic. Improving Performance Bounds in Feed-Forward Networks by Paying Multiplexing Only Once. In *Proc. of GI/ITG MMB*, 2008.

[19] K. Tindell and J. Clark. Holistic schedulability analysis for distributed hard real-time systems. *Microprocessing and Microprogramming*, 1994.

Fair workload distribution for multi-server systems with pulling strategies

Andrea Marin
Università Ca' Foscari Venezia, Italy
marin@dais.unive.it

Sabina Rossi
Università Ca' Foscari Venezia, Italy
srossi@dais.unive.it

ABSTRACT

The problem of parallel job scheduling has been widely studied in the literature with the aim of improving some performance indices, such as the throughput, the response time, the fairness or a combination of these indices (see, e.g., [3]). One can distinguish two basic approaches to the problem depending on the phase at which the dispatcher is placed. The two approaches are: *dispatching before the queues* and *dispatching after the queue*. In the first approach, the dispatcher decides how to assign a job to a server according to some scheduling discipline which takes into account the queueing state and other information about the servers. In contrast, the second approach consists in storing the jobs in a shared queue and these are assigned by the dispatcher to a server as soon as it becomes available. The scheduling policy can rely on a pushing strategy, i.e., the dispatcher takes the initiative to send a job to a specific server or on a pulling strategy, i.e., the servers decide autonomously to fetch a job from the shared queue.

In this paper we study the second approach relying on a pulling strategy. In contrast to prior works, we focus on the balance of the total number of jobs served by a set of K identical servers. We propose a stateless scheduling discipline implemented by the servers so that the difference between the number of jobs served by each unity is finite in steady-state. Our scheduling discipline is based on a server rate-adaptation algorithm. Informally, each server maintains a variable to store the difference between the total number of jobs served by itself and a neighbour. Given just this piece of information, the server may decide to slow down its maximum service speed in order to reduce this difference. As soon as the server finishes its job, it fetches a new one from the queue. We study two rate-adaptation strategies. The first one, named *bimodal* strategy, uses only two distinct service rates: the highest is used when a server has served less jobs than its neighbour, while the slowest is used otherwise. The second rate-adaptation policy, named *proportional* strategy, requires a server to reduce a fixed maximum service rate in proportion to the number of extra jobs it has served with respect to its neighbour. We propose a Markovian model for such a scheduling discipline and for both the rate-adaptation strategies described above. We show that, despite the little knowledge that each server has about the state of the system, we can derive a necessary and sufficient condition for the job balance index to have finite expectation in the bimodal strategy whereas in the proportional strategy the job balance is unconditionally finite. We derive the exact expressions for two relevant performance indices: the system's throughput and the balance index. The latter measures the differences among the total number of jobs processed by each server, hence low values imply a well balanced system. Although the Markov process underlying the models has an infinite state space, these expressions involve finite sums derived from the evaluation of hypergeometric functions.

Our findings show that maintaining reasonable low values for the balance index reduces the throughput at around 70% of the maximum. More interestingly, numerical evidences show that this value scales slowly with the number of servers, which means that the rate adaptation policy scales well with the system's size. From a theoretical point of view, to analyse our model we resort to the notion of *ρ-reversibility* [2]. Indeed, we show that although the model is in general *not* reversible [1], it satisfies the Kolmogorov's criteria for ρ-reversibility allowing us to derive an analytical product-form expression for the invariant measure.

VALUETOOLS 2016, October 25-28, Taormina, Italy

CCS Concepts

•Computing methodologies → *Modeling and simulation;*

Keywords

Fork-join queueing systems, Markov models, load balancing, rate adaptation

1. REFERENCES

[1] F. Kelly. *Reversibility and stochastic networks*. Wiley, New York, 1979.

[2] A. Marin and S. Rossi. On the relations between Markov chain lumpability and reversibility. *Acta Informatica*, 2016. Available online.

[3] I. Tsimashenka, W. Knottenbelt, and P. Harrison. Controlling variability in split-merge systems and its impact on performance. *Annals of Oper. Res.*, 239:569–588, 2016.

Optimal population mix in pool depletion systems with two-class workload

Davide Cerotti Marco Gribaudo Riccardo Pinciroli

Giuseppe Serazzi
Dip. di Elettronica, Informazione e Bioingengeria
Politecnico di Milano
Via Ponzio 34/5, 20133 Milano, Italy
{davide.cerotti, marco.gribaudo, riccardo.pinciroli, giuseppe.serazzi}@polimi.it

ABSTRACT

The evolutions of digital technologies and software applications have introduced a new computational paradigm that involves the concurrent processing of jobs taken from a large pool in systems with limited capacity. The definition of admission control policies that choose which jobs to process is crucial to improve the overall performance especially in systems with multiclass workload. In a previous work we show that in such systems, hereinafter called *pool depletion systems*, few parameters have a non-trivial impact on the processing time of the whole pool. Other performance indices, such as the energy consumption, are also deeply affected. In the present work, we further investigate such phenomenon by applying results from queueing theory, absorption time analysis and by performing discrete event simulations. We propose different techniques in order to identify the optimal or near-optimal setting. We analyze their complexity and provide guidelines to choose which of them adopt according to the application scenario characteristics.

Keywords

Stochastic models; pool depletion system; performance evaluation; optimization; multiclass models

1. INTRODUCTION

The replication concept is extensively applied by the big data technologies to achieve the expected performance improvements. The key feature of this computing framework is the parallel execution of a high number of processes, that may be, for example, replicas of the same request operating on different data sets or functions that summarize huge amount of data. A complete execution of a big data application consists of a sequence of parallel computations and their following synchronizations according to some user defined rules. Typically, the computing framework orchestrates the executions of the processes taking into consideration the configuration of the available architecture. The optimization of the distribution of the executions plays a fundamental role in the performance gains that can be obtained.

In this paper we approach one of the problems related to the optimization of the execution time of big data applications with different resource demands. Given a high number of processes (referred to as *pool*) belonging to two different applications, we study the problem of the minimization of the execution time required by their complete executions, referred to as *depletion time*. More precisely, knowing the resource demands of the two classes of applications, we are able to derive analytically the mixes of processes in concurrent execution in a system with finite capacity that minimize the global execution time of all the processes in the pool.

In the study presented we consider one system with two resources, e.g., CPU and storage. However, it will be easy to show that the optimization results achieved in this case, which is the least favorable, will be emphasized with an increased number of systems. We study the depletion system with different load conditions and we derive the analytical solutions in both cases with asymptotic and non-asymptotic load. To compute the results we use queueing networks, discrete event simulations and Markov analysis techniques.

The paper is organized as follows. Sections 2 and 3 provide a review of the background results and a description of the system architecture, software and hardware, used. Section 4 reports the derivation of the analytical results in the asymptotic case. The non-asymptotic load is studied in Section 5, where the results obtained with different techniques are also presented. Section 6 concludes the paper.

2. BACKGROUND

In this Section we emphasize some results on product-form closed queuing networks [1] with two-class workload and fixed rate single server stations that will be exploited in the analysis of depletion systems developed in the following Sections. Two-class workloads are enough simple to analitically deal with, while being representative of several realistic workload of actual systems. In this case, the workload of models with M stations can be characterized by a matrix of service demands $\mathbf{D} = [D_{rc}]$ where D_{rc} is the time required by station $r \in \{1, \ldots, M\}$ to completely process a class $c \in \{A, B\}$ request. Hereinafter, we will consider a sys-

VALUETOOLS 2016, October 25-28, Taormina, Italy

tem with two resources and the following service demands:

$$\mathbf{D} = \begin{bmatrix} 0.75 & 0.64 \\ 0.48 & 1.25 \end{bmatrix} \quad (1)$$

According to matrix (1), class A service demands on stations 1 and 2 are 0.75 and 0.48 time units, respectively, whereas class B demands on the two stations are 0.64 and 1.25 time units, respectively.

The performance of systems with multi-class workloads depends on the fraction of requests in execution of each class, referred to as *population mix*. Let β represents the fraction of requests of class A in execution. In the example of matrix D, when $\beta = 0$ we have only class B requests and the bottleneck (i.e., the saturated resource) is station 2, whereas with $\beta = 1$ (only class A requests) the bottleneck becomes station 1. Thus, varying the value of β a *bottleneck switch* occurs. In these conditions, there exists a value β^* such that both stations are equally utilized for any number of requests inside the system; such value is called the *equi-utilization point*. In addition, providing that the service demand matrix values allow the occurrence of a bottleneck switch[1] and when the number of requests is sufficiently large, it is possible to identify an interval of values of the population mix that concurrently saturate the stations. Indeed, for the values of β belonging to such *common saturation sector* (CSS) the system throughput achieves the maximum and the system response time is minimum.

In [6] it is shown that the equi-utilization point is given by:

$$\beta^* = \frac{log\frac{D_{22}}{D_{12}}}{log\frac{D_{11}D_{22}}{D_{12}D_{21}}} \quad (2)$$

and it is proved that the equi-utilization point always belongs to the CSS of edges:

$$\begin{cases} \beta^L &= D_{2A}\frac{D_{2B}-D_{1B}}{D_{1A}D_{2B}-D_{2A}D_{1B}} \\ \beta^U &= D_{1A}\frac{D_{2B}-D_{1B}}{D_{1A}D_{2B}-D_{2A}D_{1B}} \end{cases} \quad (3)$$

where β^L and β^U denote the lower and upper edges, respectively. Moreover, in the same paper the behavior of the per-class throughputs are analytically computed. In particular, we have that for values of β inside the CSS the per-class throughputs are:

$$\begin{matrix} X_A^{CSS} &=& X_A(\mathbf{K}) &=& \frac{D_{2B}-D_{1B}}{D_{1A}D_{2B}-D_{2A}D_{1B}} \\ X_B^{CSS} &=& X_B(\mathbf{K}) &=& \frac{D_{2A}-D_{1A}}{D_{1B}D_{2A}-D_{1A}D_{2B}} \end{matrix} \quad (4)$$

where $\mathbf{K} = [K_A, K_B]$ denotes the number of requests of each class. For values of β at the right of the saturation sector (i.e. with $\beta > \beta^U$) we have:

$$X_A(\mathbf{K}) = \frac{\beta}{D_{1A}} \quad X_B(\mathbf{K}) = \frac{1-\beta}{D_{1B}} \quad (5)$$

Similar equations can be derived for values of β at the left of the saturation sector, thus obtaining the overall trend of the per-class throughputs as function of the population mix.

3. SYSTEM DESCRIPTION

We consider a system where each job consists of several independent tasks. Examples of such type of workloads are video transcoding/analysis, applications of business analytics, NoSQL queries and so on. In particular, we focus on jobs composed by two types of tasks, defined as class A and class B. For example, in multimedia stream applications each chunk is processed by a single task and the two classes may represent the computation of audio and video chunks, respectively.

We assume that the tasks of a job are executed sequentially by two resources, denoted as Res_1 and Res_2, that, for example, may represent the CPU and the storage of a server. The global service time required by resource r for a complete execution of a class c task is referred to as *service demand* D_{rc}. The service demands characterize the workload in terms of total processing requirements to the resources, and their values are considered exponentially distributed. Each resource executes the concurrent tasks according to a *processor sharing* queuing discipline: all tasks are processed by the resources with a service rate proportional to the current number of tasks in service.

We call N_A the number of class A tasks, N_B the number of class B and $N = N_A + N_B$ the total number of tasks of a job. The system can execute at most K tasks concurrently. This limitation is used to model constraints on memory occupancy that prevents all the N tasks to be executed in parallel. In particular, the system is allowed to execute K_A tasks of class A and K_B of class B, with $K = K_A + K_B$. As soon as one task is completed, another task of the same class is admitted in execution, if available. When all the tasks of one class are completed, the system allows the tasks of the other class to be processed.

Figure 1 gives a visual representation of the considered scenario. We are interested in studying the total time T required to complete the execution of all the N tasks of a job that initially are in the pool. With the type of applications considered in this study we have $N_A \geq K_A$ and $N_B \geq K_B$.

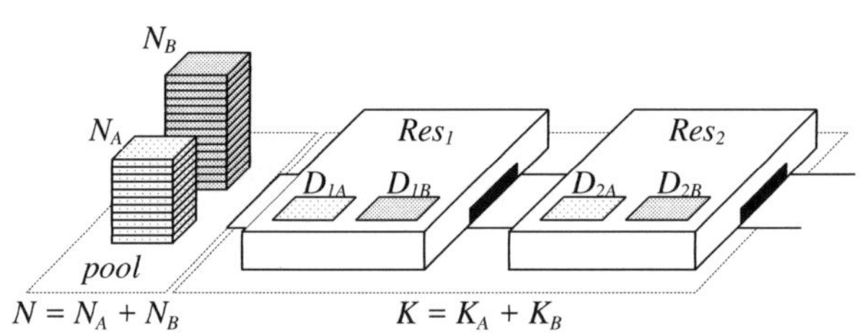

Figure 1: The considered scenario.

Figure 2 shows the temporal evolution of the number of tasks in the system. Initially, K out of N tasks immediately starts being serviced by the first resource of the system. As long as there are tasks of both classes in the pool waiting to be executed, the number of tasks in the system is constantly kept to $K = K_A + K_B$. We address this phase as Φ_{I}: after a short initial transient period, denoted with $T_{\tau 0}$, the system behaves as a closed queueing model with K_A and K_B customers, since as soon as one of the task of a class leaves the system, it is immediately replaced by another one of the same class. At time $T_{\Phi 1}$ the tasks in the pool of one class are finished and no new tasks of that class may enter the system (in Figure 2 this happens for class A tasks). At this time the system starts replacing the tasks of the exhausted class with the ones of the other class: phase Φ_{II} begins. After an initial

[1]It can be verified by checking if $D_{1A} > D_{1B}$ and $D_{2A} < D_{2B}$; see [6] for further details.

transient in which all the remaining tasks of the exhausted class are executed, the system behaves as a closed queuing model with K customers (in Figure 2 these customers are of class B). We denote the end of this transient part as $T_{\tau 12}$. After some time, the tasks in the pool that still need to be executed will end, and the system will begin to execute a decreasing number of tasks. We denote this instant of time by $T_{\Phi 2}$, and the period of time in which the server is working with less than K tasks as phase Φ_{III}. The job completes its execution when all its tasks are terminated at time T, referred to as *depletion time*.

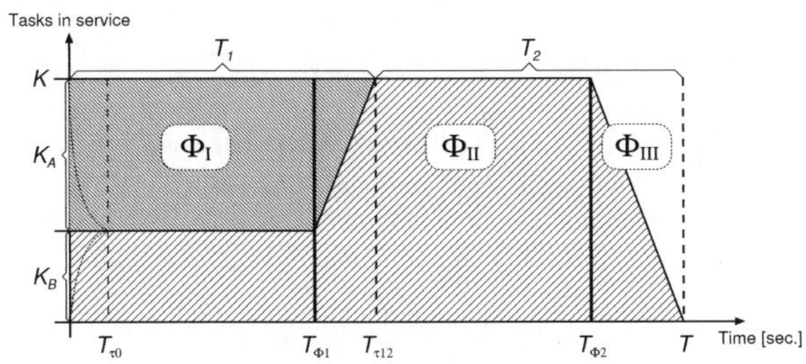

Figure 2: Behavior of the number of tasks in execution with phases characterization.

4. ASYMPTOTIC RESULTS

In this Section we describe the model used to study the asymptotic behavior of the system. This assumption is motivated by the actual big data applications in which the number of tasks that generated by a job is definetly larger than the number of tasks that can be executed concurrently in the system. Two examples of problems that can be solved through our analysis are proposed.

4.1 Asymptotic model

In order to study the asymptotic behavior of the system, let us assume that the number N of tasks in the pool is much larger than the number K of tasks admitted in execution, i.e., $N \gg K$. The region containing the resources of the system where $K = K_A + K_B$ tasks are admitted in execution is identified as Finite Capacity Region (FCR). If K is large enough to saturate the system, the per-class throughputs can be derived with closed formulas [6]. Due to the asymptotic assumption, the transient phases shown in Figure 2 are negligible and the depletion time may be computed as $T = T_1 + T_2$, since Φ_{I} and Φ_{II} are the dominant ones.

First phase Φ_{I} lasts until there is at least one task of each class in the system. Let us define the fraction of class A tasks initially in the pool, and that could be executed concurrently in the system, when available, as:

$$\alpha = \frac{N_A}{N}, \quad \beta = \frac{K_A}{K},$$

respectively. The Φ_{I} length can be derived as:

$$T_1(N, \alpha, \beta) = min\left(\frac{N_A}{X_A(\beta)}, \frac{N_B}{X_B(\beta)}\right) \tag{6}$$

where $X_c(\beta)$ is the asymptotic throughput for tasks of class $c \in \{A, B\}$ when there are $K_A = \beta K$ and $K_B = (1-\beta)K$ tasks in the FCR. Φ_{I} ends when system runs out of tasks of one class.

In phase Φ_{II}, in the asymptotic case, the system always executes a single class workload (e.g., class B in Figure 2). It starts with less than N_C tasks – where C is the remaining class – since part of them have been already served during Φ_{I} and it ends when there are no more tasks in the system. Φ_{II} phase length, that is T_2, is computed as:

$$\begin{aligned} T_2(N, \alpha, \beta) &= \frac{N_A - min\left(\frac{N_A}{X_A(\beta)}, \frac{N_B}{X_B(\beta)}\right) X_A(\beta)}{X_A(1)} \\ T_2(N, \alpha, \beta) &= \frac{N_B - min\left(\frac{N_A}{X_A(\beta)}, \frac{N_B}{X_B(\beta)}\right) X_B(\beta)}{X_B(0)} \end{aligned} \tag{7}$$

where $X_A(1)$ ($X_B(0)$) is the class A (B) throughput when there are only tasks of class A (B) in the system. One of the two equations is considered based on the remaining class. For example, if Φ_{I} ends when tasks of class A are exhausted (i.e., $\frac{N_A}{X_A(\beta)} < \frac{N_B}{X_B(\beta)}$), the second equation in (7) must be used, since the first one is 0. Instead, if system runs out of class B tasks when Φ_{I} finishes, first equation in (7) is considered.

To derive the asymptotic depletion time of the system we use the definition previously given and we sum equations (6) and (7):

$$\begin{aligned} T(N, \alpha, \beta) &= T_1(N, \alpha, \beta) + T_2(N, \alpha, \beta) \\ &= min\left(\frac{N_A}{X_A(\beta)}, \frac{N_B}{X_B(\beta)}\right) \\ &+ \frac{N_A - min\left(\frac{N_A}{X_A(\beta)}, \frac{N_B}{X_B(\beta)}\right) X_A(\beta)}{X_A(1)} \\ &+ \frac{N_B - min\left(\frac{N_A}{X_A(\beta)}, \frac{N_B}{X_B(\beta)}\right) X_B(\beta)}{X_B(0)} \end{aligned} \tag{8}$$

We may sum both equations in (7) since one of them is null based on the exhausted class. Collecting the minimum in equation (8) we have:

$$\begin{aligned} T(N, \alpha, \beta) &= \frac{N_A}{X_A(1)} + \frac{N_B}{X_B(0)} \\ &+ min\left(\frac{N_A}{X_A(\beta)}, \frac{N_B}{X_B(\beta)}\right) \cdot \left(1 - \frac{X_A(\beta)}{X_A(1)} - \frac{X_B(\beta)}{X_B(0)}\right) \end{aligned} \tag{9}$$

Finally, due to the asymptotic assumption $N \gg K$, we divide equation (9) by the initial number of tasks in the pool:

$$\begin{aligned} \frac{T(N, \alpha, \beta)}{N} &= T(\alpha, \beta) \\ &= \frac{\alpha}{X_A(1)} + \frac{1-\alpha}{X_B(0)} \\ &+ min\left(\frac{\alpha}{X_A(\beta)}, \frac{1-\alpha}{X_B(\beta)}\right) \cdot \left(1 - \frac{X_A(\beta)}{X_A(1)} - \frac{X_B(\beta)}{X_B(0)}\right) \end{aligned} \tag{10}$$

where $N_A/N = \alpha$ and $N_B/N = 1 - \alpha$.

4.2 Relative minimum depletion time

Initially we consider a configuration where all the parameters of the system (i.e., N_A, N_B, K and the D matrix) are given by the user and only the fraction of the tasks of the two classes in the FCR (i.e., K_A and K_B) varies. Referring to equation (10), only the β value can be set by the scheduler, whereas α is given as input parameter that is kept constant. In this situation, the scheduler must search for the β value such that the depletion time computed with equation (10) is minimized.

Let us assume that the input parameters given by the user are matrix (1) and $\alpha \in [0, 1]$. The scheduler must analyze all the possible $\beta \in [0, 1]$ that can be adopted by the FCR and identify the one that minimize the depletion time. Figure 3 shows the behavior of T/N, T_1/N and T_2/N as functions of β with two values of α, 0.4 and 0.8 respectively. In Figure

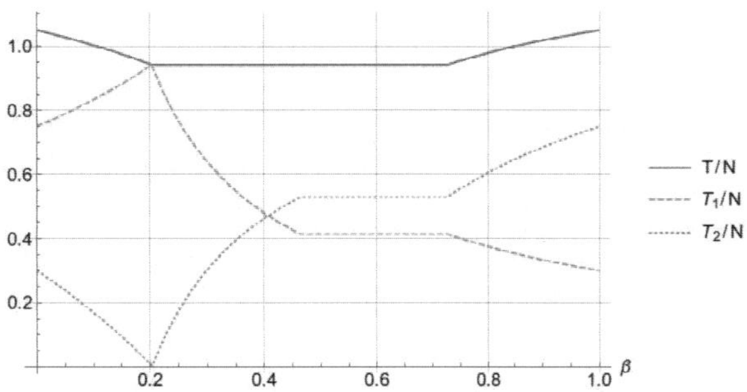

(a)

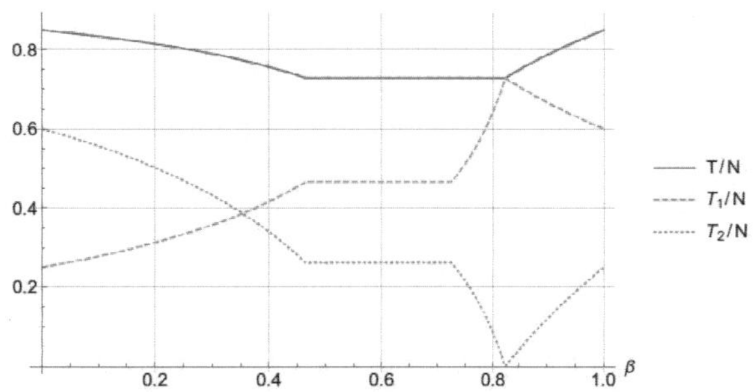

(b)

Figure 3: Asymptotic depletion time as a function of parameter β for $\alpha = 0.4$ (a) and $\alpha = 0.8$ (b).

3a T is minimum when $\beta \in [0.204, 0.725]$. The common saturation sector (CSS) [6] of the considered system (i.e., $(\beta_L, \beta_U) = (0.465, 0.725)$) is included in the interval that minimize the depletion time and both of them have the same β_U. In order to minimize T, we look for the value of β that makes the executions of all class A and class B tasks end at the same time. Let us denote such value with β^+. Thus, with β^+ we have $N_A/X_A(\beta^+) = N_B/X_B(\beta^+)$. Indeed, since the system completes the execution of both classes at the same time, we have:

$$T_1(N, \alpha, \beta) = min\left(\frac{N_A}{X_A(\beta)}, \frac{N_B}{X_B(\beta)}\right) = \frac{N_A}{X_A(\beta)} = \frac{N_B}{X_B(\beta)}$$

and $T_2 = 0$. The depletion time is minimized when $K_A/K = \beta^+$, since we defined $T = T_1 + T_2$ and T_1 and T_2 are both positive, and T_1 is maximum since it is defined as the minimum value of two functions: one of them is monotonically increasing and the other one is monotonically decreasing.

Similar considerations can be applied to results of Figure 3b. In this case, the minimum depletion time is obtained for $\beta \in [0.465, 0.824]$ and this interval is sharing its minimum value with the CSS.

It is interesting to note that when $\beta^+ < \beta_L$ (i.e., the minimum value of the CSS) the depletion time is minimum for $\beta \in [\beta^+, \beta_U]$ and if $\beta^+ > \beta_U$ (i.e., the maximum value of the CSS) the depletion time is minimum for $\beta \in [\beta_L, \beta^+]$.

As said, the value of β^+ in the asymptotic condition can be computed imposing that:

$$\frac{X_A(\beta)}{X_B(\beta)} = \frac{N_A}{N_B} \tag{11}$$

and properly using equations (4-5). In particular, if substituting equation (4) in (11) we obtain an identity, then for all the values of β in the CSS the depletion time is minimum. Otherwise, assuming that β^+ belongs to the right side of the CSS, using equation (5) and after some algebraical manipulations, we have:

$$\beta^+ = \frac{N_A D_{1A}}{N_A D_{1A} + N_B D_{1B}} \tag{12}$$

where the solution is valid only if $\beta^+ > \beta^U$. Similar equation can be derived when β^+ is on the left side of the CSS.

Since depletion time is minimum for several values of β, the scheduler can consider also other performance metrics to make better choices about the value of β to use. For example, it may consider the per-class response times shown in Figure 4. In particular, it may constraint the system to operate with the minimum T and privileging one of the two classes making its tasks exit the system faster than the tasks of the other class.

Finally, note that the minimum depletion times identified in this Section are relative to the given values of α. A more general problem is studied in next Section, where an absolute minimum is identified.

4.3 Absolute minimum depletion time

In the second problem that we study, the parameters defined by the user are the initial number of tasks N in the pool, the capacity K of the FCR, and the matrix D. In this case, the scheduler chooses the proportion of tasks both inside the FCR and in the pool. In other words, it searches for the minimum depletion time varying both parameter α and parameter β in equation (10). The scheduler operates according to the following steps: *i)* it computes the equi-utilization point $\beta^* \in [\beta_L, \beta_U]$ for the given matrix D as defined by equation (2); *ii)* it derives $X_A(\beta^*)$ and $X_B(\beta^*)$ through equations (4); *iii)* it computes the optimal initial population mix of the pool α^*. Starting from equation (11) and making some derivations we obtain:

$$1 + \frac{N_B}{N_A} = 1 + \frac{X_B(\beta^*)}{X_A(\beta^*)} \tag{13}$$

that is

$$\frac{N_A + N_B}{N_A} = \frac{X_A(\beta^*) + X_B(\beta^*)}{X_A(\beta^*)} \tag{14}$$

and inverting equation (14):

$$\alpha^* = \frac{X_A(\beta^*)}{X_A(\beta^*) + X_B(\beta^*)} \tag{15}$$

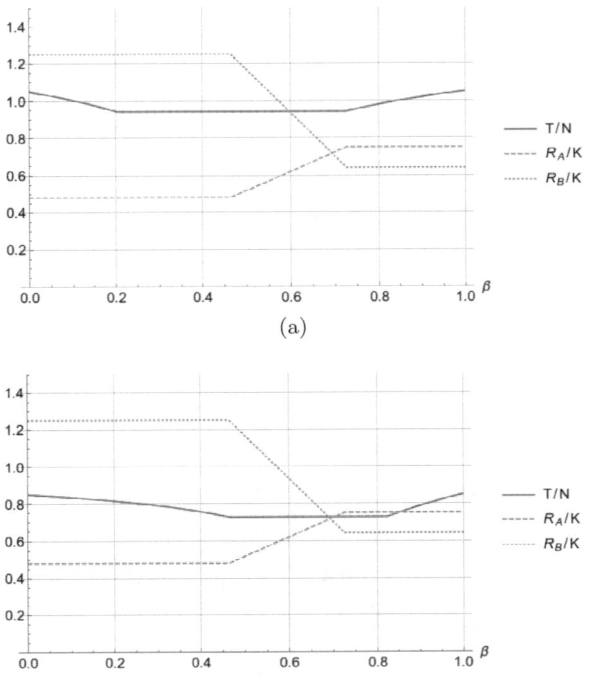

(a)

(b)

Figure 4: Depletion time and asymptotic response time as a function of β for $\alpha = 0.4$ (a) and $\alpha = 0.8$ (b).

since $\alpha^* = N_A/N$; *iv)* it forces the system work with $N_A/N = \alpha^*$ and with any number of tasks in the FCR such that $K_A/K \in [\beta_L, \beta_U]$.

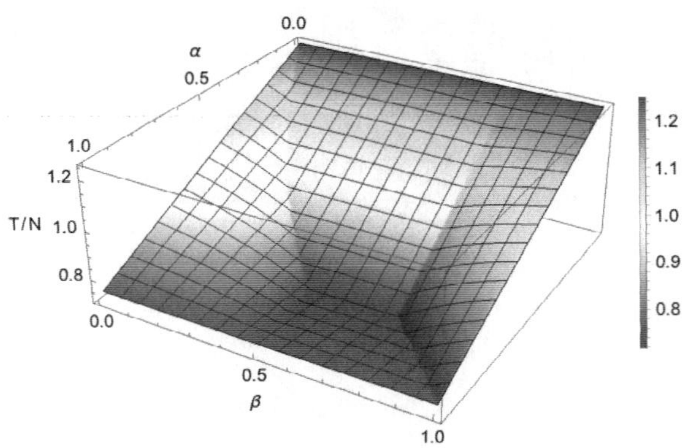

Figure 5: Depletion time as a function of α and β.

Figure 5 represents depletion time as a function of α and β, and matrix (1) has been used for the service demands of the system. It shows that an absolute minimum can be find in α^* (i.e., 0.693 for the given matrix) and for any value of $\beta \in [0.465, 0.725]$, that is, the CSS for the matrix in equation (1). If $\alpha \neq \alpha^*$ it is only possible to find a relative minimum depletion time, as seen in Section 4.2.

We also compute the gain G of the system as a function of α. It is the percentage of saved time using the best $\mathbf{K}$ – defined as $(\beta K, (1-\beta)K))$ – in the FCR for the considered value of α. The maximum and the minimum depletion times for each value of the variable α have been collected and the gain has been computed as:

$$G = \frac{T_{max} - T_{min}}{T_{min}} \tag{16}$$

Figure 6 shows the gain of the system for different proportions of the tasks in the pool, when it works with a value of β that minimizes depletion time. The system achieves the largest G when it works with α^*.

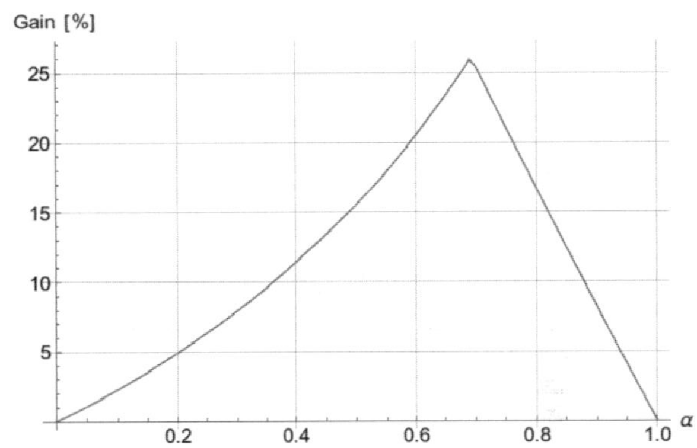

Figure 6: Gain of the system for different values of α, when it works with the best value of β.

5. NON-ASYMPTOTIC RESULTS

When the assumptions of the asymptotic results are not satisfied, the system have a slightly different behavior. In order to study the system in non-asymptotic regime, we perform both analytical evaluation using technique presented in [3], and discrete event simulation using the *JMT: Java Modeling Tool* [2]. The main differences from the asymptotic behavior come from the fact that the transient durations $T_{\tau 0}$, $T_{\tau 12} - T_{\Phi 1}$ and $T - T_{\Phi 2}$ are not negligible with respect to the total depletion time T.

5.1 Simulation model

In order to study the system under configurations with $N \gg 0$ or $K \gg 0$ that would have led to state space sizes for which the analytical technique could have not been applied, we have performed discrete event simulation using a specifically patched version of JMT. The system has been modeled by the fork/join queuing network shown in Figure 7. The model has just one job, starting in the delay station `Delay` with zero service time: the purpose of this node is to provide the reference station for computing throughput and response time, and to restart the system after one execution run. This job is immediately split into N_A class A tasks and N_B class B tasks by the fork node named `Fork`. The same node produces also one class C task, which acts as a marker to allow us to compute the duration of phase Φ_{I} in a simulation run. The job finishes when all tasks rejoins into the originating job in node `Join`. The two resources are modeled by nodes `Res 1` and `Res 2`, that act as single server processor sharing queues with exponential service times characterized by demands D_{1A}, D_{1B}, D_{2A} and D_{2B}. The service time for the marker class C is zero in both stations. The policy of the scheduler is implemented in a patched version of the finite capacity region that includes both resources. In particular, we have modified the admission policy inside FCR to: *i)* allow at most K_A and K_B jobs if there are still some jobs of both classes waiting to be served in the FCR queue (phase Φ_{I}); *ii)* allow at most K jobs if one class as finished its jobs (phase Φ_{II}); *iii)* let the marker class C task enter and pass through the system when phase Φ_{I} is ended. The average system response time corresponds to the depletion time T, and the average waiting time of the class C task in the queue of the FCR defines $T_{\Phi 1}$, the total length of phase Φ_{I}.

5.2 Validation

In order to validate the results, a continuous-time Markov chain (CTMC) of the depletion system has been developed to compare the values obtained for the depletion time with those obtained by the simulator described in Section 5.1. In the CTMC the state of the system is described by a tuple counting for each class the current number of tasks in the pool, in station Res_1 and in station Res_2. The completions of tasks change the system state and are represented in the CTMC as transitions from a value of the tuple to another. Assuming that all such events follow an exponential distribution, the whole state space of the system is built and the resulting CTMC can be analysed by standard numerical techniques. In particular, the depletion time and the duration of each phase, including the transient ones, are analytically computed through absorption time analysis. Further details can be found in [3] and [5].

The analytic analysis of the CTMC suffers of the the well-known state explosion problem: large values of K makes the resulting state space grow exponentially, thus making the solution computationally unfeasible. For such reasons, we restrict the validation to scenarios with small values of K, in particular we compared the two models for different configurations with $N = 100$ and $K = 10$. With 99% confidence intervals and 3% maximum relative error the measures obtained through simulation fit those obtained with the stochastic model.

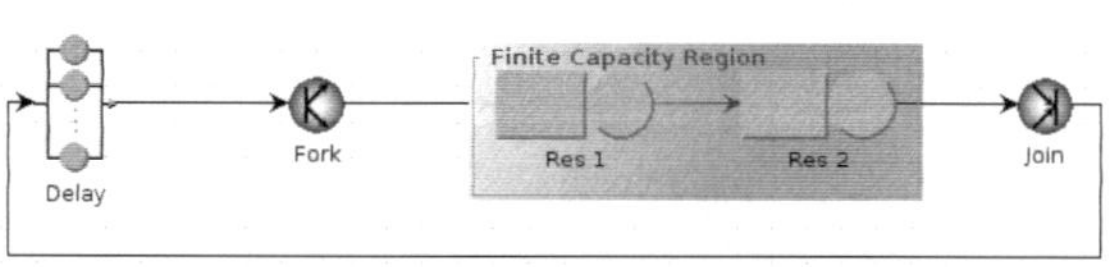

Figure 7: JMT model of the considered system.

5.3 Depletion times in non-asymptotic condition

In order to study the behavior of system in non-asymptotic regime, in this Section we use different finite values for N and K (e.g., $(N, K) = \{(100, 10),$ $(1000, 10), (1000, 100), (2000, 200)\}$). When we need to choose a value for α, we assume user is passing the closest value to α^*. For the system with matrix (1) $\alpha^* = 0.693$, as computed in Section 4.3. Let us call that system *System1*. We also analyze another system with two resources and two classes and the following service demands:

$$\mathbf{D} = \begin{bmatrix} 0.8 & 0.496 \\ 0.2 & 1.25 \end{bmatrix} \qquad (17)$$

With equation (15) we derive $\alpha^* = 0.557$ for the second system, *System2*.

First of all, we study the non-asymptotic version of the *relative minimum* problem presented in Section 4.2. Figure 8 shows the length of each phase for both the systems when $N = 100$ and $K = 10$. *System1* has been analyzed for $\mathbf{N} = (70, 30)$, whereas *System2* for $\mathbf{N} = (55, 45)$. In both cases all possible $\mathbf{K}$ are taken into consideration. Note that, the sum of all the phases is the depletion time, and it is also represented in that figure. *System1* has the minimum

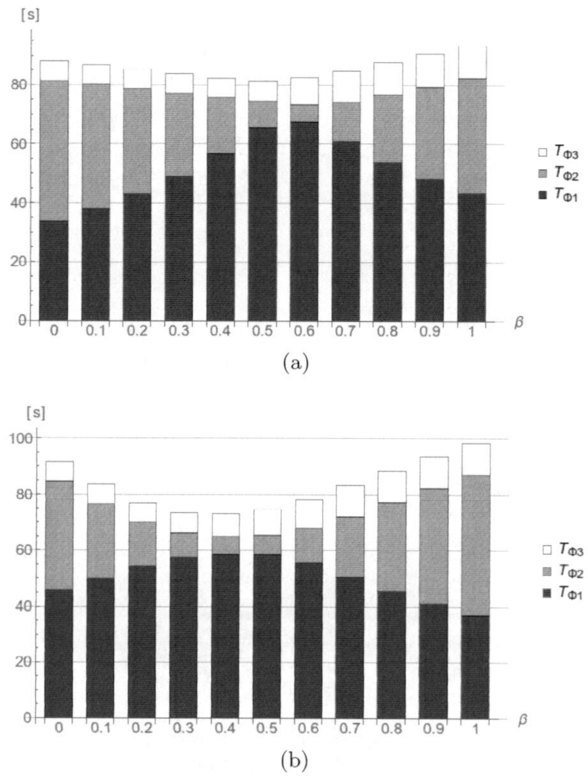

Figure 8: Length of each phase and of depletion time for *System1* when $\alpha = 0.7$ (a) and *System2* when $\alpha = 0.55$ (b).

depletion time for $\beta = 0.5$, whereas the maximum $T_{\Phi 1}$ is for $\beta = 0.6$. We have that discrepancy since now N is not asymptotically bigger than K. For this reason, transient phases (i.e., $T_{\tau 0}$, $T_{\tau 12}$ and $T_{\Phi 3}$) are now not negligible and they may affect the general system behavior. Nevertheless, this difference with respect to the asymptotic regime is not seen in all the systems. For example, in *System2* both the minimum T and the maximum $T_{\Phi 1}$ are measured for $\beta = 0.4$.

We also study the non-asymptotic behavior of the *absolute minimum* problem. For this purpose we derive β^* for both the systems (i.e., $\beta^* = 0.6$ for *System1* and $\beta^* = 0.4$ for *System2*). Then we vary α, looking for the one that make the system empty in the shortest time. The results are shown in Figure 9. Differently from the asymptotic behavior, for both

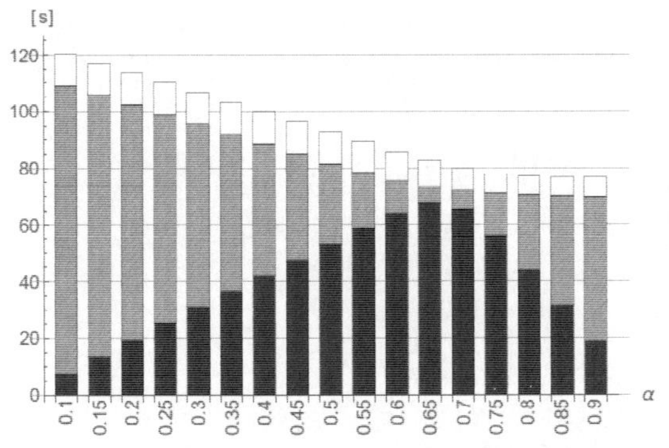

(a)

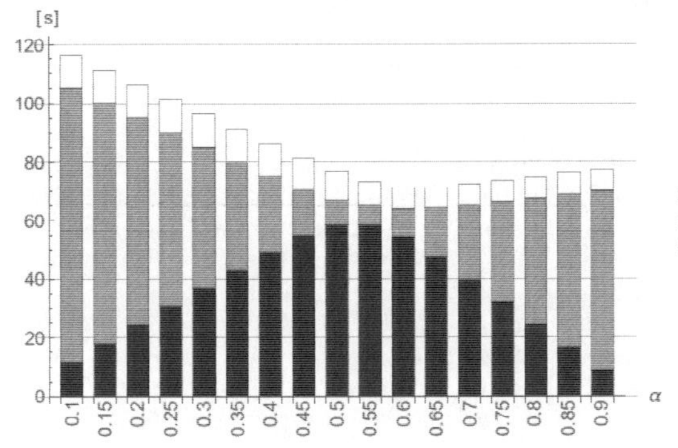

(b)

Figure 9: Length of each phase and of depletion time for *System1* when $\beta = 0.6$ (a) and *System2* when $\beta = 0.4$ (b).

the considered systems the minimum depletion time is not measured in α^*. In particular, *System1* has the minimum T for $\alpha = 0.90$, and *System2* has its minimum depletion time for $\alpha = 0.65$. Also the maximum $T_{\Phi 1}$ of the two systems is not measured for α^*, even if in both cases they are closer to the asymptotic optimal than the minimum T (i.e., $\alpha = 0.65$ for *System1* and $\alpha = 0.5$ for *System2*).

Due to the discrepancies found in previous results with respect to what has been shown in Section 4, we analyze the percentage error done by the scheduler when it uses asymptotic strategies for non-asymptotic regime. It is computed for different values of α and for the β chosen by the scheduler. The percentage error is defined as:

$$Error = \frac{|T_{min} - T_{estimated}|}{T_{min}} \tag{18}$$

where T_{min} is the real minimum value of the depletion time that can be reached with the passed parameters, and $T_{estimated}$ is the depletion time that is reached using the scheduler. For both the systems, error is never larger than 5% and for several values the asymptotic strategy used by the scheduler makes the system empty in the shortest time and the percentage error is 0%.

Also the gain in using the scheduler has been studied. In

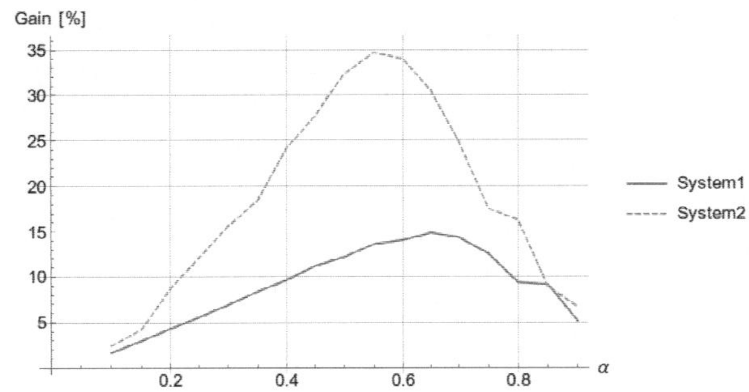

Figure 10: System gain when the scheduler is used to work with the best population mix in non-asymptitic regime.

the non-asymptotic case, it is computed as:

$$G = \frac{T_{max} - T_{estimated}}{T_{estimated}} \tag{19}$$

Results are shown in Figure 10 for both the systems as a function of α, when the β is chosen by the scheduler. *System2* has a greater gain in using the scheduler than *System1*. It depends on the service demands of the resources. Furthermore, comparing the asymptotic gain presented in Figure 6 with the non-asymptotic one for *System1* in Figure 10, we see that in asymptotic regime we have a greater gain for the same values of α. It is due both to the error done by the scheduler in a non-asymptotic regime and to the differences between the asymptotic and the non-asymptotic behaviors described at the beginning of Section 5.

Finally, in Figure 11 results obtained through simulation are shown. Here, we considered three different configurations of *System1*: $(N, K) = \{(1000, 10), (1000, 100), (2000, 200)\}$ when $\alpha = 0.7$. The confidence interval of each measure is 99% and the maximum relative error is 3%. Confidence intervals are shown in the graph. From these results we note that the larger is K, the flatter is the optimal region (i.e., the interval for which the depletion time is minimum). Indeed, if the FCR size is larger, then the system can saturate. This result supports our initial decision in considering asymptotic behavior of the system, and we expect that the larger is the value of K, the lower will be the error done by the scheduler. Since the simulation time for configuration $(N, K) = (2000, 200)$ was long, we focused only on the most interesting values of β.

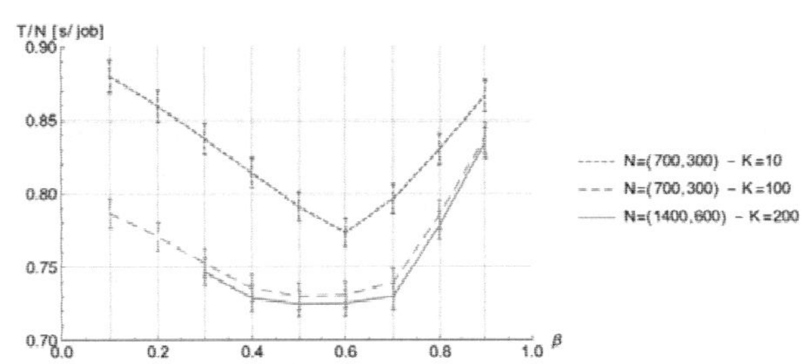

Figure 11: Simulation of different configurations of *System1* as a function of β.

5.4 Computation of the optimal class mix β

As we have seen in Section 5.3, we have verified that an appropriate choice of $\beta = \beta^+$, $K_A = \beta K$ and $K_B = (1-\beta)K$ is the one for which:

$$\frac{X_A(\beta)}{N_A} \approx \frac{X_B(\beta)}{N_B} \qquad (20)$$

This is because, when $\frac{X_A(\beta)}{N_A} = \frac{X_B(\beta)}{N_B}$ the length of phase Φ_{II} tends to zero, minimizing the effects of the transients. In the following we will see two techniques for determining β depending on the concurrent execution capacity K of the system.

If K is of moderate size (say $K < 100$), we can find β^+ in quadratic time complexity $O(K^2)$, and linear space complexity $O(K)$ using a modified version of the Mean Value Analysis (MVA) algorithm for multi-class models [4]. In particular, we can insert the exhaustive search of β^+ in the MVA algorithm, and re-use the measurements of the system performances when working with one job less to compute the throughput for all the values of β at the same time. The algorithm is sketched in 1.

Algorithm 1 Modified MVA algorithm to determine β

1: $Q_1[0][0] \leftarrow 0,\ Q_2[0][0] \leftarrow 0,\ \ldots,\ Q_M[0][0] \leftarrow 0$
2: $d \leftarrow \infty$,
3: **for** $k \leftarrow 1$ *to* K **do**
4:   **for** $k_A \leftarrow 0$ *to* k **do**
5:     $k_B \leftarrow k - k_A$,
6:     **for** $r \leftarrow 1$ *to* M **do**
7:       $R_{rA} \leftarrow D_{rA}\,(1 + Q_r[k_A - 1][k_B])$
8:       $R_{rB} \leftarrow D_{rB}\,(1 + Q_r[k_A][k_B - 1])$
9:     **end for**
10:     **for** $c \in \{A, B\}$ **do**
11:       $X_c \leftarrow \dfrac{k_c}{\sum_i^M R_{ic}}$
12:     **end for**
13:     **for** $r \leftarrow 1$ *to* M **do**
14:       $Q_r[k_A][k_B] \leftarrow \sum_{c\in\{A,B\}} R_{rc} \cdot X_c$,
15:     **end for**
16:     **if** $\left|\frac{N_A}{X_A} - \frac{N_B}{X_B}\right| < d \wedge k = K$ **then**
17:       $\beta^+ \leftarrow \frac{k_A}{K},\quad d \leftarrow \left|\frac{N_A}{X_A} - \frac{N_B}{X_B}\right|$,
18:     **end if**
19:   **end for**
20: **end for**

Lines 1-2 initialize the average queue length for the two resources Res_1 and Res_2 for the empty system, and the current measure of equality d for $\frac{N_A}{X_A}$ and $\frac{N_B}{X_B}$ to ∞. As for standard MVA, loops in lines 3-5 cycles respectively on the total population k, and on the class A population k_A, defining the corresponding class B population to $k_B = k - k_A$. Loop 6 computes the average residence time R_{rc} for each resource r and class c. Then the throughput X_c for each class c is computed in loop 10, and the average number of jobs in the stations for the current task population $Q_r[k_A][k_B]$ is computed in loop 13. When the total population K is reached, lines 16-18 updates the current values of β and d, if the considered class mix provides a better approximation for equation (20).

If $K \gg 0$, we can use the same approximation used in Section 2 to determine the throughputs $X_A(\beta)$ and $X_B(\beta)$, and find the β that satisfy equation (20). In particular, from equations (3-5) and (20), we have:

$$\beta^+ \approx \begin{cases} \frac{N_A D_{2A}}{N_A D_{2A} + N_B D_{2B}} & if\ N_B X_A^{CSS} > N_A X_B^{CSS} \\ \forall \beta \in [\beta^L, \beta^U] & if\ N_B X_A^{CSS} = N_A X_B^{CSS} \\ \frac{N_A D_{1A}}{N_A D_{1A} + N_B D_{1B}} & if\ N_B X_A^{CSS} < N_A X_B^{CSS} \end{cases} \qquad (21)$$

where the conditions specify the position of β^+ with respect to the CSS.

6. CONCLUSIONS

In this paper we have considered the problem of determining an optimal scheduling algorithm that can reduce total time required to execute a job composed of a set of tasks belonging to two different classes, by simply determining how many task per class initially allow to be concurrently executed. We have proven that this simple policy can obtain gains in the order of 30%.
Future works will extend the model to include multiple servers resource: this will allow to use the proposed framework to optimize data analytics applications based on frameworks such as Apache Spark, in which a job is split into a large number of tasks that are concurrently executed in parallel on a number of nodes. Other studies will focus on the analysis of the impact of the proposed scheduling technique on other important metrics such as power consumption.

Acknowledgment. This work was partially funded by the European Commission under the grant ANTAREX H2020 FET-HPC-671623.

7. REFERENCES

[1] F. Baskett, K. M. Chandy, R. R. Muntz, and F. G. Palacios. Open, closed, and mixed networks of queues with different classes of customers. *J. ACM*, 22(2):248–260, Apr. 1975.

[2] M. Bertoli, G. Casale, and G. Serazzi. Jmt: performance engineering tools for system modeling. *SIGMETRICS Perform. Eval. Rev.*, 36(4):10–15, 2009.

[3] D. Cerotti, M. Gribaudo, R. Pinciroli, and G. Serazzi. Stochastic analysis of energy consumption in pool depletion systems. In *Measurement, Modelling and Evaluation of Dependable Computer and Communication Systems - 18th International GI/ITG Conference, MMB & DFT 2016, Münster, Germany, April 4-6, 2016, Proceedings*, pages 25–39, 2016.

[4] E. D. Lazowska, J. Zahorjan, G. S. Graham, and K. C. Sevcik. *Quantitative System Performance.* Prentice-Hall, 1984.

[5] J. Muppala, M. Malhotra, and K. Trivedi. Markov dependability models of complex systems: Analysis techniques. In S. Ozekici, editor, *Reliability and Maintenance of Complex Systems*, volume 154, pages 442–486. Springer Berlin Heidelberg, 1996.

[6] E. Rosti, F. Schiavoni, and G. Serazzi. Queueing network models with two classes of customers. In *Modeling, Analysis, and Simulation of Computer and Telecommunication Systems, 1997. MASCOTS'97., Proc. Fifth Int. Symp. on*, pages 229–234. IEEE, 1997.

Coordinated charging strategies for plug-in electric vehicles to ensure a robust charging process

Jannik Hüls
Westfälische Wilhelms-Universität Münster
Institute of Mathematics and Computer Science
Münster, Germany
jannik.huels@uni-muenster.de

Anne Remke
Westfälische Wilhelms-Universität Münster
Institute of Mathematics and Computer Science
Münster, Germany
anne.remke@uni-muenster.de

ABSTRACT

Charging of plug-in electric vehicles is expected to heavily increase the load of the electric grid. Therefore coordinated charging strategies are proposed to facilitate a flexible charging process that may be delayed to a time when e.g. extra energy is available. The expected recurrence time of the client and the maximum speed of the charging process implicitly determine the latest possible time to start charging. This paper proposes a simple Hybrid Petri net (HPnG) model that implements a charging station based on a predicted recurrence time of the client. The impact of coordinated charging on the client is investigated by comparing three different charging strategies: (i) Immediate, (ii) Considerate and (iii) Just-in-time. Recent algorithms for model-checking HPnGs are used to compute the probability that the charging processes is finished upon the arrival of the client. This ensures that the client's charging requirements do not suffer from the created flexibility. We show that the proposed model may be used to identify system parameters for coordinated charging even though the recurrence time is not exactly known.

Keywords

Electric vehicles; Robust Coordinated charging; Hybrid Petri Nets; Stochastic Model Checking

1. INTRODUCTION

The power demand of plug-in electric vehicles (PEVs) is expected to have a huge impact on the stability of the power grid [8]. As shown in [5] PEVs cause a high power demand during their charging process. Therefore grid-coordinated charging may be used to relieve the grid. Hereby, the charging process can be delayed and started when the grid is less stressed. As motivated in [9] the available battery capacity may be used as a buffer for frequency regulation. Provided the right incentives are offered to the use, the battery may be charged from the grid (G2V) or discharged to the grid (V2G) to help maintain the appropriate frequency.

VALUETOOLS 2016, October 25-28, Taormina, Italy

Recent work mainly focuses on the optimization of coordinated charging strategies. Refs. [10, 2] investigate the optimal charge profile by minimizing power losses. They use stochastic programming to incorporate the stochastic nature of load forecasts. Optimal schedules, based on time-varying prices and target profile, for charging PEVs are introduced in [11]. Ref. [7] presents optimal strategies w.r.t. the clients' requirements. The authors extend the so-called PowerMatcher to provide long-term demand and price predictions. They are able to formulate and solve an optimal short-term bidding strategy minimizing the clients costs. However, to the best of our knowledge, none of these papers take the stochastic nature of clients recurrence times into account. Ref. [12] considers a delay-optimal charging station with multiple charging points. The uncertainty of the arrival of the EV, the intermittence of the renewable energy and the variation of the grid power price are modeled as a Markov process. They aim at minimizing the mean waiting time under the long-term constraint on the power costs. A charging system comparable to the one proposed within this paper is presented in [6]. The authors present a real-time scheduling strategy that minimizes impacts on the power grid and guarantees the satisfaction of the client's charging requirements.

We use Hybrid Petri nets with a single general one-shot transition (HPnGs) [4] to model a charging station. Once a client arrives at the station he chooses (i) whether to charge the PEV immediately or (ii) whether to allow for coordinated charging. The recurrence time can either be specified by the client or estimated by the system, e.g. from the location of the charging system and known usage patterns. Nevertheless, the actual recurrence time may differ, hence a random variable is used to model the time until recurrence. In this paper we investigate the impact of coordinated charging strategies on the charging experience of the client, i.e. the *robustness* of the charging process. For now we do not take into account the load of the grid. Instead, the presented model can be used to investigate in how far the charging process can facilitate a coordinated use without affecting the robustness of the charging process. Moreover, we are able to obtain charging system parameters that satisfy clients' requirements even though the recurrence time may vary from the expected time.

The paper is further organized as follows: Section 2 introduces the charging station and explains the parameter choices. The initial Hybrid Petri net model is shown in Section 3. Section 4 recalls the measure of interest. Results are presented in Section 5 before Section 6 concludes the paper.

2. CHARGING STATION

Coordinated charging has recently been enabled by strongly increasing charging rates, which allow to delay the charging process until a time at which the grid is less stressed and to still charge the battery in time. We use data from Tesla[1] PEVs and charging infrastructure for the model parameter setup. As presented in [1] there are three different charging stations available that differ in the maximum charging rate: (i) *Home* charger, (ii) *Public* charger and (iii) *Supercharger*. The latter provides charging rates up to 120kW and hence is well-suited to be used for a charging strategy that allows a grid-coordinated use. A PEV's battery cannot be charged with maximum rate at all times, its rate depends on the current State-Of-Charge (SOC) and on external influences, e.g. heat. In this first approach we approximate the slope of the charging rate, based on the facts gathered from [1], with a granularity of 10 minutes.

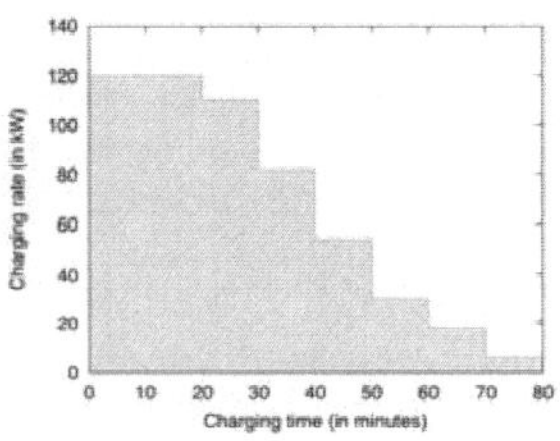

Figure 1: Charging rate

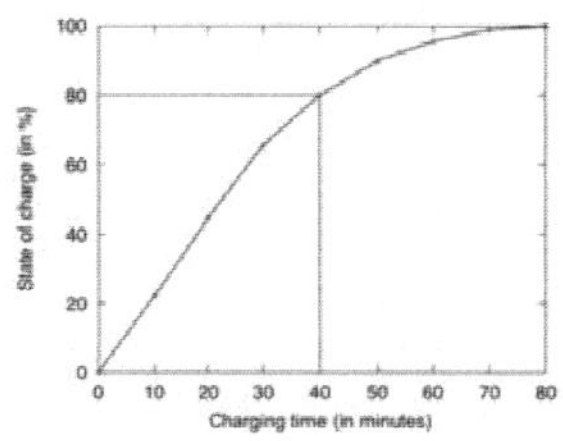

Figure 2: State of charge

Figure 1 shows the available charging rates for a Tesla Model S having a battery capacity of 90kWh. The maximum available charging rate decreases with increasing charging time due to external influences like heat, voltage level and state of charge (SOC). Figure 2 shows the resulting SOC of the PEV's battery. Note that it takes almost the same time to charge the last 20% and the first 80% of the battery.

Figure 3 presents a schematic overview of the components that are involved in the charging process. Once a *Plugin Electric Vehicle* arrives at the *Charging Station* a client is able to select in the *GUI* whether or not coordinated strategies should be used. According to the chosen strategy, the *Charging Station Controller* determines the charging process and how to use the *Power Sources*. The client is able to choose three different strategies: (i) *Immediate* charging starts charging immediately with the highest possible charging rate. (ii) *Considerate* and (iii) *Just-in-time* facilitate coordinated charging. The process is delayed based on the predicted recurrence time. Just-in-time tries to maximize the flexibility within the charging process and aims at finishing exactly at the expected recurrence time. Since the robustness may suffer, Considerate charging includes a safety margin and finishes before the client is expected to return. Figure 4 illustrates the possible SOC for the three different charging strategies. The battery is always charged immediately up to a certain minimum state of charge (`msoc`) to expand battery lifetime and preserve power for frequency regulation. Note that since it can be difficult to specify the starting time for the Considerate strategy we use a model to identify system parameters that guarantee a robust charging process, i.e., the battery is charged up to the SOC that is expected by the customer upon its return.

[1] http://www.teslamotors.com

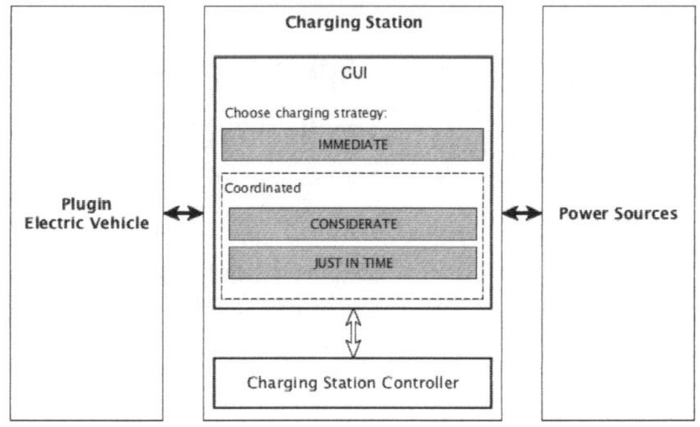

Figure 3: Schema of the charging station.

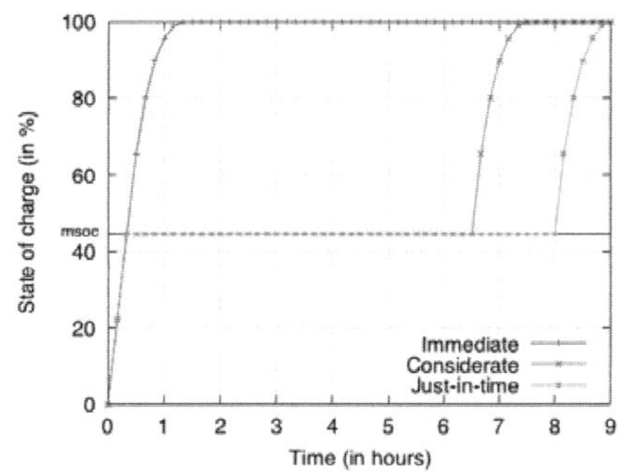

Figure 4: SOC of the three charging strategies.

3. MODEL OF THE CHARGING PROCESS

We use a Hybrid Petri Net with one general one shot transition, as introduced in [4], to model the *Charging Process*. The HPnG formalism is suitable, since we only need one general transition to model the recurrence of the client. Furthermore the system consists of a hybrid part to model the battery and a discrete part to control the system state. We approximated charging to a process with piece-wise deterministic rates to fit the HPnG formalism. Figure 5 shows an abstracted HPnG model of the charging process. The charging station is for example operated by a company and possibly powered with solar energy. We consider a setup in which a client charges the PEV during working hours, hence the general transition follows a normal distribution and is parametrized with mean μ = 9hours and varying standard deviations σ to model the variance in the duration of a working day. Charging is only possible as long as the client has not unplugged the vehicle from the charging station, i.e., the discrete place *loading* contains a token. *Battery Management* controls the flow of power, depending on the charging strategy. The model distinguishes three states of the battery, it can either be *full*, *good* or *empty*. In state *full*, G2V interaction is possible, since the battery is completely charged. The *Charging Station Controller* consists of the *G2V Controller* as well as the *V2G Controller* which are used to gather system information to regulate the charging and discharging process. Note that we focus on G2V within this paper, since adaptive V2G interaction would require a model that is able to reflect the state of the grid (e.g. voltage and frequency) to decide when the grid should be relieved.

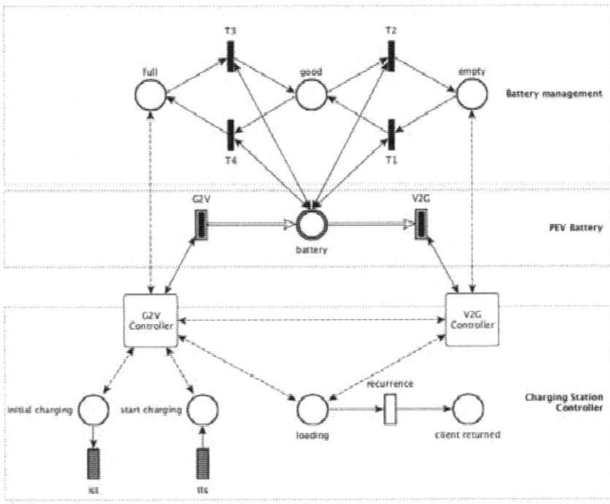

Figure 5: HPnG model of the Charging Station.

The deterministic transitions *immediate charging time* (*ict*) and *time to charge completely* (*ttc*) control the system in a time-based fashion. The *ict* is used to model the immediate charging up to the battery level *msoc*. The transition *ttc* determines the latest point in time at which the system has to start the remaining charging process.

4. MEASURE OF INTEREST

The presented charging strategies need to balance the interests of the grid-operator and the clients' interests. The first profits from a flexible battery use that is possible with coordinated charging whereas the latter requires the battery to be fully charged (if possible) when he returns. Note that the flexible battery use (`fbu`) that results from a delayed charging process with coordinated charging is a deterministic measure and can be obtained from simple computations or simulations and is not further investigated in this paper. In contrast we focus on the robustness of the charging process, which is a probabilistic measure that highly depends on the parametrization of the general transition. The robustness of the charging process describes the probability that the PEV is charged at least up to the expected SOC `esoc` when the client returns. This can be specified formally, using the so-called until operator of Stochastic Time Logic (STL) [3]:

$$\texttt{robustness} = \texttt{loading} \;\; \mathcal{U}^{[0,t]} \;\; (\texttt{battery} \geq \texttt{esoc}). \quad (1)$$

This formula holds, when the battery is charged up to at least `esoc` within t time units until the client returned, i.e. place loading contains no token any longer. In this setting the time bound t corresponds to the maximum model execution time. We use $t = 14$ hours in our example setup hence we assume that employees are not allowed to stay longer than 14 hours at work.

5. RESULTS

This section presents results obtained from the analysis of the presented Hybrid Petri net model. We investigate (i) the impact of the Just-in-time strategy on the robustness and (ii) obtain the latest possible starting time for the Considerate strategy, which still ensures robustness.

Immediate charging and Just-in-time charging represent the best and worst case scenario, respectively. The first maximizes the robustness and does not facilitate grid-coordination, whereas the latter results in a very low robustness but is expected to provide a high flexibility for grid-coordination. Figure 6 compares the robustness probability of the Immediate and Just-in-time strategy for different standard deviations σ, i.e. expected inaccuracy of the predicted recurrence time. Due to its very early charging time the robustness of Immediate charging only suffers for very high values of σ. The robustness probability of Just-in-time charging drops to 0.5 very quickly. Hence it is not suitable in case of potentially imprecise recurrence time predictions.

As mentioned above Just-in-time charging performs worse when the distribution of the general transition shows a high standard deviation. The Considerate strategy may be used to obtain a better compromise between flexible battery use and robustness. We assess possible starting time parameters and compare Just-in-time with the chosen Considerate one. Figure 7 shows the robustness probability for Considerate charging with different completion times. The different graphs correspond to completion times $t \in [0, 120]$ minutes before the expected recurrence time, which increases the robustness of the considerate strategy. Especially for deviation values smaller than 30 minutes Considerate charging performs much better than the Just-in-time strategy.

Whenever a client chooses Considerate or Just-in-time charging it is likely that the battery is not charged completely in case the client returns early. However, he may be reimbursed for the use of the battery and therefore accept slight disadvantages. Figure 8 compares the probability that the battery is charged at least to a specified percentage for the Considerate and Just-in-time strategy. We use standard deviation values of 0, 30, 60 and 90 minutes to compare the two strategies. The Just-in-time strategy suffers largely for high deviation of 60 and 90 minutes. All other strategies have a probability larger than 0.9 that the battery is charged up to at least 90%. It can be seen that it is relatively expensive to ensure a completely charged battery in case any form of a delayed charging strategy is used.

6. CONCLUSION

This paper proposes a Hybrid Petri net model that implements a PEV Charging Station process. The case study shows that the model is suitable to investigate system parameters for charging stations that introduce delayed charging, based on a predicted recurrence time, to facilitate grid-coordination. We have investigated the robustness probability of three different strategies. (i) Immediate charging, (ii) Considerate charging and (iii) Just-in-time charging. The last two facilitate grid-coordination and therefore contribute to a more stable grid. We have seen that the Considerate strategy which finishes charging some time before the expected recurrence time offers a good trade-off between possible coordination and robustness. Its robustness (c.f. Eq.1) is larger than 0.95 for all standard deviations up to 60 minutes. Note that the Just-in-time strategy results in the lowest the robustness probabilities. In a real-world system the Just-in-time strategy would only be used in case the grid is highly loaded all the time the PEV should be charged. As soon as the grid is less stressed it would advise the charging station to charge the car according to the coordinated charging policy. This initial model does not take the grid's

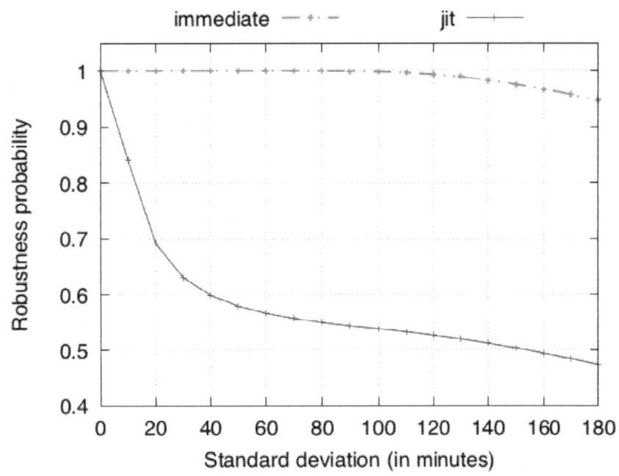

Figure 6: Probability that charging is robust for Immediate and Just-in-time and several standard deviations.

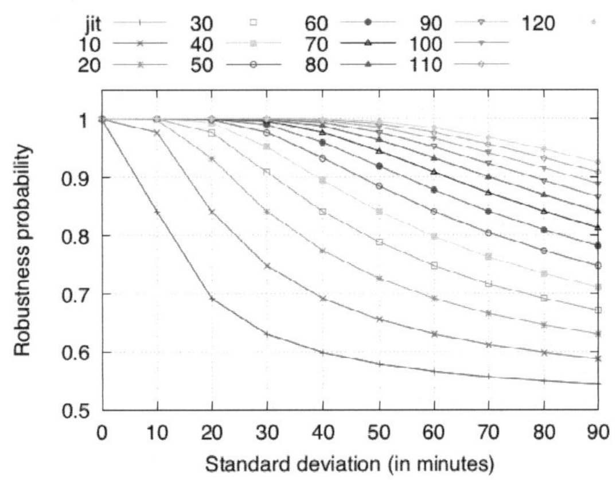

Figure 7: Probability that charging is robust for Considerate, several standard deviations and times to complete.

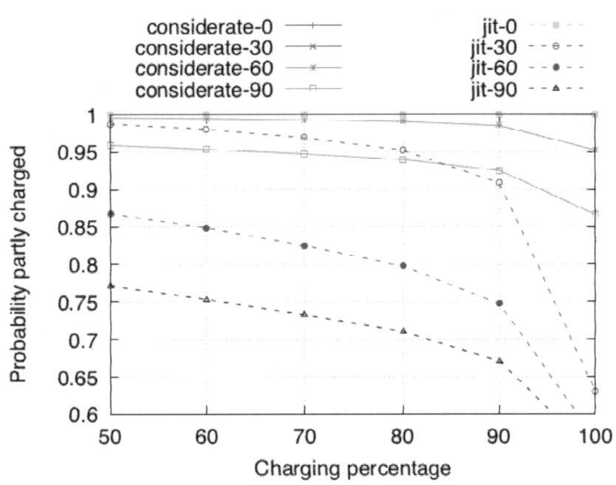

Figure 8: Probability that battery is charged up to a certain percentage for Considerate and Just-in-time.

load into account and while we are able to illustrate possible implementations of coordinated charging strategies, a more realistic model would include actual loading data. Then the static behavior of the presented model could be improved such that is adapts the chosen strategy based on the grids load. Furthermore we focused on charging (G2V) the PEV. Therefore another improvement would be to introduce the extension of discharging the PEV (V2G).

7. REFERENCES

[1] Tesla supercharger: 2016. https://www.teslamotors.com/supercharger, 2016.

[2] K. Clement, E. Haesen, and J. Driesen. Coordinated charging of multiple plug-in hybrid electric vehicles in residential distribution grids. In *Power Systems Conference and Exposition*, pages 1–7. IEEE, 2009.

[3] H. Ghasemieh, A. Remke, and B. R. Haverkort. Survivability evaluation of fluid critical infrastructures using Hybrid Petri nets. In *Pacific Rim Int. Symp. on Dependable Computing (PRDC)*, pages 152–161. IEEE, 2013.

[4] M. Gribaudo and A. Remke. Hybrid Petri nets with general one-shot transitions for dependability evaluation of fluid critical infrastructures. In *High-Assurance Systems Engineering (HASE)*, pages 84–93. IEEE, 2010.

[5] G. Hoogsteen, A. Molderink, J. L. Hurink, G. J. Smit, F. Schuring, and B. K. Liandon. Impact of peak electricity demand in distribution grids: a stress test. In *PowerTech*, pages 1–6. IEEE, 2015.

[6] J. Kang, S. J. Duncan, and D. N. Mavris. Real-time scheduling techniques for electric vehicle charging in support of frequency regulation. *Procedia Computer Science*, 16:767–775, 2013.

[7] P. Kempker, N. v. Dijk, W. Scheinhardt, H. v. d. Berg, and J. Hurink. Optimization of charging strategies for electric vehicles in powermatcher-driven smart energy grids. In *Int. Conf. on Performance Evaluation Methodologies and Tools*, pages 242–249, 2016.

[8] R. Liu, L. Dow, and E. Liu. A survey of PEV impacts on electric utilities. In *Innovative Smart Grid Technologies*, pages 1–8. IEEE, 2011.

[9] N. Nigro. Plug-in electric vehicles could help the grid: Prospects with frequency regulation: 2010, howpublished=https://goo.gl/d0hbmg.

[10] E. Sortomme, M. M. Hindi, S. J. MacPherson, and S. Venkata. Coordinated charging of plug-in hybrid electric vehicles to minimize distribution system losses. *IEEE Transactions on Smart Grid*, 2(1):198–205, 2011.

[11] T. van der Klauw, M. E. Gerards, G. J. Smit, and J. L. Hurink. Optimal scheduling of electrical vehicle charging under two types of steering signals. In *Innovative Smart Grid Technologies, Europe*, pages 1–6. IEEE, 2014.

[12] T. Zhang, W. Chen, Z. Han, and Z. Cao. Charging scheduling of electric vehicles with local renewable energy under uncertain electric vehicle arrival and grid power price. *IEEE Transactions on Vehicular Technology*, 63(6):2600–2612, 2014.

Simulation from the Normal Distribution Truncated to an Interval in the Tail

Zdravko Botev
University of New South Wales
High Street, Kensington
Sydney, NSW 2052, Australia
http://web.maths.unsw.edu.au/~zdravkobotev

Pierre L'Ecuyer
DIRO, Université de Montréal
Montréal, Canada;
and Inria–Rennes, France
http://www.iro.umontreal.ca/~lecuyer

ABSTRACT

We study and compare various methods to generate a random variate from the normal distribution truncated to some finite or semi-infinite interval, with special attention to the situation where the interval is far in the tail. This is required in particular for certain applications in Bayesian statistics, such as to perform exact posterior simulations for parameter inference, but could have many other applications as well. We distinguish the case in which inversion is warranted, and that in which a rejection method is also fine. The algorithms are implemented and available in Java, R, and MATLAB, and the software is freely available.

CCS Concepts

•**Mathematics of computing → Distribution functions; Probabilistic algorithms; Statistical software;**

Keywords

Truncated normal, normal quantile, random variate generation, inversion, exact sampling

1. INTRODUCTION

We consider the problem of generating (simulating) a standard normal random variable X, conditional on $a \le X \le b$, where $a < b$ are real numbers, and at least one of them is finite. We are particularly interested in the situation where the interval (a, b) is far in one of the tails, i.e., $a \gg 0$ or $b \ll 0$. The standard methods developed for the non-truncated case do not always work well in this case. More-over, if we insist on using inversion, the standard inversion methods break down when we are far in the tail. Inversion is preferable to a rejection method (in general) in various simulation applications, for example to maintain synchro-nization and monotonicity when comparing systems with common random numbers, for derivative estimation and op-timization, when using quasi-Monte Carlo methods, etc. [2, 11, 12, 13, 14, 16]. For this reason, a good inversion method is needed, even if rejection is faster. We examine both rejection and inversion methods in this paper.

Our motivation for this work stems from applications in Bayesian statistics and computational biology, in which one wishes to generate a random vector $\boldsymbol{X}$ from the multivariate normal or Student-t distribution conditional on $\boldsymbol{a} \le \boldsymbol{X} \le \boldsymbol{b}$ [11], or to accurately estimate the probability $\mathbb{P}[\boldsymbol{a} \le \boldsymbol{X} \le \boldsymbol{b}]$ [9]. for some rectangular box $[\boldsymbol{a}, \boldsymbol{b}]$. These problems occur in particular for the estimation of certain Bayesian regression models and for exact simulation from these models; see [6] and the references given there. More generally, the box can be replaced by a simplex, which can be transformed into a rectangular box by a change of variables (a linear transformation).

Efficient and reliable simulation methods based on importance sampling were developed recently in [4, 5] for exact simulation from such multivariate conditional distributions and to estimate the conditional probability $\mathbb{P}[\boldsymbol{a} \le \boldsymbol{X} \le \boldsymbol{b}]$. Software tools implementing these methods has been made freely available at MATLAB® Central as a toolbox (see www.mathworks.com/matlabcentral/fileexchange/53796) and as an **R** package on CRAN (see cran.r-project.org/web/packages/TruncatedNormal).

The simulation of $\boldsymbol{X}$ from these algorithms requires repeated draws from a standard normal distribution truncated to different intervals, often far in the tail. That is, we need fast and reliable algorithms to generate $X \sim \mathsf{N}(0, 1)$, conditional on $a \le X \le b$, for arbitrary real numbers $a < b$. Various methods have already been proposed to do that; see for example [6, 7, 10, 18, 21, 23]. Some methods work well when the interval $[a, b]$ contains 0 or is not far from it, but not when $a \gg 0$ or $b \ll 0$. Other methods have been designed for the right tail, i.e., when $a \gg 0$ and $b = \infty$, and use rejection. These methods may be adapted in principle to a finite interval $[a, b]$, but they may become inefficient when the interval $[a, b]$ is narrow. We also found no reliable inversion method for an interval far in the tail (say, for $a > 38$; see Section 2). To generate X from a more general normal distribution with mean μ and variance σ^2 truncated to an interval (a', b'), it suffices to apply a simple linear transformation to recover the problem studied here, so there is no loss of generality in assuming a standard normal distribution.

The aim of this paper is to review and compare the most popular methods we know for this task, propose new efficient methods for certain situations, and provide reliable software implementation of these methods. In particular, we propose a new accurate inversion method for arbitrarily large a and

VALUETOOLS 2016, October 25-28, Taormina, Italy

improvements to commonly used methods. In some of our discussion, we assume that $a > 0$. The case where $b < 0$ is covered by symmetry (just change the sign) and the case where $a \le 0 \le b$ can be handled by standard methods.

2. SETTING AND BASIC INVERSION

All over the paper, we use ϕ to denote the density of the standard normal distribution (with mean 0 and variance 1), Φ for its cumulative distribution function (cdf), $\overline{\Phi}$ for the complementary cdf, and Φ^{-1} for the inverse cdf defined as

$$\Phi^{-1}(u) = \min\{x \in \mathbb{R} \mid \Phi(x) \ge u\}.$$

Thus, if $X \sim \mathsf{N}(0, 1)$,

$$\Phi(x) = \mathbb{P}[X \le x] = \int_{-\infty}^{x} \phi(y)\mathrm{d}y = 1 - \overline{\Phi}(x).$$

Conditional on $a \le X \le b$, X has density

$$\frac{\phi(x)}{\Phi(b) - \Phi(a)} \qquad \text{for } a < x < b, \tag{1}$$

and 0 elsewhere. We denote this truncated normal distribution by $\mathsf{TN}_{a,b}(0, 1)$.

It is well known that if $U \sim U(0, 1)$, the uniform distribution over the interval $(0, 1)$, then

$$X = \Phi^{-1}(\Phi(a) + (\Phi(b) - \Phi(a))U) \tag{2}$$

has exactly the standard normal distribution conditional on $a \le X \le b$. But even though very accurate approximations are available for Φ and Φ^{-1}, (2) is sometimes useless to generate X from the desired conditional distribution.

In particular, recall that whenever computations are made under the IEEE-754 double precision standard (which is typical), any number of the form $1 - \epsilon$ for $0 \le \epsilon < 2 \times 10^{-16}$ (approximately) is identified with 1.0, any positive number smaller than about 10^{-324} cannot be represented at all (it is identified with 0), and numbers smaller than 10^{-308} are represented with less than 52 bits of accuracy. This implies in particular that $\overline{\Phi}(x) = \Phi(-x)$ is identified as 0 whenever $x \ge 39$ and is identified as 1 whenever $-x \ge 8.3$. Thus, (2) cannot work when $a \ge 8.3$. In the latter case, or whenever $a > 0$, it is much better to use the equivalent form:

$$X = -\Phi^{-1}(\overline{\Phi}(a) - (\overline{\Phi}(a) - \overline{\Phi}(b))U), \tag{3}$$

which is accurate for a up to about 37, assuming that we use accurate approximations of $\overline{\Phi}(x)$ for $x > 0$ and of $\Phi^{-1}(u)$ for $u < 1/2$. Such accurate approximations are available for example in [3] for $\Phi^{-1}(u)$ and via the error function `erf` on most computer systems for $\overline{\Phi}(x)$. For larger values of a (and x), a different inversion approach must be developed. We do it in the next section.

3. INVERSION FAR IN THE RIGHT TAIL

When $\overline{\Phi}(x)$ is too small to be represented as a floating-point `double`, we will work instead with the Mills ratio, defined as $q(x) \stackrel{\text{def}}{=} \overline{\Phi}(x)/\phi(x)$, which is the inverse of the hazard rate (or failure rate) evaluated at x. When x is large, this ratio can be approximated by the truncated series (see [1], or [22], page 44):

$$q(x) \approx \frac{1}{x} + \sum_{n=1}^{r} \frac{1 \times 3 \times 5 \times \cdots \times (2n-1)}{(-1)^n x^{2n+1}}. \tag{4}$$

For any x this series diverges when $r \to \infty$ (because the numerator increases faster than exponentially with n), but it gives a lower bound when r is odd and an upper bound when r is even, and the distance between the lowest upper bound and the highest lower bound converges to 0 rapidly when x increases. In our experiments with $x \ge 10$, we compared $r = 5, 6, 7, 8$, and we found no significant difference (up to machine precision) in the approximation of X defined by the inverse cdf in (3), by the method we now describe. In view of (3), we want to find x such that

$$\overline{\Phi}(x) = \Phi(-x) = \overline{\Phi}(a) - (\overline{\Phi}(a) - \overline{\Phi}(b))u,$$

for $0 \le u \le 1$, when a is large. This equation can be rewritten as $h(x) = 0$, where

$$h(x) \stackrel{\text{def}}{=} \overline{\Phi}(a) - \overline{\Phi}(x) + (\overline{\Phi}(b) - \overline{\Phi}(a))u \tag{5}$$

To solve $h(x) = 0$, we will start by finding an approximate solution and then refine this approximation via Newton iterations. We detail how this is achieved. To find an approximate solution, we replace the normal cdf Φ in (3) by the standard Rayleigh distribution, whose complementary cdf and density are given by $\overline{F}(x) = \exp(-x^2/2)$ and $f(x) = x\exp(-x^2/2)$ for $x > 0$. Its inverse cdf can be written explicitly as $F^{-1}(u) = (-2\ln(1-u))^{1/2}$. This choice of approximation of Φ^{-1} in the tail has been used before (see for example [3] and Section 4). It is motivated by the facts that $F^{-1}(u)$ is easy to compute and that $\bar{\Phi}(x)/\bar{F}(x) \to 1$ rapidly when $x \to \infty$. By plugging $\overline{F}$ and F^{-1} in place of $\overline{\Phi}$ and Φ^{-1} in (3), and solving for x, we find the approximate root

$$x \approx \left(a^2 - 2\ln\left(1 - u + u\exp\left((a^2 - b^2)/2\right)\right)\right)^{1/2}, \tag{6}$$

which is simply the u-th quantile of the standard Rayleigh distribution truncated over (a, b), with density

$$f(x) = \frac{x\exp(-(x^2 - a^2)/2)}{1 - \exp(-(b^2 - a^2)/2)} \qquad \text{for } a < x < b. \tag{7}$$

The next step is to improve the approximation (6) by applying Newton's method to Equation (5). For this, it is convenient to make the change of variable $x = \xi(z)$, where $\xi(z) \stackrel{\text{def}}{=} \sqrt{a^2 - 2\ln(z)}$ and $z = \xi^{-1}(x) = \exp((a^2 - x^2)/2)$, and apply Newton's method to $g(z) \stackrel{\text{def}}{=} h(\xi(z))$. Newton's iteration for solving $g(z) = 0$ has the form

$$z_{\text{new}} = z - g(z)/g'(z),$$

where

$$\begin{aligned}
\frac{g(z)}{g'(z)} &= \frac{h(\xi(z))}{h'(\xi(z))} \cdot \frac{1}{\xi'(z)}, \quad \text{(by the chain rule)} \\
&= -z\xi(z)\frac{\overline{\Phi}(a) - \overline{\Phi}(\xi(z)) + u(\overline{\Phi}(b) - \overline{\Phi}(a))}{\phi(\xi(z))} \\
&= z\xi(z)\frac{\overline{\Phi}(\xi(z)) - \overline{\Phi}(a) + u(\overline{\Phi}(a) - \overline{\Phi}(b))}{\phi(\xi(z))} \\
&= z\xi(z)\Big(q(\xi(z)) - q(a)(1-u)\exp\left(\tfrac{\xi(z)^2 - a^2}{2}\right) - \\
&\qquad - q(b)u\exp\left(\tfrac{\xi(z)^2 - b^2}{2}\right)\Big) \\
&= x\Big(zq(x) - q(a)(1-u) - q(b)u\exp\left(\tfrac{a^2 - b^2}{2}\right)\Big),
\end{aligned}$$

where the identity $x = \xi(z)$ was used for the last equality. A key observation here is that, thanks to the replacement of

$\overline{\Phi}$ by q, the computation of $g(z)/g'(z)$ does not involve extremely small quantities that can cause numerical underflow, even for extremely large a. The resulting Newton algorithm converges rapidly whenever a is large (say, $a \geq 10$).

The complete procedure is summarized in Algorithm 1, which we have implemented in Java, MATLAB®, and **R**. According to our experiments, the larger a the faster the convergence. Figure 1 shows the required number of Newton iterations to have $\delta_x \leq \delta^* = 10^{-10}$, as a function of a, where δ_x represents the relative change in x in the last iteration.

Algorithm 1 : Returns the u-quantile of $\mathsf{TN}_{a,b}(0,1)$

Require: Input $u \in (0,1)$, δ^*
- $q_a \leftarrow q(a)$
- $q_b \leftarrow q(b)$
- $c \leftarrow q_a(1-u) + q_b u \exp(\frac{a^2-b^2}{2})$
- $\delta_x \leftarrow \infty$
- $z \leftarrow 1 - u + u\exp(\frac{a^2-b^2}{2})$
- $x \leftarrow \sqrt{a^2 - 2\ln(z)}$
- **repeat**
  - $z \leftarrow z - x(zq(x) - c)$
  - $x_{\text{new}} \leftarrow \sqrt{a^2 - 2\ln(z)}$
  - $\delta_x \leftarrow |x_{\text{new}} - x|/x$
  - $x \leftarrow x_{\text{new}}$
- **until** $\delta_x \leq \delta^*$
- **return** Quantile x

Figure 1: Number n of Newton iterations necessary to achieve $\delta_x < \delta^* = 10^{-10}$ for the median of $\mathsf{TN}_{a,\infty}(0,1)$, as a function of a.

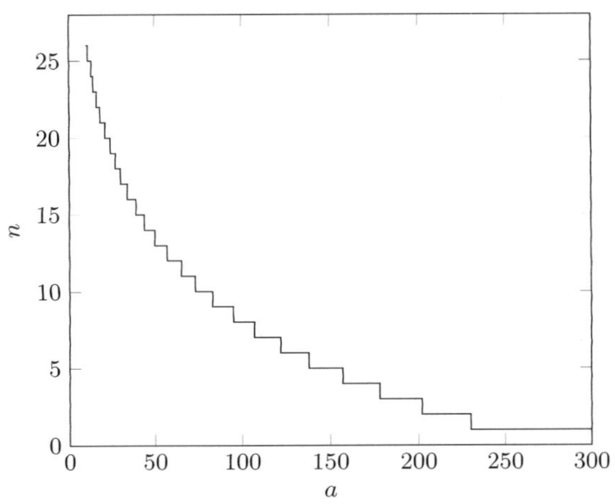

Table 1: Inversion using (3) vs using Algorithm 1: a comparison for some values of a, b, and u, with $r = 5$ and $\delta^* = 10^{-14}$.

a	b	u	using (3)	using Algo. 1
10.0	12.0	0.99	10.446272896499	10.446272896855
10.0	12.0	0.30	10.035260039588	10.035260039626
20.0	22.0	0.99	20.228389499595	20.228389499595
20.0	22.0	0.30	20.017781627473	20.017781627473
30.0	32.0	0.99	30.152946658582	30.152946658582
30.0	32.0	0.30	30.011873653870	30.011873653867
40.0	42.0	0.99	—	40.114892634811
40.0	42.0	0.30	—	40.008910319783
50.0	52.0	0.99	—	50.091982066969
50.0	52.0	0.30	—	50.007130140913

We note that for an interval $[a,b] = [a, a+w]$ of fixed length w, when a increases the conditional density concentrates closer to a. As an illustration, Table 2 gives the conditional probability $\mathbb{P}[X > a+1 \mid X > a] = \overline{\Phi}(a+1)/\overline{\Phi}(a)$ for a few values of a. The third column in the table reports the approximation (4) with $w = 1$,

$$\frac{\overline{\Phi}(a+w)}{\overline{\Phi}(a)} = \frac{q(a+w)\phi(a+w)}{q(a)\phi(a)} \approx \frac{a\exp[-w^2/2 - wa]}{a+w},$$

which shows that this conditional probability decreases as $\exp(-aw)$ when $a \to \infty$. We see that there is practically no difference between generating X conditional on $a \leq X \leq a+1$ and conditional on $X \geq a$ when $a \geq 30$, but there can be a significant difference for small a.

Table 2: Conditional probability $\overline{\Phi}(a+1)/\overline{\Phi}(a)$ and its Mill's ratio approximation for some values of a.

a	$\mathbb{P}[X > a+1 \mid X > a]$	$\frac{a}{a+1}\exp(-a-1/2)$
2	5.93×10^{-2}	5.47×10^{-2}
10	2.51×10^{-5}	2.50×10^{-5}
20	1.19×10^{-9}	1.19×10^{-9}
30	5.49×10^{-14}	5.49×10^{-14}

4. REJECTION METHODS

We now examine *rejection* (or *acceptance-rejection*) methods, which can be faster than inversion. A large collection of rejection-based generation methods for the normal distribution have been proposed over the years; see [6, 7, 10, 23] for surveys, discussions, comparisons, and tests. Most of them (the fastest ones) use a change of variable and/or precomputed tables to speedup the computations. In its most elementary form, a rejection method to generate from some density f uses a hat function $h \geq f$ and rescales h vertically to a probability density $g = h/\int_{-\infty}^{\infty} h(y)dy$, often called the proposal density. A random variate X is generated from g, is accepted with probability $f(X)/h(X)$, is rejected otherwise, and the procedure is repeated until X is accepted as the retained realization. In practice, more elaborate versions are used that incorporate transformations and partitions of the area under h.

Any of these proposed rejection methods can be applied easily if $\Phi(b) - \Phi(a)$ is large enough, just by adding a rejection step to reject any value that falls outside $[a,b]$. The acceptance probability for this step is $\Phi(b) - \Phi(a)$. When this probability is too small, this becomes too inefficient and something else must be done. One way is to define a proposal g whose support is exactly $[a, b]$, but this could be inefficient (too much overhead) when a and b change very often. Chopin [6] developed a rejection method specially adapted to this situation. It is based on a hat function defined by juxtaposing a large number of vertical rectangles of different heights but equal surface over some finite interval $[a_{\min}, a_{\max}]$, and use an exponential proposal with rate $a = a_{\max}$ (the RejectTail variant of Algorithms 2 below) for the tail above $a_{\max}$ or when $a > a'_{\max}$. The fastest implementation uses 4000 rectangles, $a_{\max} \approx 3.486$, $a'_{\max} \approx 2.605$. This method is fast, although it requires the storage of very large precomputed tables, which could actually slow down computations on certain type of hardware for which memory is limited, like GPUs.

Simple rejection methods for the standard normal truncated to $[a, \infty)$, for $a \geq 0$, have been proposed long ago. Marsaglia [19] proposed a method that uses for g the standard Rayleigh distribution truncated over $[a, \infty)$. An efficient implementation is given in [7, page 381]. Devroye [7, page 382] also gives an algorithm that uses for g an exponential density of rate a shifted by a. There two methods have exactly the same acceptance probability,

$$\alpha(a) = a\sqrt{2\pi}\exp(a^2/2)\overline{\Phi}(a),$$

which converges to 1 when $a \to \infty$. Geweke [8] and Robert [21] optimized the acceptance probability to

$$\beta(a) = \lambda\sqrt{2\pi}\exp\left(a\lambda - \lambda^2/2\right)\ \overline{\Phi}(a)$$

by taking the rate $\lambda = (a + \sqrt{a^2+4})/2 > a$ for the shifted exponential proposal. However, the gain with respect to Devroye's method is small and can be wiped out easily by a larger computing time per step. Table 3 compares these two acceptance probabilities for some values of a. For large a, both are very close to 1 and there is not much difference between them.

Table 3: Acceptance probabilities $\alpha(a)$ and $\beta(a)$ for some values of a.

a	$\alpha(a)$	$\beta(a)$
2	0.84273845	0.93364532
10	0.99028596	0.99520084
20	0.99751852	0.99876308
30	0.99889257	0.99944705

We will compare two ways of adapting these methods to a truncation over a finite interval $[a, b]$. The first one is to keep the same proposal g which is positive over the interval $[a, \infty)$ and reject any value generated above b. The second one truncates and rescales the proposal to $[a, b]$ and applies rejection with the truncated proposal. We label them by *RejectTail* and *TruncTail*, respectively. TruncTail has a smaller rejection probability, by the factor $1 - \overline{\Phi}(a)/\overline{\Phi}(b)$, but also entails additional overhead to properly truncate the proposal. Typically, it is worthwhile only if this additional overhead is small and/or the interval $[a, b]$ is very narrow, so it improves the rejection probability significantly. Our experiments will confirm this.

Algorithms 2, 3, 4, state the rejection methods for the TruncTail case with the exponential proposal with rate a [7], with the rate λ proposed in [21], and with the standard Rayleigh distribution, respectively, extended to the case of a finite interval $[a, b]$. For the RejectTail variant, one would remove the computation of q, replace $\ln(1 - qU)$ by $\ln U$, and add $X \leq b$ to the acceptance condition. Algorithm 5 gives this variant for the Rayleigh proposal.

Algorithm 2 : $X \sim \mathsf{TN}_{a,b}(0,1)$ with exponential proposal with rate a, truncated

```
K_a ← 2a²
q ← 1 − exp(−(b − a)a)
repeat
    Generate U, V ~ U(0,1), independent
    X ← −ln(1 − qU)
    E ← −ln(V)
until X² ≤ K_a V
return a + X/a
```

Algorithm 3 : $X \sim \mathsf{TN}_{a,b}(0,1)$ with exponential proposal with rate λ, truncated

```
λ ← (a + √(a² + 4))/2
q ← 1 − exp(−(b − a)λ)
repeat
    Generate U, V ~ U(0,1), independent
    X ← a − ln(1 − qU)/λ
until V ≤ exp((X − λ)²/2)
return a + X/a
```

Algorithm 4 : $X \sim \mathsf{TN}_{a,b}(0,1)$ with Rayleigh proposal, truncated

```
c ← a²/2
q ← 1 − exp(c − b²/2)
repeat
    Simulate U, V ~ U(0,1), independently.
    X ← c − ln(1 − qU)
until V²X ≤ a
return X ← √(2X)
```

Algorithm 5 : $X \sim \mathsf{TN}_{a,b}(0,1)$ with Rayleigh proposal and RejectTail

```
c ← a²/2
repeat
    Simulate U, V ~ U(0,1), independently.
    X ← c − ln(U)
until V²X ≤ a and 2X ≤ b * b
return √(2X)
```

When the interval $[a, b]$ is very narrow, it makes sense to just use the uniform distribution over this interval for the proposal g. This is suggested in [21] and shown in Algorithm 6. Generating from the proposal is then very fast. On the other hand, the acceptance probability may become very small if the interval is far in the tail and $b - a$ is not extremely small. Indeed, the acceptance probability in this case is:

$$\frac{\sqrt{2\pi}\exp(a^2/2)(\overline{\Phi}(a)-\overline{\Phi}(b))}{b-a} = \frac{q(a)-q(b)\exp((a^2-b^2)/2)}{b-a},$$

which decays at a rate of $1/a$ when $a \to \infty$ while $(b-a)$ remains constant.

Algorithm 6 : $X \sim \mathsf{TN}_{a,b}(0,1)$ with uniform proposal, truncated

```
repeat
    Simulate U, V ~ U(0,1), independently.
    X ← a + (b − a)U
until 2 ln V ≤ a² − X²
return X
```

Another choice that the user can have with those generators (and for any variate generator that depends on some distribution parameters) is to either *precompute* various constants that depend on the parameters and store them in some "distribution" object with fixed parameter values, or to *recompute* these parameter-dependent constants each time a new variate is generated. This type of alternative is common in modern variate generation software [15, 17]. The first approach is worthwhile if the time to compute the relevant constants is significant and several random variates are to be generated with exactly the same distribution parameters. For the applications in Bayesian statistics mentioned earlier, it is typical that the parameters a and b change each time a new variate is generated [6]. But there can be applications in which a large number of variates are generated with the same a and b.

For one-sided intervals $[a,\infty)$, the algorithms can be simplified. One can use the RejectTail framework and since $b=\infty$, there is no need to check if $X \le b$. When reporting our test results, we label this the *OneSide* case.

Note that computing an exponential is typically more costly than computing a log (by a factor of 2 or 3 for negative exponents and 10 for large exponents, in our experiments) and the latter is more costly than computing a square root (also by a factor of 10). This means significant speedups could be obtained by avoiding to recompute the exponential each time at the beginning of Algorithms 2, 3, and 4. This is possible if the same parameter b is used several times, or if $b=\infty$, or if we use RejectTail instead of TruncTail.

5. SPEED COMPARISONS

We report a representative subset of results of speed tests made with the different methods, for some pairs (a,b). In each case, we generated 10^8 (100 millions) truncated normal variates, added them up, printed the CPU time required to do that, and printed the sum for verification. The experiments were made in Java using the SSJ library [15], under Eclipse and Windows 10, on a Lenovo X1 Carbon Thinkpad with an Intel Core(TM) i7-5600U (single) processor running at 2.60 GHz. All programs were executed in a single thread and the CPU times were measured using the stopwatch facilities in class `Chrono` of SSJ, which relies on the `getThreadCpuTime` method from the Java class `ThreadMXBean` to obtain the CPU time consumed so far by a single thread, and subtracts to obtain the CPU time consumed between any two instructions. The measurements were repeated a few times to verify consistency and varied by about 1 to 2 percent at most. The compile times are negligible relative to the reported times. Of course, these timings depend on CPU and memory usage by other processes on the computer, and they are likely to change if we move to a different platform, but on standard processors the relative timings should remain roughly the same. They provide a good idea of what is most efficient to do.

Table 4: Time to generate $n=10^8$ random variates for $[a,b]=[3.0,3.1]$.

Method	CPU time (seconds)	
	recompute	precompute
Generation in $[a,b)$		
ExponD	6.46	6.22
ExponDRejectTail	23.04	23.20
ExponR	16.63	9.92
ExponRRejectTail	32.40	32.40
ExponRRejectTailLog	25.10	25.30
Rayleigh	10.29	4.60
RayleighRejectTail	15.23	15.33
Uniform	4.26	4.34
InverseSSJ	15.14	8.14
InverseQuickSSJ	18.80	3.31
InverseRightTail	31.12	7.66
Generation in $[a,\infty)$		
ExponDOneSide	6.43	6.46
ExponROneSideLog	7.05	6.99
RayleighOneSide	4.07	4.41
InverseSSJOneSide	18.81	8.20
InverseRightTailOneSide	18.72	7.64

Table 5: Time to generate $n=10^8$ random variates for $[a,b]=[7.0,8.0]$.

Method	CPU time	
	recompute	precompute
Generation in $[a,b)$		
ExponD	11.70	6.16
ExponDRejectTail	6.04	6.08
ExponR	15.96	8.98
ExponRRejectTail	9.20	9.09
ExponRRejectTailLog	7.03	7.02
Rayleigh	9.86	4.27
RayleighRejectTail	3.91	3.99
Uniform	25.40	25.68
InverseSSJ	30.67	8.14
InverseRightTail	31.12	7.70
Generation in $[a,\infty)$		
ExponDOneSide	5.90	5.96
ExponROneSideLog	6.80	6.71
RayleighOneSide	3.74	4.05
InverseSSJOneSide	19.00	8.19
InverseRightTailOneSide	18.76	7.59

Table 6: Time to generate $n = 10^8$ random variates for $[a, b] = [100.0, 102.0]$.

Method	CPU time	
	recompute	precompute
Generation in $[a, b)$		
ExponD	11.68	6.01
ExponDRejectTail	5.88	5.91
ExponR	15.79	8.86
ExponRRejectTail	9.13	9.02
ExponRRejectTailLog	6.93	6.96
Rayleigh	9.97	4.16
RayleighRejectTail	3.84	3.90
Uniform	650.62	656.42
InverseMillsRatio	22.31	15.97
Generation in $[a, \infty)$		
ExponDOneSide	5.77	5.82
ExponROneSideLog	6.72	6.63
RayleighOneSide	3.67	3.96
InverseMillsRatioOneSide	15.62	15.84

Table 7: Time to generate $n = 10^8$ random variates for $[a, b] = [100.0, 100.0001]$.

Method	CPU time	
	recompute	precompute
Generation in $[a, b)$		
ExponD	12.31	6.83
ExponDRejectTail	543.80	546.58
ExponR	16.47	10.65
ExponRRejectTail	865.24	865.34
ExponRRejectTailLog	651.19	648.99
Rayleigh	10.59	5.07
RayleighRejectTail	323.08	322.41
Uniform	3.59	3.62
InverseMillsRatio	18.03	12.12
Generation in $[a, \infty)$		
ExponDOneSide	5.79	5.83
ExponROneSideLog	6.74	6.63
RayleighOneSide	3.66	3.99
InverseMillsRatioOneSide	15.67	15.84

Tables 4 to 7 report the timings, in seconds. The two columns "recompute" and "precompute" are for the cases where the constants that depend on a and b are recomputed each time a random variate is generated or are precomputed once for all, respectively, as discussed earlier.

ExponD, ExponR, and Rayleigh refer to the TruncTail versions of Algorithms 2, 3, and 4, respectively. We add "RejectTail" to the name for the RejectTail versions. For ExponRRejectTailLog, we took the log on both sides of the inequality to remove the exponential in the "until" condition. Uniform refers to Algorithm 6. InversionSSJ refers to the default inversion method implemented in SSJ, which uses [3] and gives at least 15 decimal digits of relative precision, combined with a generic (two-sided) "truncated distribution" class also offered in SSJ. InverseQuickSSJ is a faster but much less accurate version based on a cruder approximation of $\overline{\Phi}$ from [20] based on table lookups, which returns about 6 decimal digits of precision. We do not recommend it, due to its low accuracy. Moreover, the implementation we used does not handle well values larger than about 5 in the right tail, so we report results only for small a. InverseRightTail uses the accurate approximation of $\overline{\Phi}$ together with (3). InverseMillsRatio is our new inversion method based on Mills ratio, with $\delta^* = 10^{-10}$. This method is designed for the case where a is large, and our implementation is designed to be accurate for $a \geq 10$, so we do not report results for it in Tables 4 and 5. For all the methods, we add "OneSide" for the simplified OneSide versions, for which $b = \infty$.

For the OneSide case, i.e., $b = \infty$, the Rayleigh proposal gives the fastest method in all cases, and there is no significant gain in precomputing and storing the constant $c = a^2/2$.

For finite intervals $[a, b]$, when $b-a$ is very small so $\overline{\Phi}(b)/\overline{\Phi}(a)$ is close to 1, the uniform proposal wins and the RejectTail variants are very slow. See Table 7. Precomputing the constants is also not useful for the uniform proposal. For larger intervals in the tail, $\overline{\Phi}(x)$ decreases quickly at the beginning of the interval and this leads to very low acceptance ratios; see Tables 5 and 6. A Rayleigh proposal with the RejectTail option is usually the fastest method in this case. Precomputing and storing the constants is also not very useful for this option. For intervals closer to the center, as in Table 4, the uniform proposal performs well for larger (but not too large) intervals, and the RejectTail option becomes slower unless $[a, b]$ is very wide. The reason is that for a fixed $w > 0$, $\overline{\Phi}(a + w)/\overline{\Phi}(a)$ is larger (closer to 1) when $a > 0$ is closer to 0.

6. CONCLUSION

We have proposed and tested both inversion and rejection methods to generate a standard normal truncated to an interval $[a, b]$, when $a \gg 0$.

In general, inversion is slower than the fastest rejection method. But as mentioned in the introduction, there are many situations where inversion is required. The new Mills ratio technique is useful for those situations when a is large (say, $a \geq 10$). For a not too large (say, $a \leq 30$), the accurate approximation of [3] implemented in InversionSSJ works well.

When inversion is not needed, the rejection method with the Rayleigh proposal is usually the fastest when a is large enough, especially if a large number of variates must be generated for the same interval $[a, b]$, in which case the cost of precomputing the constants used in the algorithm can be amortized over many calls. The RejectTail variant is usually the fastest, unless $\bar{\Phi}(b)/\bar{\Phi}(a)$ is far from 0, which happens when the interval $[a, b]$ is very narrow or a is not large (say $a \leq 5$). It is interesting to see that using the Rayleigh proposal is faster than using an exponential proposal as in the popular methods of [6, 8, 21].

7. ACKNOWLEDGMENTS

Zdravko Botev has been supported by the *Australian Research Council Discovery Early Career Researcher Award* DE140100993. Pierre L'Ecuyer received support from an NSERC-Canada Discovery Grant, a Canada Research Chair, and an Inria International Chair.

8. REFERENCES

[1] M. Abramowitz and I. A. Stegun. *Handbook of Mathematical Functions*. Dover, New York, 1970.

[2] S. Asmussen and P. W. Glynn. *Stochastic Simulation*. Springer-Verlag, New York, 2007.

[3] J. M. Blair, C. A. Edwards, and J. H. Johnson. Rational Chebyshev approximations for the inverse of the error function. *Mathematics of Computation*, 30:827–830, 1976.

[4] Z. I. Botev. The normal law under linear restrictions: simulation and estimation via minimax tilting. *Journal of the Royal Statistical Society: Series B (Statistical Methodology)*, 2016. doi: 10.1111/rssb.12162.

[5] Z. I. Botev and P. L'Ecuyer. Efficient estimation and simulation of the truncated multivariate Student-t distribution. In *Proceedings of the 2015 Winter Simulation Conference*, pages 380–391. IEEE Press, 2015.

[6] N. Chopin. Fast simulation of truncated Gaussian distributions. *Statistics and Computing*, 21(2):275–288, 2011.

[7] L. Devroye. *Non-Uniform Random Variate Generation*. Springer-Verlag, New York, NY, 1986.

[8] J. Geweke. Efficient simulation of the multivariate normal and Student-t distributions subject to linear constraints and the evaluation of constraint probabilities. In *Computing science and statistics: Proceedings of the 23rd symposium on the interface*, pages 571–578, Fairfax, Virginia, 1991.

[9] C. Hans. Model uncertainty and variable selection in Bayesian lasso regression. *Statistics and Computing*, 20(2):221–229, 2010.

[10] W. Hörmann, J. Leydold, and G. Derflinger. *Automatic Nonuniform Random Variate Generation*. Springer-Verlag, Berlin, 2004.

[11] D. P. Kroese, T. Taimre, and Z. I. Botev. *Handbook of Monte Carlo Methods*. John Wiley and Sons, New York, 2011.

[12] P. L'Ecuyer. Variance reduction's greatest hits. In *Proceedings of the 2007 European Simulation and Modeling Conference*, pages 5–12, Ghent, Belgium, 2007. EUROSIS.

[13] P. L'Ecuyer. Quasi-Monte Carlo methods with applications in finance. *Finance and Stochastics*, 13(3):307–349, 2009.

[14] P. L'Ecuyer. Random number generation with multiple streams for sequential and parallel computers. In *Proceedings of the 2015 Winter Simulation Conference*, pages 31–44. IEEE Press, 2015.

[15] P. L'Ecuyer. SSJ: Stochastic simulation in Java, software library, 2016. http://simul.iro.umontreal.ca/ssj/.

[16] P. L'Ecuyer and G. Perron. On the convergence rates of IPA and FDC derivative estimators. *Operations Research*, 42(4):643–656, 1994.

[17] J. Leydold. *UNU.RAN—Universal Non-Uniform RANdom number generators*, 2009. Available at http://statmath.wu.ac.at/unuran/.

[18] G. Marsaglia. Generating a variable from the tail of the normal distribution. *Technometrics*, 6(1):101–102, 1964.

[19] G. Marsaglia and T. A. Bray. A convenient method for generating normal variables. *SIAM Review*, 6:260–264, 1964.

[20] G. Marsaglia, A. Zaman, and J. C. W. Marsaglia. Rapid evaluation of the inverse normal distribution function. *Statistics and Probability Letters*, 19:259–266, 1994.

[21] C. P. Robert. Simulation of truncated normal variables. *Statistics and computing*, 5(2):121–125, 1995.

[22] C. G. Small. *Expansions and Asymptotics for Statistics*. Number 115 in Monographs on Statistics and Applied Probability. CRC Press, 2010.

[23] D. B. Thomas, W. Luk, P. H. Leong, and J. D. Villasenor. Gaussian random number generators. *ACM Computing Surveys*, 39(4):Article 11, Nov. 2007.

Compositional Construction of Importance Functions in Fully Automated Importance Splitting

Carlos E. Budde, Pedro R. D'Argenio, and Raúl E. Monti
FAMAF, Universidad Nacional de Córdoba – CONICET
{cbudde,dargenio,rmonti}@famaf.unc.edu.ar

ABSTRACT

Importance splitting is a technique to accelerate discrete event simulation when the value to estimate depends on the occurrence of rare events. It requires a guiding *importance function* typically defined in an *ad hoc* fashion by an expert in the field, who could choose an inadequate function. In this article we present a compositional and automatic technique to derive the importance function from the model description, and analyze different composition heuristics. This technique is linear in the number of modules, in contrast to the exponential nature of our previous proposal. This approach was compared to crude simulation and to importance splitting using typical *ad hoc* importance functions. A prototypical tool was developed and tested on several models, showing the feasibility and efficiency of the technique.

1. INTRODUCTION

Nowadays, systems are required to have a high degree of resilience and dependability. Determining properties that fail with extremely small probability in complex models can be computationally very demanding. Though such properties can be efficiently calculated using numerical tools, this is limited to finite Markov models, and, moreover, the representation through an adequate data structure needs to fit in the computer memory. Beyond this class of models, calculations are limited to Monte Carlo simulation methods. However, standard Monte Carlo simulation is impractical when the probability of the event under analysis is extremely low: it will easily require an enormous amount of sampling to obtain an acceptable confidence level of the estimated probability, in order to compensate for the high variance induced by the rare occurrences of such event.

To reduce this considerable need for simulation runs, efficient Monte Carlo simulation techniques have been tailored to deal with rare events. These can be largely divided into two conceptually different techniques: *importance sampling* and *importance splitting* methods. We focus on *importance* splitting techniques, see e.g.[14, 18, 19]. Importance splitting works by decomposing the state space in multiple levels where, ideally, the rare event is at the top level and a level is higher as the probability of reaching the rare event grows. The estimation of the rare probability is obtained as the product of the estimates of the (not so rare) conditional probabilities of moving one level up. As a consequence, the effectiveness of this technique crucially depends on an adequate grouping of states into levels. *Importance functions* are the means to assign a value to each state so that, if perfect, such value is directly related to the likelihood of reaching the rare event. It is desirable that a state in the rare set receives the highest importance and the importance of a state decreases according to the probability of reaching a rare state from it.

Usually, an expert in the area of the system provides the importance function in an *ad hoc* manner. A badly chosen function can deteriorate the effectiveness of the technique. With some notable exceptions [1,8,11,15], automatic derivation of importance functions has received scarce attention.

In [1] we presented preliminary results on an effective technique to derive automatically an importance function. The algorithm works by applying inverse breadth first search (BFS) on the underlying graph of the stochastic process, labelling each state with the shortest distance to a rare state. The importance of each state is then defined as the difference between the maximum distance and its actual distance. Though this technique is not limited to Markov models, it still requires a finite graph which fits in the computer memory. Unfortunately such graph grows exponentially with the number of modules that conform the model of the system.

In this paper, we improve on this technique by obtaining the importance function in a compositional manner. We consider the system modelled as a network of interacting modules, where each module is described in terms of an input/output stochastic automaton (IOSA) and the interaction is defined through standard parallel composition [6]. The technique we propose works by applying the method of [1] per module, previous analysis of how the local states relate to the property under study, and the final importance function is obtained by composing the modular functions. Contrarily to the technique of [1], this way of calculating the importance function grows linearly with the number of modules that conform the system model.

The paper is organized as follows. Sec. 2 explains the foundations of our specification language. Sec. 3 briefly describes the importance splitting technique and the RESTART method. In Sec. 4 we introduce our technique for the compositional derivation of importance functions. Sec. 5 re-

VALUETOOLS 2016, October 25-28, Taormina, Italy

ports the performance of our technique on four different case studies. The paper concludes in Sec. 6.

2. FORMAL SETTING

2.1 System models

We describe our models using input/output stochastic automata (IOSA) [6]. An IOSA is a variant of stochastic automata [4,5] which allows the description of stochastic decision processes in which the occurrence of events (or actions) are governed by continuous random variables called clocks. IOSA considers two disjoint type of actions: input actions and output actions, which should synchronize when different IOSAs interact in a parallel composition. Output actions are locally controlled by the IOSA modelling a particular module. Thus, the occurrence time of output actions is controlled by a random variable. Instead, inputs are externally controlled and hence their occurrence time can only depend on their interaction with outputs in a parallel composition.

Definition 1. *An* input/output stochastic automaton *(IOSA for short) is a structure* $(\mathcal{S}, \mathcal{A}, \mathcal{C}, \rightarrow, \mathcal{C}_0, s_0)$*, where* $\mathcal{S}$ *is a finite set of states,* $\mathcal{A}$ *is a finite set of labels partitioned into disjoint sets of input labels* $\mathcal{A}^I$*, and output labels* $\mathcal{A}^O$*,* $\mathcal{C}$ *is a finite set of clocks such that each* $x \in \mathcal{C}$ *has associated a continuous probability measure* μ_x *on* $\mathbb{R}$ *s.t.* $\mu_x(\mathbb{R}_{>0}) = 1$*,* $\rightarrow \subseteq \mathcal{S} \times \mathcal{C} \times \mathcal{A} \times \mathcal{C} \times \mathcal{S}$ *is a transition relation (we generally write* $s \xrightarrow{C,a,C'} s'$ *instead of* $(s, C, a, C', s)' \in \rightarrow$*),* $\mathcal{C}_0$ *is the set of clocks that are initialized in the initial state, and* $s_0 \in \mathcal{S}$ *is the initial state. In addition an IOSA should satisfy the following constraints:*

1. *If* $s \xrightarrow{C,a,C'} s'$ *and* $a \in \mathcal{A}^I$*, then* $C = \emptyset$*.*
2. *If* $s \xrightarrow{C,a,C'} s'$ *and* $a \in \mathcal{A}^O$*, then* C *is a singleton set.*
3. *If* $s \xrightarrow{\{x\},a_1,C_1} s_1$ *and* $s \xrightarrow{\{x\},a_2,C_2} s_2$ *then* $a_1 = a_2$*,* $C_1 = C_2$ *and* $s_1 = s_2$*.*
4. *If* $s \xrightarrow{\{x\},a,C} s'$ *then, for all* $t \xrightarrow{C_1,b,C_2} s$*, either* $x \in C_2$*, or* $x \notin C_1$ *and there exists* $t \xrightarrow{\{x\},c,C_3} t'$*.*
5. *If* $s_0 \xrightarrow{\{x\},a,C} s$ *then* $x \in \mathcal{C}_0$*.*
6. *For every* $a \in \mathcal{A}^I$ *and state* s*, there exists* $s \xrightarrow{\emptyset,a,C} s'$*.*
7. *For every* $a \in \mathcal{A}^I$*, if* $s \xrightarrow{\emptyset,a,C_1} s_1$ *and* $s \xrightarrow{\emptyset,a,C_2} s_2$*,* $C_1' = C_2'$ *and* $s_1 = s_2$*.*

The occurrence of an output action is controlled by the expiration of clocks. Thus, whenever $s \xrightarrow{\{x\},a,C} s'$ and the system is in state s, output action a will occur once the value of clock x reaches 0. At this point, the system moves to state s' setting the values of every clock $y \in C$ to a value sampled according to the distribution μ_y. An input transition $s \xrightarrow{\emptyset,a,C} s'$, can potentially occur at any time which will be defined once the action interacts with an output.

Restrictions 1-7 ensure that: 1. input and output behave in reactive and generative fashion, respectively, 2. the class of IOSAs is closed w.r.t. parallel composition, and 3. every *closed* IOSA (i.e., an IOSA with no input actions), is deterministic (or fully probabilistic) in the sense that it almost never reaches a state where two possible actions can be taken at the same time. See [6] for detail explanations and proofs. We remark that a closed IOSA defines a generalized semi-Markov process (GSMP). This is important since fully probabilistic models, such as GSMPs, are amenable to simulation in the general case.

Table 1: Parallel composition of IOSAs

$$\frac{s_1 \xrightarrow{C,a,C'}_1 s_1' \quad a \in \mathcal{A}_1 \backslash \mathcal{A}_2}{s_1||s_2 \xrightarrow{C,a,C'} s_1'||s_2} \qquad \frac{s_2 \xrightarrow{C,a,C'}_2 s_2' \quad a \in \mathcal{A}_2 \backslash \mathcal{A}_1}{s_1||s_2 \xrightarrow{C,a,C'} s_1||s_2'}$$

$$\frac{s_1 \xrightarrow{C_1,a,C_1'}_1 s_1' \quad s_2 \xrightarrow{C_2,a,C_2'}_2 s_2'}{s_1||s_2 \xrightarrow{C_1 \cup C_2, a, C_1' \cup C_2'} s_1'||s_2'}$$

Since we intend outputs to be autonomous (or locally controlled), we do not allow synchronization between outputs. Besides, we need to avoid name clashes on the clocks, so that the intended behaviour of each component is preserved and also to ensure that the resulting composed automata is indeed an IOSA. Thus we require to compose only *compatible* IOSAs, and only compatible IOSAs are allowed to compose.

Definition 2. *Two IOSAs* $\mathcal{I}_1$ *and* $\mathcal{I}_2$ *are said to be* compatible *if they do not share output actions nor clocks.*

Given two compatible IOSAs $\mathcal{I}_1$ *and* $\mathcal{I}_2$*, the* parallel composition $\mathcal{I}_1||\mathcal{I}_2$ *is a new IOSA* $(\mathcal{S}_1 \times \mathcal{S}_2, \mathcal{A}, \mathcal{C}, \rightarrow, \mathcal{C}_0, s_0^1||s_0^2)$ *where (i)* $\mathcal{A}^O = \mathcal{A}_1^O \cup \mathcal{A}_2^O$ *(ii)* $\mathcal{A}^I = (\mathcal{A}_1^I \cup \mathcal{A}_2^I) \backslash \mathcal{A}^O$ *(iii)* $\mathcal{C} = \mathcal{C}_1 \cup \mathcal{C}_2$ *(iv)* $\mathcal{C}_0 = \mathcal{C}_0^1 \cup \mathcal{C}_0^2$ *and* $\rightarrow$ *is the smallest relation defined by rules in Table 1 where we annotate* $s||t$ *instead of* (s,t)*.*

The parallel composition works as the usual CSP parallel composition [10]: The two IOSAs should synchronize on actions of equal name, but each component may execute independently if the action belongs only to it in an interleaving manner. Thus, the first two rules in Table 1 correspond to the interleaving case in which each component proceeds independently, while the third corresponds to the synchronization case. Due to compatibility, synchronization only happens between an input and an output. Moreover the union $C_1 \cup C_2$ of clocks in the conclusion of the third rule let the input of one component inherit the clock of the output from the other component, and moreover, this action becomes an output in the resulting composed IOSA.

So far we gave an introduction to the fundamentals of IOSA. However, our prototype tool actually implements a more friendly syntax similar to that of PRISM [13], using modules and integer and boolean variables, with guarded expressions. Thus, a local state in a module is given by particular valuations of the local variables, and a global state is given by the union of local states (w.l.o.g. we assume that different modules have different variables names).

2.2 Rare event properties

In this work we study transient and long run logical properties interpreted on the state space of an IOSA. *Transient* properties are used to calculate the probability of reaching a set G of *goal states* before visiting any *reset state* from the (disjoint) set R. (For simulation purposes the probability of reaching a state in $G \uplus R$ has to be 1.) Let $bexp_1$ and $bexp_2$ be two *propositional formulas* which, when interpreted on the states of an IOSA, identify the complement of R and the set G respectively. Then the transient property is characterized by the PCTL formula

$$\mathsf{P}(bexp_1 \; \mathsf{U} \; bexp_2) \qquad (1)$$

where U denotes the unbounded until operator from LTL and $\mathsf{P}(\Phi)$ denotes the probability of observing any state that satisfies formula Φ.

We also study the behaviour of systems in the long run or steady state situation. *Long run* analysis focuses on the quantification of a property once the system has reached an equilibrium. In particular, the steady state probability of a set G of *goal states*, identified by some propositional formula *bexp* in the state space of an IOSA, is the portion of time in which any state in G is visited in the long run and is characterized by the CSL property

$$\mathsf{S}(bexp) \tag{2}$$

Both types of properties are recurring in the literature of rare event simulation, see e.g. [3, 7, 9, 19] for the case of properties like (1), and [16, 19] for properties like (2).

3. IMPORTANCE SPLITTING

When a parameter is estimated using Monte Carlo simulation, the speed and overall efficiency of the method is highly dependent on the precision required for the estimate. Confidence intervals are commonly used to convey a notion of how far the produced estimate may be from the actual value. As a general rule, whichever the confidence interval construction method, the simulations "length" grows with the tightness desired for the interval. In particular several rare event scenarios are known to require a number of samples which grows exponentially on the model size [12].

Importance splitting (IS for short) aims to speed up the occurrence of a rare event without modifications on the system dynamics (see [14] and references therein.) The general idea in IS is to favour the "promising runs" that approach the rare event by saving the states they visit at certain predefined checkpoints. Replicas of these runs are created from those checkpoint states, which continue evolving independently from then on. Contrarily, simulation runs deemed to steer away from the rare event are identified and killed, avoiding the use of computational power in fruitless calculi. The likelihood of visiting a goal state from any other state s is called the *importance* of s. Variations in such importance determine when should a simulation run be split or killed, as the importance value crosses some given *thresholds* up or down, respectively. This procedural description of IS has a sound statistical equivalent. For a comparison see [1].

We focus on the RESTART method, a version of IS with multiple thresholds, fixed splitting and deterministic discards of unpromising simulations [16–20]. A RESTART run can be depicted as in Fig. 1 where the horizontal axis represents the simulation progress and the vertical axis the importance value of the current state. The run starts from an initial state and evolves until the first threshold T_1 is crossed *upwards*. This takes the path from zone Z_0 below threshold T_1 into zone Z_1 between T_1 and T_2. As this happens the state is saved and $s_1 - 1$ replicas or *offsprings* of the path are created. See A in Fig. 1, where the *splitting* for T_1 is $s_1 = 3$. This follows the idea of rewarding promising simulations: up-crossing a threshold suggests the path heads towards a goal state. From then on the s_1 simulations will evolve independently. As they continue, one of them may hit the upper threshold T_2, activating the same procedure: $s_2 - 1$ offsprings are generated from it and set to evolve independently. See B on T_2; here, the splitting is $s_2 = 2$.

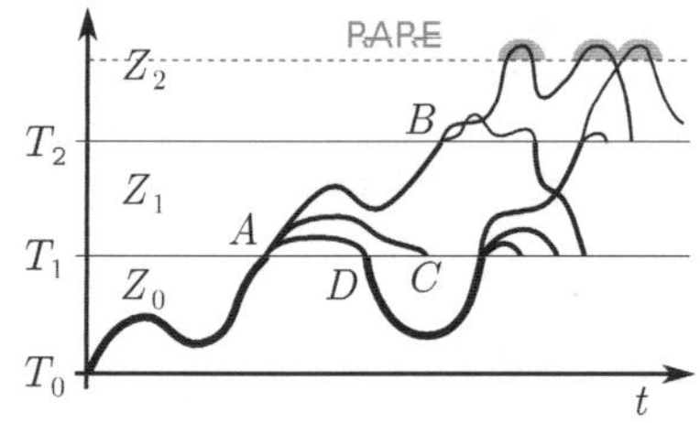

Figure 1: RESTART importance splitting

However, it could also happen that some simulation hits T_1 again, meaning the path is leading *downwards*. This simulation steers away from the goal set and RESTART deals with it discarding the run right away (see C in Fig. 1). In each zone Z_i there exists nonetheless an *original simulation*, which crossed threshold T_i upwards generating the $s_i - 1$ offsprings. This run is allowed to survive a down-crossing of threshold T_i (see D in Fig. 1).

In this setting all simulations reaching a goal state went through the replication procedure, which stacked up on every threshold crossed. Simply counting these hits would introduce a bias, because the *relative weight* of the runs in upper zones decreases by an amount equivalent to the splitting of the thresholds. In consequence, each rare event observed is pondered by the relative weight of the simulation from which it stemmed. If all the goal states exist beyond the uppermost threshold like in Fig. 1, then it suffices to divide the observed quantity of rare events by $\mathrm{SPLIT}_{\mathsf{MAX}} \doteq \prod_{i=1}^{n} s_i$. Otherwise more involved labelling mechanisms are needed.

4. MODULAR COMPUTATION OF THE IMPORTANCE FUNCTION

It is clear from Sec. 3 that importance splitting simulations are entirely guided by the *importance function* which defines the importance of each state. This function conveys the locations where the simulation effort should be intensified, and it is from its definition that many other settings of IS are usually derived. Importance functions are defined in most situations in an *ad hoc* fashion by an expert in the field of the particular system model. With a few exceptions in some specific areas ([8, 11, 15]) automatic derivation of importance functions is still a novel field for general systems.

4.1 Basic importance function derivation

Consider a single-module system $\mathcal{M}$ described in e.g. the IOSA language. The importance of each state s in $\mathcal{M}$ is formally defined as the probability of observing the rare event after visiting s. In the setting of the logical properties $\mathsf{P}(bexp_1 \,\mathsf{U}\, bexp_2)$ and $\mathsf{S}(bexp)$ presented in Sec. 2, the rare event is the set G of *goal states*, defined as the system states satisfying the boolean expressions $bexp_2$ and *bexp* respectively. Therefore if one could track or at least conjecture a path leading from s to a goal state, some notion of the distance between s and the rare event may be determined and used to choose an appropriate importance for the state.

A simultaneous backwards-reachability analysis starting from the set G serves this purpose. Each layer of states visited is labelled with decreasing importance, computing the shortest path leading from each state to G by means of a Breadth-First Search routine of complexity $\mathcal{O}(k \cdot n)$, where n is the size of the state space and k is the branching degree of the underlying graph of the model. Albeit $k = n$ in the worst case, k is normally several orders of magnitude smaller than n. The pseudocode for this algorithm is shown in Fig. 2, where s_0 stands for the initial state of $\mathcal{M}$.

Using this strategy one can indeed obtain in very short computational time a good importance function to use with the IS technique of choice [1]. The thresholds can then be selected either arbitrarily, using e.g. some fixed approach ("*set one every three importance values*"), or adaptively by means of an algorithm that exercises the model dynamics. Whenever feasible we prefer the later alternative due to its flexibility and verified efficiency. Adaptive computation of the thresholds has been observed to skip, for instance, the lowermost importance values and place the first threshold at importance $T_1 > 0$, resulting in a decrease of the splitting overflow and a consequent improvement in the estimation times/precision. A few techniques have been devised in the field of adaptive algorithms, most notably *Adaptive Multilevel Splitting* and its successor *Sequential Monte Carlo* by F. Cérou and A. Guyader in [2,3].

4.2 The modular approach

One of the strengths of the IOSA language is the possibility to describe the system as a set of simpler disjoint modules whose parallel composition captures the desired behaviour. However, the algorithm from Fig. 2 works on a single module. The question is how to apply that to a *set of modules*.

A simple *monolithic* solution is a straightforward application of IOSA's compositionality: since the parallel composition of compatible IOSA modules is itself an IOSA, we could as well construct such global module (from now on referred to as *the model*) and derive the importance function as previously described. This approach is, as a matter of fact, not only feasible but also effective, as it will be shown in Sec. 5. It is nonetheless also limited in scope since it does not scale. The BFS algorithm requires an explicit representation of the state space of the composed IOSA (and actually of the whole adjacency matrix), which grows exponentially with the number of modules involved in the composition.

In order to avoid this problem it is essential to find a modular solution, some way to compute and store the importance separately on each module. The goal is then to build *local importance functions*, that is, local to each module in the system, which will be used later to construct the

Input: module $\mathcal{M}$
Input: goal state set $G \neq \varnothing$
$g(G) \leftarrow 0$
`queue.push`(G)
repeat
  $s \leftarrow$ `queue.pop()`
  for all $s' \in \mathcal{M}$`.predecessors`(s) **do**
    if s' not visited **then**
      $g(s') \leftarrow g(s) + 1$
      `queue.push`(s')
    end if
  end for
until `queue.is_empty()` **or** s_0 visited
$g(s) \leftarrow g(s_0)$ for every non visited state s
$f(s) \leftarrow g(s_0) - g(s)$ for every state s
return importance function f

Figure 2: Basic importance function derivation

global importance function of the model.

The first challenge one finds in this direction is the identification of the rare event in the local state of each module. Recall that the propositional formulas of the properties from Sec. 2 (viz. *bexp*, $bexp_1$ and $bexp_2$) are interpreted on the state space of the composed model. The names of variables from any module can occur in the expressions of these formulas. Since we need to identify, in every module taken individually, the local states corresponding to the global rare event, the question is then how to interpret such "global formulas" locally on each module.

To illustrate the issue consider the example of a tandem-network whose queues q_1 and q_2 have capacity $C < \infty$. Declare one module per queue, as it might come naturally, and let us study the long-run property (2) for three definitions of the rare event *bexp*: (a) $q_2 = C$, (b) $q_1 = C \land q_2 = C$ and (c) $q_1 > \frac{C}{2} \Rightarrow q_2 = C$. All three definitions speak of an overflow in the second queue, but the role of the first queue is harder to grasp. In (a) variable q_1 is missing, so we ignore the module of the first queue when deriving the local importance functions, as it does not change the validity of the formula $q_2 = C$. In other words, for (a) the local importance function of the module of the first queue should be null. In (b) q_1 does appear in *bexp*; more precisely one may define the states satisfying $q_1 = C$ as the *local rares*, and apply the backwards BFS from them. Finally, (c) should be analyzed more carefully, since there $bexp \equiv \neg\left(q_1 > \frac{C}{2}\right) \lor q_2 = C$. Therefore the local rares in the module of the first queue are exactly those which *do not* satisfy $q_1 > \frac{C}{2}$.

The difficulty is hence, when standing on a single module, how to interpret the occurrence of its local variables in the atomic propositions from the formulas *bexp*, $bexp_1$ and $bexp_2$. As we have seen, it is not necessarily clear whether such occurrences should be taken positively or negatively.

To cope with this difficulty we ask for the formulas *bexp*, $bexp_1$ and $bexp_2$ to be expressed in *disjunctive normal form* (*DNF*), i.e. a disjunction of *clauses*, each of which is a conjunction of *literals* (i.e. of atomic propositions or negated atomic propositions). This approach imposes no restriction on the description of the rare event, since any propositional formula can be equivalently written in DNF. The difficulty in the interpretation of the atomic propositions is however solved since the literal clearly states if it should be interpreted positively or negatively.

The procedure to follow is now direct: first project, for the current module under study, the rare event DNF formula into the set of local variables. If the projection is empty then this module plays no role in the rare event and ought to be discarded for importance computation. Otherwise use the resulting formula, also in DNF and containing solely local variables names, to identify the local rare states in this module. Once this set is known the basic importance function derivation can be applied. The pseudocode of this algorithm is presented in Fig. 3.

This way we compute and store the local state importance in a per-module basis, which *grows linearly* with the number of modules in the model. The result is a notion of local importance functions, which still need to be combined amongst modules to compute the global importance function.

4.3 Composition of local importance functions

In the description of RESTART (Sec. 3) the technique is oblivious of the way in which the importance of the system is computed or stored. RESTART simply needs the importance of the current state of the model after every transition is taken. The same transparency is required by all known IS techniques and even by the adaptive algorithms from [2, 3]. Hence if we are to use the modular approach described in Sec. 4.2, we need a composition procedure or function to decide the importance of each state of the composed model, taking as input the local importance of each module.

One option is to let the user settle the matter via an *ad hoc* choice. He would have to provide an algebraic expression using the local importance functions as variables, which would be used at every step of the simulation to combine the local importance values. Recall for instance the tandem-network example from Sec. 4.2 and let `Queue1` and `Queue2` be the local importance functions of the modules representing the first and second queue respectively. The user could specify composition functions such as `Queue1+Queue2`, `0.5 Queue1 + Queue2`, or `(1+Queue1)*(1+Queue2)`.

Alternatively, we could use an associative binary operator to combine all local importance functions with. Natural candidates are addition, product, `max` and `min`. As an example take the first definition of the rare event in the tandem-network, $q_2 = C$. Using `+` or `max` as compositional operand would yield the same result, since the first queue has a null local importance function. If on the other hand we take the second rare event definition, $q_1 = C \wedge q_2 = C$, then `max` and `+` will behave differently, most likely in favour of the later.

The previous analysis shows the definition of the rare event, or more generally the expression of the property, may have a critical impact on the efficiency of the composition function chosen. Furthermore, since we request the properties to be expressed in DNF, we could exploit the structure of the formula to identify specific arithmetical operands or even algebraic structures to associate to each logical operand. We are currently investigating a way to automatically map the disjunctions and conjunctions to their best-match arithmetical counterparts. Our last studies are leading us towards the use of semi-rings such as `(max,+)` and `(+,*)`, which could be thought of as naturally corresponding to the $(\vee,\wedge)$ structure of DNF formulas. The results of these studies and also of the comparisons between the different ways to build the importance function (*ad hoc*, automatic monolithic and automatic per-module) are presented in Sec. 5.

As a final remark notice that using the product to combine local importance functions could lead to problems whenever a null importance value is encountered. As a workaround in such cases the functions where updated after construction, replacing every importance value i with 2^i (e.g. the values $0, 1, 2, \ldots$ map into $1, 2, 4, \ldots$) This solved the issue and set the computed importance values further apart, with interesting consequences in the IS simulations.

Input: modules set $\{\mathcal{M}_i\}_{i=1}^n$
Input: global rare event formula *bexp*
bexp.`assert_DNF`()
for all $\mathcal{M}_i$ **do**
  $bexp_i \leftarrow bexp$.`project`($\mathcal{M}_i$.`variables`())
  if $bexp_i \equiv$ **true then**
    $f_i \leftarrow$ `null`
  else
    $G_i \leftarrow \mathcal{M}_i$.`identify_states` ($bexp_i$)
    $f_i \leftarrow$ `derive_importance_function` ($\mathcal{M}_i, G_i$)
  end if
end for
return local importance functions set $\{f_i\}_{i=1}^n$

Figure 3: Local importance functions computation

5. EXPERIMENTAL VALIDATION

To validate our approach we selected four case studies from the literature and analyzed them using a self-developed software tool. We remark the tool is still in a prototypical stage, accounting for the high timeouts chosen for the executions. To validate correctness, the results estimated with IS simulation were compared against the published results in all cases where an exact IOSA reproduction of the model could be devised. Otherwise, and restricted to markovian systems, a numerical approximation by the model checking tool PRISM was used as reference value. Our estimates where also compared against the analytic solution of the problem whenever this was available.

All estimates were computed together with a confidence interval, i.e., the confidence level and precision of the estimations were taken into account. Two methods were used to build these intervals depending on the type of the property. The standard interval $\left[\, \overline{X} - z_{1-\frac{\alpha}{2}} \cdot {}^{\hat\sigma}/_{\sqrt{N}} \,,\ \overline{X} + z_{1-\frac{\alpha}{2}} \cdot {}^{\hat\sigma}/_{\sqrt{N}} \,\right]$ was used for estimates corresponding to the long run properties as in (2), where N is the number of independent simulation runs, $\overline{X}$ stands for the mean value of the sample, $100(1-\alpha)\%$ is the confidence level and ${}^{\hat\sigma}/_{\sqrt{N}} \cdot z_{1-\frac{\alpha}{2}}$ is the semi-precision or error margin. Transient properties like (1) are inherently binomial, because every simulation almost surely succeeds or fails to encounter a rare event, and one is after the (weighed) number of successful simulations. Since the samples are binomially distributed we can choose a confidence interval construction method better fitted than the standard method described above. The *Wilson score interval* [21] is specially tailored for situations when the proportion $p \doteq \frac{\#\mathsf{succ}}{N}$ takes extreme values, viz. $p \approx 0$ or $p \approx 1$, which clearly fits our situation best.

The precision of the intervals was chosen relative to the expected value of the estimate. This means that the smaller the probability of the rare event, the tighter the confidence interval built for the estimate. Even though this has an obviously negative impact on the simulation times, the goal was to generate as useful an interval as possible.

Simulations were requested to reach a specified confidence level and precision within certain time limit. The precise values of the three criteria (i.e. the confidence, the relative precision and the timeout) are subject to each particular experiment. Simulations reaching the wall time limit were truncated; in these cases the data of interest is the precision achieved at truncation. For each experiment we varied some model parameter, testing the performance of the simulation methods for decreasing values of the probability of the rare event (henceforth "p"), which overall ranged from $p \approx 1.02 \cdot 10^{-2}$ to $p \approx 2.45 \cdot 10^{-13}$. From now on IFUN will denote "importance function". To validate the performance of our approach, for each model and parameter value we tested the following simulation strategies where applicable: RESTART using the *compositional* IFUN described in Sec. 4, RESTART using the *monolithic* IFUN built from the composed model (the "monolithic solution" from Sec. 4.2), RESTART using any known or devised *ad hoc* IFUN, and *standard Monte Carlo*. All RESTART simulations were tested with different split values.

Experimentation was carried out in two computer settings: the cluster *Mendieta* featuring 8-cores 2.7 GHz Intel Xeon E5-2680 processors, each with 32 GiB 1333MHz of available DDR3 RAM; and the server *Jupiterace*, with a 12-cores 2.40GHz Intel Xeon E5-2620v3 processor and 128 GiB 2133MHz of available DDR4 RAM.

5.1 Tandem queue

Consider a tandem network consisting of two connected queues where customers arrive at the first one following a Poisson process with rate λ. After being served by server 1 at rate μ_1 they enter the second queue, where they are attended by server 2 at rate μ_2. The event of interest is an overflow in the second queue for maximum capacity $C < \infty$. This model has received considerable attention in the literature [7–9,19]. We studied this model in [1] and use it here to validate the correction of the tool used for experimentation.

We follow the setting from [7] which has an exact analytic solution. The first queue is initially empty and the second has a single customer. We measured the probability of full occupancy in the second queue before it emptied, i.e. an instance of Property (1). The model was simulated for $(\lambda, \mu_1, \mu_2) = (3, 2, 6)$. The maximum capacities studied were $C = 8, 10, 12, 14$, for which the corresponding probabilities are 5.62e-6, 3.14e-7, 1.86e-8, and 1.14e-9. Simulations had to reach a 90% confidence level with precision equal to 20% of the estimate. Estimates were successfully validated against the exact analytic solution. RESTART simulations were run for split values $2, 3, 6, 9, 12$. Experimentation was performed in Mendieta, comparing standard MC and RESTART simulations using the IS strategies *compositional*, *monolithic*, and the *ad hoc* 'q_2', viz. counting the second queue occupancy.

Standard Monte Carlo simulations were the slowest by a factor of at least 5x and failed to meet the stopping criteria for $C > 10$ within 2 hours of wall time execution. Contrarily, none of the RESTART simulations timed-out and the performance obtained with all IFUNs is comparable. Overall RESTART simulations took 2 to 17 seconds for $C = 8$ (mean time of 8.7 s), 7 to 119 s for $C = 10$ (mean: 44.7 s), 20 to 550 s for $C = 12$ (mean: 171.2 s), and 88 to 3242 s for $C = 14$ (mean: 33 m). Times varied significantly for the different split values, with no best candidate for all queue sizes and importance techniques. The automatic derivation of the importance function never took longer than 30 ms.

There was a strong similarity in performance between the automatically computed *compositional* IFUN and the *ad hoc* strategy 'q_2'. This was expected: since the property involves a variable from the module of the second queue only, the function derived by our algorithm ignores the module of the first queue and yields something very much like counting the elements of the second queue. Notice 'q_2' is the best *ad hoc* strategy reported in [1] for the tandem queue model.

We also studied the long run behaviour for the saturation of the second queue. The maximum capacities studied were $C = 10, 13, 16, 18, 21$, for which the corresponding long run probabilities are 7.25e-6, 2.86e-7, 1.12e-8, 1.28e-9, and 4.94e-11. Simulations had to reach a 90% confidence level with precision of 40%. Estimates were successfully validated against a numerical approximation by PRISM. We tested the same IS strategies mentioned above with the split values $2, 3, 6, 11$. Experiments were run in Mendieta.

Again standard Monte Carlo took always the longest, timing out after 6 hours for the two biggest queue sizes. For $C = 21$ some RESTART simulations also timed out, depending non-uniformly on the split value. Overall RESTART simulations took 1 to 4 s for $C = 10$ (mean: 2.33 s), 4 to 48 s for $C = 13$ (mean: 24.1 s), 9 to 6702 s for $C = 16$ (mean: 20 m) 1 to 166 m for $C = 18$ (mean: 33 m), and for $C = 21$ the only successful simulations within the time bound where the *ad hoc* strategy for splitting 6 and 11, the compositional strategy for splitting 3 and 11, and the monolithic strategy for splitting 6. As before the automatic derivation of the importance function never took longer than 30 ms.

Table 2: Simulation times on triple tandem queue

IFUN	Split	a	b	c	d	e	f
		h:mm	h:mm	h:mm	h:mm	h:mm	h:mm
mono.	3	0:18	0:08	0:33	0:19	*4.9e-10	0:16
	6	0:21	0:04	0:04	0:52	0:29	1:17
	11	0:11	0:02	0:04	0:05	0:02	0:08
comp.	3	0:58	0:11	0:28	1:22	1:12	1:19
	6	0:24	0:03	0:05	0:06	0:30	0:10
	11	0:15	0:03	0:09	2:28	3:41	1:51
ah_1	3	1:20	0:18	0:41	2:56	3:05	*7.4e-10
	6	0:11	0:04	0:20	0:11	1:30	0:41
	11	0:27	0:06	0:08	*1.3e-9	*4.3e-10	2:47
ah_2	3	1:15	0:10	0:57	0:36	0:58	3:45
	6	0:26	0:18	0:04	1:06	3:12	1:29
	11	0:10	0:22	0:13	0:13	0:34	3:13
MC		*4.1e-9	1:37	*4.7e-8	*8.5e-9	*1.0e-9	*2.6e-9

5.2 Triple tandem queue

Consider now a non-markovian tandem network operating under the same principles but consisting of three queues with Erlang-distributed service times. External arrivals follow a Poisson process with rate $\lambda = 1$. The shape parameter α of the service times is either 2 or 3 consistently in all queues. The load at the third queue is always $^1/_3$, meaning the scale parameter μ_3 of the Erlang in the third queue takes the values $^1/_6$ and $^1/_9$ when α is 2 and 3 respectively. The rare event of interest is the long run saturation probability at the third queue, i.e. an instance of Property (2).

This model was studied in [16] starting from initially empty queues. The scale parameters μ_1 and μ_2 at the first and second queues, as well as the threshold capacity C at the third queue, were chosen to keep the steady state probability in the same order of magnitude for all case studies. We chose a rare event probability of the order of $5 \cdot 10^{-9}$. The values $(\alpha, \mu_1, \mu_2, C)$ for the case studies **a**–**f** are $[(2, {}^1/_3, {}^1/_4, 10), (3, {}^2/_3, {}^1/_6, 7), (2, {}^1/_6, {}^1/_4, 11), (3, {}^1/_9, {}^1/_6, 9), (2, {}^1/_{10}, {}^1/_8, 14), (3, {}^1/_{15}, {}^1/_{12}, 12)]$. Simulations had to reach a 90% confidence level with precision equal to 20% of the estimated parameter within 4 hours of wall time execution. Experimentation was carried out in Jupiterace and the resulting simulation times are in Table 2, where "mono.", "comp." and "ah" stand for the IS strategies *monolithic*, *compositional* and *ad hoc* respectively. Simulations which failed to meet the confidence criteria within 4 hours are labelled '*' and the achieved precision for a 90% confidence level is reported if available.

All but one of the standard Monte Carlo simulations failed within the time bound imposed. Two *ad hoc* importance strategies were tested: counting just the occupancy in q_3 (ah_1) and counting also the occupancy in the first two queues with the weight coefficients proposed in [16] (ah_2). Our results suggest their performance is strongly dependent on the splitting used, with no clear optimal choice, see e.g. case

Table 3: **Simulation times on queue with breakdowns**

IFUN	Split	K40	K60	K80	K100	K120	K140	K160
		m:ss	*m:ss*	*m:ss*	*m:ss*	*m:ss*	*m:ss*	*m:ss*
mono.	3	0:03	0:18	6:50	315:54	2:43	*5.4e-11	6:44
	6	0:01	0:10	0:14	46:55	*4.9e-11	*6.2e-12	*-
	9	0:01	1:01	3:33	1:44	4:15	0:46	*1.5e-12
	12	0:01	0:08	40:18	0:23	0:44	1:50	6:23
comp.	3	0:03	0:19	5:04	333:23	1:04	*5.4e-11	6:19
	6	0:01	0:18	0:19	48:18	*4.9e-11	*6.2e-12	*-
	9	0:01	1:01	3:17	0:39	8:04	0:42	*1.5e-12
	12	0:01	0:09	54:42	0:39	1:22	2:30	5:58
ad hoc	3	0:03	0:18	4:51	311:15	1:04	*5.4e-11	5:51
	6	0:00	0:16	0:17	43:57	*4.6e-11	*6.2e-12	*-
	9	0:01	0:57	3:07	0:36	7:37	0:39	*1.5e-12
	12	0:01	0:08	50:37	0:36	1:14	2:08	5:23
MC		0:17	10:26	317:56	*6.5e-9	*2.8e-9	*-	*-

studies **c** and **e**. The general behaviour of the compositional IFUN resembles that of ah_1 but proved better in most scenarios. In any case and letting aside a few outliers (e.g. **d** and **f** for splitting 6 and **e** for splitting 3), the monolithic global IFUN was the fastest in all case studies. We believe this is due to the amount of information available during the iterations of the basic derivation algorithm (Fig. 2), which spreads along the whole model and thus considers the state of all three queues. The main advantage in comparison to similar *ad hoc* approaches like ah_2 is the automatization of the method, here also crowned by an excellent performance.

5.3 Queue with breakdowns

This case study is taken from [12] and models a network where the inputs come from several sources operating in parallel, which are of type $i \in \{1, 2\}$ and have exponential on/off times with parameters α_i and β_i respectively. Whenever a source of type i is active it sends packets at rate λ_i to the only system buffer. Queued packets are handled by a server which breaks down at rate γ and gets fixed at rate δ, processing at rate μ when functional. We estimate the probability of the buffer reaching maximum capacity K before emptying, i.e. an instance of Property (1).

The system starts with a single queued packet and a broken server. There are five sources of each type, all down initially except for one of type 2. The sources parameters are $(\alpha_1, \beta_1, \lambda_1) = (3, 2, 3)$ and $(\alpha_2, \beta_2, \lambda_2) = (1, 4, 6)$, the server parameters are $(\gamma, \delta, \mu) = (3, 4, 100)$ and the queue capacities tested were $K = 40, 60, 80, \ldots, 160$, for which the corresponding probabilities are 4.59e-4, 1.25e-5, 3.72e-7, 9.59e-9, 2.86e-10, 8.44e-12, and 2.45e-13.

We set the confidence level at 90%, the precision at 40% and the wall time limit at 6 hours. Results from computations performed in Mendieta are shown in Table 3. Standard Monte Carlo simulations timed-out for $K > 80$. The importance strategies used in RESTART simulations were the automatic 'compositional' and 'monolithic' variants, and the best *ad hoc* approach reported in [1], namely counting the number of queued packages. All three showed very similar performance in spite of the high variance related to the splitting value chosen. The best simulation times for $K = 40, 80, 160$ were ~1 s, 14 s, and 323 s respectively. The corresponding IFUN derivation times were below 4.4 s, 9.32 s, and 23.11 s for the monolithic approach, and below 0.17 s, 0.34 s, 0.64 s for the compositional approach.

5.4 Database with redundancy

The final case study is a database system consisting of disks arranged in clusters, disk controllers, and processors. As it was studied in [19], for redundancy 'R' the system is composed of two types of processors (with R copies of each type), two types of controllers (with R copies of each type), and six disk clusters (with $R+2$ disks each). Units lifetime is exponentially distributed with failure rates μ_d, μ_c and μ_p for disks, controllers and processors resp. A unit can fail, with equal probability, in one of two modes, whose repair rates are 1 per hour and 0.5 per hour. The system is *operational* as long as *less than* R processors of each type, R controllers of each type, and R disks on each cluster, have failed. The property of interest is the steady state probability of a system breakdown, i.e. an instance of Property (2).

From the point of view of IS this has a *flat structure* which differs from all previous models: few discrete events produce a breakdown despite the high number of system components. This is aggravated by a low failure rate of disks w.r.t. processors and controllers: a breakdown is likely to be caused by broken proc./ctrl. of the same type, rather than by failures on the clusters. There is no trivially efficient way to compute the importance.

We propose five compositional importance functions which exercise the analysis from Sec. 4.3: AC_1 is a simple addition of the local IFUN of every module; AC_2 adds the product of (the local IFUNs of) all the disks in the database, the product of all the controllers, and the product of all the processors; AC_3 follows a similar approach but is finer-grained, since it multiplies (the local IFUNs of) all components in every cluster or processor/controller of the same type, adding these together; finally AC_4 and AC_5 consider the DNF formulation of the property. The first implements the `(max,+)` semi-ring, so every failure configuration is a sum (e.g. $\mathrm{disk}_3^6 + \mathrm{disk}_4^6$ for $R = 2$), and the resulting maximum is the global system importance. AC_5 implements `(+,*)`, so every failure configuration is a product and all these are summed together. Local importance was linear for $\{\mathsf{AC}_i\}_{i=1,4}$ and exponential for $\{\mathsf{AC}_i\}_{i=2,3,5}$, e.g. a state at distance d from the rare event had importance 2^d. Interestingly, AC_4 coincides with the *ad hoc* approach followed in [19]. The monolithic approach could not be tested due to the memory requirements.

Like in [19] simulations were run for increasing redundancy values (we used $R = 2, 3, 4, 5$). However, a randomized policy of the repairman cannot be expressed in the current IOSA syntax. For that reason the estimates produced are not comparable to those reported in the cited article. Furthermore the failure rates chosen were $(\mu_p, \mu_c, \mu_d) =$ (2e-2, 2e-2, 1e-2). The resulting long run probabilities estimated with this setting were in the order of 1.10e-2, 8.68e-5, 4.47e-7, and 1.13e-9 for the indicated redundancies. Unlike previous experiments simulations were run for fixed time periods (3 s, 1 m, 1 h and 6 h, for the respective redundancies). The goal was to build the narrowest possible interval for each time budget. Simulations were run on Jupiterace and the resulting precisions for a 90% confidence level are shown in Fig. 4, where the x axis groups the different simulations per redundancies and the y axis shows the achieved interval widths. The plot shows the results using split = 3; the outcomes for split $\in \{2, 5, 6\}$ were similar.

As expected the benefits of RESTART pay off only for the higher values of R: standard Monte Carlo (MC) competed against IS for redundancies 2 and 3. However for $R = 4$ the

Figure 4: Estimation precisions on database

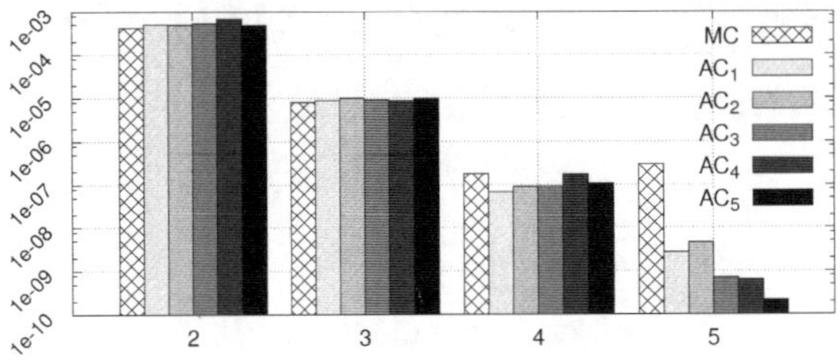

compositional IFUNs performed better, and for $R = 5$ the event is too rare for MC. Notice how in this last case the semi-ring composition variants performed best. Derivation times for all importance functions were below 2 s in all cases.

6. CONCLUSIONS

In this work we have presented a novel technique to automatically derive an importance function following a compositional construction. Though we focused on RESTART, such function could be used with any IS technique.

We studied the performance of our algorithms in case studies taken from the literature, matching or improving the performance of the best *ad hoc* alternatives to our knowledge. Overall and between the two automatic approaches proposed, the monolithic variant outperformed the compositional one to a minor extent. This was to be expected since it counts with global behaviour information, lost in the modular projections of the compositional variant.

In contrast both the computation time and memory storage requirements needed to compute the compositional importance function are orders of magnitude lower than the monolithic variant, which in particular could not be computed for the database case study. Besides, the monolithic method performs badly in graphs with high connectivity, since any rare state is close to the initial state and hence the IFUN would have a small image. Contrarily, in the compositional method, the composition of local IFUNs may yield a composed IFUN with a large image. This situation would be precisely the case in the database case study.

Experimentation shows RESTART is extremely sensitive to the split value chosen, even when measures are taken to mitigate the starvation (resp. overhead) of choosing a splitting too small (resp. big). A possible workaround would be to run the simulation tool parallelly for different splittings, stopping at the first successful estimation. When clusters like Mendieta are available this poses no major challenge.

Our research would also benefit from an extension of the IOSA syntax. The repairman model is a typical agent in rare event simulation, for which various repair policies exist. Referring to the state of the modules by means of arrays or similar constructs would help us implement such policies.

Acknowledgments

We thank José Villén-Altamirano for his help on the triple tandem queue. This work was supported by grants ANPCyT PICT-2012-1823, SeCyT-UNC 05/BP12 and 05/B497, and the ERC Advanced Grant 695614 (POWVER) while the second author visited Saarland University. Experiments were run on computers provided by CCAD and FAMAF-UNC.

7. REFERENCES

[1] C. E. Budde, P. R. D'Argenio, and H. Hermanns. Rare event simulation with fully automated importance splitting. In *EPEW 2015*, *LNCS* 9272, pages 275–290. Springer, 2015.

[2] F. Cérou, P. Del Moral, T. Furon, and A. Guyader. Sequential Monte Carlo for rare event estimation. *Statistics and Computing*, 22(3):795–808, 2012.

[3] F. Cérou and A. Guyader. Adaptive multilevel splitting for rare event analysis. *Stochastic Analysis and Applications*, 25(2):417–443, 2007.

[4] P. R. D'Argenio. *Algebras and Automata for Timed and Stochastic Systems*. PhD thesis, University of Twente, 1999.

[5] P. R. D'Argenio and J.-P. Katoen. A theory of stochastic systems part I: Stochastic automata. *Inf. Comput.*, 203(1):1–38, 2005.

[6] P. R. D'Argenio, M. D. Lee, and R. E. Monti. Input/Output Stochastic Automata - Compositionality and Determinism. In *FORMATS 2016*, *LNCS* 9884, pages 53–68. Springer, Springer, 2016.

[7] M. J. J. Garvels. *The splitting method in rare event simulation*. PhD thesis, Department of Computer Science, University of Twente, 2000.

[8] M. J. J. Garvels, J.-K. C. W. Van Ommeren, and D. P. Kroese. On the importance function in splitting simulation. *European Transactions on Telecommunications*, 13(4):363–371, 2002.

[9] P. Glasserman, P. Heidelberger, P. Shahabuddin, and T. Zajic. Multilevel splitting for estimating rare event probabilities. *Operations Research*, 47(4):585–600, 1999.

[10] C. Hoare. *Communicating Sequential Processes*. Prentice Hall, 1985.

[11] C. Jegourel, A. Legay, and S. Sedwards. Importance splitting for statistical model checking rare properties. In *CAV 13*, *LNCS* 8044, pages 576–591. Springer, 2013.

[12] D. P. Kroese and V. F. Nicola. Efficient estimation of overflow probabilities in queues with breakdowns. *Performance Evaluation*, 36:471–484, 1999.

[13] M. Kwiatkowska, G. Norman, and D. Parker. PRISM 4.0: Verification of probabilistic real-time systems. In *CAV'11*, *LNCS* 6806, pages 585–591. Springer, 2011.

[14] P. L'Ecuyer, F. Le Gland, P. Lezaud, and B. Tuffin. Splitting techniques. In *Rare Event Simulation using Monte Carlo Methods*, pages 39–61. John Wiley & Sons, Ltd, 2009.

[15] D. Reijsbergen, P.-T. de Boer, W. Scheinhardt, and B. Haverkort. Automated rare event simulation for stochastic Petri nets. In *QEST 2013*, *LNCS* 8054, pages 372–388. Springer, 2013.

[16] J. Villén-Altamirano. RESTART simulation of networks of queues with erlang service times. In *Winter Simulation Conference*, WSC '09, pages 1146–1154. Winter Simulation Conference, 2009.

[17] M. Villén-Altamirano, A. Martínez-Marrón, J. Gamo, and F. Fernández-Cuesta. Enhancement of the accelerated simulation method RESTART by considering multiple thresholds. In *Proc. 14th Int. Teletraffic Congress*, pages 797–810, 1994.

[18] M. Villén-Altamirano and J. Villén-Altamirano. RESTART: a method for accelerating rare event simulations. In *Queueing, Performance and Control in ATM (ITC-13)*, pages 71–76. Elsevier, 1991.

[19] M. Villén-Altamirano and J. Villén-Altamirano. The rare event simulation method RESTART: efficiency analysis and guidelines for its application. In *Network Performance Engineering*, *LNCS* 5233, pages 509–547. Springer, 2011.

[20] J. Villén-Altamirano. Asymptotic optimality of RESTART estimators in highly dependable systems. *Reliability Engineering & System Safety*, 130:115 – 124, 2014.

[21] E. B. Wilson. Probable inference, the law of succession, and statistical inference. *Journal of the American Statistical Association*, 22(158):209–212, 1927.

fDRIT- An Evaluation Tool for Transient Removal Methods in Discrete Event Stochastic Simulations

Sushma Nagaraj
Systems and Software Engineering
Technische Universität Ilmenau, Germany
sushma.nagaraj@tu-ilmenau.de

Armin Zimmermann
Systems and Software Engineering
Technische Universität Ilmenau, Germany
armin.zimmermann@tu-ilmenau.de

ABSTRACT

The choice of an initial state in a stochastic simulation often leads to a transient bias in the estimation results. A well-known solution for this problem is to detect and estimate this initial phase and its subsequent removal. A significant number of algorithms has been proposed in the literature for this task. Because of their heuristic nature and the stochastic experiment underlying each individual simulation run, their quality cannot be easily evaluated for a new application model or simulation tool.

The goal of this paper is a software framework for the systematic comparison of such algorithms to let tool developers evaluate and compare them for their specific needs in a fair and generic manner, and to allow researchers in the field of initial transient removal to compare and test their ideas. Along the way, a set of possible quantitative evaluation criteria is proposed. The framework is then used to evaluate and compare numerous existing algorithms.

1. INTRODUCTION

Performance evaluation of system models is done either in steady-state or at a certain transient point of time (or interval). Steady-state (or stationary) evaluations are arguably more often used in model-based systems design, as they answer questions about the general long-time behavior of a system and thus help in designing system parameters or decide about architectural choices [10, 2].

There have been various solutions proposed in the literature for the detection of the initial transient phase, explained in detail in [8], with a Run-in model for the determination of the warm-up period and the steady-state conditions, followed by the deletion of the collected warm-up data being the most accepted solution.

During a simulation run, when an underlying stochastic discrete-event model is simulated and the values of performance measures are measured, the quality of the estimation becomes crucial. This quality will improve with the number of measured samples, only when the samples come from an unbiased observation of the stochastic process. As the 'normal' setup of state variables (or a probability distribution over them) for the corresponding simulation is not known in advance, simulation models are often started empty or with default state variables. This will introduce a systematic bias in the estimated results, which will fade with a longer simulation run, and thus the estimated result will be closer to the real value if this biased initial phase is ignored. There is then a trade-off about where to cut off the initial phase: the more the discarded samples, the lower the influence of the initial bias, but, with fewer usable samples, resulting in a higher variance of the estimated result. Taking into account simulation costs and uncertainty of truncation quality in addition to this, the necessity of the truncation may even be questioned [14]. Also, sometimes when the transient detection is carried out using confidence intervals or spectral intervals, the effectiveness also depends on the stationarity of the sample distribution. Hence, when a group of samples has to be considered for discarding, the accuracy of the determined truncation point becomes very important.

Within the framework of a sequential simulation, when the simulation was carried out until a pre-specified accuracy was reached, focussing specifically on the transient removal, the results showed that there actually was no substantial difference in the point or interval estimates of the mean values, explicitly obtained from removal of the biased phase, especially considering the run lengths required for commonly used levels of accuracy [14].

There have been various methods that have been suggested in diverse scenarios and applications. Methods such has the MSER-5 [21], in combination with Schruben's test [19] and Fishman's rule [3] are known to be successful and are currently being used in various simulation software tools. However, when these methods need to be evaluated, or compared against newer methods, a re-implementation of the methods is necessary. Apart from the tried and tested methods, there have been various new algorithms such as the sequential steady state detection (online) [4] and the MSER-5Y (offline) [21], that have been suggested to perform better than the existing methods. However, unless all the methods under consideration are subject to similar testing conditions, a systematic and fair comparison between them would not be possible. This paper thus presents a software *Framework for the Detection and Removal of Initial Transients* (fDRIT) providing this platform for a comparative analysis between various transient detection and removal methods, and allowing benchmark test cases. This not only helps in the qualitative and quantitative evaluation of multiple

VALUETOOLS 2016, October 25-28, Taormina, Italy

algorithms, but also eliminates the need for separate implementations. An inspiration for such a tool was derived from the modified proposal by Schruben dating back to 1983 [19]. The main intention is to provide an accessible platform for understanding and comparing the performance of the deployed methods in a modern computing environment, and as a basis for the future development of new algorithms.

The remainder of this paper is divided as follows: Section 2 briefly explains the background of steady state simulation and its transient removal problem, illustrating an overview of some of the transient removal methods from the literature. Section 3 explains the design and software architecture of the framework. It provides a detailed explanation of how the performance metrics are currently calculated. Section 4 provides an example case and the corresponding results, with a comparison between the various implemented algorithms and their corresponding quality ratings.

2. METHODS TO DETECT THE WARM-UP PERIOD

There are various tests described in literature for dealing with transient detections. They can be classified into the following categories:

- Output Data Analysis - This classification is derived based on the manner in which the output is analyzed where a set of rules is given to handle the transient removal. A further classification may be based on the nature of the rules - heuristic methods [3] [22] [12] [16] [21] [15], graphical methods [20] [4], statistical methods [10] [1] [6], initialization bias tests [19] and hybrid methods [16] [12] [9].

- Input Data Gathering - Any of the above mentioned algorithms can be executed with either offline or online data. When the algorithm is executed with a set of data that is pre-saved, then such an analysis can be called an offline analysis. Various algorithms suggested in literature like the MCR [15], MSER [15], Schruben [19], Kalman filter [6], Conway [18], Gafarian [5] etc. belong to this category. On the other hand, online algorithms acquire and process real-time simulation data from the model and can thus be used to stop the running simulation when the required accuracy is reached. The hybrid methods used, e.g., TimeNET Simulation tool [9], Akaroa simulation tool [4], JMT simulation tool [12] etc., are all examples of online truncation point detection methods.

- Independent Replications - is a widely used approach when the size of the sample that is to be analyzed is pre-fixed before the simulation run. This method is also called as "Replications" in short and it deals with multiple runs of the same simulation, assuming independence between the runs, calculating an estimate of the mean and its corresponding variance for all the individual runs, separately. Reference [17] gives a detailed analysis of this method, with its corresponding advantages and disadvantages.

- Batch Means Methods - deals with the case of using only one long run of output data. According to Welch it "exactly parallels the method of independent replications except that the sequences are adjacent, non-overlapping sub-sequences of the output of a single simulation run" [20]. The most important part is to determine the batch size, m, necessary to indicate independence among the batches considering the fact that the batches will be independent of each other if m is long enough. Once this independence is identified, the batches can be compared as if they were separate runs, and the various model samples be evaluated. Euclidean distance algorithm, proposed by Young-Hae Lee *et al.* [11] is an example of this method.

3. FDRIT - A FRAMEWORK TO DETECT AND REMOVE INITIAL TRANSIENTS

The idea of implementing a framework in which multiple transient detection algorithms can be implemented and tested against standard tests was inspired by the modified proposal by Schruben of 1983 [19], who suggest an alternative hypothesis testing framework with a family of tests for detecting initialization bias in the mean of the simulation output series. Often, an efficient transient removal can be achieved with an individual or a combination of the methods that are already known. However, the comparative suitability of the available methods is unknown due to the lack of knowledge of the presence of the methods, or limited testing, proving it difficult to analyze the applicability of the algorithms to the situation at hand. The presented framework provides a platform for the understanding and comparison of the performance of any deployed methods.

The framework comprises three modular parts:

1. Algorithm implementation framework
2. Test framework
3. Evaluation tool

The algorithm implementation part contains an extensible number of transient removal algorithms, which are connected to the remaining software by a standardized interface for easier implementation of future algorithms. At the time of writing, we have implemented eight algorithms from the literature:

1. Euclidean Distance Method by Young-Hae Lee *et al.* [11].
2. Schruben's stationarity Rule [19].
3. Method of Cumulative means by Adam Freeth used in Akaora [4].
4. Fishman's rule or R5 Heuristic by Pawlikowski [16].
5. MSER-5 by Spratt [15], [21].
6. MSER-5Y by Saeideh Yousefi [21].
7. Initial transient detection approach used in the TimeNET tool [9, 7].
8. Initial transient detection approach used in the JMT simulator [12].

The test framework holds the definition of various dynamic test algorithms that generate random data for the input data generation of the algorithms. Its modular structure allows the easy extension by additional examples. This part is planned to be extended towards a set of benchmark data generators. The current implementation uses three M/M/1 queuing systems as first examples, which are:

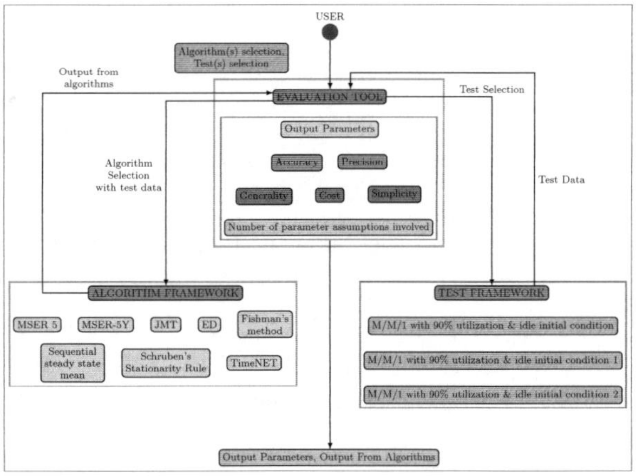

Figure 1: fDRIT software architecture

- M/M/1 queue-waiting-time process with empty-and-idle initial condition and 90% server utilization.
- M/M/1 queue-waiting-time process with 113 initial customers and 90% server utilization.
- M/M/1/LIFO queue-waiting-time process with empty and idle initial condition and 80% server utilization.

The evaluation tool defines a set of methods that calculate the quality of the executed methods. This is also a part responsible for the user interaction. The user is required to provide two inputs: an algorithm or a combination of algorithms that are to be analyzed and compared, and a test method that needs to be executed, for generating the necessary test data.

3.1 Software Architecture

The software architecture of the framework has three components: The part which contains the algorithm implementation, the test data generation framework and the part where the evaluation of the selected methods are carried based on the selected tests. A brief overview of the architecture is shown in Figure 1.

3.1.1 Algorithm Implementation

The implementation of the transient detection or removal algorithm, that needs to be evaluated is done in this module. The implementation of the algorithm is independent of any test data, isolating it from the testing environment. The main intention of separating the test framework from the algorithm implementation was to enable a dynamic evaluation of the implemented methods. A call is made from the evaluation framework to the implementation framework, to fetch the required methods under scrutiny. The job of the implementation framework will then be to run the implemented algorithm, with the test data provided by the evaluation part, and to return the calculated output values, like the steady-state mean, output or error values, or any other output calculated for the system. The only responsibility of the algorithm framework is to execute the implemented method with the provided test inputs and returning the result values. This part may be extended to accommodate as many new algorithms as necessary, with complete abstraction. A comparative result obtained from the tool for and M/M/1 queue is given in the results section of this paper.

3.1.2 Test Data Generation

The quality of algorithms implemented cannot be guaranteed with limited testing. Hence the creation of a separate framework for the purpose of testing and input data generation. The implemented algorithms have to be subjected to different test scenarios / benchmarks, to observe their performance and to draw a comparison between each other. This is an important part, especially when the choice of a suitable algorithm needs to be made for a certain individual setup. In the current implementation three variations of an M/M/1 queue are implemented. However, this needs to be further extended to provide an extensive set of tests for the purpose of the algorithm evaluation. The testing framework is also instantiated and called from the evaluation part of the tool. When the respective call is made, the job of the testing framework is to generate and supply the appropriate test-data dynamically.

3.1.3 Evaluation of the Algorithms

This is the only part of the tool with user interaction. The user must specify the algorithm(s) to be executed and select the corresponding test data for them. The tool then carries out the requests internally and provides the output and the performance metric scores to the user. The various performance metrics explained in this paper are calculated and displayed to the user. Accordingly, the decision of which algorithm should be used or a comparison between several algorithms (individually or in combination) can be drawn. The main job of the evaluation section is to gather the input, i.e., the selection of the algorithms to be compared and the test data to be used, collect test data (online) and acquire the corresponding output parameters from the selected transient removal algorithm(s) by initiating their execution with the collected test data. The evaluation engine basically acts as an interface between the user and the framework. The different criteria used for the calculation of the performance metrics are: Accuracy, Precision, Generality, Cost, Simplicity and Parameter estimation. More details about these calculations are given in Section 3.2 below.

3.2 Evaluation Parameters for the Quality of the Algorithms

The criteria proposed here represent one of the possible ways for quantifying the performance of the implemented algorithms, with a possibility of comparing them against each other. In [13], a set of performance measures like the Mean Square Error and its corresponding percentage change, Variance and its corresponding percentage change and cost calculations are explained. In [5], Gafarian *et al.* also specify five criteria to evaluate the goodness of the algorithm under consideration. Using these as a guide, we have incorporated six criteria and further devised a method for calculating the score of the respective metric, in order to quantify the performance of the various algorithms. These are elaborated below:

3.2.1 Accuracy

The parameter accuracy defines a score of the accuracy of the evaluated truncation point with respect to the theoretically exact truncation point. The accuracy can be given any score between 0 and 10. This score is assigned by calculating the accuracy percentage using Equation 1 given below and then dividing this percentage value by 10, to deduce a score between 1 and 10. The accuracy parameter has an overall weighting of 25% in the goodness measure of the algorithm. The weighting along with the score is used in the benefit analysis, which is used for the comparison of the goodness of multiple algorithms.

$$a = \frac{\text{Estimated Truncation Point}}{\text{Theoretical Truncation Point}} \times 100 \tag{1}$$

In the case of the truncation point estimate being smaller than the theoretical truncation point, i.e., if the estimated percentage is greater than 100, the score is calculated by subtracting the difference from 100 and then dividing by 10, and is also assigned a negative sign to signify the loss of useful data.

$$\text{Theoretical value} = 8.3$$
$$\text{Estimated value} = 6.7$$
$$A = \frac{\text{Estimated value}}{\text{Theoretical value}} \times 100 = 77\%$$
$$a = \frac{77}{10} = 7.7$$

Figure 2: Positive accuracy

3.2.2 *Precision*

The considered algorithm can be said to be precise if the estimated truncation point is not a varied value, i.e., the estimated value should be similar across runs. This value is obtained from the coefficient of variation which is the ratio of the standard deviation to the mean of the truncation point obtained across a pre-specified number of times, as given in Equation 2 below. Typically, any method is expected to be precise, which means that it should have a negligible variance. This means that the closer the value p from the Equation 2 is to zero, the more precise is the respective value.

$$p = \frac{\text{Standard Deviation Of The Estimated Truncation Point}}{\text{Mean Of The Estimated Truncation Point}} \times 100 \tag{2}$$

Similar to the accuracy score, the precision is also scored between 0 and 10, which is obtained by subtracting the tenth of p from the Equation 2 from 10. If the precision value is negative, then the precision score is considered to be 0. An example of the precision calculation is as shown in Figure 3.

The precision parameter also weighs 25% of the overall goodness measure for our sample evaluation. This weight, in combination with the precision score of the respective algorithm, and along with the other parameters is used in the beneficial analysis of the corresponding algorithms.

Estimated truncation points across 10 runs = {6.5, 6.0, 6.3, 6.4, 6.2, 7.0, 5.8, 7.2, 6.2, 6.0}
Mean of the Estimated truncation point = 6.36
Standard Deviation = 0.198
Coefficient of variation = 3.11%
Precision score = 10 - 0.311 = 9.7

Figure 3: Precision score calculation example

3.2.3 *Generality*

The generality parameter for any algorithm refers to the suitability of the algorithm across various scenarios. In order to set this score, the algorithm implementations have to be tested on diverse application areas, with different discrete distributions. The algorithm under scrutiny must work with similar precision and accuracy with input models from different test models. In order to calculate the generality score of a particular algorithm or a combination of models under consideration, the accuracy and precision scores for all the input models under consideration are calculated. Following this, the mean of both the score values for the respective algorithm is calculated. The generality score is the mean of all the previously calculated mean values. An example of the calculation of the generality score is as shown in Table 1 below.

Evaluated Heuristic	Heuristic 1	Heuristic 2	Heuristic 3	Heuristic 4	Heuristic 5
Accuracy Score	7	6	7.5	5.5	7.8
Precision Score	8	7	6	7	8
Mean	7.5	6.5	6.75	6.25	7.9
Generality score	$\sum Mean/5 = 6.98$				

Table 1: Generality score calculation example

3.2.4 *Cost*

The cost parameter is evaluated by calculating the amount of time required for the following three operations:

(i) Computing time for the algorithm itself i.e., the computational efficiency.

(ii) Computing time for collecting the output data before estimating the truncation point and subsequently discarding the biased data.

(iii) Computing time associated with a bias in the determination of the truncation point.

The total computing time is calculated from the implementation code, but for the beneficial analysis, we require a score between 1 and 10. This is done by assuming a grade of 10 initially and reducing 1 point for every 30 secs that the algorithm uses in our sample case. Hence the cost score will vary based on the algorithm(s) that are being executed and the respective input model used.

The cost parameter has the least weighting amongst all the evaluation parameters, with a value of 5. This value along with the score is used for the beneficial analysis during comparison of algorithms.

3.2.5 *Simplicity*

The parameter simplicity has a weighting of 10 and it signifies the understandability of the algorithm to programmers with less domain knowledge. The simplicity parameter is graded between 1 and 10, 1 being the least and 10 the highest value, i.e., an algorithm with a simplicity score of 10 is extremely simple to understand and be implemented by a non-expert.

A pre-defined simplicity score is assigned to each of the implemented algorithms based on the challenges faced during implementation. The factors considered for the assignment of this score are: conceptual complexity, extent of mathematical formulae used and the number of calculations that were to be made. The simplicity factor has a weight of 10 in the benefit evaluation of the algorithms. This weight along with the provided score is to be used in grading all the available algorithms in the framework. When the simiplicity score was calculated, all the implemented algorithms showed to have an average simplicity score of around 5.

3.2.6 Parameter Estimation

The parameter estimation score is based on the percentage of the total number of parameters in the algorithm which are assumed. This value is important because the more parameters are necessary in the algorithm, the riskier the algorithm may be in the case of wrong selections. This value is calculated by finding the number of parameters that are estimated in the execution of the algorithm and assigning a tenth of that value as the parameter estimation score.

The parameter estimation score can range between 1 and 10 and it has a weighting of 15% in the beneficial analysis of the algorithms.

3.2.7 Benefit Analysis

The performance of the various implemented algorithms is evaluated using a standard benefit analysis method from systems engineering or variant decision. The different parameters explained in Section 3.2 have been used for the analysis. A sample benefit rating matrix is as shown in the table 2. The benefit rating for the individual algorithms is computed by first computing the parameter scores for the respective heuristics. These scores are then multiplied by the corresponding parameter weights and finally summed up for each algorithm. The performance of the algorithm under consideration is directly proportional to its benefit rating. fDRIT provides this detailed analysis to the user and can thus support an informed decision between algorithms dealing with the initial transient problem.

Evaluation Statistic	Weight(w)	Truncation Algorithms					
		ED Method		Cumulative Means		TimeNET	
		Score(S)	$W * S$	S	$W * S$	S	$W * S$
Accuracy	25	3	75	6	150	4	100
Precision	25	4	100	7	175	5	125
Generality	20	3	60	7	140	7	140
Cost	5	5	25	5	25	5	25
Simplicity	10	5	50	6	60	6	60
Parameter Estimation	15	3	45	6	90	7	105
Benefit Rating	$\sum = 100$	355		640		555	

Table 2: Sample benefit rating matrix for evaluation of three truncation methods

4. EXAMPLE AND RESULTS

The framework was executed with the test data from a dynamic M/M/1 queue-waiting-time process with empty and idle initial condition and 90% server utilization. The results obtained are shown Table 3.

In Table 3, values for three of the methods are depicted in detail. The benefit rating of the other methods are given in Table 4. The benefit ratings are calculated by the tool using the parameters mentioned above. It should be noted that this criteria selection and weighting is just one possible setup that should be chosen following the intentions of a future user. If, for instance, the algorithm complexity is not significant as only the numerical results are considered important, the corresponding value can be set to 0, possibly resulting in a different algorithm to be chosen.

Evaluation Statistic	Weight(w)	Truncation Algorithms					
		ED Method		Fishman's Rule		Cumulative Batch Means	
		Score(S)	$W * S$	S	$W * S$	S	$W * S$
Accuracy	25	3	75	5	125	7	175
Precision	25	5	125	5	1275	7	175
Generality	20	5	100	5	100	7	140
Cost	5	3	15	4	20	6	30
Simplicity	10	6	60	6	60	7	70
Parameter Estimation	15	9	135	9	135	9	135
Benefit Rating	$\sum = 100$	510		565		710	

Table 3: Benefit rating matrix for evaluation of three truncation methods

The framework acts as a base evaluation and testing platform for all implemented methods. This work may be reused in any other project as a dynamic library, without the need to re-evaluate and re-implement the initial transient problem for every requirement from the scratch. The possibility of drawing a comparison and conclusion to the algorithm decision is the main idea here. When the implemented algorithms is taken into consideration, it can be seen from the benefit ratings that the rating of the combination of the Cumulative batch means method and the MSER-5Y algorithms has the highest rating, showing that it is the best of the compared lot. In a similar way, based on the requirement and the testing method, the best suitable algorithm(s) for the particular situation can be decided upon.

Truncation Algorithms	Benefit Rating
Batch Means by Euclidean Distance Method	510.0
Fishman's Rule	565.0
Cumulative Batch Means	710.0
MSER-5	687.5
MSER-5Y	695.0
Schruben's Rule	565.0
TimeNET	687.5
JMT	730.0
Cumulative Batch Means + MSER-5Y	765.0

Table 4: Benefit ratings for the experiments carried out on the framework

5. CONCLUSION

This paper presented the prototype software framework fDRIT for the evaluation and comparison of algorithms that solve the problem of the initial transient for stochastic discrete-event simulations. Several available methods from the literature have been summarized, implemented and compared with a simple first benchmark test. Criteria for the userspecific weighted benefit comparison are proposed and the set of algorithms is evaluated as an example. The framework should act as a decision help and standardized comparison to evaluate new and existing methods for certain types of application models or input data. Its software architecture is modular and extendable for future implementation of more benchmark models / data sources, and transient detection algorithms. A secondary use may be the use of the framework or parts of it inside other tools, which then do not have to reimplement a certain transient removal algorithm for themselves.

As a part of the future research, a possible feature to verify the generated output with mathematical heuristics like variance and confidence intervals and design and development of a basic user interface for the framework are considered. In the future, we plan to use the tool to select or develop on-line algorithms for the initial transient detection of stochastic Petri net models.

6. REFERENCES

[1] D. Abramson, M. Lees, V. Krzhizhanovskaya, J. Dongarra, P. M. Sloot, F. Borges, A. Gutierrez-Milla, R. Suppi, and E. Luque. 2014 international conference on computational science optimal run length for discrete-event distributed cluster-based simulations. *Procedia Computer Science*, 29:73 – 83, 2014.

[2] S. Asmussen and P. Glynn. *Stochastic Simulation: Algorithms and Analysis*, volume 57 of *Stochastic Modelling and Applied Probability*. Springer, 2007.

[3] G. S. Fishman. Bias considerations in simulation experiments. *Operations Research*, 20(4):785–790, 1972.

[4] A. Freeth. *A Sequential Steady-State Detection Method for Quantitative Discrete-Event Simulation*. PhD thesis, University of Canterbury, 2012.

[5] A. V. Gafarian, C. J. Ancker, and T. Morisaku. Evaluation of commonly used rules for detecting "steady state" in computer simulation. *Naval Research Logistics Quarterly*, 25(3):511–529, 1978.

[6] M. A. Gallagher, K. W. Bauer, and P. S. Maybeck. Initial data truncation for multivariate output of discrete-event simulations using the kalman filter. *Annals of Operations Research*, 53(1):419–441, 1994.

[7] R. German and J. Mitzlaff. Transient analysis of deterministic and stochastic Petri nets with TimeNET. In *Proc. Joint Conf. 8th Int. Conf. on Modelling Techniques and Tools for Performance Evaluation*, volume 977 of *Lecture Notes in Computer Science*, pages 209–223. Springer Verlag, 1995.

[8] K. Hoad, S. Robinson, and R. Davies. Automating warm-up length estimation. *Journal of the Operational Research Society*, 2009.

[9] C. Kelling. TimeNET-Sim—a parallel simulator for stochastic Petri nets. In *Simulation Symposium, 1995, Proceedings of the 28th Annual*, pages 250–258, Apr 1995.

[10] A. M. Law and D. M. Kelton. *Simulation Modeling and Analysis*. McGraw-Hill Higher Education, 3rd edition, 1999.

[11] Y. H. Lee, K. Hyung Kyung, and C. Sik Jung. On-line determination of steady state in simulation outputs. *Computers & Industrial Engineering*, 33(3):805–808, 1997.

[12] G. S. M. Bertoli, G. Casale. An overview of the JMT queueing network simulator. Tr 2007.2, Politecnico di Milano, DEI, 2007.

[13] P. S. Mahajan and R. G. Ingalls. Evaluation of methods used to detect warm-up period in steady state simulation. In *Proceedings of the 36th Conference on Winter Simulation*, WSC '04, pages 663–671. Winter Simulation Conference, 2004.

[14] D. McNickle, G. C. Ewing, and K. Pawlikowski. Some effects of transient deletion on sequential steady-state simulation. *Simulation Modelling Practice and Theory*, 18(2):177–189, 2010.

[15] R. Pasupathy and B. Schmeiser. The initial transient in steady-state point estimation: Contexts, a bibliography, the MSE criterion, and the MSER statistic. In *Simulation Conference (WSC), Proceedings of the 2010 Winter*, pages 184–197, Dec 2010.

[16] K. Pawlikowski. Steady-state simulation of queueing processes: Survey of problems and solutions. *ACM Comput. Surv.*, 22(2):123–170, June 1990.

[17] A. A. Pritsker. *Introduction to Simulation and SLAM II*. John Wiley & Sons, Inc., New York, NY, USA, 3rd edition, 1986.

[18] R.W.Conway. Some tactical problems in digital simulation. *Management Science*, 10(1):47–61, 1963.

[19] L. Schruben. Confidence interval estimation using standardized time series. *Operations Research*, 31(6):1090–1108, 1983.

[20] P. D. Welch. *Computer Performance Modeling Handbook*. Academic Press, Inc., Orlando, FL, USA, 1983.

[21] S. Yousefi. MSER-5Y: An improved version of MSER-5 with automatic confidence interval estimation. Master's thesis, North Carolina State University, 2011.

[22] A. Zimmermann. Modeling and evaluation of stochastic Petri nets with TimeNET 4.1. In *Performance Evaluation Methodologies and Tools (VALUETOOLS), 2012 6th International Conference on*, pages 54–63, Oct 2012.

Parametric Sensitivity and Uncertainty Propagation in Dependability Models

Riccardo Pinciroli
DEIB, Politecnico di Milano
Milano, 20133, Italy
riccardo.pinciroli@polimi.it

Kishor S. Trivedi
Department of ECE, Duke University
Durham, NC 27708, USA
ktrivedi@duke.edu

Andrea Bobbio
DISIT, Universita' del Piemonte Orientale
Alessandria, 15121, Italy
andrea.bobbio@uniupo.it

ABSTRACT

Input parameters of dependability models are often not known accurately. Two principal methods of dealing with such parametric uncertainty are: sensitivity analysis and uncertainty propagation. This paper is an initial attempt to link the two approaches. The case-study used here (i.e., the multi-voltage propulsion system for the Italian High Speed Railway) also enhances the model presented in [6].

Keywords

Epistemic uncertainty propagation; Parametric sensitivity analysis; Homogeneous and Non-Homogeneous Markov models; Hierarchical models; Railway system dependability

1. INTRODUCTION

Simple and accurate models are fundamental for a good system analysis. Modellers are required to consider different features of the system and to incorporate them to make the stochastic model as similar as possible to the real system. Furthermore, they are also asked to keep the model simple in order to get fast results and possibly fully symbolic solutions. In addition to modeling errors in the stochastic model (i.e., errors due to a bad representation of the system), epistemic uncertainty [26] must also be taken into consideration if good results are desired. Epistemic uncertainty is introduced into a model because of the way in which the input parameters of the model are derived (i.e., finite number of samples in measurement campaigns). Because of this uncertainty, output measures are conditional on the parameter values used.

Generally, a trade-off between simplicity of the model and other features such as accuracy and ease of deriving solutions exists. For example, when the modellers want to include dependencies using a state space approach: it is possible to model the system with a continuous time Markov chain (CTMC), but it is often impractical to solve a model with a large number of states, and the ease of deriving solutions decreases. Thus, it can be hard to model a real system trying to provide all these features together.

Uncertainty propagation analysis is used to distinguish between errors in model output due to bad modeling assumptions and low accuracy due to epistemic (parametric) uncertainty. The method consists in propagating epistemic uncertainty in the input parameters through the model, in order to compute the uncertainty in the output measures. Unfortunately, it is not always easy to study the uncertainty propagation. Indeed, for large and complex models it is often not practical to analytically or numerically computing the uncertainty. On the other side, parametric sensitivity analysis is a method that lets modeller identify the parameters for which the smallest variation most affects the model output measures. This analysis can be done also with complex models in short time. Different techniques in sensitivity function computation can be adopted in order to deal with different model types [4, 5, 11, 19, 22].

In this paper, we consider as a case study the model of a multi-voltage propulsion system proposed in [6] for the Italian High Speed Railway. We focus on two different aspects of modeling. First, we propose some enhancements to the original model, in order to show how it is possible to add some features to the model, while trying to keep it as simple as possible. The purpose of the added features is to make the model more accurate and yet easier to solve. Then, we consider accuracy of the same model with particular interest in epistemic uncertainty propagation and parametric sensitivity. This is the first step to find a relationship between these two aspects of the model in order to identify the parameters that have the greatest impact on the output measures and thus need to be known with higher accuracy.

The remainder of this paper is structured as follows. In Section 2 prior work on uncertainty propagation is discussed. In Section 3 a first description of the system is given through a reliability block diagram (RBD) and then the Markov model used in [6] is presented. Section 4 describes the improvements introduced in the original model in order to make it more accurate and yet easier to derive fully symbolic solutions. In Section 5 we study the accuracy of the input parameters of the model, looking for a relationship between parametric sensitivity and epistemic uncertainty. Finally, Section 6 concludes the paper.

VALUETOOLS 2016, October 25-28, Taormina, Italy

2. RELATED WORK

There are two main kinds of uncertainty [29]: epistemic uncertainty that is due to lack of knowledge [8, 31] and aleatory uncertainty due to the natural variations of the physical phenomenon [25,27]. For the purpose of this paper, we are interested in epistemic uncertainty since it can be reduced [1]. It has been studied both in stochastic simulation [2,24,30] and in analytic models [20,21,23].

Simulation optimization has been largely analyzed in order to take into consideration uncertainty propagation. For example, Yi, Xie and Zhou [30] proposed a seuqential experiment design to identify the samples that contribute the most to the percentile estimation. Song et al. [24] analyzed how indifference-zone formulation of ranking and selection – a procedure used to choose the best among a set of simulated alternatives – works with epistemic uncertainty. Authors of [2] estimated the input uncertainties that minimize the cost of data collection and comply with a given bound. For that purpose, they proposed a technique (i.e., inverse uncertainty propagation) to find the optimal input uncertainties so that the given bound on the simulation output uncertainty is satisfied.

Analytic methods for uncertainty propagation derive variance or confidence interval (exact or approximate) manipulating the closed-form solutions of the model output measures. Several papers in literature [9, 12, 17] only considered non-state-space models (simple series-parallel systems or fault tree), with a small number of input parameters. Author of [23] studied the uncertainty propagation through a multidimensional integration. Even if several analytical and numerical methods can be applied, the computation of integrals can be hard for large and complex models. Alternatively, Monte Carlo sampling methods have also been proposed to propagate the uncertainty through the model in order to compute the quantiles of the distribution of the model output. Some of them assume that the input parameters follow a given epistemic distribution [14], some others derive the epistemic distribution from a given confidence interval [20].

We wish to provide an easy and quick way to identify, through parametric sensitivity analysis, which parameter must be more carefully measured in order to get a tighter confidence interval on the output measures. For this purpose, we identify a relationship between uncertainty propagation and parametric sensitivity.

3. MODEL DESCRIPTION

The multi-voltage propulsion system, originally proposed in [6] and [7], consists of three equivalent modules in a parallel redundant configuration. In Figure 1 the RBD of the system is shown. Each module is composed of transformer (T), filter (F), inverter (I) and motor (M) in series with two parallel converters (C_1 and C_2). In [6], the component times to failure are assumed to be exponentially distributed with the failure rate values reported in Table 1. Denote by $\lambda = \lambda_T + \lambda_F + \lambda_I + \lambda_M$ the total failure rate of the series components and γ the failure rate of each parallel component. The propulsion system works until one of the three parallel modules is up, but the available power capacity (i.e., the rewards of each state, see Section 3.1) depends on the number of working modules and components.

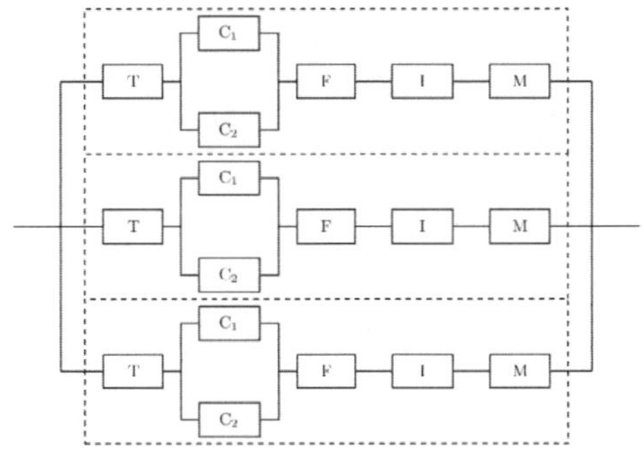

Figure 1: RBD of the propulsion system.

Table 1: System block failure rate.

Component	Failure rate [f/h]
Transformer	$\lambda_T = 2.2 \cdot 10^{-6}$
Converter	$\gamma = 2.8 \cdot 10^{-5}$
Filter	$\lambda_F = 4.0 \cdot 10^{-7}$
Inverter	$\lambda_I = 3.8 \cdot 10^{-5}$
Motor	$\lambda_M = 3.2 \cdot 10^{-5}$

3.1 Continuous time Markov chain

The Markov chain model for the system is reported in Figure 2. Each state represents a possible configuration of the system by means of a label that has three rows, one for each parallel module, and two columns. The first column of the label is 1 if all the series components in the module (row) are working, 0 otherwise. The second column of the label indicates how many parallel converters are working. If one series component or both the parallel ones are down, the module fails and the two digits of the label are set to 0. Each arc is labelled with a time-independent failure rate (no repair operations can be provided while the train is travelling) and hence we are dealing with a homogeneous CTMC. To compute the power capacity delivered by the multi-voltage propulsion system as a function of time, we assign to each state a reward rate indicating the power delivered in that state.

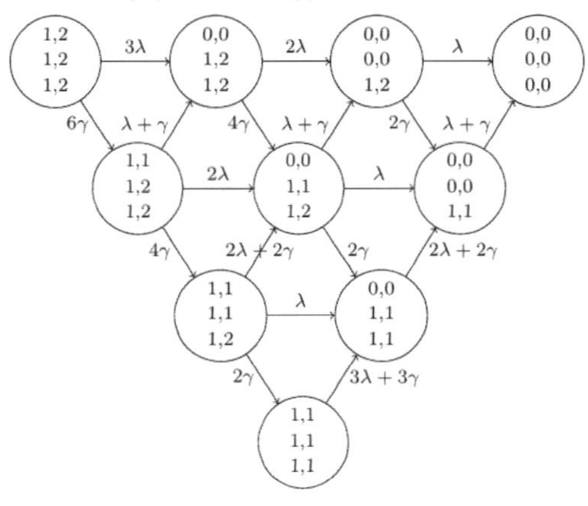

Figure 2: Original CTMC as described in [6].

Due to the state-space dimension of the CTMC of Figure 2, it is impractical to get a fully symbolic transient solution [18]. We could derive semi-symbolic or numerical solutions. Instead, in Section 4 we develop a hierarchical model that will enable us to produce a fully symbolic solution.

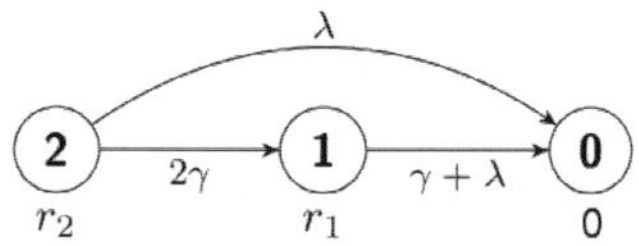

Figure 3: Markov Reward Model for one module.

4. MODEL IMPROVEMENTS

We show the steps to arrive to a fully symbolic solution while removing the constraint of constant failure rates.

4.1 Single module analysis

We start representing one single module by means of the three-state Markov reward model (MRM) shown in Figure 3. In *State 2* all the components are working, the module is fully operational and delivers a power represented by the reward rate r_2. In *State 1* only one of the two converters is operative and the module delivers a reduced power [6] represented by the reward rate r_1. *State 0* is the down state and no power is delivered. The CTMC arrives to *State 0* from *State 1* if one of the series components fails, or from *State 1* if the second converter fails.

Since the MRM has only three states, we can derive the fully symbolic transient solution, for example by resorting to Laplace transforms:

$$\begin{cases} \pi_2(t) = e^{-(2\gamma+\lambda)t} \\ \pi_1(t) = 2e^{-(\gamma+\lambda)t} - 2e^{-(2\gamma+\lambda)t} \\ \pi_0(t) = 1 - \pi_1(t) - \pi_2(t) \end{cases} \tag{1}$$

The module reliability is

$$R(t) = \pi_2(t) + \pi_1(t) = 2e^{-(\gamma+\lambda)t} - e^{-(2\gamma+\lambda)t}.$$

Denote by $X(t)$ the power delivered by the module at time t and by $Y(t)$ the energy delivered up to time t. The expected values $E[X(t)]$ and $E[Y(t)]$ of these quantities can be computed by combining the obtained state probabilities with the reward rates.

$$\begin{aligned} E[X(t)] &= \sum_{i=0}^{2} r_i \pi_i(t) = r_2\pi_2(t) + r_1\pi_1(t) \\ &= (r_2 - 2r_1)e^{-(2\gamma+\lambda)t} + 2r_1 e^{-(\gamma+\lambda)t} \end{aligned}$$

$$\begin{aligned} E[Y(t)] &= \sum_{i=0}^{2} \int_0^t r_i \pi_i(x)dx \\ &= r_2 \int_0^t \pi_2(x)dx + r_1 \int_0^t \pi_1(x)dx \\ &= \frac{(r_2 - 2r_1)(1 - e^{-(2\gamma+\lambda)t})}{2\gamma+\lambda} + \frac{2r_1(1 - e^{-(\gamma+\lambda)t})}{\gamma+\lambda} \end{aligned} \tag{2}$$

Following [6], we assume $r_2 = 2200\ kW$ and $r_1 = 1100\ kW$.

The Cdf of the total energy delivered till absorption $Y(\infty)$ can be derived using the method proposed by Beaudry in [3]. The method consists in changing the domain representation of the process from a time domain to a reward domain representation, scaling the transition rates by the reward rates. Consider that in a state with reward rate r, in a time interval of length t the system accumulates a reward $y = rt$. After differentiation and manipulation we get $dt = dy/r$. Given a transition rate λ_i from a state i with reward rate r_i, the new transition rate in reward unit is λ_i/r_i as shown in Figure 4. Solving the CTMC of Figure 4, we can derive

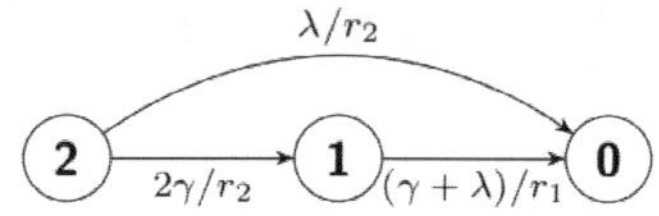

Figure 4: CTMC of the reward domain representation.

the new state probabilities in the reward domain (denoted by a superscript (R)):

$$\begin{cases} \pi_2^{(R)}(r) = e^{-\frac{(2\gamma+\lambda)}{r_2}r} \\ \pi_1^{(R)}(r) = 2r_1\gamma \cdot \dfrac{e^{-\frac{(\gamma+\lambda)}{r_1}r} - e^{-\frac{(2\gamma+\lambda)}{r_2}r}}{\gamma(2r_1 - r_2) + \lambda(r_1 - r_2)} \\ \pi_0^{(R)}(r) = 1 - \pi_1^{(R)}(r) - \pi_2^{(R)}(r) \end{cases} \tag{3}$$

and finally we compute the Cdf of the accumulated reward till absorption as:

$$\begin{aligned} Pr(Y(\infty) \geq y) &= \pi_1^{(R)}(y) + \pi_2^{(R)}(y) \\ &= \frac{[(r_1 - r_2)\lambda - r_2\gamma]e^{-\frac{2\gamma+\lambda}{r_2}y} + 2r_1\gamma e^{-\frac{\gamma+\lambda}{r_1}y}}{(2r_1 - r_2)\gamma + (r_1 - r_2)\lambda} \end{aligned} \tag{4}$$

Figure 5 depicts $Pr(Y(\infty) \geq y)$ as a function of y.

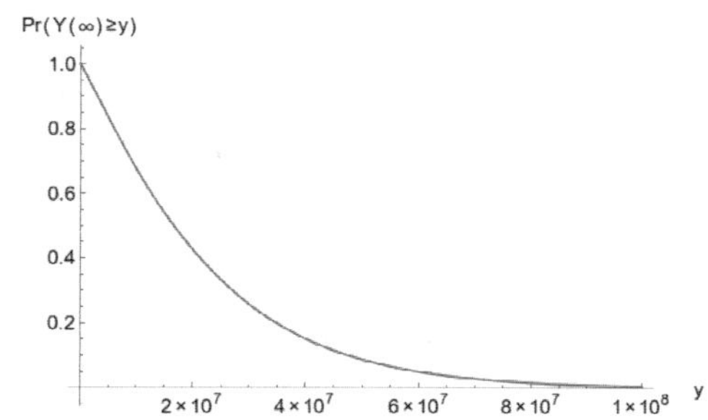

Figure 5: $Pr(Y(\infty) \geq y)$ computed as in Equation 4.

A simple algorithm to obtain the mean time to absorption in a transient CTMC is based on the computation of the expected state occupancy in the transient states before absorption. Given that τ_i is the expected state occupancy in state i and $\boldsymbol{\tau}$ the vector grouping the τ_i, we can compute the mean time to failure (MTTF), from equation [28]:

$$\boldsymbol{\tau Q}_u = -\boldsymbol{\pi}_u(0) \tag{5}$$

where $\boldsymbol{Q}_u$ is the partition of the infinitesimal generator matrix of the CTMC over the transient states and $\boldsymbol{\pi}_u(0)$ the partition of the initial probability vector over the transient states. We compute τ_i solving (5) and then the MTTF is the sum of the τ_i over the transient states. In our case:

$$\begin{aligned} MTTF_{module} &= \tau_2 + \tau_1 = \frac{1}{2\gamma+\lambda} + \frac{2\gamma}{(2\gamma+\lambda)(\gamma+\lambda)} \\ &= \frac{3\gamma+\lambda}{(2\gamma+\lambda)(\gamma+\lambda)} \end{aligned}$$

With the values of Table 1 $MTTF_{module} = 12104.7\,hr$. Combining expected time spent in state i before absorption, τ_i, and the reward rate of the same state, r_i, we can compute the mean energy delivered till failure (MEDF) as:

$$MEDF_{module} = r_2\tau_2 + r_1\tau_1 = \frac{r_2}{2\gamma+\lambda} + \frac{2r_1\gamma}{(2\gamma+\lambda)(\gamma+\lambda)}$$
$$= \frac{(r_2+2r_1)\gamma + r_2\lambda}{(2\gamma+\lambda)(\gamma+\lambda)}$$

With the assigned numerical values we get $MEDF_{module} = 2.18688 \cdot 10^7\ Wh$.

4.2 Non-Homogeneous CTMC

One of the weaknesses of the original model is that the failure rates are time-independent. In order to include aging phenomena of the components, all the rates should depend on time. For this purpose, the model presented in Section 4.1 is extended as shown in Figure 6 where rates are now time dependent. The underlying stochastic process is now a Non-Homogeneous CTMC (NHCTMC) and the entries of the generator matrix can vary over the same global time. The Markov property is still satisfied, but the homogeneity requirement is not satisfied. Kolmogorov differential equations [28] is used to define the transient behavior of a NHCTMC:

$$\frac{d\boldsymbol{\pi}(t)}{dt} = \boldsymbol{\pi}(t)\boldsymbol{Q}(t)$$

with $\boldsymbol{\pi}(t_0)$ the given initial state probability vector. The probability vector $\boldsymbol{\pi}(t)$ is subject to the normalization condition for any time $\sum_{i=1}^{n} \pi_i(t) = 1\ (t \geq 0)$.

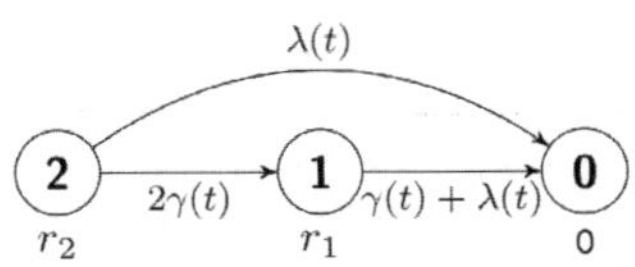

Figure 6: Markov Reward Model for one module with time dependent failure rates.

Since the NHCTMC is acyclic, we can use the *convolution integration approach* [10, 28] to derive the state probability expressions for the three states:

$$\pi_2(t) = e^{-\int_0^t (\lambda(x)+2\gamma(x))dx}$$
$$= e^{-\int_0^t \lambda(x)dx} \cdot e^{-\int_0^t 2\gamma(x)dx} = e^{-(\Lambda(t)+2\Gamma(t))} \tag{6}$$

where

$$\Lambda(t) = \int_0^t \lambda(x)dx \ , \quad \Gamma(t) = \int_0^t \gamma(x)dx$$

$$\pi_1(t) = \int_0^t \pi_2(x) \cdot 2\gamma(x) \cdot e^{-\int_x^t (\lambda(y)+\gamma(y))dy} dx$$
$$= \int_0^t e^{-(\Lambda(x)+2\Gamma(x))} \cdot 2\gamma(x) \cdot e^{-\int_x^t (\lambda(y)+\gamma(y))dy} dx$$
$$= 2\int_0^t e^{-\int_0^t (\lambda(y)+\gamma(y))dy} \cdot \gamma(x) \cdot e^{-\Gamma(x)} dx \tag{7}$$
$$= 2e^{-(\Lambda(t)+\Gamma(t))} \cdot (1 - e^{-\Gamma(t)})$$
$$= 2e^{-(\Lambda(t)+\Gamma(t))} - 2e^{-(\Lambda(t)+2\Gamma(t))}$$

$$\pi_0(t) = 1 - \pi_2(t) - \pi_1(t)$$
$$= 1 + e^{-(\Lambda(t)+2\Gamma(t))} - 2e^{-(\Lambda(t)+\Gamma(t))} \tag{8}$$

Once we have derived the state probability expressions, we can compute the expected power available at time t and the expected energy delivered in the interval $(0, t]$ using the reward rates r_1 and r_2:

$$E[X(t)] = r_2\pi_2(t) + r_1\pi_1(t)$$
$$= (r_2 - 2r_1)e^{-(\Lambda(t)+2\Gamma(t))} + 2r_1 e^{-(\Lambda(t)+\Gamma(t))}$$

$$E[Y(t)] = r_2 \int_0^t \pi_2(x)dx + r_1 \int_0^t \pi_1(x)dx \tag{9}$$
$$= r_2 \int_0^t e^{-(\Lambda(x)+2\Gamma(x))} dx$$
$$+ r_1 \int_0^t 2e^{-(\Lambda(x)+\Gamma(x))} - 2e^{-(\Lambda(x)+2\Gamma(x))} dx$$

4.3 Hierarchical model

The models described in Sections 4.1 and 4.2 still refer to one single module of the three lines of the multi-voltage propulsion system. Now we extend our argument to consider the whole system with the goal of arriving to a fully symbolic solution not easily obtained from the CTMC of Figure 2.

To build up a model for the whole system of Figure 1, we assume statistical independence among the three parallel modules, and we use a hierarchical approach whose structure is depicted in Figure 7. The highest level of the hierarchy is implemented with a multivalued Fault Tree, in which the top event is the system failure. The top event is the output of an AND gate whose inputs are the module failures. At the lower level of the hierarchy there are the NHCTMC of Figure 6 modeling the module failures. The top event occurs when all the inputs occur, i.e., all the three modules fail. Each basic event can be in one of the three states of Figure 6 and we indicate by n_i the number of modules in state i ($i = 0,\ 1,\ 2$) where $0 \leq n_0, n_1, n_2 \leq 3$ and $n_0 + n_1 + n_2 = 3$. Hence, the state of the top event can be described by a triple $\{n_0, n_1, n_2\}$ indicating how many modules are in state 0, in state 1 and in state 2.

The probability of each possible output configuration is derived as:

$$\pi_{n_0,n_1,n_2} = \binom{3}{n_0, n_1, n_2} \cdot [\pi_2(t)]^{n_2} \cdot [\pi_1(t)]^{n_1} \cdot [\pi_0(t)]^{n_0}$$
$$= \frac{3!}{n_0!\ n_1!\ n_2!} \cdot [\pi_2(t)]^{n_2} \cdot [\pi_1(t)]^{n_1} \cdot [\pi_0(t)]^{n_0} \tag{10}$$

where the $\pi_i(t)$ in the r.h.s. of Equation (10) are those derived in Equations (6), (7) and (8).

From the hierarchical model we can compute the expected power delivered at time t, the total energy supplied during the interval $(0, t]$ and the system MTTF. For the sake of simplicity, we consider time-independent transition rates in the lower level model i.e., the homogeneous CTMC of Figure 3 and we use the results of Equation (1) in Equation (10).

Thus, the expected power delivered at time t and the total energy supplied during the interval $(0, t]$ are:

$$E[X(t)] = \sum_{n_2=0}^{3}\sum_{n_1=0}^{3-n_2}(r_2n_2 + r_1n_1)\binom{3}{3-n_1-n_2, n_1, n_2} \cdot [\pi_2(t)]^{n_2} \cdot [\pi_1(t)]^{n_1} \cdot [\pi_0(t)]^{3-n_1-n_2} = 3e^{-(2\gamma+\lambda)t} \cdot [2(e^{\gamma t} - 1)r_1 + r_2]$$

$$E[Y(t)] = \sum_{n_2=0}^{3}\sum_{n_1=0}^{3-n_2}(r_2n_2 + r_1n_1)\binom{3}{3-n_1-n_2, n_1, n_2} \cdot \int_0^t [\pi_2(x)]^{n_2} \cdot [\pi_1(x)]^{n_1} \cdot [\pi_0(x)]^{3-n_1-n_2}dx = \frac{3e^{-(2\gamma+\lambda)t}}{(\gamma+\lambda)(2\gamma+\lambda)} \cdot \Big[(e^{(2\gamma+\lambda)t} - 1)(\gamma+\lambda)r_2 + 2r_1[(1 - 2e^{\gamma t} + e^{(2\gamma+\lambda)t})\gamma + \lambda - \lambda e^{\gamma t}]\Big] \quad (11)$$

To derive the MTTF, we start computing the reliability

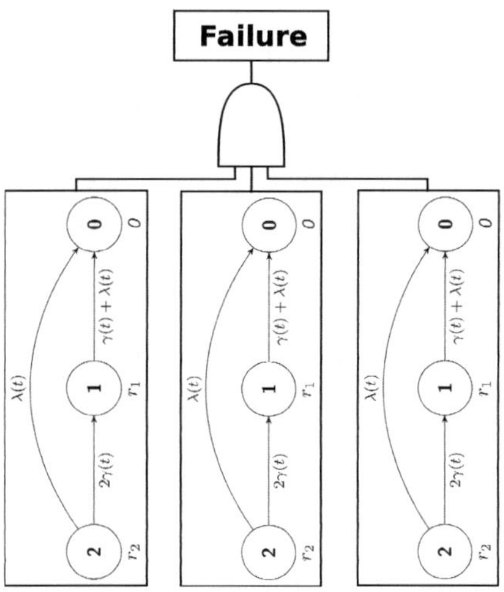

Figure 7: Hierarchical model for the multi-voltage system.

of the whole system represented by the model in Figure 7. Given the system configuration, the reliability can be derived from the equation $R_{sys}(t) = 1 - \pi_{3,0,0}$, where $\pi_{3,0,0}$ is the down state and is computed from Equation (10). In this case, the reliability is:

$$\begin{aligned} R_{sys}(t) &= 1 - [1 - 2e^{-(\gamma+\lambda)t} + e^{-(2\gamma+\lambda)t}]^3 \\ &= 12e^{-(3\gamma+2\lambda)t} + 6e^{-(5\gamma+3\lambda)t} - 12e^{-(4\gamma+3\lambda)t} \\ &\quad - 3e^{-(2\gamma+\lambda)t} - 3e^{-2(2\gamma+\lambda)t} - e^{-3(2\gamma+\lambda)t} \\ &\quad + 6e^{-(\gamma+\lambda)t} - 12e^{-2(\gamma+\lambda)t} + 8e^{-3(\gamma+\lambda)t} \end{aligned} \quad (12)$$

Due to the simplicity of this model, same result could have been obtained by a direct application of the series/parallel reduction rules to the RBD of Figure 1. MTTF of the whole system is computed integrating the reliability as follows:

$$\begin{aligned} MTTF &= \int_0^\infty R_{sys}(t)dt \\ &= \frac{8}{3(\gamma+\lambda)} - \frac{29}{6(2\gamma+\lambda)} + \frac{12}{(3\gamma+2\lambda)} \\ &\quad - \frac{12}{(4\gamma+3\lambda)} + \frac{6}{(5\gamma+3\lambda)} \end{aligned} \quad (13)$$

Substituting the numerical values given in Table 1 to λ and γ, we obtain $MTTF = 21662.9$ hours.

5. ACCURACY ANALYSIS

In this section we study how to evaluate the accuracy of the results and how to find a convenient strategy to improve the accuracy. For this purpose, we first investigate the parametric sensitivity to identify the most affecting parameters for a chosen significant measure (the MTTF in our case), then we study how the uncertainty in the knowledge of the input parameters is propagated to the output measures. Finally, we investigate a possible relation between sensitivity and uncertainty.

5.1 Parametric sensitivity

Parametric sensitivity is a technique used to identify components that most affect an output measure. In this paper we focus on the MTTF whose expression, for the system with time-independent failure rates, is given in Equation (13).

Differential analysis [13, 19] is the basis of many sensitivity analysis techniques. The sensitivity $S_\theta(MTTF)$ of the MTTF with respect to the model parameter θ is obtained by computing the partial derivative of the metric of interest with respect to the parameter, as in Equation (14):

$$S_\theta(MTTF) = \frac{\partial MTTF}{\partial \theta}, \quad \theta = \{\lambda_T, \lambda_F, \lambda_I, \lambda_M, \gamma\} \quad (14)$$

The dimensionless scaled sensitivity is defined as follows [11]:

$$SS_\theta(MTTF) = \frac{\partial MTTF}{\partial \theta} \cdot \frac{\theta}{MTTF} \quad (15)$$

Adoption of scaled or unscaled sensitivity depends on several factors: type of the output metrics; the range of values of the output and input parameters; etc. In this paper we use the scaled sensitivity as computed in Equation (15). For one of the series components with rate λ_X with $X = \{T, I, F, M\}$, the scaled sensitivity in Equation (15) becomes:

$$SS_{\lambda_X}(MTTF) = -\lambda_X \cdot \frac{\frac{8}{3(\gamma+\lambda)^2} - \frac{29}{6(2\gamma+\lambda)^2} + \frac{24}{(3\gamma+2\lambda)^2} - \frac{36}{(4\gamma+3\lambda)^2} + \frac{18}{(5\gamma+3\lambda)^2}}{\frac{8}{3(\gamma+\lambda)} - \frac{29}{6(2\gamma+\lambda)} + \frac{12}{3\gamma+2\lambda} - \frac{12}{4\gamma+3\lambda} + \frac{6}{5\gamma+3\lambda}} \quad (16)$$

Expanding Equation (15) for a parallel converter with failure rate γ, we obtain:

$$SS_\gamma(MTTF) = -\gamma \cdot \frac{\frac{8}{3(\gamma+\lambda)^2} - \frac{29}{3(2\gamma+\lambda)^2} + \frac{36}{(3\gamma+2\lambda)^2} - \frac{48}{(4\gamma+3\lambda)^2} + \frac{30}{(5\gamma+3\lambda)^2}}{\frac{8}{3(\gamma+\lambda)} - \frac{29}{6(2\gamma+\lambda)} + \frac{12}{3\gamma+2\lambda} - \frac{12}{4\gamma+3\lambda} + \frac{6}{5\gamma+3\lambda}} \quad (17)$$

In Table 2, numerical values of the scaled sensitivity of MTTF computed through Equations (16) and (17) are reported. They have been sorted from the most to the least sensitive. Note that all the values are negative meaning that if the value of the parameter θ increases, the MTTF decreases. The most influential component in affecting the MTTF is the inverter which is the component with the largest failure rate value.

Figure 8 shows the variation of the MTTF as a function of the variation of the failure rate of one single component, keeping all the other failure rates constant. The larger is the parametric sensitivity in absolute value, as reported in Table 2, the greater is the benefit that is possible to obtain if the considered component failure rate is improved. The straight line in Figure 8 is the current value of MTTF, as computed with Equation (13).

Table 2: Ranking based on scaled sensitivities of MTTF.

θ	$SS_\theta(MTTF)$
λ_I	$-4.16997 \cdot 10^{-1}$
λ_M	$-3.51155 \cdot 10^{-1}$
γ	$-2.03316 \cdot 10^{-1}$
λ_T	$-2.41419 \cdot 10^{-2}$
λ_F	$-4.38944 \cdot 10^{-3}$

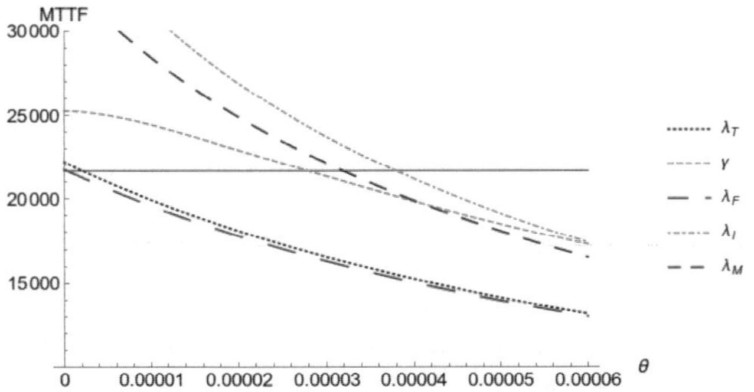

Figure 8: MTTF of the system computed varying the failure rate of one component at a time. Each curve is obtained varying the considered parameter between 0 and $6 \cdot 10^{-5}$, and keeping constant all the other failure rates. The straight line is the current value of MTTF, as computed from Equation (13).

5.2 Uncertainty propagation

We derive the uncertainty propagation through the analytic closed-form approach described in [20, 21], then we compare the results with those obtained from the parametric sensitivity analysis of Section 5.1.

Input parameters of a model have uncertainty associated with them (called epistemic uncertainty [26]), since they are derived from a finite number of observations in measurement campaigns. Authors of [21] describe a closed-form approach to compute how the uncertainty in the model input parameters propagates to the model output affecting the reliability of the system. The same procedure can be applied to compute the uncertainty propagation for other output measures, like the MTTF considered in this paper. Let the input parameters of the model be the random variables $(\Lambda_1, \Lambda_2, \ldots, \Lambda_\ell)$. The MTTF can be viewed as a random function of the ℓ input parameters $MTTF(\Lambda_1, \Lambda_2, \ldots, \Lambda_\ell)$ indicated, for short, as $MTTF(\bullet)$. The technique derived from [20, 21] consists in computing the unconditional expected MTTF through the following equation:

$$E[MTTF] = \int \ldots \int MTTF(\bullet) f(\bullet) d\lambda_1 \ldots d\lambda_\ell \qquad (18)$$

where the input parameters are set to $\Lambda_1 = \lambda_1$, $\Lambda_2 = \lambda_2$, ..., $\Lambda_\ell = \lambda_\ell$ and $f(\bullet)$ is the joint epistemic density $f_{\Lambda_1, \Lambda_2, \ldots, \Lambda_\ell}(\lambda_1, \lambda_2, \ldots, \lambda_\ell)$ of the input parameters

Let X be an exponentially distributed random variable of rate Λ and let $f_\Lambda(\lambda)$ be the prior density of Λ. We observe a sample of k independent and identically distributed (iid) random realizations of X, say $X_1, X_2, \ldots, X_k$. Setting $S = \sum_{i=1}^{k} X_i$, the conditional density of Λ given $S = s$ can be derived from the continuous version of Bayes's theorem and it is shown to be [21] a k-stage Erlang distribution with parameter s:

$$f_{\Lambda|S}(\lambda|s) = \frac{\lambda^{k-1} s^k e^{-\lambda s}}{(k-1)!} \qquad (19)$$

Since we are considering exponentially distributed time to failures, the maximum likelihood estimate for the rate λ in Equation (19) is $\hat{\lambda} = k/s$. In this setting, the unconditional expected MTTF is computed from:

$$E[MTTF] = \int_0^\infty \int_0^\infty \int_0^\infty \int_0^\infty \int_0^\infty MTTF(\bullet) \cdot \prod_\theta \frac{\theta^{k_\theta - 1} s_\theta^{k_\theta} e^{-\theta s_\theta}}{(k_\theta - 1)!} d\theta \qquad (20)$$

where $\theta = \{\lambda_T, \gamma, \lambda_I, \lambda_F, \lambda_M\}$ and k_θ and s_θ are the values of k and s computed for the component with rate θ. In Equation (20) we can define the joint pdf $f(\bullet)$ as a product of the marginal pdfs since we assume that the model input parameters are independent random variables.

Figure 9a shows $E[MTTF]$ of the considered system computed from (20) as a function of the sample size k. The dashed line at the bottom of the graph is the MTTF computed with the parameter values of Table 1, to which the expected MTTF tends asymptotically as $k_\theta \to \infty$. Note that, for simplicity, the value of k_θ is kept the same for all the parameters.

The variance of the MTTF can be computed from

$$Var[MTTF] = E[MTTF^2] - (E[MTTF])^2 \qquad (21)$$

and is depicted in Figure 9b. In this case, for $k_\theta \to \infty$ the variance tends to zero. The smaller is the variance, the tighter will be the confidence interval of the considered output measure.

With equation:

$$E[MTTF] = \int_0^\infty MTTF \frac{\theta^{k_\theta - 1} s_\theta^{k_\theta} e^{-\theta s_\theta}}{(k_\theta - 1)!} d\theta \qquad (22)$$

it is possible to evaluate the uncertainty introduced in the MTTF by the single parameter θ, while all the other parameters are assumed to have the constant value of Table 1. Variance can still be derived through Equation (21). Results are depicted in Figure 10. Each curve represents the $E[MTTF]$ ($Var[MTTF]$) of the system that is computed through Equation (22) for the considered parameter. For $k \to \infty$ the expected MTTF tends to the MTTF computed with the parameters of Table 1, whereas the variance tends to zero.

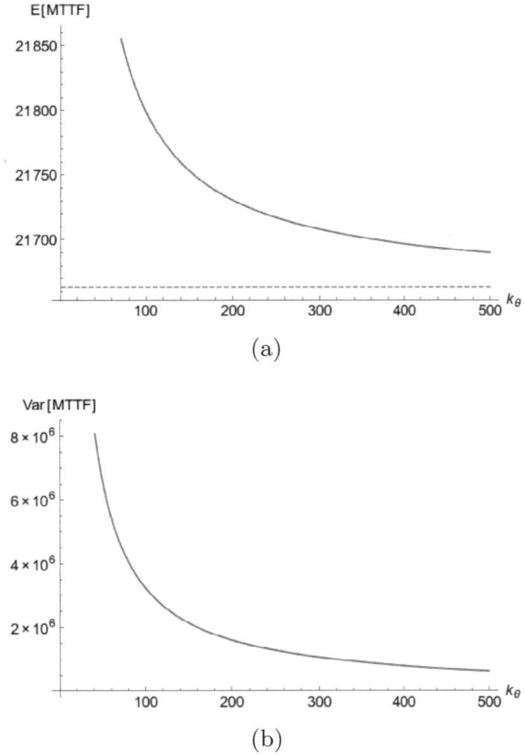

Figure 9: Expected value (a) and variance (b) of MTTF of the multi-voltage propulsion system.

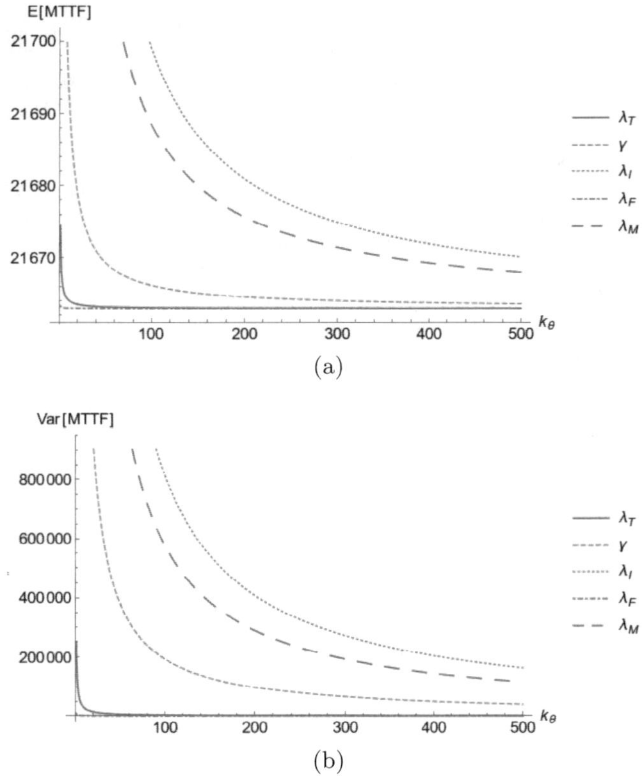

Figure 10: Expected value (a) and variance (b) of the MTTF varying the estimated parameter.

5.3 Sensitivity vs. Uncertainty Propagation

The closed-form approach to the uncertainty propagation requires the computation of a multiple integral for each parameter; symbolic or numerical computation of such integral becomes impractical for complex and large models [20]. Moreover, this technique also requires us to specify the joint epistemic density of all the parameters: this step may be difficult even if it can be simplified considering independent parameters (as we have done in this paper).

From Table 2 and Figure 10 it is possible to observe that for the parameters with a larger absolute value of the sensitivity a larger number of samples is needed to reach the same tight confidence interval. Results obtained in Sections 5.1 and 5.2 show that a relationship between parametric sensitivity and uncertainty propagation exists. Parametric sensitivity evaluation through partial derivatives is easier and quicker to carry out than uncertainty propagation through integral computation. The same observation remains valid for other parametric sensitivity computation methods, such as percentage difference [15] and Design of Experiments [16].

The above mentioned relationship allows us to use parametric sensitivity analysis to identify the parameters that need tighter confidence interval to get more accurate output measures. This method is less affected by the largeness and complexity of the system than the uncertainty propagation technique.

6. CONCLUSIONS

The multi-voltage propulsion system proposed in [6] and developed for the Italian High Speed Railway is the case study analyzed in this paper. Some techniques to simplify the derivation of fully symbolic solution and to get more accurate results are presented. In the considered case study, it is possible to model the whole system with a hierarchical model to obtain a symbolic solution for the model measures like the reliability and the MTTF. In addition, adopting a MRM it is possible to evaluate measures related to the delivered power. Further, time dependent failure rates can be included in the model by still deriving a symbolic solution.

In this paper, parametric sensitivity and epistemic uncertainty of the input parameters are also considered. A relevant result shows that a relationship between these two evaluation methods exists. It means that, for more complex models it is possible to use the parametric sensitivity analysis instead of the uncertainty propagation to identify the parameters that need a larger number of samples to reach the same accuracy. Note, however, that the same method cannot predict how many samples are needed to attain a given level of accuracy because the parametric sensitivity does not depend on the number of samples.

This paper is the first attempt to find a relationship between parametric sensitivity and uncertainty propagation. We wish to formalize this relationship and investigate possible generalizations. Two different ways can be envisaged to extend the paper in this direction: to analyze other output measures (e.g, reliability, availability, etc.) and to consider different applications. A more challenging direction of our research is toward building an optimization problem. Indeed, since a larger number of observations entails increased costs for the measurement campaign, a trade-off between cost and accuracy of the output measures exists and can be analyzed.

Acknowledgement

This research was supported in part under US NSF grant number CNS-1523994, by US Navy under grant N00174-16-C-0036, by IBM under a faculty grant, by NATO under Science for Peace project number 984425 and by DiSit-UniUpo local research Project.

7. REFERENCES

[1] H. R. Bae, R. V. Grandhi, and R. A. Canfield. Epistemic uncertainty quantification techniques including evidence theory for large-scale structures. *Computers & Structures*, 82(13–14):1101–1112, 2004.

[2] P. Baumgärtel, G. Endler, A. M. Wahl, and R. Lenz. Inverse uncertainty propagation for demand driven data acquisition. In *Proceedings of the 2014 Winter Simulation Conference*, pages 710–721. IEEE, 2014.

[3] M. D. Beaudry. Performance-related reliability measures for computing systems. *Computers, IEEE Transactions on*, 100(6):540–547, 1978.

[4] J. T. Blake, A. L. Reibman, and K. S. Trivedi. Sensitivity analysis of reliability and performability measures for multiprocessor systems. *ACM SIGMETRICS Performance Evaluation Review*, 16(1):177–186, 1988.

[5] A. Bobbio and A. Premoli. Fast algorithm for unavailability and sensitivity analysis of series-parallel systems. *IEEE Transactions on Reliability*, R-31:359–361, 1982.

[6] G. Cosulich, P. Firpo, and S. Savio. Power electronics reliability impact on service dependability for railway systems: a real case study. In *Industrial Electronics, 1996. ISIE'96., Proceedings of the IEEE International Symposium on*, volume 2, pages 996–1001. IEEE, 1996.

[7] G. Dazi, S. Savio, and P. Firpo. Estimate of components reliability and maintenance strategies impact on trains delay. In *Proc 21st European Conf on Modelling and Simulation ECMS*, 2007.

[8] A. De Galizia, C. Simon, P. Weber, B. Iung, C. Duval, and E. Serdet. Modelling non-deterministic causal mechanisms involving resilience in risk analysis. In *8th IFAC Conference on Manufacturing, Management & Control, MIM 2016*, 2016.

[9] R. G. Easterling. Approximate confidence limits for system reliability. *Journal of the American Statistical Association*, 67(337):220–222, 1972.

[10] T. E. Fortmann and K. L. Hitz. *An introduction to linear control systems*. Crc Press, 1977.

[11] R. Fricks and K. Trivedi. Importance analysis with markov chains. In *Proceedings IEEE Annual Reliability and Maintainability Symposium*, pages 89–95, 2003.

[12] M. A. S. Guth. A probabilistic foundation for vagueness and imprecision in fault-tree analysis. *IEEE Transactions on Reliability*, 40(5):563–571, Dec 1991.

[13] D. Hamby. A review of techniques for parameter sensitivity analysis of environmental models. *Environmental monitoring and assessment*, 32(2):135–154, 1994.

[14] B. R. Haverkort and A. M. Meeuwissen. Sensitivity and uncertainty analysis of markov-reward models. *IEEE Trans Reliability,*, 44(1):147–154, 1995.

[15] F. Hoffman and R. Gardner. Evaluation of uncertainties in radiological assessment models. In *Radiological Assessment: A Textbook on Environmental Dose Analysis*, pages 11.1–11.55. United States Nuclear Regulatory Commission Washington, DC, 1983.

[16] R. Jain. *The art of computer systems performance analysis*. John Wiley & Sons, 2008.

[17] G. Lieberman and S. Ross. Confidence intervals for independent exponential series systems. *J American Statistical Association*, 66(336):837–840, 1971.

[18] R. A. Maire, A. L. Reibman, and K. S. Trivedi. Transient analysis of acyclic markov chains. *Performance Evaluation*, 7(3):175–194, 1987.

[19] R. Matos, J. Araujo, D. Oliveira, P. Maciel, and K. Trivedi. Sensitivity analysis of a hierarchical model of mobile cloud computing. *Simulation Modelling Practice and Theory*, 50:151–164, 2015.

[20] K. Mishra, K. Trivedi, and R. Some. Uncertainty analysis of the remote exploration and experimentation system. *J. of Spacecraft and Rockets*, 49(6):1032–1042, 2012.

[21] K. Mishra and K. S. Trivedi. Closed-form approach for epistemic uncertainty propagation in analytic models. In *Stochastic Reliability and Maintenance Modeling*, pages 315–332. Springer, 2013.

[22] J. K. Muppala and K. S. Trivedi. Gspm models: sensitivity analysis and applications. In *Proc 28th Ann Southeast Regional Conf*, pages 25–33. ACM, 1990.

[23] N. D. Singpurwalla. *Reliability and risk: a Bayesian perspective*. John Wiley & Sons, 2006.

[24] E. Song, B. L. Nelson, and L. J. Hong. Input uncertainty and indifference-zone ranking & selection. In *Proceedings of the 2015 Winter Simulation Conference*, pages 414–424. IEEE, 2015.

[25] O. Strack, R. Leavy, and R. M. Brannon. Aleatory uncertainty and scale effects in computational damage models for failure and fragmentation. *International Journal for Numerical Methods in Engineering*, 102(3-4):468–495, 2015.

[26] L. Swiler, T. Paez, and R. Mayes. Epistemic uncertainty quantification tutorial. In *Proceedings of the IMAC-XXVII*. Society for Experimental Mechanics Inc., 2009.

[27] D. Tannenbaum, C. R. Fox, and G. Ülkümen. Judgment extremity and accuracy under epistemic vs. aleatory uncertainty. *Management Science*, 2016.

[28] K. S. Trivedi. *Probability & statistics with reliability, queuing and computer science applications*. John Wiley & Sons, 2008.

[29] R. L. Winkler. Treatment of aleatory and epistemic uncertainty uncertainty in probabilistic risk assessment. *Reliability Engineering & System Safety*, 54(2):127–132, 1996.

[30] Y. Yi, W. Xie, and E. Zhou. A sequential experiment design for input uncertainty quantification in stochastic simulation. In *Proc. of the 2015 Winter Simulation Conference*, pages 447–458. IEEE, 2015.

[31] K. Zwirglmaier and D. Straub. A discretization procedure for rare events in bayesian networks. *Reliability Engineering & System Safety*, 153:96–109, 2016.

Sensitivity of Application Performance to Resource Availability

Boris Penev
School of Informatics
University of Edinburgh, UK
s1249355@sms.ed.ac.uk

Ajitha Rajan
School of Informatics
University of Edinburgh, UK
arajan@staffmail.ed.ac.uk

ABSTRACT

Existing literature has extensively explored and analysed the effects of shared resource contention to improve system throughput and resource utilisation. Nevertheless, a systematic study varying different resource availabilities and examining their combined effect on the performance of an individual application has not been conducted earlier. In this paper, we perform global sensitivity analysis using Monte Carlo simulations of three resource parameters – CPU availability, RAM availability and number of cores, and examine their effect on execution time of industry standard benchmark programs. In addition to understanding application performance sensitivity, our study also lends itself to identifying threshold levels of required resources, below which severe application performance degradation occurs.

1. INTRODUCTION

Users, whether on a desktop, laptop or mobile device, tend to have several applications running concurrently. The performance of any one of these applications, given a hardware platform, is heavily dependent on the resources available, which in turn relies on the resource demands of applications and processes running at that time, shared resource contention and the operating system's resource allocation priorities and decisions. It is common knowledge that resource contention directly impacts application performance [6]. Mars et al. show more than 30% degradation in application performance (from running alone) when run alongside with another application on a multicore chip due to contention for the last level cache. However, varying levels of resource contention and, therefore, resource availability and its resulting impact on application performance is not well understood. Additionally, the user receives little to no feedback on the extent of expected performance degradation of an application due to resource contention and reduced availability.

Previous work has extensively explored and analysed the effects of shared resource contention [6],[11],[5]. The aim in all these studies has been to use the understanding of resource contention to improve system throughput, resource usage, and to enforce QoS and fairness across *all* running applications. *System*, rather than an *individual application*, performance has been the optimisation goal. Bhadauria et al. performed Parsec Benchmark characterisation for cache performance, DRAM speed and bandwidth, thread scalability for solo benchmark execution (no other running applications) [1]. Dey et al. and Zhuravlev et al. study L1, L2 cache and front side bus contentions for multi-threaded applications individually and with one other co-running application [2],[12]. They show performance degradation occurs in the presence of certain co-running applications but not others. The effect of reduced resource availability as a result of one other co-running application was studied, however the effect of systematically varying different resource availabilities across the whole range (from 0 to 100%) has not been studied. The experiments presented in this paper attempts to fill this gap. The goal in understanding this effect with respect to an application is to inform the user dynamically of when the performance of the application is expected to fall below acceptable levels due to lack of availability in required resources. The user can use this feedback to guide their actions, which might be to kill other running applications, or to have the operating system prioritise resources to the application of interest, or to simply accept the below par performance. Techniques in existing literature have never actively involved the user in the decision for resource allocation. This work is an attempt to give the user, if they choose, information and ultimately control in managing the performance of an application dynamically.

In this paper, we examine the effect on the execution or completion time of an application when the percentage of available CPU, RAM and number of cores *simultaneously* change. Other resources, such as cache, memory bus, network, I/O decives will also potentially impact the performance of an application. However, in this initial study we do not examine the effect of these other resources. We plan to consider them in the future.

We use global sensitivity analysis [10] to assess the impact of resource availability on application performance since parameter sensitivity is dependent on the interactions and influences of all parameters considered together on application performance rather than one parameter at a time. Sensitivity analysis can be achieved through Monte Carlo sampling [3] – repeated random sampling of input parameters from given distributions. In our setting, in each iteration, we randomly sample values for the three hardware parameters, set the resource availability to the respective values and record execution time of the application for each such setting. The input and output distributions are useful in assessing influence of input parameters on the overall output performance.

VALUETOOLS 2016, October 25-28, Taormina, Italy

We used industry standard benchmarks in our experiments. For 5 of the 6 benchmarks, we found CPU availability was the most influential of the three resource parameters on execution time. For one of the benchmarks, number of cores was the most influential parameter. Our experiment results revealed that it is possible to set and monitor for threshold levels of required resources to avoid performance degradation of an application below user expectations.

2. EXPERIMENT

In our experiment, we use applications from EEMBC [9] benchmark suite, SPEC CPU 2006 [4] and a Linux kernel compilation program to study performance degradation from limited resource availability. In actual settings, limited resource availability arises from shared resource contentions with other running applications. We artificially set limits to availability of different resources in our experiments so we can systematically explore a large sample of values in the range of resource availabilities. We ran our experiments on a desktop running Scientific Linux 7.1 with 8 GB RAM, Intel i5-3470 quad core CPU at 3.20GHz. In the following sections, we discuss the tools we use to limit available resources, the Monte Carlo approach we use to understand the effect of limited resources, and finally the benchmark applications used in our experiment.

2.1 Setting Hardware Parameters

We consider application performance as its completion time and measure it using the time module in the python script used to run the benchmark and workload. Other performance measures can also be used in place of execution time, but we have not considered them in this paper. In addition to monitoring the output performance, we need to control and vary the input parameters which is amount of available resources–(1) **CPU**, (2) **Memory (RAM)**, and (3) **number of cores** – for the application of interest. Cgroups is a kernel feature to limit the resource usage for a group of processes [7] and creates little to no overhead since it is a kernel tool. We use Cgroups to modify all three hardware parameters using the `cpuset, cpu` and `memory` subsystems. To achieve limits on cpu availability and number of cores, the `cpu` and `cpuset` subsystem manipulates the scheduler and its policy with respect to the group of processes in cgroup. The memory subsystem manipulates the memory allocation policy to achieve limits on the memory parameter.

2.2 Random Sampling of Parameters

In our experiments, we sample and generate random settings of the parameters– CPU availability, #cores and RAM availability, using their gaussian distributions. The CPU availability(in %) has a mean 50, deviation 20, left limit 25 and right limit 100. Number of cores parameter has a mean 2, deviation 1.5, left limit 1 and right limit 4. The memory parameter has a mean 1 GB, deviation 0.4 GB, left limit 1KB and right limit 3 GB. These limits have been chosen based on the hardware configuration and application characteristics (mainly for memory limits). Our base case environment has 50% CPU availability, 2 cores and 1GB memory and we use this as the mean of the normal distribution. The deviation in the distribution corresponds to the variation in the resource availability.

2.3 Subject Programs

We used the Embedded Microprocessor Benchmark Consortium (EEMBC) [9] that provides a diverse suite of benchmarks for microprocessors, microcontrollers and embedded devices with a total of 32 programs and workloads from the automotive, telecommunications, office, networking, and image processing domains. We also used the integer benchmarks from the SPEC CPU 2006 suite [4] (SPECint benchmarks), an industry standard benchmark suite to test CPU performance, with a total of 12 programs and corresponding reference workload for each. We also use Linux kernel compilation(`build_kernel`) as a benchmark. We disable non-essential drivers, networking, cryptography and virtualisation options. This lowers the number of dependencies, making it more tractable for our initial evaluation. We compile it using multiple cores to assess the sensitivity of execution with respect to cores.

3. RESULTS AND ANALYSIS

We ran Monte Carlo simulation over the three hardware parameters for all 45 programs. Owing to space limitations, we show the results for only six of the 45 programs in the paper– `build_kernel`, `matrix01` from the EEMBC suite, `astar, bzip2, gobmk, h264` from the SPEC CPU2006 benchmarks, whose descriptions are shown in Table 1. Results for the remaining 39 programs from EEMBC and SPEC CPU 2006 benchmark suites can be accessed at "`http://homepages.inf.ed.ac.uk/arajan/results-MC.pdf`".

Parameter sensitivity can be determined qualitatively by plots of input vs output values, or quantitatively by calculations of correlation coefficients [3]. Table 3 shows scatter plots for the 6 programs, plotting each resource availability against execution time. It is worth noting that although each plot only shows one resource at a time, all three resource availability values have been changed and sampled at the points in the plots.

Program	ρ CPU avail.	ρ #Cores	ρ RAM
matrix01	-0.55	0.05	0.03
build kernel	-0.46	-0.61	0.19
astar	-0.92	-0.07	0.09
bzip2	-0.93	-0.02	-0.01
gobmk	-0.92	0.04	-0.03
h.264	-0.93	0.02	-0.07

Table 2: Sensitivity indices of resource availability (Correlation Coeff. with exec. time)

We compute sensitivity indices for the parameters using Pearson's correlation coefficient (ρ) which represents the sensitivity of the output to input parameter variations [3]. The larger the absolute value of ρ the stronger the degree of linear relationship between the input and output values. A negative value of ρ indicates the output is inversely related to the input. Table 2 shows the sensitivity indices for CPU availability, number of cores and RAM with respect to a program's execution time. Negative values of ρ for resource availability is to be expected since execution time is typically lesser when there is more resource available.

From the plots in Table 3, we find that for all benchmarks, except `build_kernel`, CPU availability has the most effect on performance – increased CPU availability results in decreased execution time. This is also reflected by its significantly higher sensitivity index in Table 2 when compared to the other two resources, RAM and #cores. We checked the sensitivity values for CPU availability over the different benchmarks were valid by artifically simulating CPU load and comparing the execution time with our results in Table 3. For each benchmark, we performed 300 runs setting CPU load to different values (based on the CPU availability values used in our Monte Carlo Sampling) using a CPU load

Program	Description	Benchmark Suite	# Samples
`matrix01`	Matrix operations	EEMBC	1438
`build_kernel`	Building Linux kernel	n/a	101
`astar`	Pathfinding library for 2D maps	SPEC CINT2006	500
`bzip2`	File compression	SPEC CINT2006	500
`gobmk`	Plays the *GO* game	SPEC CINT2006	500
`h.264`	Video encoding	SPEC CINT2006	500

Table 1: Benchmarks and their desciption

generator [8]. We compare the execution times using CPU load generator with the execution times for the corresponding CPU availability set in our experiment. We found the mean absolute percentage error between the execution times were within 5% to 8% for all benchmarks.

For benchmark programs other than `build_kernel`, the sensitivity indices for #cores and RAM is small (absolute values in the range of 0.01 to 0.09) and only marginally different. As can be seen in the `Cores` and `Memory` plots for the 5 programs in Table 3, there is no discernible effect on execution time with increased availability. This is because the 5 benchmark programs are not optimised to run on multiple cores (designed as single core benchmarks) and have low memory requirements. Nevertheless, we found that for the `gobmk` benchmark when the available RAM was sampled at values less than 30MB, execution time increased dramatically – by 2 times for 24.1 MB RAM to 1195 times for 0.82 MB. We confirmed the effect was because of the RAM, rather than the other resources, by fixing the values for #cores at 2 and CPU available at 100%. Among available RAM values beyond 30MB, the difference in execution time was negligible. This implies that performance degradation is rapid when RAM available is below a certain threshold, which is 30MB for `gobmk`. We can use this information to notify the user when available RAM nears the threshold, using performance monitoring tools, to avoid this performance degradation. We did not see this phenomenon with available RAM for the other 4 benchmarks.

`build_kernel` exhibited a different trend from the other benchmarks. We find that execution time is most affected by changes in #cores (highest sensitivity index) – an increased number of CPU cores results in decreased build time. This is seen in the plot for `build_kernel Cores` in Table 3 as the number of cores increases from 1 to 4, the execution time reduces significantly. The make tool and the Linux kernel build processes are well optimised for multi-threaded execution on multicore processors. Although not as high as #cores, CPU availability also has a significant impact. Increased CPU availability results in decreased build time as seen in the `build_kernel Availability` plot. Thus, #cores and CPU availability are both important for `build_kernel` execution time. Changes in RAM availability produced no noticeable result in the build time and this may be because memory requirements for `build_kernel` are not high.

Using the information on parameter sensitivity, the plots in Table 3 and the raw data from running the experiment, one can identify thresholds for the different parameters beyond which performance degradation is unacceptable for the user. Identifying the threshold of unacceptability will require knowledge of expected performance levels (as per user) which can be inferred using historical data or user input. For instance, for `bzip2`, if we assume unacceptable performance is execution slowdown (from best case time) greater than 33%, then we pick threshold 60% for CPU availability (see plots in Table 3), since execution time increases by more than 33% for lower than 60% available CPU. RAM and # cores do not have a profound effect on execution time, so we do not pick thresholds for these resources for `bzip2`.

4. CONCLUSION

For the industry standard benchmarks used in this paper, we found that varying the input parameters using Monte Carlo simulations and examining the effect on execution time was an effective way to study application performance sensitivity to availability of different resources. Systematically analysing global resource sensitivity has not been studied previously. We found that such a study helps in identifying thresholds of unacceptable performance degradation. Resources can be monitored for these threshold values and the information communicated to the user or the system to act upon as needed.

5. REFERENCES

[1] M. Bhadauria, V. Weaver, and S. McKee. Understanding parsec performance on contemporary cmps. In *IISWC 2009*, pages 98–107. IEEE, 2009.

[2] T. Dey, W. Wang, J. Davidson, and ML Soffa. Characterizing multi-threaded applications based on shared-resource contention. In *ISPASS 2011*, pages 76–86. IEEE, 2011.

[3] DM Hamby. A review of techniques for parameter sensitivity analysis of environmental models. *Environmental monitoring and assessment*, 32(2):135–154, 1994.

[4] John L Henning. Spec cpu2006 benchmark descriptions. *ACM SIGARCH Computer Architecture News*, 34(4):1–17, 2006.

[5] H. Jin, R. Hood, J. Chang, J. Djomehri, D. Jespersen, K. Taylor, R. Biswas, and P. Mehrotra. Characterizing application performance sensitivity to resource contention in multicore architectures. *NASA Ames Research Center, Tech. Rep. NAS-09-002*, 2009.

[6] J. Mars, N. Vachharajani, R. Hundt, and ML Soffa. Contention aware execution: online contention detection and response. In *Proceedings of the 8th CGO*, pages 257–265. ACM, 2010.

[7] P. Menage, P Jackson, and C Lameter. Cgroups. *Available on-line at: http://www. mjmwired. net/kernel/Documentation/cgroups. txt*, 2008.

[8] Boris Penev. CPU Load Generator. https://github.com/boris-penev/CPULoadGenerator.

[9] J.A. Poovey, M Levy, S Gal-On, and T Conte. A benchmark characterization of the eembc benchmark suite. *Micro, IEEE*, PP(99):1–1, 2009.

[10] H. Wagner. Global sensitivity analysis. *Operations Research*, 43(6):948–969, 1995.

[11] C. Xu, X. Chen, R. Dick, and Z. Mao. Cache contention and application performance prediction for multi-core systems. In *ISPASS 2010*, pages 76–86.

[12] S. Zhuravlev, S. Blagodurov, and A. Fedorova. Addressing shared resource contention in multicore processors via scheduling. In *ACM Sigplan Notices*, volume 45, pages 129–142. ACM, 2010.

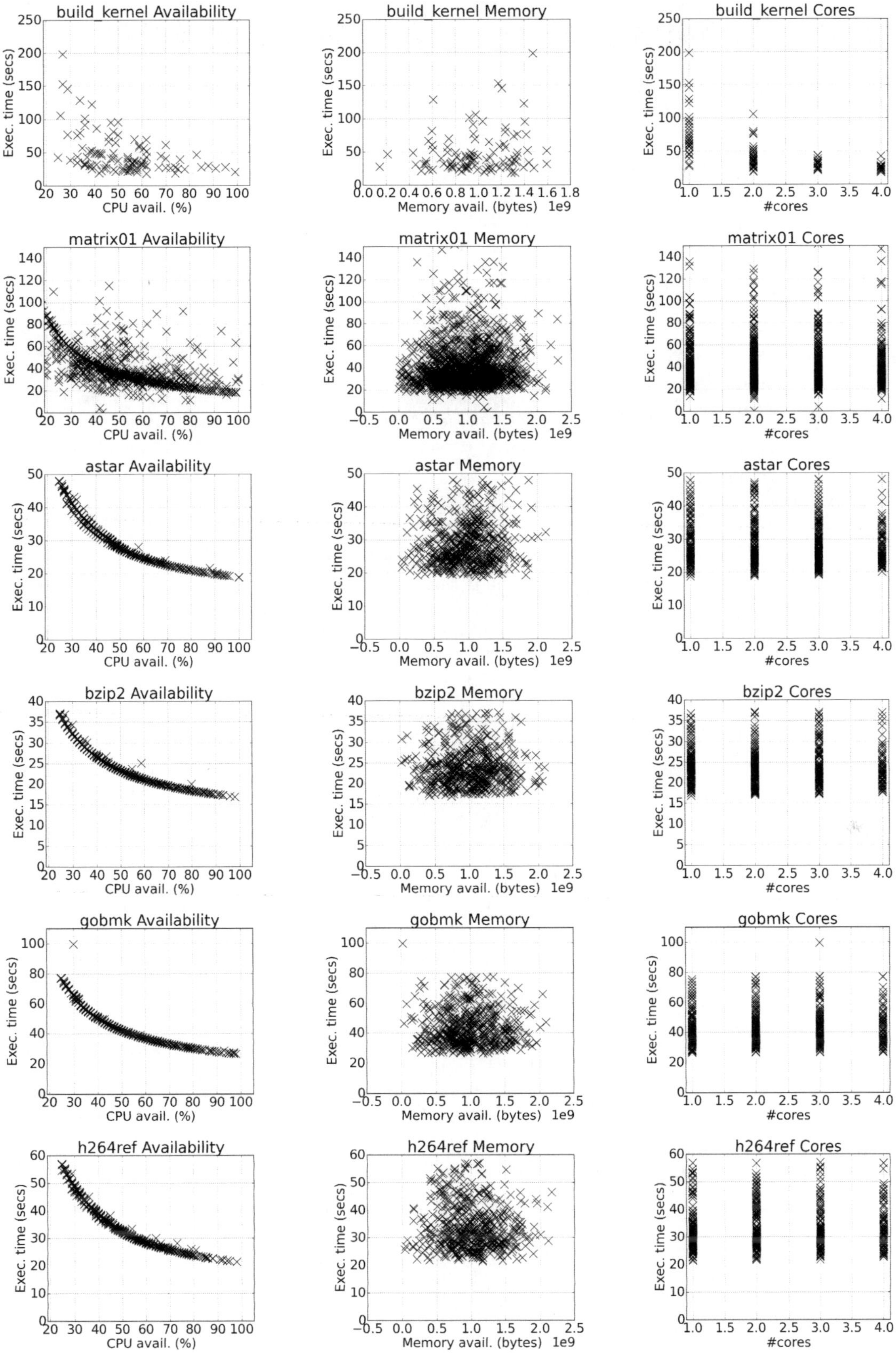

Table 3: Scatter plots of execution time versus resource availability (CPU, RAM, #cores) for build_kernel, 1 EEMBC and 4 SPEC benchmarks

Simulation Modeling for Speed Scaling Designs

[Extended Abstract]

Maryam Elahi Carey Williamson
Department of Computer Science, University of Calgary
Calgary, Alberta, Canada T2N 1N4
{bmelahi, carey}@ucalgary.ca

ABSTRACT

This paper introduces an extensible simulation tool for the study of speed scaling designs for a single server with variable service rates. This simulator facilitates detailed performance analysis of scheduling and speed scaling policies under different background settings. Our component-based design separates the system configuration, like the power consumption model and the incoming workload, from the policy components for scheduling and speed scaling. Furthermore, the simulator allows for custom implementations of the data logger, so the instrumentation could be fine tuned to the desired level of detail for each run of the simulation. We present the design of the main components of our simulator. We then show example results to highlight the versatility of the simulator for studying different speed scaling configurations.

CCS Concepts

•**Computing methodologies** → **Simulation tools;** •**Mathematics of computing** → *Queueing theory;*

Keywords

Speed Scaling, Scheduling, Energy Consumption, Discrete Event Simulation

1. INTRODUCTION

Modern CPUs have over a dozen processing rates, which enable system designers to balance speed and power consumption based on the required performance. This tradeoff is of interest both for mobile devices, which have limited power, and for datacenters, for which heat and cost man-agement are key considerations. Recently, there has been increased attention to the study of scheduling policies for servers with adjustable service rates both in the systems and theory communities [2, 12]. For a single-speed server, several analytical and simulation studies quantify the propertie

VALUETOOLS 2016, October 25-28, Taormina, Italy

ing policies. In particular, commonly used scheduling polices like First-Come-First-Serve (FCFS) and Processor Sharing (PS) were compared to size-based scheduling policies like Shortest-Remaining-Processing-Time (SRPT) with regard to queueing delay, response time, and fairness [9, 14].

For datacenters, optimizing the monetary cost of operation is the main goal. This could be translated into some combination of energy cost and the cost of losing customers or money for violating the service level aggreements (SLAs). These two metrics are inherently at odds with each other. Running at lower speeds consumes less energy, but degrades the performance. Furthermore, optimizing the average performance could have undesirable side effects like poor tail behavior, or decreased robustness in face of flash loads.

The tradeoffs between optimality, robustness, and fairness in speed scaling was first studied in [12]. For the cost function represented by the linear combination of the average response time and average energy consumption per job, [12] shows that SRPT with queue-length-based speed scaling is optimal in the worst case. The idea of queue-length-based speed scaling (*coupled speed scaling* for the rest of this paper), wherein the service rate is a function of the instantaneous system occupancy, was introduced in earlier literature [2]. In [12], the optimal speed function is shown to be the inverse of the power-consumption function.

There are many interesting questions still remaining about the interplay of scheduling and speed scaling. For example, [12] shows that coupled speed scaling magnifies unfairness for policies like SRPT and all the non-preemptive policies. However, the level of unfairness for these polices under different types of workloads is unknown.

In spite of the growing interest in the study of speed-scaling policies, to the best of our knowledge there is no public-domain tool for the simulation of scheduling with speed scaling. There are a number of simulation results presented for speed scaling designs in recent literature [7,12,13]. A recent public-domain simulation tool for a single speed server has been developed to study size-based scheduling when exact knowledge of job sizes is not available [5]. However, the simulator does not support variable service rates.

Our work: We have developed an extensible simulation tool for the study of speed scaling designs, which facilitates detailed performance analysis of scheduling and speed scaling policies under different background settings.

Design of a speed scaling simulator has several challenges. Special care is required to separate the scheduling and speed scaling decisions in order to allow for simulation of new approaches with minimal effort, and without introducing

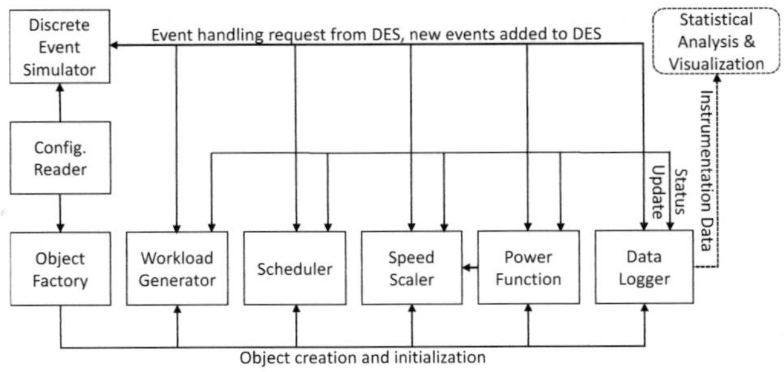

Figure 1: Data flow between the main components of the simulator.

bugs or inconsistencies into the simulation. Decoupling the scheduling decisions from speed scaling decisions was first presented in [7]. The idea was presented in the context of FSP with speed scaling, but was later generalized to other policies [6–8].

We developed our simulation tool to study the interplay between the speed scaler and the scheduler under different load regimes and power consumption models. For this reason, the extensibility of the simulation tool has been the main design focus. Furthermore, due to high variability of sampled metrics in many scenarios, long simulation runs are necessary in order to obtain statistically significant results. Therefore, efficiency in terms of run-time, memory, and storage requirements was considered in the design.

The simulator has an abstract design that models a single server with variable service rates. An infinite stream of jobs arrive to the system to receive service in some order specified by the scheduler and with some speed specified by the speed scaler. Energy consumption of the system is computed according to some power function. The entire operation of the server is tracked by the logger. Each of these components and the operation of the simulator is presented in more detail in Section 2.2.

We have used this simulator to verify previous analytical and simulation results presented in [13]. We have also gained insight into the autoscaling effect of coupled speed scaling systems under heavy load [6]. For cases where the analytical study of policies is challenging, like the average busy period length under coupled SRPT or average response time under FSP, the simulation study can be used to investigate the expected behavior of the system.

To illustrate the application of this abstract design, we present selected simulation results for coupled and decoupled speed scaling systems in Section 3.

2. SIMULATOR

This section provides an overview of the simulator (see Figure 1). We briefly discuss the design choices and then present the main components and their dependencies.

2.1 Design overview

The main focus in our design is two-fold: ease of extensibility, and efficiency for large-scale simulations. Simulating a new scheduling policy should only require the implementation of the abstract class Scheduler, without any changes to other components or the core of the simulator. The abstract design of the Logger class makes it possible to change the instrumentation targets and level of detail based on the focus of the simulation study, again without any changes required to other components. The ability to change the instrumentation level is important in order to reduce the execution time and storage requirements for long simulation runs.

Execution time for a single run of the simulator depends on the following factors: (1) duration of the run; (2) expected queue length; (3) step complexity of the scheduler and speed scaler components for handling each event; and (4) complexity of the instrumentation by the logger. The first three factors have direct dependence on the workload and the simulated policies, and usually dominate the overall complexity of the simulation. Memory usage is dominated by the implementation of the logger. The minimum requirement depends on the expected queue length, since the logger has to keep track of all jobs in the queue.

Our implementation of the simulator is written in C++, and it only uses the C++ standard libraries. The current code base is developed and compiled on a Windows machine, but could be compiled on other platforms with minimal effort [1].

The simulation scenario specifications are all modified via the configuration file, which is a human-readable text file with easy-to-interpret value pair format.

2.2 Main components

A single run of the simulator is comprised of three stages. First, the configuration file is read and the policy components and the background component objects are created and initialized. Second, the Discrete Event Simulator (DES) and the Logger are initialized. Third, according to the user specified configurations, the simulation is run until all the first N_{MAX} arrivals have departed the system, at which point the simulation terminates. If jobs are serviced in the order of their arrival (FCFS), this is at the time of departure number N_{MAX}. However, depending on the policies and the workload, termination time could be much later.

For the probe-based sampling of the response times, the third stage is repeated with a probe job inserted at random into the workload stream (similar to the algorithm presented in [9]). For each probe size, the probing is repeated until the user-specified desired confidence interval is achieved. The range of probe job sizes are also specified in the simulation configuration.

Figure 1 illustrates the main components in our simulator. Figure 2 shows selected abstract classes and example implementations.

Simulator Configuration The Simulation scenario specifications are read from a human-readable text file (`configuration.txt`). These specifications include the scheduling and speed scaling policies, the power function, the workload, and their corresponding parameters. It also specifies the logger and its parameters that include the metrics of interest and granularity of measurements.

Object Factory To make the simulator extensible, and to separate different policies from the background settings, all policy and background setting components are defined by abstract classes. The configuration component calls the Object Factory to create and initialize the objects required to execute the specified simulation scenario.

Discrete Event Simulator (DES)

The DES maintains a priority queue of events. In each iteration of the main loop, the event with the smallest timestamp is removed from the priority queue and passed on to

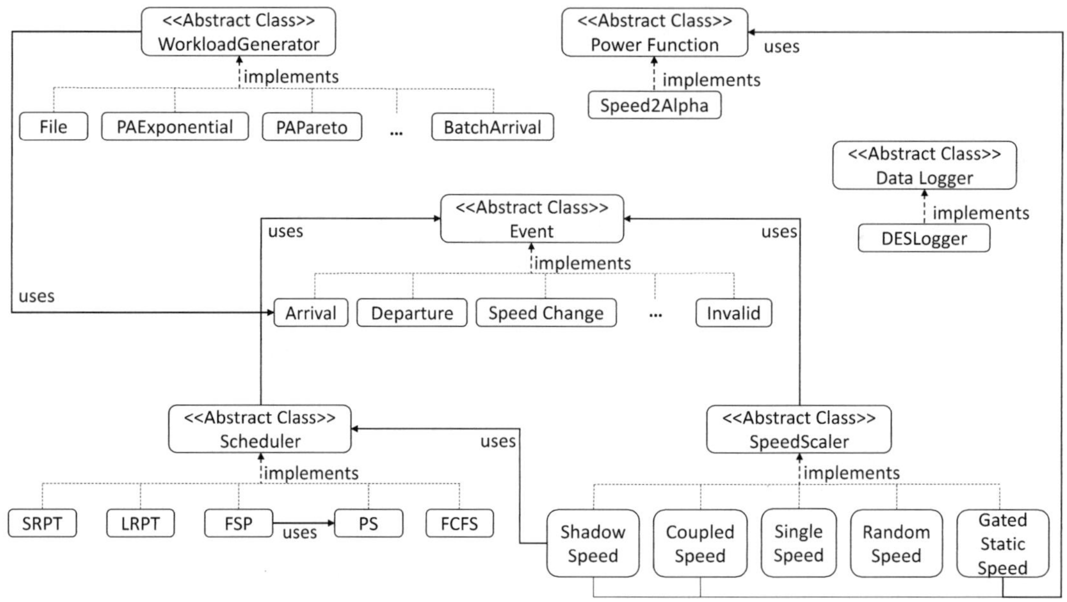

Figure 2: Abstract classes and example implementations.

the proper handlers depending on the type of the event e.g., *Arrival*, *Departure*, *Speed Change*, etc. (see Figure 2). New events may be generated as a result of handling the current event. These are inserted into the priority queue. The loop stops when all the first N_{MAX} arrivals complete their work.

Logger The logger component keeps track of the changes in the state of the system by receiving updates when other components have a status change. It plays the role of the omniscient observer. When other components need information about the current status of the system, they call the interfaces provided by the logger. For example, upon each arrival and departure, the coupled speed scaler queries the logger object for the number of jobs in the system in order to set the speed. Our *Comprehensive Logger* implementation records the status of the entire queue upon each event. For long simulations, however, the amount of data generated could be several gigabytes. For this reason, we have other implementations of the logger that only record a subset of the instrumentation such as queue length and the remaining work in the system upon each arrival and departure.

Workload Generator The arrival process is generated by the workload generator in the form of arrival events. At the initialization of the DES, the generator is asked for the first arrival event. Upon removing an arrival from the priority queue, the DES asks the workload generator to create the next arrival event. Each arrival event includes a timestamp and a job object. The job object must be initialized with the arrival time of the job, and optionally other properties like deadline and priority. Different implementations of the workload generator class allow alternative sources for the arrival sequence. For example, the workload could be generated from a trace file, or could be a Poisson process with job sizes drawn from an Exponential or a Pareto distribution.

Scheduler The scheduler component determines the order in which jobs receive service. Our current implementations include First-Come-First-Serve (FCFS), Processor Sharing (PS), Shortest Job First (SJF), Shortest Remaining Processing Time (SRPT), Longest Remaining Processing Time (LRPT), and Fair Sojourn Protocol (FSP).

Speed Scaler The speed scaling component decides the rate at which the server is processing jobs at each point in time during the simulation. This could be decided based on the system status, such as the system occupancy, or could be completely independent, like a single-speed system. The current implementations include *SingleSpeed*, *CoupledSpeed* (sets the speed to the inverse of the power function of the number of jobs in the system), *ShadowSpeed* (determines the speed based on the occupancy of a shadow scheduler that works on the same arrival process).

Power Function The power function component computes the energy consumption based on the speed of the system. It has two interfaces: one that returns the energy consumption as a function of speed, and one to compute the inverse of the power function.

Statistical Analysis and Visualization The simulator output depends on the implementation of the logger. Our current implementations output three types of log files: metric reports, job reports, and queue progress reports.

Metric reports are text files with timestamp and value pairs. This type of log records the evolution of a metric over time. For example, the `speedprofile.txt` records every speed change event, and the `byteprofile.txt` records the remaining work in the system at the time of every arrival, departure and speed change event.

Job report logs are text files in which each line shows the report of a job upon its departure. We record the size, arrival, departure, energy consumption and time under execution for each job. Metrics like response time and slowdown can be directly derived from the above. The logger could generate this report for any subset of the jobs. For example, the `probereport.txt` contains the job report for only the probe jobs inserted into the workload stream.

Queue progress reports are text files in which every line has a timestamp followed by the status of the queue at that timestamp. This log records the evolution of the remaining sizes of jobs in the queue. Figure 5 shows an excerpt from

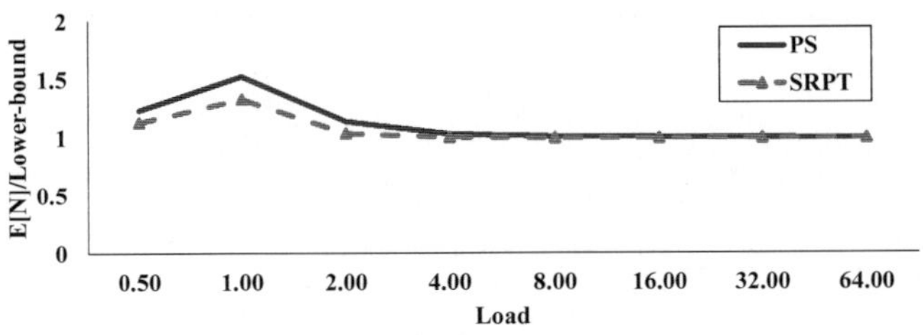

Figure 3: Comparison of queue occupancy under heavy load for coupled PS and SRPT with $s(t) = P^{-1}(n(t))$. The job sizes are Pareto(2.2)

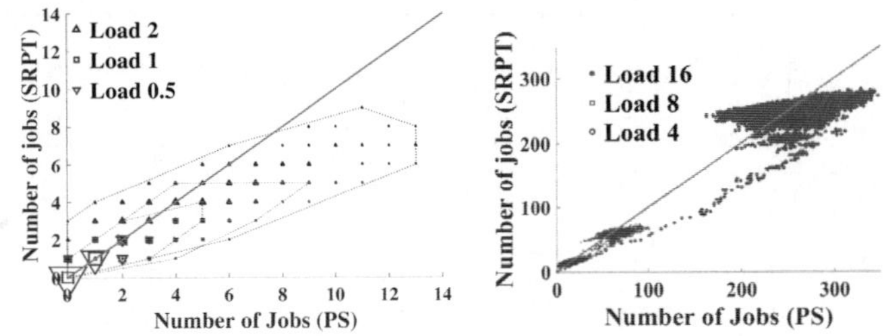

Figure 4: Occupancy $n(t)$ under coupled SRPT vs. coupled PS when the two system work on the same workload stream. Size of the marker indicates the frequency of sampled occupancy.

this log.

We have implemented separate C++ programs to perform further statistical analysis on the output, including mean, variance, and frequencies for recorded metrics. We also have implemented Matlab scripts for further statistical analysis and generation of plots. A Java-based visualization of the queue progress report has been implemented by an undergraduate summer student.

3. EXAMPLE RESULTS

In this section, we show selected simulation results to demonstrate the versatility of the simulation tool for the study of a range of speed scaling policies under different settings and with different metrics.

3.1 Occupancy under heavy load

It is well known that SRPT optimizes the average occupancy, $E[N]$, in single-speed systems [11]. In fact, given any speed sample path, SRPT yields the minimal average occupancy among all work conserving scheduling policies [3].

In coupled speed scaling systems, the speed $s(t)$ at time t is based on the number of jobs in the system. The interdependency of average speeds and system occupancy results in a lower-bound for the occupancy [6]. In order to guarantee stability in the system, the average speed must be at least that of the incoming load, $\bar{s} \geq \rho$. In [13], it is observed that if the power function is convex, then by Jensen's inequality we have $E[N] = E[P(s(t))] \geq P(E[s(t)]) \geq \rho^2$.

With our simulation tool, we can investigate how far the average occupancy is from the lower-bound. Figure 3 shows the comparison of queue occupancy under heavy load for coupled PS and SRPT. As load increases, the average occupancy under PS and SRPT both converge to the lower-bound. This is in high contrast to the results in the single-speed setting, where the average occupancy under PS grows quickly in comparison to SRPT.

Figure 4 shows a snapshot of system occupancy under coupled PS and SRPT, sampled at the same points in time when the two systems work on the same workload stream. We see that with the increase of load, the occurrences where SRPT has higher occupancy than PS increases. This is counter-intuitive, since SRPT in single-speed systems always runs at lower queue occupancy (i.e., the sampled points would always remain below the 45 degree line).

3.2 Queue Progress Log

In order to better understand why the queue occupancy under SRPT exceeds that under PS, we investigate the detailed queue progress log. Figure 5 shows an excerpt of this log for PS and SRPT on the same workload stream with load $\rho = 4$. In this short excerpt, the total remaining work under PS is much lower than under SRPT. Furthermore, the number of jobs that have not even started service is larger under SRPT. This hints at the compensation effect that PS benefits from [6]. By running at higher occupancy prior to this excerpt, PS can cope with the load in this episode at lower speed. Conversely, SRPT needs to compensate for running at lower speed prior to this excerpt in order to keep up with the incoming load.

An interesting observation is the difference in the distribution of remaining sizes in the two queues. Not surprisingly, SRPT tends to accumulate jobs with larger remaining sizes in its queue. The surprising part is the large difference in the work backlog in the two queues, and the high number of jobs that have not started service under SRPT. This hints at the possibility that coupled SRPT is nearly starving larger jobs.

3.3 Remaining bytes in the system

We further investigate the byte backlog in the queue under SRPT and PS by looking at the total remaining sizes vs. the queue occupancy. Figure 6 and 7 show the remaining bytes and the queue occupancy over time under SRPT and PS respectively. These three workloads all have average load $\rho = 4$ but with different job size distributions. For the case of Pareto job sizes, the average job size is 1 (Figure 6(c) and 7(c)). For SRPT, the job size distribution greatly influences the shape of the work backlog, while queue occupancy is less sensitive to the job size distribution. Note that the occupancy stays close to the lower-bound of ρ^2 under all the considered workloads for both SRPT and PS.

Figure 8 shows the average remaining bytes in the system as a function of load. The backlog under coupled SRPT grows very quickly with the increase of load, while the increase is much more moderate under PS.

3.4 Fairness Study

Our simulation results for remaining bytes in the system under coupled SRPT reconfirms the theoretical result on adverse effect of coupled speed scaling on slowdown of large jobs under SRPT [12]. It further shows that in comparison to coupled PS, the difference in the backlog grows rapidly with the increase of load. This suggests that the slowdown disadvantage of larger jobs under SRPT worsens under heavy load.

We can study the slowdown of different policies with the help of our probe-based simulation. Figure 9 shows the slow-

Time	Arrival (A) Departure (D) Preemption (P)	Num. started service	Num. not yet started	Sum of rem. sizes started service	Sum of rem. sizes not started service	Remaining sizes of jobs in queue (PS)												
876.991	P(0.032)	12	1	42.922	0.032	0.032	0.063	0.320	0.487	1.029	1.102	1.602	2.504	3.785	4.031	4.296	11.155	12.548
877.106	D	12	0	42.540	0.000	0.031	0.288	0.455	0.997	1.070	1.570	2.472	3.753	3.999	4.264	11.123	12.516	
877.214	D	11	0	42.165	0.000	0.257	0.424	0.966	1.039	1.539	2.441	3.722	3.968	4.233	11.092	12.485		
877.350	P(5.344)	11	1	41.716	5.344	5.344	0.216	0.383	0.925	0.998	1.498	2.400	3.681	3.927	4.192	11.051	12.444	
878.098	D	11	0	44.467	0.000	0.167	0.709	0.782	1.282	2.184	3.465	3.711	3.976	5.128	10.835	12.228		
878.611	P(4.979)	11	1	42.766	4.979	4.979	0.012	0.554	0.627	1.127	2.029	3.310	3.557	3.821	4.974	10.680	12.073	
878.649	P(1.343)	12	1	47.611	1.343	1.343	0.001	0.543	0.616	1.116	2.018	3.299	3.545	3.810	4.962	4.968	10.669	12.062
878.653	D	12	0	48.942	0.000	0.542	0.615	1.115	1.342	2.017	3.298	3.544	3.809	4.961	4.967	10.668	12.061	
880.532	D	11	0	42.434	0.000	0.073	0.573	0.800	1.475	2.756	3.002	3.267	4.419	4.424	10.126	11.519		
880.773	D	10	0	41.633	0.000	0.500	0.727	1.402	2.683	2.929	3.194	4.346	4.352	10.053	11.446			
880.877	P(2.398)	10	1	41.306	2.398	2.398	0.467	0.695	1.369	2.650	2.897	3.161	4.314	4.319	10.021	11.413		

(a) PS

Time	Arrival (A) Departure (D) Preemption (P)	Num. started service	Num. not yet started	Sum of rem. sizes started service	Sum of rem. sizes not started service	Remaining sizes of jobs in queue (SRPT)														
876.991	P(0.032)	1	12	7.877	231.066	0.032	7.877	17.683	18.134	18.250	18.478	19.455	20.297	20.497	20.643	22.898	23.050	31.649		
877.000	D	1	11	7.877	231.034	7.877	17.683	18.134	18.250	18.478	19.455	20.297	20.497	20.643	22.898	23.050	31.649			
877.350	P(5.344)	1	12	6.666	236.378	5.344	6.666	17.683	18.134	18.250	18.478	19.455	20.297	20.497	20.643	22.898	23.050	31.649		
878.611	A(4.979)	2	12	7.462	236.013	0.796	4.979	6.666	17.683	18.134	18.250	18.478	19.455	20.297	20.497	20.643	22.898	23.050	31.649	
878.649	A(1.343)	2	13	7.318	237.356	0.652	1.343	4.979	6.666	17.683	18.134	18.250	18.478	19.455	20.297	20.497	20.643	22.898	23.050	31.649
878.818	D	1	13	6.666	237.356	1.343	4.979	6.666	17.683	18.134	18.250	18.478	19.455	20.297	20.497	20.643	22.898	23.050	31.649	
879.177	D	1	12	6.666	236.013	4.979	6.666	17.683	18.134	18.250	18.478	19.455	20.297	20.497	20.643	22.898	23.050	31.649		
880.558	D	1	11	6.666	231.034	6.666	17.683	18.134	18.250	18.478	19.455	20.297	20.497	20.643	22.898	23.050	31.649			
880.877	P(2.398)	1	12	5.561	233.432	2.398	5.561	17.683	18.134	18.250	18.478	19.455	20.297	20.497	20.643	22.898	23.050	31.649		

(b) SRPT

Figure 5: Comparison of queue progress log for coupled PS and SPRT given the same workload stream with load 4.

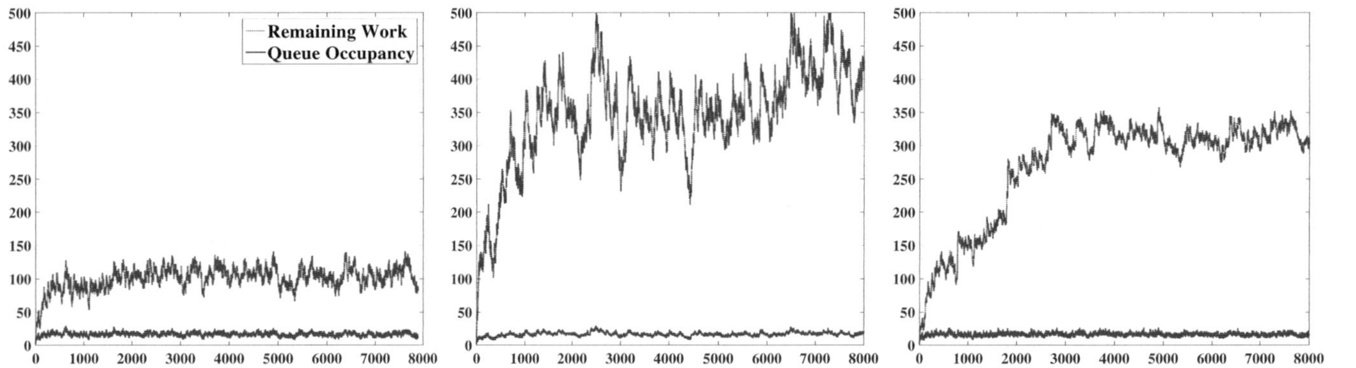

(a) EXP(1) (b) EXP(4) (c) Pareto(2.2)

Figure 6: The remaining bytes vs. queue occupancy in coupled SRPT given average load 4 with different job size distributions.

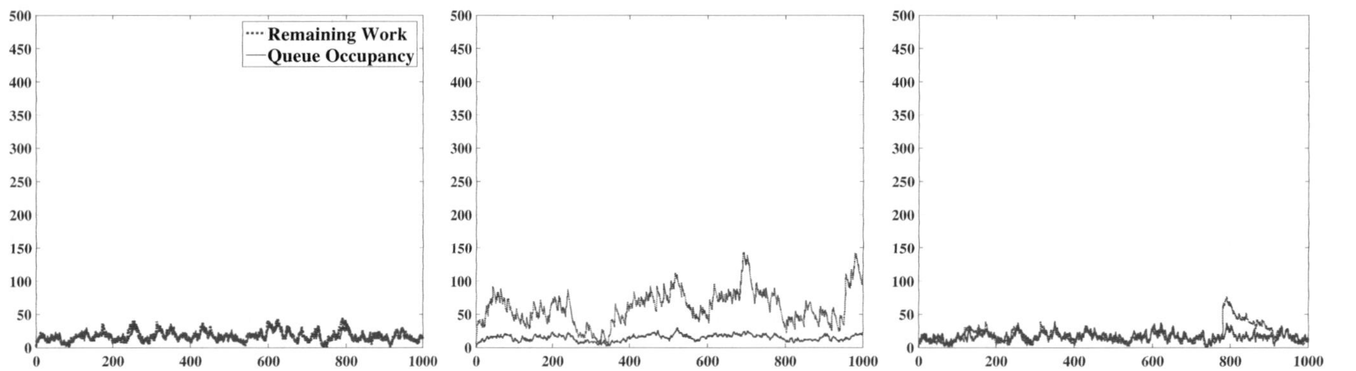

(a) EXP(1) (b) EXP(4) (c) Pareto(2.2)

Figure 7: The remaining bytes vs. queue occupancy in coupled PS given average load 4 with different job size distributions.

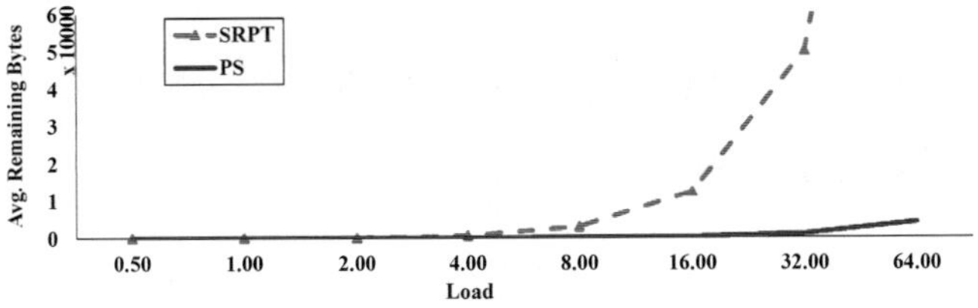

Figure 8: Comparison of average remaining bytes under coupled SRPT and PS, Pareto(2.2) job sizes.

down for 6 different policies when $\rho = 2$ with Pareto(2.2) job sizes. Note that coupled PS is a symmetric queue and therefore has constant slowdown for all job sizes [10, 13]. In Figure 9(a) the slowdown under SRPT for jobs larger than 5 is already more than double the slowdown under PS. Figure 9(b) highlights the slowdown disadvantage of SRPT. Under SRPT with load 2, slowdown of jobs larger than 250 is greater than slowdown of jobs under PS with load 64.

In Figure 9(a), SRPT-PS and FSP-PS dominate PS (i.e., always maintain slowdown no worse than that under PS). These decoupled speed scaling policies determine the speed based on the occupancy of a shadow PS scheduler that works on the same arrival process. The analytical result in [7] shows that for all load configurations, FSP-PS performs at least as well as PS for both slowdown and the sum of average response time and energy consumption (i.e., the cost). Further investigation is required to quantify the improvement under different load regimes.

3.5 Cost

We study the cost improvements under FSP-PS and SRPT-PS in comparison to coupled PS. Figure 10 shows the ratio of cost to the lower-bound. The cost is the linear combination of average response time and energy consumption. For load ρ, the lower bound $max(2\rho, \rho^2)$ is shown in [13]. Under heavy load, both FSP-PS and SRPT-PS greatly improve the cost in comparison to PS. SRPT-PS has a slight edge on FSP-PS, but there is a slowdown tradeoff for this gain in cost (see Figure 9(a)).

4. CONCLUSIONS

This paper presented an extensible simulation tool for the study of speed scaling designs. Through example results, we have shown the versatility of the simulation tool for the study of a range of policies under different speed scaling configurations. We are further investigating the behavior of coupled and decoupled SRPT under heavy load. For future work, more policies can be implemented and studied. The current implementation of FSP could be greatly improved by incorporation of the algorithm proposed in [4].

Acknowledgments

Financial support for this work was provided by Canada's Natural Sciences and Engineering Research Council (NSERC). The authors are grateful to Philipp Woelfel for insightful discussions about speed scaling systems, and to Jennifer Williamson for building a Java-based visualization of our queue progress log output.

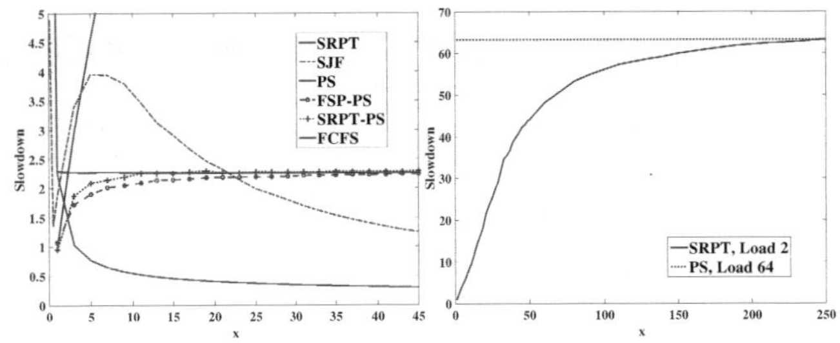

(a) (b)

Figure 9: Slowdown under different coupled and decoupled scheduling polices. (a) Load 2 and job sizes are Pareto(2.2).

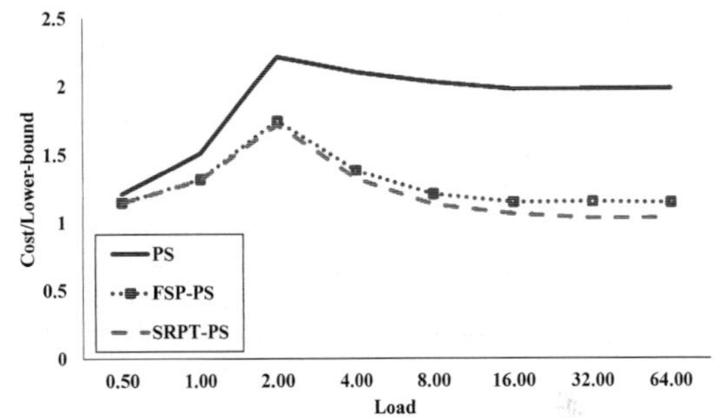

Figure 10: Comparison of cost of Coupled PS and Decoupled SRPT and FSP with speeds of PS. Pareto(2.2) job sizes.

5. REFERENCES

[1] Versatile Speed Scaling Simulator. https://github.com/bmelahi/SpeedScalingSimulator.

[2] S. Albers. Energy-efficient algorithms. *Commun. ACM*, 53(5):86–96, May 2010.

[3] N. Bansal, H.-L. Chan, and K. Pruhs. Speed scaling with an arbitrary power function. In *Proc. ACM-SIAM Symposium on Discrete algorithms (SODA)*, pages 693–701, 2009.

[4] M. Dell'Amico, D. Carra, and P. Michiardi. PSBS: practical size-based scheduling. *IEEE Trans. Computers*, 65(7):2199–2212, 2016.

[5] M. Dell'Amico, D. Carra, M. Pastorelli, and P. Michiardi. Revisiting size-based scheduling with estimated job sizes. In *MASCOTS*, pages 411–420, 2014.

[6] M. Elahi and C. Williamson. Autoscaling effects in speed scaling systems. In *MASCOTS 2016*, pages 307–312, 2016.

[7] M. Elahi, C. Williamson, and P. Woelfel. Decoupled speed scaling. *Perform. Eval.*, 73:3–17, 2014.

[8] M. Elahi, C. Williamson, and P. Woelfel. Turbocharged speed scaling: Analysis and evaluation. In *MASCOTS*, pages 41–50, 2014.

[9] M. Gong and C. Williamson. Revisiting unfairness in web server scheduling. *Comput. Netw.*, 50(13):2183–2203, 2006.

[10] F. Kelly. *Reversibility and Stochastic Networks*. Cambridge University Press, 2011.

[11] L. Schrage. A proof of the optimality of the shortest remaining processing time discipline. *Oper. Res.*, 16:678–690, 1968.

[12] A. Wierman, L. Andrew, and M. Lin. Speed scaling: An algorithmic perspective. In *Handbook of Energy-Aware and Green Computing - Two Volume Set.*, pages 385–405. 2012.

[13] A. Wierman, L. Andrew, and A. Tang. Power-aware speed scaling in processor sharing systems: Optimality and robustness. *Perform. Eval.*, 69(12):601–622, 2012.

[14] A. Wierman and M. Harchol-Balter. Classifying scheduling policies with respect to unfairness in an M/GI/1. In *Proc. ACM SIGMETRICS*, pages 238–249, 2003.

Testing spnps perfect sampling tool on fork-join queueing networks (tool paper)

Simonetta Balsamo
DAIS - Università Ca' Foscari
Venezia
via Torino, 155
Venice, Italy
balsamo@dais.unive.it

Andrea Marin
DAIS - Università Ca' Foscari
Venezia
via Torino, 155
Venice, Italy
marin@unive.it

Ivan Stojic
DAIS - Università Ca' Foscari
Venezia
via Torino, 155
Venice, Italy
ivan.stojic@unive.it

ABSTRACT

Stochastic Petri nets (SPNs) are widely used for the performance evaluation of computer and telecommunication systems. They inherit from their untimed version the capability of modeling parallel computations in a simple, graphical way. Simulation of SPNs is an important way to assess the performance of a system measured as throughput, response time or expected number of customers/resources in some places. Perfect sampling allows for the selection of the initial state of a simulation with a probability which corresponds to its stationary probability and hence the warm-up period is not required any more. In this paper we present performance tests of spnps, a tool based on some previous works that implements perfect sampling algorithm for SPNs by using decision diagrams. We test performance of the tool on a class of stochastic models of great importance in the quantitative evaluation of distributed systems and communication networks: the fork-join queueing networks.

Categories and Subject Descriptors

C.4 [**PERFORMANCE OF SYSTEMS**]: Modeling techniques

General Terms

Performance

Keywords

Stochastic Petri nets, Simulation, Perfect sampling

Permission to make digital or hard copies of all or part of this work for

VALUETOOLS 2016, October 25-28, Taormina, Italy

1. INTRODUCTION

Performance evaluation of parallel and distributed systems requires the capability of modeling the evolution of different tasks and their competition or their synchronization on sets of finite resources. In the literature, Timed Petri nets have been used for the performance evaluation of microprocessor systems [16], communication networks [14, 20] and other fields such as biological systems [1]. Stochastic Petri nets (SPNs) [18] are a subset of timed Petri nets for which firing delays associated with Petri net transitions are independent of each other (but they may depend on the model's state) and are exponentially distributed. It can be shown that the stochastic process underlying an SPN is a continuous-time Markov chain (CTMC). Unfortunately, in the literature, very few analytical results are available for the solution of SPNs and in general the exact computation of the stationary performance indices is extremely inefficient. For this reason, SPN models are usually studied by means of simulation [11]. Several tools are available for simulating SPNs among which we recall Timenet [22], GreatSPN [8], SPNP [13]. One of the problems in the stationary simulation of stochastic models (including SPNs) is the detection of the so called *warm-up* period, i.e., the period required by the model to move from its initial condition to the equilibrium (if it exists). There are several statistical approaches for the detection of the length of transient phase in a simulation which can be formulated for SPNs (see e.g., [15]); however, they usually depend on the users' skills (such as the Welch's graphical method) and hence are prone to errors. For ergodic models with finite state spaces, perfect sampling is a method to sample a reachable state of the model with a probability that corresponds to its stationary probability, i.e., we sample a reachable state according to the steady-state distribution of the SPN.

In this paper we present performance tests of a tool called Stochastic Petri Nets Perfect Sampling (spnps) that implements *coupling from the past* [19] algorithm for SPNs with finite state spaces. Spnps uses decision diagrams to contain the problem of the state space explosion and its strength lies in the generality of the models that it can handle. Although in the worst case the time and space complexities of spnps are more than exponential with respect to the net structure (since the whole net state space must be built), we observed that in many practical cases the structure of the model's underlying reachability graph has regularities that can be efficiently exploited by decision diagrams. For this reason, we test spnps on a class of models which are known to play an important role in the analysis of distributed systems and telecommunication systems: fork-join queueing networks [12, 7]. For these models very few exact results are known [2] mainly relying on product-form theory. Therefore, the definition of techniques for approximation and simulation are the principal approaches for the estimation of their stationary performance indices. In [9, 5] the authors present algorithms for perfect sampling on restricted classes of fork-join queueing networks (in the former case consisting of one node, in the latter with limitation on the probabilistic routing). They take advantage of the reachability graph properties in order to improve the efficiency of the algorithms. Similarly, another approach [6] is applicable to a different class of fork-join queueing networks; however, in the queueing networks considered there, customer routing cannot depend on the total number of customers in a set of queues, while in the models that we consider, queues can have a shared capacity (i.e., restriction on the total number of customers in a set of queues) and a customer that cannot enter a destination queue due to shared capacity being full is blocked. Further research is needed in order to assess the possibility of applying to the models considered here the general method proposed in [6]. While spnps is less efficient than these approaches for particular classes of models, its generality allows for studying SPNs (and hence fork-join queueing networks that are representable as SPNs) with a more general structure. In particular, we show that for fork-join queueing networks, the time required for performing a perfect sampling is acceptable even for relatively large nets.

The paper is structured as follows. In Section 2 we briefly describe the tool interface and the supported class of SPNs and we outline the algorithm implemented by the tool. Next, in section 3 we introduce models used in testing, describe the testing procedure and discuss the performance of the tool. Finally, Section 4 concludes the paper.

2. SPNPS: TOOL DESCRIPTION

Spnps is a command-line tool that takes in input an SPN model specified in PNML [21], place marking bounds, i.e., the maximum number of tokens that a place can contain, and an ordering of places for the construction of the decision diagram.

When used for its main purpose, perfect sampling, the output of the tool is a specified number of perfect samples from the reachability set of the input SPN. In addition, the user can specify as a stopping criterion the maximum cardinality of the final set $\mathcal{A}_0$ in Algorithm 1 (1 is the default value) and in this case the sampling runs are stopped before completion and the entire set $\mathcal{A}_0$ is returned as the result. Performing such incomplete perfect sampling runs can be useful in the analysis of models that exhibit multimodal behaviour.

Spnps is a stand-alone tool and as such can be used in a preprocessing step to provide initial markings for stationary simulation runs that can then be performed by other tools. C++ source code of the tool can be obtained at the web page of one of the authors[1]. For a more detailed description of the tool, the interested reader can refer to [4].

2.1 Assumptions on the SPN

The class of SPNs that we consider are those introduced in [18] that are standard Petri nets in which each transition is associated with a firing delay that may depend on the model's state. The firing delays are exponentially distributed random variables. It can be shown that under these assumptions the stochastic process underlying the SPN is a CTMC and that the reachability set of the untimed Petri net is identical to the state space of the CTMC underlying the model. Spnps works on SPNs with finite state spaces and whose transitions implement one of the following firing semantics. *Single server (SS) semantics*, i.e., the firing delay is set when the transition is first enabled and a new delay is sampled in case the same transition is enabled after the firing. In other words, the firing rate of an enabled transition is state independent. *Infinite server (IS) semantics*, i.e., every enabling set of tokens is processed in parallel as soon as they arrive at the input places. Each of these concurrent delays associated with a transition are i.i.d. exponentially distributed random variables. According to the race policy, this corresponds to a single server semantics in which the firing rate depends on the marking of the transition's input places.

2.2 The algorithm behind spnps

This subsection contains a high-level overview of the perfect sampling algorithm as implemented in the present tool, while the details and a version of the algorithm that supports more general transition firing semantics can be found in a previous paper by the same authors [3]. The algorithm is based on coupling from the past [19], which is an algorithm for sampling from the stationary distributions of discrete time Markov chains (DTMC)—the tool simulates the DTMC obtained by uniformization of the original CTMC starting from all states and performs the simulation until all states couple into a single state. Algorithm 1 outlines main steps of the algorithm implemented in the present tool.

Algorithm 1: PERFECT_SAMPLING

Data:
- SPN $(\mathcal{P}, \mathcal{T}, I, O, W, \boldsymbol{m}_0)$,
- function $S : \mathcal{T} \to \{\mathrm{SS}, \mathrm{IS}\}$ defining transitions' firing semantics,
- vector of place marking bounds $\boldsymbol{B} \in \mathbb{N}^{|\mathcal{P}|}$,
- function $V : \mathcal{P} \to \{0, 1, \ldots, |\mathcal{P}| - 1\}$ defining ordering of places,
- i.i.d. uniform on $[0, 1]$ random variables $U_0, U_{-1}, \ldots$

Result: Sample from the stationary distribution of the SPN

1 **begin**
2   $\mathcal{RS} \leftarrow$ GENERATE_STATE_SPACE(SPN, $\boldsymbol{B}, V$);
3   $\phi \leftarrow$ GENERATE_UPDATE_RULE(SPN, $S, \boldsymbol{B}, V$);
4   $m \leftarrow 1$;
5   **repeat**
6     $\mathcal{A}_{-m} \leftarrow \mathcal{RS}$;
7   **for** $i = -m + 1$ *to* 0 **do**
8       $\mathcal{A}_i \leftarrow \phi(\mathcal{A}_{i-1}, U_i)$;
9     $m \leftarrow 2m$;
10   **until** $|\mathcal{A}_0| = 1$;
11   **return** $s \in \mathcal{A}_0$;

In line 2 state space $\mathcal{RS}$ of the CTMC underlying the SPN is generated and encoded by a multi-way decision diagram (MDD). The generation of the state space is performed by saturation algorithm [17] which can efficiently generate

[1] http://www.dais.unive.it/~stojic/soft.html

MDDs encoding very large state spaces for many types of practical models. Then, in line 3, several MDDs that together encode a simulation update rule $\phi : 2^{\mathcal{RS}} \times [0,1] \to 2^{\mathcal{RS}}$ are generated. Simulation update rule ϕ respects step probabilities of a DTMC that is obtained by uniformization from the CTMC underlying the SPN model: i.e., if $s_i, s_j \in \mathcal{RS}$ are two states of the DTMC with the corresponding single step probability p_{ij} and U is uniformly on $[0,1]$ distributed random variable then the following holds:

$$\Pr\{\phi(\{s_i\}, U) = \{s_j\}\} = p_{ij}.$$

To generate MDDs that encode ϕ we exploit the specific structure of a CTMC underlying an SPN, namely that there is only a limited number of ways that the marking can change (one for each transition) and that there is only a limited number of different transition rates in the CTMC (one for each combination of a transition and its enabling degree). Given an MDD that encodes a set of states $\mathcal{A}_{i-1} \subseteq \mathcal{RS}$ and a sample from U, the update rule ϕ performs one simulation step (of the DTMC obtained by uniformization of the CTMC) from all states in the set $\mathcal{A}_{i-1}$, producing an MDD that encodes set $\mathcal{A}_i$ of states that are reached from some state in $\mathcal{A}_{i-1}$ by the simulation step. Since the simulation step can couple some of the states in $\mathcal{A}_{i-1}$ (i.e., performing the simulation step from different states can produce the same state), the resulting set has equal or smaller cardinality, $|\mathcal{A}_i| \leq |\mathcal{A}_{i-1}|$. This process can then be continued until a set containing only a single state is obtained. Lines 4 to 10 perform such simulations for increasing number m of steps until the resulting set $\mathcal{A}_0$ contains only a single state $s \in \mathcal{RS}$ which is returned as the sample. Update rule ϕ and the algorithm are constructed so that the probabilities of sampling each of the states in $\mathcal{RS}$ are equal to their stationary probabilities in the CTMC underlying the SPN. The number m of steps that produces the coupling depends on the properties of the model and on the update rule ϕ, and its expected value is finite for all SPNs with finite state spaces [3]. Thus the algorithm terminates in a finite expected time.

3. TESTING THE TOOL ON FORK-JOIN QUEUEING NETWORKS

Fork-join queueing networks allow the jobs to be split into several tasks that are processed in parallel. Once all the tasks have been served, a join operation is performed and we consider the original job served. These models are very useful for the performance evaluation of distributed systems with task concurrency and synchronization. In this section we test spnps on a fork-join queueing network and discuss the performance of the perfect sampling algorithm that it implements.

3.1 The testing model

We consider the fork-join queueing network depicted in Figure 1. The model is described by parameters: n, m, r. Figure 1 shows the leftmost service station Q_0 that initially contains m jobs. Once a job is served, it is forked into n sub-tasks which are enqueued in $Q_1, \ldots, Q_n$, respectively. After being served by station Q_i, the sub-task i is routed to one of the stations $Q_{i1f}, \ldots, Q_{inf}$ according to a uniform probabilistic choice: this is the first phase of service. The second phase is performed by stations $Q_{i1s}, \ldots Q_{ins}$ with a constraint on the available resources: at most r sub-tasks can simultaneously be in the queues $Q_{i1s}, \ldots, Q_{ins}$ for each $i = 1, \ldots, n$. All the service times are independent and exponentially distributed and the stations are equipped with a single server. We assume a processor sharing queueing discipline.

The queueing network for parameters $n = 2$, $m = 3$, $r = 1$ is modeled by the Petri net in Figure 2. There are $m = 3$ tokens in place P_0, representing jobs. Transition T_1 models the fork and T_{14} the join. The resources are modelled as tokens in places P_{r1} and P_{r2}. Places P_{1j} and P_{2j} model the waiting room for sub-tasks which have been served and are waiting to be joined. The remaining places model the waiting/service rooms of the corresponding queueing stations. The resulting Petri net has $2n^2 + 3n + 1$ places and $3n^2 + 2$ transitions.

We make two important observations on the model of Figure 2: the first is that the SPN for $n \geq 2$ is *not* a free choice SPN. In fact, in a free choice Petri net if there is an arc from a place s to a transition t, then there must be an arc from any input place of t to any output transition of s [10]. Now, consider the net of Figure 2 and let s be for example P_{r1} and t be transition T_4. Consider the input place P_{11f} of T_4 and the output transition T_5 of P_{r1}: since there is no arc from P_{11f} to T_5 the net is not free choice. Therefore, the optimised algorithms for perfect sampling of free choice SPNs cannot be applied (see [5] and the references therein). The second observation is on the semantics of the join specified in terms of SPN. In fact T_{14} does not guarantee that the join occurs among the sibling sub-tasks since a sub-task may overtake another sub-task that was previously forked. The more detailed representation of the join operation requires a much more complicated stochastic process and is out of the scope of this paper.

3.2 Performance evaluation

To test the performance of spnps on the fork-join model we performed two groups of tests.

In the first group of tests, we study how the performance scales with number of initial jobs. We fixed the size of the SPN by setting $n = 2$ and run the tests for parameter m ranging from 2 to 40 with step 2 and with number of resources per fork equal to half the number of jobs, $r = m/2$.

In the second group, we examine how the performance scales with the size of the SPN by fixing the number of jobs to $m = 2$ and number of resources per fork to $r = 1$ and running the tests for parameter n ranging from 2 to 16.

For each of these $20 + 15 = 35$ sets of parameters, 50 independent tests were run by performing the perfect sampling procedure with different random seeds. Rates of all transitions of the tested SPN models were set to 1. We report the results as 95% confidence intervals for the means of measured values.

Testing was done on a GNU/Linux system with Intel(R) Core(TM) i5-2310 CPU with maximum clock of 3.2 GHz and with 8GB of main memory.

The results of the testing are shown in Table 1 and 2 for the first and second batch of tests, respectively. The meaning of the columns is the following:

- n_P: number of places of the SPN.
- n_T: number of transitions of the SPN.
- $|\mathcal{RS}|$: cardinality of reachability set of the SPN.

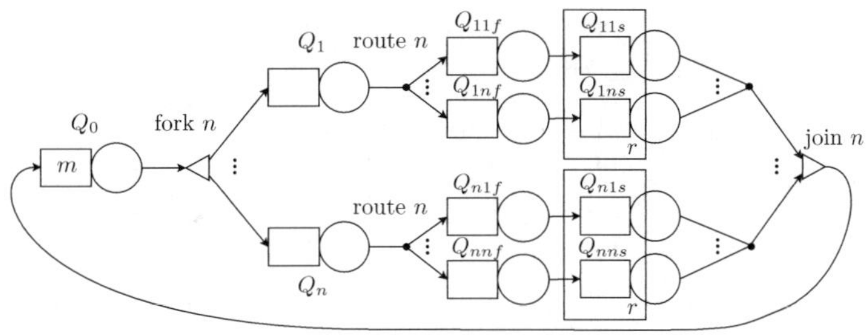

Figure 1: Example of fork-join queueing network.

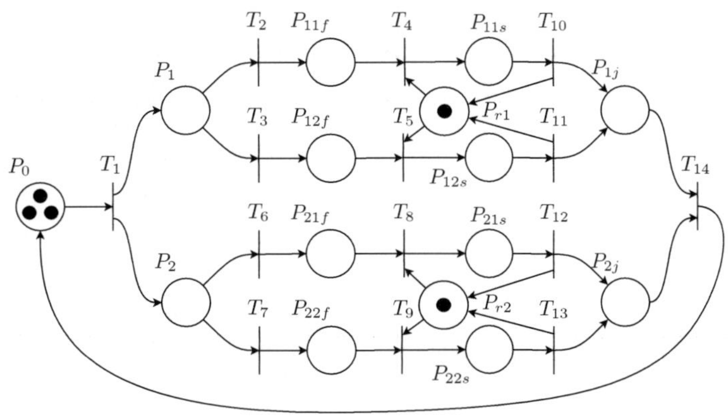

Figure 2: SPN associated with the fork-join queueing network of Figure 1 for $n = 2$, $m = 3$ and $r = 1$.

- init time (s): time in seconds spent in generating decision diagrams that encode the reachability set and simulation update rule used in perfect sampling. If multiple samples are generated, this needs to be done only once and these decision diagrams can be reused in different sampling runs (i.e., this time can be amortized over the sampling runs). The init times are independent of the random seed, resulting in very tight confidence intervals; we therefore report only the means.
- sampling time (s): 95% confidence interval for mean time in seconds spent in a perfect sampling run.
- iterations: 95% confidence interval for mean number of simulation steps in a perfect sampling run.
- peak memory (kB): 95% confidence interval for mean peak memory use in kilobytes for the entire program. The program loads the SPN from a PNML file, parses it and runs the perfect sampling. The non-sampling parts use about 5MB of memory.

Common magnitudes of intervals' boundaries are shown outside the intervals.

We observe that the tool scales very well with the size $|\mathcal{RS}|$ of the reachability set when we vary the size of the net (second group of tests), but not as well when we vary the size of the initial marking (first group of tests). Figure 3 shows log-log plots of memory use on the left and sampling time on the right as functions of the reachability set size. For the model from the first group of tests with largest tested reachability set size $|\mathcal{RS}| \approx 4.857 \times 10^{12}$, the memory consumption is comparable to the model from the second group of tests for which $|\mathcal{RS}| \approx 1.152 \times 10^{26}$, and the sampling time is comparable to the model from the second group of tests with the largest tested $|\mathcal{RS}| \approx 3.882 \times 10^{42}$.

As performance of the algorithm depends in large part on efficiency of MDDs that are used to encode subsets of the reachability set and the simulation update rule, and efficiency of MDDs depends on the properties of the sets or functions that they encode, the observed difference in performance between the two groups of tests is likely in part due to the structure of the reachability sets. If we consider the reachability sets of the n SPN components between fork and join transitions, then for $m = 1$ the reachability set of the entire SPN is equal to the union of a singleton set containing initial marking (where the single token is in the initial place) and the Cartesian product of the n components' reachability sets restricted to the case when the initial place is empty. This is highly structured and is well suited to representation using decision diagrams (but note that the high symmetry of the reachability sets is not exploited in the decision diagram representation, only the high decomposability; i.e., the important property is that the reachability set is similar to a Cartesian product and not that the sets in the Cartesian product are equal). Similar considerations apply for other small values of m. In contrast, for small n and large m, the reachability set is not as well structured (we obtain a large union of $m + 1$ Cartesian products over components).

In addition, because the implementation encodes reachability sets and their subsets by decision diagrams in which

m	r	$\|\mathcal{RS}\|$	init time (s)	sampling time (s)	iterations	peak memory (kB)
2	1	361	3.204×10^{-3}	$[3.735, 4.489] \times 10^{-3}$	$[2.386, 3.169] \times 10^{2}$	$[5.638, 5.682] \times 10^{3}$
4	2	14207	5.294×10^{-3}	$[1.530, 1.754] \times 10^{-2}$	$[3.124, 4.095] \times 10^{2}$	$[5.900, 5.945] \times 10^{3}$
6	3	214492	8.835×10^{-3}	$[4.449, 4.929] \times 10^{-2}$	$[4.134, 5.286] \times 10^{2}$	$[6.618, 6.659] \times 10^{3}$
8	4	1.865×10^{6}	1.372×10^{-2}	$[1.068, 1.181] \times 10^{-1}$	$[5.372, 6.711] \times 10^{2}$	$[7.836, 7.981] \times 10^{3}$
10	5	1.130×10^{7}	2.134×10^{-2}	$[2.250, 2.472] \times 10^{-1}$	$[5.998, 7.723] \times 10^{2}$	$[7.897, 8.074] \times 10^{3}$
12	6	5.290×10^{7}	3.101×10^{-2}	$[4.277, 4.707] \times 10^{-1}$	$[6.945, 8.415] \times 10^{2}$	$[1.053, 1.062] \times 10^{4}$
14	7	2.045×10^{8}	4.568×10^{-2}	$[7.911, 8.528] \times 10^{-1}$	$[0.888, 1.057] \times 10^{3}$	$[1.057, 1.141] \times 10^{4}$
16	8	6.809×10^{8}	6.338×10^{-2}	$[1.434, 1.568]$	$[1.101, 1.357] \times 10^{3}$	$[1.546, 1.606] \times 10^{4}$
18	9	2.012×10^{9}	8.897×10^{-2}	$[2.255, 2.441]$	$[1.219, 1.505] \times 10^{3}$	$[1.583, 1.597] \times 10^{4}$
20	10	5.392×10^{9}	1.185×10^{-1}	$[3.861, 4.229]$	$[1.728, 2.246] \times 10^{3}$	$[2.072, 2.379] \times 10^{4}$
22	11	1.332×10^{10}	1.554×10^{-1}	$[5.724, 6.221]$	$[1.563, 2.000] \times 10^{3}$	$[2.721, 2.747] \times 10^{4}$
24	12	3.071×10^{10}	1.998×10^{-1}	$[9.056, 9.640]$	$[2.242, 2.796] \times 10^{3}$	$[2.739, 3.011] \times 10^{4}$
26	13	6.673×10^{10}	2.606×10^{-1}	$[1.286, 1.389] \times 10^{1}$	$[2.359, 3.089] \times 10^{3}$	$[3.620, 4.244] \times 10^{4}$
28	14	1.378×10^{11}	3.263×10^{-1}	$[1.854, 2.021] \times 10^{1}$	$[2.896, 3.822] \times 10^{3}$	$[4.916, 5.118] \times 10^{4}$
30	15	2.719×10^{11}	4.086×10^{-1}	$[2.607, 2.824] \times 10^{1}$	$[3.399, 4.466] \times 10^{3}$	$[5.150, 5.164] \times 10^{4}$
32	16	5.158×10^{11}	5.004×10^{-1}	$[3.521, 3.757] \times 10^{1}$	$[3.759, 4.843] \times 10^{3}$	$[5.207, 5.737] \times 10^{4}$
34	17	9.446×10^{11}	6.199×10^{-1}	$[4.481, 4.871] \times 10^{1}$	$[4.043, 5.378] \times 10^{3}$	$[6.514, 7.456] \times 10^{4}$
36	18	1.676×10^{12}	7.517×10^{-1}	$[6.095, 6.723] \times 10^{1}$	$[4.641, 6.869] \times 10^{3}$	$[8.265, 8.833] \times 10^{4}$
38	19	2.890×10^{12}	9.036×10^{-1}	$[8.086, 8.860] \times 10^{1}$	$[4.897, 6.694] \times 10^{3}$	$[9.042, 9.256] \times 10^{4}$
40	20	4.857×10^{12}	1.080	$[1.011, 1.106] \times 10^{2}$	$[5.392, 7.552] \times 10^{3}$	$[9.651, 9.976] \times 10^{4}$

Table 1: First group of tests with $n = 2$, m ranging from 2 to 40 and $r = m/2$. The net has 15 places and 14 transitions.

n	n_P	n_T	$\|\mathcal{RS}\|$	init time (s)	sampling time (s)	iterations	peak memory (kB)
2	15	14	361	3.204×10^{-3}	$[3.589, 4.216] \times 10^{-3}$	$[2.189, 2.829] \times 10^{2}$	$[5.645, 5.679] \times 10^{3}$
3	28	29	27513	9.316×10^{-3}	$[2.081, 2.523] \times 10^{-2}$	$[5.947, 8.389] \times 10^{2}$	$[6.654, 6.691] \times 10^{3}$
4	45	50	4.111×10^{6}	2.401×10^{-2}	$[7.792, 9.251] \times 10^{-2}$	$[1.342, 1.812] \times 10^{3}$	$[8.101, 8.181] \times 10^{3}$
5	66	77	9.927×10^{8}	5.041×10^{-2}	$[2.329, 2.687] \times 10^{-1}$	$[2.295, 3.030] \times 10^{3}$	$[1.123, 1.129] \times 10^{4}$
6	91	110	3.513×10^{11}	9.699×10^{-2}	$[6.775, 7.887] \times 10^{-1}$	$[3.848, 5.245] \times 10^{3}$	$[1.698, 1.726] \times 10^{4}$
7	120	149	1.714×10^{14}	1.656×10^{-1}	$[1.572, 1.925]$	$[5.368, 7.657] \times 10^{3}$	$[2.754, 2.771] \times 10^{4}$
8	153	194	1.103×10^{17}	2.890×10^{-1}	$[3.153, 3.755]$	$[7.363, 9.594] \times 10^{3}$	$[3.229, 3.460] \times 10^{4}$
9	190	245	9.065×10^{19}	5.198×10^{-1}	$[5.843, 6.849]$	$[0.889, 1.176] \times 10^{4}$	$[5.155, 5.226] \times 10^{4}$
10	231	302	9.261×10^{22}	7.359×10^{-1}	$[1.087, 1.298] \times 10^{1}$	$[1.432, 1.911] \times 10^{4}$	$[9.214, 9.395] \times 10^{4}$
11	276	365	1.152×10^{26}	1.223	$[1.715, 2.031] \times 10^{1}$	$[1.697, 2.203] \times 10^{4}$	$[1.009, 1.025] \times 10^{5}$
12	325	434	1.714×10^{29}	1.616	$[2.683, 3.184] \times 10^{1}$	$[1.991, 2.793] \times 10^{4}$	$[1.522, 1.585] \times 10^{5}$
13	378	509	3.006×10^{32}	2.558	$[3.772, 4.537] \times 10^{1}$	$[2.097, 2.785] \times 10^{4}$	$[1.888, 1.920] \times 10^{5}$
14	435	590	6.141×10^{35}	3.175	$[6.133, 7.234] \times 10^{1}$	$[3.093, 4.247] \times 10^{4}$	$[2.101, 2.114] \times 10^{5}$
15	496	677	1.445×10^{39}	4.103	$[8.546, 9.790] \times 10^{1}$	$[3.386, 4.216] \times 10^{4}$	$[2.653, 3.148] \times 10^{5}$
16	561	770	3.882×10^{42}	6.012	$[1.067, 1.259] \times 10^{2}$	$[3.452, 4.675] \times 10^{4}$	$[3.798, 4.173] \times 10^{5}$

Table 2: Second group of tests with n ranging from 2 to 16, $m = 2$ and $r = 1$.

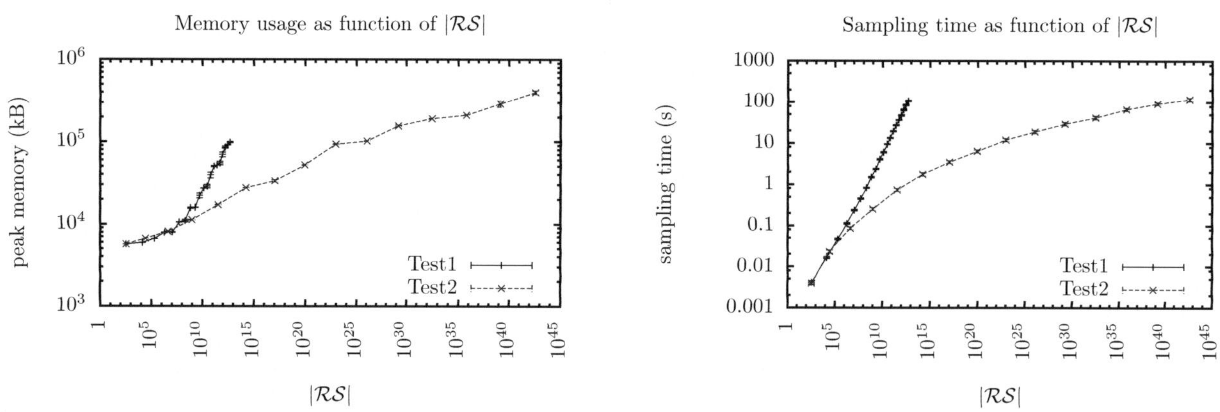

(a) Memory consumption (b) Time consumption

Figure 3: Comparison of the memory usage and the sampling time for the first and the second batch of tests.

levels correspond to Petri net places, enlarging the net makes the decision diagrams taller (more levels), while enlarging the marking makes them wider (more pointers per node). Since the decision diagrams gain efficiency, in comparison to a tree representation of the reachability set, by reusing nodes on lower levels, this makes them likely to be more efficient in the former case—in taller diagrams there are more levels and reusing nodes deeper in the diagram is often more profitable for efficiency.

4. CONCLUSION

We have presented the tool spnps which implements a variant of the coupling from the past algorithm for perfect sampling in bounded SPNs. Spnps uses decision diagrams as a data structure to perform the perfect sampling and we have shown that when the SPN has a certain regularity in its reachability set, the sampling can be done efficiently even in nets with very large state spaces.

We have evaluated the performance of the tool on SPN models of fork-join queueing networks with some resource competition. The results of our tests suggest that the algorithm as implemented is likely to be more efficient for sampling in models that are composed of many loosely coupled components. Future work will explore the possibility of improving the tool performance by using different encodings. In fact, as mentioned before, currently each SPN place is encoded by a single level in the decision diagram, while multiple levels per place or multiple places per level could be used.

Acknowledgements

Work partially supported by MIUR fund Fondo per il sostegno dei giovani "Programma strategico: ICT e componentistica elettronica".

5. REFERENCES

[1] Baldan, P., Cocco, N., Marin, A., and Simeoni, M. Petri nets for modelling metabolic pathways: a survey. *Natural Computing 9*, 4 (2010), 955–989.

[2] Balsamo, S., Harrison, P. G., and Marin, A. Methodological Construction of Product-form Stochastic Petri-Nets for Performance Evaluation. *J. of System and Software 85*, 7 (2012), 1520–1539.

[3] Balsamo, S., Marin, A., and Stojic, I. Perfect sampling in stochastic Petri nets using decision diagrams. In *Proc. of 23rd Int. Symp. on Modeling, Analysis and Simulation of Computer and Telecommunication Systems (MASCOTS)* (2015), pp. 126–135.

[4] Balsamo, S., Marin, A., and Stojic, I. *Spnps: A Tool for Perfect Sampling in Stochastic Petri Nets.* Springer International Publishing, Cham, 2016, pp. 163–166.

[5] Bouillard, A., and Gaujal, B. Backward coupling in bounded free-choice nets under Markovian and non-Markovian assumptions. *Discrete Event Dynamic Systems 18*, 4 (2008), 473–498.

[6] Bušić, A., Gaujal, B., and Vincent, J.-M. Perfect simulation and non-monotone Markovian systems. In *Proceedings of the 3rd International Conference on Performance Evaluation Methodologies and Tools* (ICST, Brussels, Belgium, 2008), ValueTools '08, ICST (Institute for Computer Sciences, Social-Informatics and Telecommunications Engineering), pp. 27:1–27:10.

[7] Chen, R. An upper bound solution for homogeneous fork/join queueing systems. *IEEE Trans. on Parallel and Distributed Systems 22*, 5 (2011), 874–878.

[8] Chiola, G., Franceschinis, G., Gaeta, R., and Ribaudo, M. GreatSPN 1.7: Graphical editor and analyzer for timed and stochastic Petri nets. *Perf. Eval. 24* (1995), 47–68.

[9] Dai, H. Exact simulation for fork-join networks with heterogeneous service. *Int. J. of Statistics and Probability 4*, 1 (2015).

[10] Desel, J., and Esparza, J. *Free choice Petri nets.* Cambridge Tracts in Theoretical Computer Science 40. Cambridge University Press, 1995.

[11] Haas, P. *Stochastic Petri Nets: Modelling, Stability, Simulation.* Springer Series in Operations Research. Springer, 2002.

[12] Heidelberger, P., and Trivedi, K. Analytic queueing models for programs with internal concurrency. *IEEE Trans. Comput. C-32* (1983), 73–82.

[13] Hirel, C., Tuffin, B., and Trivedi, K. S. SPNP: stochastic Petri nets. Version 6.0. In *Computer Performance Evaluation: Modelling Techniques and Tools, 11th International Conference, TOOLS 2000, Schaumburg, IL, USA, March 27-31, 2000, Proceedings* (2000), pp. 354–357.

[14] Kant, K. *Introduction to Computer System Performance Evaluation.* McGraw-Hill, 1992.

[15] Law, A. M., and Kelton, W. D. *Simulation modeling and analysis*, 3rd ed. McGraw-Hill, 2000.

[16] Marsan, M. A., Conte, G., and Balbo, G. A class of generalized stochastic Petri nets for the performance evaluation of multiprocessor systems. *ACM Trans. Comput. Syst. 2*, 2 (1984), 93–122.

[17] Miner, A. Saturation for a general class of models. In *Proc. of Quantitative Evaluation of Systems (QEST)* (2004), pp. 282–291.

[18] Molloy, M. K. Performance analysis using stochastic Petri nets. *IEEE Trans. on Comput. 31*, 9 (1982), 913–917.

[19] Propp, J. G., and Wilson, D. B. Exact sampling with coupled Markov chains and applications to statistical mechanics. *Random Struct. Algorithms 9*, 1-2 (1996), 223–252.

[20] Tutsch, D. *Performance analysis of network architectures.* Springer, 2006.

[21] Weber, M., and Kindler, E. The Petri net markup language. In *Petri Net Technology for Communication-Based Systems*, vol. 2472 of *Lecture Notes in Computer Science.* Springer Berlin Heidelberg, 2003, pp. 124–144.

[22] Zimmermann, A., Freiheit, J., German, R., and Hommel, G. Petri net modelling and performability evaluation with TimeNET 3.0. In *TOOLS '00: Proc. of the 11th Int. Conf. on Computer Performance Evaluation: Modelling Techniques and Tools* (London, UK, 2000), Springer-Verlag, pp. 188–202.

J2CBROKER: A Service Broker Simulation Tool For Cooperative Clouds

Maurizio Giacobbe
Department of Engineering
University of Messina
Contrada Di Dio - 98166, Messina
mgiacobbe@unime.it

Riccardo Di Pietro
Department of Engineering
University of Messina
Contrada Di Dio - 98166, Messina
rdipietro@unime.it

Carlo Puliafito
DIEEI
University of Catania
Viale Andrea Doria 6 - 95100, Catania
carlopulia@gmail.com

Marco Scarpa
Department of Engineering
University of Messina
Contrada Di Dio - 98166, Messina
mscarpa@unime.it

ABSTRACT

The Internet and digital technologies are transforming our world, but existing barriers, mainly due to obsolete Information Technologies (IT), lead citizens to miss out on goods and services, enterprises and start-ups to limit their horizons, and businesses and governments to cannot fully benefit from digital tools. Recently, *Cloud computing* emerged as hot topic in IT, both in industrial and academic area, in order to overcome the above barriers. Its use in large scale distributed infrastructure, platform or software services is motivated by the possibility to promote a new economy of scale in different contexts. Such scenario demands timely, repeatable, and controllable methodologies for evaluation of algorithms, applications and policies before the development of Cloud services or products, especially to achieve a good compromise between several performance indicators. To this end, **simulations-based environments** allow to evaluate the hypothesis prior to the software development, thus reducing the risk of economic losses, scarce *Quality of Service* or *Quality of Experience.* In this paper we present and discuss a simulation-based approach for **Cloud Brokerage ecosystems**. More specifically, we propose the **J2CBROKER** *Simulation Tool*, mainly based on *JAVA* and *JavaScript Object Notation (JSON)* technologies. Its architecture, functionalities and technological choices are discussed and motivated. Moreover, we present a *case of study* to evaluate the goodness of the proposed approach.

Keywords

Broker, Cloud Brokerage, Cloud Computing, Cooperative Clouds, Digital Single Market, Key Performance Indicator, JAVA, JavaScript Object Notation, Simulation Tool.

VALUETOOLS 2016, October 25-28, Taormina, Italy

1. INTRODUCTION

Nowadays, Cloud computing represents the reference technology for delivering distributed, scalable, heterogeneous, reliable, fault-tolerant, and sustainable computational services. They are generally presented as Infrastructure, Platform, or Software as a Services (IaaS, PaaS, SaaS). However, recently the XaaS acronym emerged as a collective term signifying "X as a Service", "anything as a Service" or "everything as a Service", thus referring to services that are delivered over the Internet rather than locally or on-site, especially in presence of the emerging *Internet of Things (IoT)* paradigm. Moreover, services may be offered by *Cloud Service Providers (CSPs)* in private Data Centers (DCs), i.e. by *private Clouds*, or they can be commercially offered for customers, i.e. by *public Clouds*, or yet it is possible that both public and private Clouds are combined forming *hybrid Clouds.*

The above wide set of Cloud architectures demands timely, repeatable, and controllable methodologies for evaluation of algorithms, applications, and policies before the development of Cloud services or products, especially with the increasing demand for energy-efficient *IT* solutions. Since the use of real testbeds limits the experiments to the scale of the testbed, thus making the reiteration of results an extremely difficult undertaking, alternative approaches need to be considered both for Clouds and traditional IT systems. Among these possible alternatives, **simulations tools** allow researchers and practitioners to evaluate working hypothesis before the software development. In this manner it is possible to set environment variables and parameters defining models, reproducing tests and providing results (textual and/or graphical) to analyze. Specifically, the use of a simulation-based approach is fundamental for Cloud environments, because access the infrastructure incurs payments in real currency (*pay-as-you-go* system) At the customer side, simulation tools can offer significant benefits, for example by allowing Cloud customers to test their services in repeatable and controllable environment, without paying Cloud services. At the provider side, instead, simulators can allow evaluation of different scenarios where to allocate computational resources under varying performances, workload conditions, and monetary cost distributions. CSPs can proceed in their *business analysis* thus to optimize the resource access cost with a special focus on improving profits. In the absence of such simulation-based environments, both Cloud customers and providers risk to commit serious errors of assessment, or to refer to non-objective evaluations resulting in inefficient service performance and economic losses.

2. MOTIVATIONS

Within the *Digital Single Market* [1] *European Commission* priority, Cloud computing plays a key role through the *data-driven innovation* initiatives, *data ownership, access* and *usability ownership, portability of data* and *switching* of service providers. In this complex context, customers' discovery of the services and selection of the one which best suits their needs is not a trivial issue and might be very time-consuming and/or ineffective. Moreover, customers need to be assisted during this process. A **Cloud Service Broker (CSB)** might be the solution to this problem. Essentially, a CSB is an additional computing layer which acts as an intermediary between service customers on one side and service providers on the other. *Gartner* [14], the world's leading information technology research and advisory company, identifies three areas in which Cloud brokerage might play an important role towards service customers, but also service providers. The first area is *aggregation*, that is to manage multiple services, possibly from different providers, presenting them as an unified service. Complex relationships and agreements among providers define the level of criticality. The second area is *integration* to make applications, which are independent at first, work nicely together and cooperate in order to fulfill the customer's needs. The third and last area is the *customization* one, which consists in the tweaking of services in order to best suit users' needs.

Other applications of CSB, which still come under the concept of service selection, are the *ranking* of services according to parameters provided by users (e.g. services ordered by cost) and the *selection* of the best DC (or site), among the N available, to execute a certain job.

Cloud Brokerage Enablers are software platforms which enable Cloud Brokerage. According to *MarketsandMarkets* [2], a market research firm, the Cloud Service Brokerage and Enablement market size is estimated to grow from USD 7.44 billion in 2016 to USD 26.71 billion by 2021. Some of the most important CSB companies are, in alphabetical order: *Appirio*, *ComputeNext* and *Dell Boomi.*

3. RELATED WORKS

Due to the great interest and importance played by CSB, many researches have been carried out in this field, surveying the possible approaches and algorithms for the service selection [16], [17], [13], but also the Cloud simulators which can be used to evaluate a CSB's performances [15]. In fact, the evaluation of performances in a real Cloud environment is too cost-and-time-consuming. This is why, very often, researchers and businesses prefer to use simulation tools to evaluate their proposals.

Probably, **CloudSim** [7] is the most popular and complete framework for the modeling and simulation of Cloud environments. It was developed at the *CLOUd computing and Distributed Systems (CLOUDS) Laboratory*, in the *University of Melbourne, Australia.* It is open source, entirely written in *JAVA* and provides basic classes for modeling DCs, users, brokers, computational resources, policies and virtual machines. CloudSim is built on top of another open source framework, named **GridSim** [6], used for large scale Grid systems and P2P networks.

Thanks to its success, CloudSim has been extended by researchers and thus other products using it as their core have been developed. The most important example of these is **CloudAnalyst** [18], which is a JAVA based simulation tool. It was developed for a precise purpose, which is that of dealing not just with a tool, but with an easy to use tool.

GreenCloud [11] is an open source simulation environment built as an extension of the *NS2* network simulator, which is written in *C++* and *OTcl.* The peculiarity which distinguishes this environment from all the others is the focus on the energy consumed by all the computing and communication components of a DC in a simulated Cloud environment. GreenCloud is a packet level simulator, meaning that whenever a packet has to be transmitted, all the relative protocol processing is performed. On the other hand, CloudSim and CloudAnalyst are event-based simulators: they avoid to process packets individually and they capture the overall effect of interaction instead. The result is that even if GreenCloud is more accurate, it is slower in simulating and is able to simulate systems with a lower number of nodes. Unlike CloudAnalyst, GreenCloud does not have a GUI for an easy simulation setup, nor for the representation of the simulation results as tables or charts. It uses the Nam animation tool to visualize the simulated topology and the packet flow after the simulation is completed.

iCanCloud [12] is an open source simulation platform entirely written in C++ and developed as an extension of the *OMNET* network simulator. The main purpose of iCanCloud is to estimate the trade-off between costs and performances, thus to help users in to optimize it. iCanCloud has a feature that the previously discussed environments do not have: if there is a cluster of nodes available to carry out an experiment, it is possible to perform a parallel simulation among them.

However, even if many simulator tools that can be used for studying Cloud systems, we can not establish what is the best simulator to use because the evaluation depends upon actual requirement.

4. THE J2CBROKER SIMULATION TOOL

Based on the above considerations, we thought of a tool capable of simulating different cooperative Cloud Brokerage scenarios across different metrics and evaluation criteria included in *models* such as *sustainability* and *availability* in a single "multi-criteria" model.

4.1 Architecture and Technological Choices

We thought of a tool capable of managing **JSON** documents and written in **JAVA**: hence the name *Java Json Cloud BROKER (J2CBROKER).* The main goal is to provide a simulation-based tool that: *i)* dynamically manages JSON documents as inputs simulating both requests and offers by CSPs; *ii)* calculates the best choices (i.e., offers) on the basis of specific parameters through different multi-

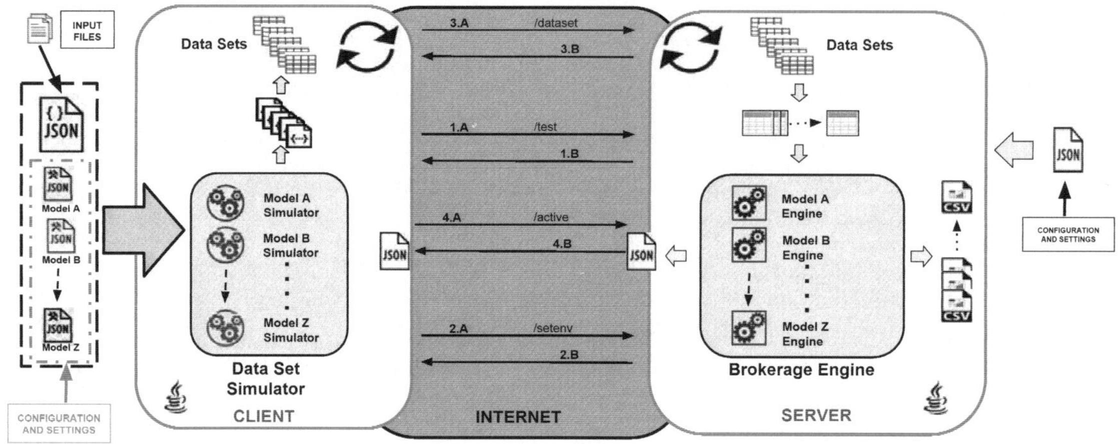

Figure 1: A general architecture of the *J2CBROKER* Simulation Tool.

criteria engines (i.e., multi-criteria algorithms implemented in JAVA language); *iii)* provides the resulting best offers of its calculation as outputs, both in the form of JSON documents and *on-screen* (results can be also provided in many other forms, such as *CSV*).

JSON is a lightweight, text-based, language-independent data interchange format derived from the *ECMAScript Programming Language Standard*. It defines a small set of formatting rules for the portable representation of structured data [3]. It has a simple syntax, which results, for example, in less "markup" overhead, more compact and more readable if it is compared to the *eXtensible Markup Language (XML)* alternative [9].

The J2CBROKER **general architecture** is shown in Figure 1, where we introduced the concept of **model**. A model is essentially a JSON file which contains all the *input* metrics describing the basic characteristics of a given Scenario.

The JAVA client-server architecture uses a stateless *RESTful* approach for its communication. The client and the server can operate on different machines across the Internet. The server is modeled as a perpetual process that waits for clients to receive requests, and then processes them. The server offers resources through *REST API*. The use of the JAVA *object-oriented, class-based* and *general-purpose* computer programming language [10] is an advantage. It allows to run the same program on many different systems by being platform-independent at both the source and binary levels. Moreover, it is ideal to create modular programs and reusable code. Before starting their activities, both the client and the server have a mandatory JSON configuration file called *json-conf-file* that the user have to fill in with the appropriate information. At the client side, the configuration file contains besides the client/server configuration settings, the specific information of the Model that the user wants to use during the simulation. At the server side, this file contains only the server configuration settings. These two configuration files allow the user to set up the client-server architecture and to dynamically configure the behavior of the simulation tool at each new simulation session.

For each model, the architecture provides two specific components: the related Model Simulator at the client side, and the related Model Engine at the server side. More specifically, referring to Figure 1, we mainly distinguish two blocks: the **Data Set Simulator** at the client side and the **Brokerage Engine** at the server side, both containing several Models (respectively Simulators and Engines).

4.1.1 The Data Set Simulator

The Data Set Simulator is the "core" of the client application. It consists of a modular structure which contains different Model Simulators. The result is a general purpose tool which allows anyone to create and connect his own Model Simulator. Each Model Simulator implements different specific behaviors. Those latter depend on both the directives received from the *json-conf-file* and the characteristic dedicated for the simulation. If the user uses the client-server application according to the directives of the Random Simulation Mode, the Data Set Simulator creates specific Data Sets according to a dedicated Model. Otherwise (i.e., according to the directives of the Guided Simulation Mode) the Data Set Simulator gathers and parses the information from the JSON absolute paths listed inside the *json-input-list-file*. In any case, the expected behavior at the server side will be the same. It will store all the Data Sets and, when it will receive the *active request*, it will elaborate the Data Sets according to the Model Engine predetermined in the simulation. Finally the server will send a JSON file to the client with the result of the calculation at the Brokerage Engine. In such a context, each Data Set represents a simulated offer by a CSP at a specific Cloud site.

4.1.2 The Brokerage Engine

The "Brokerage Engine" represents the "core" of the Server application. It consists of a modular structure that contains different Model Engines. This is important because it makes this client-server application a general purpose tool, which allows anyone to create and connect his own Model Engine. However, each Model Engine implements different specific behaviors. Those latter depend on both the directives received from the client through the HTTP POST "/setenv" request, and on the characteristic of the dedicated brokerage scenario.

4.1.3 The Client/Server Communication

The communication phase between the client and the server is done in four different steps (see Figure 1). First of all, the client verifies if the server is alive by sending to it an *HTTP POST* request for the resource "/test" **(1.A)**. If the server returns a response containing the status code equal to 200 **(1.B)**, which means that the test is successfully done, then the client can move to the next step **(2.A)**.

In order to set some server side environment parameters, the client sends an *HTTP POST* request to the server for the resource "/setenv" and specifies those parameters inside the *Headers* of the HTTP request **(2.A)**. If the server returns a response that contains the status code equal to 200 **(2.B)**, which means that the set-environment request is successfully done, then the client can move to the next step **(3.A)**.

In order to transfer all the Data Sets to the server, the client uses one *HTTP POST* request for each Data Set. All these requests are for the resource "/dataset" **(3.A)** and each one will contain all the information about a particular Data Set the client wants to transfer at that moment. All these information are parameters stored as Headers inside the HTTP request. If the server returns a response that contains the status code equal to 200 **(3.B)**, which means that the dataset request was successfully done, then the client will send another dataset request, and so on, until the end. Then the client can move to the next step **(4.A)**.

To start the server side processing phase, the client sends *HTTP POST* request to the server for the resource "/active" **(4.A)**. When the server will complete the processing with success, it will return a response with the status code equal 200 and the JSON file containing the output of the processing phase **(4.B)**.

4.1.4 Simulation Modes

The J2CBROKER can work in two different modes: the **Random Simulation Mode** and the **Guided Simulation Mode**. Both the above simulation modes are part of the setting at client-side.

During the *Random Simulation Mode*, the client reads the information of the specific Model described inside the related *json-conf-file*. According to the reported information, the client simulates the Data Sets and takes care of sending them, one per time, to the server, along with other directives addressed to the related Model Engine. Once the server received all the information needed, it will elaborate them and returns the output through a new JSON file.

In order to be run in the *Guided Simulation Mode*, the client needs the above-mentioned *json-conf-file*, along with another mandatory JSON configuration file called *json-input-list-file*. This latter needs to be filled with the absolute paths of all the JSON files representing the Data Sets that the user wants to use in this guided Simulation. The client reads all the absolute paths indicated inside the *json-input-list-file*, understands what Model they are related to and makes a parsing operation to extract all the information needed to create the correspondent Data Sets. Therefore, the client sends one Data Set per time, along with other directives addressed to the related Model Engine, to the server. At this time, the server will do the same processing as in the Random Simulation Mode.

5. CASE OF STUDY: SUSTAINABILITY-ORIENTED MODEL

In this Section, we present a *case-of-study* to prove the goodness of the proposed methodology. By referring to Figure 1, we introduce a **sustainability-oriented Model** to make the best choice in *resource allocation* thus to push down environmental pollution (sustainability), and contemporary taking into account the availability and the **monetary cost** criterion in a *multi-criteria approach*.

We started the J2CBROKER application server on a *Virtual Machine* equipped with *Ubuntu Server 14.04* and hosted in a *IBM BladeCenter LS21* at the *Cloud Laboratory DC - University of Messina*. We tested the application server by running several application clients, hosted in different machines both inside and outside the above-mentioned DC.

5.1 The Sustainability Metric

We refer to *sustainability* as part of the concept of *sustainable development* [8] that is "the development that meets the needs of the present, without compromising the ability of the future generations to meet their own needs" [4]. For our energy-aware purposes, in the following we express sustainability through several sub-metrics (Table 1 to follow) which are generally used to define "how green is a DC".

5.2 The Monetary Cost Criterion

Monetary Cost is a quantifiable criterion that addresses customers and organizations in their business. By referring to IT services it is generally expressed in $\$/h$ (i.e., dollars-per-hour) or $\$/GB$ (i.e., dollars-per-GigaByte). Usually providers offer instance placement services with a fixed price in the service maintenance time at a site. Therefore, we can express cost for an instance i at a site node s, as follows:

$$cost_{s,i} = service\_price_{s,i} * \Delta_t \quad (1)$$

where Δ_t is the *running time* of the $i-th$ instance at the $s-th$ site node.

5.3 Scenario

The proposed tool simulates a scenario where the main goal is to reduce *carbon dioxide emissions* (i.e. the *CO2*) through a Cloud brokerage ecosystem, where *Cloud Service Providers (CSPs)* cooperate in a *centralized brokerage environment* to run *instance workloads* at the most convenient Cloud sites. An instance is a temporary virtual server that needs to be allocated in order to run services. More specifically, we developed a sustainability-oriented Model Data Set at client side and a sustainability-oriented Model Engine at server side.

5.3.1 Roles

The entire simulated process mainly consists into three roles (*applicant (A), brokering (B)* and *offering (O)*).

Role A. When a Cloud provider receives some instances to run it generates a request to B for computation, and

Sustainability-oriented Model Data Set	
Service Data Set	
Parameter	**Range**
Instance workload (watts)	200-300
Power basic (watts)	100
Running time (hours)	10, 24, 360, 750
Number of instances in each request	1, 10, 20, 50
Number of instances in each offer	12, 14, 16, 18, 20
Availability (%)	99.90-99.99
Service price ($/h)	0.007-0.112
Sustainability Data Set	
Parameter	**Range**
ITEU	0.3-0.6
ITEE	0.1-3.9
PUE	1.4-2.3
GEC	0.0-0.003
CDIE (kgCO2/kWh)	*source: https://www.ipcc.ch*

Table 1: The Sustainability-oriented Model Simulator Data Set.

cooperates within the ecosystem to determine where the load should run.

Role B. At each new event concerning the status of requests or offers, it gathers the requests from A profiles and evaluates the offers (sent by the O profiles) by using its Model Engine (i.e. the algorithm). Finally, the resulting best offers, where an instance has to run, are presented to the A profiles.

Role O. Each CSP creates one or more offers, each one based on sustainability, availability and cost factors at the involved site. Therefore, it sends its offer to B.

The J2CBROKER allows the user to simulate the above-mentioned roles' tasks by configuring and executing the sustainability oriented Model Data Set and the sustainability oriented Model Engine, where a developed energy-aware algorithm runs.

5.3.2 The Sustainability-oriented Model Simulator

The proposed simulation environment presents a modeling of both service and Cloud site, i.e. the **Model Data Set**, thus to provide *input* data for the related Model Engine. Each offer is modeled by a *JSON* document, i.e. the Model Data Set, which includes two main collections: the first one defines a service data set describing the service parameters and among these availability and cost; the second one defines the sustainability metrics and factors at each Cloud site.

The service data set is obtained from a survey on several "top" providers of IT technologies (e.g., Dell blade servers), Cloud services and solutions (e.g., Amazon Web Services (AWS)). The sustainability data set, instead, is based on the measurement results of a real scenario, from the METI Japan project [5] on enhancing the energy efficiency and the use of green energy in DCs.

Table 1 shows the Model Data Set: the simulator selects a random value between the range set for each metric in order to characterize each offer by its sustainability, availability and monetary cost values.

5.3.3 The Sustainability-oriented Model Engine

The Brokerage Engine consists of a modular structure that contains different Model Engines. Among these, in the presented case of study, we refer to the sustainability-oriented Model Engine. This one is mainly based on a decision making algorithm in the perspective of an energy-aware instance allocation in a centralized brokerage Cloud environment. The algorithm provides a ranking of the offers (i.e., Data Sets as previously mentioned in the Paragraph 4.1.1) calculated on the basis of the inputs from the sustainability-oriented Model Simulator, and contemporary taking into account all the parameters reported in Table 1. The description of the algorithm is not the objective of this paper.

However, in order to introduce the experimental results thus to prove the goodness of the proposed approach, we briefly describe the main *formula* of the algorithm. It results in the *opt* value, which is an "optimum" index computed by the algorithm to weight each offer in terms of carbon dioxide emission (sustainability in gCO2) and cost ($-per-hour) as follows:

$$opt_{nProvider,nDataset} = A*(gCO2_{nProvider,nDataset}/gCO2_{worst}+ B*(cost_{nProvider,nDataset}/cost_{worst}); \quad (2)$$

where $A + B = 1$.

In that Formula, *nProvider* is an unique number which identifies the CSP' site, *Dataset* is an unique number identifying the offer of that CSP, *gCO2* quantifies the related CO2 emission to run an instance workload, *cost* is the service price in $-per-hour.

The A and B coefficients respectively represent the weight chosen for sustainability and for cost. Both CO2 emission and cost are normalized to the respective worst case calculated at each iteration on all the offers by all the CSPs.

5.4 Experimental Results

The resulting best offers of the J2CBROKER calculation are provided at each computation as ranking, both in the form of JSON documents and *on-screen*. In particular, each output reports three blocks, each one identifying a different ranking of offers based on the calculated *opt* values. The first one shows a ranking based on the best "green" offers (A=1;B=0); the second one results in a compromise between sustainability and cost (A=0.5;B=0.5); the last instead ranks offers ordered according to the service price (A=0;B=1).

Figure 2 allows the reader for a quick visual feedback about the confidence interval of the above-mentioned *opt* index to allocate a number N of 10 instances, with $A = 0.5$, $B = 0.5$, a number of 1000 samples and a 95% *confidence*. The *x-axis* reports the required *running time* in *hours (h)*. The values reported in Figure 2 are the result of a post-processing phase, by getting as input all the best *opt* values calculated at each run step. If we consider that for each run in our simulation, the worst case results in an *opt* index close to 1000, the energy-aware algorithm at Broker is able to select offers with an *opt* index very low when compared with the worst case. The result is a good compromise between sustainability and cost since it is as better as it is closer to zero.

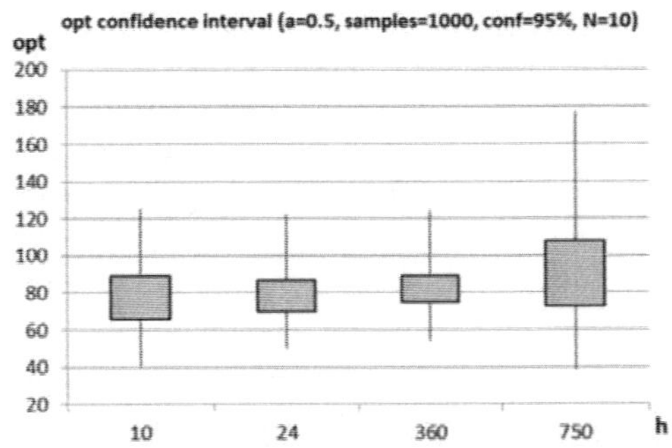

Figure 2: Confidence interval of the *opt* index for the allocation of ten instances.

6. CONCLUSIONS AND FUTURE WORK

The evaluation of performances in a real Cloud environment is too cost-and-time-consuming. This is why simulation tools can help researchers, Cloud Service Providers and customers to evaluate their proposals. In this paper we presented and discussed a multi-criteria Brokering Simulation Tool, we name *J2CBROKER*, able to simulate the discovering at a Cloud Broker of the most convenient offers delivered by Cloud Service Providers in cooperative Cloud ecosystems. By modeling different Cloud sites and the related economic offers on several criterion, we demonstrate how the proposed approach can accommodate different scenarios characterized by a different number of instances to allocate and based on both performance and business parameters. These last may also come from real datasets, and thanks to an "optimum" balance between them, it is possible analyze possible scenarios where a cooperative Cloud ecosystem can reduce the gap in competition with larger providers. Actually, the J2CBROKER is managed via command line. The results provided by the Brokerage Engine are available both through a JSON file and displayed on the screen at the user side.

In future works, we plan to realize an administrative dashboard which allows users to setup the simulation in a user-friendly manner. Furthermore we plan to develop a JAVA module to automatically show the results in a graphical way, by choosing between different representations.

7. ACKNOWLEDGMENTS

This work has been carried out in the framework of the CINI Smart Cities National Lab.

8. REFERENCES

[1] The Digital Single Market. https://ec.europa.eu/digital-single-market/en/digital-single-market.

[2] MarketsandMarkets. http://www.marketsandmarkets.com/.

[3] Standard ECMA-404. http://www.ecma-international.org/publications/standards/Ecma-404.htm.

[4] United Nations General Assembly (1987) Report of the World Commission on Environment and Development: Our Common Future. http://www.un-documents.net/wced-ocf.htm.

[5] The Ministry of Economy Trade and Industry (METI) Japan Project - Enhancing the Energy Efficiency and Use of Green Energy in Data Centers. http://home.jeita.or.jp/greenit-pc/sd/pdf/ds2.pdf.

[6] R. Buyya and M. Murshed. Gridsim: A toolkit for the modeling and simulation of distributed resource management and scheduling for grid computing. *CONCURRENCY AND COMPUTATION: PRACTICE AND EXPERIENCE (CCPE*, 14(13):1175–1220, 2002.

[7] R. N. Calheiros, R. Ranjan, A. Beloglazov, C. A. F. De Rose, and R. Buyya. Cloudsim: A toolkit for modeling and simulation of cloud computing environments and evaluation of resource provisioning algorithms. *Softw. Pract. Exper.*, 41(1):23–50, Jan. 2011.

[8] M. Giacobbe, A. Celesti, M. Fazio, M. Villari, and A. Puliafito. A sustainable energy-aware resource management strategy for iot cloud federation. In *1st IEEE International Symposium on Systems Engineering, ISSE 2015 - Proceedings*, pages 170–175, 2015.

[9] M. Giacobbe and M. Villari. Tecniche avanzate di data management per la diagnostica avanzata in campo navale. In *SEA-MED Conference Proceedings*, pages 234–248. DIECII, 2014.

[10] J. Gosling, B. Joy, G. Steele, G. Bracha, and A. Buckley. The java language specification, java se 8 edition, 2015.

[11] D. Kliazovich, P. Bouvry, and S. U. Khan. Greencloud: a packet-level simulator of energy-aware cloud computing data centers. *The Journal of Supercomputing*, 62(3):1263–1283, 2012.

[12] A. Núñez, J. L. Vázquez-Poletti, A. C. Caminero, G. G. Castañé, J. Carretero, and I. M. Llorente. icancloud: A flexible and scalable cloud infrastructure simulator. *J. Grid Comput.*, 10(1):185–209, Mar. 2012.

[13] I. Patiniotakis, Y. Verginadis, and G. Mentzas. Pulsar: preference-based cloud service selection for cloud service brokers. *Journal of Internet Services and Applications*, 6(1):1–14, 2015.

[14] D. C. Plummer, B. J. Lheureux, M. Cantara, and T. Bova. Cloud services brokerage is dominated by three primary roles. *Gartner doc*, 2011.

[15] M. Radi. Efficient service broker policy for large-scale cloud environments. *CoRR*, abs/1503.03460, 2015.

[16] L. Sun, H. Dong, F. K. Hussain, O. K. Hussain, and E. Chang. Cloud service selection: State-of-the-art and future research directions. *Journal of Network and Computer Applications*, 45:134 – 150, 2014.

[17] S. Sundareswaran, A. Squicciarini, and D. Lin. A brokerage-based approach for cloud service selection. In *Cloud Computing (CLOUD), 2012 IEEE 5th International Conference on*, pages 558–565, June 2012.

[18] B. Wickremasinghe, A. Prof, and R. B. Contents. Cloudanalyst: A cloudsim-based tool for modelling and analysis of large scale cloud computing environments, 2009.

jSSTL - A Tool to Monitor Spatio-Temporal Properties*

Luca Bortolussi
DMG, University of Trieste, Italy. MOSI, Saarland University, Germany. ISTI-CNR, Pisa, Italy
luca@dmi.units.it

Michele Loreti
University of Florence, Italy
michele.loreti@unifi.it

Laura Nenzi
IMT, Lucca, Italy
laura.nenzi@imtlucca.it

ABSTRACT

Controlling and designing spatio-temporal behaviours requires proper formal tools to describe such properties, and to monitor and verify whether, and how robustly, they are satisfied by a system. In this paper, we introduce jSSTL, a Java tool for the specification of *Signal Spatio-Temporal Logic* (SSTL) properties and their robust monitoring on spatio-temporal trajectories. The tool consists of a jSSTL API and a front-end, integrated in ECLIPSE. We describe in details the framework and the use of the plugin, exploiting a running example of a cholera outbreak.

Keywords: Monitoring, Spatio-temporal Logic, Signal Temporal Logic, Java Tool, Eclipse.

1. INTRODUCTION

With the advent of Internet-of-Things and the diffusion of many cyber-physical devices, the problem of designing and validating complex systems composed of many heterogeneous interacting entities, distributed in space, is getting more and more central. Examples include smart cities (e.g. bike sharing, intelligent transport), robot swarms, self-driving vehicles.

Model-based development (MBD) will play a central role in the design stage, but the ability to program and analyse efficiently such models has to be complemented with suitable languages to specify requirements, and with algorithmic methods to check them.

Modal logics are an obvious candidate in this respect, owing to their widespread use and the presence of many model checking tools. However, the fundamental role of space in several Cyber-Physical Systems (CPS) requires us to use a spatio-temporal logic, which is more expressive and complex to analyse than standard temporal logic languages.

Linear time spatio-temporal logics can also be monitored in real time, and may then be used to control and guide adaptation of these systems. Monitoring (namely verification of a property on a single system trace) can also be useful in the MBD process for statistical analysis of complex stochastic hybrid models of CPS. To this end, efficient monitoring tools and libraries for expressive spatio-temporal logics need to be developed and deployed.

*Work partially funded by the EU-FET project QUANTICOL (nr. 600708) and FRA-UniTS.

VALUETOOLS 2016, October 25-28, Taormina, Italy

Signal Spatio-Temporal Logic (SSTL) [13, 14] is a linear-time temporal logic, recently designed, suitable to describe behaviours of traces generated from simulations or measured from real systems. It spatially extends *Signal Temporal Logic* (STL) with a number of spatial modality that permit to specify metric and topological properties in a discrete space. In [13, 14], the authors provide a Boolean and quantitative semantics of SSTL, efficient monitoring algorithms for both semantics and interesting case studies, showing the usefulness of the logic.

In order to make this logic usable in practice, there is the need of an efficient and usable implementation. For this reason, we developed jSSTL, a Java-based tool for the specification and the verification of SSTL properties. The tool consists of a Java library (jSSTL API) and a front-end, integrated in ECLIPSE. Both the library and the ECLIPSE plugin can be downloaded from `http://quanticol.sourceforge.net/`. The source code is available at `https://bitbucket.org/LauraNenzi/jsstl`. The ECLIPSE plugin provides a user friendly interface to the tool, whereas the library can be used to integrate jSSTL within other applications and tools, as it has been done in [2]. Furthermore, the modular approach of the implementation allows to develop different front-end for jSSTL.

In this paper, we describe jSSTL and show its usage to analyse spatio-temporal behaviours of complex models. We will use a running example throughout paper. In particular, we will consider a model of a cholera outbreak, a prominent example of a waterborne disease [4, 12]. We presented this case study in [13] to describe some potentialities of the logic. We will use it here to introduce the type of models that we can consider, to give some examples of SSTL properties and to show the tool at work.

The spread of a cholera infection. The model describes the spread of a Cholera infection along the communities that live close to a river. The space is represented as a weighted graph, see Figure 1. The nodes ℓ_1, ..., ℓ_7 represent the communities; the edges describe the connection between the communities through the river. The graph is equipped with a weight function $w : E \to \mathbb{R}$ that returns the cost of each edge; for this model we interpret the cost $w(\ell_i, \ell_j)$ of an edge as the distance between the locations ℓ_i and ℓ_j.

There are two agent classes: the bacteria and the individuals. The bacteria have only one state (B) but they can be transported to different nodes via the river. An individual, instead, can be in three different states: susceptible (S) infected (I) and recovered (R), but cannot change location. The simplification is justified by the fact that we are not presenting a complete realistic model but just a simple example exploited later to illustrate the tool. We can easily extend the model to more complex scenarios as [12], for which we can specify and verify more complex spatio-temporal behaviours. Beside the inter-node movement of the bacteria, the dynamic of individuals is specified by natality and mortality and by transitions encoding the epidemic behaviour. The model of this system has state variables $\vec{X} = X_S, X_I, X_R, X_B$, counting the number of susceptible, infected, and recovered individuals, and the concentration of the bacteria in each location. The dynamics is specified by a list of transitions, each corresponding to an event and changes the system according to the transition rule (e.g,. $I \to R$ means an infected individual becomes recovered). Each transition has a speed governed by a rate function, that can depend on the concentration of the bacteria and individuals in each state . Below, we will list all the transitions (see [13] for a more detailed description of the model):

⋆ *Infection* : $S + B \to I + B$;
⋆ *Natality*: $\varnothing \to S$;
⋆ *Mortality* of a susceptible: $S \to \varnothing$;
⋆ *Mortality* of an infected: $I \to \varnothing$;
⋆ *Recovery*: $I \to R$
⋆ *Death* of bacteria: $B \to \varnothing$;
⋆ *Bacterial growth*: $\varnothing \to B$.

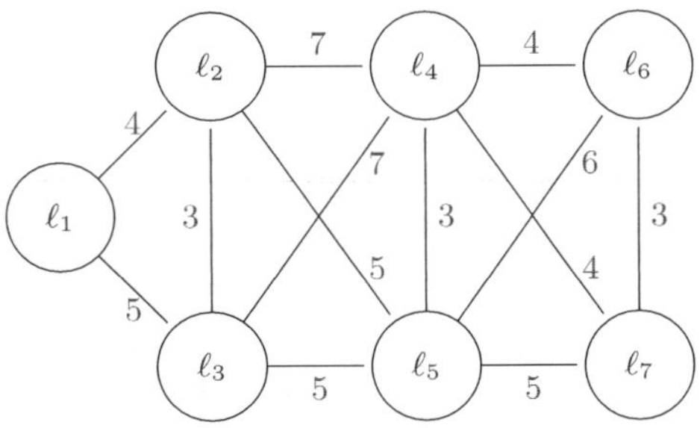

Figure 1: Representation of the space of the epidemic model. The nodes ℓ_1, ..., ℓ_7 represent the different communities; the edges represent the link between the communities through the water basin. The green numbers correspond to the values w of the weight function for each edge.

For such a description, we can derive both a deterministic model (a set of ODEs) or a stochastic one (a patch CTMCs), that can respectively be integrated with an ODE solver or simulated with standard algorithms as SSA or Gibson-Bruck. The solution of the integration/simulation is a spatio-temporal trace $\vec{x}(t,\ell) = (x_S(t,\ell), x_I(t,\ell), x_R(t,\ell) x_B(t,\ell))$ that describes the concentration of susceptible, recovered, infected individuals and bacterias, at each time, in each location.

Such spatio-temporal trajectories are the input of our jSSTL tool. This means that SSTL specifies properties directly over the spatio-temporal traces of the system. An interesting consideration about this is that we do not necessarily need a mathematical model but just observable traces of some process, including real observations. Hence, the tool can be used also for the analysis of black box systems for which we do not have a model but only informations about their behaviour.

The rest of the paper is organised as follows. In Section 2, we introduce SSTL. The features of the jSSTL Plug-In and how they can be exploited to identify and analyse SSTL properties are described in Section 3. In Section 4, we report the architecture of the tool. Finally, in Section 5, we present some related works and we conclude with final remarks and directions for future works.

2. SSTL

Signal Spatio Temporal Logic (SSTL) [13, 14] is a spatial extension of STL [7, 11]. SSTL integrates the temporal modalities of STL with two spatial operators. The logic is interpreted on spatio-temporal signals with continuous time and discrete space.

The space representation. As we have seen in the example, we consider a discrete representation of space, modelled as a weighted graph, with populations of interacting components evolving in each location (node) and with entities migrating from one location to another one (connected via edges). Formally, a weighted graph is a tuple $G = (L, E, w)$ where L is a set of nodes, E is a set of edges and $w : E \to \mathbb{R}_{\geq 0}$ is the function that returns the cost/weight of each edge. The space is also equipped with a metric, i.e., a function $d : L \times L \to \mathbb{R}_{\geq 0}$ that returns a positive real value for each pair of elements in L; in particular, the metric is the *shortest weighted path distance*, i.e., the cost of the shortest path between two different locations. So, for example, in Figure 1, $d(\ell_1, \ell_5) = w(\ell_1, \ell_2) + w(\ell_2, \ell_5) = 9$.

The signal. A *spatio-temporal signal*, is a function $\vec{s} : \mathbb{T} \times L \to \mathbb{E}$, where $\mathbb{T}$ is a dense real interval, L is a discrete set of locations and $\mathbb{E}$ is a subset of $\mathbb{R}^* = \mathbb{R} \bigcup \{+\infty, -\infty\}$. Signals with $\mathbb{E} = \mathbb{B} = \{0, 1\}$ are called *Boolean signals*, whereas those where $\mathbb{E} = \mathbb{R}^*$ are called real-valued or *quantitative signals*. A *spatio-temporal trace* is a function $\vec{x} : \mathbb{T} \times L \to \mathbb{D}$, s.t. $\vec{x}(t,\ell) := (x_1(t,\ell), \cdots, x_n(t,\ell)) \in \mathbb{D} \subseteq \mathbb{R}^n$, where each $x_i : \mathbb{T} \times L \to D_i \subseteq \mathbb{R}$, for $i = 1, \ldots, n$, is the projection on the ith coordinate/variable. Note that these projections have the form of quantitative signals. They are called the *primary signals* of the trace. We can thus see the trace as a set of primary signals. In particular, this means that SSTL can specify property of spatio-temporal traces.

The syntax of SSTL is given by

$$\varphi := \mu \mid \neg\varphi \mid \varphi_1 \wedge \varphi_2 \mid \varphi_1 \mathcal{U}_{[t_1,t_2]} \varphi_2 \mid \diamondsuit_{[d_1,d_2]} \varphi \mid \varphi_1 \mathcal{S}_{[d_1,d_2]} \varphi_2.$$

where μ is an atomic predicate (inequalities of the form $\mu_j(x_1, \ldots, x_n) \equiv (f_j(x_1, \ldots, x_n) \geq 0)$, for $f_j : \mathbb{R}^n \to \mathbb{R}$), negation and conjunction are the standard Boolean connectives, and $\mathcal{U}_{[t_1,t_2]}$ is the temporal *until* operator, where $[t_1, t_2]$ is a real positive closed intervals with $t_1 < t_2$. The spatial operators are the *somewhere* operator, $\diamondsuit_{[d_1,d_2]}$, and the *bounded surround* operator $\mathcal{S}_{[d_1,d_2]}$, where $[d_1, d_2]$ is a closed real interval with $d_1 < d_2$. There are also three derivable operators: the *eventually* operator $\mathcal{F}_{[t_1,t_2]} \varphi := \mathbf{true} \mathcal{U}_{[t_1,t_2]} \varphi$, the *always* operator $\mathcal{G}_{[t_1,t_2]} \varphi := \neg \mathcal{F}_{[t_1,t_2]} \neg \varphi$ and the *everywhere* operator $\boxdot_{[d_1,d_2]} \varphi := \neg \diamondsuit_{[d_1,d_2]} \neg \varphi$. Temporal operators are like in standard metric temporal logic, while spatial operators will be described in the next subsection. For more details, we refer the reader to [13, 14]. Below, we give an idea of what the logic can specify giving some examples.

Examples of SSTL properties. The idea for the definition of the somewhere and everywhere operators came from the necessity to describe behaviours at a certain distance from a specific point, e.g., "from a bike sharing station, in a radius of 100 meters, there are more than 30 bikes" or "in all the positions around my location, at a distance less the 1 km, there are no infected individuals". Let us see some more specific examples. Let us consider the epidemic model described in Section 1, with an infection that starts from location ℓ_1. We want then describe the diffusion of the epidemic along the communities. In particular, we want to check whether the infection has propagated at a certain distance from ℓ_1 after a certain time. This behaviour can be captured by the SSTL formula:

$$\varphi_1 = F_{[0,T_{inf}]} \diamondsuit_{[d_1,d_2]} (X_I > c_{inf}), \tag{1}$$

verifying it in location ℓ_1. The exact meaning of the formula is: eventually, in less than T_{inf} unit time, the number of infected individual becomes more than c_{inf} in a location ℓ with $d(\ell_1, \ell) \in [d_1, d_2]$, i.e., at a distance from location ℓ_1 equal or greater than d_1 and equal or less than d_2.

Let us see also a more complicated property:

$$\varphi_2 = \boxdot_{[0,d_{max}]}(\psi_1 \longrightarrow \psi_2), \tag{2}$$

where:

$$\psi_1 = F_{[0,T_{start}]}(\diamondsuit_{[0,d_{near}]}(X_I > c_{inf})))$$
$$\psi_2 = (F_{[T_{start},T_{start}+DT]} \diamondsuit_{[d_{far},d_{max}]} (X_I > c_{inf}))$$

The property stating that a large infection (with at least c_{inf} individuals) happening at some time $t \in [0, T_{start}]$ and localised within distance d_{near} from a given reference point, will spread further away, at a location at distance between d_{far} and d_{max}, at some time $t' \in [T_{start}, T_{start} + DT]$. Furthermore, this is true for every reference point (say at distance at most d_{max} from ℓ_1).

The surround operator $\varphi_1 \mathcal{S}_{[d_1,d_2]} \varphi_2$, instead, expresses the topological notion of being surrounded by a φ_2-region, while being in a φ_1-region, with additional metric constraints. The idea is that one cannot escape from a φ_1-region without passing from a node that satisfies φ_2 and, in any case, one has to reach a φ_2-node at a distance between d_1 and d_2. For example, this operator permits to describe properties as "there are many infected individuals in my community but all the communities directly connected with me have a very low concentration of infected individuals". For more example of surround properties we refer the reader to [14].

The semantics. Similarly to STL, SSTL has two semantics, the classical *boolean* semantics and a *quantitative* semantics.
The boolean semantics returns true or false depending on whether the trace satisfies the SSTL property, i.e. $(\vec{x}, t, \ell) \models \varphi$ is true if and only if the trace $\vec{x}(t, \ell)$ satisfies φ. The whole trace satisfies a property in location ℓ iff it satisfies the property at time zero, i.e. $(\vec{x}, \ell) \models \varphi \Leftrightarrow (\vec{x}, 0, \ell) \models \varphi$. This because we are working with *future* temporal modalities that talk about true *now* as a function of some true in the future. Furthermore, the trace is verified in each point in space, as we assume no privilege direction or location.

The quantitative semantics, instead, returns a real value $\rho(\varphi, \vec{x}, t, \ell)$ that quantifies the level of satisfaction of the formula by the trajectory $\vec{x}$ at time t in location ℓ. The absolute value $|\rho(\varphi, \vec{x}, t, \ell)|$ can be interpreted as measure of the robustness of the satisfaction or dissatisfaction. Furthermore, the sign of $\rho(\varphi, \vec{x}, t, \ell)$ is related to the truth of the formula: if $\rho(\varphi, \vec{x}, t, \ell) > 0$, then $(\vec{x}, t, \ell) \models \varphi$, and similarly if $\rho(\varphi, \vec{x}, t, \ell) < 0$, then $(\vec{x}, t, \ell) \not\models \varphi$. In accordance with the boolean semantics, the quantitative value of the whole trace in location ℓ is given by its value at time zero, i.e. $\rho(\vec{x}, \ell) = \rho(\vec{x}, 0, \ell)$.

Given a spatio-temporal trace $\vec{x}(t, \ell)$ and a property φ, the logic has specific algorithms to compute the boolean and the quantitative signal of the formula. Each formula's parse tree is seen as a network of signal transducers, taking as input the primary signals of the trace at the leaves, processing them bottom up, and returning the satisfaction value at the root. For details about monitoring algorithms we refer the reader to [13, 14].

3. ECLIPSE PLUGIN

The ECLIPSE plugin provides a simple user interface to specify and verify SSTL properties of spatio-temporal trajectories generated from the simulation of a system or from real observations. We can specify the properties, describe a model of the space (i.e., its graph structure), import the trajectories and then verify if such trajectories satisfy the specified properties. The instructions to download the plugin and to create a jSSTL Project are reported in `http://quanticol.sourceforge.net/`.

In Figure 2, we can see a snapshot of the ECLIPSE plugin. It provides an *editor*, containing the script with the SSTL properties that we want to analyse in our scenario (on the left) and a *view* to visualise the space model, the data and the results of the analyses (on the right).

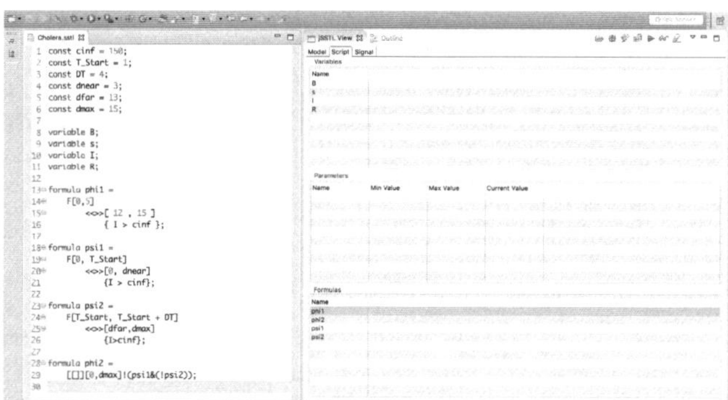

Figure 2: The jSSTL ECLIPSE plugin

In the **jSSTL editor**, it is possible to define a script that contains the list of properties that we want to analyse using jSSTL. The editor is based on Xtext[1], a framework for development of programming languages and domain-specific languages. The syntax of the script of our language is reported in Figure 3. Besides the list of formulae, each script contains the list of the variables considered in the model, a set of constants, and a list of parameters that may occur in the formula. The parameters can be declared to take values in an interval. When the monitoring procedure is performed, the user can select a specific value for each parameter in the corresponding interval. Standard expression can be used to define both constant and parameter intervals. In the script, each formula is associated with a name, that is used to select the specific property during the monitoring procedure.

We can see, on the left of Figure 2, the file Cholera.sstl containing the script of properties (1) and (2), described in the previous section. First, we have the declaration of the value of each parameter (const cinf= 150, ...), then the declaration of the variables (variable I,..), and finally the description of each property, e.g., property (1) is defined as: formula phi1 = F[0,5]«»[12,15] { I > cinf }.

As we can see in Figure 2 (where the panel with the Script is selected), the **jSSTL view** provides three different panels: to visu-

[1] `https://eclipse.org/Xtext/`

script	::=	element*
element	::=	variableDec | constDec | parameterDec | formulaDec
variableDec	::=	**variable** $name$
constDec	::=	**const** $name$ = expr
parameterDec	::=	**parameter** $name$ **in** interval
interval	::=	[expr, expr]
expr	::=	baseExpr | expr + expr | expr × expr | ···
baseExpr	::=	int | float | literalExpr
formulaDec	::=	**formula** $name$ = formula
formula	::=	formula**&**formula | formula|formula
	|	formula**U**interval formula | **G**interval formula
	|	**F**interval formula | formula**S**interval formula
	|	<<>> interval formula | [[]]interval formula
	|	!formula | relExpr
relExpr	::=	expr<expr | expr≤expr | expr>expr | expr≥expr
	|	expr==expr | ! =expr

Figure 3: jSSTL formula syntax.

alise the spatial models (*Model* panel), to summarise the relevant data declared in a script (*Script* panel), and to plot the system's trajectories and the Boolean and quantitative satisfaction signals (*Signal* panel). The icons on the right top of the jSSTL view serve to: open a graph model, create a grid model, open an SSTL script, open a signal data (the trajectory), execute the monitor, display the signal and clear the data.

The *Model* panel can be used to see a graph-based representation of the spatial model. The spatial model can be can be imported as a .tra file or, in case of regular grid, can be directly created, selecting the number of rows and columns. In Figure 4, we can see, in the model panel, the representation of the space for the Cholera model that corresponds to the graph reported in Figure 1.

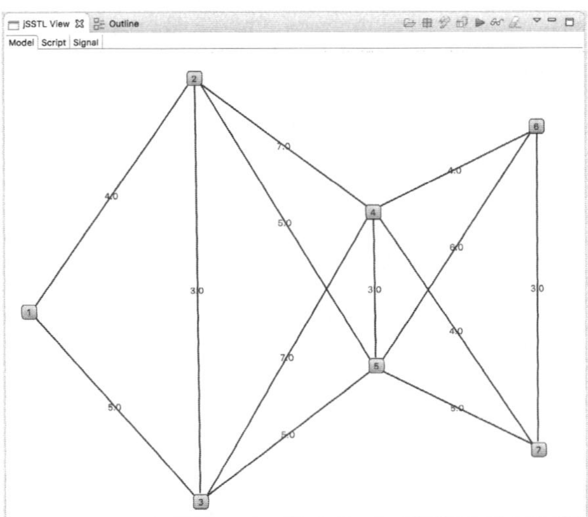

Figure 4: Visualisation of the space in the jSSTL ECLIPSE plugin.

The *Script* panel outlines the main informations of our scenario. We can see here the list of variables, parameters and formulae names. Currently, CSV and tabular based ASCII files are supported for both input and output of signals. The traces have to be imported with a single file for each variable and location, e.g., for the infected individual I we will have the files values_i_I.dat, with $i \in \{1, .., 7\}$. Having selected the space model, the trajectory and the property, we can compute the related Boolean and quantitative satisfaction signals. To do that, we have to select from the Script panel which property we want to verify, and to chose the specific values for the parameters for which we considered a range.

In the *Signal* panel, the spatio-temporal trajectories and the Boolean and quantitative signals can be visualised. We can choose which variables and which locations to plot. In Figure 5, we can see the trace x_I, the variation in time of the number of infected individuals in each location. We can observe as, at time 0, we have infected individuals only in ℓ_1. The temporal trajectories of each location are indicated adding @i to each variable, e.g., $x_I(t, \ell_1)$ is indicated in the plot as I@1.

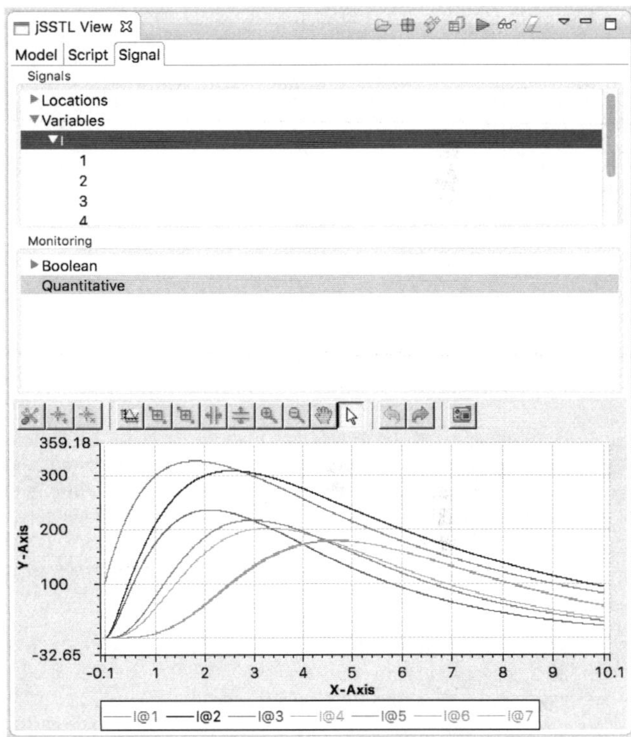

Figure 5: Plot of x_I, number of infected individual in each location.

Figure 6 shows Boolean satisfaction of the property psi1 (in each location). Instead, in Figure 7, we can see the quantitative satisfaction of the only location ℓ_1 of the properties phi1 and psi1. We can see from the plot that the trajectories satisfy both properties, but that property psi1 is much robust than property phi1 . The different length of the signals is due to the different temporal intervals in the two formulas. Indeed, in the monitoring procedure, if the signal has duration T, and a formula has temporal horizon h (i.e. its truth depends on what happens in h units of time in the future), then the duration of the Boolean/ satisfaction signal will be $T - h$.

In any case, we remind that the satisfaction of a formula for the whole trace is determined at time zero and for a specific location; hence, we can say that the $\vec{x}$ satisfies φ_1 in location ℓ_1 iff phi1@1 at time 0 is greater than 0.

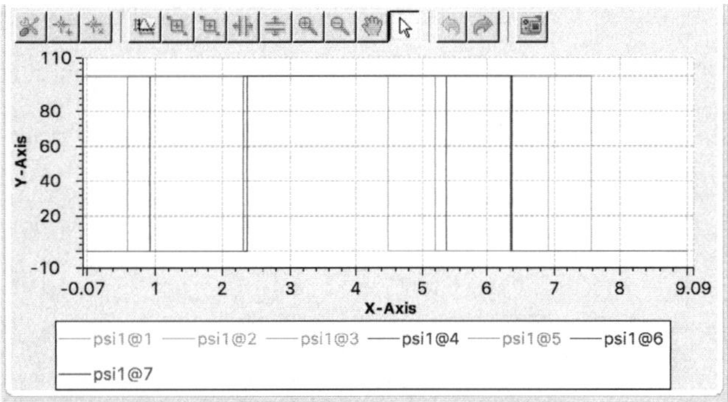

Figure 6: Plot of the Boolean semantics of the properties psi1.

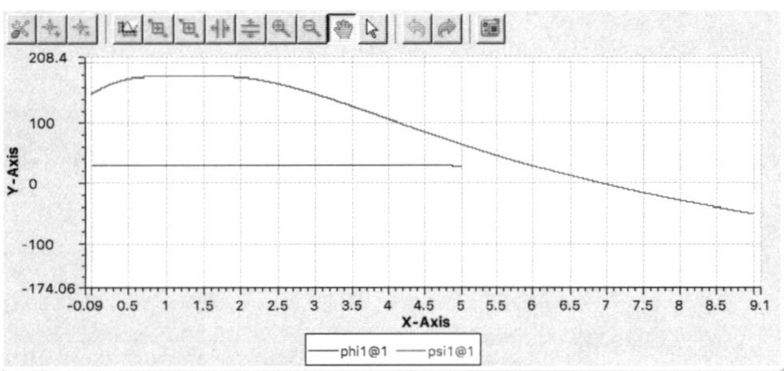

Figure 7: Plot of the quantitative semantics of the properties phi1 and psi1 for location 1.

Both the plots of the trajectories of Boolean and quantitative signals can be easily exported. Furthermore, the tool permits also to import a set of trajectories, instead of a single one, to compute the Boolean and quantitative satisfaction signals of such trajectories for a specific property and then to evaluate their mean (the average robustness) and their variance. This can be very useful when we want to analyse stochastic systems.

We stress that the plug in and the library work with much more complex models, like the one in [14], than the one presented here, which has been kept simple for the sake of clarity.

4. JSSTL JAVA LIBRARY

Our library, available at `https://bitbucket.org/LauraNenzi/jsstl`, has been designed in a modular way, which allows us to change/improve specific classes without changing the overall behaviour. It consists of three main packages: util, core, and io (Figure 8).

Package util handles the temporal signals of the logic. Its class BooleanSignal defines the temporal Boolean signals of the logic. They are represented as a sequence of time intervals with value true or false. The class BooleanSignalTransducer implements a method to compute the interval covering of a set of Boolean signals, a method to convert piecewise constant signals into Boolean signals and the methods to perform operations between temporal signals:

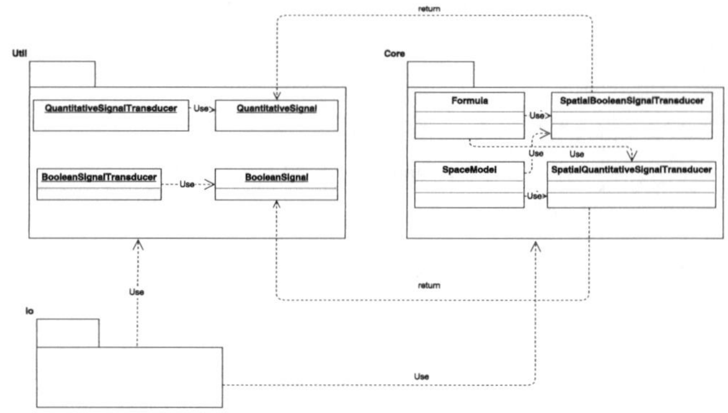

Figure 8: jSSTL: UML Package Diagram.

and, or, not, until, eventually, always. The class QuantitativeSignal defines the temporal quantitative signals of the logic, represented as piecewise constant signals. The class QuantitativeSignalTransducer implements the same methods as the Boolean case, for the operations between quantitative signals.

Package core is divided in three subpackages: space, monitor and formula.

In the space subpackage, the class SpaceModel is an interface that represents a generic space model. It is parametrised with respect to the type of data that represents the nodes and the edges. It provides three methods to obtain informations about nodes, edges and the external border of the model. The GraphModel class implements the interface as a space model based on a graph, and contains the methods to design, work, and have informations about the graph. It exploits the JGraphT[2] package to compute the matrix distance of the graph.

The monitor package handles the spatial Boolean and quantitative signals of the logic. They are treated as an HashMap that associates a temporal (Boolean or quantitative) signal to each location of the graph. The classes SpatialBooleanSignalTransducer and SpatialQuantitativeSignalTransducer contains all the methods to make operations between spatio-temporal signals: surround, somewhere, everywhere, and, or, not , until, always, eventually.

The third subpackage, formula, provides the classes used to represent SSTL formulae. These classes mimic the *abstract syntax tree* of formulas. The base interface is the class formula, it contains the methods booleanCheck and quantitativeCheck that compute the spatial Boolean and quantitative signals, taking as input the GraphModel and the Signal. The Signal class contains the method to translate the data, i.e., the primary signals, in a spatial Boolean or quantitative signal. Each operator has a specific class formula parametrised over one or two sub-formulae (depending on whether the operator is unary or binary) and an interval for some operators. The methods in each subformula refer to the methods in the SignalTransducer class of the specific operator. For example, the SurroundFormula class has the method booleanCheck that returns the monitoring evaluation SpatialBooleanSignalTransducer.surround of the signals of the two subformulae for the given (spatial) interval. Hence, the Monitoring algorithm is implemented following the *visitor pattern*. It is performed via a visit of a formula

[2] `http://jgrapht.org`

that implements a bottom-up evaluation. It is important to remark that the use of this pattern simplifies the integration of possible alternative monitoring algorithms.

Package io provides a set of classes that can be used to read graph models and input signals from an input stream and to write monitoring results to an output stream. Currently, CSV and tabular based ascii files are supported for both input and output of signals. Specific interfaces are also provided to simplify the integration of new specific input/output data formats.

The library can be easily integrated in other Java project, as we have done in [2], or used inside Matlab, exploiting Xtext for the specification of the property.

5. DISCUSSION

Related Works. There already exist useful tools to specify and monitor behaviours of systems with a temporal dynamics, as `Breach` [6] for STL properties or `S-TaLiRo` [1] for MTL specifications.The situation is very different, instead, when spatio-temporal dynamics are considering.

In [5], a *Spatial Logic for Closure Spaces* (STLCS) is proposed for a discrete and topological notion of space, based on closure spaces [9]. It is a spatial extension of the branching logic CTL, where the temporal aspects are considering as "snapshot" models. The logic cannot be used to monitor properties of spatio-temporal trajectories and, furthermore, it does not have a quantitative semantics. The related model-checker can be found at `https://github.com/vincenzoml/topochecker`.

`Mudi` [15], available at `http://mudi.modelchecking.org/`, is a spatio-temporal model checker employed for the automatic validation of complex biological systems. Their consider only regular discrete spaces, in particular a pseudo-3D representation of space (2D space plus a density measure). The properties are specified using the *Probabilistic Bounded Linear Spatial Temporal Logic* (PBLSTL) that presents only a boolean semantics. The essential difference between their approach and ours is that their logic considers space properties only as atomic predicates, i.e., the logic restricts the spatial specification to only the number of different predicates that have been designed, it does not have spatial operators that can be nested between them and with temporal ones. This allows us to express more complex spatio-temporal properties.

The only linear-time spatio-temporal logic with a robust monitoring procedure for checking properties directly over spatio-temporal trajectories that we are aware of is *Spatial-Temporal Logic* (SpaTeL) [10], in which spatial properties are expressed using ideas from image processing, namely *quad trees* [8]. This allows one to capture very complex spatial structures, but at the price of a complex formulation of spatial properties, which are in practice only learned from some template image. To our knowledge, a proper tool for the logic is not yet available.

Conclusions and Future Works. In this paper, we presented a Java-based tool to specify spatio-temporal properties in the linear time spatio-temporal logic SSTL, and to monitor trajectories coming from simulations or from measurements of real systems. The tool can be used stand-alone, via an ECLIPSE plug-in interface, or as a Java library. We stress here few features of the tool.
⋆ It can handle traces coming from different sources, hence it can be used to monitor simulations but also real systems.
⋆ The parametrisation of formulae enables to integrate the tool to perform parameter synthesis and estimation, see for instance [2].
⋆ The possibility to directly check a set of trajectories can simplify the statistical analysis of stochastic systems.
⋆ It has a quantitative semantics that can be used to evaluate the robustness of the satisfaction and to drive the behaviour of the system, see for instance [3].

The plugin is still in development and new features will be integrated. For instance, we are working on new kinds of formats and sources for input and output of data, and on a better integration with `Matlab`. We are also developing better monitoring algorithms and extending the logic with new operators, implementing them in the tool. In particular, we are developing an online monitoring procedure where trajectories are collected from external data sources, and a semantics to incorporate uncertainty in measurements.

6. REFERENCES

[1] Y. Annpureddy, C. Liu, G. Fainekos, and S. Sankaranarayanan. S-TaLiRo: A Tool for Temporal Logic Falsification for Hybrid Systems. *In Proc. of TACAS*, 2011.
[2] E. Bartocci, L. Bortolussi, D. Milios, L. Nenzi, and G. Sanguinetti. Studying Emergent Behaviours in Morphogenesis Using Signal Spatio-Temporal Logic. In *Proc. of HSB*, 2015.
[3] E. Bartocci, L. Bortolussi, L. Nenzi, and G. Sanguinetti. System design of stochastic models using robustness of temporal properties. *Theoretical Computer Science*, 2015.
[4] E. Bertuzzo, S. Azaele, A. Maritan, M. Gatto, I. Rodriguez-Iturbe, and A. Rinaldo. On the space-time evolution of a cholera epidemic. *Water Resources Research*, 2008.
[5] V. Ciancia, S. Gilmore, G. Grilletti, D. Latella, M. Loreti, and M. Massink. An Experimental Spatio-Temporal Model Checker. In *SEFM*, 2015.
[6] A. Donzé. Breach, A Toolbox for Verification and Parameter Synthesis of Hybrid Systems. In *Proc. of CAV*, 2010.
[7] A. Donzé and O. Maler. Robust satisfaction of temporal logic over real-valued signals. In *Proc. of FORMATS*, 2010.
[8] R. A. Finkel and J. L. Bentley. Quad trees a data structure for retrieval on composite keys. *Acta Informatica*, 1974.
[9] A. Galton. The mereotopology of discrete space. In *Spatial Information Theory. Cognitive and Computational Foundations of Geographic Information Science*, 1999.
[10] I. Haghighi, A. Jones, J. Z. Kong, E. Bartocci, Grosu R., and C. Belta. SpaTeL: A Novel Spatial-Temporal Logic and Its Applications to Networked Systems. In *Proc. of HSCC*, 2015.
[11] O. Maler and D. Nickovic. Monitoring temporal properties of continuous signals. In *Proc. FORMATS*, 2004.
[12] L. Mari, E. Bertuzzo, L. Righetto, R. Casagrandi, M. Gatto, I. Rodriguez-Iturbe, and A. Rinaldo. Modelling cholera epidemics: the role of waterways, human mobility and sanitation. *Journal of The Royal Society Interface*, 2012.
[13] L. Nenzi and L. Bortolussi. Specifying and monitoring properties of stochastic spatio-temporal systems in signal temporal logic. In *Proc. of VALUETOOLS*, 2014.
[14] L. Nenzi, L. Bortolussi, V. Ciancia, M. Loreti, and M. Massink. Qualitative and Quantitative Monitoring of Spatio-Temporal Properties. In *Proc. of RV*, 2015.
[15] O. Pârvu and D. Gilbert. Automatic validation of computational models using pseudo-3d spatio-temporal model checking. *BMC Systems Biology*, 2014.

Performance Analysis of SDN Switches with Hardware and Software Flow Tables*

Piotr Rygielski
Institute of Computer Science
University of Würzburg,
Germany
piotr.rygielski@uni-wuerzburg.de

Marian Seliuchenko
Dept. of Telecommunication
Lviv Polytechnic National
University, Ukraine
m.seliuchenko@gmail.com

Samuel Kounev
Institute of Computer Science
University of Würzburg,
Germany
samuel.kounev@uni-wuerzburg.de

Mykhailo Klymash
Dept. of Telecommunication
Lviv Polytechnic National
University, Ukraine
mklimash@lp.edu.ua

ABSTRACT

Nowadays data centers are increasingly becoming larger and dynamic due to virtualization. Software-Defined Networking is the leading approach to network virtualization and flexible management. The wide variety of hardware implementations have brought strong heterogeneity to the market of networking devices which are different in terms of OpenFlow features and performance. In this paper we address the issue of heterogeneity of four hardware OpenFlow switches by characterizing selected performance relevant parameters for the hardware and software flow tables. We characterize maximum size of hardware flow tables for each switch including the behavior of a rule promotion engine that moves the rules between tables. We show that in the worst case forwarding packets using software table decreases the throughput by two orders of magnitude (from 940 to 14 Mbit/s). Our results can help the developers of SDN applications to account performance limitations of hardware and software processing as well as limited hardware support for a specific rule types.

CCS Concepts

•Networks → Network performance analysis; Network measurement;

Keywords

Software-defined networking; switching; flow tables; performance.

* This work was funded by the German Research Foundation (DFG) under grant No. KO 3445/18-1.

VALUETOOLS 2016, October 25-28, Taormina, Italy

1. INTRODUCTION

Software-Defined Networking (SDN) has established a new standard for network virtualization by separating data plane from control plane and letting the user to develop custom software for the latter. OpenFlow [13] has become the standard protocol for communication between OpenFlow-enabled switches and SDN controllers. Many hardware vendors already offer OpenFlow-enabled network devices that support various versions of the OpenFlow protocol. The diversity of OpenFlow implementations (including both hardware capabilities and control plane software behaviors) makes understanding and control over a network difficult. As a result, the network performance becomes affected by the heterogeneity of OpenFlow switches and should be investigated to better understand the consequences of the design and configuration decisions of an SDN-based deployments.

In this paper, we focus on the influence of the heterogeneity of switch implementations on the performance of a software-defined network. We observe different behaviors and performance characteristics of OpenFlow-enabled devices. The main issue that motivates this work and concerns currently available devices is a change in the performance that depends on the state of the switch flow table [11]. Not all devices handle the rules in the flow tables in the same way; capacity of flow tables and rule compatibility differ among switch models. As shown in [10], different switches place the same rules differently as well as optimize the rules placement during the runtime. This can result in an unpredictable behavior where forwarding speed may drop drastically. The authors observed that most of hardware is still not mature enough for the performance to be predicted in the repeatable manner, because "each switch under test has many quirks which result in unexplained performance changes." They conclude that "the switch performance is difficult to predict—a single rule can degrade the update rate of a switch by an order of magnitude". The authors stress high diversity of the performance of the switches. On the other hand, the authors of [5] have shown that "The results also show that a more complicated SDN (...) does not necessarily mean performance degradation. Performance reflects the specific implementation of the SDN." These statements, among others, are our main incentive for investigating the heterogeneity of the switches and its influence on the performance.

Our goal is to investigate the heterogeneity of four models of OpenFlow-enabled switches by the means of their: flow table types and capacities, behaviour of the rule insertion and promotion engines, flow tables compatibility with the various rule types and finally the switching performance. We manipulate the switch parameters and install forwarding rules into various flow tables to observe the performance of the switch. We aim to identify parameters that have strong influence on the performance. In particular, we answer the question about the performance of a switch when the hardware flow table is full. Additionally, we investigate what happens when some rules are removed from the tables and the rule placement can be reorganized. We focus on a proactive rule insertion, where controller installs rules before the matching packets arrive to the switch.

The main contributions of this paper are the following: (1) we investigate four models of physical switches and characterize their SDN capabilities, (2) we analyze the throughput performance of the switches in various SDN modes, and (3) we characterize the behavior of the rule management engines implemented in the switches.

This paper is organized as follows. In Section 2, we introduce the background of OpenFlow switch components that are relevant further in the paper. We present selected related work in Section 3. In Section 4, we show the testbed setup and describe how we measured the switches. In Section 5, we discuss the experiments and their results in details to finally conclude the paper in Section 6.

2. FOUNDATIONS OF SDN SWITCH PERFORMANCE

Software-defined networking assumes separation of the data plane and the control plane. In the data plane, a switch forwards the packets, whereas in the control plane, algorithms make decisions where the packets should be forwarded. The decisions are converted to a forwarding rules stored in the flow tables of the respective switches.

2.1 Hardware and Software Flow Tables

The rules saved in the switch can be exact-match (all match fields are specified) or wildcard-match (some fields have a value *any*). Exact match rules are stored in BCAM memory (binary content-addressable memory). The wildcard rules are saved in the TCAM (ternary content-addressable memory) that allows each cell to have three states: 1, 0, and $*$. Hardware flow tables based on TCAM usually have very limited capacity and capabilities because this memory is power hungry and expensive. The rules that do not fit to the *hardware flow tables* (either in BCAM or TCAM memory) are placed in the switch SDRAM—so called *software flow table*. As a rule of thumb, the hardware flow tables offer usually nearly the full line switching speed (do not inflict delay) but their volume is limited. We elaborate more on this in Section 5.

2.2 Reactive and Proactive Rule Insertion

If an arriving packet cannot be matched against any rule, the switch forwards the packet to the controller that reacts with inserting new rules. We call this a *reactive rule insertion*. In contrast, *proactive rule insertion* implies that the switches are preconfigured with the rules to handle all flows without reactive interaction with the controller. The *proactive rule insertion* fits better large scale data center scenarios where the paths usually stay constant, whereas the *reactive rule insertion* fits better smaller but highly dynamic networks (e.g., access networks or sensor networks [14]).

Although currently available SDN controllers do no scale well (as shown in, e.g., [14]), the authors of [12] point that the current commodity switches are unable to process all flows in hardware. For example, the authors of [2] point out that for large-scale delivery content networks there can be up to 16 million flows. This limits the performance of the reactive SDN on one hand (due to controller scalability issues) but also challenges proactive SDN setups on the other hand (as the capacity of the hardware flow tables is limited).

3. RELATED WORK

The topic of SDN performance attracts many researchers and some aspects have been already investigated in the literature. However, various authors usually focus on selected parts of SDN architecture so they miss the overall picture of the system (e.g., they focus on the performance of control path, data path, or a controller [10, 6, 3]), or model a network in a coarsely black-box manner [7]. Additionally, many authors (e.g., [5]) do not investigate physical switches but theorize their findings based on simulators or emulators. The relatively young concept of SDN resulted in multiple various hardware products that offer the support for the OpenFlow protocol. This variety resulted in different implementations and thus the offered performance can differ among the vendors or even among the switch models of the same vendor.

The authors of [9] reviewed almost 600 works concerning SDN and its aspects, among others the performance. They found out that "understanding the performance and limitation of the SDN concept is a requirement for its implementation in production networks. There are very few performance evaluation studies of OpenFlow and SDN architecture. Although simulation studies and experimentation are among the most widely used performance evaluation techniques, analytical modelling has its own benefits as well." In this Section, we extend their findings and propose an overview of the state-of-the-art in SDN performance.

As presented in [9], many authors use simulation techniques to solve performance models. In [8], the authors investigate various performance-related parameters of an SDN system. The system is modeled and examined in the OF-Sim simulator. The authors divide the process of packet forwarding into four stages: data plane, data-to-control plane, control plane, and control-to-data plane processing. They identify parameters correlated with the performance and examine the dependencies between achieved performance, table sizes and various message rates (*packetIn*, *flowmod*). The authors also note that "performance bottleneck may be located in the existing switches, and the flow table entry installation delay is a pressing issue." Unfortunately, they do not validate their simulator against a setup with physical switches, and support for data center networks are in their future plans. Moreover, the authors assume that the flow tables have size up to 20 thousand entries which is normally not the case for hardware forwarding tables, which deliver high performance. Using real hardware, the authors would install the most of the rules in the software forwarding tables or their rules would be rejected by the switch.

The authors of [3] analyze the Linux implementation of the OpenFlow on a commodity server investigating the performance of the data plane. Their setup is similar to the NFV approach where the networking hardware is replaced by commodity servers. The analysis is conducted for single- and multi-flow case, so that the forwarding performance can be examined *with* (for single flow) and *without* the presence of the limited size of forwarding table (for multi-flow). Additionally the authors test the packet processing delays for exact-match and wildcard rules as well as for different types of flow tables and their sizes (usually 25-29μs). Although their results are relevant for a combination of SDN and NFV, they lack the context of a data center, where usually hardware network switches are used.

Similarly, the authors of [5] do not examine hardware switches to investigate the performance. They "indicate that SDN does have a performance penalty; however, it is not necessarily related to the complexity level of the underlying SDN infrastructure". In their paper, they compare performance of an SDN setup with performance of non-SDN networking devices. They use software SDN switch and Linux-based ProGFE which is an alternative to OpenFlow.

On the other hand, the authors of [6], investigate four various SDN switches (including the software OpenvSwitch) in a simple experimental testbed. Their aim is to design an emulator of an OpenFlow switch. They "focus primarily on vendor-specific variations in the control plane, although data planes can also be different across vendors." Their findings focus on the controller performance and thus are not applicable to proactive rule insertion that we focus on. They observe that network switch "emulators do not attempt to reproduce vendor-specific details of particular pieces of hardware, as end-to-end performance is typically dominated by implementation-agnostic features like routing (choice of links), link contention, and end-system protocols (application or transport-layer)." Moreover, they find out "that an appropriately calibrated emulation infrastructure can approximate the behaviour of the switches we study." Although their findings do not concern our point of view at the performance analysis directly (they focus mainly on control plane), their findings support our statement that a medium-grained end-to-end performance model of SDN-based data center can be built disregarding the heterogeneity of the switches.

On the other hand, there exist analytical performance models of OpenFlow switches. Jarschel et al. [7] model SDN using two queues (M/M/1-S and M/GI/I-S) and thus specify two processing paths having different performance—with and without the controller. The selection of the controller and non-controller path is modelled in a probabilistic manner. Unfortunately, the path over the software flow table that involves CPU processing on a switch is not modelled making the results applicable to an abstract SDN switch with unlimited TCAM capacity or to small use cases (cf. [12]).

Another analytical performance model was introduced by Azodolmolky et al. in [1]. The authors propose a model based on network calculus as "In contrast to queuing theory, network calculus is concerned with worst case (upper bounds) instead of average (equilibrium) behaviour and therefore does not deal with arrival and departure processes themselves but with bounding processes called arrival and service curves." [1]. They validate their model against the results obtained in the literature, namely in [15]. In [15], the authors propose a benchmark for OpenFlow switches and demonstrate it using three hardware switches of which one has full OpenFlow support and the rest run experimental firmware. The authors did not mention the models of the switches under test, however one of the two switches with incomplete OpenFlow support seems to use the software flow table (switching latency was reported as $\approx 300\mu s$). Unfortunately, in [1], the authors do not investigate the performance of the switching using software flow tables.

Many other authors, for example [11, 4] stress the diversity of switch capabilities and behaviors what makes network harder to understand and control. Current OpenFlow switch implementations may lead to performance bottlenecks with respect to the CPU load. Also the flow tables where the rules are inserted may be non-deterministic—on some switches rules may be rejected whereas on the others, rules may be installed into the software or hardware flow table.

It is important to stress that the understanding of the SDN performance with software and hardware flow tables is as important as understanding the behavior of the SDN controllers. Faced by the fact, that the flow tables are simply too small to accommodate enough flows for production scenarios, we investigate the performance and characteristics of four heterogeneous switches to provide more insight towards building a complete performance model. The currently available performance models usually investigate the performance of SDN controllers, but the forwarding performance using the software flow table is not addressed, although it cannot be neglected.

4. SWITCHES UNDER TEST AND EXPERIMENTAL ENVIRONMENT

In this paper, our ultimate goal is to investigate the behavior of hardware OpenFlow switches in various configurations, especially in the switching that uses the software flow table. In this Section, we present our testbed, its setup, and measurement methodology.

4.1 Switches Under Test

We evaluate the performance of four hardware OpenFlow switches. The exact models and their specifications are presented in Table 1. We investigate four heterogeneous HP switches. We characterize briefly the main differences between them. The models 2920 and 3500*yl* use *ProVision* operating system, whereas 5130 and 5700 use *Comware*. The switches based on *ProVision* system have two flow tables: one hardware and one software flow table. The 2920 supports only OpenFlow v1.0, whereas 3500*yl* supports OpenFlow *v1.0* and *v1.3*. The 2920 exposes both hardware and software table as a single abstract table that is reported by HP VAN SDN controller as table with *n/a*. Thus, the controller is not aware of multiple tables and cannot manipulate the rules location directly. The only possibility to distinguish the flow location is to query the switch operating system directly over console. The switch 3500*yl* acts identically to 2920 if configured to support OpenFlow *v1.0*. For OpenFlow *v1.3* it exposes each table with the preconfigured ID, unfortunately without any reference to the type of the table (hardware or software). The switches 5700 and 5130 support only OpenFlow *v1.3* and contain four hard-

Table 1: Switches under test: models and switching performance in native non-SDN mode (source: vendor data sheet).

Switch Model	Firmware Version	Switching Capacity	Switching Throughput
HP 2920-24G (J9726A)	WB.15.12.0015	92.2 *Mpps*	128.0 *Gbps*
HP 3500yl-24G (J8692A)	K.15.17.0007	75.7 *Mpps*	101.8 *Gbps*
HPE FF 5700-32XGT-8XG-2QSFP+ (JG898A)	2422P01	714.2 *Mpps*	960.0 *Gbps*
HPE 5130-24G-4SFP+ EI (JG932A)	3111P03	96.0 *Mpps*	128.0 *Gbps*

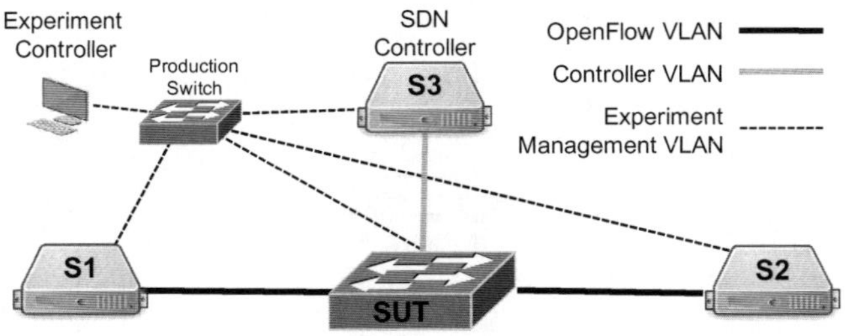

Figure 1: The overview of the experimental testbed.

ware flow tables which are: *extensibility*, *mac-ip*, *egress-vlan* and *ingress-vlan*. Both switches do not contain software flow tables. The ingress-vlan and egress-vlan tables provide support for tunnelling as defined by IEEE 802.1q, however, when any of these tables is in use, the connection to the controller is lost. The extensibility table supports all OpenFlow-mandatory matching fields, in contrast MAC-IP table supports only *vlan_vid*, *eth_dst* and *ip_dst*.

4.2 Experimental Testbed

Our experimental environment consists of the switch under test (SUT) and four servers that are connected to the production switch. The overview of the testbed is presented in Figure 1. The non-SDN production switch is used to control the experiment management VLAN. It connects all devices of the testbed using separate VLAN and separate physical cables so the OpenFlow network is isolated from the experiment management network. In this way, we can assure that the measured performance is not influenced by the experiment control traffic.

We use two servers ($S1$ and $S2$) to generate, receive, and measure the forwarding performance. The servers are connected to the SUT over a dedicated OpenFlow VLAN using the one gigabit copper interface and the Cat 6 cable. The third server $S3$ hosts HP SDN VAN Controller (version 2.5.15.1175) and is connected to the SUT over the controller VLAN. Finally, the fourth server—experiment controller—hosts the experiment control software that we developed to automate the experiments. The experiment controller connects to the generator and receiver servers over the SSH protocol and controls the traffic generation leveraging *iperf* and *ping* tools to measure SUT's throughput and the packet round-trip time. The experiment controller connects additionally to the SUT over *ssh* and polls hardware parameters (e.g., CPU load, the number of flows in the software and hardware tables, and the location of a given flow) that are not available over the controller. The experiment controller uses the REST API of the HP VAN SDN Controller to manipulate the flow tables of the SUT.

5. RESULTS

In this Section, we present the results of performance characterization measurements for the four switches under test. We focus on three distinguished aspects: hardware flow table capacities, forwarding performance and the behavior of the rule promotion engine.

5.1 Hardware Flow Table Capacities

The flow tables that handle the SDN forwarding rules have limited capacity. We identify this limit as the most important factor that influences the behavior of the switches. In this Section, we measure their maximal capacities with respect to the rule type.

5.1.1 Measurement Procedure

In order to measure maximal number of supported rules by a flow table we used standard 12 tuple matching structure with *output to port* action. For each switch we created set of rules supported by its hardware flow table. The rules are sorted by the number of wildcarded fields in descending order in every set. At the beginning we select the first rule form the respective set (i.e., having as many exact-match fields as possible). Then, we restart the OpenFlow instance at the switch to clear all flow tables and assure identical initial settings before every measurement. We use the direct ssh connection to the switch operating system to assure its clean state. Since the flow table contains rules that controller installs by default (e.g., redirecting packet to controller or to the software table), we pull the rules number and store this number as a reference. Next, we insert one rule and pull the rules number to verify if the rule was inserted properly. If the rule counter does not change then the table is full. We report the table capacity for the given rule structure. Next, we repeat this procedure for all rules in the respective set.

5.1.2 Capacities of Hardware Flow Tables

Results of the measurements for all switches are shown in Table 2. Table 2 should be read as follows. We assume that all fields are wildcarded, except the fields specified in the *match field* column. So, for example in row #6, the switch 3500 can store maximally 1526 rules having the following matching structure: fields *in_port*, *vlan_vid*, *vlan_pcp*, *eth_src*, *eth_dst*, *eth_type* are defined (except of *eth_src* and *eth_dst* that are required to be left empty), whereas the rest of the match fields are wildcarded. Zeros mean incompatibility with the given switch model.

Concerning the hardware limitations, the switch 2920 can store maximally 460 rules if all fields are wildcarded (except the *in_port* and *vlan_vid* that are not allowed to be wildcarded for this model). Considering the rest of the fields, any combination of those allows to create maximum of 460 unique rules in hardware. All rules that are not supported

Table 2: **Hardware flow table capacities for various rule structures.**

	Switch	2920	3500	3500	5130	5130	5700	5700
	OpenFlow Version	$v1.0$	$v1.0$	$v1.3$	$v1.3$	$v1.3$	$v1.3$	$v1.3$
	Flow Table				*EXT*	*MAC-IP*	*EXT*	*MAC-IP*
Row	Match field							
#1	*in_port*	460	381	0	384	0	640	0
#2	*vlan_vid*	460	381	0	384	0	640	0
#3	*vlan_pcp*	460	0	0	384	0	640	0
#4	*eth_src*	0	0	0	384	0	640	0
#5	*eth_dst*	0	0	0	384	16000	640	65535
#6	*eth_type*	460	1526	1526	384	16000	512	65535
#7	*ip_dscp*	460	1526	1526	512	0	512	0
#8	*ip_src*	460	1526	1526	512	0	512	0
#9	*ip_dst*	460	1526	1526	512	16000	512	65535
#10	*ip_proto*	460	1526	1526	512	0	512	0
#11	*tcp_src*	460	1526	1526	512	0	512	0
#12	*tcp_dst*	460	1526	1526	512	0	512	0

in the hardware flow table are propagated to the software flow table. The capacity of the hardware table of the 3500*yl* switch depends on the OpenFlow version. If we set the version of OpenFlow to *v1.0* and the matching structure contains only *in_port*, the hardware flow table can store 381 rules with different priorities. This is also true for the *in_port* and *vlan_vid* fields together or just the *vlan_vid* alone. The maximum number of rules with any combination of the rest of the fields is 1526. In OpenFlow $v1.3$, the switch discards rules that contain at least one of the fields: *in_port*, *vlan_id*. For any other combination of fields, the hardware flow table can store maximally 1526 rules. The firmware of 5700 switch allows to configure the maximal size of extensibility table up to 65535 entries, however in practice the limitations are significantly lower. Maximal number of rules that do not include the field *eth_type*, IP fields and TCP fields is 512. In all other cases, the maximal rules number is 640. The *MAC-IP* table of the 5700 has maximum size of 65535 rules. The extensibility table of the *5130* can contain maximum 384 rules if all IP and TCP fields are wildcarded. Otherwise, the maximum equals 512. The *MAC-IP* tables in 5130 can hold up to 16000 rules.

5.1.3 Sharing Hardware Resources in Hybrid Switches

Both *ProVision* switches (i.e., 2920 and 3500*yl*) are hybrid and can process packets using OpenFlow and non-OpenFlow pipelines simultaneously. The switch summary reported by the HP SDN VAN Controller contains an option *hybrid mode*. If it is enabled, then the controller inserts an extra rule in the last table of the pipeline—so called *table-miss* rule that wildcards all match fields and has the lowest priority 0. This rule forwards packet to the standard pipeline if no match is found for the packet in any flow table. The *ProVision* switches share their hardware memory between various types of rules (e.g., OpenFlow, ACL, QoS). We investigated the behavior of the *rule policy engine* that reserves a given share of rules (expressed in percent) for the OpenFlow use (command: `openflow limit policy-engine-usage 100`).

The procedure for measuring the shared OpenFlow table capacity consists of the following steps: (1) disable the OpenFlow instance, (2) change the policy engine usage value, (3) enable the OpenFlow instance, and (4) fill up the table with rules that have the maximum number of exact match fields specified (not wildcarded). The results are presented in Figure 2. As expected, the dependency is linear. The OpenFlow policy engine usage can be set with granularity of 1%. When policy engine usage value equals 0, no resources are allocated to OpenFlow pipeline, i.e, no rules can be inserted. Value of policy engine usage can be changed only when the OpenFlow instance in the operating system of the switch is disabled, therefore it is not possible to scale flow table size during runtime.

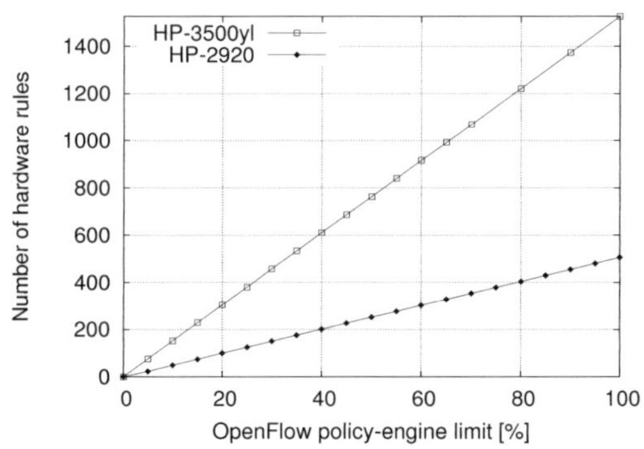

Figure 2: Maximal number of 8/2 wildcard rules (8 fields exact, 2 wildcarded) in the hardware table for varying OpenFlow share of the rule policy engine.

For the 3500*yl* switch, we observe a bug that results in the system failure when the policy engine value exceeds 60−65% and flow table size contains over 900 rules. Under these conditions, the OpenFlow instance of the switch hangs, packets are not forwarded, the connection to the controller is lost and any CLI command related to OpenFlow functionality freezes the console session. However, at the same time all other parts of the switch operate normally and CPU load is negligible low. The switch needs to be restated to function properly again.

5.2 SDN Forwarding Performance

In this section, we characterize the process of switching and describe our findings regarding the forwarding performance. Our observations concern mainly the differences among the following two cases: forwarding using a rule placed in the hardware flow table and forwarding using a rule placed in the software flow table. In this paper, we do not investigate the forwarding performance with reactive rule insertion that involves sending *packet_in* message to the SDN controller and processing of the *flow_mod* reply. Instead, we focus on forwarding performance with proactive rule insertion, where rules are installed before the traffic arrives at the switch.

5.2.1 Measurement Procedure

We measure the maximal switching throughput and the CPU load for the switching using every flow table available in the given switch model. In this part, we generate traffic for 60 seconds using *iperf* and measure average throughput using the topology presented in Fig. 1. We make sure that the number of the installed rules is constant over the experiment, so that the *rule promotion engine*, which we describe in Section 5.3, does not affect the measurements.

5.2.2 Forwarding Performance for the Software and Hardware Flow Tables

The results for the forwarding throughput are presented in Figure 3. For the 2920 and 3500*yl*, we observe a drastic drop

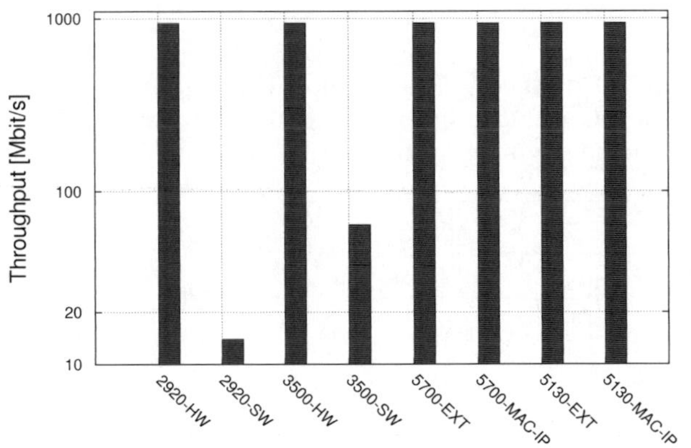

Figure 3: Maximal throughput obtained for the switches using various flow tables.

of the forwarding performance when a rule is installed in the software flow table (shortly denoted as SW in Fig. 3). The forwarding throughput of the hardware flow tables results in the full line-speed of the switch (about 941 Mbit/s) for all models, tables and OpenFlow versions. The performance in the non-OpenFlow mode is identical as when switching using the hardware OpenFlow table.

Forwarding using the software flow table causes the performance to drop from one (for the 3500*yl*) up to two orders of magnitude (for the 2920). A rule is placed in the software flow table (assuming it exists) if: (1) the rule is incompatible with the hardware flow table, or (2) the hardware flow table is full. This inflicts a serious constraint for the design of the software installed in the SDN controllers.

The switch forwarding capacity (expressed in packets per second) may be configured manually by changing *software-rate* parameter in the switch operating system. The switching capacity is expressed in packets per second. We changed the switching capacity using the *software rate* parameter (command: `openflow instance name limit software-rate <X>`) and observed the switch CPU load and the throughput. The maximum value of the *software rate* parameter is hard-coded in the switch and equals 2000 for the 2920 and 10000 for the 3500*yl*. In Figures 4 and 5, we present how the throughput and the switch CPU load depend on the limited switching capacity for the 2920 and 3500*yl* switches respectively.

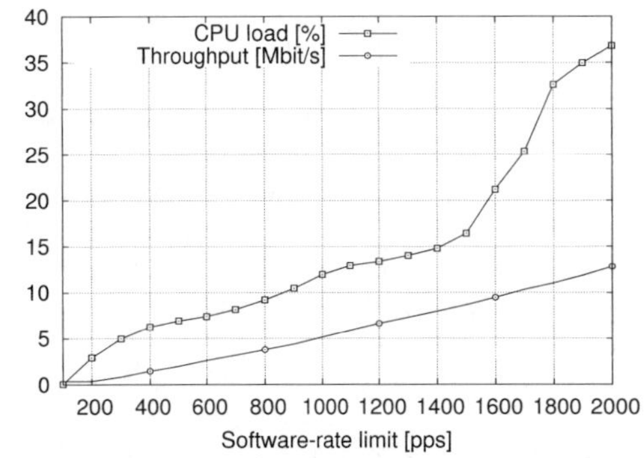

Figure 4: Throughput and switch CPU load for the software flow table of the switch 2920.

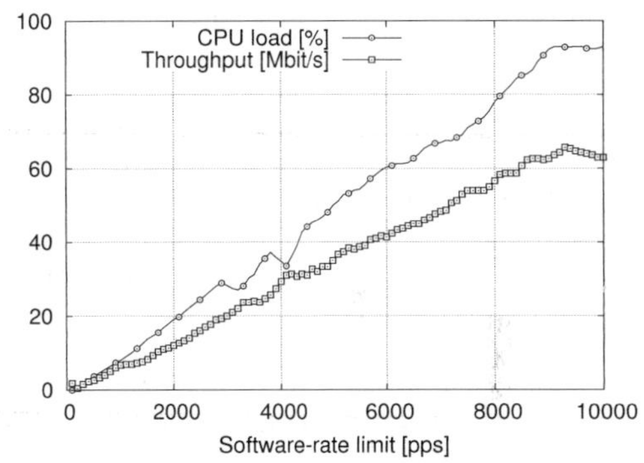

Figure 5: Throughput and switch CPU load for the software flow table of the switch 3500*yl*.

Using the software flow table, the switches offer performance that practically eliminates them from the production environments. The 3500*yl* offers only about 6% of the maximum advertised throughput, whereas the 2920 provides less than 2%. This means that the developers of the SDN applications that control the behavior of an SDN-based network should be aware of the switch limitations and avoid filling the hardware flow table at all costs.

5.3 Rule Promotion Engine Behavior

Finally, we conduct experiments to investigate the behavior of the rule promotion and rule insertion engines. The *rule promotion engine* is responsible for moving the rules between the hardware and the software flow tables that are used simultaneously by the *ProVision*-based switches (3500*yl* and 2920). The *rule insertion engine* is responsible for selecting the flow table where a new rule should be placed. In this Section, we focus on the *rule promotion engine*.

5.3.1 Measurement Procedure

The behavior of the rule promotion engine has not been officially documented, so we set up an experiment to investigate its behavior in details. As the rule promotion engine operates only in the *ProVision*-based switches, we will experiment in this Section with the 2920 and 3500*yl* switches only.

In this experiment, we configure the 3500*yl* to operate in OpenFlow *v1.0*, since we observe, that for OpenFlow *v1.3* the switch does not move the rules between tables. For both switches, we set a software limit of the hardware table size to 76 for 3500*yl* and to 23 for 2920 by setting the *openflow policy-engine usage* to 5%. We want to install forwarding rules into the software flow table and then observe if the rules are promoted to the hardware flow table when occasion arises. Unfortunately, this is not possible since we cannot place the rules directly in the software flow table (the table does not have an *ID*). Thus, we first fill the hardware flow table with dummy rules (i.e., rules that can never be matched) and then install the two active rules that enable the *iperf* traffic in both directions between the experiment servers ($S1$ and $S2$ in Fig. 1). As a result, the *iperf* rules are installed in the software flow table as we aimed. We start to measure the forwarding throughput exactly as described in Section 5.2.

During the bandwidth measurement, the switch does not move the active rules between tables and the bandwidth stays low—none of the rules in the hardware flow table is actively matched. Then, we start removing the dummy rules from hardware table and the rules from the software flow table are being moved one by one to the hardware table as the space in the hardware flow table is freed. According to the OpenFlow specification, the less wildcarded rules should be matched first and should be placed at the beginning of any flow table. Therefore, we expect the switch to promote the rules with more exact-match structure in the first turn.

5.3.2 Prioritizing of the Rule Promotion

To determine the order in which the rules are promoted from the software table to the hardware one, we filled completely the hardware flow table of the 3500*yl* switch with dummy rules (76 rules) and inserted the same number of dummy rules in the software flow table.

For each dummy rule, we set the *timeout* parameter value calculated according to the following formula: *timeout=time offset+ order number of the rule*. The *time offset* prevents the switch from removing the rules from the table until we finish inserting all the rules necessary for the experiment, i.e., the parameter defines when the action of the rule promotion engine may be triggered. In the last step, we insert the *iperf* rules and start the throughput test. The *iperf* rules are more exact than all dummy rules. Every second during the measurement, we poll the switch for the current number of rules in the software and hardware flow tables. Additionally, we record the load level of switch CPU.

As shown in Figure 6, we observe that from the $\approx$ 36-th second, the 3500*yl* starts removing the rules from the hardware flow table (due to the timeout set to $30s$ and about $6s$ warm-up time) and replaces them with rules from the software flow table. At the $\approx$ 65-th second, both *iperf* rules are promoted to the hardware flow table and the CPU load drops down to 2%.

At the same moment—see Figure 7—the throughput of the 3500*yl* increased from 64 to 940 Mbit/s. Even though the *iperf* rules are the most exact, they were moved to the hardware flow table in the last turn. Therefore, the rules are moved from the software table to the hardware table in the reverse order than they were inserted. This statement is always true and does not depend on how many wildcarded fields the rules contain or what priority they have. This may lead to many performance drawbacks—e.g., the rules cannot be ordered for the promotion from the hardware flow table to the software flow table, because the rule promotion engine works in a first-come-first-served fashion. The analogous results for the 2920 are illustrated in Figure 8.

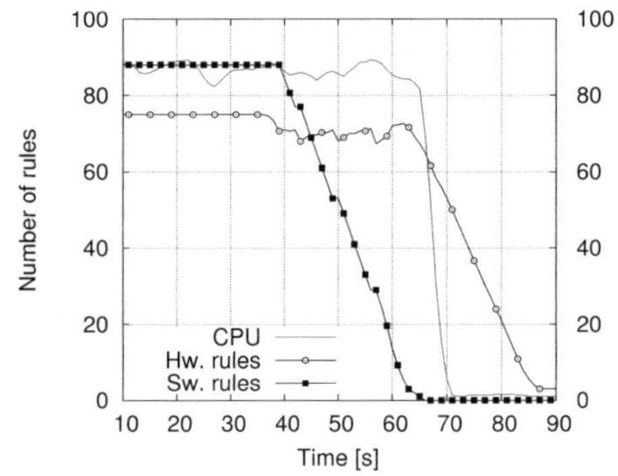

Figure 6: Behavior of the rule promotion engine for the 3500*yl*: numbers of rules in the flow tables. This Fig. has the x axis aligned with the Fig. 7.

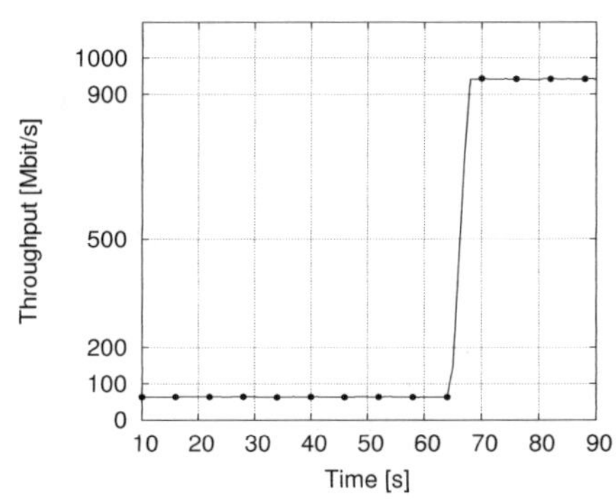

Figure 7: Behavior of the rule promotion engine for the 3500*yl*: throughput. This Fig. has the x axis aligned with the Fig. 6.

The experiments with the switch 2920 show that after the *iperf* rules are replaced from software to hardware, the throughput drops to 0 and the connection between the experiment servers is lost. The port counters in the switch detect arriving packets, however the packets are not forwarded between ports and no notification is sent to the controller. To restore the communication it is necessary to send a new *flow_mod* message and install the rules again.

6. CONCLUSIONS AND FUTURE WORK

In this paper we have investigated the parameters that influence the performance of four heterogeneous OpenFlow-

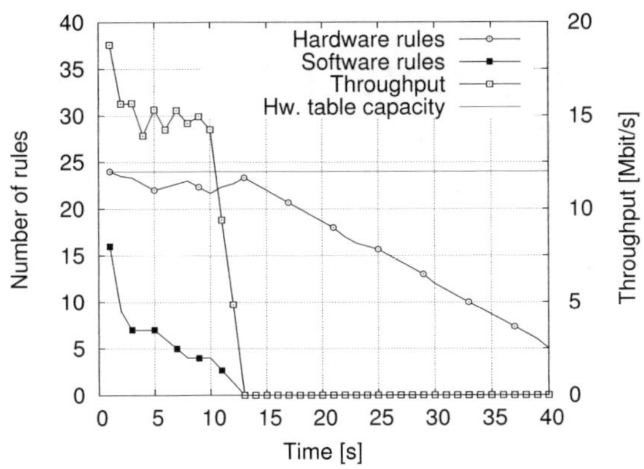

Figure 8: Behavior of the rule promotion engine for the 2920: throughput

enabled switches. In particular, we focused on capacities and forwarding performance of the hardware and software flow tables. We observed that the forwarding performance depends mainly on the location of the active rule. If the active rule is located in the software flow table, the performance is degraded by up to two orders of magnitude (941 vs. 14Mbit/s). The knowledge about the location of the active rule is thus crucial for the performance and should be acquired by every developer of the SDN controller applications. The location of a rule is influenced by many parameters such as: capacities of the TCAM and BCAM memories, behaviors of the rule promotion and insertion engines, and the compatibility of a given rule with the TCAM memory used in a given model of switch. This stresses the heterogeneity of OpenFlow-enabled switches—even if they are delivered by the same vendor. As a part of our future work, we plan to build a descriptive model that supports the modeling of the performance heterogeneity of SDN switches including their software and hardware flow tables.

7. REFERENCES

[1] S. Azodolmolky, R. Nejabati, M. Pazouki, P. Wieder, R. Yahyapour, and D. Simeonidou. An analytical model for software defined networking: A network calculus-based approach. In *Global Communications Conference (GLOBECOM 2013)*, pages 1397–1402. IEEE, Dec 2013.

[2] T. Benson, A. Akella, and D. A. Maltz. Network traffic characteristics of data centers in the wild. In *Proceedings of the 10th ACM SIGCOMM Conference on Internet Measurement*, IMC '10, pages 267–280, New York, NY, USA, 2010. ACM.

[3] A. Bianco, R. Birke, L. Giraudo, and M. Palacin. OpenFlow Switching: Data Plane Performance. In *IEEE International Conference on Communications (ICC 2010)*, pages 1–5, May 2010.

[4] A. R. Curtis, J. C. Mogul, J. Tourrilhes, P. Yalagandula, P. Sharma, and S. Banerjee. Devoflow: Scaling flow management for high-performance networks. In *Proceedings of the ACM SIGCOMM 2011 Conference*, pages 254–265. ACM, 2011.

[5] A. Gelberger, N. Yemini, and R. Giladi. Performance Analysis of Software-Defined Networking (SDN). In *IEEE 21st International Symposium on Modeling, Analysis Simulation of Computer and Telecommunication Systems (MASCOTS)*, pages 389–393, Aug 2013.

[6] D. Y. Huang, K. Yocum, and A. C. Snoeren. High-fidelity switch models for software-defined network emulation. In *Proceedings of the Second ACM SIGCOMM Workshop on Hot Topics in Software Defined Networking*, HotSDN '13, pages 43–48, New York, NY, USA, 2013. ACM.

[7] M. Jarschel, S. Oechsner, D. Schlosser, R. Pries, S. Goll, and P. Tran-Gia. Modeling and Performance Evaluation of an OpenFlow Architecture. In *23rd International Teletraffic Congress (ITC 2011)*, San Francisco, CA, USA, 2011.

[8] X. Kong, Z. Wang, X. Shi, X. Yin, and D. Li. Performance evaluation of software-defined networking with real-life isp traffic. In *Computers and Communications (ISCC), 2013 IEEE Symposium on*, pages 000541–000547, July 2013.

[9] D. Kreutz, F. M. Ramos, P. Esteves Verissimo, C. Esteve Rothenberg, S. Azodolmolky, and S. Uhlig. Software-defined networking: A comprehensive survey. *Proceedings of the IEEE*, 103(1):14–76, 2015.

[10] M. Kuzniar, P. Peresíni, and D. Kostic. What You Need to Know About SDN Flow Tables. In *Proceedings of the 16th International Conference on Passive and Active Measurement*, pages 347–359, 2015.

[11] A. Lazaris, D. Tahara, X. Huang, E. Li, A. Voellmy, Y. R. Yang, and M. Yu. Tango: Simplifying SDN Control with Automatic Switch Property Inference, Abstraction, and Optimization. In *Proceedings of the 10th ACM International on Conference on Emerging Networking Experiments and Technologies*, CoNEXT '14, pages 199–212, New York, NY, USA, 2014. ACM.

[12] D. S. Marcon and M. P. Barcellos. Predictor: Providing fine-grained management and predictability in multi-tenant datacenter networks. In *2015 IFIP/IEEE International Symposium on Integrated Network Management (IM)*, pages 71–79, May 2015.

[13] N. McKeown, T. Anderson, H. Balakrishnan, G. Parulkar, L. Peterson, J. Rexford, S. Shenker, and J. Turner. Openflow: Enabling innovation in campus networks. *SIGCOMM Comput. Commun. Rev.*, 38(2):69–74, 2008.

[14] R. Pries, M. Jarschel, and S. Goll. On the usability of openflow in data center environments. In *2012 IEEE International Conference on Communications (ICC)*, pages 5533–5537, June 2012.

[15] C. Rotsos, N. Sarrar, S. Uhlig, R. Sherwood, and A. W. Moore. Oflops: An open framework for openflow switch evaluation. In *Proceedings of the 13th International Conference on Passive and Active Measurement (PAM 2012)*, pages 85–95, Berlin, Heidelberg, 2012. Springer.

Caching Games between Content Providers and Internet Service Providers

Vaggelis G. Douros[1], Salah Eddine Elayoubi[1], Eitan Altman[2], Yezekael Hayel[3]
[1] Orange Labs, Châtillon, France; {evangelos.douros, salaheddine.elayoubi}@orange.com
[2] INRIA, Sophia Antipolis, France; eitan.altman@sophia.inria.fr
[3] University of Avignon, Avignon, France; yezekael.hayel@univ-avignon.fr

ABSTRACT

We consider a scenario where an Internet Service Provider (ISP) serves users that choose digital content among M Content Providers (CP). In the status quo, these users pay both access fees to the ISP and content fees to each chosen CP; however, neither the ISP nor the CPs share their profit. We revisit this model by introducing a different business model where the ISP and the CP may have motivation to collaborate in the framework of caching. The key idea is that the ISP deploys a cache for a CP provided that they share both the deployment cost and the additional profit that arises due to caching. Under the prism of coalitional games, our contributions include the application of the Shapley value for a fair splitting of the profit, the stability analysis of the coalition and the derivation of closed-form formulas for the optimal caching policy.

Our model captures not only the case of non-overlapping contents among the CPs, but also the more challenging case of overlapping contents; for the latter case, a non-cooperative game among the CPs is introduced and analyzed to capture the negative externality on the demand of a particular CP when caches for other CPs are deployed.

CCS Concepts

•Networks → Network economics; •Theory of computation → Solution concepts in game theory;

Keywords

Coalitional game theory, Shapley value, Nash Equilibrium

1. CONTRIBUTIONS

The goal of our work (the full version has been selected to be published in [1]) is to analyze a business model where the ISP and the CPs collaborate by sharing the cache cost/ profit deployment. We use coalitional game theory to model the interactions between them.

VALUETOOLS 2016, October 25-28, Taormina, Italy

Initially, we consider a scenario with one ISP that serves J users and one CP that offers additional content to these users. We compute the profit for the ISP and the CP, expressed as a utility function that captures the difference between the income minus the expenses. Then, we examine the impact of caching on the utility functions of the ISP and the CP. We show that the deployment of the cache incurs always a positive externality for the income of CP, since his profit will increase (in the worst case, it will remain stable). On the other hand, the deployment of the cache is beneficial for the ISP if and only if the backhaul bandwidth savings are larger than the cache cost deployment.

We propose a different business model where the CP and the ISP are willing to split the cost/profit that arises due to caching. Therefore, they are willing to form a coalition; We compute the Shapley value showing that, in our model, the ISP and the CP share equally the additional cache cost/profit. Then, we analyze the stability of the Shapley value, showing under which conditions it belongs to the core of the game; if this is the case, neither the ISP nor the CP have motivation to leave the coalition. Finally, we compute the optimal caching policy that maximizes the revenue of both the ISP and the CP.

We then examine the more general case, where there is a unique ISP and M CPs. A key issue is that the caches of the other CPs create a negative externality to the demand of the CP i; there is a coalitional game between the CP i and the ISP. As previously, we compute the Shapley value. Then, we analyze the non-cooperative game that arises due to the competition among the CPs. We prove that this game admits always a Nash Equilibrium (NE). Finally, we examine the uniqueness of the NE and we make the following contributions: i) We prove a necessary and sufficient condition for the uniqueness of the NE. ii) We propose a best-response dynamics scheme, where each CP i updates iteratively his cache size C_i aiming at maximizing his utility function, that is guaranteed to converge to the unique NE. iii) Simulations show that the scheme converges fast to the NE.

2. ACKNOWLEDGMENT

This work has been performed in the framework of the H2020 project METIS-II co-funded by the EU.

3. REFERENCES

[1] V. G. Douros, S.-E. Elayoubi, E. Altman, and Y. Hayel. Caching Games between Content Providers and Internet Service Providers. *Elsevier Perfomance Evaluation (PEVA) Journal*, 2016 (to appear).

Performance of Data Traffic in Small Cells Networks with Inter-Cell Mobility *

Philippe Olivier
Orange Labs
44 avenue de la République
92320 Châtillon, France
phil.olivier@orange.com

Alain Simonian
Orange Labs
44 avenue de la République
92320 Châtillon, France
alain.simonian@orange.com

ABSTRACT

We analyze the impact of inter-cell mobility on data traffic performance in dense networks with small cells. To this end, a Markovian queuing model with impatience is proposed as a generic tool that captures mobility through the sojourn time of users in the cell. An approximate model, based on Quasi-Stationary assumptions, is developed to speed up computation. We then show how the performance of a network of small cells is amenable to the application of the generic model to each individual cell; the analysis of a homogeneous network is further reduced to that of a single representative cell. Our approach is applied to derive the throughput of both mobile and static users, along with the probability of handover. Numerical evaluation and simulation results are provided to assess the accuracy of the approach and we show, in particular, that both classes of users benefit from a throughput gain induced by the "opportunistic" displacement of mobile users among cells.

CCS Concepts

•Mathematics of computing → Markov processes; •Networks → Network performance analysis; Mobile networks;

Keywords

Cellular networks; mobility; traffic; performance evaluation

1. INTRODUCTION

To address the permanent increase of mobile traffic, the capacity of networks can be upgraded by a massive deployment of small cells. This is a solution envisaged by network operators in the framework of LTE-A heterogeneous networks [8] or Ultra Dense Networks scenarios for future 5G networks [13]. In such dense networks, however, the amount of handover generated by users mobility will significantly increase with a notable impact on signaling overhead, thus counterbalancing possible throughput gains.

In this context, the present paper aims at evaluating the impact of *inter-cell mobility* on the performance of data traffic in dense networks. Specifically, considering small cells enables us to neglect the possible spatial variations of intra-cell capacities and thus to focus on the impact of inter-cell mobility itself. Furthermore, we decouple the performance evaluation problem from the modeling of the user displacement in the plane, the latter topic being out of scope of the present paper (see [11, 14] for current displacement models). Mobility is here supposed to be captured through the distribution of the users residual sojourn time in a cell, that is, the time a mobile user is physically present in the cell once its transmission has started; this distribution can be seen as the output of user displacement models.

Given this distribution, we construct a flow-level queuing model that allows us to derive the essential performance metrics in each cell, namely the mean throughput and the handover probability. The generic tool of our model is a multi-class Processor Sharing (PS) queue with "impatient" customers; the impatience here accounts for the mobility of customers from cell to cell. An approximate model is derived for this queue in order to replace the exact Markovian model when the latter requires exceeding computation time. This generic model can then be applied to each individual cell to solve the set of flow equations, which characterize the handover rates between cells, and compute the performance indicators.

The PS queue with impatience and one customer class has been early addressed in [7], where several asymptotic regimes are given for the reneging probability. For the multi-class PS queue in overload condition (with identical impatience rates but distinct service rates), an asymptotics for the reneging probability has been provided in [9]. The analysis of the stable multi-class PS queue with distinct impatience rates, however, has not received so far a significant contribution.

In the literature, throughput gains induced by mobility in cellular networks are generally related to the spatial variations of capacity inside the cells, which permits an opportunistic use of favorable transmission conditions by mobile users [1, 3, 4, 6, 10]. These papers also base their evaluation on flow-level traffic modeling but address mobility through a spatial Markov process where users jump between distinct capacity zones in the cells. In [1], throughput gains are ob-

*Part of this work has been carried out in the framework of IDEFIX project, funded by the ANR under the contract number ANR-13-INFR-0006

VALUETOOLS 2016, October 25-28, Taormina, Italy

served for the Round-Robin and opportunistic "max C/I" scheduling schemes with a main focus on intra-cell mobility. In [3, 4], the average throughputs of different classes of users are estimated through upper and lower bounds associated with fluid limits and quasi-stationary regimes, respectively. By means of an approximate model, [10] computes the mean flow throughput of a single class of users and highlights a throughput gain created by intra- and inter-cell mobility altogether. In a complementary way, [6] focuses on the characterization of network capacity with different scenarios of intra-cell and inter-cell mobility.

The present work is an attempt to analyze a queuing model to derive multi-class performance indicators, namely the throughput gains as well as the handover rates induced by inter-cell mobility alone, and to apply it to a whole network of small cells. In the following, a generic one-cell Markovian model is first constructed in Section 2 to derive such indicators; a heuristic Quasi-Stationary approximation is then proposed to alleviate computation. Section 3 presents our approach to model networks with mobility. Section 4 provides numerical results, including simulation experiments, to validate the approach. Finally, Section 5 draws conclusions and summarizes our main achievements.

2. GENERIC QUEUEING MODEL

As a first step, we consider a single cell whose performance model may be used as the generic tool to further analyze the impact of inter-cell mobility in a network. This section is an extension of the single cell model proposed in [2] and proposes a different approximation, the so-called *QS approximation model* developed in Section 2.2, which allows us to quantify the performance of various classes of customers.

2.1 A PS Queue with Impatience

The considered cell is supposed to be "small", i.e., of limited range so that its transmission capacity C can be assumed spatially constant; this capacity is viewed as an input parameter accounting for radio and interference conditions in the considered cellular network. We handle downlink traffic only and suppose that capacity C is equally shared among all active users present in its service area, as implemented by means of a Round-Robin scheduling. Following this fair sharing policy, the system occupancy (defined by the number of active transmissions at any time) can then be modeled by a Processor-Sharing (PS) queue [5].

We consider K classes of users which may have different traffic characteristics and mobility behaviours. The users generate requests for transmission in the cell according to Poisson processes with respective arrival rate λ_k, $k = 1, ..., K$. In this open queuing system, the arrival rates are supposed to be exogenous input parameters. How the arrival rates may account for the handover traffic flows from cell to cell will be addressed in Section 3. Class-k users have i.i.d. transmission requests of data volume Σ_k with mean σ_k, hence a service rate $\mu_k = C/\sigma_k$. Since customers may actually leave the cell during their communications, we call T_k the *remaining* sojourn time of a mobile user, i.e., the time duration he physically stays in the cell after the transmission has started. We finally denote by $\theta_k = 1/\mathbb{E}(T_k)$ the mean cell departure rate of class-k users, called class-k *mobility rate*; any class k where $\theta_k = 0$ will be called *static*.

Given this framework, the cell occupancy can be described by the K-dimensional process $\mathbf{N}(t) = (N_1(t), ..., N_K(t))$, $t \geq 0$, where $N_k(t)$ denotes the number of ongoing class-k data transfers in the cell at time t. The evolution of this process is represented by a Processor-Sharing queue with impatience, the "impatient" customers here corresponding to mobile users that may leave the system before their service completion within the given cell.

We assume that Σ_k and T_k are exponentially distributed with parameters $1/\sigma_k$ and θ_k, respectively. The process $(\mathbf{N}(t))_{t\geq 0}$ is then Markovian in the state space $\mathbb{N}^K$; from state $\mathbf{n} = (n_1, ..., n_K)$ and for $\mathbf{e}_k = (0, ..., 1, ...0)$ with 1 at the k-th component, we can reach state $\mathbf{n}+\mathbf{e}_k$ with transition rate λ_k, or state $\mathbf{n}-\mathbf{e}_k$ with transition rate $n_k\mu_k/L(\mathbf{n})+n_k\theta_k$ if $n_k > 0$, $L(\mathbf{n}) = \sum_{1\leq j\leq K} n_j$ denoting the total number of active users.

PROPOSITION 2.1. ***Let $\rho_k = \lambda_k/\mu_k$ be the offered load of class k. The Markov occupancy process $(\mathbf{N}(t))_{t\geq 0}$ has a stationary regime if and only if***

$$\rho_S = \sum_{k\in S} \rho_k < 1, \tag{1}$$

where S is the set of static user classes.

Although condition (1) is intuitive, its derivation is not straightforward; we refer to [12] for the detailed proof which exhibits a proper Lyapounov function ensuring the sufficiency of (1). Now, given (1), the equilibrium equations of process $(\mathbf{N}(t))_{t\geq 0}$ in stationary regime read

$$\sum_{k=1}^{K} \left[\lambda_k + n_k\left(\frac{\mu_k}{L(\mathbf{n})} + \theta_k\right)\right] \Pi(\mathbf{n}) = \sum_{k=1}^{K} \lambda_k \Pi(\mathbf{n} - \mathbf{e}_k) +$$

$$\sum_{k=1}^{K} (n_k + 1)\left(\frac{\mu_k}{L(\mathbf{n}) + 1} + \theta_k\right) \Pi(\mathbf{n} + \mathbf{e}_k) \tag{2}$$

where $\Pi(\mathbf{n}) = \mathbb{P}(\mathbf{N} = \mathbf{n})$ and with $\sum_{n\in\mathbb{N}^K} \Pi(\mathbf{n}) = 1$. For given k, multiplying each equation of (2) by n_k and then summing over all state vectors $\mathbf{n} \in \mathbb{N}^K$ provides the following relation.

COROLLARY 2.1. ***For any class k, the average arrival and departure rates verify the conservation law***

$$\lambda_k = \mu_k \mathbb{E}\left(\frac{N_k \mathbf{1}_{N_k>0}}{L(\mathbf{N})}\right) + \theta_k \mathbb{E}(N_k). \tag{3}$$

Process $(\mathbf{N}(t))_{t\geq 0}$ is not reversible unless all classes are static; its stationary distribution $\Pi(\cdot)$ is thus not amenable to a simple closed form. Though we can evaluate this distribution by solving system (2) numerically and derive the performance indicators of interest. We define two performance indicators per user-class, the *average throughput* and the *handover probability*. Considering data (elastic) traffic, the user-perceived QoS can be measured by the average throughput defined as the ratio of the mean volume of transferred data to the mean transfer time [5]. We also define the *handover probability* for class-k users as the proportion of users that exit the cell before the completion of their transmission, i.e., the ratio of the mean handover rate λ_k^{Out} to the mean flow arrival rate λ_k. The latter definitions read

$$\gamma_k \triangleq \frac{\mathbb{E}(X_k)}{\mathbb{E}(\Delta_k)}, \quad H_k \triangleq \frac{\lambda_k^{Out}}{\lambda_k}, \quad \forall\, k = 1, ..., K, \tag{4}$$

where X_k denotes the part of the total data volume Σ_k which is actually transferred by a class-k user during its transmission time Δ_k (less than or equal to T_k) in the cell.

PROPOSITION 2.2. ***For any class k, the throughput γ_k and the handover probability H_k are given by***

$$\gamma_k = C\left(\frac{\rho_k}{\mathbb{E}(N_k)} - \frac{\theta_k}{\mu_k}\right), \qquad H_k = \frac{\mathbb{E}(N_k)\,\theta_k}{\lambda_k}, \tag{5}$$

which depend on the mean number of class-k users only. Moreover, the relation

$$H_k = \frac{\theta_k\,\sigma_k}{\gamma_k + \theta_k\,\sigma_k} \tag{6}$$

holds between H_k and γ_k.

PROOF. By Little's law, $\mathbb{E}(N_k)/\lambda_k$ equals the mean time $\mathbb{E}(\Delta_k)$ to transfer the average volume $\mathbb{E}(X_k)$, hence

$$\gamma_k = \frac{\lambda_k \mathbb{E}(X_k)}{\mathbb{E}(N_k)}. \tag{7}$$

The average transferred volume $\mathbb{E}(X_k)$ is not directly computable from distribution $\Pi(\cdot)$. We can nevertheless observe that $\lambda_k\mathbb{E}(X_k)$ represents the *carried* traffic intensity for class k. In a way similar to the derivation of Little's formula, this traffic intensity can be shown to equal the mean bandwidth $\mathbb{E}(\phi_k)$ allocated to class-k users, so that (7) eventually reads

$$\gamma_k = \frac{\mathbb{E}(\phi_k)}{\mathbb{E}(N_k)} = \frac{C}{\mathbb{E}(N_k)}\,\mathbb{E}\left(\frac{N_k\,\mathbf{1}_{N_k>0}}{L(\mathbf{N})}\right). \tag{8}$$

Using conservation law (3), expression (5) for γ_k then follows. As to the handover probability, the mean handover rate λ_k^{Out} is by definition $\mathbb{E}(N_k)\,\theta_k$, hence (5) for H_k.

Relation (6) directly follows from eliminating $\mathbb{E}(N_k)$ between both expressions (5). □

2.2 Quasi-Stationary Approximation

Consider now the important case where users are gathered into two classes, namely static users (with class index "S") and mobile users (with index "M"). We thus set $\theta_S = 0$, $\theta_M > 0$, and define loads $\rho_S = \lambda_S/\mu_S$, $\rho_M = \lambda_M/\mu_M$.

Although the Markovian model can be solved numerically, it does not provide explicit expressions for performance indicators. To also circumvent the explosive computation time of either the simulation or the numerical resolution when the load increases, we here develop an approximation framework suitable for this two-class scenario. The results of this approach can be summarized as follows.

PROPOSITION 2.3. ***Let $A > 0$ be the solution to***

$$e^{-A}\,(1-\rho_S) = \frac{\theta_M}{\mu_M}A + 1 - \rho_S - \rho_M. \tag{9}$$

The throughputs γ_S and γ_M can be approximated by

$$\gamma_S \approx \frac{C(1-\rho_S)}{1+A}, \quad \gamma_M \approx \sigma_M\left(\frac{\lambda_M}{\mathbb{E}(N_M)} - \theta_M\right) \tag{10}$$

with $\mathbb{E}(N_M) = \sum_{(\ell,m)\in\mathbb{N}^2} m\Psi(m|\ell)q(\ell)$, where

$$\left[\begin{array}{l} q(\ell) = e^{-A\rho_S}\,\rho_S^\ell(1-\rho_S)\displaystyle\sum_{k=0}^{\ell}\binom{\ell}{k}\frac{[A(1-\rho_S)]^k}{k!}, \\ \\ \Psi(m|\ell) = \Psi(0|\ell)\left(\dfrac{\rho_M}{\rho_\theta}\right)^m \dfrac{1}{m!}\displaystyle\prod_{k=1}^{m}\frac{\ell+k}{\ell+k+1/\rho_\theta} \end{array}\right. \tag{11}$$

for all $(\ell,m) \in \mathbb{N}^2$, with constant $\rho_\theta = \theta_M/\mu_M$ and where the factor $\Psi(0|\ell)$ is determined by the normalization condition $\sum_{m\geq 0}\Psi(m|\ell) = 1$ for all ℓ.

The handover H is calculated by applying (6) to the value γ_M given in (10).

PROOF. As a preamble, applying conservation law (3) to each class, we obtain

$$\rho_S = \mathbb{E}\left(\frac{N_S\mathbf{1}_{N_S>0}}{L(\mathbf{N})}\right), \rho_M = \mathbb{E}\left(\frac{N_M\mathbf{1}_{N_M>0}}{L(\mathbf{N})}\right) + \frac{\theta_M}{\mu_M}\mathbb{E}(N_M).$$

Then, noting that (with $L(\mathbf{N}) = N_S + N_M$)

$$\mathbb{E}\left(\frac{N_S\,\mathbf{1}_{N_S>0}}{L(\mathbf{N})}\right) + \mathbb{E}\left(\frac{N_M\,\mathbf{1}_{N_M>0}}{L(\mathbf{N})}\right) = \mathbb{E}(\mathbf{1}_{\mathbf{N}\neq(0,0)}),$$

we obtain the relation

$$\mathbb{E}(N_M) = \frac{\mu_M}{\theta_M}\left(\rho_S + \rho_M + \Pi(0,0) - 1\right). \tag{12}$$

Now, the underlying idea for the proposed approximation is a Quasi-Stationary (QS) assumption which can be applied in two steps.

(I) First, note that the largest the load, the highest tendency of mobile users to leave the cell before the end of their transmission. The stationary distribution of their number N_M may thus be approximated by that of a queuing system without any constraint, i.e., a Poisson distribution describing the occupancy of an M/G/∞ queue. The mean value $A = \mathbb{E}(N_M)$ of this Poisson distribution remains to be evaluated. Given a number $N_M = m$ of mobile users in the cell, we assume it to remain constant in time (*Quasi-Stationary*) so that the number N_S of static users evolves as the occupancy process of a Processor Sharing queue with a set of m permanent customers. This enables us to obtain the conditional distribution $\Phi(\cdot|m)$ of N_S, which is readily derived from the local balance equations of the one-dimensional Markov process $(N_S(t))$, that is,

$$\Phi(\ell|m) = \Phi(0|m)\,\rho_S^\ell\,\frac{(\ell+m)!}{\ell!\,m!}, \quad \ell \geq 0, \tag{13}$$

where $\Phi(0|m)$ is determined by the normalization condition $\sum_{\ell\geq 0}\Phi(\ell|m) = 1$, hence $\Phi(0|m) = (1-\rho_S)^{m+1}$. Deconditioning on N_M, the joint distribution of (N_S, N_M) is then

$$\Pi^{(1)}(\ell,m) = e^{-A}\,\frac{A^m}{m!}\binom{\ell+m}{m}\rho_S^\ell(1-\rho_S)^{m+1} \tag{14}$$

for $(\ell,m) \in \mathbb{N}^2$ and, in particular, $\Pi(0,0) = e^{-A}\,(1-\rho_S)$. Using relation (12) and the latter value of $\Pi(0,0)$, we deduce that the unknown mean A is determined as the unique positive solution to the implicit equation (9).

Applying relation (5) with $\mathbb{E}(N_M) = A$ then provides the expression (10) for γ_M. As regards static users, we use the distribution (14) to derive $\mathbb{E}(N_S) = \rho_S\mathbb{E}(N_S)+\rho_S\mathbb{E}(N_M+1)$, hence $\mathbb{E}(N_S) = (1+A)\rho_S/(1-\rho_S)$ and the application of (5) with $\theta_S = 0$ eventually leads to formula (10) for γ_S.

(II) This first step, however, does not provide accurate enough values for throughputs (in particular, γ_M) when comparing them to that of the exact Markovian Model. We thus iterate the QS approximation scheme by considering now that mobile users "see" a succession of stationary regimes conditioned on the number of static users. We first compute the marginal distribution $q(\cdot)$ of N_S from the joint distribution (14) as

$$q(\ell) = \sum_{m\geq 0} e^{-A}\,\rho_S^\ell(1-\rho_S)\binom{\ell+m}{m}\frac{[A(1-\rho_S)]^m}{m!}$$

for all $\ell \geq 0$. The latter formula reduces after simple manipulations to the expression for $q(\ell)$ given in (11). For any given $N_S = \ell$, the number N_M is then supposed to evolve as the occupancy process of a Processor Sharing queue with impatient (mobile) customers and a set of ℓ permanent customers. The conditional distribution $\Psi(\cdot|\ell)$ for the number of mobile users thus verifies the local balance equations

$$\lambda_M \Psi(m-1|\ell) = m\left(\frac{\mu_M}{\ell+m} + \theta_M\right)\Psi(m|\ell) \tag{15}$$

for all $m > 0$. By recursion, we obtain expression (11) for $\Psi(m|\ell)$, $m \geq 0$, with $\Psi(0|\ell)$ given by the normalization condition. By deconditioning on N_S, the joint distribution of (N_S, N_M) is now given by

$$\Pi^{(2)}(\ell, m) = \Psi(m|\ell)\, q(\ell), \quad (\ell, m) \in \mathbb{N}^2. \tag{16}$$

The throughput γ_S in this second step QS approximation will leave expression (10) unchanged, since $\gamma_S = C\rho_S/\mathbb{E}(N_S)$ and the marginal distribution $q(\cdot)$ of N_S is now known *a priori*. Besides, relations (3) and (5) again enable us to write γ_M as in (10) where the mean $\mathbb{E}(N_M)$ has to be re-evaluated from the joint distribution (16). □

The latter evaluations associated with the second step distribution $\Pi^{(2)}$ indeed provide more accurate results (see Sections 4.1.6 and 4.2) than that obtained at the first step. Besides, it has been observed that further iterations of this QS approximation scheme do not bring better accuracy.

3. NETWORK WITH MOBILITY

3.1 A closed network of queues

Consider now a cellular network of I cells with possibly distinct capacities. Users from K traffic classes may appear and move during their communications. When leaving a cell during transmission, users join one of the neighboring cells according to some routing probabilities. They consequently generate supplementary flows of new arrivals, hereafter called *handover arrivals*, which are to be added to *fresh arrivals* in each cell.

We assume that class-k users generate requests for transmission in cell i according to a Poisson process with rate $\lambda^0_{i,k}$, $i = 1, ..., I$, $k = 1, ..., K$; this corresponds to the fresh traffic offered to cell i. To account for class-k users that became active outside cell i and experienced one or more handovers, the total flow arrival to cell i is written as

$$\lambda_{i,k} = \lambda^0_{i,k} + \lambda^{In}_{i,k} \tag{17}$$

where $\lambda^{In}_{i,k}$ denotes the handover arrival rate from neighboring cells. For all i and k, we will assume that the handover arrival process to cell i from class-k users can be approximated by a Poisson process so that it can be superposed to the fresh arrivals to build up a total Poisson arrival process with rate $\lambda_{i,k}$ given in (17). All Poisson processes introduced above are assumed to be mutually independent.

This Poisson assumption is fundamental in our modeling approach, which allows a local description of the traffic flows at each cell as explained below. This notably simplifies the global description of the system by reducing it to a network of queues which is *closed* regarding the handover flows. This is, in particular, in contrast to the overall multi-class multi-cell process considered in other papers quoted in the Introduction.

The handover arrival rate $\lambda^{In}_{i,k}$ to cell i results from the superposition of handovers departing from neighboring cells according to routing probabilities $p_k(j, i)$ from cell $j \neq i$ to cell i for class-k users. We can write the flow equation

$$\lambda^{In}_{i,k} = \sum_{j \neq i} p_k(j, i) \cdot \lambda^{Out}_{j,k} \tag{18}$$

where $\lambda^{Out}_{j,k}$ is the handover departure rate from cell j emanating from class k-users. Rate $\lambda^{Out}_{j,k}$ can in turn be considered as an output of a queuing model for cell j (typically, the generic queuing model studied in Section 2) and calculated by means of some *performance function* $\mathcal{F}_{j,k}(.)$, that is,

$$\lambda^{Out}_{j,k} = \mathcal{F}_{j,k}\left(\lambda^{In}_{j,1}, ..., \lambda^{In}_{j,K}\right) \tag{19}$$

for $j = 1, ..., I$ and $k = 1, ..., K$. In (19), only handover arrival rates are considered as variables, all other intrinsic parameters (such as cell capacities, per-class offered traffic and mobility rates) being kept constant. From (18)-(19), it follows that a stationary network regime can be characterized by a system of $I \times K$ flow equations with unknowns, the handover arrival rates $\lambda^{In}_{i,k}$, namely

$$\lambda^{In}_{i,k} = \sum_{j \neq i} p_k(j, i) \cdot \mathcal{F}_{j,k}\left(\lambda^{In}_{j,1}, ..., \lambda^{In}_{j,K}\right). \tag{20}$$

The problem of existence and uniqueness of a solution to the non-linear system (20) for a general network is out of the scope of the present paper. As the performance functions $\mathcal{F}_{j,k}$ may not be explicit in terms of input parameters, the practical determination of a solution to (20) involves a numerical iterative procedure, e.g. a fixed-point algorithm.

3.2 The case of a homogeneous network

Now assume that the network is *homogeneous*, with identical cells, in the following sense:

(i) all intrinsic parameters (capacities, arrival rates, ...) are the same for all cells, so that performance functions do not depend on the cell index, that is, $\mathcal{F}_{j,k}(.) = \mathcal{F}_k(.)$;

(ii) handover routing is symmetric, i.e., for each class k, cell i receives handover traffic from a set $\mathcal{J}_k(i)$ of neighboring cells with identical probability $p_k(j, i) = 1/J_k$, where J_k is the common cardinal of sets $\mathcal{J}_k(i)$.

Clearly, any solution to the simpler system

$$\begin{cases} \lambda^{In}_{i,k} = \lambda^{In}_{j,k} = \lambda^{In}_k, & \forall\, i, j, k, \\ \lambda^{In}_k = \lambda^{Out}_k = \mathcal{F}_k\left(\lambda^{In}_1, ..., \lambda^{In}_K\right), & \forall\, k, \end{cases} \tag{21}$$

will provide a particular solution to (20), hence *the* solution if uniqueness is ensured. For a homogeneous network, the problem thus reduces to the study of a single cell, hereafter called the *representative cell.* System (21) expresses the fact that the outgoing handover traffic is fed back in a balanced way as a supplementary traffic to the ingress of this cell.

In this homogeneous network model with inter-cell mobility, we will define the total and per-class loads by referring to the fresh offered traffic, that is,

$$\rho^0_k = \frac{\lambda^0_k \sigma_k}{C} \quad (k = 1, ..., K), \quad \rho^0 = \sum_{k=1}^{K} \rho^0_k.$$

We conjecture that the stability region is now characterized by $\rho^0 < 1$. This can be understood since mobile users re-enter the system until their transfer is completed.

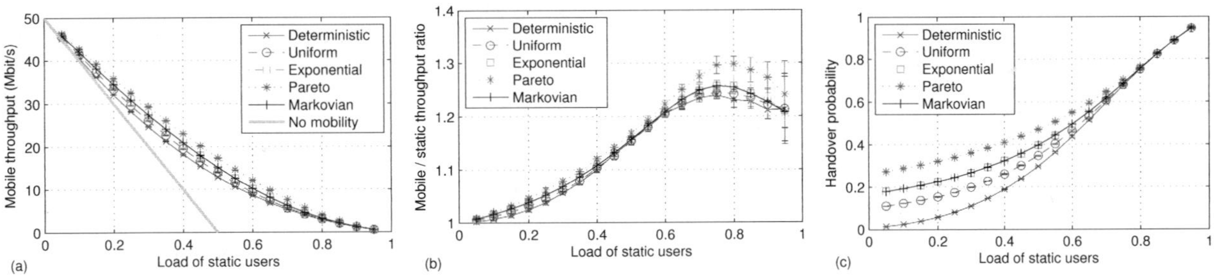

Figure 1: Impact of the mobile sojourn time distribution on (a) mobile user throughput, (b) mobile throughput to static throughput ratio and (c) handover probability, computed from simulation and the Markovian IM (proportion of 50% mobile users and mobility rate $\theta_M = 0.1$ s^{-1}).

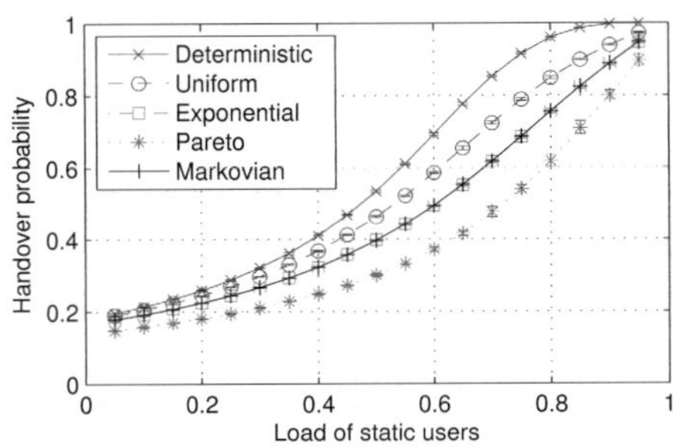

Figure 2: Impact of the flow volume distribution on the handover probability, computed from simulation and the Markovian IM for a proportion of 50% mobile users and a mobility rate $\theta_M = 0.1$ s^{-1}.

CONJECTURE 3.1. ***In the homogeneous network with inter-cell mobility, the condition $\rho^0 < 1$ ensures the existence of a fixed-point solution to equilibrium equation (21), that is, $\lambda_k^{In} = \lambda_k^{Out}$, $\forall\, k = 1, ..., K$.***

Note that, for simplicity, this condition will still be called a *stability condition*, as it translates the fact that the resource must have enough capacity to handle all offered traffic. Although the proof of its sufficiency is open, its necessity is straightforward: in fact, applying conservation equation (3) to any class k and recalling that $\lambda_k = \lambda_k^0 + \lambda_k^{In}$ with $\lambda_k^{In} = \lambda_k^{Out} = \theta_k\, \mathbb{E}(N_k)$, we obtain

$$\rho_k^0 = \mathbb{E}\left(\frac{N_k \mathbf{1}_{N_k>0}}{L(\mathbf{N})}\right), \quad k = 1, ..., K,$$

hence $\rho^0 = \sum_{k=1}^{K} \rho_k^0 = \mathbb{E}(1_{L(\mathbf{N})>0}) = 1 - \Pi(\mathbf{0}) < 1$.

4. NUMERICAL RESULTS

In this section, we validate the robustness of the proposed approach regarding some important assumptions. For the sake of clarity, we distinguish

- the *Impatience Model* (IM) consisting in the generic Markovian model analyzed in Section 2, where the arrival rate λ_k for any class k is an exogenous input parameter,

- the *Mobility Model* (MM) consisting in the same Markovian model but where, as discussed in Section 3.2, λ_k is the sum of a given exogenous arrival rate λ_k^0 (the fresh offered traffic) and the handover arrival rate λ_k^{In} which exactly balances the outgoing handover rate λ_k^{Out}.

Moreover, we focus on the two-class model introduced in Section 2.2, with all customers gathered either in a static class or in a mobile class with a single mobility rate.

4.1 Impatience Model

4.1.1 Numerical set-up

Event-driven simulations have been performed at the flow level (i.e., neglecting detailed packet-scale phenomena and assuming all system level parameters are summarized in the cell capacity). The purpose of such experiments is to test the sensitivity to the Markovian assumptions made on the users' traffic and mobility. We fix a cell capacity $C = 50$ Mbit/s, a proportion of 50% mobile users and a mean flow volume $\sigma =$ 12.5 MB (100 Mbit) for both classes. The mobile users speed is set to $v = 36$ km/h and the mean distance crossed by a mobile user, after its data transfer has started, is $\mathbb{E}(D) =$ 100 m, hence a mean exit rate $\theta_M = v/\mathbb{E}(D) = 0.1$ s^{-1}.

The accuracy of results drawn from simulation has been tightly controlled. Specifically, in every configuration, ten independent simulation runs have been performed, generating around 1 million discrete events each, so as to guarantee a confidence interval with range equal to two standard deviations around the mean. The confidence intervals plotted on Fig. 1 and 2 are very small and can hardly be distinguished in most cases. Thus, for simplicity, such confidence intervals will not be represented anymore in further figures.

4.1.2 Influence of sojourn time distribution

We envisage several theoretical distributions for T_M so as to obtain a wide range of values for its variance (with given mean). Beside the exponential distribution, we thus consider the Deterministic, the Uniform and the Pareto distribution with power index 2.

For such distributions of T_M, Fig. 1 depicts the variations of γ_M, γ_M/γ_S and H with varying static load ρ_S. We observe that the throughput of each class is only marginally impacted by the distribution of T_M, indicating that results derived in the Markovian framework remain valid for more realistic sojourn time distributions. The handover H is, however, noticeably more impacted (particularly at low load) and increases with the variance of T_M.

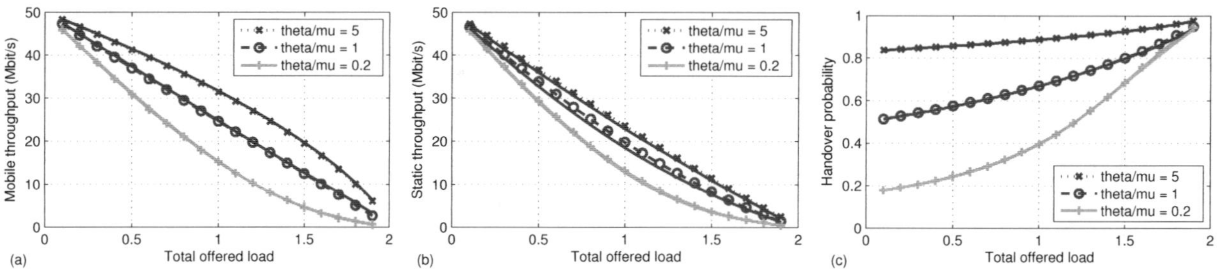

Figure 3: Comparison of the (a) mobile throughput, (b) static throughput and (c) handover probability obtained from the Markovian IM (marks) with those from the QS approximation (lines), for a proportion of 50% mobile users and a normalized mobility rate of 0.2, 1, or 5.

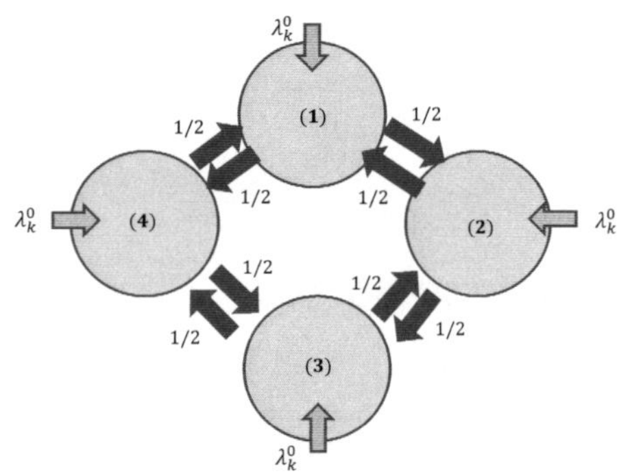

Figure 4: A homogeneous ring network of four identical cells with symmetric routing.

4.1.3 Influence of flow volume distribution

Sensitivity tests have also been performed regarding the distribution of the flow volume. Surprisingly, the impact of this distribution (applied to both mobile and static users) on γ_S and γ_M is the same as that of Fig. 1 with an identical parameter setting (discrepancies are indistinguishable and so results are not shown here). On the other hand, the impact on H is reversed, as shown in Fig. 2: the greater the distribution variability, the lower H.

4.1.4 Throughput gains

Fig. 1(a) shows a significant throughput gain for mobile users compared to a scenario where all users would be static; besides, Fig. 1(b) highlights a significant gain of mobile users throughput over that of static users. Such throughput gains are expected in this open-loop system: they result from the impatient nature of mobile users who may leave the system without re-entering it, thus decreasing the load (hence the gain w.r.t. the all-static scenario) and tend to do it especially when local congestion occurs (hence the gain mobile/static). As indicated by Fig. 1(c), these throughput gains are obtained at the expense of larger handover.

In relation with these observations, note that the stability region is $\rho_S < 1$, as expected from Proposition 2.1, while it is limited to $\rho_S < 0.5$, in this scenario with 50% static users, when no mobility occurs (the system in that case is a genuine multi-class PS queue).

4.1.5 Other scenarios

We have also considered different proportions of mobile users and different values of θ_M. Qualitatively, the corresponding performance curves show a behavior quite similar to that of the above scenario. Based on these observations, we will further pay no more attention to the sensitivity of performance indicators and always refer to the Markovian framework with exponential distributions. We have further observed that the throughput gain of mobile over static users appears to be the greatest when the mobility rate is large (say, more than twice the service rate for mobile users) and when the proportion of mobile users is small (say, 20%).

4.1.6 Validation of the QS Approximation

The QS approximation is compared in Fig. 3 to the results of the Markovian IM with the same parameter setting, but all random variables are now supposed to be exponentially distributed and we consider a series of three normalized mobility rates: θ_M equals 0.2, 1 or 5 times the service capacity $\mu_M = 0.5$ s^{-1}. The accuracy of the approximation appears very good for all performance indicators. This has also been checked for other parameter settings and, in particular, for other proportions of the mobile user class.

Interpreting the previous results and figures helps us to assess the impact of the cell size. In fact, assuming a constant speed v, the mean distance the mobile user travels in the cell is $\mathbb{E}(D) = v/\theta_M$; this mean distance is typically of order the radius R of a circular cell. Thus if $v = 90$ km/h for example, the values of θ_M considered above, namely $5\,\mu_M$, μ_M and $0.2\,\mu_M$ (with $\mu_M = 0.5$ s^{-1}) respectively correspond to a radius of 10 m, 50 m and 250 m, typical of a Femto, Pico, and Micro cell. As expected, users in Femto cells experience the largest throughput since their mobility rate is the highest. As a counterpart, the handover probability they generate is much higher than that in other types of cells.

4.2 Mobility Model in a Network

To handle mobility in a network, first consider the homogeneous four-cell ring network represented in Fig. 4, where all cells are equivalent with the same capacity and traffic parameters as that used in Section 4.1. All random variables are still assumed to be exponentially distributed, and we consider a series of three normalized mobility rates: θ_M equals 0.1, 1 or 10 times the service capacity $\mu_M = 0.5$ s^{-1}.

Fig. 5 depicts the performance indicators obtained from

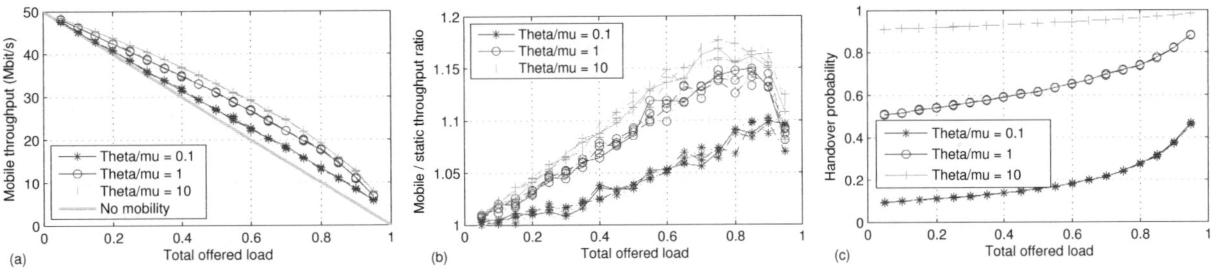

Figure 5: Homogeneous ring network: performance indicators, (a) mobile user throughput, (b) mobile throughput to static throughput ratio and (c) handover probability, obtained from simulation versus the total offered load in each cell (initial proportion of 50% mobile users and $\theta_M/\mu_M = 0.1, 1, 10$).

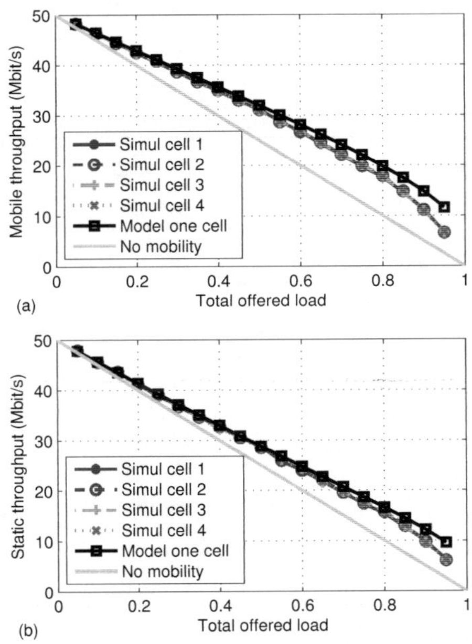

Figure 6: Homogeneous ring network: (a) mobile and (b) static throughput obtained from simulation and the Markovian MM ($\theta_M/\mu_M = 1$).

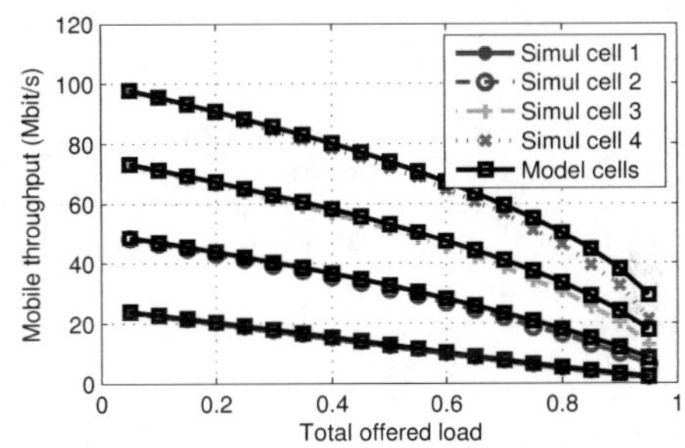

Figure 7: Heterogeneous ring network: mobile throughput obtained from simulation and the generic model ($\theta_M/\mu_M = 10$).

simulation. For each value of θ_M, the four curves (each corresponding to a given cell) are plotted with the same color code; note that they are almost indistinguishable from each other, except for the ratio γ_M/γ_S.

We observe that the stability region is characterized by $\rho^0 < 1$, as predicted by Conjecture 3.1. From Fig. 5(a)(b), we note that the throughput gains due to mobility increase with the mobility rate. Other complementary results have shown that the mobile/static throughput gain is all the more important that the proportion of mobile users is weak.

The latter simulation results are compared in Fig. 6 to the Markovian MM (applied to the *representative cell*) in the case when $\theta_M = \mu_M$. We observe that the representative cell model provides slightly optimistic throughputs compared to those obtained from simulation. From plots obtained for other values of θ_M/μ_M, we have noted that these discrepancies generally increase with the mobility rate.

The good match between model and simulation results validates our approach for reducing a homogeneous network of small cells to a single representative cell: the critical assumption that the handover traffic flow re-enters the representative cell as a supplementary Poisson flow appears reasonable. We now check this assumption in the case of a heterogeneous network by considering the ring network of Fig. 4 but with different cell capacities: 25, 50, 75 and 100 Mbit/s for cell 1 to 4, respectively. The static/mobile user classes generate fresh traffic in each cell proportionally to its capacity, and mobile users have a mobility rate which is also proportional to the service rate in each cell. The performance indicators are computed for each cell, either from simulation or from the generic model used to solve iteratively the handover flow equations (20). For concision, results are given in Fig. 7 for the mobile throughput only, in the case of 50% mobile users and a ratio $\theta_M/\mu_M = 10$; they again show that our proposed approach (to decorrelate mobility from performance computations in each cell) works quite well.

Note finally that the values of the mobility rate θ_M can be interpreted in terms of various mobile speeds for a given cell size. Specifically, Fig. 8 depicts the static and mobile users throughputs and the handover in terms of the speed v for different values of the total offered load (0.2, 0.5, and 0.8) in

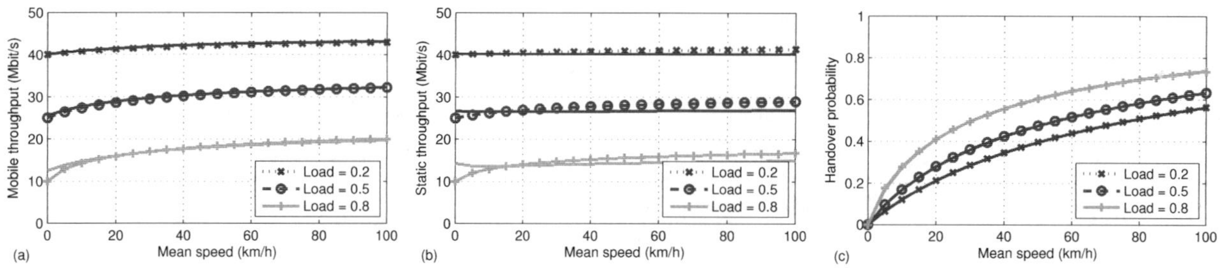

Figure 8: Impact of the users speed on (a) mobile throughput, (b) static throughput and (c) handover probability, obtained from the Markovian MM (marked points) and the QS approximation (plain lines), for an initial proportion of 50% mobile users, cell radius 50 m, and total offered load 0.2, 0.5 or 0.8.

the MM framework. The initial proportion of mobile users is still 50% and the cell radius is 50 m (a Pico cell). Results are derived from the exact Markovian model as well as from the QS approximation, which is shown once again to work nicely enough, and notably for predicting the performance of mobile users. As expected, all performance indicators are increasing functions of the speed. In particular, $H \to 1$ when $v \to \infty$ as predicted by (6); for $v = 0$, both static and mobile users throughputs equal $C(1 - \rho^0)$, the throughput achieved when all users are static.

5. CONCLUSION

We have investigated the impact of inter-cell mobility on the performance of dense networks with small cells. Our approach relies on two main ideas: (1) a simple performance model can be developed to capture mobility on the basis of the multi-class Processor-Sharing queue with impatience; (2) the performance of a network of small cells can be handled by applying the generic model to each individual cell. The main outcomes are: **(i)** the two-class (static / mobile) PS queue can be treated by means of the QS approximation with quite a good level of accuracy; **(ii)** as a step beyond available studies, the handover probability has been evaluated so as to assess the trade-off between throughput gain and signaling overhead due to mobility; **(iii)** both classes of users are shown to benefit from a throughput gain induced by inter-cell mobility; this gain is created by the opportunistic displacement of mobile users within the network according to local load variations in individual cells.

Further work on this topic can be envisaged in two directions: generalize the QS approximate model to an arbitrary number K of traffic classes; extend the performance analysis to cellular networks with spatially varying cell capacities.

6. ACKNOWLEDGMENTS

The authors thank colleagues from the IDEFIX project, and notably Thomas Bonald from Telecom ParisTech, for very fruitful discussions on the considered model.

7. REFERENCES

[1] N. Abbas, T. Bonald, and B. Sayrac. Opportunistic Gains of Mobility in Cellular Data Networks. In *Proc. of WiOpt 13th Intl. Symposium "Modeling and Optimization in Mobile, Ad Hoc and Wireless Networks"*, 2015.

[2] B. Baynat, R.-M. Indre, N. Nya, P. Olivier, and A. Simonian. Impact of Mobility in Dense LTE-A Networks with Small Cells. In *Proc. of VTC2015-Spring Workshop*, Glasgow, Scotland, May 2015.

[3] T. Bonald, S. Borst, and N. Hegde. How Mobility Impacts the Flow-level Performance of Wireless Data Systems. In *Proc. of IEEE Infocom*, 2004.

[4] T. Bonald, S. Borst, N. Hegde, M. Jonckheere, and A. Proutière. Flow-level Performance and Capacity of Wireless Networks with User Mobility. *Queueing Systems*, 63:131–164, 2009.

[5] T. Bonald and A. Proutière. Wireless Downlink Data Channels: User Performance and Cell Dimensioning. In *Proc. of MobiCom'03*, San Diego, USA, Sept. 2003.

[6] S. Borst, A. Proutière, and N. Hegde. Capacity of Wireless Data Networks with Intra- and Inter-cell Mobility. In *Proc. of IEEE Infocom*, 2006.

[7] E. G. Coffman, A. A. Puhalskii, M. I. Reiman, and P. E. Wright. Processor-Shared Buffers with Reneging. *Performance Evaluation*, 19:25–46, 1994.

[8] E. Dahlman, S. Parkvall, and J. Skold. *4G: LTE/LTE-Advanced for Mobile Broadband (2nd ed.)*. Academic Press, 2013.

[9] F. Guillemin, S. ElAyoubi, C. Fricker, P. Robert, and B. Sericola. Controlling Impatience in Cellular Networks Using QoE-aware Radio Resource Allocation. In *Proc. of 27th International Teletraffic Congress*, 2015.

[10] M. K. Karray. User's Mobility Effect on the Performance of Wireless Cellular Networks Serving Elastic Traffic. *Wireless Networks*, 17:247–262, 2011.

[11] X. Lin, R. K. Ganti, P. J. Fleming, and J. G. Andrews. Towards Understanding the Fundamentals of Mobility in Cellular Networks. *IEEE Transactions on Wireless Communications*, 12(4), April 2013.

[12] P. Olivier and A. Simonian. User Performance in Small Cells Networks with Inter-Cell Mobility. arXiv document http://arxiv.org/abs/1605.08353, May 2016.

[13] A. Osseiran et al. Scenarios for 5G Mobile and Wireless Communications: the Vision of the METIS Project. *IEEE Communications Magazine*, 52(5):26–35, 2014.

[14] C. Schindelhauer. Mobility in Wireless Networks. In *Proc. of SOFSEM 2006: Theory and Practice of Computer Science*, Merin, Czech Republic, Jan. 2006.

Delay Efficient Load Balancing Scheme for Component Carrier Selection in Carrier Aggregation in LTE-A

Aditi Gupta
Bharti School of Telecommunication Technology and Management
IIT Delhi, New Delhi 110016, India
gaditi80@gmail.com

Selvamuthu Dharmaraja
Bharti School of Telecommunication Technology and Management
IIT Delhi, New Delhi 110016, India
dharmar@maths.iitd.ac.in

Subrat Kar
Bharti School of Telecommunication Technology and Management
IIT Delhi, New Delhi 110016, India
subrat@ee.iitd.ac.in

ABSTRACT

In Long Term Evolution-Advanced (LTE-A), Carrier Aggregation (CA) allows user to simultaneously transmit and receive data on multiple carriers resulting in increased throughput. Carriers need to be selected to maximize load balancing and the spectral efficiency. In this paper, a load balancing CC selection scheme which can be optimized for the Quality of Service (QoS) required by users is proposed. Feedback fluid queue model has been used to analyze and optimize the performance of the proposed scheme.

Keywords

LTE-A, Carrier Aggregation, Component Carrier, Load Balancing, Disjoint Queue Scheduler, Feedback Fluid Queue

1. INTRODUCTION

The objectives of Long Term Evolution (LTE) are reduced latency, higher user data rate, improved system capacity and coverage [1]. Long Term Evolution-Advanced (LTE-A) targets for 1 Gbps downlink speed for each user. To achieve this, increase in bandwidth is required as, a single carrier of 20MHz in LTE is not sufficient. Carrier Aggregation (CA), a feature of LTE-A aggregates more than one carrier together to provide higher bandwidth. With CA, upto five carriers can be combined together to provide 100 MHz bandwidth. Each carrier is called Component Carrier (CC). The CC can be of two types, Primary Component Carrier (PCC) and Secondary Component Carrier (SCC). PCC is always connected to the user while SCCs can be activated or deactivated. A smart load balancing algorithm for CC selection can be utilized to maintain spectral efficiency and QoS requirements. In this paper, an adaptive load balancing algorithm for LTE-A CA based system is proposed. The proposed algorithm is capable of balancing the load across different carriers and also considering the service requirements of user.

VALUETOOLS 2016, October 25-28, Taormina, Italy

The rest of the paper is organized as follows. In Section 2, research in CC selection methodologies in Radio Resource Management (RRM) framework and the motivation behind this research work are discussed. In Section 3, performance model is proposed and the fluid queue analysis is presented. The performance analysis of the proposed model is numerically illustrated in Section 4. Finally concluding remarks and future work are given in Section 5.

2. RELATED WORK

In RRM framework of LTE-A [2], first, PCC is selected for a user and then depending on traffic load and QoS requirements, SCC's are allotted. CC selection plays an important role in optimizing the system performance with CA. There have been different scheduling algorithms proposed in the literature for CA based systems. In [3], it is proposed to assign maximum CCs to the LTE-A user to achieve maximum efficiency. In [4], least load method is introduced in which the data is assigned to the CC that has the least amount of load. The users however, arrive randomly with different sizes of files for transmission and it is difficult to completely avoid the idle CCs. To overcome this issue, CC coupling schemes have been modeled in [5] [6]. In CC coupling, if any of the CC is in busy state the user can be switched to the other CC. There are two challenges. First, handling the CC switch delay and second, development of the efficient coupling methods for multiple CC.

Lesser scheduling delay is also a required factor, especially for real time data. A scheduler algorithm has been designed to meet the QoS level of real time traffic in [7]. The data arriving will first be classified into Real Time (RT) (e.g., live streaming) and Non Real Time (NRT) (e.g. emails) traffic by a classifier and divided in RT and NRT queue respectively. The algorithm proposed aims at optimizing the system overall throughput while maintaining the required QoS of the RT traffic by providing more RB's (Resource Block) to it. Each RB constitutes 12 sub-carriers providing a bandwidth of 180 KHz. It also corresponds to a sub-frame in time domain, with Transmission Time Interval (TTI) of 1 ms. To best of our knowledge, an efficient scheme for load balancing across different carriers has not been proposed. In real time networks, the scenario is quite dynamic and one carrier may be overloaded while the others idle. On switching the data there would be scheduling delay and overhead incurred which would add to the delay and bandwidth consumed.

Therefore, the scheduling algorithm should be devised such that there is always an even balance across the carriers to maximize the efficiency. Since LTE-A focuses on reducing the packet delay, it is important to keep the scheduling delay minimum. Keeping these requirements in mind, we have proposed a load balancing CC selection scheme that reduces the delay of the network.

3. PROPOSED SCHEME AND ITS PERFORMANCE MODEL

3.1 Load Balancing CC Selection Scheme

The first scheduler has the information of the CCs load and on the basis of the buffer content (the buffer content rises above a certain level), the data should be switched to other carriers. In this paper, we propose a model with two thresholds for CC selection. The two thresholds divide the buffer into three regimes, the rate of the data input to the carrier depending on the regime of the buffer. If the data is above the first threshold denoted by $T^{(1)}$, the rate of the input data should be decreased and routed to another carrier. If the input data rate increases further above the second threshold, denoted by $T^{(2)}$, the input rate turns down to 0, i.e., the data inflow to the carrier is stopped completely. To provide adaptable service according to the class of traffic, the parameters (input rate in different regimes, the two thresholds value) of the model should be adjusted. We have analysed performance model through the feedback fluid queue.

In fluid queue model, instead of individual customers, a continuous entity, fluid is considered. The fluid flows into the a fluid reservoir according to a background Markov process, and flows out dependent on the output rate of the server [8]. Depending on the state of the background process, the input rate to the buffer content changes. Fluid queues are particularly useful in telecommunication systems because the bursts of data is transmitted in smaller sized cells or data packets and can be considered as fluid.

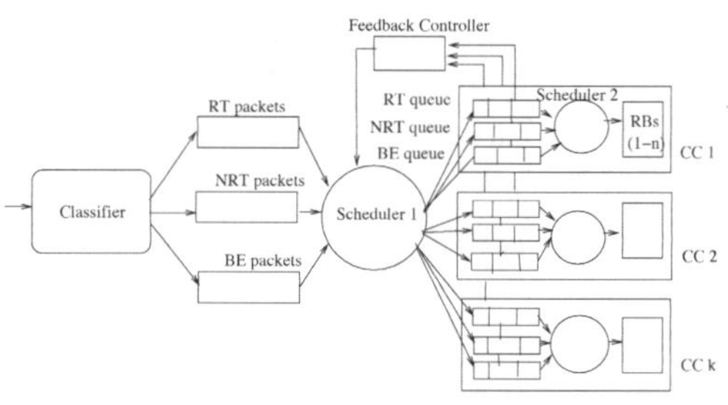

Figure 1: Schematic of the proposed performance model

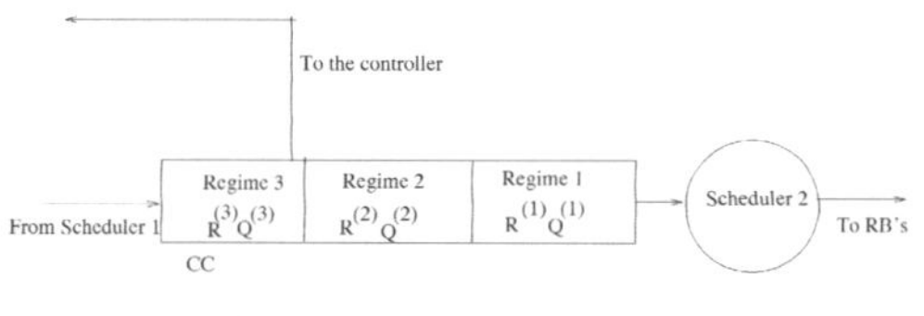

Figure 2: Buffer obtained for corresponding CCs

Feedback fluid queue is the type of fluid queue where the input rate to the buffer content depends on the background process and the behaviour of the background process depends on the content present in the buffer [9]. The meaning of feedback here is completely different from the traditional queueing systems. The feedback in fluid queue refers to control signals being sent to originating process depending on the buffer content unlike sending the data back in the conventional systems. In proposed model the input rate to the CC depends on the content of its buffer so feedback fluid queues are appropriate to model its behaviour.

3.2 Feedback Fluid Queueing Model

A feedback fluid queue with an infinite buffer content and a constant output rate c is considered to analyse the proposed performance model. In the proposed model there wouldn't be any overflows or losses, infinite buffer system can provide good approximations for the finite buffer. Figure 2 shows each CC's buffer corresponding to the users of a particular class of traffic. Let $W(t)$ be the content in the buffer for a class of traffic per CC at time t. The rate at which fluid enters the queue per unit time is dependent on the current state of a background irreducible continuous time Markov chain $\{X(t), t \geq 0\}$, defined on a state space $\{1, 2, \ldots, d\}$ for $d \in D$ where D is the total number of states in the background process.

In this performance model, the background process is the first scheduler that assigns the data to a particular CC. The background process or the first scheduler operates in two states, either it gives data to the CCs buffer (ON state) or it does not (OFF state). The $(i,j)th$ element of the scheduler generator is given by elements of matrix $Q_{ij}^{(k)}(\tilde{Q}_{ij}^{(k)}$ at the threshold) such that the sum of row elements is 0. Q_{ij} for $j = i$ is the transition rate at which the background process jumps from states i to j. $R^{(k)}$ for a regime k is defined as the diagonal matrix with its ith diagonal element be given by $ir - c$, where r is the input rate to the buffer (r_h and 0 in regime 1, r_l and 0 in regime 2) and c is the constant output rate of the fluid outflow from the buffer. The output rate is constant, because some RBs are usually kept reserved for a class of traffic and continuous scheduling for those is carried out. While the output rate is constant, the value of r depends on two parameters. First, on the state of the system, whether it is ON or OFF. If it is ON then the rate depends on the second parameter, i.e., the regime of buffer. The two threshold model divides the buffer into three regimes. The input rate is high (in regime 1) as long as the lower threshold $T^{(1)}$ has not crossed. If that happens input rate is made low (in regime 2). If the higher threshold $T^{(2)}$ is reached the input flow is stopped completely (in regime 3) and the content is let to flow out until comes back to $T^{(2)}$ (in regime 2) wherein the input flow is started again.Thus, on the basis of the amount of fluid, content in the buffer at times t, the system is divided into three different regimes for our model.

For all the regimes, the subsets of D consisting of ON state, OFF state respectively are defined as:

$$D_{+}^{(k)} = \{i \in D | r_i^{(k)} > 0\}$$

$$D_{-}^{(k)} = \{i \in D | r_i^{(k)} < 0\}$$

where $k = 1, 2, 3$ depending on the regime of the buffer content. It is assumed that the input rate is not equal to the output rate for the sake of calculations. The stability condition for the system is given by:

$$\sum_{i=1}^{D} \pi_i^{(k)} r_i^{(k)} < 0$$

where $\pi_i^{(k)}$ is the stationary distribution of the Markov process with generator $Q^{(k)}$.

Now, we find the expression for distribution of the buffer content, to calculate the performance measures like throughput, delay etc. Let $F^{(k)}(x)$ be the equilibrium distribution of the buffer where $k = 1, 2, 3$ depending on the regime of the buffer. i.e.,

$$F^{(k)}(x) = \lim_{t\to\infty} Prob\{W(t) \leq x\}, x \geq 0, k = 1, 2, 3.$$

The differential equations satisfied by the distribution can be expressed in matrix form as [10]:

$$\frac{d\mathbf{F}^{(k)}(x)}{dx} R^{(k)} = \mathbf{F}^{(k)}(x)Q^{(k)} + \mathbf{F}^{(k)}(T^{(k-1)})(\tilde{Q}^{(k-1)} - Q^{(k)}) +$$

$$\mathbf{F}^{(k)}(T^{(k-1)}-)(Q^{(k)} - \tilde{Q}^{(k-1)}) + \ldots + \mathbf{F}^{(1)}(T^{(1)}-)(-Q^{(1)} - \tilde{Q}^{(1)})$$

$$+\mathbf{F}^{(1)}(0)(\tilde{Q}^{(0)} - Q^{(1)}), k = 1, 2, 3. \quad (1)$$

The solution of the above differential equations is given by:

$$\begin{aligned}
\mathbf{F}_i^{(1)}(x) &= a^{(1)} exp[z_{(1)}^{(1)} x]\mathbf{v}_{(1)}^{(1)} + b^{(1)}\mathbf{v}_{(2)}^{(1)} + \mathbf{c}^{(1)} \text{ for regime 1} \\
\mathbf{F}_i^{(2)}(x) &= a^{(2)} exp[z_{(1)}^{(2)} x]\mathbf{v}_{(1)}^{(2)} + b^{(2)}\mathbf{v}_{(2)}^{(1)} + \mathbf{c}^{(2)} \text{ for regime 2} \\
\mathbf{F}_i^{(3)}(x) &= a^{(3)} exp[z_{(1)}^{(3)} x]\mathbf{v}_{(1)}^{(3)} + \mathbf{c}^{(3)} \text{ for regime 3}
\end{aligned}$$

$(z_i^{(k)}, v_i^{(k)})$ are the eigen value vector pair of $z_i^{(k)} v_i^{(k)} R^{(k)} = v_i^{(k)} Q^{(k)}$ and $a^{(k)}, c^{(k)}$ are the unknown coefficients for $k = 1, 2, 3$, $b^{(k)}$ for $k = 1, 2$ and $i = 1, 2$ depending on the regime of the buffer and on-off state of the system. We obtain total eleven unknown coefficients in the solution above whose values can be found by the following conditions:

1. $F_1^{(1)} = 0$. We get one equation from this condition.
2. $F_i(T^{(k)}-) = F_i(T^{(k+1)})$ for $i = 1, 2$ and $k = 1, 2$ This gives four equations from the continuity conditions at the thresholds $T^{(1)}$ and $T^{(2)}$.
3. $0 = \mathbf{c}^{(3)}Q^{(K)} + \mathbf{F}^{(K)}(T^{(K-1)})(\tilde{Q}^{(K-1)} - Q^{(K)}) + \mathbf{F}^{(K)}(T^{(K-1)}-)(Q^{(K)} - \tilde{Q}^{(K-1)}) + \ldots + {} + \mathbf{F}^{(1)}(T^{(1)}-)(-Q^{(1)} - \tilde{Q}^{(1)}) + \mathbf{F}^{(1)}(0)(\tilde{Q}^{(0)} - Q^{(1)})$ will give another equation.
4. $\sum_{i=1}^{3} c^{(i)} = 1$ is the normalization condition.
5. Substitution of the solution of the balance equations for $k = 1, 2$ in equation (1) gives four more equations.

The unique solution for the stationary distribution of the buffer content is obtained by which the performance measures have been calculated in the following section.

4. PERFORMANCE ANALYSIS

In this section, the performance measures are calculated and then some issues are discussed. Is the two threshold models better than the single threshold model, if so then how? What should be the relation between the thresholds to achieve the optimal performance of the model? How should the threshold and rates be varied according to the QoS required? To find the answers to above questions, we plot buffer content, throughput, mean delay with respect to the lower threshold $T^{(1)}$ by keeping different values of $T^{(2)}$. For illustration purpose, the generator matrices and rate vectors are given as follows:

$$Q^{(1)} = Q^{(2)} = Q^{(3)} = \tilde{Q}^{(0)} = \tilde{Q}^{(1)} = \tilde{Q}^{(2)} = \begin{pmatrix} -2 & 2 \\ 1 & -1 \end{pmatrix},$$

$$R^{(1)} = \begin{pmatrix} 15 \\ 0 \end{pmatrix}, R^{(2)} = \begin{pmatrix} 7 \\ 0 \end{pmatrix}.$$

With these values and different values of thresholds, the density distribution is found and then the performance measures are calculated.

4.1 Mean Buffer Content

Mean Buffer content is given by $\int_0^\infty (1 - F(x)dx$. It is plotted in Figure 3 and for increasing values of thresholds the buffer content increases as the accumulations in it increase.

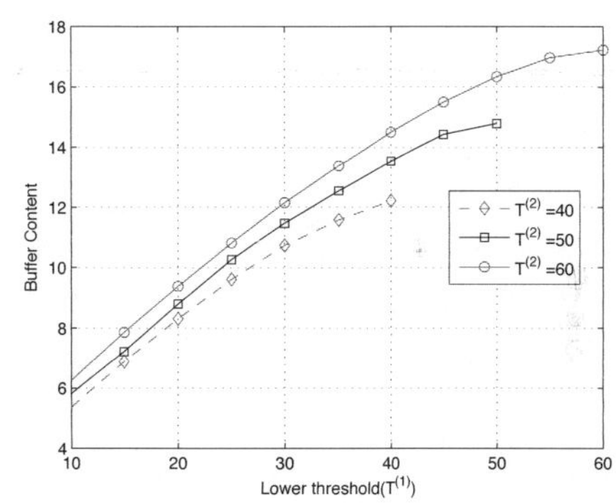

Figure 3: Mean buffer content Vs thresholds

4.2 Mean Throughput

Mean throughput is given by $c * (1 - F(0))$ where $F(0)$ is the density when the buffer content is 0. It is observed from Figure 4 that, for a given value of $T^{(2)}$, the throughput increases as the $T^{(1)}$ increases. Also, when $T^{(1)} = T^{(2)}$, which is the maximum limit for $T^{(1)}$, the throughput becomes maximum. This is also the case of a single threshold as both $T^{(1)} = T^{(2)}$ can be considered there. Hence, it is concluded on comparing with a single threshold model (in which the input is given at a single constant rate), proposed model will give lower throughput.

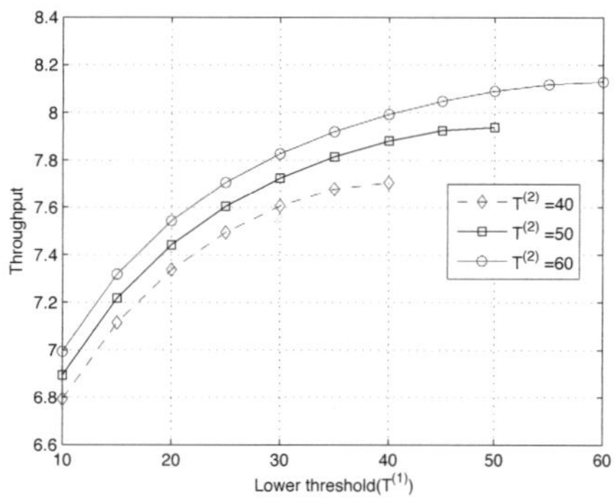

Figure 4: Throughput Vs thresholds

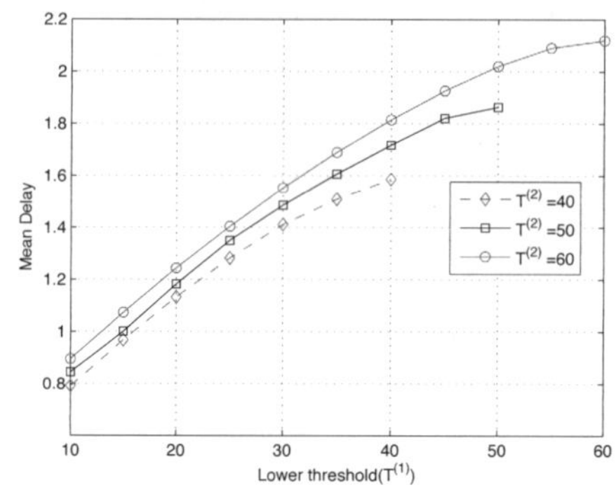

Figure 5: Delay Vs thresholds

4.3 Mean Delay

Mean Delay is given by average buffer content divided by throughput. In Figure 5, mean delay is plotted against the threshold. It is observed that as the two thresholds get closer, delay increase. Delay in a single threshold system would be thus higher than proposed model of two thresholds. Hence, it can be concluded that the proposed model results in lower delay and lower throughput as compared to model where the CC is assigned based on the single threshold. Apart from throughput and delay, number of feedback signals sent to the first scheduler also play role in adjusting the parameters for the incoming traffic. The feedback signals being sent result in causing overheads so it is an important factor while designing the system. Further, it is observed from the above results that, throughput increases when the difference between $T^{(1)}$ and $T^{(2)}$ increases though leading to more feedback signals being sent.

Keeping in mind the delay, throughput and amount of feedback involved in the model which can be designed. The real time data has the minimum delay requirement, thus for those packets, a lesser value higher threshold should be chosen. In other words, the switching of data to other users should be done even for low values of buffer content. The lesser the value of lower threshold is kept, lesser would be the delay. The bigger the difference between the thresholds, the lesser will be the feedback signals sent. The data sent as the best effort on the network such as emails, file sharing which do not require as least as delay possible, thus the other parameters such as throughput can be maximized for this class of data. Since, the data does not require minimal delay, the higher threshold can be kept more in this case. Thus, even a single carrier is sufficient for such data packets.

5. CONCLUSIONS AND FUTURE WORK

In this paper, a delay efficient load balancing scheme for CC selection in CA in LTE-A is proposed. Proposed scheme involving double threshold can be adapted according to different QoS requirement of user. Performance analysis of the proposed model is presented with fluid queue and the measures such as throughput and mean delay are compared with single threshold system. The proposed scheme is capable of balancing load across carriers while keeping the delay lesser than the single threshold model. The impact of this model and implementation on higher layers such as TCP can be studied as future work.

6. REFERENCES

[1] A. Hashimoto, H. Yoshino, and H. Atarashi. Roadmap of IMT-advanced development. *Microwave Magazine, IEEE, 9(4),* 80-88, 2008.

[2] K. I. Pedersen, F. Frederiksen, C. Rosa, H. Nguyen, L. G. U Garcia, and Y. Wang. Carrier aggregation for LTE-advanced: functionality and performance aspects.*Communications Magazine, IEEE, 49(6),* 89-95, 2011.

[3] Y. Wang, K. I. Pedersen , P.E. Mogensen, and T.B. Sorensen. Carrier load balancing methods with bursty traffic for LTE-Advanced systems. In *20th International Symposium on Personal, Indoor and Mobile Radio Communications,* 22-26. IEEE, 2008.

[4] L. Chen, W. Chen, X. Zhang, and D. Yang. Analysis and simulation for spectrum aggregation in LTE-advanced system. In *70th Vehicular Technology Conference Fall (VTC 2009-Fall),* 1-6. IEEE, 2009.

[5] L. Zhang, F. Liu, L. Huang, and W. Wang. Traffic load balance methods in the LTE-Advanced system with carrier aggregation. In *International Conference on Communications, Circuits and Systems (ICCCAS),* 63-67. IEEE, 2010.

[6] Y. Li, L. Zhange, X. Tan, and B. Cao. An advanced spectrum allocation algorithm for the across-cell D2D communication in LTE network with higher throughput. In *China Communications,* to appear, 2016.

[7] Y. L. Chung, L. J. Jang, and Z. Tsai. An efficient downlink packet scheduling algorithm in LTE-Advanced systems with Carrier Aggregation. In *Consumer communications and networking conference (CCNC),* 632-636. IEEE, 2011.

[8] D. Anick, D. Mitra, and M. M. Sondhi. Stochastic theory of a data-handling system with multiple sources. *Bell System Technical Journal, 61(8),* 1871-1894, 1982.

[9] W. R. W. Scheinhardt. *Markov-modulated and feedback fluid queues.* Universiteit Twente, 1998.

[10] M. Mandjes, D. Mitra, and Scheinhardt. Models of network access using feedback fluid queues.*Queueing Systems, 44(4),* 365-398, 2003.

Efficient Computation of the Mean Time to Security Failure in Cyber Physical Systems *

Jose M. Martinez
ECE Department
Duke University
Durham, NC, USA
j.m.martinez@duke.edu

Kishor S. Trivedi
ECE Department
Duke University
Durham, NC, USA
ktrivedi@duke.edu

Benny N. Cheng
Naval Surface Warfare Center
Corona Division
Norco, CA, USA
benny.cheng@navy.mil

ABSTRACT

In this paper, we present a computationally efficient technique for calculating the mean time to security failure (MTTSF) of a mobile cyber physical system (CPS). The CPS analyzed here has been comprehensively studied by other authors using stochastic reward nets (SRN). In simple terms, the CPS is composed of a collection of communicating nodes, which are subject to security attacks. An intrusion detection mechanism is used to detect such attacks based on a voting scheme of some selected nodes. Three sources of failure are considered: successful inside attacks, Byzantine failure condition and energy exhaustion. The numerical solution technique proposed here takes advantage of the acyclic structure of the underlying Markov chain (MC) that captures the CPS dynamics. The proposed approach avoids the generation of the actual state-space of the MC, by performing a direct recursive computation with a space complexity proportional to a fraction of the number of nodes considered, which is orders of magnitude smaller than in previous works. This enables the calculation of the MTTSF for systems composed of several thousands of nodes without using parallelism.

CCS Concepts

•Security and privacy → Mobile and wireless security; Intrusion detection systems; •Computer systems organization → Reliability; •Mathematics of computing → Markov processes;

Keywords

Cyber Physical System, Security, MTTF, Markov Chain, Stochastic Reward Net.

*DISTRIBUTION A. Approved for public release; distribution is unlimited.

VALUETOOLS 2016, October 25-28, Taormina, Italy

1. INTRODUCTION

We revisit a security model developed in [7] which considered a mobile cyber physical system (CPS) consisting of a number of communicating (mobile) nodes, subject to security attacks. The aim of that work was to analyze the reliability (security) of the system by calculating the mean time to security failure (MTTSF) under two main conditions: intrusion attacks and energy exhaustion.

A comprehensive Markov model of such a system was also developed in [7]. Since the state space will increase exponentially as the number of nodes being modeled, the original authors used a high level modeling formalism based on Stochastic Petri Nets known as Stochastic Reward Nets (SRN) [1]. Such a formalism allows a concise specification and automated generation/solution of underlying continuous time Markov chain (CTMC) model. Nevertheless, such a largeness tolerance approach is limited in the size of the system it can handle.

In this paper, we develop an efficient numerical technique for calculating the MTTSF or, equivalently, the MTTF (mean time to failure) from the reliability context [4], by exploiting the special structure of the underlying continuous time Markov chain (CTMC). We propose a scalable solution to the original model, in order to gain a tremendous advantage in time and space required for the computation. We note, to the best of our knowledge, that algorithms for the transient state probability computation for acyclic CTMC have been published [6] [5] [8], but algorithms for the computation of MTTF have not.

The rest of the paper is organized as follows. Section 2 gives a brief description of the cyber phyisical system under study. Section 3 presents a model of the system using stochastic reward nets (SRN). Section 4 describes the underlying continuous time Markov chain generated from the SRN model. Section 5 develops the fundamentals of the calculations of the MTTSF. Section 6 presents the recursion scheme for calculating the MTTSF, the main result of this paper. Section 7 describes the computational and numerical aspects of the new approach. Finally, Section 8 presents the conclusions and outlines some future research.

2. CYBER PHYSICAL SYSTEM

The CPS reference model, in general terms, is based on a real-world architecture system [11], which is composed of a certain number of mobile nodes (128 in the original paper). Each node uses sensors for localization, ranging its neighbors (periodically), and for measuring and communicating any detectable phenomena nearby.

The intrusion detection system functionality is distributed to all nodes in the system for intrusion and fault tolerance. A control node manages the mobile sensors (nodes) and is able to respond to the sometimes changing conditions (e.g., different types and strength of attacks). This control unit is considered fault and intrusion free.

The intrusion detection mechanism involves two main steps/parts: 1) the selection of a group of detectors and 2) a time interval for the periodic invocation of the mechanism. In broad terms, each node exchanges information about its location and identification periodically. A coordinator is chosen among the neighbor nodes, then this node selects m detectors randomly that will participate in the voting procedure (including itself). Finally, a node is considered as good or bad based on the majority vote.

The attack model described here considers a node capture attack which involve taking control of a good node by deceiving authentication and turning it into a bad node that will be able to generate inside attacks. The attackers primary objective is to cause impairment failure by performing persistent, random, or insidious attacks. To prevent these types of attacks, some intrusion detection mechanism is necessary. Furthermore, any detection mechanism is subject to false alarms; therefore, some level of tolerance is necessary within this mechanism.

The Byzantine fault model [3] is used to define a security failure; that is, if 1/3 or more of the nodes are compromised, then the system fails. The reason is that once the system contains more than 1/3 captured nodes, it is impossible to reach a consensus, therefore causing a security failure.

A system (security) failure can occur due to a security condition or due to an energy-exhaustion condition. In terms of security failure, two conditions are considered: 1) a Byzantine failure condition [3]; and 2) an impairment failure condition. A Byzantine failure occurs when one-third or more of the nodes have been captured by the attacker, causing the system to fail. On the other hand, an impairment failure occurs when the system is prevented from working properly due to undetected compromised nodes performing successful attacks. In terms of energy-exhaustion condition, the periodic sensing procedure (part of the intrusion detection mechanism) plays an important role, besides the normal power consumption of the nodes, in causing a system failure due to nodes running out of energy.

Our focus in this paper is to calculate the expected time until the whole system fails, the MTTSF, assuming that all nodes are working properly at the beginning of the analysis.

3. STOCHASTIC REWARD NET MODEL

Following the development in [7], Figure 1 shows the SRN model that describes the behavior of the system under analysis, where the different variables are defined as follows: N_G is the number of good nodes (nodes that have not been captured by an attacker); N_B is the number of nodes that have been turned bad; N_E is the number of evicted nodes; i.e., nodes that have been detected as bad ones by the intrusion detection mechanism; N_F is a binary variable, indicating with 1 a security failure and with 0 that there is no failure of that type (yet); and N_D is a binary variable that indicates with 1 a system energy exhaustion failure and with 0 that there is still energy available. The definition of the transition firing rates in term of the parameters of the system are given in Table 1.

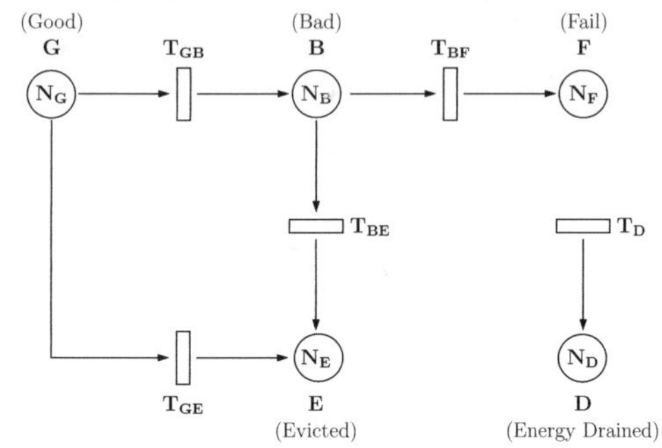

Figure 1: SRN model

Transition Name	Rate
T_{GB}	$N_G\,\lambda_c$
T_{GE}	$N_G\,\dfrac{P_{\text{fp}}}{T_{\text{IDS}}}$
T_{BF}	$N_B\,p_a\,\lambda_f$
T_{BE}	$N_B\,\dfrac{(1-P_{\text{fn}})}{T_{\text{IDS}}}$
T_D	$\dfrac{1}{N_{\text{IDS}}\,T_{\text{IDS}}}$

Table 1: SRN transition firing rates

The dynamics of the system is captured by the following SRN input parameters:

- The initial state of the system is given by the condition that all nodes are good; i.e., $N_G = N$ (and $N_B = N_D = N_E = N_F = 0$).
- Transition T_{GB} models the capture of a good node by an attacker. Transition T_{BE} models a bad node being detected correctly and evicted. Transition T_{GE} models a good node being detected as a bad one and being evicted (false positive detection).
- A capture rate λ_c characterizes the process that a good node is being compromised; therefore the firing rate of T_{GB} is given by $N_G\lambda_c$. A token in place B (*bad*) means that a node is compromised but is still undetected.
- A transition from place B (*bad*) to E (*evicted*) is characterized with a rate $N_B\,\frac{1-P_{fn}}{T_{IDS}}$ which considers a false negative probability (P_{fn}) of the voting-based intrusion detection mechanism. This transition models the eviction of a detected bad node. The intrusion detection procedure is carried out periodically, with period T_{IDS}.
- A transition from place G (*good*) to E (*evicted*) has a firing rate $N_G\,\frac{P_{fp}}{T_{IDS}}$ which accounts for the probability (P_{fp}) of having a false positive detection by the voting-based mechanism. That node will be taken out (evicted) from the system.
- When a node is captured, it will perform attacks with a probability p_a. The success of such attacks (from

N_B compromised nodes) is modeled through the rate λ_f. Consequently, the transition T_{BF} has a firing rate $N_B\, p_a\, \lambda_f$ leading the system to be irreversibly compromised (placing a token in F).

- A transition from place D (*energy drained*) accounts for the exhaustion of the system energy. The transition rate is given by $\frac{1}{N_{IDS}\, T_{IDS}}$, where N_{IDS} is the number of intrusion detection intervals completed before exhausting its energy, due to energy consuming tasks performed by the voting-based intrusion detection mechanism.

To complete the SRN model, we need to consider the conditions that induce a system failure (an undetected bad node performing an attack, a Byzantine failure or a energy drained condition); i.e.,

- When the number of bad nodes (N_B) is at least 1/3 of the total number of nodes ($N_B + N_G$), or equivalently $N_G \leq 2N_B$, the system fails because of a Byzantine failure. This condition is modeled by disabling all transitions in the SRN, under these conditions. SRN has a feature known as halting condition to be able to indicate this easily.
- The voting-based intrusion detection mechanism works properly by selecting m nodes; therefore a system (security) failure will occur if the number of good nodes and undetected bad nodes is smaller than m; i.e., $N_G + N_B < m$. This condition can be also modeled by disabling all transitions in the SRN under this condition.
- A token in place F means that a system failure occurred due to a captured node performing a successful attack.
- A token in place D means that enough energy was drained from the system to cause a system failure.

As was described in Section 2, a false alarm can be triggered by the security detection mechanism, which is characterized by probabilities P_{fp} and P_{fn}. The system false-positive, P_{fp}, and system false-negative, P_{fn}, detection probabilities are two characteristics of the intrusion detection mechanism that account for the possibility of detecting a good node as a bad one or a bad node as a good one, respectively. They both depend on the proportion of bad nodes in the system at the moment of performing the majority voting. Equations (1), (2), (3), and (4) below describe these probabilities. We show here the expressions allowing the calculation of these probabilities, in order to illustrate the complexity involved in their computation, but we have left out the detailed explanation of the terms since it is out of the scope of this paper. We refer to the reader to [7] for a deeper description of the expressions:

$$P_{\text{fp}}(N_G, N_B) = \sum_{i=0}^{\lfloor (m-1)/2 \rfloor} A(N_G, N_B, p_a, m, i) + \sum_{j=0}^{\lfloor (m-1)/2 \rfloor} B(N_G, N_B, p_a, m, j, p_{\text{fp}})\,, \tag{1}$$

$$P_{\text{fn}}(N_G, N_B) = \sum_{i=0}^{\lfloor (m-1)/2 \rfloor} A(N_G, N_B, p_a, m, i) + \sum_{j=0}^{\lfloor (m-1)/2 \rfloor} B(N_G, N_B, p_a, m, j, p_{\text{fn}})\,, \tag{2}$$

where $A(\cdot)$ and $B(\cdot)$ are given by:

$$A(N_G, N_B, p_a, m, i) = \frac{\binom{N_B p_a}{\lceil (m+1)/2 \rceil + i}\binom{N_G + N_B(1-p_a)}{m - \lceil (m+1)/2 \rceil - i}}{\binom{N_G + N_B}{m}}\,, \tag{3}$$

$$B(N_G, N_B, p_a, m, j, p_{\text{x}}) = \binom{N_B p_a}{j} \cdot \sum_{k=\lceil (m+1)/2 \rceil - j}^{m-j} \left[\frac{\binom{N_G + N_B(1-p_a)}{k}\binom{N_G + N_B(1-p_a) - k}{m-j-k}}{\binom{N_G+N_B}{m}} \cdot p_{\text{x}}^k (1-p_{\text{x}})^{m-j-k} \right], \tag{4}$$

where p_x is replaced with p_{fp} or p_{fn}, accordingly; and p_{fp} and p_{fn} are the per-host false-positive and per-host false-negative probabilities of the intrusion detection system.

Note that the calculation of P_{fn} and P_{fp} gets very complex as the number of nodes increases. Infinite precision software (e.g., Mathematica [12]) is currently used for the implementation of these expressions. In Section 7, we will revisit this issue in terms of the overall computation of the MTTSF.

4. UNDERLYING STOCHASTIC PROCESS

The underlying stochastic process of the SRN given in Figure 1 is a continuous time Markov chain (CTMC). Considering a state definition given by the 5-tuple (N_G, N_B, N_E, N_F, N_D), a general description of the state transition diagram corresponding to the CTMC is given in Figure 2, where the failure states (absorbing) due to a captured node performing a successful attack and due to energy exhaustion are shown with thick rectangles, and where $\gamma_e = \frac{P_{fp}}{T_{IDS}}$, $\gamma_{be} = \frac{(1-P_{fn})}{T_{IDS}}$, $\gamma_f = p_a \lambda_f$, and $\gamma_d = \frac{1}{N_{IDS}\, T_{IDS}}$. Note that γ_e and γ_{be} are state dependent through the probabilities P_{fp} and P_{fn}, respectively.

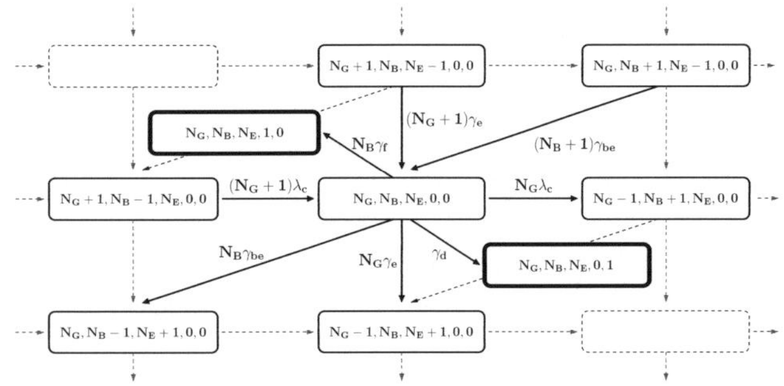

Figure 2: State transition diagram for state $(N_G, N_B, N_E, N_F, N_D)$. Absorbing states are shown with a thick border

In order to graphically describe the Byzantine condition and the minimum number of nodes required for the voting-based mechanism, we will consider a small running example given by a total number of nodes, $N = 8$, and the number of nodes necessary for the voting-based intrusion detection mechanism, $m = 5$. The resulting Markov chain state diagram is shown in Figure 3.

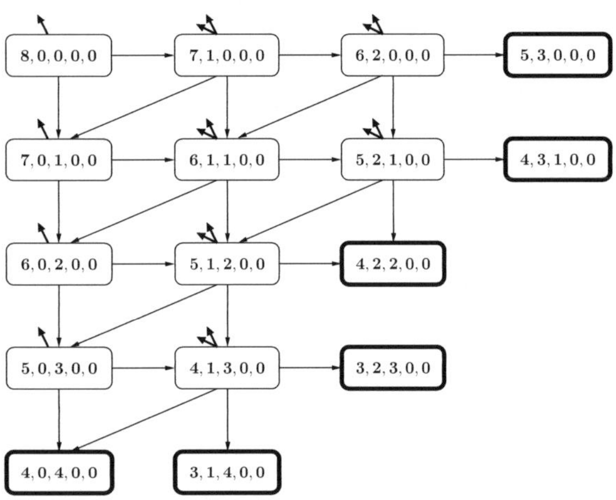

Figure 3: Example of underlying Markov chain for N = 8 and m = 5

For purposes of clarity, in Figure 3 we left out those absorbing states corresponding to the conditions given when $N_F = 1$ or $N_D = 1$ from the SRN model, although the transitions to those states are shown with small thick arrows coming out from the non-absorbing states. Note that in the case of states corresponding to $N_B = 0$ there is only one of such transition since only the possibility of $N_D = 1$ is present. The remaining absorbing states are shown with a thick border and correspond to the Byzantine failure condition ($N_G \leq 2\,N_B$), which are shown on the right hand side of Figure 3, and to the condition of having a number of detectors smaller than necessary for performing the voting-based intrusion detection ($N_G + N_B < m$), which are shown on the bottom of Figure 3.

Next, we will consider a simplification of the Markov chain by collecting all the absorbing states into just one, denoting the system failure condition. This will allow us to facilitate our analysis in order to compute the MTTSF. Figure 4 shows how this state space reduction is carried out in the running example.

Examining Figure 4 we can conclude, without loss of generality, that the underlying stochastic process is an acyclic Markov chain. In what follows we will use the acyclic characteristic of this CTMC to devise a recursive scheme for evaluating the MTTSF.

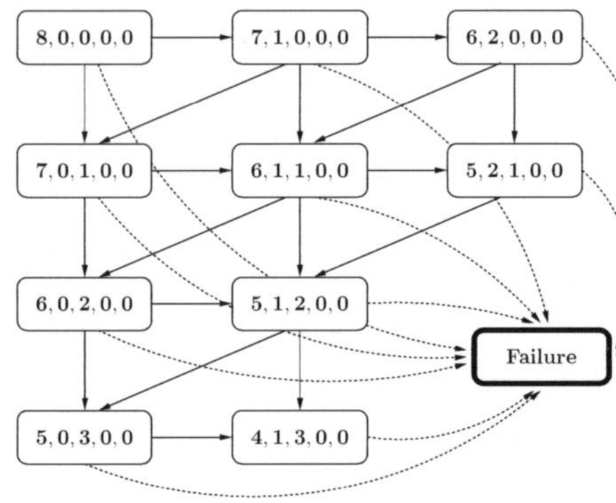

Figure 4: Reduced Markov chain for N = 8 and m = 5 (one absorbing state)

5. MEAN TIME TO SECURITY FAILURE

In Section 4, we saw that the underlying stochastic process is an acyclic Markov chain. Let us consider now a topological sort [2] of the states given by traversing the chain (see Figure 4) from top to bottom and from left to right and leaving the "Failure" state (absorbing) for last; i.e., in our running example, the ordered set $\{(8,0,0,0,0), (7,1,0,0,0), (6,2,0,0,0), (7,0,1,0,0), (6,1,1,0,0), (5,2,1,0,0), (6,0,2,0,0), (5,1,2,0,0), (5,0,3,0,0), (4,1,3,0,0), (\text{Failure})\}$ corresponds to the state numbering from 1 to 11. It is easy to see that the underlying infinitesimal generator matrix is upper triangular, as is shown in Figure 5, where the nonzero entries are shaded. This implies that the calculation of the MTTSF can be greatly simplified, as we will explain below.

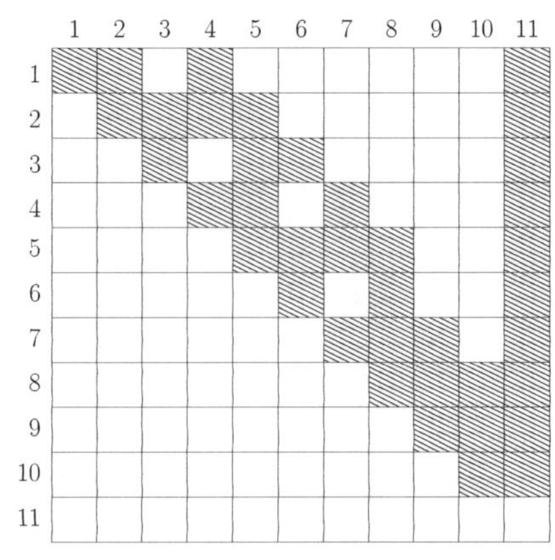

Figure 5: Infinitesimal generator matrix for N = 8 and m = 5 (with one absorbing state)

The calculation of the MTTSF is equivalent to the one of MTTF (concept from reliability analysis) applied to the security context. In [10] a MTTF computation method of a CTMC with failure states considered as absorbing states is shown. We use that result here to derive our efficient recursion scheme for the evaluation of MTTSF.

Let $\mathcal{X} = \{\mathcal{X}(t), t \geq 0\}$ be a CTMC with finite state space $\mathcal{S} = \{1, 2, \ldots, |\mathcal{S}|\}$. Let $\mathbf{Q} = [q_{i,j}]_{i,j \in \mathcal{S}}$ be the infinitesimal generator matrix that characterizes $\mathcal{X}$, where $q_{i,j}$, with $i \neq j$, denotes the transition rate from state i to state j, and where $q_{i,i} = -\sum_{j \neq i} q_{i,j}$. Let $L_i(t)$ be the expected cumulative time that the CTMC spends in state i during the interval $(0, t]$. Let $\vec{L}(t)$ be the row vector such that $\vec{L}(t) = [L_i(t)]_{i \in \mathcal{S}}$. Then, the following system of differential equations holds:

$$\frac{d}{dt}\vec{L}(t) = \vec{L}(t)\,\mathbf{Q} + \vec{\pi}(0)\ , \tag{5}$$

where $\vec{\pi}(0) = [\pi_i(0)]_{i \in \mathcal{S}}$ is the initial probability vector of $\mathcal{X}$.

Next, consider that the state space $\mathcal{S}$ is partitioned in two sets: the set $\mathcal{T}$ of transient (non-absorbing) states and the set $\mathcal{A}$ of absorbing states. Let $\hat{\mathbf{Q}}$ be a submatrix of $\mathbf{Q}$ and let $\hat{\vec{\pi}}(0)$ be a subvector of $\vec{\pi}(0)$, where their elements correspond to states in $\mathcal{T}$ (in our running example, $\mathcal{T} = \{1, \ldots, 10\}$, see Figure 5). Then, by defining $\tau_i = \lim_{t \to \infty} L_i(t)$ and assuming that this limit exists for $i \in \mathcal{T}$, the following result can be deduced from Eq. (5):

$$\hat{\vec{\tau}}\,\hat{\mathbf{Q}} = -\hat{\vec{\pi}}(0)\ , \tag{6}$$

where $\hat{\vec{\tau}} = [\hat{\tau}_i]$, with $i = \{1, \ldots, |\mathcal{T}|\}$, is a subvector of $\vec{\tau}$ where its elements correspond to states in $\mathcal{T}$. Consequently, the MTTF can be obtained as follows:

$$MTTF = \sum_{i \in \mathcal{T}} \tau_i \tag{7}$$

Computation of Eq. (6) is carried out (usually) by using iterative methods (e.g., Jacobi, Gauss-Seidel, SOR) [9]. One of the key results of this paper is the simplification of the computation of $\hat{\vec{\tau}}$ when $\hat{\mathbf{Q}}$ is upper triangular, as is the case of the CTMC we consider here.

Consider $\hat{\mathbf{Q}} = \hat{\mathbf{D}} + \hat{\mathbf{U}}$, with $\hat{\mathbf{D}}$ being a diagonal matrix and $\hat{\mathbf{U}}$ being an strictly upper triangular matrix. Then, Eq. (6) can be written as:

$$\hat{\vec{\tau}}\,(\hat{\mathbf{D}} + \hat{\mathbf{U}}) = -\hat{\vec{\pi}}(0) \tag{8}$$

Reordering terms, we obtain:

$$\hat{\vec{\tau}}\,\hat{\mathbf{D}} = -\hat{\vec{\tau}}\,\hat{\mathbf{U}} - \hat{\vec{\pi}}(0) \tag{9}$$

Reuniting to get $\hat{\vec{\tau}}$ on the left hand side of Eq. (9):

$$\hat{\vec{\tau}} = -\hat{\vec{\tau}}\,\hat{\mathbf{U}}\,\hat{\mathbf{D}}^{-1} - \hat{\vec{\pi}}(0)\,\hat{\mathbf{D}}^{-1} \tag{10}$$

Assuming that $\hat{\pi}_1(0) = 1$ (i.e., all N nodes are working properly initially), we can derive a recursive formulation for the computation of $\hat{\tau}_i$ by writing Eq. (10) in scalar form, i.e.,

$$\hat{\tau}_i = \begin{cases} \dfrac{1}{-\hat{q}_{1,1}}\ , & i = 1\ , \\[2ex] \dfrac{1}{-\hat{q}_{i,i}} \displaystyle\sum_{j=1}^{i-1} \hat{\tau}_j\,\hat{q}_{j,i}\ , & 1 < i \leq |\mathcal{T}|\ . \end{cases} \tag{11}$$

Notice that the terms involved in the calculation of $\hat{\tau}_i$ depend only on: 1) the input and output rates of the state i, and 2) the $\hat{\tau}_j$s associated to states j with a direct arc to state i.

Next, it will be shown that this recursive scheme for computing $\hat{\tau}_i$ will allow us to devise an efficient calculation approach for the MTTSF without requiring the generation of the whole state-space of the underlying SRN, allowing savings of orders of magnitude in space and time, thus making the computation of MTTSF for CPS with thousands of nodes feasible.

6. MTTSF RECURSIVE COMPUTATION

Following the same topological structure of the running example (Figure 4), the graph-based description of Eq. (11) is depicted in Figure 6, where each cell corresponds to a value $\hat{\tau}_i$, expressed now in terms of N_E and N_B, as $\hat{\tau}_{N_E,N_B}$. The computation proceeds by levels (given by N_E) and in each level the calculation is performed from left to right (from $N_B = 0$ to $N_B = \lceil (N - N_E)/3 - 1 \rceil$. Each $\hat{\tau}_{N_E,N_B}$ depends on some previous values, indicated with directed arcs. The output transitions, from each cell to the (unique) absorbing state, are shown with an arc pointing to a small shaded circle.

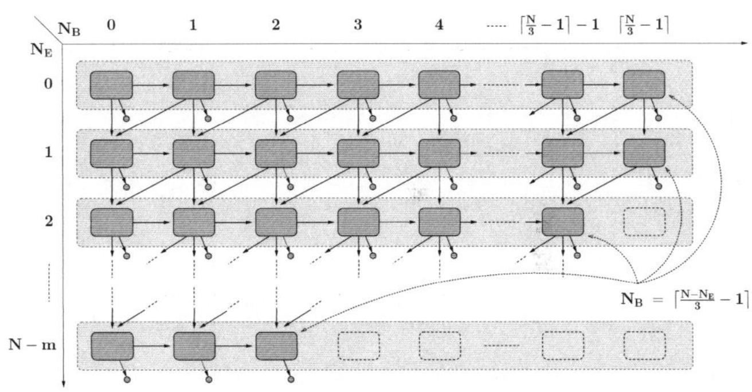

Figure 6: Recurrence graph for the calculation of $\hat{\tau}_i$ in terms of coordinates N_E and N_B.

Based on the above recurrence description, the MTTSF formula in Eq. (7) and the corresponding $\hat{\tau}_i$ recursion formulation given in Eq. (11) can be both rewritten in terms of $\hat{\tau}_{N_E,N_B}$:

$$MTTSF = \sum_{N_E=0}^{N-m} \sum_{N_B=0}^{\left\lceil \frac{N-N_E}{3} - 1 \right\rceil} \hat{\tau}_{N_E,N_B}\ , \tag{12}$$

where the index of the innermost summation moves within a level (fixed value of N_E) and the index of the outermost one moves along the N_E values (from 0 to $N - m$).

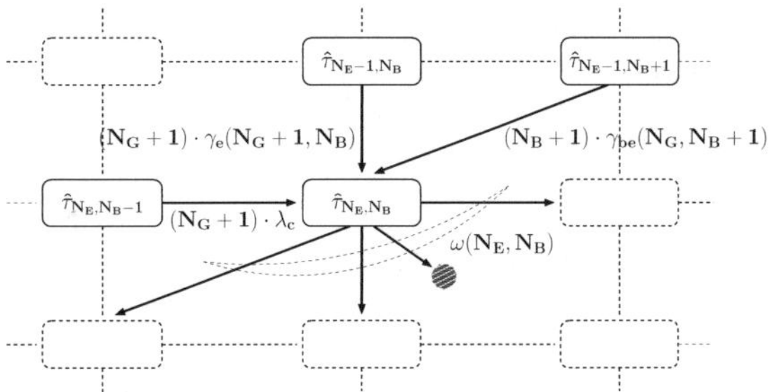

Figure 7: Detailed $\hat{\tau}_{N_E,N_B}$ evaluation

Recalling that $N_G = N - N_B - N_E$ and considering the detailed description of the computation of $\hat{\tau}_{N_E,N_B}$ in Figure 7 (where γ_e and γ_{be} depend on the current state through the current values of N_G and N_B), the following recursive expression for $\hat{\tau}_{N_E,N_B}$ can be easily obtained:

$$
\begin{aligned}
\hat{\tau}_{N_E,N_B} = {} & \frac{1}{\omega(N_E,N_B)} \\
& \cdot \Big[(N_G+1)\cdot\gamma_e(N_G+1,N_B)\cdot\hat{\tau}_{N_E-1,N_B} \\
& + (N_B+1)\cdot\gamma_{be}(N_G,N_B+1)\cdot\hat{\tau}_{N_E-1,N_B+1} \\
& + (N_G+1)\cdot\lambda_c\cdot\hat{\tau}_{N_E,N_B-1} \Big]
\end{aligned}
\quad (13)
$$

where the accompanying factor of $\hat{\tau}_{N_E-1,N_B}$, $\hat{\tau}_{N_E-1,N_B+1}$ and $\hat{\tau}_{N_E,N_B-1}$ are the transition rates from states $(N_G+1, N_B, N_E-1, 0, 0)$, $(N_G, N_B+1, N_E-1, 0, 0)$ and $(N_G+1, N_B-1, N_E, 0, 0)$, respectively; and $\omega(N_E, N_B)$ corresponds to the transition rate out from state $(N_G, N_E, N_B, 0, 0)$, see Figure 2, i.e.,

$$
\begin{aligned}
\omega(N_E,N_B) = {} & N_G\cdot\gamma_e(N_G,N_B) + N_G\cdot\lambda_c \\
& + N_B\cdot\gamma_{be}(N_G,N_B) + N_B\cdot\gamma_f + \gamma_d
\end{aligned}
\quad (14)
$$

Finally, the boundary conditions necessary to complete this recursion are:

$$
\hat{\tau}_{N_E,-1} = 0, \quad \hat{\tau}_{-1,N_B} = 0, \quad \hat{\tau}_{N_E,\lceil \frac{N-N_E}{3}-1\rceil+1} = 0. \quad (15)
$$

Equations (12), (13), (14) and (15) define an efficient computation approach for calculating the MTTSF of the CPS model given in Figure 1, without generating the underlying CTMC.

7. COMPUTATIONAL COMPLEXITY

Computing the MTTSF involves calculating all the $\hat{\tau}_{N_E,N_B}$ within the different levels (N_E) as depicted in Figure 6. It can be easily seen that this can be accomplished by only using two arrays of size $\lceil N/3\rceil$. The total number of levels that has to be computed is $N - m$, and in each level the actual number of $\hat{\tau}_{N_E,N_B}$ that must be calculated is $\lceil (N-N_E)/3\rceil$. Consequently, the approximate total number of $\hat{\tau}_i$ terms needed to be computed is $(\lceil N/3\rceil + \lceil m/3\rceil)(N-m)/2$.

The calculations involved within each $\hat{\tau}_{N_E,N_B}$ include the factors P_{fn} and P_{fp}, which get very complex as the number of nodes N and detectors m increase. In our algorithm implementation we have used infinite precision software (e.g., Mathematica). A recursion scheme for calculating P_{fn} and P_{fp} can be envisioned using the state transition diagram structure. This will be done in the future. Note that the complexity in calculating these factors stays the same as with the original paper.

Our technique yields exactly the same results as with the original SRN and the solution technique used in [7]. That is, there is no sacrifice in accuracy in achieving the scalability.

Furthermore, we must emphasize that our technique completely avoids the generation and storage of the infinitesimal generator matrix **Q**. Consequently, we also avoid the application of an iterative solution technique such as Jacobi, Gauss-Seidel or SOR, for solving the linear system given in Eq. (6), as it was done in the original paper, where the number of equations could be in the order of millions.

The enormous savings in space can be appreciated in Table 2 where the state-space cardinality in the original paper is compared with the space requirements of our recursion. The first column shows the number of nodes considered, the second and third columns show the number of states and transitions generated by the SRN in Figure 1, respectively, and the fourth column shows the total size of the vectors (arrays) that are needed during the whole computation of the recursion. It can be easily appreciated that using the original approach (solving the SRN) imposes a great demand on memory resources when just a few thousands of nodes are analyzed. On the other hand, with our approach, the memory requirement are upper-bounded by the number of nodes, making it possible to analyze systems with thousands of nodes in a single machine.

N	No. States (approx.)	No. Transitions (approx.)	Recursion (No. values)
100	5 000	8 350	67
200	20 000	33 400	134
500	125 000	208 700	334
1 000	500 000	835 000	667
2 000	2 000 000	3 340 000	1 334
5 000	12 500 000	20 875 000	3 334
10 000	50 000 000	83 500 000	6 667
20 000	200 000 000	334 000 000	13 334
50 000	1 250 000 000	2 087 500 000	33 334

Table 2: No. States/No. Transitions as a function of N in the original SRN, compared with the storage needed for the proposed recursion

Table 3 shows the computation time for several combinations of number of nodes (N) and number of detectors (m), considering that the parameters used (for the rest of the variables) are the same as in the original paper. We must note that the computation time greatly depends on the calculation of P_{fn} and P_{fp}, a cost that is inherited from the original paper, keeping open the possibility for future improvement since it was not the focus of our contribution. The implementation of the algorithm was done completely using Mathematica [12].

8. CONCLUSIONS

In this paper, we developed a numerical approach to efficiently compute the mean time to system failure of a cy-

N	Time (sec)	
	m = 3	m = 5
1 000	3	4
5 000	83	90
10 000	349	370
20 000	1 388	1 981
50 000	8 796	9 247

Table 3: Computation time of the implemented recursion in Mathematica (2.8GHz Intel Core i5)

ber physical system composed of a network of communicating/sensing mobile nodes, where a system (security) failure is caused by either a security intrusion attack or due to energy exhaustion.

The numerical technique presented here takes advantage of the underlying structure of the continuous-time Markov chain that captures the CPS behavior. It computes the MTTSF precisely and recursively, without generating the actual Markov chain, allowing enormous savings in space and time compared to the original procedure based on modeling and solving an SRN, where a linear system of equations (with millions of equations, eventually) has to be solved in order to compute such a measure. The approach presented here allow us to calculate the MTTSF for CPS models consisting on thousands of nodes using a single machine and with just a few lines of code.

Our efficient numerical technique takes the computation of the MTTF (from the reliability context) and adapts it for the case of an acyclic Markov chain with an upper triangular infinitesimal generator matrix.

In terms of future work, one task considers extending the MTTF calculation technique in order to include general acyclic Markov chains; i.e., not necessarily with an upper triangular infinitesimal generator matrix. Another task considers the efficient computation of the false alarm probabilities P_{fn} and P_{fp}, using a recursion scheme that also takes advantage of the state transition diagram structure of the underlying Markov chain. And another direction of improvement would be to consider other type of security failure condition different from the Byzantine condition.

9. ACKNOWLEDGMENTS

We thank Robert Mitchell, Ph.D., from Sandia National Laboratories, for early discussions related to his original work.

This research was partially supported by US NSF grant number CNS-1523994, by US Navy NEEC grant number N00174-16-C-0036, by IBM under a faculty grant, and by NATO under Science for Peace project number 984425.

10. REFERENCES

[1] G. Ciardo, A. Blakemore, P. F. Chimento, J. K. Muppala, and K. S. Trivedi. Automated generation and analysis of markov reward models using stochastic reward nets. In C. D. Meyer and R. J. Plemmons, editors, *Linear Algebra, Markov Chains, and Queueing Models*, pages 145{191. Springer New York, New York, NY, 1993.

[2] T. H. Cormen, C. E. Leiserson, R. L. Rivest, and C. Stein. *Introduction to Algorithms*. The MIT Press, 3rd edition, 2009.

[3] L. Lamport, R. Shostak, and M. Pease. The byzantine generals problem. *ACM Transactions on Programming Languages and Systems (TOPLAS)*, 4(3):382{401, July 1982.

[4] E. E. Lewis. *Introduction to Reliability Engineering*. Wiley, 2nd edition, 1996.

[5] C. Lindemann, M. Malhotra, and K. S. Trivedi. Numerical methods for reliability evaluation of Markov closed fault-tolerant systems. *IEEE Transactions on Reliability*, 44(4):694{704, December 1995.

[6] R. A. Marie, A. L. Reibman, and K. S. Trivedi. Transient solution of acyclic Markov chains. *Performance Evaluation*, 7(3):175{194, August 1987.

[7] R. Mitchell and I.-R. Chen. Effect of intrusion detection and response on reliability of cyber physical systems. *IEEE Transactions on Reliability*, 62(1):199{210, March 2013.

[8] H. Nabli. Performability measure for acyclic Markovian models. *Computers & Mathematics with Applications*, 35(8):41{51, 1998.

[9] W. J. Stewart. *Introduction to the Numerical Solution of Markov Chains*. Princeton University Press, 1994.

[10] K. S. Trivedi. *Probability and Statistics with Reliability, Queuing, and Computer Science Applications*. Wiley, 2nd edition, 2001.

[11] US Department of Homeland Security. BAA-09-02 geospatial location accountability and navigation system for emergency responders (GLANSER), 2009.

[12] Wolfram Research, Inc. Mathematica, Version 10.4. Champaign, Illinois, 2016. http://www.wolfram.com.

Stationary solutions of discrete and continuous Petri nets with priorities*

Xavier Allamigeon
INRIA and CMAP, École polytechnique, CNRS
xavier.allamigeon@inria.fr

Vianney Bœuf
INRIA and CMAP, École polytechnique, CNRS, École des Ponts ParisTech, Brigade de sapeurs-pompiers de Paris
vianney.boeuf@inria.fr

Stéphane Gaubert
INRIA and CMAP, École polytechnique, CNRS
stephane.gaubert@inria.fr

ABSTRACT

We study a continuous dynamics for a class of Petri nets involving priorities. We initially studied this class in [1] in the discrete setting, motivated by an application to the performance analysis of an emergency call center. In the discrete setting, limit time-periodic behaviors can occur. They may lead to asymptotic throughputs different from the affine stationary solutions of the dynamics, a pathology which motivates our study of a continuous version of the dynamics.

In a Petri net equipped with a continuous dynamics, the circulation of tokens is fluid, so that the dynamics can be represented by a system of ordinary differential equations or differential inclusions. Here, we address the situation in which the routing is specified by priority or preselection rules which are independent of the processing rates. To do so, it is convenient to attach times to places, instead of attaching firing rates to transitions, as in the standard continuous model, see [3].

The continuous dynamics of our class of Petri nets is piecewise linear, discontinuous. The nonlinearity arises from minimization operations corresponding to synchronization and priority configurations. We show that the continuous dynamics can be expressed in terms of *policies*. A policy is a map associating with every transition one of its upstream places. In this way, the dynamics of the Petri net can be written as an infimum of the dynamics of subnets induced by the different policies. The policies reaching the infimum indicate the places which are bottleneck in the Petri net. On any time interval in which a fixed policy reaches the infimum, the dynamics reduces to a linear dynamics.

Our main theorem provides a characterization of the stationary solutions in terms of the policies of the net. This allows us to set up a correspondence between the (ultimately affine) stationary solutions of the discrete dynamics that were described in [1] and the stationary solutions of the continuous dynamics. In particular, the stationary throughputs are proven to be the same for well-chosen initial markings.

An important problem is to relate the stationary flow to the initial marking. Difficulties arise from the nonmonotonicity of the dynamics (due to the priority routing rule). We present a partial result relating the continuous stationary solutions to the initial marking of the Petri net, under the assumption that the trajectory is associated with a constant policy. This result requires the semi-simplicity of the eigenvalue 0 of a matrix depending on the policy.

We finally provide some numerical simulations of the continuous dynamics. Our case of study is a model of emergency call center with two hierarchical levels for handling calls, taken from [1]. On this Petri net, numerical experimentations are led using the SpaceEx verification tool [2], which provides certified bounds on the trajectory of hybrid automata. Results illustrate the convergence of the trajectory towards the stationary solution, so that the pathological behavior observed in the discrete setting vanishes. We leave it for further work to see under which generality the convergence to the stationary solution can be established.

CCS Concepts

•**Networks** → *Network performance modeling;* •**Theory of computation** → *Timed and hybrid models;*

Keywords

Continuous Petri nets; Timed discrete event systems

1. REFERENCES

[1] X. Allamigeon, V. B., and S. Gaubert. Performance evaluation of an emergency call center: tropical polynomial systems applied to timed Petri nets. In *Formal Modeling and Analysis of Timed Systems*, pages 10–26. Springer, 2015.

[2] G. Frehse, C. Le Guernic, A. Donzé, S. Cotton, R. Ray, O. Lebeltel, R. Ripado, A. Girard, T. Dang, and O. Maler. SpaceEx: Scalable verification of hybrid systems. In *International Conference on Computer Aided Verification*, pages 379–395. Springer, 2011.

[3] C. R. Vázquez, C. Mahulea, J. Júlvez, and M. Silva. Introduction to fluid Petri nets. In *Control of Discrete-Event Systems*, pages 365–386. Springer, 2013.

*This work was partially supported by ANR through the CSOSG Democrite project, ANR-13-SECU-0007

VALUETOOLS 2016, October 25-28, Taormina, Italy

Quantitative assessment of workflow performance through PH reduction

Salvatore Distefano
University of Messina, Italy
sdistefano@unime.it
Kazan Federal University, Russia
sdistefano@kpfu.ru

Marco Scarpa
University of Messina, Italy
Department of Engineering
Contrada di Dio, S. Agata, 98166 Messina, Italy.
mscarpa@unime.it

ABSTRACT

Workflows are logical abstraction of processes widely adopted in several contexts. Design and operation of workflows are critical stages where issues not manifested by the single block arise from compositions. To deal with such issues, proper techniques and tools should be implemented as support for workflow designers and operators. This paper proposes a solution for the evaluation of the workflow performance starting from the components' ones. Based on the stochastic characterization of the workflow tasks, phase type distributions and stochastic workflow reduction rules, our approach allows to overcome the limits of existing solutions, considering general response time distributions while providing parametric analysis on customer usage profiles and design alternatives. To demonstrate the effectiveness of the proposed solution an example from literature is evaluated.

Keywords

Workflow, non-Markovian behaviors, usage profile, design alternatives, phase type, performance.

1. INTRODUCTION

A workflow is usually composed of tasks or activities orchestrated through connectors specifying the process logic. The process design is therefore usually split in two phases: i) workflow logic specification and ii) task selection. Once defined, the *workflow management system* (WfMS) is in charge of setting-up, executing and monitoring the workflow based and acting on its components [22].

For a workflow development and operation both functional and non-functional requirements and properties are of strategic importance. This is particularly challenging because of the properties of a system usually emerge from those of its components, often providing functionalities not implemented by any component itself and manifesting behaviors that are not just the summation of components' ones. From a functional perspective this is the *"added value"* but, from a non-functional perspective, it introduces uncertainty and complexity to deal with. To investigate on workflow non functional properties is therefore a quite challenging goal. This is highlighted by the scientific literature, where different solutions are available. Related work mainly focuses on mathematical models such as Queueing Networks [7], Petri Nets [11], simulation [24], UML-based [9, 18], and graph-based [5] ones.

Focusing on performance, a solution should properly take into account the behavior of the system in time, consequently characterizing tasks in statistical-stochastic terms through adequate service time distributions (in general non-Markovian). To support the enforcement of service level agreement policies, it should also be able to deal with different classes of end users-customers (multi-class). Furthermore, different design alternatives have to be taken into account to support the design phase.

In this paper we propose a methodology to support a designer in workflow design and operation. The proposed framework allows to take into account different design alternatives and customer classes, providing a proper model able to deal with general distributions expressed in form of phase types. To the best of our knowledge, this is the first attempt in providing a framework for parametric workflow design. Other works mainly address these issues separately. For example, in [8], different customer classes have been considered in a service oriented computing context. On the other hand, in [13] a technique for dealing with different design alternatives in software families and software product lines is proposed. None of them deal with general, non-Markovian, distributions, mainly providing solutions in the Markovian case. However, starting from these approaches, here we propose to relax this assumption while merging their goals. We base our solution on the lightweight stochastic workflow reduction approach [5], characterizing the service time through distributions dealt with by the phase type expansion, then reduced through random variable algebra and related properties. This way a parametric phase type is obtained for the overall process, which could provide insights on it by posing and solving specific optimization problems targeting optimal design, deployment and operation.

The paper is organized as follows. In Section 2 the rationale and the related work are discussed. Then the proposed technique is presented and detailed in Section 3. Its effectiveness is demonstrated by a case study reported in Section 4 while conclusions are in Section 5.

VALUETOOLS 2016, October 25-28, Taormina, Italy

2. PROBLEM STATEMENT

2.1 Rationale

To characterize the problem in formal terms, we start from an abstract workflow considered as a set of activities, interconnected through directed arcs.

DEFINITION 1. *A generic workflow W is a bipartite, connected, directed, rooted graph represented by the tuple*

$$W = \{\mathbf{T}_W, \mathbf{C}_W, \mathbf{E}_W\}$$

where:

- $\mathbf{T}_W \subseteq \mathcal{T}$ *is a non-empty set of tasks, and* $\mathcal{T}$ *is the task space set.*
- $\mathbf{C}_W \subseteq \mathcal{C}$ *is a set of workflow connectors, and* $\mathcal{C}$ *is the connector space set. At least two distinguished elements belong to* $\mathbf{C}_W$*,* C_s *and* C_e*. They represent the* W *initial and final connectors, respectively, corresponding to the graph root and sink.*
- $\mathbf{E}_W \subseteq (\mathbf{C}_W \times \mathbf{C}_W) \cup (\mathbf{C}_W \times \mathbf{T}_W) \cup (\mathbf{T}_W \times \mathbf{T}_W) \cup (\mathbf{T}_W \times \mathbf{C}_W) \equiv \mathcal{E}$ *is a set of directed arcs connecting workflow elements, and* $\mathcal{E}$ *is the arc space set.*

Task nodes have *indegree* 1 and *outdegree* 1. On the other hand, workflow connector nodes may have either 0, 1 or greater indegree and outdegree. Indeed, the root C_s is the only node with indegree 0 and outdegree 1 while the sink C_e has indegree 1 and outdegree 0. After the above definition, we have to characterize workflow elements in terms of performance. To this purpose, considering a workflow W, we define a task T as follows:

DEFINITION 2. *A generic task* $T \in \mathbf{T}_W$ *is represented by its service time distribution*

$$T = \{F_T\}$$

where:

- $F_T : \mathbb{R}^+ \to [0, 1] \subset \mathbb{R}$ *is the cumulative distribution function (CDF) of the* T *service time.*

Workflow connectors are logic elements that can be considered *instantaneous*. Thus, they can be formally represented as follows.

DEFINITION 3. *A generic workflow connector* $C \in \mathbf{C}_W$ *can be represented by the tuple:*

$$C = \{Id, \mathbf{In}, \mathbf{Out}, Class, Op, \mathbf{\Pi}\}$$

where:

- $Id \in \mathbb{N}^+$ *is the connector unique identifier;*
- $\mathbf{In} \subseteq \mathbf{T}_W \cup \mathbf{C}_W \cup \emptyset$ *is the set of input tasks and/or connectors such that* $\forall In_i \in \mathbf{In} \Rightarrow (In_i, C) \in \mathbf{E}_W$*;*
- $\mathbf{Out} \subseteq \mathbf{T}_W \cup \mathbf{C}_W \cup \emptyset$ *is the set of output tasks and/or connectors such that* $\forall Out_o \in \mathbf{Out} \Rightarrow (C, Out_o) \in \mathbf{E}_W$*;*
- $Class \in \{Start|End|Split|Join\}$ *identifies the specific connector type among the 4 here defined;*
- $Op \in \{AND|XOR|\emptyset\}$ *specifies the operation applied to connectors;*
- $\mathbf{\Pi}$ *is the* weight vector*, which generic element* $\mathbf{\Pi}[h]$ *characterizes the h-th input or output in case of multiple inputs or outputs.*

Given a connector, its **In** and **Out** sets are such that $\mathbf{In} \cap \mathbf{Out} = \emptyset$. A connector of type *Start* has no input arcs ($\mathbf{In} = \emptyset$) and only one output arc, while connectors in the class *End* have only one input arc and no output arcs ($\mathbf{Out} = \emptyset$). We denote such kind of connectors with C_s and C_e, respectively, and they are characterized by $OP = \emptyset$. *Split* and *Join* connectors are associated with logical operations: AND represents *concurrent* executions of all the multiple branches while XOR represents the *exclusive choice* of just a branch among the available ones. A connector in class *Split* is characterized by one incoming arc and multiple outgoing arcs, while a connector in class *Join* has multiple incoming arcs and just one outgoing arc. The weight vector $\mathbf{\Pi}$ is related to the set **In** for *Join* connectors and to the set **Out** for *Split* connectors. In the case of conditional patterns (XOR split and join), $\mathbf{\Pi}$ of the XOR split corresponds to a probabilistic choice and its elements must sum to 1. For parallel patterns (AND split), $\mathbf{\Pi}$ of the AND split is a vector of 1 $\mathbf{\Pi} = \{1, .., 1\}$. In the case of loops ($XOR$ split and join), the XOR split $\mathbf{\Pi}$ is the same of conditional choices, while the XOR join includes the information of the matching split in $\mathbf{\Pi}[0] = XORS.Id$. Furthermore, if the loop has fixed number of iterations $r \in \mathbb{N}^+$, this parameter is specified in the XOR join $\mathbf{\Pi}[1] = r$, while all the other elements of the XOR join $\mathbf{\Pi}$ are 0. In all the other cases the join $\mathbf{\Pi} = \{0, .., 0\}$.

2.2 Parametric workflow

To ensure a proper quality of service able to satisfy SLA constraints, it is often required to discriminate among customers. In terms of the overall process, this implies an in depth investigation on its workflow aiming at characterizing the *usage profile* of a class of customers knowing the corresponding workload. This means to identify the paths, the alternatives selected by the customer of a class, by mainly quantifying and stochastically characterizing conditional choices and branches. This way the usage profile of a customer class can be specified by a vector composed of the probabilities associated with all the conditional patterns in the workflow.

It could also be of interest to include possible *design options or alternatives.* Typical examples are software families and software product lines, where specific variability modeling solutions are used to perform parametric evaluations. Such alternatives can be included on a workflow as a special kind of conditional statements, which branches represent the design choices available thus turning the workflow into a parametric one. Also in this case the design parameters can be represented by a vector composed of the parameter associated with the design alternatives in the workflow.

An interesting feature of the proposed technique is the possibility of performing parametric analysis, taking into account both the usage profile of customers and different, alternative options in the workflow design. These options, identifying alternative workflow solutions for the composite process or parts of it, can be represented through extra exclusive choices and thus included in the main workflow containing the process choices characterizing the usage profile thus obtaining a single, parametric model. The multiple exclusive choice $XOR-Split/XOR-Join$ pattern is therefore the key pattern for expressing both usage and design alternative parameters into the workflow.

To this end, a parameter vector can be associated with a $XOR-Split/XOR-Join$ connector of the workflow, characterized by the $\mathbf{\Pi}_i$ weight vector of the ith $XOR-Split$. This way, a parameter set $\mathbf{V}=\{\mathbf{\Pi}_i\}$ is specified. Such parameters can be categorized into two groups, the usage profile and the design alternative ones, thus identifying a partition of $\mathbf{V}$ into two subsets $\mathbf{U}$ and $\mathbf{Z}$, respectively, such that $\mathbf{V}=\mathbf{U}\cup\mathbf{Z}$. In the case of a design alternative parameter the weight vector associated with the $XOR-Split$ of the corresponding exclusive choice is a binary stochastic vector where the element related to the selected branch (e.g. the jth one with $1\leq j\leq m$) is 1 and the others are 0, i.e. $\mathbf{\Pi}=\{\underbrace{0,..,0}_{j-1},1,\underbrace{0,..,0}_{m-j}\}$.

2.3 Related work

Several methods have been proposed in the literature to evaluate workflow performance, including simulation [24], process calculi [18], queuing networks [7], Petri nets [11] and graphs (DAG, workflow graphs, control flow graph, process flow graphs) [5]. However, the most widely adopted formalism for workflow performance evaluation is queuing networks. In [7], workflow performance requirements and specifications are expressed by P-WSDL (Performance-enabled WSDL) and then QoS parameters such as average response time and utilization are evaluated by a layered queueing network (LQN) model generated by the proposed tool. Similarly, in [15], the performance of a Web service workflow are evaluated through bound analysis, while [14] performed bottleneck analysis of a personnel application modeled as a LQN with three different customer classes, thus allowing to take into account different usage profiles.

Even if less investigated than others, there are some interesting work on design alternatives available in literature. In [20], a delta-oriented approach is adopted to deal with variants in a software product line model. This technique is also applied to the performance evaluation of workflows expressed as performance annotated activity diagrams in [13]. However, most of the above referred techniques, and in particular those based on state space models, have the problem of state space explosion, thus limiting the applicability of related techniques to low complexity problem. To relax this restriction, workflow reduction techniques, sometimes combined with simulation, have been proposed in [5, 10] to estimate WS workflow QoS parameters.

The main problem to deal with in the above mentioned work is related to complexity and state space explosion. Furthermore, one of the goal of this work is to take into account both usage profiles and design alternatives altogether, which introduce further complexity on the overall model. To this purpose a solution should base on workflow reduction, which anyway does not allow to represent workflow performance with stochastic behaviors and related quantities such as cumulative distribution functions. The main goal of this paper is therefore to relax these assumptions, allowing, on the one hand, to deal with complex problems including usage profiles and design alternatives through workflow reduction while, on the other hand, taking into account the stochastic behavior of a system not limiting to Markovian/exponential distributions.

3. WORKFLOW REDUCTION AND EVALUATION

Since the model we are dealing with is in general non-Markovian, we approach the problem by using phase type distributions (PHs); we assume that the CDFs in $\mathbf{F}$ are approximated by the corresponding phase types through specific fitting algorithms. When PHs are obtained, we apply a reduction step in order to obtain a PH distribution representing the whole process in a parametric form.

After introducing symbols and definitions used in the rest of the paper, we give the algebraic expressions describing all the possible patterns defined; they are used to perform the reduction step.

3.1 PH expansion

Let us consider a continuous time Markov chain $\mathcal{X}$ with $\nu+1$ states, of which states $1,\cdots,\nu$ are transient and state $\nu+1$ is *absorbing*. Let us suppose $\boldsymbol{\pi}(0)=[\alpha_1,\cdots,\alpha_\nu,\alpha_{\nu+1}]$ is the Markov chain initial probability distribution. Let ξ denote the random variable that gives the time until absorption of $\mathcal{X}$. Then we say, according to the definition given in [17], that ξ has a *phase-type distribution.* More formally:

Definition 1. *A continuous PH distribution (*CPH*) [17] is defined as the CDF of the time till absorption of a continuous time Markov chain (CTMC) with ν transient states and one absorbing state $(\nu+1)$, given an initial probability vector.*

More specifically, we say that ξ is distributed according to a phase type distribution with *representation* $(\boldsymbol{\alpha},\boldsymbol{G})$ and order ν, where $\boldsymbol{\alpha}$ and $\boldsymbol{G}$ are defined as follows:

- let $\boldsymbol{\pi}(0)=[\,\boldsymbol{\alpha},\ \alpha_{\nu+1}\,]$ be the $(\nu+1)$ initial probability (row) vector, then the following holds: $\alpha_{\nu+1}=1-\sum_{i=1}^{\nu}\alpha_i$.
- let $\widehat{\boldsymbol{G}}$ (of dimension $(\nu+1)\times(\nu+1)$) be the infinitesimal generator matrix of the CTMC $\mathcal{X}$. $\widehat{\boldsymbol{G}}$ can be partitioned in the following way:

$$\widehat{\boldsymbol{G}}=\left[\begin{array}{c|c}\boldsymbol{G} & \boldsymbol{B}\\ \hline \mathbf{0} & 0\end{array}\right],$$

  where, $\boldsymbol{G}$ is a $(\nu\times\nu)$ matrix that describes the transient behavior of the CTMC and $\boldsymbol{B}$ is a $(\nu\times 1)$ column vector grouping the transition rates to the absorbing state. Since the matrix $\widehat{\mathbf{G}}$ must be stochastic, we have $\boldsymbol{B}=-\boldsymbol{G}\cdot\mathbf{e}$, where $\boldsymbol{e}$ is a $(\nu\times 1)$ column vector with all the entries equal to 1.

Definition 1 implicitly assumes that the system is absorbed (i.e. reaches state $\nu+1$) with probability 1. This can be guaranteed irrespective of the value of $\boldsymbol{\alpha}$ if state $\nu+1$ is reachable from every other state. Using this notion and the basic properties of the matrix $\boldsymbol{G}=[g_{ij}]$ (i.e. $g_{ii}<0$, $g_{ij}\geq 0$ for $i\neq j$, and $|g_{ii}|\geq\sum_{j\neq i}g_{ij}$), it can be showed that $\boldsymbol{G}$ must be non singular [12]. This means that all the eigenvalues of $\boldsymbol{G}$ must be non positive [16].

Given a CPH with representation $(\boldsymbol{\alpha},\boldsymbol{G})$, its CDF is $F(t)=1-e^{\boldsymbol{G}t}\mathbf{1}$, and its k moment is written as

$$E(\xi^k)=k!\ \boldsymbol{\alpha}(-\boldsymbol{G})^{-k}\mathbf{1}.$$

Other relevant properties involves operation among CPHs; in particular, in the following of this paper, we exploit summation, mixture, maximum and minimum, thus we briefly recall the related expressions.

Let us consider two CPHs, X_1 and X_2, with representation $(\boldsymbol{\alpha}_1, \boldsymbol{G}_1)$ and $(\boldsymbol{\alpha}_2, \boldsymbol{G}_2)$ respectively and such that the initial probabilities to the absorbing state ν_{i+1} are null; thus the following properties hold:

1. the summation $X_S = X_1 + X_2$ is a CPH with representation $(\boldsymbol{\alpha}_S, \boldsymbol{G}_S)$, where $\boldsymbol{\alpha}_S = (\boldsymbol{\alpha}_1, \mathbf{0})$ and $\boldsymbol{G}_S = \left[\begin{array}{c|c} \boldsymbol{G}_1 & \boldsymbol{B}_1\boldsymbol{\alpha}_2 \\ \hline \mathbf{0} & \boldsymbol{G}_2 \end{array}\right]$;

2. the mixture $X_T = \begin{cases} X_1 & \textit{with probability } p \\ X_2 & \textit{with probability } (1-p) \end{cases}$ is a CPH with representation$(\boldsymbol{\alpha}_T, \boldsymbol{G}_T)$, where $\boldsymbol{\alpha}_T = (p\boldsymbol{\alpha}_1, (1-p)\boldsymbol{\alpha}_2)$ and $\boldsymbol{G}_T = \left[\begin{array}{c|c} \boldsymbol{G}_1 & \mathbf{0} \\ \hline \mathbf{0} & \boldsymbol{G}_2 \end{array}\right]$;

3. the minimum $X_m = \min(X_1, X_2)$ is a CPH with representation $(\boldsymbol{\alpha}_m, \boldsymbol{G}_m)$, where $\boldsymbol{\alpha}_m = \boldsymbol{\alpha}_1 \otimes \boldsymbol{\alpha}_2$ and $\boldsymbol{G}_m = \boldsymbol{G}_1 \oplus \boldsymbol{G}_2$;

4. the maximum $X_M = \max(X_1, X_2)$ is a CPH with representation $(\boldsymbol{\alpha}_M, \boldsymbol{G}_M)$, where $\boldsymbol{\alpha}_M = \left[\begin{array}{c|c|c} \boldsymbol{\alpha}_1 \otimes \boldsymbol{\alpha}_2 & \mathbf{0} & \mathbf{0} \end{array}\right]$ and $\boldsymbol{G}_M = \left[\begin{array}{c|c|c} \boldsymbol{G}_1 \oplus \boldsymbol{G}_1 & \boldsymbol{B}_1 \oplus \boldsymbol{I} & \boldsymbol{I} \oplus \boldsymbol{B}_2 \\ \hline 0 & \boldsymbol{G}_2 & 0 \\ \hline 0 & 0 & \boldsymbol{G}_1 \end{array}\right]$.

In the expression above, we used the symbols $\otimes$ and $\oplus$ to denote the Kronecker multiplication and Kronecker sum respectively.

The use of CPHs is justified because most of generally distributed continuous r.v. can be approximated by a CPH distribution by using appropriate fitting algorithms [2,3,21].

3.2 Reduction rules

The evaluation performed at this step has to deal with the high complexity of the process, especially when its workflow has branches and nesting that can also represents alternative design choices as discussed above. The evaluation technique is based on well known aggregation-reduction techniques [5, 6]. This section deals with the analytic formulas expressing the service time of each workflow basic pattern in terms of those of its tasks. Both one branch and multiple branch patterns are investigated. In the latter case, for the sake of readability and clarity, we just consider two branches, $T_1 = \{F_{T_1}, C_{T_1}\}$ and $T_2 = \{F_{T_2}, C_{T_2}\}$, characterized by the corresponding service time random variable (r.v.) X_1 and X_2 with their CPH distributions $F_{T_1} = (\boldsymbol{\alpha}_1, \mathbf{G}_1)$ and $F_{T_2} = (\boldsymbol{\alpha}_2, \mathbf{G}_2)$ and costs, respectively. Anyway, complex multi-branch patterns with more than two branches can be easily decomposed into 2-branch nested patterns and thus reduced by iteratively applying the following rules.

In the following, we evaluate the aggregation reduction formulas for the main process workflow single and multi-branch patterns $W = \{\mathbf{T}_W, \mathbf{C}_W, \mathbf{E}_W\}$ in terms of the involved T_1 and T_2 task service time CDFs and related kth moments $E(X_1^k)$ and $E(X_2^k)$.

3.2.1 Sequence

Considering a workflow composed of the *sequence* $S = \{\mathbf{T}_S, \mathbf{C}_S, \mathbf{E}_S\}$ of two tasks T_1 and T_2, such that $\mathbf{T}_S = \{T_1, T_2\}$ (where T_1 and T_2 are the same above specified), $\mathbf{C}_S = \{C_s, C_e\}$ and $\mathbf{E}_S = \{(C_s, T_1), (T_1, T_2), (T_2, C_e)\}$. Since S returns control when the tasks complete following the sequence order, we have that

$$X_S = X_1 + X_2 \,. \tag{1}$$

The sequence pattern S CPH representation $(\boldsymbol{\alpha}_S, \mathbf{G}_S)$ can be thus expressed as:

$$\boldsymbol{\alpha}_S = [\boldsymbol{\alpha}_1, \mathbf{0}]\,, \qquad \mathbf{G}_S = \begin{bmatrix} \mathbf{G}_1 & \boldsymbol{B}_1\boldsymbol{\alpha}_2 \\ \mathbf{0} & \mathbf{G}_2 \end{bmatrix} \tag{2}$$

3.2.2 Multi branch patterns

According to the definitions of Section 2.1, three possible combinations are meaningful for split/join multibranch patterns: XOR/XOR, AND/AND, AND/XOR, while the XOR/AND configuration is semantically wrong.

XOR/XOR.

XOR/XOR patterns implement conditional exclusive choices among alternative paths each associated with the corresponding task or subworkflow. The 2-way XOR/XOR exclusive choice $XOR/XOR = \{\mathbf{T}_{XOR/XOR}, \mathbf{C}_{XOR/XOR}, \mathbf{E}_{XOR/XOR}\}$ is expressed as

$$\mathbf{T}_{XOR/XOR} = \{T_1, T_2\}, \mathbf{C}_{XOR/XOR} = \{C_s, C_{XORS}, C_{XORJ}, C_e\}$$

and

$$\mathbf{E}_{XOR/XOR} = \{(C_s, C_{XORS}), (C_{XORS}, T_1), (C_{XORS}, T_2), (T_1, C_{XORJ}), (T_2, C_{XORJ}), (C_{XORJ}, C_e)\}.$$

If the X_c r.v. identifies the selected branch and thus $X_c \in \{1, 2\}$, the service time r.v. of the XOR/XOR pattern $X_{XOR/XOR}$ can be expressed as follows:

$$X_{XOR/XOR} = \begin{cases} X_1 \text{ if } X_c = 1 \\ X_2 \text{ if } X_c = 2 \end{cases} . \tag{3}$$

Assuming that all such random variables are statistically independent and also that the probability to choose T_1 is given by $\mathbf{\Pi}_{XORS}[1] = Pr\{X_c = 1\} = p_c$ while the T_2 one is $\mathbf{\Pi}_{XORS}[2] = Pr\{X_c = 2\} = 1 - p_c$ the CPH describing the XOR/XOR multiple branch $(\boldsymbol{\alpha}_{XOR/XOR}, \mathbf{G}_{XOR/XOR})$ is

$$\boldsymbol{\alpha}_{XOR/XOR} = [p_c\boldsymbol{\alpha}_1, (1-p_c)\boldsymbol{\alpha}_2], \boldsymbol{G}_{XOR/XOR} = \begin{bmatrix} \mathbf{G}_1 & \mathbf{0} \\ \mathbf{0} & \mathbf{G}_2 \end{bmatrix} \tag{4}$$

The XOR/XOR pattern could also have a *null* task of one its branches. In this case the CPH associate is smaller since it is defined by the transient behavior of the non null task that is executed with a given probability. Let us suppose X_1 is the r.v. associated to the non null task, thus the representation is:

$$\boldsymbol{\alpha}_{XOR/XOR} = p_c\boldsymbol{\alpha}_1, \qquad \boldsymbol{G}_{XOR/XOR} = \boldsymbol{G}_1 \tag{5}$$

We point out that the non null activity modifies the structure of the resulting CPH that does not start from a transient phase with probability 1.0 because the $\nu+1$-th element of its initial probability vector is $(\alpha_{XOR/XOR})_{\nu+1} = 1 - p_c \neq 0$.

A *null* task is instead semantically without sense for the other multi-branch patterns.

AND/AND.

The AND/AND pattern is the simplest concurrent pattern splitting the main flow into parallel threads and finally synchronizing them through the join. It thus terminates only when *all* the parallel threads return control regardless the order. The 2-way AND/AND concurrent pattern $AND/AND = \{\mathbf{T}_{AND/AND}, \mathbf{C}_{AND/AND}, \mathbf{E}_{AND/AND}\}$ is expressed as $\mathbf{T}_{AND/AND} = \{T_1, T_2\}$, $\mathbf{C}_{AND/AND} = \{C_s, C_{ANDS}, C_{ANDJ}, C_e\}$ and $\mathbf{E}_{AND/AND} = \{ (C_s, C_{ANDS}), (C_{ANDS}, T_1), (C_{ANDS}, T_2), (T_1, C_{ANDJ}), (T_2, C_{ANDJ}), (C_{ANDJ}, C_e)\}$. The service time r.v. of an AND/AND concurrent pattern $X_{AND/AND}$ with 2 parallel branches T_1 and T_2 characterized by the X_1 and X_2 service time r.v. is therefore identified by the maximum among such random variables. Let $\mathbf{X}^{AND/AND}$ be the set or the *largest order statistic*

$$X_{AND/AND} = \mathbf{X}_{(2)}^{AND/AND} = \max\{X_1, X_2\} \; . \tag{6}$$

Then, the AND/AND CPH with representation

$$(\boldsymbol{\alpha}_{AND/AND}, \mathbf{G}_{AND/AND})$$

is expressed as:

$$\boldsymbol{\alpha}_{AND/AND} = \left[\; \boldsymbol{\alpha}_1 \otimes \boldsymbol{\alpha}_2, \quad \mathbf{0}, \quad \mathbf{0} \; \right] \tag{7}$$

and

$$G_{AND/AND} = \begin{bmatrix} \mathbf{G}_1 \oplus \mathbf{G}_2 & \boldsymbol{B}_1 \otimes \mathbf{I}_2 & \mathbf{I}_1 \otimes \boldsymbol{B}_2 \\ \mathbf{0} & \mathbf{G}_2 & \mathbf{0} \\ \mathbf{0} & \mathbf{0} & \mathbf{G}_1 \end{bmatrix} \tag{8}$$

AND/XOR.

Another concurrent pattern is the AND/OR one, where all the threads concurrently start and the first completing closes the pattern. The 2-way AND/XOR concurrent pattern $AND/XOR = \{\mathbf{T}_{AND/XOR}, \mathbf{C}_{AND/XOR}, \mathbf{E}_{AND/XOR}\}$ is expressed as $\mathbf{T}_{AND/XOR} = \{T_1, T_2\}$, $\mathbf{C}_{AND/XOR} = \{C_s, C_{ANDS}, C_{XORJ}, C_e\}$ and $\mathbf{E}_{AND/XOR} = \{(C_s, C_{ANDS}), (C_{ANDS}, T_1), (C_{ANDS}, T_2), (T_1, C_{XORJ}), (T_2, C_{XORJ}), (C_{XORJ}, C_e)\}$. This way, if $\mathbf{X}_{AND/XOR}$ r.v. is the *first order statistic* (or smallest order statistic), i.e. the minimum between X_1 and X_2, we can describe the AND/XOR pattern service time r.v. by the following formula:

$$X_{AND/XOR} = \mathbf{X}_{(2)}^{AND/XOR} = \min\{X_1, X_2\}. \tag{9}$$

Then, the AND/XOR CPH $(\boldsymbol{\alpha}_{AND/XOR}, \mathbf{G}_{AND/XOR})$ is expressed by:

$$\alpha_{AND/XOR} = \boldsymbol{\alpha}_1 \otimes \boldsymbol{\alpha}_2, \qquad G_{AND/XOR} = \mathbf{G}_1 \oplus \mathbf{G}_2 \tag{10}$$

3.2.3 Loop

According to the usual notion, we define the *Loop* pattern as a structure able to execute a number of iterations. The number of performed iterations could be either fixed or undefined and probabilistically controlled. In the following, the rules for both cases will be introduced.

Fixed number of iterations.

The loop pattern is composed of the body task T that has to be executed a r times. It is therefore represented as a sequence of the task T and the following loop condition, and can be unrolled into a sequence of task T repeated r times. Formally, the loop pattern $L = \{\mathbf{T}_L, \mathbf{C}_L, \mathbf{E}_L\}$ is composed of just one task to be iterated, and thus expressed as $\mathbf{T}_L = \{T\}$, $\mathbf{C}_L = \{C_s, C_{XORS}, C_{XORJ}, C_e\}$ and $\mathbf{E}_L = \{(C_s, C_{XORS}), (C_{XORS}, T), (C_{XORS}, C_{XORJ}), (T, C_{XORJ}), (C_{XORJ}, C_e)\}$. Thus, assuming the iteration service times X_T r.v. are independent and identical distributed, the loop CPH $(\boldsymbol{\alpha}_L, \mathbf{G}_L)$ can be iteratively described by

$$\boldsymbol{\alpha}_L = (\boldsymbol{\alpha}, \underbrace{\mathbf{0}, .., \mathbf{0}}_{r}) \tag{11}$$

and

$$G_L = \begin{bmatrix} \mathbf{G}_L^{r-1} & \boldsymbol{B}_L^{r-2}\boldsymbol{\alpha} \\ \mathbf{0} & \mathbf{G}_L^{r-1} \end{bmatrix} \tag{12}$$

where:

$$G_L^{r-1} = \begin{bmatrix} \mathbf{G}_L^{r-2} & \boldsymbol{B}^{r-3}\boldsymbol{\alpha} \\ \mathbf{0} & \mathbf{G}_L^{r-2} \end{bmatrix}$$

and

$$G_L^2 = \begin{bmatrix} \mathbf{G} & \boldsymbol{B}\boldsymbol{\alpha} \\ \mathbf{0} & \mathbf{G}_L \end{bmatrix}$$

for $r > 1$, while if $r = 1$ then $\boldsymbol{\alpha}_L = \boldsymbol{\alpha}$ and $\mathbf{G}_L = \mathbf{G}$, corresponding to the T CPH distribution attributes.

Probabilistic iterations.

In the general case the loop pattern is composed of the body task T_b followed by the loop condition characterized by the iteration probability p_l[1]. When the random choice selects a new iteration, another task T_e could be eventually executed. It is therefore represented as a sequence of the task T_b, the following loop condition and the task T_e. It can be considered as a sequence of tasks repeated a random number of times. Formally, the loop pattern $L = \{\mathbf{T}_L, \mathbf{C}_L, \mathbf{E}_L\}$ is composed of two tasks to be iterated, and thus expressed as $\mathbf{T}_L = \{T_b, T_e\}$, $\mathbf{C}_L = \{C_s, C_{XORS}, C_{XORJ}, C_e\}$ and $\mathbf{E}_L = \{(C_s, C_{XORS}), (C_{XORS}, T_b), (T_b, C_{XORJ}), (C_{XORJ}, T_e), (T_e, C_{XORS}), (C_{XORJ}, C_e)\}$ If no task has to be executed when a new iteration starts the task T_e could be considered *null*.

Let X_b and X_e the service time r.v. of T_b and T_e tasks; the loop L service time r.v. is distributed according to a CPH computed as a sequence of X_b followed by X_e with probability p_L after which it start again; the task L completes with probability $(1 - p_L)$. Thus the loop service time is expressed by a CPH with representation $(\boldsymbol{\alpha}_L, \boldsymbol{G}_L)$ where

$$\boldsymbol{\alpha}_L = [\boldsymbol{\alpha}_b, \mathbf{0}], \qquad \mathbf{G}_L = \begin{bmatrix} \boldsymbol{G}_b & p_L \boldsymbol{B}_b \boldsymbol{\alpha}_e \\ \boldsymbol{B}_e \boldsymbol{\alpha}_b & \boldsymbol{G}_e \end{bmatrix} \tag{13}$$

The representation of X_L become simpler when the task T_e is null. In fact, in that case, after the probabilistic selection the task T_b starts again with probability p_L, thus $\boldsymbol{\alpha}_L$ and $\mathbf{G}_L$ are:

$$\boldsymbol{\alpha}_L = \boldsymbol{\alpha}_b, \qquad \boldsymbol{G}_b + p_L \boldsymbol{B}_b \boldsymbol{\alpha}_b \tag{14}$$

3.3 Reduction algorithm and evaluation

The formulas thus obtained in eq. (1)-(14) can be applied to a complex structured workflow hierarchically combining and nesting the above patterns into an ordered rooted tree as detailed in the Algorithm 1. It assumes a workflow W is specified as an ordered *workflow tree*, WFT, where tasks appear only on leaves and connectors are internal nodes [4,23], removing *Start* and *End* connectors. This way the reduction

[1] In this work, we assume the iteration probability is not dependent on the number of the already performed iterations.

algorithm mainly consists in a left to right in-order traversal of WFT to preserve the workflow connector order, resulting in the reduced workflow phase type distribution $(\mathbf{G}_W, \boldsymbol{\alpha}_W)$ representing the W service time. Function $ReduceWF$ is invoked to apply the formulae above specified to the corresponding patterns, thus returning the corresponding CPH distribution (step 6). In the leaf case, $CWFT[]$ is an empty vector and $ReduceWF$ returns the task CPH.

Algorithm 1: $WFTSWR$

input : a tree WFT corresponding to a non-null workflow
output: reduced workflow CPH $(\mathbf{G}_W, \boldsymbol{\alpha}_W)$
local : the $CWFT[]$ vector storing partial reduction, index i initialized to 0

```
1 begin
2   if WFT is not a leaf then
3     foreach C ∈ {the ordered set of children of WFT} do
4       CWFT[i] ⟵ WFTSWR(C);
5       i ⟵ i + 1;
6   return ReduceWF(WFT, CWFT[]);
```

This way, the workflow service time CPH $(\mathbf{G}_W, \boldsymbol{\alpha}_W)$ is obtained as a function of its task parameters $(\mathbf{G}_i, \boldsymbol{\alpha}_i)$ and C_i $\forall i = 1, .., n$, i.e.

$$\mathbf{G}_W = f_{\mathbf{G}_W}(\mathbf{G}_1, .., \mathbf{G}_n) = f_{\mathbf{G}_W}(\mathbf{Z}, \mathbf{U})$$

$$\boldsymbol{\alpha}_W = f_{\boldsymbol{\alpha}_W}(\boldsymbol{\alpha}_1, .., \boldsymbol{\alpha}_n) = f_{\boldsymbol{\alpha}_W}(\mathbf{Z}, \mathbf{U})$$

which can be expressed in parametric form in terms of $\mathbf{U}$ and $\mathbf{Z}$ parameters.

The reduction algorithm together with the reduction rules (2)-(14) generate a block matrix representing an irreducible Markov chain with one absorbing state whose evaluation gives the CDF of the workflow response time. Due to the structure of the stochastic process a semi-symbolic analysis algorithms [19] can be used and an expression giving the completion time probability could be obtained as a function of usage and design parameters. Generally speaking the result of the evaluation is a function $F(t; \boldsymbol{u}, \boldsymbol{z})$, with $\boldsymbol{u} \in \mathbf{U}$ and $\boldsymbol{z} \in \mathbf{Z}$, and the $F(t; \boldsymbol{u}, \boldsymbol{z})$ has the shape of an expolynomial expression.

4. AN EXAMPLE

In order to explain the proposed technique and demonstrate its effectiveness, we applied it to an example taken from literature [13]. A high-level representation of the example workflow through activity diagrams is shown in Figure 1. It represents a logical workflow, composed of a *do while* loop iterating a sequence of three tasks where a conditional choice identifies the second one (Figure 1a). Therefore, in the main workflow there are two conditional choices C1 and C2, the former associated with the loop while the latter with the inner condition, which characterizes its usage profile. After performing the process design the designer has to select tasks and orchestrate the overall workflow. In this stages, starting from functional properties, but also based on non functional ones, tasks are selected and eventual possible project alternatives identified. The resulting workflow is thus reported in Figure 1b, including 2 design alternatives D1 and D2. As highlighted in this figure they are correlated, since branches associated with the same letter (**a** or **b**) correspond, thus identifying in total two possible combinations among the four available.

Par. i	1	2	3	4	5
γ_i	0.5775	0.4331	0.2887	0.2475	0.8663
β_i	2.0	2.0	2.0	2.0	2.0

Table 1: Distribution associated with the ith task ($i = 1, .., 5$) of the example workflow.

The completion time distributions associated with the five tasks composing this workflow are reported in Table 1. These are all Weibull distributions in the form $F_i(t, \gamma_i, \beta_i) = 1 - e^{-(x/\gamma_i)^{\beta_i}}$, where γ_i is the scale parameter and β_i the shape one, with $i = 1, .., 5$. These parameters have been specified according to the [13] ones, preserving the mean completion time but considering here non exponential distributions.

The distributions thus identified in Table 1 have been then represented by a 2-stage CPHs in canonical form CF-A [1] as the one showed in Figure 2a, whose representation is $(\boldsymbol{\alpha}_i, \boldsymbol{G}_i)$. This means that each of such distributions are characterized by the three parameters $\lambda_{12}^i, \lambda_{13}^i, \lambda_{23}^i$, whose numerical values are reported in Table 2.

Par. i	1	2	3	4	5
λ_{12}	3.986494	5.315632	7.974369	9.301820	2.657509
λ_{13}	0.000923	0.001230	0.001845	0.002153	0.000615
λ_{23}	3.964869	5.286798	7.931112	9.251362	2.643094

Table 2: CPH rates associated with the ith task of the workflow example.

After that, we have to specify the workflow tree corresponding to the example workflow. By applying the rules discussed in Section 3.3 the workflow tree shown in Figure 2b is obtained. In particular, since conditional constructs needs at least two branches, a *null* fictitious task is inserted in the conditional choice D2. The loop is composed by two branches: the direct branch made by a sequence of composed tasks and the reverse branch containing two tasks depending on the design alternative. We used a *null* task to model the design alternative **a** in the reverse task.

Given that we can obtain the full matrix representing the whole process by just apply the workflow reduction rules identified in Section 3.2. Starting from the leaves of the tree in Figure 2b, the matrices characterizing the CPHs of the XOR/XOR pattern C_2 and D_2 are built:

$$\boldsymbol{\alpha}_{C_2} = [p_{C_2}\boldsymbol{\alpha}_2, (1 - p_{C_2})\boldsymbol{\alpha}_3], \quad \boldsymbol{G}_{C_2} = \begin{bmatrix} \boldsymbol{G}_2 & \mathbf{0} \\ \mathbf{0} & \mathbf{G}_3 \end{bmatrix}$$

and

$$\boldsymbol{\alpha}_{D_2} = p_b\boldsymbol{\alpha}_5, \quad \boldsymbol{G}_{D_2} = \boldsymbol{G}_5$$

where p_{C_2} is the probability that the task 2 is selected in the branch C_2 ($p_{C_2} \in \mathbf{U}$), and $p_b \in \mathbf{Z}$ is the binary quantity used to select the design alternative **b**. We point out that when the alternative **b** is under evaluation $p_b = 1$ and correspondingly $p_a = 0$; at the opposite when the design alternative **a** is evaluated $p_a = 1$ and $p_b = 0$, thus the vector $\boldsymbol{\alpha}_{D_2}$ will be null deselecting the corresponding branch.

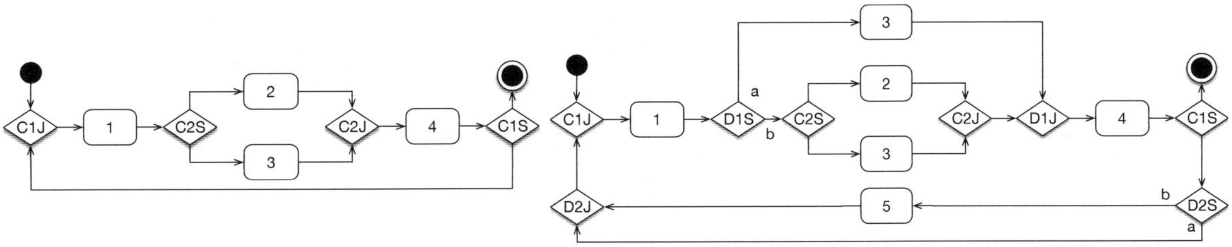

(a) Original

(b) With design aternatives

Figure 1: The example workflow.

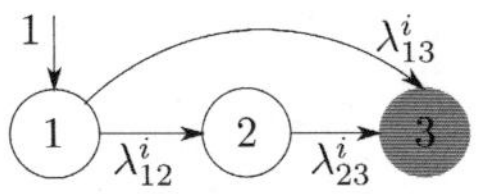

$\alpha_i = [1, 0]$

$$\mathbf{G}_i = \begin{bmatrix} 1 - \lambda_{12}^i - \lambda_{13}^i & \lambda_{12}^i \\ 0 & -\lambda_{23}^i \end{bmatrix}$$

(a)

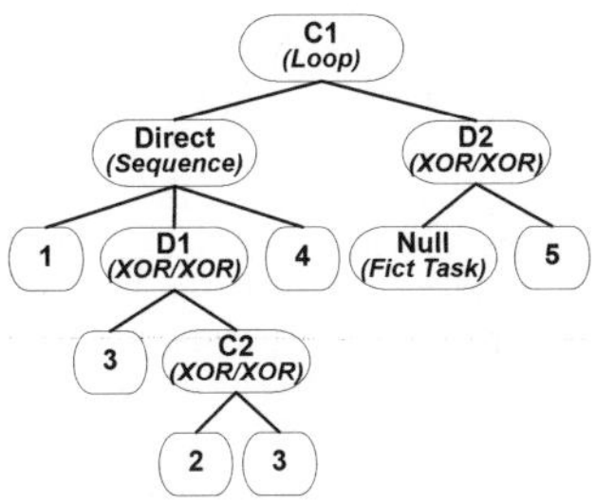

(b)

Figure 2: The example CPH (a) and workflow tree (b).

Iteratively visiting the tree toward the root node, the block matrices of the global CPH are similarly obtained:

$$\boldsymbol{\alpha}_{Direct} = [\boldsymbol{\alpha}_1, \mathbf{0}, \mathbf{0}], \quad \boldsymbol{G}_{Direct} = \begin{bmatrix} \boldsymbol{G}_1 & \boldsymbol{B}_1\boldsymbol{\alpha}_{D_1} & \mathbf{0} \\ 0 & \boldsymbol{G}_{D_1} & \boldsymbol{B}_{D_1}\boldsymbol{\alpha}_4 \\ \mathbf{0} & \mathbf{0} & \boldsymbol{G}_4 \end{bmatrix}$$

$$\boldsymbol{\alpha}_{D_1} = [p_a\boldsymbol{\alpha}_3, p_b\boldsymbol{\alpha}_{C_2}], \quad \boldsymbol{G}_{D_1} = \begin{bmatrix} \boldsymbol{G}_3 & \mathbf{0} \\ \mathbf{0} & \mathbf{G}_{C_2} \end{bmatrix}$$

$$\boldsymbol{\alpha} = [\boldsymbol{\alpha}_{Direct}, \mathbf{0}],$$

$$\boldsymbol{G} = \begin{bmatrix} \boldsymbol{G}_{Direct} + p_a p_{C_1} \boldsymbol{B}_{Direct}\boldsymbol{\alpha}_{Direct} & p_b p_{C_1} \boldsymbol{B}_{Direct}\boldsymbol{\alpha}_5 \\ \boldsymbol{B}_5\boldsymbol{\alpha}_{Direct} & \boldsymbol{G}_5 \end{bmatrix}$$

The parameter sets of the workflow are $\mathbf{U} = \{p_{C_1}, p_{C_2}\}$ and $\mathbf{Z} = \{p_a, p_b\}$.

User class	p_{C_1}	p_{C_2}
$U1$	0.5	0.3
$U2$	0.5	0.7
$U3$	0.2	0.3
$U4$	0.2	0.7

Table 3: User classes definition.

Given the matrices $\boldsymbol{G}$ and $\boldsymbol{\alpha}$, we evaluated the response time distribution of the considered workflow, $Fw(t)$, assuming four different classes of users characterized by the values as in Table 3. The user class U1 is the same evaluated in [13]. We evaluated the different classes with respect to the two design choices also. Other interesting measure could be derived, but we omit them for lack of space.

The resulting CDFs are depicted in Figure 3. The graph in Figure 3a shows the CDFs for the users classes considered in the case of design choice **a**. As clearly shown the parameter p_{C_2} does not affect the behavior of the system because the C_2 pattern is not used in this design choice while p_{C_1} is the same for $U1$ and $U2$, as well as for $U3$ and $U4$, respectively, thus identifying just two curves. When the design choice **b** is considered the parameter p_{C_2} has some effect slightly worsening the performances by increase as shown in Figure 3b. At the opposite, the analysis reveals a great impact of the parameter p_{C_1} on both the design choices: response time increases when the value of p_{C_1} increases. This is due to increased number of iterations in the loop.

5. CONCLUSIONS

Workflow design and orchestration are critical phases where issues may arise from task composition compromising the overall process. Modeling and evaluation technique can be a valid support to reduce the impact of such issues in early stage, predicting design flows or defects.

In this paper a technique for dealing with performance evaluation of workflows is proposed. It allows to take into account different customer classes, characterized by their usage profiles, and design alternatives as well. These are probabilistically characterized in a parametric workflow by conditional choices, which analysis parameters are the split probabilities. The proposed technique also allows to take into account the full stochastic characterization for the time behavior of components considering generic distributions. Based on stochastic workflow reduction rules, phase type distributions and related properties, it is able to provide parametric analyses of the worklow on different usage profiles and design choices.

6. REFERENCES

[1] A. Bobbio and A. Cumani. *ML estimation of the parameters of a PH distribution in triangular canonical form*, pages 33–46. Elsevier Science Publishers, 1992.

[2] A. Bobbio, A. Horvath, M. Scarpa, and M. Telek. Acyclic discrete phase type distributions: properties and a parameter estimation algorithm. *Performance Evaluation*, 54(1):1 – 32, 2003.

[3] A. Bobbio and M. Telek. A benchmark for PH estimation algorithms: results for acyclic-PH. *Communications in Statistics. Stochastic Models*, 10(3):661–677, 1994.

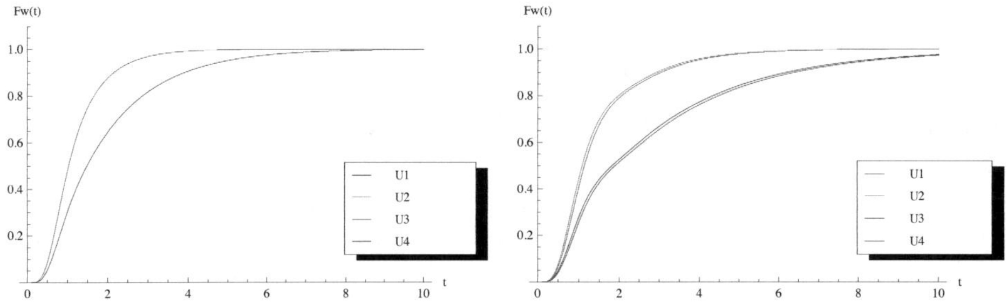

(a) Design alternative **a** (b) Design alternative **b**

Figure 3: Workflow completion time distributions.

[4] D. Bruneo, S. Distefano, F. Longo, and M. Scarpa. Stochastic Evaluation of QoS in Service-Based Systems. *IEEE Trans. Parallel Distrib. Syst.*, 24(10):2090–2099, 2013.

[5] J. Cardoso, A. Sheth, J. Miller, J. Arnold, and K. Kochut. Web semantics: Science, services and agents on the world wide web; quality of service for workflows and web service processes. *Journal of Web Semantics, Elsevier*, 1(3):281–308, 2004.

[6] J. A. Cardoso. *Quality of Service and Semantic Composition of Workflows.* PhD thesis, Graduate School of the University of Georgia, Athens, Georgia, Aug 2002.

[7] A. D'Ambrogio and P. Bocciarelli. A model-driven approach to describe and predict the performance of composite services. In *WOSP '07: Proceedings of the 6th international workshop on Software and performance*, pages 78–89, New York, NY, USA, 2007. ACM.

[8] S. Distefano and G. Serazzi. Performance driven WS orchestration and deployment in service oriented infrastructure. *J. Grid Comput.*, 12(2):347–369, 2014.

[9] K. H. HAN, S. K. YOO, and B. KIM. Qualitative and quantitative analysis of workflows based on the uml activity diagram and petri net. *WSEAS Transactions on Information Science and Applications*, 6(7):1249–1258, July 2009.

[10] S.-Y. Hwang, H. Wang, J. Tang, and J. Srivastava. A probabilistic approach to modeling and estimating the qos of web-services-based workflows. *Inf. Sci.*, 177(23):5484–5503, 2007.

[11] G. Janssens, J. Verelst, B., and Weyn. Techniques for modeling workflows and their support of reuse. In W. Van der Aalst, J. Desel, and A. Oberweis, editors, *Business Process Management: Models Techniques and Empirical Studies-LNCS1806*, pages 2–15, London, UK, 2000. Springer-Verlag.

[12] K. Kant. *Introduction to Computer System Performance Evaluation.* Mc Graw-Hill, 1992.

[13] M. Kowal, I. Schaefer, and M. Tribastone. Family-based performance analysis of variant-rich software systems. In *Proceedings of the 17th International Conference on Fundamental Approaches to Software Engineering - Volume 8411*, pages 94–108, New York, NY, USA, 2014. Springer-Verlag New York, Inc.

[14] M. Litoiu, J. Rolia, and G. Serazzi. Designing process replication and activation: a quantitative approach. *Software Engineering, IEEE Transactions on*, 26(12):1168 –1178, dec 2000.

[15] M. Marzolla and R. Mirandola. Performance prediction of web service workflows. In *Proceedings of the Quality of software architectures 3rd international conference on Software architectures, components, and applications*, QoSA'07, pages 127–144, Berlin, Heidelberg, 2007. Springer-Verlag.

[16] M. Neuts. Probability distributions of phase type. In *Liber Amicorum Prof. Emeritus H. Florin*, pages 173–206. University of Louvain, 1975.

[17] M. Neuts. *Matrix Geometric Solutions in Stochastic Models.* Johns Hopkins University Press, Baltimore, 1981.

[18] S.-C. Oh, D. Lee, and R. T. Kumara. Misq:a framework to analyze and optimize web service composition in business service networks. *INTERNATIONAL JOURNAL OF CASES ON ELECTRONIC COMMERCE*, 1(4):35–55, 2005.

[19] R. Sahner, K. Trivedi, and A. Puliafito. *Performance and reliability analysis of computer systems.* MKluwer Academic Publisher, Norwell, Massachusettes, 02061, USA, 1st edition, 1996.

[20] I. Schaefer. Variability modelling for model-driven development of software product lines. In *VaMoS*, pages 85–92, 2010.

[21] A. Thummler, P. Buchholz, and M. Telek. A novel approach for phase-type fitting with the em algorithm. *IEEE Transactions on Dependable and Secure Computing*, 3(3):245–258, July 2006.

[22] W. Van Der Aalst and K. M. Van Hee. *Workflow management: models, methods, and systems.* MIT press, 2004.

[23] M. Wimmer, M.-C. Albutiu, and A. Kemper. Optimized workflow authorization in service oriented architectures. In *Emerging Trends in Information and Communication Security*, pages 30–44. Springer, 2006.

[24] H. P. Zhu, S. W. Xiao, and Z. Che. Research on workflow simulation supported business process analysis. *Mini-Micro Systems*, 28(8):1531–1535, 2006.

Efficient solution of extended Multiple-Phased Systems

Elvio Gilberto Amparore
Dipartimento di Informatica
Università di Torino
Torino, Italy
amparore@di.unito.it

Susanna Donatelli
Dipartimento di Informatica
Università di Torino
Torino, Italy
donatelli@di.unito.it

ABSTRACT

Multiple-Phased Systems (MPS) are systems whose behaviour can be split in a set of successive periods, called phases. We concentrate on the Phase Petri nets (PPN) formalism for the representation of state-based MPS, whose state space is a Markov Regenerative Process (MRP). MPS have been traditionally evaluated using an ad-hoc method. In this paper we show how the recently developed *Component Method* for general MRP deals with MPS. The application of this method also allows for more general MPS system, namely where the phases can be interrupted or influenced by the behaviour of the modeled system The advantages of this approach is assessed on a Scheduled Maintenance Systems model using two tools, DEEM and GreatSPN.

1. INTRODUCTION AND STATE OF ART

Multiple-Phased Sytems (MPS) [1] are systems whose behaviour can be split in a set of successive periods, called phases. Also called Phased Mission System (PMS) in other works, as in [2], since they can easily describe systems in which the behaviour is described as a mission, structured into multiple *phases*, each described by a different duration, system configuration, desired task, etc. MPS have been shown to be useful also in modelling systems with scheduled maintenance [3] (Scheduled Maintenance Systems - SMS). In a MPS, the standard question is to compute the reliability of the system, i.e. the probability that the system survives the mission, but optimization also plays a role [4], especially for SMS to determine the best maintenance policy, as well as sensitivity analysis [3, 5] to allow to reason about the structure of the mission and their parameters.

There has been a significant amount of work, especially in the late nineties and also more recently, on MPS. Different techniques have been used for modelling and solving these systems, from combinatorial methods like reliability blocks and fault trees to state-based techniques. Combinatorial approaches based on reliability blocks and fault trees have been reported for example in [6, 7]. State-based approaches build Markovian systems either through an ad-hoc language as in EHARP [6] or through a high level modelling formalism as Stochastic Petri Nets as in [8]. It is well known what are the relative advantages and disadvantages of combinatorial methods over state-based ones, but when the objective of the MPS analysis goes beyond the computation of the reliability of the system at the end of the mission, state-based approaches can provide a plus, like computing the probability of the system states at time t or associate a reward structure to the system states.

The use of a high level formalism based on Petri nets, as promoted in [8], seems to have a good trade-off between the modelling power (class of systems that can be specified) and the amount of human intervention in the definition of the model, as claimed in the same paper.

In this paper we start from the class of MPS generated by Stochastic Petri Nets as in [2]: the phases are described as a Petri net (the *Phase Net*) which only includes deterministic transitions and immediate ones, with exactly one deterministic transition enabled in each phase; And the system behaviour is again a Petri nets (the *System Net*) that only includes exponential and immediate transitions. Transition enabling and firing rates in the System Net may depend on the marking of the Phase Net and this permits a description of the system that is compact (a single net) but that is able to describe a behaviour that may differ from phase to phase.

An MPS net is indeed a *Deterministic and Stochastic Petri Net* (DSPN) [9, 10], or more precisely, a non-ergodic DSPN, since phases (the mission) always come to an end. DSPNs have the requirement that at most one deterministic transition is enabled in any one state, which is indeed true for MPS. The stochastic process of a DSPN is a *Markov Regenerative Process* (MRP) [11] which has been widely used in the modelling community since it can describe more complex behaviours than a continuous time Markov chain, while still allowing an analytical solution.

A MRP is a stochastic process defined by a sequence of time instants called *renewal times* in which the process loses its memory, i.e. the age of non-exponential (general) events is 0. The behaviour between these points is then described by a time-limited stochastic process, and we consider MRP in which the time limited stochastic process is a CTMC. MRPs have been studied extensively in the past [10, 12], and many solid analysis techniques exists.

The limitations imposed on the Phase net allow Mura et al. to show in [2] that the solution of the MPS can be decomposed in a sequence of transient solutions of Markov chains. The DEEM tool [1] implements this method. Although not

VALUETOOLS 2016, October 25-28, Taormina, Italy

recent, DEEM can still be considered the state of the art tool for MPS definition and solution.

In [13] a component-based solution technique for non-ergodic MRP has been defined. The MRP process is decomposed into smaller components that are solved in isolation with the cheapest possible technique. Indeed there are cases in which the solution of a component is equivalent to the transient solution of a CTMC. The method has been implemented inside the GreatSPN tool [14] as a solver for non-ergodic DSPNs and it is also part of the model-checker MC4CSLTA [15] of the stochastic logic CSL^{TA} [16].

This paper shows that the Component Method applied to MPS nets identifies the same components and has the same time complexity as the ad-hoc techniques developed for MPS and implemented in DEEM. Moreover we show that the Component Method can solve an extended class of MPS, that we shall term X-MPS. This extension has a practical relevance since it lifts many of the limitation imposed on MPS, for example an event in the system net may now stop and/or restart a phase, and the Phases net can also include exponential transitions.

On the other side the memory requirement of the DEEM solver is smaller, since the state spaces of the single phases are built in isolation and the state space of phase i is built, used and destroyed before the one for the $i+1$ phase. Basically DEEM builds the state space by chunks, only when needed, in a sort of on-the-fly solution. The Component Method is a general technique for non-ergodic MRPs and DSPNs, and therefore cannot build the system phase by phase since it does not know about phases.

An important aspect of DEEM is that it is specifically designed for MPS, so it has a lot of interesting features that makes the modeller activity simpler (like the separation of the description of the phases and of the basic system, the heavy use of marking dependencies and the rich reward structure). The result of this investigation indicates that a good way to follow is the integration of the best MPS characteristics of DEEM and GreatSPN in a single tool.

The paper develops as follows: Section 2 defines the necessary background on the Component Method for MRP solution (in 2.1) and on MPS and the DEEM tool (in 2.2). Section 3 shows the application of the Component Method to MPS, enlightening the extension to the current MPS DEEM models in Section 4. Section 5 studies the efficacy of the proposed technique through a set of numerical experiments on a standard and extended MPS models. Finally Section 6 concludes the paper and outlines future possible extensions and integration activities.

2. BACKGROUND

2.1 Component based solution of MRP

We assume the reader is familiar with the definition of Markov renewal sequence and of (time-homogeneous) Markov regenerative process built on a Markov Renewal sequence. A full description can be found in [17] and in [10] for a definition and notation of MRP related to DSPN. In this paper we use German's notation as in [10] and [13]. In MRP the process behaviour among regeneration points is a discrete-time Markov chain, called the *embedded Markov chain* (EMC), while the process behaviour between two regeneration points is described by a continuous-time process, called the *subordinated process*. In this paper we consider only the class of MRP where the subordinated process is a CTMC.

A MRP can be represented as a discrete event system (like in [18]) with a finite state space, where in each state a general event g is taken from a set G. As the time flows, the age of g being enabled is kept, until either g fires ($\mathbf{\Delta}$ event), or a Markovian transition, concurrent with g, fires. Markovian events may actually disable g (preemptive event, or $\bar{\mathbf{Q}}$ event), clearing its age, or keep g running with its accumulated age (non-preemptive event, or $\mathbf{Q}$ event). Matrix $\mathbf{Q}$ accounts for the rates of the exponential transitions whose firing does not disable any general (deterministic) transition; Matrix $\bar{\mathbf{Q}}$ accounts for the rates of the exponential transitions whose firing disables a general (or deterministic) one; And matrix $\mathbf{\Delta}$ has, for each entry $\mathbf{\Delta}_{i,j}$, the probability of ending in state j when the general transition fires in state i.

The *embedded Markov chain* (EMC) $\mathbf{P}$ is defined in terms of the $\mathbf{Q}$, $\bar{\mathbf{Q}}$, and $\mathbf{\Delta}$ in a standard manner (see [10] for example), but even if the three matrices are sparse, matrix $\mathbf{P}$ is usually dense and expensive to compute, due to the matrix exponential terms. This problem has been solved in [10] with the *matrix-free* technique (actually $\mathbf{P}$-free), based on the idea that $\mathbf{P}$ can be substituted by a function of the $\mathbf{Q}$, $\bar{\mathbf{Q}}$, and $\mathbf{\Delta}$ (sparse) matrices of the MRP. These functions are used in vector×matrix products with $\mathbf{P}$ so that they can be computed without the need of constructing and storing $\mathbf{P}$.

A non-ergodic EMC allows to distinguish transient and recurrent states, and specialized solution methods can be devised to compute the probability distribution of recurrent states. The work in [13, 19] introduces an efficient steady-state solution for non-ergodic MRPs, called *Component Method*, which computes the outgoing probability flow from transient to recurrent subsets of states, called *components*. In graph terms components corresponds to the union of one or more strongly connected components (SCC) of the MRP state space and they must satisfy the requirement that the component graph (the condensed graph in which each component is condensed in a single node) is a directly acyclic graph (DAG). The method is also given in matrix-free terms, so the components and their characteristic matrices are computed directly on the state space and on the $\mathbf{Q}$, $\bar{\mathbf{Q}}$, and $\mathbf{\Delta}$ matrices of the MRP, and there is no need to compute the expensive and dense matrix $\mathbf{P}$.

The basic idea of the Component Method is readily explained unrealistically assuming that matrix $\mathbf{P}$ is available. If the MRP is non-ergodic it is indeed possible to rearrange the order of its states so that the EMC matrix $\mathbf{P}$ is in upper-triangular form (the *reducible normal form*, or RNF):

$$\mathbf{P} = \begin{bmatrix} \mathbf{T}_1 & \boxed{\quad\mathbf{F}_1\quad} & & \\ & \ddots & \ddots & \\ & & \mathbf{T}_k & \boxed{\quad\mathbf{F}_k\quad} \\ & & & \mathbf{R}_{k+1} \\ & & & \quad\ddots \\ & & & \qquad\mathbf{R}_m \end{bmatrix} \qquad (1)$$

Matrix $\mathbf{P}$ has $k \geq 0$ transient subsets and $(m-k)$ recurrent subsets of states, with $m > k$. Let $\mathcal{S}_i \subseteq \mathcal{S}$ be the set of states in subset i, hereafter called the *component i*. Alternatively, the upper triangular form of $\mathbf{P}$ can be seen as if the $\mathcal{S}_i$ subsets form a DAG of components. A standard way to build an RNF for a non-ergodic process is to take as $\mathcal{S}_i$ sets the set of *strongly connected components* (SCC) [20] of the graph built by considering $\mathbf{P}$ as an adjacency matrix. Transient

SCCs are the $\mathcal{S}_i$ for $i \leq k$, and bottom SCC (BSCC) are the $\mathcal{S}_i$ for the recurrent classes ($k < i \leq m$). Indeed SCCs are the finest partition of $\mathbf{P}$ that result in an acyclic set of components. A convenient numbering of the $\mathcal{S}_i$ can then be found visiting in topological order the component graph.

When $\mathbf{P}$ is in RNF, the steady-state probability of being in the recurrent states can be computed using the outgoing probability vectors $\boldsymbol{\mu}_i$. The *outgoing probability* vector $\boldsymbol{\mu}_i$ gives for each state $s \in (\mathcal{S} \setminus \mathcal{S}_i)$ the probability of reaching s in one jump while leaving $\mathcal{S}_i$. Vector $\boldsymbol{\mu}_i$ is given by:

$$\boldsymbol{\mu}_i = \Big(\boldsymbol{\alpha}_i + \sum_{j<i}(\mathbf{I}_i \cdot \boldsymbol{\mu}_j)\Big) \cdot (\mathbf{I} - \mathbf{T}_i)^{-1} \cdot \mathbf{F}_i, \quad i \leq k \tag{2}$$

where $\boldsymbol{\alpha}_i$ is the vector of initial probability for the states in $\mathcal{S}_i$. We adopt the *matrix filter* notation of [10] where: $\mathbf{I}^g$ is the matrix derived from the identity matrix of size $|\mathcal{S}|$ where each row corresponding to states that do not enable g are set to zero; And $\mathbf{I}^E$ is the same for states that do not enable any general transition (exponential states). Since matrix inversion is usually expensive, a product of a generic vector $\mathbf{u}$ with $(\mathbf{I} - \mathbf{T}_i)^{-1}$ can be reformulated as a linear equations system $\mathbf{x} \cdot (\mathbf{I} - \mathbf{T}_i) = \mathbf{u}$. This system can be computed iteratively using vector×matrix products with $\mathbf{T}_i$. Each vectors $\boldsymbol{\mu}_i$ may depend on the previous $(i-1)$ outgoing probability vectors, implicitly defining a computational order. Given the $\boldsymbol{\mu}_i$ vectors, the steady state probability of the recurrent subsets $\mathcal{S}_i$ is given by:

$$\boldsymbol{\pi}_i = \Big(\boldsymbol{\alpha}_i + \sum_{j=1}^{k}(\mathbf{I}_i \cdot \boldsymbol{\mu}_j)\Big) \cdot \lim_{n\to\infty} (\mathbf{R}_i)^n, \quad k < i \leq m \tag{3}$$

The Component Method computes first equation (2) for all transient components, taken in an order that respects the condition $j < i$ of the formula, and then computes the probability for the recurrent subsets based on equation (3).

When the $\mathbf{P}$ matrix is available in RNF, the computation of (2) and (3) is straightforward.

In [13] the matrix-free method is generalized for the case of the reducible normal form of Eq. 1 giving rise to a *matrix-free component method*, Component Method for short. This generalization provides: 1) a derivation of the m subsets $\mathcal{S}_i$ (components) which is based only on $\mathbf{Q}$, $\bar{\mathbf{Q}}$ and $\boldsymbol{\Delta}$; 2) the matrix-free form of the sub-terms $\mathbf{T}_i$, $\mathbf{F}_i$ and $\mathbf{R}_i$, to be used in Eq. (2) and (3). The computation of the products of a generic vector $\mathbf{u}$ with the matrix-free form of $\mathbf{T}_i$ and $\mathbf{F}_i$ is given by:

$$\mathbf{u}\mathbf{T}_i = \mathbf{I}_i \cdot (\mathbf{a}_{\widehat{i}}(\mathbf{u}) + \mathbf{b}_{\widehat{i}}(\mathbf{u}) + \mathbf{c}_i(\mathbf{u})) \tag{4}$$

$$\mathbf{u}\mathbf{F}_i = (\mathbf{I} - \mathbf{I}_i) \cdot (\mathbf{a}_{\widehat{i}}(\mathbf{u}) + \mathbf{b}_{\widehat{i}}(\mathbf{u}) + \mathbf{c}_i(\mathbf{u})) \tag{5}$$

where $\mathbf{I}_i$ is a matrix derived from $\mathbf{I}$ where rows of states not in $\mathcal{S}_i$ are zeroed, $\mathbf{I}_{\widehat{i}}$ is the same for the augmented set $\widehat{\mathcal{S}}_i$, and $\boldsymbol{\Delta}_{\widehat{i}} = \mathbf{I}_{\widehat{i}} \cdot \boldsymbol{\Delta}$, $\bar{\mathbf{Q}}_{\widehat{i}} = \mathbf{I}_{\widehat{i}} \cdot \bar{\mathbf{Q}}$. The *augmented set* $\widehat{\mathcal{S}}_i$ of component i is the closure over $\mathbf{Q}$ of the states $\mathcal{S}_i$ of components i, that is to say the augmented set of a component is made by the states of the components plus all the states that can be reached through Markovian events that do not disable any general (that is to say all states that are reachable before the next regeneration point).

The vector terms $\mathbf{a}_{\widehat{i}}(\mathbf{u})$, $\mathbf{b}_{\widehat{i}}(\mathbf{u})$ and $\mathbf{c}_i(\mathbf{u})$ are:

$$\begin{aligned}
\mathbf{a}_{\widehat{i}}(\mathbf{u}) &= \mathbf{u} \cdot \Big(\sum_{g\in G} \mathbf{I}^g_{\widehat{i}} \cdot e^{\mathbf{Q}_{\widehat{i}}\delta^g}\Big) \cdot \boldsymbol{\Delta}_{\widehat{i}} \\
\mathbf{b}_{\widehat{i}}(\mathbf{u}) &= \mathbf{u} \cdot \Big(\sum_{g\in G} \mathbf{I}^g_{\widehat{i}} \cdot \int_0^{\delta^g} e^{\mathbf{Q}_{\widehat{i}}x}\, dx\Big) \cdot \bar{\mathbf{Q}}_{\widehat{i}} \\
\mathbf{c}_i(\mathbf{u}) &= \mathbf{u} \cdot \Big(\mathbf{I}^E_i - \text{diag}^{-1}(\mathbf{Q}^E_i)\mathbf{Q}^E_i\Big)
\end{aligned}$$

with $\mathbf{Q}^E_i = \mathbf{I}_i \cdot \mathbf{Q}^E = \mathbf{I}_i \cdot \mathbf{I}^E \cdot \mathbf{Q}$. These terms describe how the process evolves between two regeneration points. Vector $\mathbf{a}_{\widehat{i}}(\mathbf{u})$ and $\mathbf{b}_{\widehat{i}}(\mathbf{u})$ are the probability distribution of the next regeneration state reached with the firing of the general event ($\mathbf{a}$), or with the preemption of it ($\mathbf{b}$). Vector $\mathbf{c}_i(\mathbf{u})$ is the probability distribution of the next regeneration state when there are no general events enabled in the starting state. Note that the computation of $\mathbf{a}$ and $\mathbf{b}$ on a subset $\mathcal{S}_i$ of states has to consider all the states in the augmented set $\widehat{\mathcal{S}}_i$. Eq. (4) and (5) assumes that the subsets $\{\mathcal{S}_i\}$ have been identified.

The advantage of working at the component level is not only the trivial one of solving many small models instead of a single much bigger one, but that the cheapest available solution for each component can be used. It is sometimes possible that the component's solution do not bear the full complexity of the solution of a MRP.

Although it is intuitive and usually true that solving many small matrices is less expensive than solving a big one, in the matrix-free Component Method this is not always true. Indeed as the solution of a single components may actually require to consider states that are not part of that components (due to the construction of the augmented set), so that often it is convenient to aggregate small components into a bigger one. The work in [19, 21] already identifies a need for aggregating the components into bigger ones, and often the performance of the algorithm depends on the number, size, and solution complexity of the components. The aggregation is defined through a set of rules, to decide which components can be aggregated together, and could be done using a greedy heuristic (fast) or integer linear programming (ILP) [22] (optimal but slower). The Component Method, including the component optimization and the greedy heuristics, have been implemented as part of the GreatSPN solver for non-ergodic DSPNs. GreatSPN [14] is a tool for Petri net definition and analysis developed mainly at the University of Torino during the last 30 years. GreatSPN has been recently renovated to include a new Java-based interface with colored and plain token game simulation, model checking for branching and stochastic logics, a new solver for DSPN, and additional facilities for model composition and for performing multiple experiments. GreatSPN, including the solution used in this paper, is available upon request visiting its web page [23].

2.2 Background: MPS and DEEM

In this paper we consider definition and notation of MPS in [1, 8], in which the mission is divided into m phases of deterministic duration δ_i, and the system behavior in each phase is described by a CTMC with state space $\mathcal{S}_i$ and rate matrix $\mathbf{Q}_i$. The MPS is defined using a restricted class of DSPN called *Phased Petri net* (PPN) [24].

In a PPN the system is described by two Petri nets [25]: a *phase net* (PhN), which defines the phase structure and a *system net* (SN), which describes the stochastic behavior of the system components during each phase of the mission. Marking dependent rates and guards can be used to make the SN behaviour dependent from a specific phase, and the probability of immediate transitions in the PhN can depend from the marking of the SN: this allows the choice of the next phase to depend upon the state of the SN.

A number of limitations have been imposed on the PhN and SN and on their dependency, partly to provide a guideline to the modeller, and partly to allow for a decomposable solution [1,2]: *L1*) The PhN can only have deterministic and immediate transitions - no exponential delays are allowed, *L2*) the reachability graph of the PhN should be a DAG (directed acyclic graph), *L3*) each phase is described by a single tangible marking of the PhN which enables a single deterministic transition, *L4*) an event occurring in the SN cannot disable a phase (the firing of a transition in the SN cannot preempt a deterministic transition). Note that condition 2 implies that the whole stochastic process is non-ergodic.

Under the above limitations the work in [2] observes that the time at which the deterministic transitions of the PhN fire correspond to regeneration instants, and the markings after the firing are markings in which the system regenerates. Moreover since there is no preemption of the deterministic and the state space of the PhN is acyclic, it is possible to devise a decomposed solution approach, from regeneration point to regeneration point, approach that we explain in the following according to the schema described in [1].

The first step consists in generating the state space of the PhN. By definition each phase i is characterized by a single marking m_i and by a deterministic transition of delay δ_i, therefore it is possible to solve the whole system as follows (at the beginning $i = 0$):

- Compute the state space $\mathcal{S}_i$ of the SN when the PhN is in state m_i and build the associated rate matrix $\mathbf{Q}_i$
- Compute the transient solution at time δ_i of the CTMC specified by $\mathbf{Q}_i$ (which gives the distribution of the markings of the SN at the time phase i ends)
- Compute the $\mathbf{\Delta}_{i,j}$ matrices, the branching probability matrix of size $|\mathcal{S}_i| \times |\mathcal{S}_j|$ of going to the states of phase j at the end of phase i. This requires to build the state spaces of the SN for two successive phases
- The solution at time δ_i of $\mathcal{S}_i$ is mapped, through $\mathbf{\Delta}_{ij}$ to the initial probability of the successive components

The above sequence is repeated for successive phases until the target time t of the analysis has been reached. If t is greater than the sum of the duration of all the phases (complete duration of the mission) this corresponds to the distribution of the absorbing states of the system at the end of the mission. If t is smaller, let's say between the end of phase $i-1$ and i then $\mathbf{Q}_i$ is solved at time $t - t'$, where t' is the sum of all the duration of the previous phases.

The theory summarized above has been implemented inside the prototype tool DEEM [1]. Although not recent, DEEM can still be considered the state of the art tool for MPS definition and solution based on Petri nets. DEEM is not only a solver but also has a GUI for the definition of the PhN and of the SN, including facilities for the definition of marking dependent rates, transitions' guards and a reward structure.

For what concerns the time complexity, if there are N phases DEEM generates and computes the transient solution of N CTMCs. The space complexity is determined by the need of building N state spaces for the SN (one per phase) and the corresponding N CTMCs, and $N-1$ state spaces for pairs of successive phases (of size $|\mathcal{S}_i| + |\mathcal{S}_j|$) to build the $\mathbf{\Delta}_{i,j}$ matrices.

3. COMPONENT METHOD VS DEEM

From now on we use the MPS term to mean a MPS model defined through a DSPN that follows the PPN limitations *L1-L4*. Since a MPS is a non-ergodic DSPN, it makes sense to compare the solution approach of DEEM with the Component Method,. The comparison is organized as a set of questions for which to provide an answer. Given an MPS: *Q1*) do the two techniques consider the same components? *Q2*) do they solve the components with techniques of comparable complexity? *Q3*) do they use comparable amounts of memory?

A first step is to better understand the characteristics of the MRP produced by a MPS. If we consider the embedded Markov chain transition matrix $\mathbf{P}$ in RNF form, what are the block matrices involved? Since the state space of the PhN forms a DAG, we can certainly find a RNF form for the embedded Markov Chain transition matrix $\mathbf{P}$, in which the states of phase i corresponds to the subset i in the matrix of Eq. 1, as it was shown in [2] that the end of a phase corresponds to a regeneration point. For ease the notation each $\mathbf{F}_i$ matrix is split into multiple $\mathbf{F}_{i,j}$ submatrices, with $i < j \leq m$. We can then observe that:

$$\begin{aligned} \mathbf{T}_i &= \mathbf{0} \\ \mathbf{F}_{i,j} &= \mathrm{e}^{\mathbf{Q}_i \delta_i} \cdot \mathbf{\Delta}_{i,j} \\ \mathbf{R}_i &= \mathbf{I}_i - \mathrm{diag}^{-1}(\mathbf{Q}_i) \cdot \mathbf{Q}_i \end{aligned} \tag{6}$$

each $\mathbf{T}_i$ will be zero, since $\mathbf{T}_i$ is the submatrix of the probability of remaining in $\mathcal{S}_i$ at the end of the phase, but this is not allowed since the PhN is a DAG. The $\mathbf{F}_{i,j}$ matrices describe the probability of moving from the start of phase i to the start of phase j, and this involves the solution at time δ_i and the probability among phases (terms $\mathrm{e}^{\mathbf{Q}_i \delta_i}$ and $\mathbf{\Delta}_{i,j}$). The $\mathbf{R}_i$ terms corresponds to the recurrent terminal phases (phases with no successors), and the steady state solution can be applied. Note that, when DEEM solves an MPS at time t also the terminal phases are solved in transient.

A second step for the comparison is to recall the component classification of the Component Method and the associated computational costs when general transitions are restricted to deterministic ones. Table 1, re-elaborated from [13, Table 2], follows the classification of components in [22] and defines three component types.

Class C_E identifies components in which there is no state that enables a general transition. Their solution requires a fixed point iteration over the portion of the $\mathbf{Q}$ matrix that corresponds to $\mathcal{S}_i$. The $\mathbf{a}$ and $\mathbf{b}$ terms of (4) are zero, and a product with $(\mathbf{I}_i - \mathbf{T}_i)^{-1}$ has the same cost of a steady state solution of a CTMC.

Class C_g identifies components in which 1) there is a single deterministic g enabled; and 2) no preemption of g, if any, keeps the system inside the component. Their solution cost is that of a transient solution at time δ_g of a CTMC, over the augmented set $\widehat{\mathcal{S}}_i$. Since any preemptive Markovian or deterministic event takes the system out of the component, then $\mathbf{T}_i$ is empty, and $(\mathbf{I}_i - \mathbf{T}_i)^{-1}$ reduces to $\mathbf{I}_i$.

Finally class C_M identifies components in which either different general transitions are enabled (of course in different states) or there are preemptive events that keep the system inside the component. The process structure of the component is a MRP.

Coming back to the questions, to answer to *Q1* (do the two techniques consider the same components?) we should consider that DEEM generates the CTMC of each phase in isolation, doing a state space generation in which the marking of the PhN is kept fixed and equal to the marking that enables the deterministic transition of phase i. Let g be such a transition. In the Component Method the criteria behind the definition of an optimal partition of the MRP [13, 22] is that, starting from the initial definition of components as SCCs, two components are aggregated together only if they belong to the same complexity class and if the resulting complexity class is the same, given that the component graph after the aggregation is still a DAG. The component construction will indeed put together all states that enable g, whether they correspond to one or more SCCs, since all those SCC are of class C_g, and their union is still of class C_g, since no preemption of the deterministic transitions can take place in a MPS and the firing of the deterministic takes the system outside of all SCCs that enable g (since g is not enabled any longer).

The answer to *Q2* (time complexity) is straightforward given that there is a component per phase, and the component is of type C_g. The $\boldsymbol{\mu}_g$ vector of Eq. 2 is therefore computed with a transient solution at time δ_g, that is to say at the time the phase ends, as does the solver of DEEM.

The answer to *Q3* (memory) shows a difference in the maximum amount of storage used. Both techniques computes the same $\mathbf{Q}_i$ and $\boldsymbol{\Delta}_{ij}$ matrices, but the Component Method builds all of them beforehand, to be able to compute the components, while DEEM can exploit the knowledge of the PhN state space to build the SN of the phases one by one and the $\boldsymbol{\Delta}_{ij}$ using pair of phases. So the maximum amount of memory for the Component Method is the size of the whole system, and for DEEM is the maximum size of a pair of SN of two consecutive phases. The difference is linear in the number of phases.

In summary we can say that the more general method (the Component Method) when applied to the MPS with the limitations required by DEEM performs the same computations as DEEM which has instead an ad-hoc solver for MPS. The Component Method uses at most N times more memory than DEEM.

4. EXTENDED MPS MODELS

The Component Method is a general technique for non ergodic DSPN, so we can envision to lift all the limitations imposed by MPS and simply keep the requirement that the DSPN has to be non-ergodic. But this is an approach that may not be very useful for a designer that wants to use Petri nets to study a phased system, for which a more structured approach in the description of the system can be useful. We propose therefore to define an extended class of MPS, called X-MPS by simply lifting the limitation imposed on MPS.

Definition 1. An X-MPS is a non-ergodic DSPN composed of two nets, a Phase net, which is a DSPN, and a System Net, which is a GSPN [26] (only exponential and immediate transitions with associated priorities and inhibitor arcs).

X-MPS models can be solved efficiently with the Component Method, by devising the structure of the solution directly at the MRP level. Note that to ensure non-ergodicity in an easy manner we can re-insert limitation *L2* (the reachability graph of the PhN should be a DAG), but it is not required if the modeller is expert enough in Petri net modelling and, for example, stops a phase as a consequence of a SN event.

Lifting limitation *L1* and *L3* allows a richer description of phases in which phase duration may include some non-deterministic duration and more complex behaviour than a single marking, as in MPS. Removing limitation *L4* allows the SN to stop and restart a phase before its end, or to stop a phase and go to the next one (for example in a scheduled maintenance system a failure of a certain severity in the SN can interrupt the scheduled maintenance phase to start a more extensive maintenance activity).

The modelling power of X-MPS are shown in the next section through a number of examples of a SMS of increased complexity.

5. NUMERICAL RESULTS

In this section we consider an example of a *Scheduled Maintenance System* (SMS) model, inspired by [3], and represented using the PPN formalism. We shall first consider it in a standard MPS and then we show how it could be modified into an X-MPS to account for more complex features.

Fig. 1 shows the model of the SMS drawn with DEEM (upper part), which explicitly supports PPN, and with GreatSPN (lower part), in which the SMS is modeled as a DSPN. The SMS model represents an alternation between a factory work phase and a maintenance phase. The PhN and the SN are drawn into separate boxes, both in DEEM and in GreatSPN. The PhN models the alternation between work and maintenance, for *NP* consecutive cycles. During the production, raw pieces are loaded from a warehouse, are transformed following a sequence of steps with one of the M available machines, and are then moved back in a storage as finished products. Machines may break, and are therefore subject to a continuous maintenance that is scheduled at fixed intervals during the maintenance phase. In addition, workers have S spare parts to fix the machines between each maintenance cycle, parts that are replenished during maintenance.

In DEEM, each transition may have a guard condition that determines in which phase it is available. This feature, part of the PPN formalism, is not available in GreatSPN. Thus, the GreatSPN model has additional test/inhibitor arcs to model such guards.

Table 2 shows a comparison of the MPS method with the Component Method. The comparison is done for an increasing value of the parameter *NP*, which controls the number of phases. The table reports the PPN parameters, and the results of the MPS solver of DEEM and of the Component Method. For DEEM, the table reports the total number of phases, the maximum number of states per phase, and the total time. For the Component Method, the table reports the total number of states, the number and types of components obtained, and the total time. The last two columns report the expected number of completed products and failures of the machines after running for *NP* phases, computed with both tools, that, as expected, compute the same values.

Table 1: Classification of MRP components.

Class	*Component identification*	*Component characteristics*	*Cost of computing Eq.* (2)
C_E	No general enabled.	CTMC.	Steady state CTMC solution.
C_g	$\bar{\mathbf{Q}}_{i,i} = 0 \wedge \mathbf{\Delta}_{i,i} = 0$; g enabled and no internal $\bar{\mathbf{Q}}/\mathbf{\Delta}$ events.	CTMC under general event g.	Transient CTMC solution at time δ^g.
C_M	$\bar{\mathbf{Q}}_{i,i} \neq 0 \vee \mathbf{\Delta}_{i,i} \neq 0$, g enabled, internal $\bar{\mathbf{Q}}/\mathbf{\Delta}$ events. Mixed enabling of general events	MRP.	Steady state MRP solution.

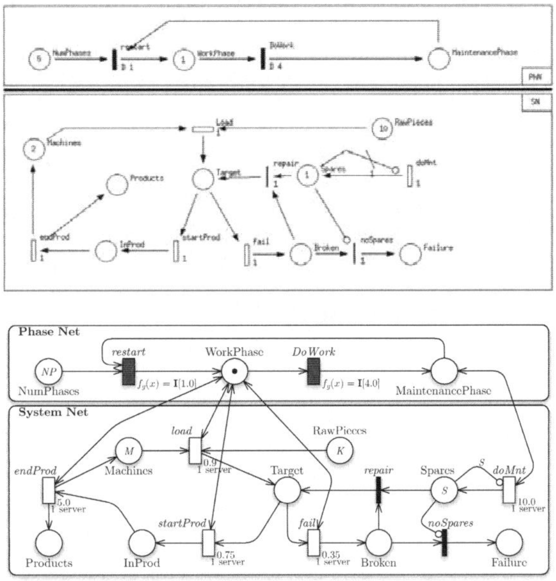

Figure 1: Scheduled Maintenance System drawn in DEEM (above, as a PPN) and in GreatSPN (below, as a DSPN).

The first observation is that DEEM execution times are much slower than expected. This is presumably due to a combination of two factors: DEEM is a prototype implementation, moreover it has been executed inside a virtual machine. For what concerns the memory requirements, from the upper table it is clear that GreatSPN builds the whole state space in a single shot (column States), while DEEM builds the state space of one phase at a time. Actually the maximum memory required by DEEM is not 389 but $2 * 389$ since two phases are needed to build the $\mathbf{\Delta}_{ij}$ matrices, but what is relevant is that this value does not increase with the number of phases.

A second observation is that, as shown in Section 3, the Component Method computes a number of components of type C_g which is equal to the number of phases, plus a final C_E component that includes all absorbing states. In this terminal component no deterministic or exponential is enabled (indeed matrix $\mathbf{Q}_i$, $\bar{\mathbf{Q}}_i$, and $\mathbf{\Delta}_i$ are empty).

The lower part of Table 2 reports in more details the structure of the phases and of the components for the two methods. Since the components correspond to the MPS phases, they are listed together. For the Component Method the component size is split into the states used in the solution (column tangible states) and the states of the frontier (state reached by a C_g component after the firing of g.

Table 2: MPS method compared to Component Method.

M=3, S=1			MPS method (DEEM)			Component method (GreatSPN)						
Model time	NP	K	Num phases	max states per phase	Time	States	C_E	C_g	C_M	Time	E[Failures]	E[Products]
14	2	10	5	389	39.9	2257	1	5	0	0.2	0.74	4.81
24	4	10	9	389	73.0	3813	1	9	0	0.2	1.11	7.38
34	6	10	13	389	118.6	5369	1	13	0	0.3	1.38	9.27
44	8	10	17	389	237.8	6925	1	17	0	0.4	1.55	10.55
54	10	10	21	389	372.8	8481	1	21	0	0.6	1.62	11.20
64	12	10	25	389	465.1	10037	1	25	0	0.8	1.65	11.41

Details for the phases/components of case NP=2, K=10:

	MPS method		Component method			
Phase num	tangible states	non-zero entries	tangible states	frontier states	total comp. states	type
1 Work	312	539	312	312	624	C_g
2 Maintenance	389	1166	389	389	778	C_g
3 Work	389	1230	389	389	778	C_g
4 Maintenance	389	1166	389	389	778	C_g
5 Work	389	1230	389	389	778	C_g
6 (system blocked)	-	-	389	0	389	C_E

X-MPS model of the SMS.

The original SMS model of interest has some additional rules that cannot be expressed as MPS, but corresponds to X-MPS. Since phases have deterministic duration, it may happen that the maintenance phase starts when the machines are processing some item. The maintenance phase needs to wait for their completion before starting. This makes the PhN dependent on a condition of the SN, which is not expressible in standard MPS. In addition maintenance could take a varying quantity of time, and thus is not represented anymore with a fixed-delay transition, but by the exponential transiton *restart*. Fig. 2 shows the Petri nets of the modified SMS as an X-MPS form, drawn with GreatSPN.

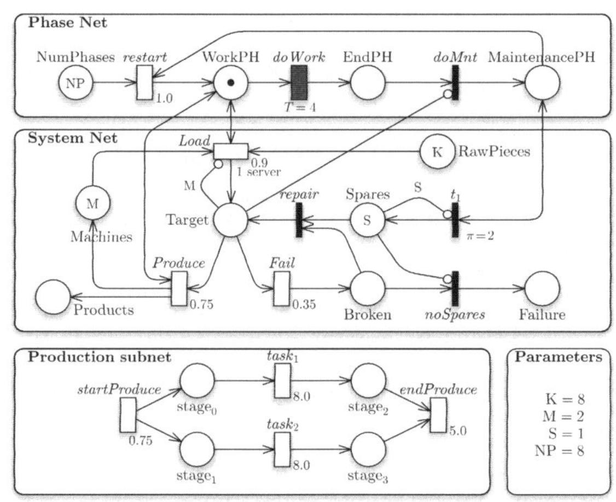

Figure 2: SMS extended with delayed maintenance rule.

Transition *Produce* is actually a subnet, shown in the lower part of Fig. 2), that models two parallel stages of the production. The delayed start of the maintenance phase is modeled using the inhibitor arc from place Target (and any place in the production subnet) to the transition *doMnt*.

The SMS in X-MPS form is tested in four different configurations. In configuration (A) a fixed number of phases is performed before the system stops. Configuration (B) is similar, runs are performed for an increasing number of both pieces and phases. Configuration (C) allows for an unbounded number of maintenance cycles: place *NumPhases* has been removed and the net is modified so that the work phase is interrupted when there are no more raw pieces. Tests are done on a varying number of parallel working machines and spare parts available to compute the probability distribution of machines into the *Failure* place at the time the system has consumed 10 raw pieces. Finally, configuration (D) has both unbounded phases and pieces, and computes the distribution of the states when all machines have failed. The net of configuration (D) can also be used to tests the duration of the *maintenance free operating period* (MFOP) of the system [24, 27]. Table 3 shows the results of the four configurations of the SMS for varying parameters.

Table 3: Component method on the extended SMS model.

(A) Finite number of phases set to NP=8:

				Standard		Component method			
K	States	SCC	BSCC	Iter.	Time	C_E	C_g	C_M	Time
20	16146	16146	99	30	23.8	9	9	0	2.9
40	32906	32906	199	31	52.6	9	9	0	6.1
60	49666	49666	299	31	79.8	9	9	0	9.1
80	66426	66426	399	31	108.4	9	9	0	12.3
100	83186	83186	499	31	134.1	9	9	0	15.5

(B) Increasing number of phases NP and pieces K, four machines:

					Standard		Component method			
K	NP	States	SCC	BSCC	Iter.	Time	C_E	C_g	C_M	Time
10	5	29877	29877	79	26	70.7	6	6	0	7.0
20	10	128407	128407	169	54	596.6	11	11	0	31.7
30	15	294237	294237	259	206	4943.6	16	16	0	74.6
40	20	527367	527367	349	-	-	21	21	0	136.4
50	25	827797	827797	439	-	-	26	26	0	215.5

(C) Unbound number of phases, waits for K=10 pieces completed:

					Standard		Component method			
M	S	States	SCC	BSCC	Iter.	Time	C_E	C_g	C_M	Time
10	2	830	467	13	25	1.0	9	9	18	2.6
10	3	3055	1796	17	30	6.4	10	9	18	18.1
10	4	8542	5219	23	42	31.4	10	9	18	76.2
20	2	1770	967	23	42	3.6	19	19	38	10.9
20	3	6865	3906	27	59	27.0	20	19	38	84.6
20	4	20432	12059	33	84	149.9	20	19	38	395.9

(D) Closed system, unbounded number of phases, ends with *Failure*:

				Standard		Component method			
K	States	SCC	BSCC	Iter.	Time	C_E	C_g	C_M	Time
20	5123	293	1	57	25.7	0	3	4	15.4
40	10683	613	1	85	81.7	0	3	4	65.8
60	16243	933	1	119	177.5	0	3	4	146.1
80	21803	1253	1	171	356.5	0	3	4	246.0
100	27363	1573	1	213	565.9	0	3	4	391.1

Note that, if we release the condition of delayed maintenance and of exponential duration of transition *restart*, configurations (A) and (B) simplify to an MPS, but configurations (C) and (D) are X-MPS system, since they have an unbounded number of phases. As we shall see, this type of net generates components of class C_M, which cannot be modeled using regular MPS.

Each table reports the test parameters, the number of MRP states, and the number of SCCs and BSCCs in the non-ergodic state space $\mathcal{S}$. Since we cannot compare with DEEM, we compare the matrix-free Component Method with a standard matrix-free solution of MRP [28] ("Standard" columns), that solves the whole system as a single component. Finally, the last four columns report the number of components obtained using the method described in this paper, divided per class type, and the time to compute the steady state distribution of absorbing states.

Case (A) is a non-ergodic MRP where the entire process can be decomposed into a constant number of C_E and C_g components (half of the phases have an exponential duration). Case (B) is similar, but the number of components grows with the parameters. In these two cases the Component Method behaves significantly better than the standard matrix-free one. Note that the aggregation of SCC into components has a significant impact: these systems have hundreds of thousands of SCCs: treating them one at a time would result in prohibitive matrix management costs. Both (A) and (B) are totally irreversible nets (no loop among states), as can be seen by the fact that the number of SCCs is the same as the number of MRP states.

Case (C) is a MRP where the aggregated components form an intermix of components of all three classes, including the C_M. The number of C_M components is rather high and this is a typical case in which the Component Method costs more than the standard matrix-free method, due to the cost of matrix management and to some inefficiency of the implementation. Case (D) has a structure made with few components, where C_M ones are still present in a small number. The method performance are similar to that of case (C), except that the smaller number of C_M components makes the overall solution process more efficient than the standard matrix-free .

6. CONCLUSIONS AND FUTURE WORK

This paper extends the class of MPS systems that can be efficiently solved in an analytical manner thanks to the Component Method for non-ergodic MRPs. It also shows that, when applied to standard MPS behaves similarly to the ad-hoc MPS solver implemented in DEEM, despite using more memory. The Component Method implemented in GreatSPN also allows for transitions with (a limited number of different) general distributions, as far as there is at most one enabled in each state: a possible future extension is to include generally distributed transitions into the PhN definition.

We have seen that DEEM saves memory by building the state space of SN one phase at a time: recent work on on-the fly generation of MRP in the context of the MC4CSLTA model-checker, which is part of GreatSPN, can be a line to follow for the on-the-fly generation of the MPS state space.

Although we believe that the extensions introduced in this paper are of practical significance, as the possibility of an unbounded number of phases, the introduction of exponential delays in the PhN or the possibility for the SN to disable a phase, we should remark that certain features of DEEM not available in GreatSPN also have a practical relevance, in particular the separation in the definition of the PhN and SN net, the guards (to avoid too many crossing arcs), the reward structure and the computation of the probability at time t of the whole MPS. This last feature is strictly related to the choice of including only deterministic timings in the

PhN. The ideal MPS tool should include features of both tools, and in particular it would be very useful to have a tool in which the user can choose his/her own trade-off among modelling power and computable performance indices.

7. REFERENCES

[1] A. Bondavalli, S. Chiaradonna, F. Di Giandomenico, and I. Mura, "Dependability modeling and evaluation of multiple-phased systems using DEEM," *IEEE Transactions on Reliability*, vol. 53, no. 4, pp. 509–522, 2004.

[2] I. Mura and A. Bondavalli, "Markov Regenerative Stochastic Petri Nets to Model and Evaluate the Dependability of Phased Missions," *IEEE Transactions on Computers*, vol. 50, no. 12, pp. 1337–1351, 2001.

[3] A. Bondavalli, I. Mura, and K. S. Trivedi, *Dependability Modelling and Sensitivity Analysis of Scheduled Maintenance Systems*. Berlin, Heidelberg: Springer Berlin Heidelberg, 1999, pp. 7–23.

[4] Z. Peng, Y. Lu, and A. Miller, "Uncertainty analysis of phased mission systems with probabilistic timed automata," in *7th IEEE International Conference on Prognostics and Health Management (PHM'16)*, 2016.

[5] H. Choi, V. Mainkar, and K. S. Trivedi, "Sensitivity analysis of Deterministic and Stochastic Petri Nets," in *International Workshop on Modeling, Analysis, and Simulation On Computer and Telecommunication Systems (MASCOTS)*, San Diego, USA, 1993, pp. 271–276.

[6] A. K. Somani, J. A. Ritcey, and S. H. Au, "Computationally-efficient phased-mission reliability analysis for systems with variable configurations," *IEEE Transactions on Reliability*, vol. 41, no. 4, pp. 504–511, 1992.

[7] L. Xing and S. Amari, "Reliability of Phased-mission Systems," in *Handbook of Performability Engineering*, K. Misra, Ed. Springer London, 2008, pp. 349–368.

[8] I. Mura, A. Bondavalli, X. Zang, and K. S. Trivedi, "Dependability modeling and evaluation of Phased Mission Systems: a DSPN approach," in *Int. Conference on Dependable Computing for Critical Applications*. IEEE Press, 1999, pp. 299–318.

[9] M. Ajmone Marsan and G. Chiola, "On Petri nets with deterministic and exponentially distributed firing times," in *Advances in Petri Nets*, ser. Lecture Notes in Computer Science, vol. 266/1987. Springer Berlin / Heidelberg, 1987, pp. 132–145.

[10] R. German, *Performance Analysis of Communication Systems with Non-Markovian Stochastic Petri Nets*. New York, NY, USA: John Wiley & Sons, Inc., 2000.

[11] R. Pyke, *Markov Renewal Processes with Finitely Many States*. New York: Columbia University, 1959. [Online]. Available: http://books.google.it/books?id=ZFn7ygAACAAJ

[12] W. J. Stewart, *Probability, Markov chains, queues, and simulation : the mathematical basis of performance modeling*. Princeton (N.J.), Oxford: Princeton University Press, 2009.

[13] E. G. Amparore and S. Donatelli, "A component-based solution for reducible markov regenerative processes," *Performance Evaluation*, vol. 70, no. 6, pp. 400 – 422, 2013.

[14] E. G. Amparore, G. Balbo, M. Beccuti, S. Donatelli, and G. Franceschinis, *30 Years of GreatSPN*. Cham: Springer International Publishing, 2016, pp. 227–254.

[15] E. G. Amparore and S. Donatelli, "MC4CSL^{TA}: an efficient model checking tool for CSL^{TA}," in *International Conference on Quantitative Evaluation of Systems*. Los Alamitos, CA, USA: IEEE Computer Society, 2010, pp. 153–154.

[16] S. Donatelli, S. Haddad, and J. Sproston, "Model checking timed and stochastic properties with CSL^{TA}," *IEEE Transactions on Software Engineering*, vol. 35, no. 2, pp. 224–240, 2009.

[17] K. S. Trivedi, *Probability and Statistics with Reliability, Queuing, and Computer Science Applications*. 605 Third Avenue, New York, USA: John Wiley and Sons, Ltd., 2002.

[18] C. G. Cassandras and S. Lafortune, *Introduction to Discrete Event Systems*. Secaucus, NJ, USA: Springer-Verlag New York, Inc., 2006.

[19] E. G. Amparore and S. Donatelli, "A component-based solution method for non-ergodic Markov Regenerative Processes," in *Computer Performance Engineering*, ser. Lecture Notes in Computer Science. Springer Berlin Heidelberg, 2010, vol. 6342, pp. 236–251.

[20] R. Tarjan, "Depth-first search and linear graph algorithms," in *Proceedings of the 12th Annual Symposium on Switching and Automata Theory (SWAT 1971)*. Washington, DC, USA: IEEE Computer Society, 1971, pp. 114–121.

[21] E. G. Amparore and S. Donatelli, "Improving and assessing the efficiency of the MC4CSL^{TA} model checker," in *Computer Performance Engineering*, ser. LNCS. Springer Berlin Heidelberg, 2013, vol. 8168, pp. 206–220.

[22] ——, "Optimal aggregation of components for the solution of Markov Regenerative Processes," to appear in QEST2016, August 2016.

[23] U. of Torino, "The greatspn tool homepage," http://www.di.unito.it/~greatspn/index.html.

[24] S. Chew, S. Dunnett, and J. Andrews, "Phased mission modelling of systems with maintenance-free operating periods using simulated petri nets," *Reliability Engineering & System Safety*, vol. 93, no. 7, pp. 980 – 994, 2008, bayesian Networks in Dependability.

[25] H. Choi, V. G. Kulkarni, and K. S. Trivedi, "Markov regenerative stochastic Petri nets," *Performance Evaluation*, vol. 20, no. 1-3, pp. 337–357, 1994.

[26] M. Ajmone-Marsan, G. Balbo, G. Conte, S. Donatelli, and G. Franceschinis, *Modelling with Generalized Stochastic Petri Nets*. Wiley Series in Parallel Computing, John Wiley and Sons, 1995.

[27] C. Hockley, "Design for success," *Journal of Aerospace Engineering*, vol. 212, no. 6, pp. 371–378, 1998.

[28] R. German, "Iterative analysis of Markov regenerative models," *Performance Evaluation*, vol. 44, pp. 51–72, April 2001.

Optimising Hidden Stochastic PERT Networks

Tommi Pesu
Imperial College London
Department of Computing, Imperial College London, South Kensington Campus, SW7 2AZ
London, United Kingdom
ttp09@imperial.ac.uk

William J. Knottenbelt
Imperial College London
Department of Computing, Imperial College London, South Kensington Campus, SW7 2AZ
London, United Kingdom
wjk@imperial.ac.uk

ABSTRACT

This paper introduces a technique for minimising subtask dispersion in hidden stochastic PERT networks. The technique improves on existing research in two ways. Firstly, it enables subtask dispersion reduction in DAG structures, whereas previous techniques have only been applicable to single-layer split–merge or fork–join systems. Secondly, the exact distributions of subtask processing times do not need to be known, so long as there is some means of generating samples. The technique is further extended to use a metric which trades off subtask dispersion and task response time.

Keywords

Stochastic PERT, Subtask dispersion, Task response time

1. INTRODUCTION

Project **E**valuation and **R**eview **T**echnique (PERT) is a widely used scheduling technique in industry [1, 8, 2]. PERT networks are DAG structures which define restrictions on the completion times of activities comprising some overall task. In stochastic PERT, the service times of activities are represented by probability distributions instead of numerical constants. *Hidden* in our context indicates that the user does not know the underlying structure of the PERT network.

In parallel processing systems, there are two useful metrics for describing performance: subtask dispersion [9, 7] (difference in time between the subtask that completes first and the subtask that completes last) and task response time [5, 11] (time for all the subtasks of the task to complete). If subtask dispersion and task response time are both important, a trade-off product metric can be used [10].

Minimising subtask dispersion in hidden stochastic PERT networks is useful in scenarios where information is distributed to multiple competing parties and receiving the information before others gives an edge to a party. An example of this happens in online games that require fast reflexes. Players who have a lower than average lag have an advantage, as they are able to react first to in-game events [12]. In this example the underlying routing structure between the computers taking part is a PERT-like network but the user is typically not aware of its structure or the performance characteristics of individual activities (in this case sending a message between two routers). Here the server's *task* is to broadcast a message to the clients. This comprises in turn several *subtasks*, each of which involves the delivery of the message to one of the clients. The server wishes that all the clients receive the information with a low subtask dispersion and a low task response time. The server can control subtask dispersion and task response time by adding delays to the transmission of messages. However, as the server does not have control of the whole network, it can only add delays to a limited set of neighbouring routers.

This paper presents a new technique for minimising subtask dispersion – or a trade-off product metric involving subtask dispersion and task response time – in hidden stochastic PERT networks. The technique approximates subtask dispersion and task response time by simulation for a given set of added delays – a decision made because analytical techniques such as [6] cannot be applied when specifics of the underlying PERT network are unknown. The Covariance Matrix Adaptation Evolution Strategy (CMA-ES) algorithm [4], noted for its ability to cope with noise, is used to minimise the approximation function.

VALUETOOLS 2016, October 25-28, Taormina, Italy

2. PRELIMINARIES

2.1 Stochastic PERT

A stochastic PERT network is a DAG that describes a processing network for completing a task. Figure 1 shows an example. An activity is a edge between two nodes. Each sink node in the PERT defines a subtask. A subtask is considered complete once all activities that can be used to reach it from the source node are completed. The task is completed when all activities in the PERT network are completed. The service time of an activity is denoted by the probability distribution f_n. Service of an activity cannot begin before all activities pointing to the node where the activity starts from have been serviced.

2.2 Task Response Time

Task response time measures the time it takes to service all activities. As the user often does not know exact details of the topology or service time distributions of activities in the PERT network, the user is not able to construct a analytical solution to the problem. Therefore in this paper, task response time is calculated via Monte Carlo simulation.

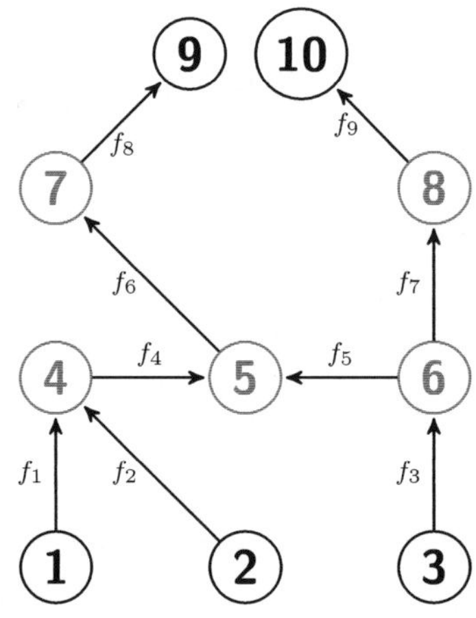

Figure 1: An example of a stochastic PERT DAG

2.3 Subtask Dispersion

For a stochastic PERT network, subtask dispersion is defined as the difference in time between the subtask that was last to complete and the subtask that was first to complete. It is possible to calculate subtask dispersion analytically, if the exact details of the PERT network are known [9, 6].

However, we consider settings where the exact topology and service time distributions are not known. Therefore calculation of subtask dispersion is simulated via Monte Carlo method, as was the case for task response time.

If it is possible to reschedule delays of the network to take into account completion of activities in the PERT network then the technique in this paper has the potential to generate even better results. For an example of how this knowledge can be used to reduce subtask dispersion see [7].

2.4 Trade-off Metric

It is possible to measure the overall performance of the system with a trade-off metric defined as the product of subtask dispersion and task response time [10], i.e.

$$T(\mathbf{d}) = E[D]E[R] \tag{1}$$

Here we extend this with a weight $0 \leq \alpha \leq 1$ which indicates the relative importance of the two metrics:

$$\mathrm{T}(\mathbf{d}, \alpha) = E[\mathrm{D}]^{1-\alpha} E[\mathrm{R}]^{\alpha}, 0 \leq \alpha \leq 1 \tag{2}$$

3. METHOD

The method presented here differs significantly from past techniques used to reduce subtask dispersion. Past works have focused on single-level parallel processing systems and have assumed full knowledge of system parameters to construct analytical functions which are minimised [9, 7, 10]. However, these techniques are manifestly unsuitable for application in the context of hidden PERT networks.

Our new technique not only works on more general DAG structures, but also does not require knowledge of the underlying probability distributions of activity service times. Instead it only needs to be able to randomly sample these. It is assumed that the user has control over a subset of the activities in the system S_c by being able to apply non-negative delays before the processing of activities in that set.

The optimisation technique has two main phases. First, subtask dispersion – for a given set of n subtasks and delays for activities in S_c – is calculated via repeated simulation of t tasks. When t is increased, accuracy increases at the expense of computation effort and *vice versa* when it is reduced. Second, CMA-ES is applied on the approximation function to find optimal delays. CMA-ES was chosen due to it being considered something of a standard in blackbox optimisation [3] which performs better in the context of non-convex optimisation than many classical methods. This is an important feature as the estimates generated via random sampling contain noise.

Where it is desired to trade off subtask dispersion and task response time, we can similarly apply CMA-ES to minimise the penalty function $\mathrm{T}(\mathbf{d}, \alpha)$, i.e.

$$\begin{aligned} &\min_{\mathbf{d}\geq 0} \mathrm{T}(\mathbf{d}, \alpha) \\ &\text{s.t. } \mathbf{d}_i = 0 \quad i \notin S_c \end{aligned} \tag{3}$$

in which the two main components of $T(\mathbf{d})$ are generated as averages of Monte Carlo simulations of t tasks.

4. RESULTS

We apply our technique in the context of the stochastic PERT network of Figure 1. It has three sources $(1, 2, 3)$ and two sinks $(9, 10)$. The user-controlled activities have distributions f_1, f_2 and f_3.

Distributions of the f_i are as follows[1]:

$$f_i = \begin{cases} \text{exponential}(0.2) & \text{i=1} \\ \text{exponential}(0.5) & \text{i=2} \\ \text{normal}(1, 0.5) & \text{i=3} \\ \text{uniform}(0.2, 0.7) & \text{i=4} \\ \text{power}(3) & \text{i=5} \\ \text{normal}(0.5, 1) & \text{i=6} \\ \text{power}(2) & \text{i=7} \\ \text{uniform}(0.75, 0.8) & \text{i=8} \\ \text{normal}(5, 1) & \text{i=9} \end{cases}$$

The durations of the two subtasks T_9 and T_{10} can be derived from the component activities as follows:

$$T_9 = \max(\max(f_1, f_2) + f_4, f_3 + f_5) + f_6 + f_8 \tag{4}$$

$$T_{10} = f_3 + f_7 + f_9 \tag{5}$$

Method 1 Optimised task response time

The results for no delays were calculated using a zero delay vector for 10^7 tasks. Metrics were averaged over 10 runs, which resulted in the following:

Subtask dispersion:	3.300 time units
Task response time:	6.677 time units
Trade-off, $\alpha = 0.5$:	4.694 time units

Method 2 Optimised subtask dispersion.

Here 1 000 samples per measurement point were taken. The CMA-ES algorithm was run on the problem 10 times and the subtask dispersion and task response time for each set of delays was calculated via simulation of 10^7 tasks.

[1]For specifics about each function please refer to Python's `numpy.random` library.

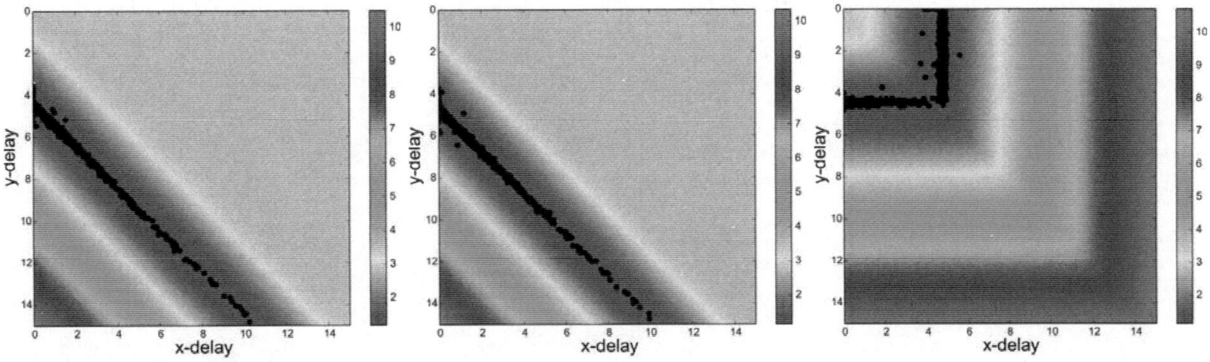

Figure 2: Subtask dispersion with delay vectors $(0, x, y)$ (left), $(x, 0, y)$ (middle) and $(x, y, 0)$ (right)

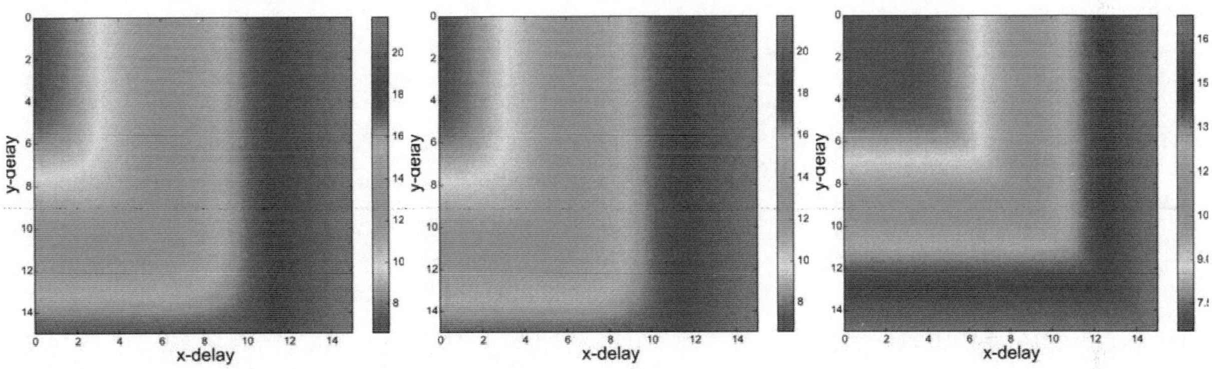

Figure 3: Task response time with delay vectors $(0, x, y)$ (left), $(x, 0, y)$ (middle) and $(x, y, 0)$ (right)

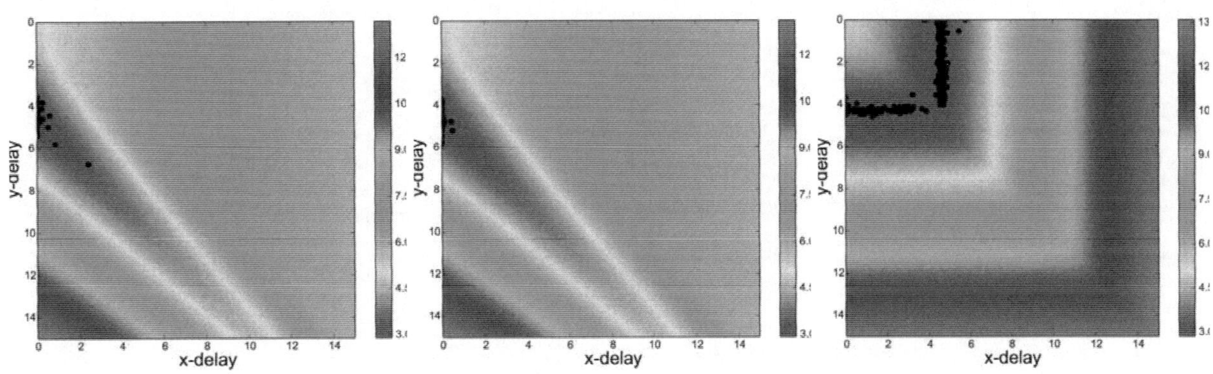

Figure 4: Trade-off ($\alpha = 0.5$) with delay vectors $(0, x, y)$ (left), $(x, 0, y)$ (middle) and $(x, y, 0)$ (right)

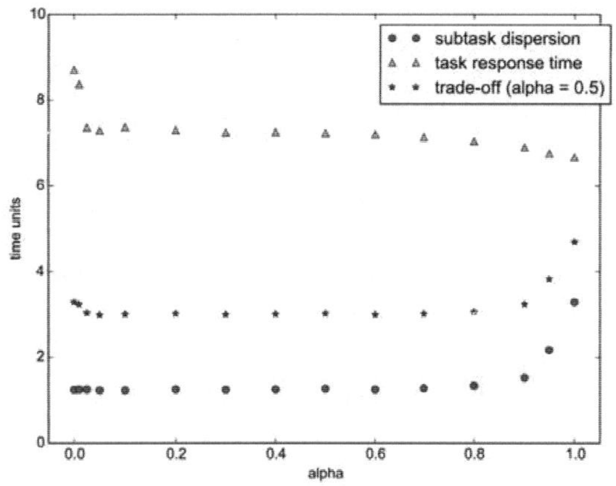

Figure 5: Influence of α on optimisation metrics

This resulted in the following:

Subtask dispersion:	1.247 time units
Task response time:	8.711 time units
Trade-off, $\alpha = 0.5$:	3.296 time units

Method 3 Optimised trade-off with $\alpha = 0.5$.
Again 1 000 samples per measurement point were taken. The CMA-ES algorithm was run on the problem 10 times and the subtask dispersion and task response time for each set of delays was calculated via simulation of 10^7 tasks.

This resulted in the following:

Subtask dispersion:	1.267 time units
Task response time:	7.233 time units
Trade-off, $\alpha = 0.5$:	3.027 time units

Figures 2, 3 and 4 display how task response time, subtask dispersion and trade-off ($\alpha = 0.5$) behave as the set of delay vectors is varied. In each picture one of the three delays of the controlling set S_c is set to 0 and the two others are allowed to vary between 0 and 15 with a stepsize of 0.1. The colouring of the image represents the resulting subtask dispersion (averaged over 1 000 samples) given the corresponding delay vector. The black dots in the images show the solutions produced by the CMA-ES technique. These are consistently located in the middle of the red band, suggesting near-optimal results.

Figure 5 shows how metrics vary as α is varied. All three metrics approach near-optimal values when α is between 0.2 and 0.8. When α approaches 1 the lowest possible task response time is found; however, this comes at the expense of subtask dispersion. Similarly, when α approaches 0 the lowest possible subtask dispersion is found; however, this comes at the expense of task response time.

5. CONCLUSION

Our method appears able to robustly control subtask dispersion in our case study hidden stochastic PERT network. Broader experimentation could establish whether these promising results hold more generally. Procedures for obtaining accurate confidence intervals should also be investigated.

6. REFERENCES

[1] V. Adlakha and V. Kulkarni. A classified bibliography of research on stochastic PERT networks: 1966–1987. *INFOR: Information Systems and Operational Research*, 27(3):272–296, 1989.

[2] D. R. Fulkerson. Expected critical path lengths in PERT networks. *Operations Research*, 10(6):808–817, 1962.

[3] N. Hansen, A. Auger, R. Ros, S. Finck, and P. Pošík. Comparing results of 31 algorithms from the black-box optimization benchmarking BBOB-2009. In *Proc. 12th Annual Conference Companion on Genetic and Evolutionary Computation*, pages 1689–1696, 2010.

[4] N. Hansen, S. D. Müller, and P. Koumoutsakos. Reducing the time complexity of the derandomized evolution strategy with covariance matrix adaptation (CMA-ES). *Evolutionary Computation*, 11(1):1–18, 2003.

[5] P. Harrison and S. Zertal. Queueing models of RAID systems with maxima of waiting times. *Performance Evaluation*, 64(7):664–689, 2007.

[6] P. G. Harrison and W. J. Knottenbelt. Passage time distributions in large Markov chains. In *ACM SIGMETRICS Performance Evaluation Review*, volume 30, pages 77–85. ACM, 2002.

[7] T. Pesu and W. J. Knottenbelt. Dynamic subtask dispersion reduction in heterogeneous parallel queueing systems. *Electronic Notes in Theoretical Computer Science*, 318:129 – 142, 2015.

[8] D. Sculli. The completion time of PERT networks. *Journal of the Operational Research Society*, 34(2):155–158, 1983.

[9] I. Tsimashenka, W. Knottenbelt, and P. Harrison. Controlling variability in split-merge systems. In *Proc. ASMTA 2012*, pages 165–177, Grenoble, France, June 2012.

[10] I. Tsimashenka and W. J. Knottenbelt. Trading off subtask dispersion and response time in split-merge systems. In *Proc. ASMTA 2013*, pages 431–442, Ghent, Belgium, July 2013.

[11] E. Varki. Response time analysis of parallel computer and storage systems. *IEEE Transactions on Parallel and Distributed Systems*, 12(11):1146–1161, 2001.

[12] S. Zander, I. Leeder, and G. Armitage. Achieving fairness in multiplayer network games through automated latency balancing. In *Proc. 2005 ACM SIGCHI ACE*, pages 117–124, 2005.

BuTools 2: a Rich Toolbox for Markovian Performance Evaluation

[Tool Paper]

Gábor Horváth
Budapest Univ. of Technology and Economics
Department of Networked Systems and Services
ghorvath@hit.bme.hu

Miklós Telek
MTA-BME Information Systems Research Group
Magyar Tudósok krt. 2, 1117 Budapest, Hungary
telek@hit.bme.hu

ABSTRACT

BuTools 2 is collection of computational methods that are useful for Markovian and non-Markovian matrix analytic performance analysis. It consists of various packages. There are packages to obtain, analyze, transform and minimize discrete and continuous time phase-type (PH) distributions and Markovian arrival processes (MAP); to fit empirical measurement data and to evaluate the result; to solve many performance measures of various Markovian queueing systems; and to solve block-structured Markov chains. All three major mathematical frameworks are supported: BuTools is released for MATLAB, Mathematica and NumPy/IPython as well, with the same features, with the same call interfaces. Every function is documented, the documentation is supplemented by many examples and the related citations. BuTools uses the state-of-the art algorithms and apart of the basic functionalities it contains several unique, difficult to implement procedures as well.

1. INTRODUCTION

Most researchers have their own set of tools that they use for the every day research activity. Collaboration between researchers can sometimes be difficult because everybody uses his/her own set of tools, and because everybody has his/her own preference of mathematical framework or programming language.

The authors of this paper had faced the same problem several years ago. They were working on very similar area, but the collaboration was difficult because everybody was sticking to his own set of tools. To address this issue, the first version of BuTools has been released in 2012 with the contribution of many colleges and students[1]. BuTools turned out to be very useful, but had some drawbacks: the source code quality was not homogeneous, and the feature parity between the three supported mathematical environments was only partial.

The aim of the second version was to address these issues. Almost every function has been rewritten from the ground up with efficiency and usability being the first priorities, and has been supplemented by unit tests. A special framework has been developed to generate the documentation, the examples, and the test scripts for the three supported environments automatically from a common source.

The second version has been finalized in September, 2015, and only very small changes were made since then. The homepage of BuTools is http://webspn.hit.bme.hu/~butools, and the source code repository is located at https://github.com/ghorvath78/butools. BuTools V2 is being used by our research group in the every day work with satisfaction. The goal of this paper is to introduce this toolbox and demonstrate its capabilities in the hope that others find it useful as well and make the results presented in the related literature easily accessible for practical computations.

2. INSTALLATION, BASIC CONCEPTS

BuTools is portable, no installation is needed. The packages of BuTools can be loaded individually, but there are convenience functions available to load every package in a single step as well. If BuTools is located in directory `<BT-Dir>`, all BuTools packages can be loaded by

- `run('<BTDir>/Matlab/BuToolsInit.m')` in Matlab,
- `%run "<BTDir>/Python/BuToolsInit"` in an IPython console,
- `AppendTo[$Path,"<BTDir>/Mathematica"]; <<BuTools`` in Mathematica.

There are three global variables used by BuTools, summarized by Table 1.

Setting `verbose` to True allows the functions to print as many useful messages to the output console as possible. Turning it off avoids bloating the console. The default value is False, but for the examples of the reference documentation we have set it to True.

If `checkInput` is set to True, the functions of BuTools perform as many checks on the input parameters as possible. This can be very useful to recognize typos as soon as

[1]This version of BuTools was available on the internet and announced through some professional mailing lists, but never got published as a tool paper. A non exhaustive list of contributors include: Levente Bodrog, Peter Buchholz, Armin Heindl, Andr´as Horv´ath, Istv´an Kolossv´ary, Andr´ Mészáros, Zoltán Németh, János Papp Philipp Reinecke, Miklós Vécsei.

VALUETOOLS 2016, October 25-28, Taormina, Italy

Name in MATLAB	Name in Mathematica	Name in Python	Default value
`BuToolsVerbose`	`BuTools'Verbose`	`butools.verbose`	False
`BuToolsCheckInput`	`BuTools'CheckInput`	`butools.checkInput`	True
`BuToolsCheckPrecision`	`BuTools'CheckPrecision`	`butools.checkPrecision`	10^{-12}

Table 1: Global variables in BuTools

possible, but can be a waste of computational effort in case of a computationally demanding application.

The `checkPrecision` serves as the tolerance when the validity of the input parameters are checked.

3. WORKING WITH PH DISTRIBUTIONS

Continuous time phase-type (PH) distributions [15] are characterized by two parameters, the initial probability vector α and the transient generator matrix of a continuous time (transient) Markov chain. The PH distribution represents the absorption time of this transient Markov chain starting from α. The cumulative distribution function (cdf) is $F_{PH}(t) = 1 - \alpha e^{\mathbf{A}t}\mathbb{1}$, where $\mathbb{1}$ is the column vector of ones.

Matrix exponential (ME) distributions [2] are the generalizations of PH distributions. Formally, the cdf is $F_{ME}(t) = 1 - be^{\mathbf{B}t}\,e$ and all further formulas for the statistical quantities are very similar to the ones of PH distributions, however, $b, \mathbf{B}$ and e can hold general numbers, the entries do not have to be valid probabilities or transition rates. ME distributions therefore lack the simple stochastic interpretation that PH distributions have. Vector b is called "starting operator", matrix $\mathbf{B}$ is the "process rate operator" and vector e is the "summing operator". BuTools uses a special form of ME distributions, where the summing operator is a vector of ones, thus $e = \mathbb{1}$. This is not a restriction, as all ME distributions defined with general summing operator can be easily transformed to this representation [16]. Assume we have an ME distribution in the general form with parameters $b, \mathbf{B}, e$. The necessary similarity transform is obtained by calling the `T = TransformToOnes(e)` procedure of the BuTools reptrans package. The parameters of the ME distribution used by all related BuTools tools can be calculated by $b' = b \cdot \mathbf{T}^{-1}$ and $\mathbf{B}' = \mathbf{T}\mathbf{B}\mathbf{T}^{-1}$.

BuTools provides several tools for both distribution classes in the `ph` package. Of course, functions for obtaining the cdf, the pdf, moments are available as well as functions to check the validity of the representations.

With the inverse characterization tools BuTools can create APH distributions from any 2 moments and from any 3 moments by the `APHFrom2Moments` and `APHFrom3Moments` functions, the size of the necessary representation is determined automatically ([4]). Furthermore, by the `PH2From3Moments` and `PH3From5Moments` functions order 2 and order 3 PH distributions can be obtained from 3 and 5 moments, respectively, if the given moments are feasible with PH(2) and PH(3) distributions ([23],[12]). An interesting procedure is `MEFromMoments` ([26]), that returns an order N ME distribution from any $2N-1$ moments, however, there is no guarantee that the result is a valid ME distribution. To check that the density is non-negative for all points it is possible to call the `CheckMEPositiveDensity` function afterwards (this is a very non-trivial procedure, which relies on the transformation to mono-cyclic representation) [22].

An other category of functions are able to transform between various PH and ME representations. `CanonicalFromPH2` creates an order 2, `CanonicalFromPH3` an order 3 canonical representation from any PH(2) and PH(3) distributions (potentially given by non-Markovian representation). The `PHFromME` function tries to find a PH(N) representation for the given ME(N) one by applying elementary similarity transformations iteratively (note however, that this function is not able to increase the order in the hope for a Markovian representation).

One of the most valuable tool in the `ph` package is the `MonocyclicPHFromME` function, which transforms *any* ME distributions (that fulfil the eigenvalue constraint (eigenvalues with maximal real part are real) and do not touch the x axis apart from the origin) to a PH distribution ([22], [19]). The required size of the representation is determined automatically. The resulting PH distribution is returned in a monocyclic representation.

With a useful set of functions it is possible to analyze the redundancy of PH distributions and to obtain the minimal representation. `MEOrder` can return the order of the PH/ME based on the analysis of the parameters of the distribution, while `MEOrderFromMoments` returns the ME order necessary to realize the moments given. Several properties of various systems can be characterized through Laplace transform expressions, from which the moments are easy to obtain. From these moments, `MEOrderFromMoments` can tell if there is a matrix-exponential-like (ME-like) behavior in the background, and if the answer is yes, what is the order of that ME distribution. Function `MinimalRepFromME` gives the minimal representation of the given ME distribution, thus the ME distribution returned is the same as the input, but can be smaller.

The `dph` package provides similar tools for the discrete counterparts of PH and ME distributions, the discrete PH (DPH) distributions and matrix-geometric (MG) distributions. The basic set of functions to obtain the moments, the probability mass function and the cdf are available, of course, however, the set of inverse characterization and representation transformation tools are less comprehensive than in the continuous case due to the lack of research results. BuTools can create order-2 and order-3 DPH distributions from 3 and 5 moments (`DPH2From3Moments` and `DPH3From5Moments` based on [21] and [14]), and the moment matching method of [26] has also been adapted to the discrete case (`MGFromMoments`). Unfortunately, flexible order procedures like `APHFrom3Moments` for DPH are not available in the literature yet.

Transforming DPHs to canonical forms for the order-2 and order-3 cases are possible (`CanonicalFromDPH2` and `CanonicalFromDPH3`), and the iterative transformation based `DPHFromMG` is also included, but the discrete equivalent to monocyclic representation is unfortunately unknown, hence we can not transform any MG distribution to DPH yet.

Finally, both the `ph` and `dph` packages contain functions

to generate random PH and DPH distributions (RandomPH and RandomDPH), and functions to generate random samples from PH and DPH distributions (SamplesFromPH and SamplesFromDPH) for simulation purposes.

4. TOOLS FOR MAPS

Continuous time Markovian arrival processes (MAPs, [15]) are commonly characterized by two matrices, $\mathbf{D_0}$ and $\mathbf{D_1}$. Arrivals by a MAP are modulated by a background continuous time Markov chain with generator $\mathbf{D} = \mathbf{D_0} + \mathbf{D_1}$. Markov chain transitions in $\mathbf{D_0}$ ($\mathbf{D_1}$) do not generate (generate) arrival events. As a result MAPs are capable of generating correlated arrivals.

Rational arrival processes (RAPs, also known as matrix-exponential processes, MEPs) are generalizations of MAPs [1]. Formally, all formulas for the statistical quantities are the same to the ones of MAPs. However, both $\mathbf{D_0}$ and $\mathbf{D_1}$ can hold negative real numbers, the entries do not have to be valid transition rates. RAPs therefore lack the simple stochastic interpretation that MAPs have.

Both MAPs and RAPs can be generalized to multi-type arrival processes. If there are K different arrival types, marked MAPs (MMAPs) and marked RAPs (MRAPs) defined by matrices $\mathbf{D_0}, \ldots, \mathbf{D_K}$ are able to describe the multi-type arrival process.

BuTools provides several tools for MAPs, RAPs and their marked variants in the map package.

With the appropriate function BuTools can return basic properties like the marginal distribution (the parameters of the corresponding PH distribution), the marginal moments, the lag auto-correlations, and the lag-k joint moments ([24]) of MAPs and MMAPs.

With the set of inverse characterization tools it is possible to obtain order N RAPs or MAPs from $2N-1$ marginal moments and $(N-1)^2$ lag-1 joint moments (RAPFromMoments and MRAPFromMoments, using the method of [24]); or from $2N-1$ marginal moments and $2N-3$ auto-correlations (RAPFromMomentsAndCorrelations, based on [18]). The method for creating an order-2 MAP from 3 moments and 1 correlation parameter published in [5] is implemented by the MAP2FromMoments function. The only flexible matching procedure (that can adjust the order of the result automatically, based on the input parameters) is MAPFromFewMomentsAndCorrelations, that implements [9].

As for representation transformation, BuTools is able to transform a RAP(2) to a canonical form (CanonicalFromMAP2), transform a MRAP(N) to MMAP(N) (MAPFromRAP and MMAPFromMRAP, by successive similarity transformations, achieving a MAP is not guaranteed), and can minimize a RAP representation with functions MinimalRepFromRAP and MinimalRepFromMRAP ([6]).

The dmap package intends to provide the same functionality for discrete time arrival processes (DMAPs and DRAPs) and their marked variants (DMMAPs and DMRAPs), however, several results present for MAPs and RAPs are not available for DMAPs and DRAPs in the literature yet.

From the inverse characterization tools only DRAPFromMoments/DMRAPFromMoments and DMAP2FromMoments are available (see [17] for the latter one).

Both the map and dmap packages contain functions to generate random MAPs, MMAPs, DMAPs, DMMAPs and to generate random samples from these processes.

5. FITTING TOOLS

5.1 The trace package

The ph, dph, map and dmap packages provide several functions to obtain PH distributions and MAPs from statistical quantities, like moments, auto-correlations and joint moments. The trace package has tools to obtain these kinds of quantities from empirical data traces.

The traces are vectors consisting of measurements. After loading them from a file, cdf, pdf, moments, joint moments, and lag-k auto-correlations can be computed by invoking the CdfFromTrace, PdfFromTrace, MarginalMomentsFromTrace, LagkJointMomentsFromTrace and LagCorrelationsFromTrace functions.

Most of these functions can cope with weighted traces as well, where each measurement data is supplemented by a weight.

5.2 Likelihood based fitting

BuTools has a fitting package, that contains two kinds of functions: procedures for likelihood (EM) based fitting, and tools to evaluate the result of the fitting.

The PHFromTrace is the implementation of the G-FIT procedure ([25]) to create a hyper-Erlang distribution by EM-algorithm. G-FIT is one of the best performing PH fitting method at the moment. While MATLAB, Mathematica and Python are known for not being efficient for such computationally demanding algorithms, BuTools has a reasonably fast, vectorized implementation capable of processing traces with millions of data.

The MAPFromTrace function implements [11], which is similar to G-FIT. The MAP it creates has Erlang components, and a switching probability matrix determining the order of these Erlang components providing the subsequent inter-arrival times. Note however, that this fitting procedure is much slower than the one for PH fitting.

The likelihood of a PH distribution or a MAP regarding a trace can be evaluated by LikelihoodFromTrace.

The functions SquaredDifference and RelativeEntropy measure the difference between two vectors (e.g., probability mass functions, lag-k autocorrelations, etc.), while EmpiricalSquaredDifference and EmpiricalRelativeEntropy are the equivalents to be used for continuous quantities (e.g., for pdf or cdf of continuous time PH variables, where they are given by a number of points only).

5.3 Application example

The usage of BuTools for trace fitting is demonstrated in Figure 1. The first line loads a trace file consisting of 1.78 million inter-arrival time samples. The next line calculates the marginal moments of the trace. Then, a PH(3) distribution is created by matching 5 moments, finally a PH(5) is obtained by fitting (G-FIT). The fitting step took 113 seconds on a PC with a 3.4 GHz CPU and 4 GB of RAM. After obtaining the PH distributions, the approximations are evaluated. First the moments are compared, then the likelihood.

After the comparison the density functions are obtained and plotted. (In case of the PH distributions the IntervalPdfFromPH function is used, which, instead of evaluating the pdf at the given points, returns the probability of falling into intervals divided by the interval lengths. This is the correct way to compare it with the empirical pdf of the trace.)

```
>> trace = dlmread('lbltcp3_iat.txt');
>> trmoms = MarginalMomentsFromTrace (trace,5);
>> [alpha3,A3] = PH3From5Moments(trmoms(1:5));
>> [alpha5,A5] = PHFromTrace (trace, 5);
>> disp(trmoms);
            1 2.942 16.84 150.73 1876.8
>> disp(MomentsFromPH(alpha3,A3));
            1 2.942 16.84 150.73 1876.8
>> disp(MomentsFromPH(alpha5,A5,5));
            1 2.8827 15.074 112.2 1062.3
>> disp(LikelihoodFromTrace(trace,alpha3,A3));
    -0.94802
>> disp(LikelihoodFromTrace(trace,alpha5,A5));
    -0.9343
>> [xt,yt] = PdfFromTrace (trace, (1:0.1:3));
>> [xp3,yp3] = IntervalPdfFromPH (alpha3, A3, (1:0.1:3));
>> [xp5,yp5] = IntervalPdfFromPH (alpha5, A5, (1:0.1:3));
>> plot (xt,yt,xp3,yp3,xp5,yp5);
```

Figure 1: Application example for fitting

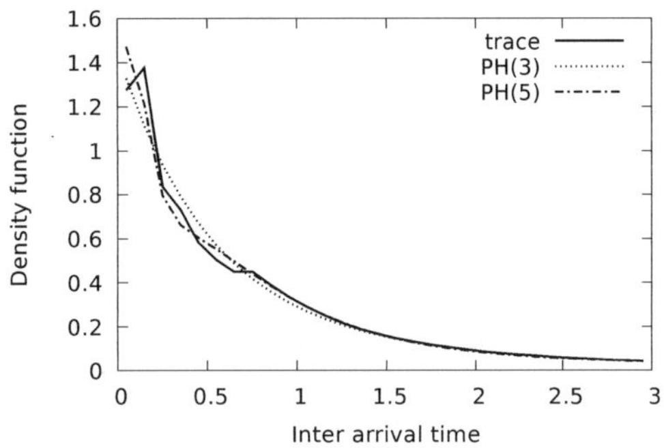

Figure 2: The output of the example of Figure 1

The result is depicted in Figure 2.

6. ANALYSIS OF QUEUES

The **queues** package heavily relies on the matrix-analytic methods.

6.1 Support for Matrix-Analytic Methods

The **mam** package of BuTools provides solution methods for problems based on non-linear matrix equations.

Functions solving the three diagonal block-structured Markov chains, namely the quasi birth-death processes (QBDs), Markov chains skip-free to the left, M/G/1 type Markov chains, and Markov chains skip-free to the right, G/M/1 type Markov chains ([15]) are included. The underlying algorithms are from the SMCSolver toolbox ([3]). The MATLAB version of BuTools requires the presence of SMCSolver, while the Mathematica and the NumPy/IPython versions include the necessary parts of SMCSolver ported to these environments.

The fundamental matrices for QBDs are returned by the **QBDFundamentalMatrices** function (matrices $\mathbf{R}, \mathbf{G}$ and $\mathbf{U}$ [15]). Matrix $\mathbf{G}$, the fundamental matrix of M/G/1 type Markov chains is provided by **MG1FundamentalMatrix**, and the $\mathbf{R}$ matrix of G/M/1 type systems is given by **GM1FundamentalMatrix**. Based on the fundamental matrices the stationary solutions are provided by functions **QBDStationaryDistr**, **MG1StationaryDistr** and **GM1StationaryDistr**, respectively, that return the stationary probabilities themselves. For QBDs the ingredients of the stationary matrix-geometric solution (the initial vector and the coefficient matrix) are returned by **QBDSolve**.

BuTools also supports the solution of continuous queueing systems, Markovian fluid flows ([7]). A large part of the related literature considers *canonical* Markovian fluid flows, where the rate at which the fluid level increases or decreases is always 1. For these systems **FluidFundamentalMatrices** returns the most important matrices, $\mathbf{\Psi}, \mathbf{K}$ and $\mathbf{U}$ [7]. The stationary solution for the fluid level at the requested points is given by **FluidStationaryDistr**, and the components of the matrix-exponential solution (intial vector, matrix exponent) can be obtained by **FluidSolve**. For fluid systems, however, we find it more useful to use **GeneralFluidSolve**, which, based on the generator of the background Markov chain and the diagonal matrix of fluid rates returns the probability mass at level 0, and for positive levels the initial vector, matrix exponent and closing matrix of the matrix-exponential solution.

6.2 Queueing models

Building upon the **mam** package, the **queues** package provides functions to obtain many performance measures of several queueing systems. The following queues are supported:

- The MAP/MAP/1 queue (**MAPMAP1**). Special cases of this queue are the PH/MAP/1, the MAP/PH/1, the PH/PH/1, etc. (see [15] and [8]).
- The QBD queue (**QBDQueue**). In this queue the arrival and the service process are not independent of each other, they share the same background process. Marked transitions of this background process are accompanied by a level increase, other marked transitions by a level decrease event. The MAP/MAP/1 queue is the special case of the QBD queue, however, several performance measures are more demanding to compute for the QBD queue. The implementation is based on [15] and [20].
- The MMAP[K]/PH[K]/1-FCFS queue (**MMAPPH1FCFS**). This is a multi-type queue with K types of customers. Each customer type can have a different (PH) service time distribution. The solution is based on [8].
- The MMAP[K]/PH[K]/1 queue with non-preemptive and preemptive resume priority service (**MMAPPH1NPPR** and **MMAPPH1PRPR**). This is a multi-type queue with preemptive service, the efficient solution is based on a recent result [10].
- The fluid queue (**FluidQueue**). In this queue there is a common background Markov chain, a diagonal matrix of fluid arrival rates and a diagonal matrix of fluid service rates in each state of the background process. The queue length and the sojourn time of the fluid drops are the two most interesting performance measures (based on [7] and [13]). This is the continuous counterpart of the QBD queues.
- The Flu/Flu queue (**FluFluQueue**), which is similar to the ordinary fluid queue, but the fluid input and output processes are independent, they are modulated by two separate background Markov chains. This independence is exploited in the solution, thus Flu/Flu queues are easier and faster to solve than the general fluid queues. This is the continuous counterpart of the MAP/MAP/1 queues.

The performance measures that can be obtained from these queues are summarized by Table 2. The abbreviation of the performance measures are

- `ncMoms/flMoms`: Stationary moments of the number of customers (in case of discrete queues) / fluid level (in case of fluid queues).
- `ncDistr/flDistr`: Stationary distribution of the number of customers / the fluid level.
- `ncDistrMG/flDistrME`: The parameters of the MG/ME distribution of the number of customers / fluid level.
- `ncDistrDPH/flDistrPH`: The parameters of the DPH/PH distribution of the number of customers / fluid level. The DPH/PH representation is obtained from the MG/ME one, which is always possible. However, in some rare cases (when a phase has a very low probability) this transformation can introduce numerical errors, hence `ncDistrMG/flDistrME` are safer to use.
- `stMoms`, `stDistr`, `stDistrME`, `stDistrPH`: the same as above for the sojourn time of the customers/fluid drops. Again, `stDistrME` behaves better numerically than `stDistrPH`.

When calling these functions, the performance measures to compute are listed in the function arguments. Several performance measures can be computed at the same function call, and BuTools will save as much computational effort as possible by avoiding repeated re-computation of some demanding steps.

6.3 Application example

The example in Figure 3 demonstrates how well the different packages of BuTools play nicely together. First the arrival process is created based on three moments and the lag-1 auto-correlation, then the service time distribution is obtained by matching two moments. The next two lines calculate the $\mathbf{S_0}$ and $\mathbf{S_1}$ matrices representing the service MAP of the queue. All the performance measures are obtained by the same function call. According to the function arguments, 3 moments of the number of customers, the distribution of the number of customers up to 20, and the PH representation of the sojourn time are requested, and the `MAPMAP1` function returns them in the same order. After that, the solution is displayed either on the screen or in a plot (the mean number of customers and the mean sojourn times are equal in this example since the mean arrival rate is 1). Figure 4 depicts the distribution of the number of customers in the system.

```
>> trace = dlmread('lbltcp3_iat.txt');
>> trmoms = MarginalMomentsFromTrace (trace,3);
>> tracf1 = LagCorrelationsFromTrace(trace,1);
>> [D0,D1]=MAP2FromMoments(trmoms,tracf1);
>> [alpha,A] = APHFrom2Moments([0.8,6.5]);
>> S0=A;
>> S1=sum(-A,2)*alpha;
>> [ncm,ncd,beta,B]=MAPMAP1(D0,D1,S0,S1,...
'ncMoms',3,'ncDistr',20,'stDistrPH');
>> disp(ncm);
       21.359 1245.1 1.0969e+05
>> plot(ncd);
>> disp(MomentsFromPH(beta,B,3));
       21.359 1172.3 97262
```

Figure 3: Usage example for queueing

7. SOME FURTHER, SMALL PACKAGES

7.1 The `moments` package

Several moment expressions are being used in various publications related to PH distributions. Most works rely on the ordinary (raw) moments, while others are able to arrive to simpler formulas by introducing some alternative moment expressions, like reduced moments, normalized moments, Hankel moments. Furthermore, in case of discrete systems transform domain techniques make it easy to obtain the factorial moments. The `moments` package provides conversion routines between these moment expressions. Additionally, it provides the `CheckMoments` function to determine if a sequence of real numbers is a valid moment sequence (there exists a distribution with the given moments), or not.

7.2 The `mc` package

A couple of basic functions to obtain the stationary distribution of Markov chains is mandatory in a tool devoted to Markovian performance analysis. The `CTMCSolve` and `DTMCSolve` functions return the stationary distribution of continuous and discrete time Markov chains, respectively, based on the direct (non-iterative) solution of the corresponding set of linear equations.

Two further functions, `CRPSolve` and `DRPSolve` provide the same functionality on rational processes, which are similar to Markov chains without the restrictions on the sign of the elements of the generator matrices. These functions are mostly used internally by the procedures operating on ME distributions and RAPs.

8. CONCLUSION

BuTools collects the implementations of many research results related to stochastic models with Markov background process. This way it makes several complex research results of the field easily accessible for practical application. BuTools is heavily used by our research group and found to be efficient for practical computations. The reader is encouraged to check and use BuTools, which is facilitated with online documentation and application demo.

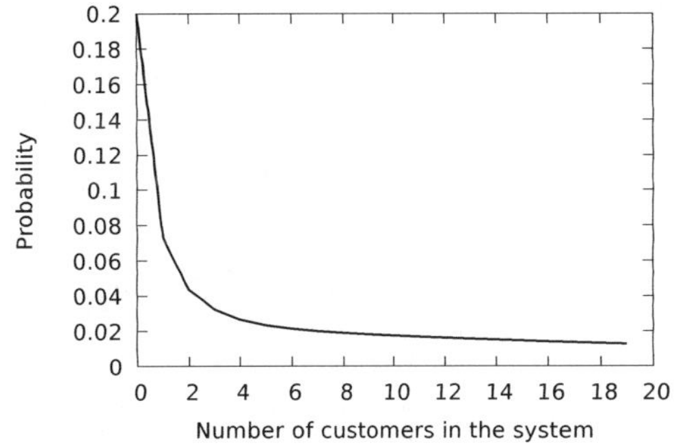

Figure 4: The output of the example of Figure 3

Perf. meas.	QBDQueue	MAPMAP1	MMAPPH1FCFS	MMAPPH1-Prio	FluidQueue	FluFluQueue
ncMoms	✓	✓	✓	✓	✓	✓
ncDistr	✓	✓	✓	✓	✓	✓
ncDistrMG	✓	✓	–	–	✓	✓
ncDistrDPH	✓	✓	–	–	✓	✓
stMoms	✓	✓	✓	✓	✓	✓
stDistr	✓	✓	✓	✓	✓	✓
stDistrME	✓	✓	✓	–	✓	✓
stDistrPH	✓	✓	✓	–	✓	✓

Table 2: Performance measures that can be computed

The authors would be glad to receive any related ideas, comments, feature requests or bug fixes.

9. REFERENCES

[1] S. Asmussen and M. Bladt. Point processes with finite-dimensional probabilities. *Stochastic Processes and their Applications*, 82(1):127Ű142, 1999.

[2] Soren Asmussen and Colm Art O'Cinneide. *Matrix-Exponential Distributions*. John Wiley & Sons, Inc., 2004.

[3] D Bini, B Meini, S Steffé, and B Van Houdt. Structured Markov chains solver: software tools. In *Proceeding from the 2006 workshop on Tools for solving structured Markov chains*, page 14. ACM, 2006.

[4] A. Bobbio, A. Horváth, and M. Telek. Matching three moments with minimal acyclic phase type distributions. *Stochastic models*, 21(2-3):303–326, 2005.

[5] Levente Bodrog, Armin Heindl, Gábor Horváth, and Miklós Telek. A Markovian canonical form of second-order matrix-exponential processes. *European Journal of Operational Research*, 190(2):459–477, 2008.

[6] Peter Buchholz and Miklós Telek. On minimal representations of rational arrival processes. *Annals of Operations Research*, 202(1):35–58, 2013.

[7] A. da Silva Soares. *Fluid Queues: Building Upon the Analogy with QBD Processes*. PhD thesis, Université Libre de Bruxelles, 2005.

[8] Qi-Ming He. Age process, workload process, sojourn times, and waiting times in a discrete time SM[K]/PH[K]/1/FCFS queue. *Queueing Systems*, 49(3-4):363–403, 2005.

[9] Gábor Horváth. Matching marginal moments and lag autocorrelations with MAPs. In *Proceedings of the 7th International Conference on Performance Evaluation Methodologies and Tools*, pages 59–68, 2013.

[10] Gábor Horváth. Efficient analysis of the MMAP[K]/PH[K]/1 priority queue. *European Journal of Operational Research*, 246(1):128–139, 2015.

[11] Gábor Horváth and Hiroyuki Okamura. A fast EM algorithm for fitting marked Markovian arrival processes with a new special structure. In *European Workshop on Performance Engineering*, pages 119–133. Springer, 2013.

[12] Gábor Horváth and Miklós Telek. On the canonical representation of phase type distributions. *Performance Evaluation*, 66(8):396–409, 2009.

[13] Gábor Horváth and Miklós Telek. Sojourn times in fluid queues with independent and dependent input and output processes. *Performance Evaluation*, 79:160–181, 2014.

[14] Illés Horváth, János Papp, and Miklós Telek. On the canonical representation of order 3 discrete phase type distributions. *Electronic Notes in Theoretical Computer Science*, 318:143–158, 2015.

[15] Guy Latouche and Vaidyanathan Ramaswami. *Introduction to matrix analytic methods in stochastic modeling*, volume 5. Siam, 1999.

[16] Lester Lipsky. *Queueing Theory: A linear algebraic approach*. Springer Science & Business Media, 2008.

[17] András Mészáros and Miklós Telek. Canonical representation of discrete order 2 MAP and RAP. In *European Workshop on Performance Engineering*, pages 89–103. Springer, 2013.

[18] Kenneth Mitchell and Appie van de Liefvoort. Approximation models of feed-forward G/G/1/N queueing networks with correlated arrivals. *Performance Evaluation*, 51(2):137–152, 2003.

[19] Ştefăniţă Mocanu and Christian Commault. Sparse representations of phase-type distributions. *Stochastic Models*, 15(4):759–778, 1999.

[20] Toshihisa Ozawa. Sojourn time distributions in the queue defined by a general QBD process. *Queueing Systems*, 53(4):203–211, 2006.

[21] János Papp and Miklós Telek. Canonical representation of discrete phase type distributions of order 2 and 3. In *Proc. of UK Performance Evaluation Workshop, UKPEW*, volume 2013, 2013.

[22] Philipp Reinecke and Miklós Telek. Does a given vector–matrix pair correspond to a PH distribution? *Performance Evaluation*, 81:40–51, 2014.

[23] Miklós Telek and Armin Heindl. Moment bounds for acyclic discrete and continuous phase type distributions of second order. In *In Proceedings of UK Performance Evaluation Workshop*, 2002.

[24] Miklós Telek and Gábor Horváth. A minimal representation of Markov arrival processes and a moments matching method. *Performance Evaluation*, 64(9):1153–1168, 2007.

[25] Axel Thummler, Peter Buchholz, and Miklós Telek. A novel approach for fitting probability distributions to real trace data with the EM algorithm. In *2005 International Conference on Dependable Systems and Networks (DSN'05)*, pages 712–721. IEEE, 2005.

[26] A Van de Liefvoort. The moment problem for continuous distributions. *Unpublished technical report, University of Missouri, WP-CM-1990-02*, 1990.

A Short Tutorial On Using SGsim Framework For Smart Grid Applications

Abdalkarim Awad
Department of Electrical and Computer Engineering
Birzeit University, Palestine
akarim@ieee.org

Peter Bazan and Reinhard German
Computer Networks and Communication Systems
University of Erlangen, Germany
{peter.bazan, reinhard.german}@fau.de

ABSTRACT

Extensive usage of information and communication technology (ICT) characterizes the next generation power grid. ICT supports diverse smart grid applications from the level of energy management, all the way down to control and protection approaches. The evaluation of a smart grid application requires multidisciplinary tools that capture its versatile nature. In this paper, we present a short tutorial on the use of the open source co-simulation framework SGsim for smart grid applications. The framework combines two main simulators. On the one hand, it uses OMNeT++ to simulate data communication networks and to control the operation of the components. On the other hand, it uses OpenDSS to simulate the power grid.

1. INTRODUCTION

The enrichment of the power grid with ICT enables new applications which eventually will make it possible to run the power grid in an efficient, secure, reliable, sustainable, and economic way. For instance, applications such as Conservation Voltage Reduction (CVR) and Volt/VAR optimization have the potential to reduce the power consumption and optimize the operation of the power grid. The rapidly increasing penetration of fluctuating renewable energy sources (RES) brings new challenges to the power grid, especially inside the distribution network. For example, on a sunny day with high penetration of photostatic, the voltage can exceed the allowed limits (over-voltage) because of a low demand at midday. Therefore, it is important to coordinate the available components to avoid abnormal situations. In addition to the loads, a typical electricity distribution grid contains also components such as transformers and distributed energy resources. Additionally, energy storage elements will be part of future power electricity distribution grid. Connecting these components together through a data communication network is very crucial for the future power grid. It will make it possible to operate the power grid in an optimal way. Moreover, it will be possible to react very fast to emergency conditions. Smart grid applications include [5]:

- Volt and VAR control (VVC): Control of voltage regulation devices and reactive power compensation devices for the purpose of reducing consumer demand and energy loss, and maintain voltages at various points in the distribution network within acceptable limits.
- Fault detection, isolation and restoration (FDIR): This application aims at automating the field switching devices. It will use microprocessor based intelligent electronic devices (IEDs) and high-speed communication connections to enhance the reliability of the system and reducing the restoration time.
- Demand response (DR) management: DR can be used to shave the peak at high demand periods. This can be achieved by introducing a variable price in which the electricity will be expensive at high demand periods and cheap at low demand periods.
- Distributed energy resources (DER) integration and management: DER provides energy inside its local vicinity. With high penetration of DER, problems such as over-voltage appear and therefore suitable solutions should be provided. This application aims at improving the integration of DER in the power grid.
- Wide area monitoring, protection and control (WAMPC): This application extends the time resolution of traditional monitoring systems down to the subsecond time scale, making it capable of monitoring and reacting to dynamic instabilities in the grid.

Because testing new approaches and algorithms inside real electricity networks is difficult and sometimes impossible, simulation plays a key role to explore the benefits and risks of applying new smart grid applications. Through simulation, it is possible to perform comprehensive simulation experiments for different scenarios and approaches and this will eventually provide answers for specific questions. It is extremely difficult to seize the many-sided nature of smart grid in one tool. Through co-simulation it is possible to capture and evaluate different aspects of smart grids.

In this paper we provide a tutorial on SGsim. The co-simulation framework SGsim [3,4] uses the open source power simulator OpenDSS [1] to simulate electric power networks and it uses OMNeT++ [21] to simulate data communication networks as well as to build several components.

VALUETOOLS 2016, October 25-28, Taormina, Italy

2. RELATED WORK

Smart grids are complex systems over multiple domains and for a number of these domains there already exist appropriate simulation tools. The coupling of such tools to a tailor-made smart grid co-simulation is part of the ongoing work. SGsim couples an electric power network simulator with a data communication network simulator and has two open source optimization tools integrated together with an interface to attach real phasor data concentrators. Other co-simulation frameworks are focused on different combinations of domains.

One example of a smart grid simulation tool used for co-simulation is GridLAB-D [7]. It is an agent-based hybrid simulation tool using continuous simulation for the energy part of the model and discrete event simulation for the communication part. There are no standard communication protocols implemented for the communication part. Only simplified network properties can be used such as bandwidth, latency, buffer size, and congestion.

GridLAB-D is used by the simulation platform GridSpice, together with MatPOWER and Amazon Web Services, for the distributed simulation of smart grids [2]. The integration of GridLAB-D in a co-simulation environment based on open source software is presented in [20]. Physical components like batteries are modeled with OpenModelica, the power system analysis is realized with the open source tool PSAT. In [14], the authors have used the commercial tool PowerFactory instead of PSAT and in [19] the co-simulation environment consists of PowerFactory for the power system, OMNeT++ for the communication infrastructure, and 4DIAC for the control system. In all three cases they investigated the smart charging of electric vehicles.

The focus of the co-simulation presented in [13] is on the coupling of the power distribution network simulator OpenDSS with the communication network simulator OMNeT++. This work is extended in [12] by a preliminary implemented information technology simulator. In general the authors suggest the use of tools like the multi-agent smart grid simulation platform MASGriP.

The MOSAIK framework controls the creation of the simulation models and the data flow between different simulators [11,16]. The simulation models are agent-based and the simulation execution is event-based with the possibility to manage different step sizes for the simulators. The framework provides an application programming interface for controlling commercial and open source simulation software. Simulators with a Functional Mock-up Interface (FMI) as well as those with a proprietary interface can be integrated. In the past, there was a lack of integrated communication network protocol simulators in the MOSAIK co-simulation framework. Therefore, the authors suggest in [8] a preliminary system architecture of integrating OMNeT++.

The co-simulation tool presented in [17] uses OPNET instead of OMNeT++ for the communication part and MATLAB/Simulink for the power system. The tool is then used for the detection of cyber-intrusion into the information infrastructure. Also, this tool provides only a part of the functionality of SGsim.

3. SGSIM

In this section we introduce SGsim framework. At the beginning we provide a detailed description of the simulator.

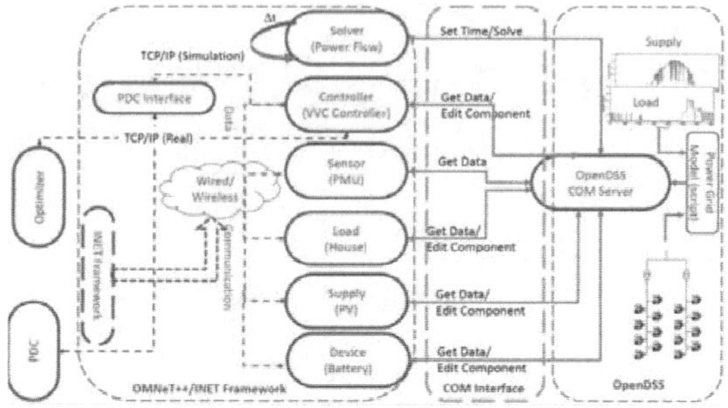

Figure 1: Structure of the SGsim framework with the connections between the components

Then we list the steps in order to install the software. At the end of this section we provide a simple example.

3.1 Description

SGsim [3,4] is a co-simulation framework, which is based on two main simulators OpenDSS [9] and OMNeT++ [21]. OpenDSS provides an in-process Component Object Model (COM) server DLL designed to be driven from an external software. OMNeT++ is discrete event simulator which is used mainly as a data communication simulator. Additionally, several frameworks, such as the INET framework have been developed with well-tuned data communication components such as TCP/IP, 802.11, and Ethernet. Figure 1 shows the different components of the SGsim framework. Through the COM interface, the user is able to control the execution of the circuit and to change/add/remove different components. This is very helpful when simulating time-dependent scenarios. The main components of the simulator are:

- Power Grid Model: The OpenDSS is fed with a script that describes the components of the power grid and the interconnections. Time-dependent loads and supplies can be provided as text files. For household demand and photovoltaic supply real data from Pecan Street [15] will be used. This database provides a 1-min resolution aggregated power usage signal and the power consumption of individual devices. This can be very suitable in exploring applications such as DR.

- Solver: It controls the OpenDSS execution through the COM interface. It ensures time synchronization between OpenDSS and OMNeT++.

- Load: This is the OMNeT++ component of the load in the power grid, e.g., a house. It can measure power grid parameters such as voltage, current and power at a specific time through the COM interface. It is also possible to change load parameters, e.g., running time for Demand Response (DR) applications.

- Supply: Represents a power generation unit in OMNeT++, e.g., a DER. It is also possible to change supply parameters, e.g., regulate the output power (active and reactive power).

- Device: It represents power grid devices (e.g., battery, switch, capacitor bank, ...). Through the COM interface, it is possible to change the parameters, e.g., power factor.

- Sensor: It can only read data on a specific component (e.g., bus, load, DER) and send it to other components. For instance Phasor Measurement Unit (PMU) is considered as a sensor and it sends data to the Phasor Data Concentrator (PDC) Interface using simulated TCP/IP packets. The data is formatted using a standard (IEEE c37.118) so that the real PDC can interpret the packets.

- Controller: it represents an intelligent unit within the system. It receives data from other components and then, based on specific algorithms it can adapt system parameters. For instance, a CVR controller can change the voltage settings of a Load Tap Changer (LTC) in order to change the voltage of the transformer. In the SGsim framework, we integrated the open source optimization tools NLopt [10] and lpSolve [6]. It is possible also to call an external optimizer through a TCP/IP connection.

- PDC interface: It receives simulated packets inside the simulator and forwards it to real software components such as OpenPDC. In this case, the simulation should be run using the real-time mode.

We have implemented a DLL library to access the elements through the COM interface. The library provides the following functions:

- `run_command(char * command)` makes it possible to run a command. For instance, the command `edit load.LD1 kw=0.329 kvar=0` will set the active and reactive power values at LD1.

- `get_values_active_object(char * activeobject)` returns back different electricity measurements (e.g. voltage, current and active, and reactive Power) on a specific element.
  E.g., `values= fun_ptr(Load.LD1);` returns back the measurements at load LD1. `fun_ptr` is a pointer to the function `get_values_active_object`.

- `get_total_losses()` returns back the total losses in the network.

- `get_energy_active_object(char * Battery)` returns back the energy of a storage element (Battery).

OMNeT++ is a discrete event simulation and consequently, SGsim is a discrete event simulator in which OpenDSS is called periodically to solve the power flow in the electricity network.

3.2 Installation

The program is tested under a windows environment (Windows 7)

- OpenDSS: Install OpenDSS. Make sure the the `OpenDSSEngine.DLL` is registered. Usually it is installed automatically if you use the installer. You can manually register the server
  - run cmd to open a command prompt
  - go to the folder with the files
  - run the command `Regsvr32 OpenDSSEngine.DLL`

- OMNeT++: Install OMNeT++ (tested with version 4.4).

- INET Framework: Install the INET framework (tested with version 2.3.0)

- `SGsimLib.dll`: Store this file and give the full path in omnetpp.ini, for example:

  `C:\\Users\\user1\\workspace`
  `\\SGsim\\simulations`
  `\\example1\\SGsimLib.dll`

- Store the DSS file in the same folder!

- Provide the full path of the DSS file in omnetpp.ini file

  Important: you have to install Visual Studio or make sure you have the following DLL files: {msvcp120d.dll, msvcr100d.dll, msvcr120d.dll}.

3.3 Simple Example

Figure 2 depicts a simple network that consists of 5 houses equipped with photovoltaic systems , and a storage element. At the beginning we have to provide a script that describes the topology of the network. The values of the parameters are not important because we can change the values from OMNeT++ during the run time. Listing 1 shows an OpenDSS script for the simple network. The script should start with `clear` so that there is no other networks in the memory. Then we create a voltage source (Line 3). After that we define the transformer and its terminals. We add here a controller for the transformer so that we can change the output voltage of the transformer. The parameters of the transmission line can be defined with `Linecode`. Then we define the connection between the buses. In OpenDSS, there are several models to represent loads. We used model 8 to represent the load which is suitable to study applications such as CVR. This load model use ZIP coefficients to represent loads as in Equations 1 and 2. The photovoltaic is defined with the keyword `PVsystem`. Additional parameters such as the relation between the efficiency and temperature can be included. The battery can be defined with the key word `storage`. Through OMNeT++ we can change the values of the parameters of a specific component, add new components or remove components.

$$P_{Li} = P_{0i}\left[Z_P\left(\frac{v_i}{v_0}\right)^2 + I_P\left(\frac{v_i}{v_0}\right) + P_P\right] \quad (1)$$

$$Q_{Li} = Q_{0i}\left[Z_q\left(\frac{v_i}{v_0}\right)^2 + I_q\left(\frac{v_i}{v_0}\right) + P_q\right] \quad (2)$$

Listing 1: OpenDSS code of a simple network

```
1 clear
2 // VSOURCE
3 new circuit.example1 basekV=11 pu=1.00 angle=0
      frequency=50 phases=3
4 set defaultBasefrequency=50
5 // TRANSFORMERS
6 new transformer.TR1 phases=3 windings=2 buses=(
      sourcebus, B0) conns=(wye, wye) kvs=(11,
      0.4) kvas=(250, 250) taps=(1,1)
7 //TRANSFORMER CONTROLLER
```

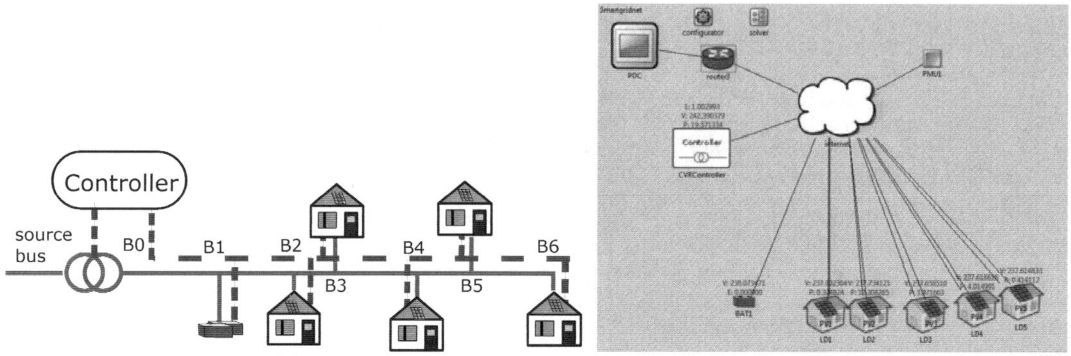

(a) (b)

Figure 2: The topology of the electricity and communication networks

```
new regcontrol.TR1 transformer=TR1 winding=2
     vreg=(242) ptratio=(1) band=1
// LINECODE AND LINES
new Linecode.LCode nphases=3 R1=0.320 X1=0.075
     C1=0 units=km
new line.Line01 bus1=B0 bus2=B1 Linecode=LCode
     length=0.5 units=km
new line.Line12 bus1=B1 bus2=B2 Linecode=LCode
     length=0.02 units=km
//repeat this line for the lines which
//connect Buses B2, B3, B4, B5, B6
// LOADS
new load.LD1 bus1=B2 kV=0.4 kW=2 PF=1 Model=8
     ZIPV=[0.85 -1.12 1.27 10.96 -18.73 8.77
     0.8]
//repeat this line for LD2 to LD5
// PV
new PVsystem.PV1 bus1=B2 phases=3 kV=0.4 KVA=10
     irrad=0.0 Pmpp=10
//repeat for PV2 to PV5
// BATTERY
New Storage.BAT1 Phases=3 Bus1=B1 kV=0.4
     kWRated=15 kWhRated=100 %stored=0 pf=1
// P.U.
Set voltagebases="11 0.4"
Calcvoltagebases
```

INET framework has been used to build the data communication network. The network consists of a model that represents the internet. Each element is equipped with a NIC that supports Ethernet, WLAN and PPP protocols. The houses are connected using PPP protocols that represents DSL connections. The NED language which is used in OMNeT++ has been used to describe the network. The source files of the network can be found at the sourceforge page [18]. Figure 2(b) shows a screenshot of the OMNeT++ simulation environment. It is preferred to use the same names in both OMNeT++ and OpenDSS. This makes the access to the components and their parameters more convenient. Some measurements are shown above each component. For instance, the voltage at the transformer (V) equals 242 volt, Power (P) is about 19 kW and the energy consumption (E) from the start of simulation is about 1 kWh. Each component produces a text file that contains the voltage and power at each time step. Of course, it is possible to include other measurements in this file.

Table 1: Parameters

Parameter	Value
PV	10 kVA
Battery power	15 kVA
Battery capacity	100 kWh
v_{thr1}, v_{thr2} ,v_{thr3} ,v_{thr4}	249, 215, 220, 244 volt
r+xj	$(0.320 + 0.075j)/km$
l_1	500 m
l_2	20 m

4. CASE STUDY: VOLTAGE CONTROL OF ELECTRICITY DISTRIBUTION GRID

Algorithm 1 The house application

Require: Get Voltage (V_i) at load i
Ensure: Sending current voltage value
if (V_i) $\leq v_{thr1}$ **then**
    send an under-voltage warning message to the controller
else if (V_i) $\geq v_{thr2}$ **then**
    send an over-voltage warning message to the controller
else
    send a normal-voltage periodic message
end if
repeat

Voltage control is an important task of the distribution grid automation. Traditionally voltage control is limited to the Tap Changer. The tap changer increases or decreases the winding ratio of the upper/lower voltage side of the transformer. The value of the transformer ratio is a task of the network planning and has to ensure that all customers all the time are served with a voltage within the allowed band. Therefore, the ratios have to be selected and fixed based on extreme load conditions and the voltage drop along the feeder. This type of planning is no longer suitable for the next generation power grid where bi-directional power flows occur. The voltage profile in a traditional power grid is shown in Figure 3(a). As can be seen, the voltage declines along the feeder. The voltage profile becomes more com-

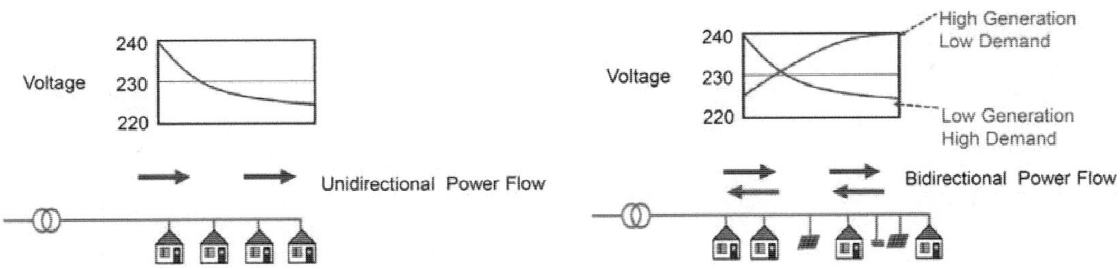

(a) (b)

Figure 3: Voltage profiles in traditional networks (a) and in current and future networks (b)

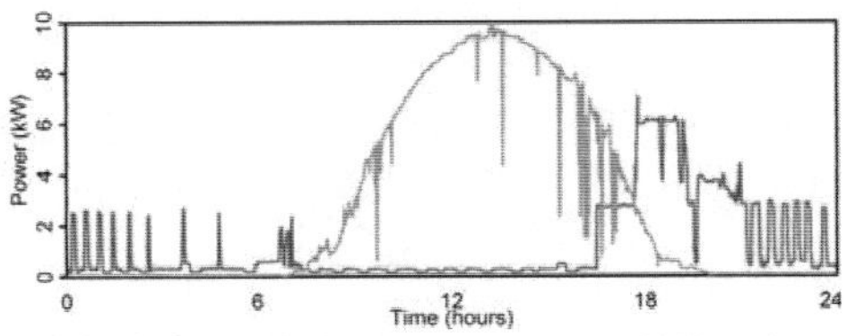

(a)

Figure 4: Demand (red) and supply (green) profiles

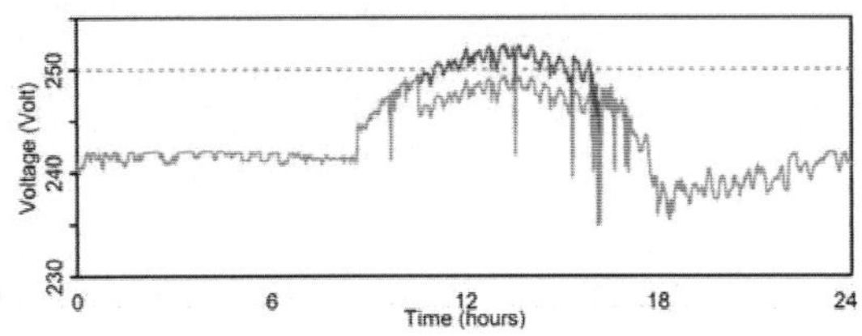

(a)

Figure 5: Voltage levels at the house at the end of the feeder without a battery (red) and with a battery (green)

plex as shown in Figure 3(b). The conditions are no longer strong/weak demand but instead are weak load/strong supply and strong supply/weak supply. New algorithms are required that are able to coordinate the operation of the different components on the power grid such as storage units, elastic loads, as well as transformers. For this purpose, the voltage measurements at end users is required. Traditionally, the voltage measurements at the customer side is not available. Here two approaches are possible: either installing measurement units or installing smart meters. Controlling the active/reactive power can be used to control the voltage at the customer side. This can be done by several methods. Introducing a variable tariff can increase the demand during the high power injection and reduce the demand during the low power injection. Another approach is to control the active/reactive power of distributed energy resources. Batteries can also be used to control the voltage at the customer side. They can be charged at high power injection periods and discharged at low power injection periods.

Algorithm 2 The controller application

Require: Receive warning voltage messages from houses
Ensure: Transformer Output Voltage v_{TR}

```
if Under − Voltage then
    send a DISCHARGE signal to the battery
    State=DISCHARGE
else if Over − Voltage then
    send a CHARGE signal to the battery
    State=CHARGE
else if (V_i ≥ v_thr3)&(State == DISCHARGE) then
    send an IDLE signal to the battery
else if (V_i ≤ v_thr4)&(State == CHARGE) then
    send an IDLE signal to the battery
end if
```

In this case study we use the network shown in Figure 2(a). The distance between the transformer and the first house (l_1) is 500 m and between two houses (l_2) 20 m. A community storage unit is located inside the network. We exploit the available storage element to decrease the voltage at the high supply/low demand period and increase the voltage at low supply/high demand period. We use power demand and supply profiles from the Pecan street database [15]. The red line in in Figure 4(a) depicts a typical household load and the green line depicts a typical supply. Every house sends periodically its measured voltage (Algorithm 1). This algorithm is implemented as C++ program inside the house component. These measurements can be used to implement smart grid applications such as CVR and VVC. Yet, if the voltage at a house is above or below specific limits, a warning message will be sent. Upon receiving these messages, the controller can take actions to prevent unacceptable voltage values. In this case study, the controller will send a charge command for an over-voltage warning message and a discharge command for a low-voltage warning message as shown in Algorithm 2, which is implemented inside the controller component. The implementation of the algorithms can be found at [18]. The discharging process will continue until the voltage is raised above a specific value (v_{thr3}) and the charging process will continue until the voltage is below a specific value (v_{thr4}). Table 1 summarizes the simulation parameters. The parameters can be set in the omnetpp.ini configuration file.

Figure 5(a) shows the voltage at the last house at the end of feeder with and without using the battery units. As can be seen, the voltage raises during the midday to high levels (red line). This occurs because of the high electricity injection from the solar panels and the low demand. Exploiting the available storage system reduces the voltage to acceptable limits (green line).

The approach is based on simple rules to react to abnormal voltage levels. A more complex approach which can employ optimization, can be used. For instance, it is possible to use demand response or control the distributed energy resources to maintain the voltage within acceptable limits as well as to improve the operation of the system.

5. CONCLUSION

In this paper we presented a tutorial on SGsim that enables the investigation of smart grid applications inside power distribution networks. SGsim is a framework that consists of the data communication simulator OMNeT++ and the power grid OpenDSS. This way, it is possible to investigate the impact of data communication systems on the electricity networks. Through a case study with real data, we have shown the possibility to mitigate over-voltage through controlling the storage units.

Acknowledgment

Peter Bazan is also a member of "Energie Campus Nürnberg", Fürther Str. 250, 90429 Nürnberg. His research was performed as part of the "Energie Campus Nürnberg" and supported by funding through the "Aufbruch Bayern (Bavaria on the move)" initiative of the state of Bavaria.

6. REFERENCES

[1] EPRI Electrical Power Research Institute. http://sourceforge.net/projects/electricdss/, 2016. [Online; accessed 20-July-2016].

[2] K. Anderson, J. Du, A. Narayan, and A. E. Gamal. GridSpice: A distributed simulation platform for the smart grid. *IEEE Transactions on Industrial Informatics*, 10(4):2354–2363, Nov. 2014.

[3] A. Awad, P. Bazan, and R. German. SGsim: a Simulation Framework for Smart Grid Applications. In IEEE, editor, *Proceedings of the IEEE International Energy Conference (ENERGYCON 2014)*, pages 730–736, Dubrovnik, Croatia, May 2014.

[4] A. Awad, P. Bazan, and R. German. SGsim: Co-Simulation Framework for ICT-Enabled Power Distribution Grids. In *18th International GI/ITG Conference on Measurment, Modelling and Evaluation of Computing Systems and Dependability and Fault-Tolerance (MMB & DFT 2016)*, Münster, Germany, April 2016.

[5] L. T. Berger and K. Iniewski, editors. *Smart Grid Applications, Communications and Security*. John Wiley & Sons, 2012.

[6] M. Berkelaar et al. lpSolve: interface to *Lp_solve* v. 5.5 to solve linear/integer programs. http://cran.r-project.org/web/packages/lpSolve/lpSolve.pdf, 2015. [Online; accessed 20-July-2016].

[7] D. P. Chassin, J. C. Fuller, and N. Djilali. GridLAB-d: An agent-based simulation framework for smart grids. *Journal of Applied Mathematics*, 2014:1–12, 2014.

[8] J. Dede, K. Kuladinithi, A. Förster, O. Nannen, and S. Lehnhoff. Omnet++ and mosaik: Enabling simulation of smart grid communications. *arXiv preprint arXiv:1509.03067*, 2015.

[9] EPRI Electrical Power Research Institute. Home page, Oct. 2016.

[10] S. G. Johnson. The NLopt nonlinear-optimization package. http://ab-initio.mit.edu/nlopt, 2016. [Online; accessed 20-July-2016].

[11] S. Lehnhoff, O. Nannen, S. Rohjans, F. Schlogl, S. Dalhues, L. Robitzky, U. Hager, and C. Rehtanz. Exchangeability of power flow simulators in smart grid co-simulations with mosaik. In *2015 Workshop on Modeling and Simulation of Cyber-Physical Energy Systems (MSCPES)*, pages 1–6. Institute of Electrical & Electronics Engineers (IEEE), Apr. 2015.

[12] M. Lévesque, C. Béchet, E. Suignard, M. Maier, A. Picault, and G. Joos. From co- toward multi-simulation of smart grids based on HLA and FMI standards. *The Computing Research Repository (CoRR)*, 2014.

[13] M. Lévesque, D. Q. Xu, G. Joós, and M. Maier. Communications and power distribution network co-simulation for multidisciplinary smart grid experimentations. In *Proceedings of the 45th Annual Simulation Symposium*, page 2. Society for Computer Simulation International, 2012.

[14] P. Palensky, E. Widl, M. Stifter, and A. Elsheikh. Modeling intelligent energy systems: Co-simulation platform for validating flexible-demand EV charging management. In *2014 IEEE PES General Meeting | Conference & Exposition*, page 1. Institute of Electrical & Electronics Engineers (IEEE), July 2014.

[15] Pecan street database. Home page, Oct. 2016.

[16] S. Rohjans, S. Lehnhoff, S. Schutte, S. Scherfke, and S. Hussain. mosaik-a modular platform for the evaluation of agent-based smart grid control. In *IEEE Innovative Smart Grid Technologies Europe (ISGT EUROPE)*, pages 1–5, 2013.

[17] M. A. H. Sadi, M. H. Ali, D. Dasgupta, and R. K. Abercrombie. OPNET/simulink based testbed for disturbance detection in the smart grid. In *Proceedings of the 10th Annual Cyber and Information Security Research Conference on - CISR 15*, page 17. ACM, Association for Computing Machinery (ACM), 2015.

[18] SGsim. Home page, April 2016. https://sourceforge.net/projects/sgsim/.

[19] M. Stifter, J. H. Kazmi, F. Andren, and T. Strasser. Co-simulation of power systems, communication and controls. In *2014 Workshop on Modeling and Simulation of Cyber-Physical Energy Systems (MSCPES)*, pages 1–6. Institute of Electrical & Electronics Engineers (IEEE), Apr. 2014.

[20] M. Stifter, E. Widl, F. Andrén, A. Elsheikh, T. Strasser, and P. Palensky. Co-simulation of components, controls and power systems based on open source software. In *2013 IEEE Power & Energy Society General Meeting*, pages 1–5. IEEE, Institute of Electrical & Electronics Engineers (IEEE), 2013.

[21] A. Varga. The OMNeT++ Discrete Event Simulation System. In *European Simulation Multiconference (ESM 2001)*, Prague, Czech Republic, June 2001.

Modeling Security Requirements for VNE algorithms

Andreas Fischer, Ramona Kühn, Waseem Mandarawi, Hermann de Meer
University of Passau
Faculty for Computer Science and Mathematics
Innstraße 43, 94032 Passau, Germany
{andreas.fischer,ramona.kuehn,waseem.mandarawi,hermann.demeer}@uni.passau.de

ABSTRACT

Public and private Infrastructure as a Service (IaaS) clouds are widely used by individuals and organizations to provision flexible virtual computing resources on demand. Virtual Network Embedding (VNE) algorithms are employed in this context to provide an automated resource assignment. With multiple involved parties, security-aware Virtual Machine (VM) placement becomes highly relevant for production environments. Moreover, VNE algorithms should also consider the security requirements of the interconnections between VMs, thereby extending the problem to networks. This paper discusses security requirements of Virtual Networks (VNs) and shows how they can be modeled in VNE to map them to the provided security mechanisms in the physical network. The paper also presents an implementation of this security-aware VNE model in the public simulation platform ALEVIN, demonstrating the applicability with a realistic use case of such a model.

CCS Concepts

•Networks → Network domains; Cloud computing; Data center networks; Overlay and other logical network structures; •Computing methodologies → Modeling and simulation; Simulation tools; •Security and privacy → *Security requirements; Formal security models; Security services; Firewalls;*

Keywords

Virtual network embedding; Cloud computing; Security; Virtual network, Substrate network, Network virtualization

1. INTRODUCTION

Network virtualization is the primary enabling technology to overcome ossification effects in todays networks. It allows network administrators to deploy multiple VNs on a single Substrate Network (SN). The respective resource assignment problem is called VNE. It describes how a VN can be embedded or mapped on the given SN. The networks can be represented as a graph with nodes connected by links, where the virtual nodes or links pose demands for certain resources. Then, they have to be mapped on appropriate hardware components offering these resources.

So far, VNE approaches focus mostly on optimizing the performance of the embedding. Approaches to make the embedding more secure remain mostly abstract and do not easily lend themselves to practical application. Nevertheless, security is a major request nowadays, either to meet legal requirements, to protect own data, or for a network provider to satisfy the needs of the customers. In contrast to other approaches, this paper focuses on concrete security mechanisms like firewalls, Network Intrusion Detection Systems (NIDSs), and Trusted Hardware (TH), and discusses how they can be taken into account during the embedding process. It considers VNE problems with unsplittable links and focuses on offline evaluation of VNE algorithms.

In this setting, it is analyzed to what extent common security mechanisms require new constraints that have to be considered for the embedding process. The paper demonstrates how these constraints can be incorporated into the common algorithm evaluation process with minimal changes to the embedding algorithms themselves. This enables researchers to easily extend their evaluations to include new problems including security requirements, thereby speeding up research in this area. This paper shows the implementation and a proof-of-concept embedding that uses a common VNE simulator tool called ALEVIN [9, 3]. The paper presents the concepts of VNE and an overview of ALEVIN, then an extension to the tool to support security requirements of VNs. An overview of typical security requirements and a use case are discussed to show the usability of the tool to support security in virtual environments.

The remainder of this paper is structured as follows: In Section 2, background information about the VNE problem is provided and the related work on the modeling of security mechanisms for VNE is discussed. Section 3 describes the problem of modeling security mechanisms for VNE. An example use case is presented, highlighting the relevance of security-aware embedding algorithms. The modeling of the respective security requirements with appropriate constraints is analyzed in Section 4. Different types of requirements are identified and the formulation as embedding constraints is presented. The concrete implementation of the security mechanisms and constraints in a common VNE simulation framework is described in Section 5. In addition, the necessary changes to the simulation framework and the em-

VALUETOOLS 2016, October 25-28, Taormina, Italy

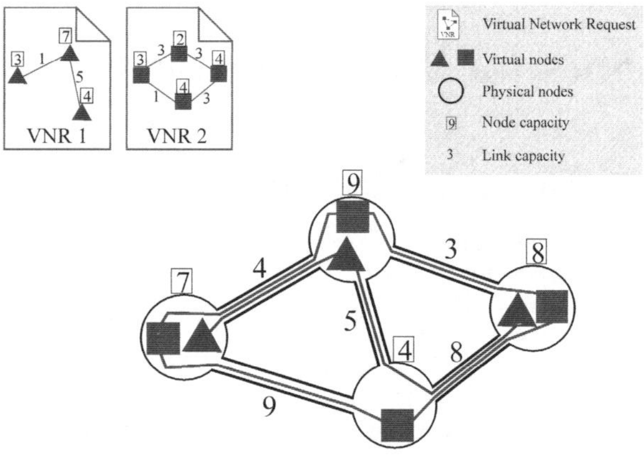

Figure 1: Example for a VNE scenario (adapted from Fischer et al. [8])

bedding process are presented. Finally, Section 6 provides a conclusion and a discussion of next steps.

2. BACKGROUND AND RELATED WORK

The VNE problem deals with the question how nodes and links of a VN should be mapped to the nodes and links of a SN. Both nodes and links are considered to provide resources in the case of substrate elements, and pose respective demands in the case of virtual elements.

VNs come in the form of Virtual Network Requests (VNRs): requests of users for instantiation of a particular network. It is the task of a VNE algorithm to decide whether all requests can be supported by the given SN, and if so, how the individual elements should be mapped.

Fig. 1 shows an example for this problem with two VNRs to be mapped onto a SN with four nodes. A possible embedding is already depicted. Each virtual element poses a demand on its respective substrate element, and the sum of the demands of all virtual elements hosted on a substrate element may not exceed the available resources. If not enough resources are left to support a VNR, it is rejected and only a partial solution can be found. Solutions (partial or complete) are not necessarily unique.

The VNE problem is known to be $\mathcal{NP}$-hard [2, 1]. Efficient approaches, therefore, require the application of heuristics. Many VNE algorithms have been proposed up to now in the literature [8]. Most VNE algorithms are performance-oriented, optimizing for cost or for the number of VNRs to be mapped onto a SN. In contrast, security considerations have been a relatively new addition to that topic [10, 12]. Often, these approaches model only abstract security requirements in a sense of different security levels or classes. One application of this is data protection: It is shown that the concept of such security classes can help to define a control flow for different kinds of data (business or personal) and define a location-based resource allocation to fulfill legal requirements [7]. This means that the virtual resources are mapped on hardware resources that comply with an adequate level of protection. However, the definition of such security classes often remains abstract. In contrast, the concrete definition of common security mechanisms and requirements such as firewalls, NIDS, or specific TH are considered in this paper. Respectively, their modeling for use in common VNE simulation software is described.

Multiple simulation frameworks are available for VNE evaluation. Yu et al. propose the VNE Simulator [15]. Chowdhury et al. describe Vineyard [6, 5]. Papagianni et al. propose CVI-Sim [14]. In this paper, the ALEVIN simulator [9, 3] is used, due to its flexibility and extensibility. It provides in particular a flexible resource/demand model that can be adapted to model security requirements. ALEVIN also offers a broad variety of functions such as developing new algorithms and defining new metrics for the comparison and evaluation of VNE algorithms. A wide set of algorithms and metrics are already implemented. Furthermore, ALEVIN is in principle scalable for large networks. This scalability depends, however, on the embedding algorithms being used. In addition, ALEVIN provides different methods for creating physical and virtual networks and assigning resources and demands to network entities. These methods are Graphical User Interface (GUI), input data files (XML), and random network generators with the required parameters.

3. PROBLEM DESCRIPTION

The implementation of security mechanisms and constraints is highly relevant for experimentation with VNE algorithms. This requires a proper formulation of these requirements for VNE simulation. In this section, first an overview is provided, specifying the necessity to formulate concrete security features. A motivational example helps to delineate the problem. The respective requirements are extracted and classified as node-based, link-based, and topology-based requirements.

3.1 Overview

Network security requirements are substantially different from conventional embedding constraints such as bandwidth or CPU time. They typically do not refer to a consumable resource, but rather to a specific set of features that need to be available. For example, a customer might require one of his virtual nodes to be executed in a particularly safe environment, requiring specific protection from the underlying substrate node.

An abstract approach to this problem is to define security levels for substrate and virtual nodes, requiring the embedding algorithm to match these levels appropriately (cf. [10, 12, 13]). However, in practice the concept of strictly hierarchical levels proves to be too abstract. In an environment with multiple involved parties (as it is common in cloud computing), it is difficult to find a comprehensive definition of levels that can satisfy each party.

Instead, it is more likely that customers specify a particular set of security requirements, defining for example that a certain node should be protected by intrusion detection software, or that a set of nodes should be protected by a firewall. A cloud provider, on the other hand, can label its equipment such that the customer's requests can be mapped appropriately. However, a customer cannot easily prove that the provider actually implements the required mechanisms. In this paper, we assume a trusted provides and that the provider conforms to the security aspects of the Service-level-agreement (SLA).

3.2 Motivational example

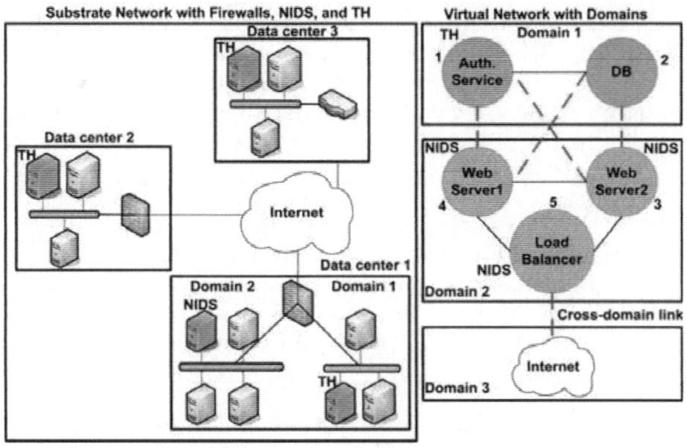

Figure 2: Cloud provider infrastructure and a VN for a web service

A motivational example is presented here to illustrate the application of security requirements in VNE. This example is depicted in Fig. 2. A cloud provider offers computing resources distributed over three data centers. Two of those data centers are protected by a firewall. One of those data centers offers two separated subnets. A client wants to implement a web service which consists of a load balancer, two web servers, a data base, and an authentication service. These components are interconnected and should be deployed in the cloud infrastructure.

Each of the components has its specific demands which have to be adhered to by the cloud provider. Some of these demands reflect the security requirements of the underlying software. For example, the web servers have to be protected from the internet by a firewall. Since a firewall cannot prevent all attacks, a NIDS should provide information about potential malicious actions. The authentication service requires TH, as it is highly security critical. Both the authentication service and the data base should be protected from the web servers by a firewall.

VNE algorithms can help to identify how the virtual infrastructure can be mapped while adhering to these requirements. However, a suitable model applicable for VNE algorithms must be found. This paper discusses how these requirements can be modeled in a public VNE simulator for experimentation with VNE algorithms.

3.3 Classification of requirements

The VNE constraints commonly investigated up to now focus mostly on quantitative values—node and link resources and demands. Popular examples are bandwidth for links and CPU capacity for nodes. Security mechanisms, in contrast, are typically qualitative in nature: A particular feature or mechanism is required from the SN. This feature or mechanism is not consumed by a virtual entity, but remains available for further nodes or links.

Security mechanisms, such as demanded by the discussed web service, can be roughly classified into three different types. There are requirements that are specific to a single node and requirements that are specific to a single link—similar to conventional constraints. However, in addition there are also more complex requirements that refer to a part of the topology. In the following, these three types are discussed in detail.

3.3.1 Node requirements

When a virtual node demands a security mechanism, the physical node has to offer this mechanism to be a possible candidate for mapping. Examples for this node-to-node mapping are TH, encrypted data storage and Virtual Machine Introspection (VMI). For the purpose of this paper, TH is used as an exemplary mechanism in the motivational example.

This means, if a virtual node demands TH, it can only be mapped on a physical node that offers TH. It is, however, possible to map an arbitrary number of virtual nodes on the same substrate node, as long as other resources are not exceeded. Moreover, if a virtual node does not demand the mechanism, a mapping on a physical node offering it is still possible. The virtual node does not have to use the property of the physical node. However, it has to be ensured that for all further virtual nodes demanding TH there are still enough physical nodes offering it, so that a mapping of the VN on the SN is possible.

3.3.2 Link requirements

There are also security mechanisms that affect the links between two nodes. A virtual link might demand that it can only be mapped on a physical link that offers a specific security mechanism. As an example, a requirement of a virtual link can be that it is only mapped on a physical link that provides data encryption.

3.3.3 Topological requirements

A new kind of requirement describes security mechanisms that affect not only an individual network entity, but a part of the topology. Both nodes and links are affected and the topological structure has to be taken into account. Firewalls and NIDSs are examples for these kinds of security mechanisms.

In the motivational example, several components demand the protection by a firewall. They have to be grouped into domains that identify the parts of the affected topology. For example, it is not allowed that one node protected by the firewall is connected to another node in a different domain of the network via a link that does not pass the firewall. If this were the case, the protection of the firewall would be obsolete. Therefore, this has to be prevented during embedding.

To handle this constraint, the network has to be separated explicitly into different network domains. On the one hand, there are domains which have to be protected by a firewall or a NIDS. On the other hand, there may also be domains where such a security mechanism is not needed. The traffic between those domains has to be exclusively routed through the firewall for example.

A security-aware VNE takes the requirements described above into account. Therefore, it has to recognize the topology of the network to be able to divide it such that the firewall offers full protection and is not circumvented. The way the presented requirements have to be translated so that VNE simulation frameworks are able to understand and implement them is discussed in the next section.

4. MODELING SECURITY REQUIREMENTS WITH RESOURCE-DEMAND PAIRS

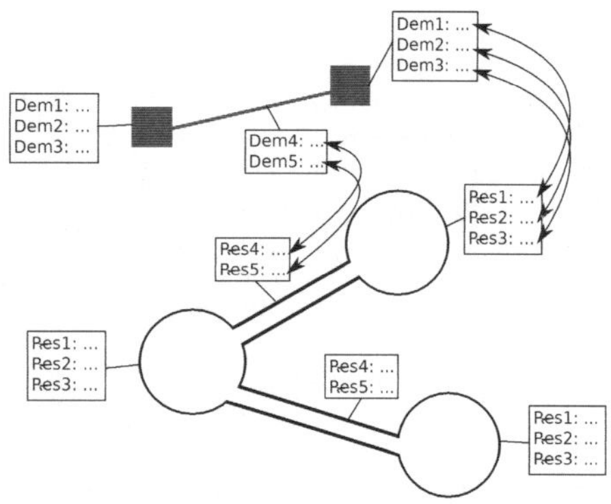

Figure 3: Resource and demand pairs

A VNE model encompasses the SN and the VNs that are mapped on it. They are modeled as graphs where nodes represent active network elements (e.g., routers) and edges represent the connectivity among them. In VNE, the consumable capabilities of the physical network entities are represented as resources that are attached to physical nodes and links, such as CPU, memory, and bandwidth. The basic model presented in Section 2 can be easily extended to contain multiple types of node and link resources.

This approach can be extended to also model specific properties of the physical network elements such as security mechanisms available in physical nodes. Likewise, the requirements of the VNs can be modeled as demands attached to virtual entities in the VNR.

In this paper, a demand is formulated to request a certain capacity of a consumable resource or request a certain property in the physical network entity. The resource/demand model is used to represent the relationship between a virtual demand and a physical resource. Resources and demands form pairs: Each demand corresponds to its respective resource.

The relationship between arbitrary resources and demands is depicted in Fig. 3. The figure shows a VN with two nodes and a link between them, and a SN with three physical nodes and two links. Each virtual node and link has demands for certain resources and each physical node and link offers certain resources. The demands and resources in the figure are depicted as Dem[ID] and Res[ID] identifiers for simplicity. The embedding algorithm has to make sure for nodes and links to pair any demand $DemN$ with the corresponding resource $ResN$.

This concept can be further extended to provide a base for modeling security capabilities and their corresponding demands. This allows to model security requirements of VNs. Here, the same resource/demand methodology is used to build a prototype that represents the security requirements. Mapping of these demands does not occupy capacity. The mapping of security requirements of virtual nodes rather depends on available properties in the corresponding physical nodes. Likewise, the mapping of the security requirements of the virtual links depends on the type of the requirements and has to check for certain properties along the physical path that maps a particular virtual link.

Here, the concepts described in the motivational example are discussed and it is shown how the resource/demand model can be adapted to implement them. The concept of resources is re-interpreted to create "pseudo-resources" that are not consumed by their corresponding demand. This allows to model THs, NIDSs, and firewalls:

- TH: A TH provides a trusted computing base to the hosted VMs such as a virtualized Trusted Platform Module (TPM) (Berger et al. [4]), for example. This is a simple node-based requirement that can be modeled by creating a special resource/demand pair "trusted hardware" in which the demand does not consume the resource.
- NIDS: A NIDS, as discussed above, represents a topological requirement. However, when the requirement is reformulated from "A NIDS is present" to "The node is protected by a NIDS", the requirement can actually be reformulated as a node-based requirement. It is then modeled similar to a TH node.
- Firewall: The firewall is more complex to model. It is not defined explicitly in the VNR. Instead, the VNR has to specify the respective network domains that should be protected and separated from each other. Using this information, Cross-domain Links (CDLs) can be identified by the embedding algorithm. As such, the demands in the VNR actually refer to domains.

  The SN, on the other hand, provides firewall nodes. This can be simply modeled with a "firewall" resource. Any CDLs is required to cross such a firewall node to ensure that nodes are properly separated. Intra-domain links, on the other hand, are preferably mapped to the same subnet.

The resource/demand model can be used to model these requirements. While TH and NIDS are straightforward to implement, the concept of firewalls requires more work. The disparate resource/demand pair has to be combined properly. Appropriate checks for CDLs have to be performed. An implementation of these mechanisms in a public VNE simulation framework is described in the following section.

5. IMPLEMENTATION OF SECURITY REQUIREMENTS CHECKS FOR VNE SIMULATION

The evaluation of VNE algorithms under security constraints requires the implementation of security requirements checks in the employed simulation framework. Here, the implementation in the ALEVIN framework is discussed and the realization of the use case presented in Subsection 3.2 is demonstrated.

5.1 Implementation of resource/demand pairs

The resource/demand model is implemented in ALEVIN using the visitor pattern to represent the occupying relationship between a virtual demand and a physical resource. ALEVIN has a generic structure that makes it easy to add new resource/demand pairs. Here, a set of resource/demand pairs that represent the basic security requirements needed for the motivational example is added.

As discussed in Section 4, security requirements that are specific to individual nodes and links can be modeled by adapting the concept of resource/demand pair. Qualitative security requirements such as "*needs protection by a NIDS*" are matched with respective security features such as "*offers protection by a NIDS*". For the presented scenario, a NIDS demand and a TH demand are implemented.

Topological requirements prove to be more involved, though. Here, the simple resource/demand model has to be extended. The simulator has to check the validity of a particular mapping between a virtual link and its respective path in the SN. The mapping is considered valid only if the path can satisfy the security requirements of the virtual link. Firewall demands are implemented through the definition of different domains. These domains are represented as identifiers that are attached to the nodes. Firewall resources are attached to the respective substrate nodes.

However, in addition to this, a check for CDLs is necessary. As an example, a check for firewall constraints is presented in Fig. 4. The check is performed during the link mapping stage and forces all CDLs to go through a firewall. First, the algorithm filters the VNR to find CDLs by comparing the domain identifiers of the source and destination nodes of the link. Then, for each link, a set of possible physical paths is selected according to the link mapping method. The possible paths are then checked to assert if at least one of the nodes along the path provides a firewall service.

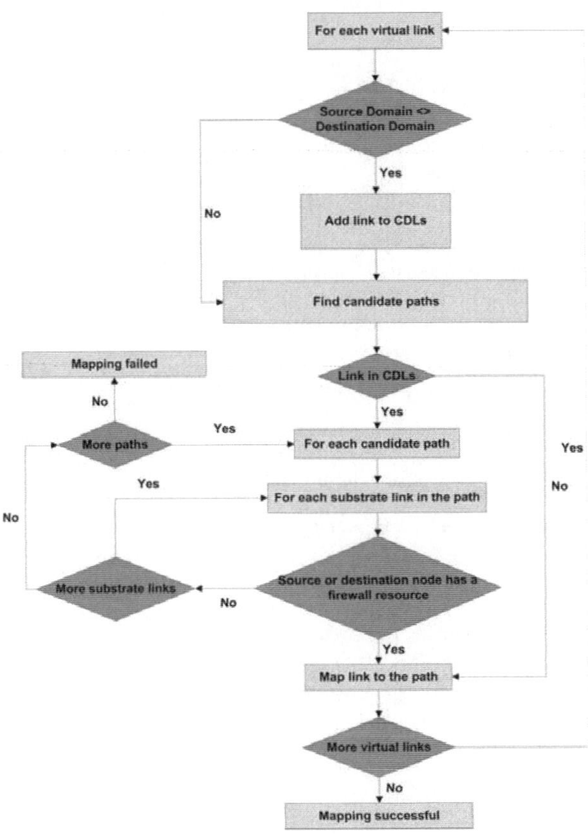

Figure 4: Embedding algorithm for CDLs

The generic embedding algorithm enforces in particular the following embedding constraints: The virtual domain is not split by a firewall and is mapped in one physical domain. CDLs are forced to go through a firewall. Virtual nodes that require a TH are mapped only to substrate nodes that offer it. Virtual nodes that require a NIDS are mapped only in domains in which at least one substrate node offers NIDS.

The implementation in the simulator itself allows to stay agnostic of the employed VNE algorithm. It is, thus, possible to evaluate scenarios with security constraints with any VNE algorithm[1].

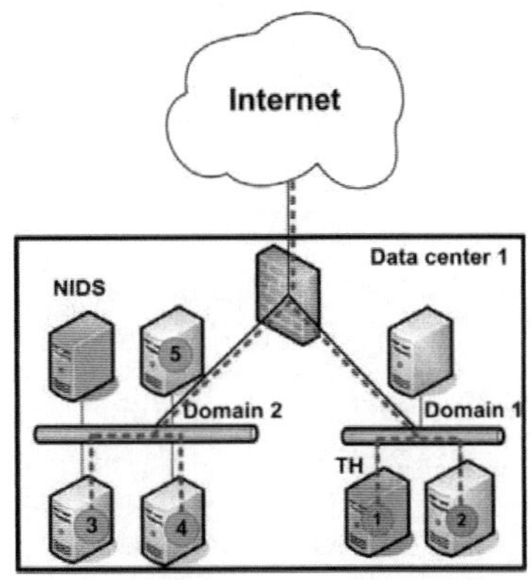

Figure 5: Motivational scenario for security-aware VNE

5.2 Realization of the motivational scenario

Fig. 5 shows the results of the mapping when implementing the motivational scenario for security-aware VNE showed in Fig. 2. In the original figure, the SN includes three different data centers. Domains are defined to identify the subnets that are protected by a firewall. Two nodes in the SN are labeled as firewall nodes and three other nodes are labeled as providing TH. The virtual network represents the specified web service with three different domains: Authentication and database, load balancer and web servers, and the general internet. The load balancer should connect to the internet to receive the web requests from users of the service. Intra- and inter-domain virtual links are depicted. The authentication server demands a node with TH. The mapping results of the VN on the SN are depicted in Fig. 5. To ensure readability, only mapped CDLs are represented.

The depicted scenario is realized in ALEVIN to test the functionality of the new security-aware VNE structure and algorithm. For demonstration, a commonly known mapping algorithm is used to perform the actual embedding. Here, the vnmFlib algorithm by Lischka and Karl [11] has been chosen. When the original topology does not contain firewall resources, the mapping procedure will not succeed since CDLs can only be mapped over nodes containing a firewall. However, when a firewall is added to the node that connects the first data center to the internet, the mapping is successful. Fig. 6 depicts the ALEVIN GUI with the constructed example topology and the procedure of adding the property of a firewall to a substrate node. For simplicity, only CDLs are shown in the VNR, and only links to the firewall in the

[1]It should be noted, though, that algorithms that do not optimize for security constraints will likely produce suboptimal results in many cases

data centers and internet links are shown in the SN. The CPU and bandwidth capacities and demands are included in the topology and allow the mapping, but are neglected from the figure for clarity.

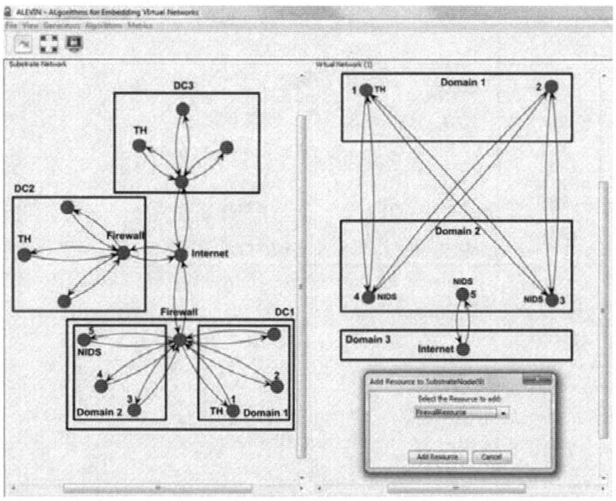

Figure 6: Adding a firewall-resource to ALEVIN

6. CONCLUSION AND FUTURE WORK

Security requirements are highly relevant for VNs deployed in public environments. It is necessary to extend VNE to incorporate these requirements and the respective security capabilities of the SN so that the embedding algorithms can satisfy them. Preferably, this is done without having to change the embedding algorithms, themselves. This paper introduced some security requirements of VNs and presented a generic methodology for modeling them. Topological constraints were identified as a new type of constraint that requires additional support by the simulation framework. The paper demonstrated a proof-of-concept implementation of a security-aware VNE model in the ALEVIN simulator, showing that, with some modifications, the existing resource/demand model can be adapted to implement security requirements. A motivational scenario that represents a web service has been discussed and implemented to demonstrate the applicability of the concept.

Future work will focus on generalizing the security constraint model to be able to adapt to more types of security requirements. Moreover, now that a generic implementation is available, multiple VNE algorithms can be evaluated in a security-aware environment.

7. ACKNOWLEDGMENTS

The research leading to these results was supported by the "Bavarian State Ministry of Education, Science and the Arts" as part of the FORSEC research association.

8. REFERENCES

[1] E. Amaldi, S. Coniglio, A. M. Koster, and M. Tieves. On the computational complexity of the virtual network embedding problem. *Electronic Notes in Discrete Mathematics*, 52:213–220, 2016. {INOC} 2015 – 7th International Network Optimization Conference.

[2] D. G. Andersen. Theoretical approaches to node assignment. Unpublished Manuscript, Dec. 2002.

[3] M. T. Beck, A. Fischer, F. Kokot, C. Linnhoff-Popien, and H. De Meer. A simulation framework for virtual network embedding algorithms. In *6th International Telecommunications Network Strategy and Planning Symposium (Networks 2014)*, pages 1–6. IEEE, Sept. 2014.

[4] S. Berger, R. Cáceres, K. A. Goldman, R. Perez, R. Sailer, and L. van Doorn. vtpm: Virtualizing the trusted platform module. In *Proceedings of the 15th Conference on USENIX Security Symposium - Volume 15*, USENIX-SS'06, Berkeley, CA, USA, 2006. USENIX Association.

[5] M. Chowdhury, M. Rahman, and R. Boutaba. Vineyard: Virtual network embedding algorithms with coordinated node and link mapping. *Networking, IEEE/ACM Transactions on*, 20(1):206–219, Feb 2012.

[6] N. Chowdhury, M. Rahman, and R. Boutaba. Virtual network embedding with coordinated node and link mapping. In *INFOCOM 2009, IEEE*, pages 783–791, April 2009.

[7] B. Doll, D. Emmerich, R. Herkenhöner, R. Kühn, and H. de Meer. *On Location-determined Cloud Management for Legally Compliant Outsourcing*, pages 61–73. Springer Fachmedien Wiesbaden, Wiesbaden, 2015.

[8] A. Fischer, J. F. Botero, M. T. Beck, H. De Meer, and X. Hesselbach. Virtual network embedding: A survey. *IEEE Communications Surveys and Tutorials*, 15(4):1888–1906, 2013.

[9] A. Fischer, J. F. Botero, M. Duelli, D. Schlosser, X. Hesselbach, and H. De Meer. ALEVIN - a framework to develop, compare, and analyze virtual network embedding algorithms. *Electronic Communications of the EASST*, 37:1–12, 2011.

[10] A. Fischer and H. De Meer. Position paper: Secure virtual network embedding. *Praxis der Informationsverarbeitung und Kommunikation*, 34(4):190–193, 2011.

[11] J. Lischka and H. Karl. A virtual network mapping algorithm based on subgraph isomorphism detection. In *VISA '09: Proceedings of the 1st ACM workshop on Virtualized infrastructure systems and architectures*, pages 81–88, New York, NY, USA, 2009. ACM.

[12] S. Liu, Z. Cai, H. Xu, and M. Xu. Security-aware virtual network embedding. In *Communications (ICC), 2014 IEEE International Conference on*, pages 834–840, June 2014.

[13] S. Liu, Z. Cai, H. Xu, and M. Xu. Towards security-aware virtual network embedding. *Computer Networks*, 91:151 – 163, 2015.

[14] C. Papagianni, A. Leivadeas, S. Papavassiliou, V. Maglaris, C. Cervello-Pastor, and A. Monje. On the optimal allocation of virtual resources in cloud computing networks. *Computers, IEEE Transactions on*, 62(6):1060–1071, June 2013.

[15] M. Yu, Y. Yi, J. Rexford, and M. Chiang. Rethinking virtual network embedding: Substrate support for path splitting and migration. *SIGCOMM Comput. Commun. Rev.*, 38(2):17–29, Mar. 2008.

An Integrated Model-driven Framework for Simulation, Analysis, and Testing Based on OMG Standards

Vitali Schneider, Anna Deitsch, Reinhard German
Friedrich-Alexander University of Erlangen-Nürnberg
Department of Computer Science 7
Martensstr. 3, D-91058 Erlangen, Germany
{vitali.schneider, anna.deitsch, reinhard.german}@fau.de

ABSTRACT

Model-driven engineering techniques are becoming increasingly popular for cost-effective and highly productive software development. Particularly, approaches and tools based on the standards provided by the Object Management Group (OMG), first of all on its famous Unified Modeling Language (UML), are already widespread throughout both the industry and the research community. Following this trend, the approach for Test-driven Agile Simulation (TAS) combines model-driven engineering, simulation, and testing techniques, based on OMG standards, to allow for advanced performance analysis and validation at early design stages. Among others, by deriving executable simulations from a system model and test specifications, this approach provides a cheap and agile technique for quantitative assessments and quality assurance of the system under design. In this paper, we present the current state of the SimTAny framework that provides a versatile, integrated, and standard-based tool chain to support the TAS approach. In particular, SimTAny facilitates the creation of model specifications, based on UML and several standardized profiles like SysML, MARTE, and UTP, the automated transformation to executable simulations, as well as testing and analysis activities. We demonstrate the main features of the SimTAny framework and illustrate the application of TAS on an example monocular vision system for the autonomous approach and landing that uses a low-budget micro aerial vehicle system.

CCS Concepts

•General and reference → Performance; Validation; Verification; •Computing methodologies → Modeling methodologies; Model verification and validation; *Discrete-event simulation;* **•Software and its engineering → Software design engineering;** *Traceability;*

VALUETOOLS 2016, October 25-28, Taormina, Italy

Keywords

Test-driven agile simulation, model-driven engineering, performance analysis, UML, model-driven testing

1. INTRODUCTION

Model-driven engineering (MDE) [6] is a promising approach for a cost-effective and high-productive development of complex software-intensive systems. It focuses on models as a primary artifact during the engineering process and is essentially based on two technologies: modeling languages and transformation mechanisms [17]. Besides the benefits of an increasing productivity due to the automated code generation from specification models, MDE provides a lot of advantages. To mention just a few examples: it helps to overcome the complexity hurdle by increasing the abstraction level during system design, it supports precise documenting of software architectures, and leads to significant improvements in the area of quality assurance.

As recent studies show, the principals of MDE are already practiced across a wide range of industries [5, 20]. Thereby, the standards provided by the *Object Management Group* (OMG)[1] find a very wide application. This concerns in particular the OMG's *Unified Modeling Language* (UML) [15], especially for software development. Even if domain-specific modeling languages (DSML) are applied, they are often implemented as an extension profile for UML or used in combination with it. Based on UML, several standardized profiles are offered by OMG to cover specific modeling issues. Thus, for instance, the *System Modeling Language* (SysML) [13] allows modeling of system specifications and requirements, the profile for *Modeling and Analysis of Real-time and Embedded systems* (MARTE) [12] can be used to express non-functional properties, time and analysis aspects, while the *UML Testing Profile* (UTP) [9] considers testing issues. Furthermore, dedicated transformation languages MOFM2T [10] and QVT [11], respectively for model-to-text and model-to-model transformations, are also offered by OMG.

As a logical consequence of MDE, the approach of *Test-driven Agile Simulation* (TAS) [2] aims to combine model-driven engineering, simulation, and testing to a holistic approach by building upon the common modeling and transformation standards of OMG mentioned above. Using UML as a basic modeling language and coupling it with appropriate standardized extension profiles, the TAS approach effectively allows for seamless inspection of the involved models at early design stages. Thus, besides the static validation

[1] http://omg.org

of models, TAS also focuses on automated generation of executable simulations in order to analyze the performance and to validate the dynamic behavior of the designed system. This helps to improve the quality of the system under design as well as to reduce development and lifecycle costs potentially caused by insufficient designs.

Related MDE techniques based on OMG standards were partially approved in several European research projects, like COMPLEX [4] and MADES [16]. Quite similar ideas of coupling model-driven engineering, simulation, and testing are also embraced by some commercial development environments like SCADE[2] or IBM Rational Rhapsody[3]. However, in contrast to these projects, TAS is calling for a more holistic and solely standard-based approach, including not only system design but also simulation-based testing and performance analysis. A more detailed description of the TAS approach as well as a discussion about related work have been recently published in [18].

In this paper, we primarily provide an updated overview about our framework SimTAny, which implements a versatile, integrated, and seamlessly standard-based tool environment to support the TAS approach. Particularly, in section 2 of this paper we focus on presenting the main features of this framework, like for instance modeling support, simulation code generation, traceability, and design of experiments. Subsequently, in section 3 we demonstrate how modeling, analysis, and validation issues can be performed with SimTAny on an example monocular vision system for the autonomous approach and landing using a low-cost micro aerial vehicle (MAV) system.

2. SIMTANY FRAMEWORK

In order to provide a technical support for the suggested TAS approach, the framework SimTAny (formerly introduced in [2] as 'VeriTAS') has been developed. This framework integrates relevant tools with newly developed components in a common environment based on a popular and open platform Eclipse RCP[4]. Among others, SimTAny integrates a UML modeling tool, a transformation framework, a simulation engine, and an analysis tool (see Fig. 1). Furthermore, due to a service-oriented architecture of the framework and mostly open source tools used, SimTAny provides a versatile environment that can be easily adapted for specific domains allowing integration in a distributed development environment. In the following sections, we describe the main features of our framework in some more details.

Modeling

As previously mentioned, our TAS approach utilizes UML as a basic modeling language that provides a general-purpose notation for object-oriented modeling. Using annotations from specialized extension profiles for UML, such as SysML, MARTE and UTP, it is further possible to express specific aspects like requirements, non-functional properties and tests (see examples in section 3). Thus, UML forms a fundamental basis for a holistic modeling methodology with only one common modeling language, as intended for TAS to cover system design, analysis and validation aspects.

[2]http://www.esterel-technologies.com/products/

[3]http://www.ibm.com/software/awdtools/rhapsody/

[4]http://wiki.eclipse.org/Rich_Client_Platform

In order to enable standard conform modeling using different profiles mentioned above, SimTAny integrates the open source modeling tool Papyrus[5]. We preferably use Papyrus since it most precisely implements several OMG standards and provides an advanced modeling support for UML including SysML and MARTE profiles. Nevertheless, all other modeling tools can also be used instead of Papyrus, provided that they are able to exchange models via the OMG' interchange format XMI consistently.

SimTAny also offers some extensions to Papyrus in order to improve the modeling efficiency. This primarily concerns the modeling of detailed behaviors and expressions with textual editors. For this purpose, we apply the standardized *Action Language for Foundational UML* (ALF) [14], which alternatively allows the specification of detailed behaviors by means of a higher programming language. Such textual representation is often much more compact, faster, and intuitive than standard UML behavior diagrams.

Static Validation and Verification

In order to achieve static validation and verification of modeled specifications, SimTAny provide several constraints to check for inconsistencies in each model separately and for incompatible relations between models. Since such checks are easily performable on very early design stages, this helps to eliminate the propagation of modeling errors and thus to increase the efficiency of the development process. This feature has been realized in SimTAny by means of the Eclipse EMF validation framework[6]. The detected defects are listed in the Eclipse' problems view and the affected elements are marked as erroneous in the model editor as well. It is further possible to navigate from problems view to corresponding elements in the model editor. Currently only a few constraints for most typical failures are implemented in SimTAny. Nevertheless, new constraints can be easily added.

Transformation to Simulation Code

One of the most important tasks of TAS, and thus also of SimTAny, is to enable for validation and analysis of the dynamic system behavior. For this purpose, our framework provides a transformation module for automated generation of the executable simulation code from system and test models. Since a solid methodology with extensive tool support is required to perform this task, we build our code generators upon the OMG's standard MOFM2T [10] and its reference implementation, i.e. the Eclipse Acceleo[7] framework.

Using Acceleo, we have implemented model-to-text transformation templates, as prescribed by MOFM2T. This enables us to derive executable simulations for OMNeT++[8] - an open source discrete-event simulator that is quite popular for simulation of communication networks. Furthermore, our transformation module is designed to be extendable for other simulation engines too.

During the execution of the generated simulation model, one can observe the behavior of system components, especially focusing on their communication patterns. Beside this, quantitative measurements are collected during the execution and can be analyzed afterwards.

[5]http://eclipse.org/papyrus

[6]http://eclipse.org/modeling/emf/?project=validation

[7]http://eclipse.org/acceleo

[8]http://omnetpp.org

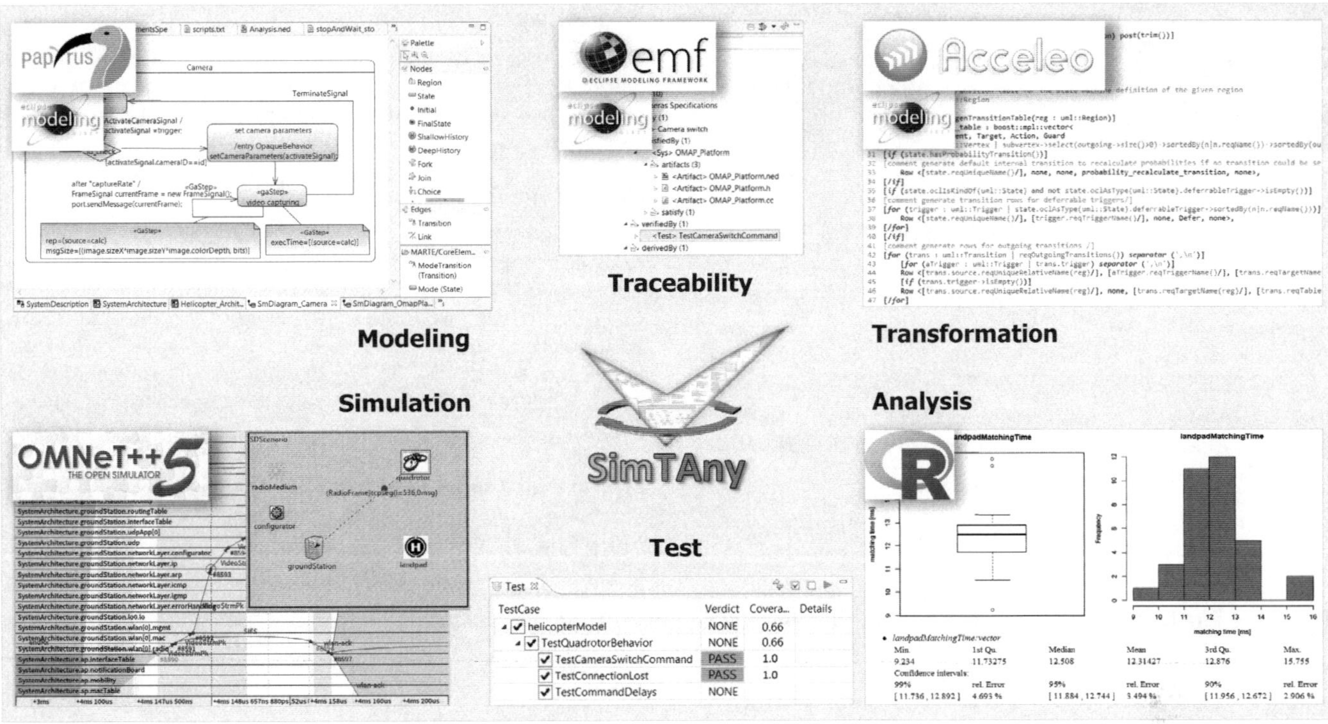

Figure 1: Main features of the SimTAny framework and integrated tools (Reproduced from [18])

Analysis

In order to simplify the access to output data collected during the simulation runs, SimTAny provides a dedicated perspective where the simulation results can be imported and visualized. It allows for calculation of a number of key statistical measures as well as creation of various graphical plots for the selected data. Therefore, it is possible to perform first analyses without leaving the SimTAny environment.

Test

Along with the generation of simulation code from the system model our framework also provides the generation of executable OMNeT++ simulations for each test case contained in the test model. Within a dedicated test view the user may obtain an overview of all test contexts and test cases defined in the model. Once the simulation code has been generated for the model, tests can be performed from this view. The test view also presents the verdict and eventual error reports of each completed test run.

Traceability

Further on, SimTAny provides a dedicated model for collecting of traceability information. Initially traceability links are created in the specification models. Thus, using the SysML profile, the designer has to assign test cases to requirements they are intended to verify or to assign system model elements to requirements they satisfy. These traceability links are automatically transformed by SimTAny to its own traceability meta-model utilizing the additional OMG standard for model-to-model transformations QVT and the Eclipse modeling framework EMF[9]. On the one side, a dedicated traceability model allows to put all relevant information together in a more compact form. On the other side, it can be enriched with additional information that is outside of the scope of specification models, like for example traceability links to code or simulation artifacts generated from models.

In order to provide an overview about all available traceability information, SimTAny implements a special traceability view. This view enables the user to inspect relationships between elements in all directions starting either from requirements, from system or test model elements, or even from artifacts. The traceability view also provides filters to detect potential deficiencies such as unsatisfied or untested requirements.

Design of Experiments

In order to inspect alternative system configurations, experiments with different combination of parameters have to be defined and performed. It is worth noting that using SimTAny an experiment can be defined in two ways: (1) Directly in the analysis model as a class annotated with MARTE's stereotype *GaAnalysisContext* and providing default values for each property that represent an experiment parameter; (2) Using our additional design of experiments module for more advanced and automated generation, management, execution control as well as result analysis of experiment studies. The module for method (2) has been initially set up in [21] applying model-driven development techniques based on the EMF framework. Among others, it allows designing parameter variation rules and automated generation of concrete experiment iterations according to various design-of-experiments (DOE) methods, like for instance *full factorial* or *latin hypercube* designs. More details about DOE can be found in [8] or [7].

[9]http://eclipse.org/modeling/emf

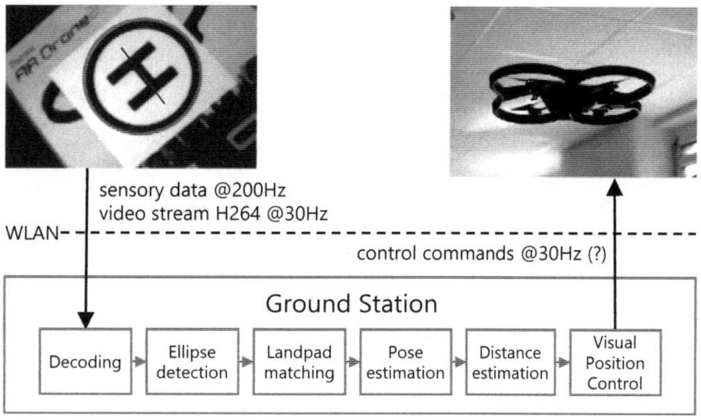

Figure 2: Concept of a monocular vision system for autonomous approach and landing using a low-budget quadrotor (Reproduced from [3])

3. CASE STUDY

In this section we introduce a system to exemplify a use case of the SimTAny framework. The system that is shown in Fig. 2 presents a monocular vision system for autonomous approach and landing using an off-the shelf Parrot A.R.Drone 2.0 quadrotor MAV. This system enables the quadrotor to autonomously detect a typical helicopter landpad consisting of a letter "H", approach it, and land on it. A detailed description as well as the implementation details of this system have been illustrated in [3].

In this work we selected only few factors that pose challenges for development of applications for this system. The detection of a landpad is performed by analyzing video stream frames captured using one of the two cameras installed on the quadrotor. Due to quadrotor's hardware restrictions the image processing pipeline cannot be performed directly onboard. Instead, the quadrotor must communicate with a ground station that receives sensory and video data, performs the computations, and generates steering commands. Quadrotors are generally very unstable systems that must react in a timely manner. To achieve smooth drone movements, steering commands have ideally to be sent every 30ms. However, delays between different kinds of sensors, delays introduced by the detection of the landpad, as well as delays arising during the communication between the quadrotor and the ground station can occasionally cause the quadrotor to drift while hovering over the landpad since the steering commands cannot be sent fast enough.

In order to support the development of this application, we first provide specification models which represent all relevant requirements, system's architecture and behavior aspects as well as formal tests for further validation. The application of the TAS approach using the SimTAny framework allows then to derive executable simulations. By means of simulation of the system behavior and communication aspects, we aim at resolving these problem statements where we investigate system's properties and compare alternative design solutions. For this case study in particular, we focus on the estimation of network latencies and detection of performance bottlenecks for variable system configurations regarding different camera resolutions and network transport protocols. The goal is therefore to determine which system configuration produces the best landpad detection rate and hence the steering rate close to 30Hz.

Modeling

Based on the modeling guidelines defined in our previous work [19, 1], we will now focus on modeling of some basic aspects like requirements, functional system behavior and test cases.

Requirements Modeling

Our design specification typically starts with the definition and modeling of system requirements by means of SysML. Some exemplary requirements, that need to be considered in order to achieve a satisfying control of the quadrotor, including sending steering commands and video capturing, are illustrated in Fig. 3. For example, the requirements on quadrotor's cameras include restrictions according activation and switching time between cameras.

Based on the specified requirements model, the functional system model as well as the test model may be created independently from each other in order to ensure their utilization for mutual validation.

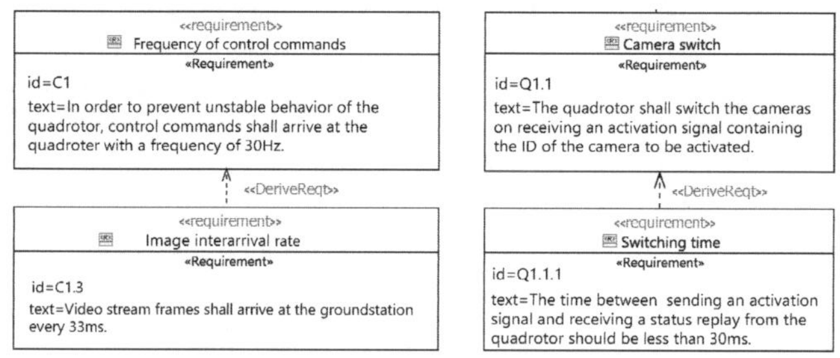

Figure 3: Example of system requirements model

Functional Modeling

The aim of a functional system model is to design the generic topology of the system architecture in terms of functional blocks. The structural and behavioral aspects of blocks can be expressed by means of SysML block definition, internal block, and state machine diagrams. For example, Fig. 4 presents the internal structure of the *Quadrotor* block from our example system. It consists of two cameras, a video encoder, controller, and a network component. By using the SysML concepts of flow ports and connectors, one is able to express communication links between these various components.

To model the behavior of system components, we primarily use UML state diagrams. An example state machine that represents the behavior of cameras is shown in Fig. 5.

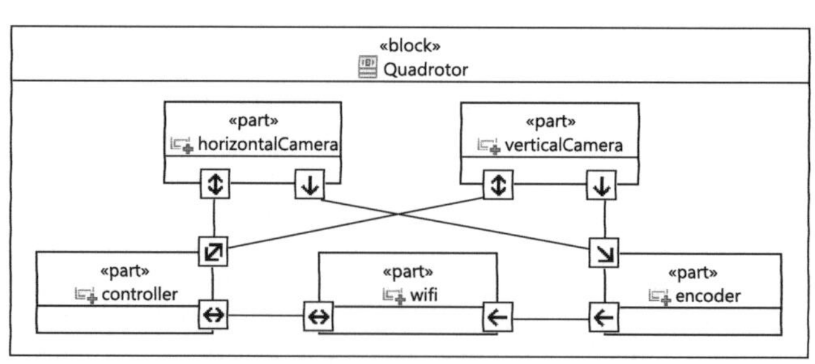

Figure 4: Example of a composite structure for quadrotor

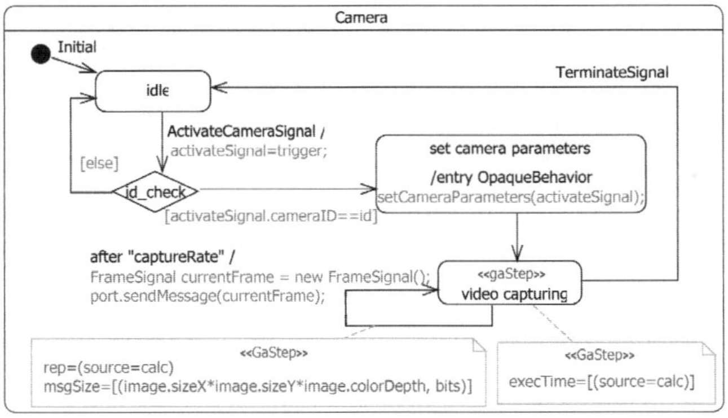

Figure 5: Example of modeling component behavior

In order to express non-functional performance attributes of behavior steps, we apply the MARTE's stereotype *GaStep*. For instance, we specify that the video frame size in bits can be measured as follows: resolution of frame × color depth. To collect the statistic of interest during the simulation, one just has to apply an additional MARTE expression *source=calc* on the corresponding property value.

Test Modeling

Similar modeling paradigm as used for functional system specification can also be applied for test specifications. Derived from common requirements the objective in this phase is to provide test cases for validation of the modeled system. As shown in Fig. 6, we utilize UML sequence diagrams to specify a test case. To identify several test aspects, i.e. test configurations, test cases, components under test, as well as test components, we apply the corresponding stereotypes of the UTP profile.

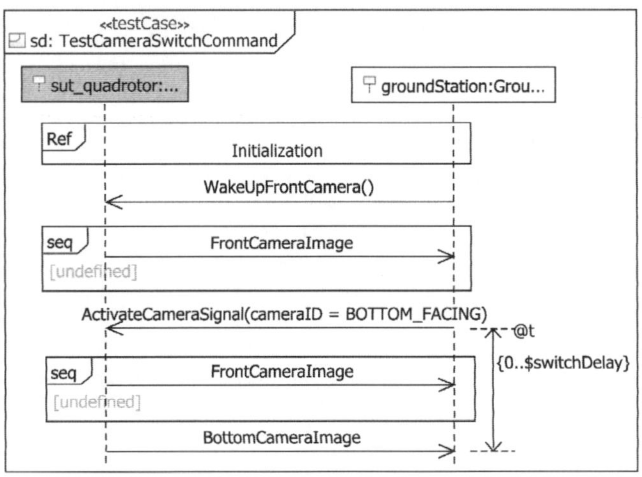

Figure 6: Example of modeling test case

Simulation Experiments and Results

The specification models, some parts of which have been presented in the previous sections, can finally be transformed with the help of SimTAny to executable simulation code for OMNeT++. Subsequently, simulation experiments and tests can be performed to examine and to validate these models.

As mentioned previously, one of the primary goals in this case study was to estimate the expected performance and network latency for the given application. In order to inspect alternative system configurations, different experiments have been defined and performed. Due to space limitation, we omit to show the complete overview of all experiments and just focus on a few of them.

Thus, among others, we analyzed the effects on the total image transmission delay and the detection rate by different frame resolutions and transport protocols for video streaming. In Fig. 7, we exemplarily show some averaged results of our simulation experiments. In particular, Fig. 7a displays varying proportions for image delays, i.e. the buffering and encoding delay on the quadrotor, network transmission delay, and decoding delay on the ground station. Thereby, two transmission protocols (TCP and UDP) and two resolutions of frames captured by quadrotor's cameras are considered in this example: SD with 640x360 pixels and HD with 1280x720 pixels. The distributions of time between arrivals of subsequent frames on the ground station are shown in Fig. 7b for different resolutions in case of using TCP as a transmission protocol. Furthermore, the resulting landpad detection rates for both SD and HD resolutions can be seen in Fig. 7c.

To summarize the results, we can exclude using of higher resolutions than SD because the required detection rate cannot be satisfied sufficiently in that case. Even if we could omit buffering on the quadrotor, which is automatically activated for HD encoding, the large remaining delay and rather big variations in inter-arrival times can lead to an unstable flight behavior of the quadrotor since steering commands cannot be sent on time. On the other side, the configuration with the SD resolution lets expect a sufficient detection rate above 24Hz in conjunction with an overall image delay of about 33ms. A further promising design solution would be to apply UDP as a transport protocol since the delay as well as the deviation of transmission times can be reduced significantly. Unfortunately, this option is not available for the Parrot AR.Drone 2.0 quadrotor.

The results obtained by the simulation for the SD/TCP configuration have already been successfully validated by the prototype implementation of the system. Furthermore, during the iterative modeling process we could repeatedly use validation and testing capabilities of SimTAny and could detect some modeling errors in the system model as well as in the test model itself.

4. CONCLUSIONS

One of the main objectives of the TAS approach and, by association, of its supporting framework SimTAny is to enable for efficient and qualitative development of complex systems. The combination of model-driven engineering, simulation and testing techniques based on common standards helps to improve the overall quality of the development process. On the one side, the models provide a good support in understanding, communicating and documenting of different engineering aspects. On the other side, simulation-based analysis and validation provide a cheap and agile possibility to investigate performance and to approve the functionality of the modeled system behavior.

In the presented work we offered an updated overview about main features of our framework SimTAny. Furthermore, on an example application for autonomous landpad

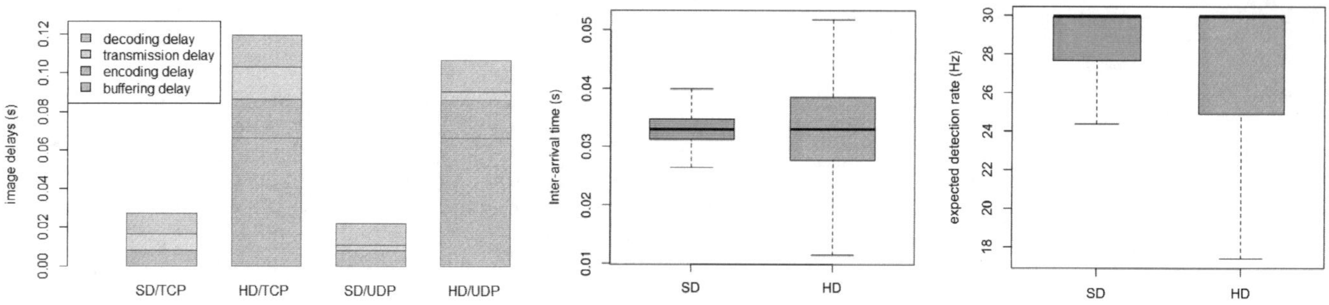

(a) Image delays (b) Inter-arrival times of frames (TCP) (c) Landpad detection rates (TCP)

Figure 7: Results of the simulation study

approaching of a quadrotor MAV, we demonstrated a practical application of SimTAny for modeling, performance analysis, and validation of a system under development.

In our ongoing efforts to improve the modeling efficiency we are working on the clarification of the holistic modeling methodology by introducing the concept of viewpoints and implementing a view-specific wizard modeling support. Furthermore, we intend to offer a domain specific modeling language and modeling library for the special domain of image processing systems.

5. REFERENCES

[1] A. Deitsch, V. Schneider, J. Kane, W. Dulz, and R. German. Towards an Efficient High-Level Modeling of Heterogeneous Image Processing Systems. In *Proceedings of the Symposium on Theory of Modeling & Simulation - DEVS Integrative (DEVS '16)*, Pasadena, CA, USA, Apr. 2016.

[2] A. Djanatliev, W. Dulz, R. German, and V. Schneider. VeriTAS - a Versatile Modeling Environment for Test-driven Agile Simulation. In *Proceedings of the Winter Simulation Conference*, WSC '11, pages 3662–3671, Phoenix, AZ, USA, Dec. 2011.

[3] S. Dotenco, F. Gallwitz, and E. Angelopoulou. Autonomous Approach and Landing for a Low-Cost Quadrotor Using Monocular Cameras. In L. Agapito, M. M. Bronstein, and C. Rother, editors, *Computer Vision - ECCV 2014 Workshops*, pages 209–222. Springer International Publishing, Cham, 2015.

[4] F. Herrera, H. Posadas, P. Peñil, E. Villar, F. Ferrero, R. Valencia, and G. Palermo. The COMPLEX methodology for UML/MARTE Modeling and design space exploration of embedded systems. *Journal of Systems Architecture*, 60(1):55–78, Feb. 2014.

[5] J. Hutchinson, J. Whittle, M. Rouncefield, and S. Kristoffersen. Empirical Assessment of MDE in Industry. In *Proceedings of the 33rd International Conference on Software Engineering*, ICSE '11, pages 471–480, New York, USA, 2011. ACM.

[6] S. Kent. Model Driven Engineering. In M. Butler, L. Petre, and K. Sere, editors, *Integrated Formal Methods*, Lecture Notes in Computer Science, pages 286–298. Springer Berlin Heidelberg, 2002.

[7] J. P. C. Kleijnen. *Design and Analysis of Simulation Experiments*, volume 111. Springer-Verlag, 2008.

[8] A. Law and W. Kelton. *Simulation Modeling and Analysis*. McGraw-Hill, 2000.

[9] Object Management Group (OMG). UTP: UML Testing Profile 1.2. http://omg.org/spec/UTP.

[10] OMG. MOF Model to Text Transformation Language (MOFM2T). http://omg.org/spec/MOFM2T, 2008.

[11] OMG. MOF Query/View/Transformation (QVT). http://omg.org/spec/QVT, 2011.

[12] OMG. UML Profile for MARTE Modeling and Analysis of Real-Time and Embedded Systems. http://omg.org/spec/MARTE, 2011.

[13] OMG. Systems Modeling Language (SysML). http://omg.org/spec/SysML, 2012.

[14] OMG. Action Language for Foundational UML (ALF). http://omg.org/spec/ALF/, 2013.

[15] OMG. UML Unified Modeling Language. http://omg.org/spec/UML, 2015.

[16] I. R. Quadri, A. Bagnato, and A. Sadovykh. MADES EU FP7 Project: Model-Driven Methodology for Real Time Embedded Systems. In M. A. Khan, S. Saeed, A. Darwish, and A. Abraham, editors, *Embedded and Real Time System Development: A Software Engineering Perspective*, pages 57–89. Springer Berlin Heidelberg, 2014.

[17] D. C. Schmidt. Model-Driven Engineering. *IEEE Computer*, 39(2):25–31, Feb. 2006.

[18] V. Schneider, A. Deitsch, W. Dulz, and R. German. Combined Simulation and Testing Based on Standard UML Models. In L. Fiondella and A. Puliafito, editors, *Principles of Performance and Reliability Modeling and Evaluation*, Springer Series in Reliability Engineering. Springer International Publishing, 2016.

[19] V. Schneider, A. Yupatova, W. Dulz, and R. German. How to Avoid Model Interferences for Test-driven Agile Simulation based on Standardized UML Profiles. In *Proceedings of the Symposium on Theory of Modeling and Simulation - DEVS Integrative (TMS/DEVS '14)*, Tampa, FL, USA, Apr. 2014.

[20] J. Whittle, J. Hutchinson, and M. Rouncefield. The State of Practice in Model-Driven Engineering. *IEEE Software*, 31:79–85, 2014.

[21] T. Zangl. Management and Control of Experiments in the Test-driven Agile Simulation. Master's thesis, Friedrich-Alexander-Universität Erlangen-Nürnberg, 2015.

Dispatching fixed-sized jobs with multiple deadlines to parallel heterogeneous servers

Esa Hyytiä
University of Iceland
esa@hi.is

Rhonda Righter
UC Berkeley
rrighter@ieor.berkeley.edu

Olivier Bilenne
Aalto University
olivier.bilenne@aalto.fi

Xiaohu Wu
Aalto University
xiaohu.wu@aalto.fi

ABSTRACT

We study the M/D/1 queue when jobs have firm deadlines for waiting (or sojourn) time. If a deadline is not met, a job-specific deadline violation cost is incurred. We derive explicit value functions for this M/D/1 queue that enable the development of efficient cost-aware dispatching policies to parallel servers. The performance of the resulting dispatching policies is evaluated by means of simulations.

Keywords

Dispatching problem; Parallel computing; Deadlines; M/D/1

1. INTRODUCTION

In the dispatching problem, each arriving job is routed to one of the available servers immediately upon arrival. Even though a single fast server would often be preferred, the parallel servers are needed to match increasing capacity demands. Moreover, short latency, in the absence of preemptive scheduling, requires parallel servers.

We consider a cost structure based on (firm) deadlines. Each job has a certain deadline for the waiting time it can tolerate. If this waiting time is exceeded, a deadline violation cost is incurred, but the job must still be served. This cost structure stems from quality-of-experience metrics, where customers observe a good service level whenever the waiting time is "short" [1]. Similarly, service level agreements (SLAs) are often defined in terms of acceptable waiting times [3].

We use our results for the M/D/1 queue and policy iteration to obtain efficient dispatching heuristics. This basic setting has been studied recently in [2] in the context of M/G/1 queues. However, the results given there are either asymptotic or in the form of differential equations. In contrast, we derive exact closed-form expressions for the value function and admission cost for the M/D/1 queue subject to a general deadline-based cost structure. Even though the service times are assumed to be fixed, we allow multiple deadlines each with a unique (additive) violation cost.

2. MODEL AND RESULTS

Let λ denote the arrival rate and d the constant service time of a job so that the offered load is $\rho = \lambda d$. Jobs whose waiting time in queue, W, reach time τ, referred to as the deadline, incur a unit cost. The mean cost rate is $r = \lambda\,\mathrm{P}\{W \geq \tau\}$, and $\mathrm{P}\{W \geq \tau\}$ is available, e.g., from [4]. In the general case, we have multiple classes of jobs, each with its own arrival rate λ_i, target deadline τ_i and i.i.d. deadline violation cost H_i. First we derive the so-called value function with respect to the deadline cost structure. Formally, the value function is defined as $v(u) \triangleq \lim_{t\to\infty} \mathrm{E}[V(u,t) - rt]$, where u is the current backlog (unfinished work) in the queue, and the random variable $V(u,t)$ denotes the deadline violation costs during time $(0,t)$ when the system is initially in state u. Given $\rho < 1$, the system is stable and ergodic, and the above limit is well-defined.

The value function for the M/D/1 queue with a single deadline takes the form of a double sum with a finite number of terms. This result is then generalized for multiple job classes, each having its own target deadline and violation cost. The value function enables policy iteration when developing cost-aware dispatching strategies for parallel servers. This is illustrated in numerical examples.

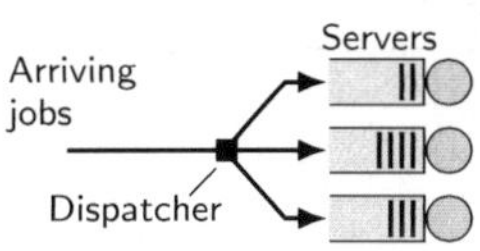

Figure 1: Dispatching system with parallel servers.

Acknowledgements

This work was supported by the Academy of Finland in the FQ4BD project (grant nos. 296206).

3. REFERENCES

[1] J. Dean and L. A. Barroso. The tail at scale. *Commun. ACM*, 56(2):74–80, Feb. 2013.

[2] E. Hyytiä and R. Righter. Routing jobs with deadlines to heterogeneous parallel servers. *Operations Research Letters*, 44(4):507–513, 2016.

[3] Z. Liu, M. S. Squillante, and J. L. Wolf. On maximizing service-level-agreement profits. In *Proc. of the 3rd ACM Conference on Electronic Commerce*, NY, USA, 2001.

[4] R. Syski. *Introduction to congestion theory in telephone systems.* North-Holland, 1986.

Dynamic Parameter Substitution for solution of Layered Queueing Networks with Timeout Decisions

Lianhua Li
Department of Systems and Computer Engineering
Carleton University
Ottawa, ON Canada
lianhua@sce.carleton.ca

Greg Franks
Department of Systems and Computer Engineering
Carleton University
Ottawa, ON Canada
greg@sce.carleton.ca

ABSTRACT

Solving performance models using queueing networks poses a challenge because parameters such as service times and routing are fixed and must be known prior to solution. Models which involve *decisions* based on performance quantities must therefore often be solved using a state-based model, through simulation, or a hybrid combination of these approaches. However, state-based approaches suffer from state space explosion for even moderately sized models, while simulation can be time consuming. This paper broadens Layered Queueing Networks (LQN) to handle a subset of models with state-based behaviour, namely systems with timeouts and aborts. The approach, called dynamic parameter substitution (DPS), updates the parameters of the underlying queueing networks of a LQN model as the model is being solved. This approach in this paper is both fast and highly scalable, compared to simulations (LQSIM and CSIM) and a hybrid solution.

CCS Concepts

•Computing methodologies → Modeling methodologies; •Software and its engineering → Software performance; System modeling languages; Model-driven software engineering; *Layered systems;*

Keywords

dynamic parameter substitutions; timeout; abort decisions; layered queueing network; performance modelling

1. INTRODUCTION

In the field of Software Performance Analysis, analytic performance modeling has many advantages. It can be done at any stage of the development process, the time required for the analysis is small, and it is of relative low cost compared to other methods [9, 18]. Analytic solutions to performance models can be found using a wide variety of methods, though queuing models were found to be the preferred approach [2, §4.1.1]. Queueing models scale well, solve quickly and have sufficient accuracy [18, §3.2].

The downside of queueing models is their inability to model arbitrary dynamic data-dependent behaviour. One important form of behaviour that fits this category is exception handling. Exceptions are defined as *"Of the conditions detected while attempting to perform some operation, exception conditions are those brought to the attention of the operation's invoker. The invoker is then permitted (or required) to respond to the condition."* [8]. From the standpoint of a performance model exceptions can be raised as a result of trying to acquire a resource.

The exception pattern considered in this paper is the *timeout* pattern, shown in the sequence diagram in Figure 1. This pattern arises when the response time for a service request exceeds some value, T_{timeout}, then simply gives up. Note that there may be some additional costs in giving up, so this action can also affect the performance of the system. The abort decision [20], is considered a special case of a *timeout* decision when the threshold of timeout, $T_{timeout} = 0$.

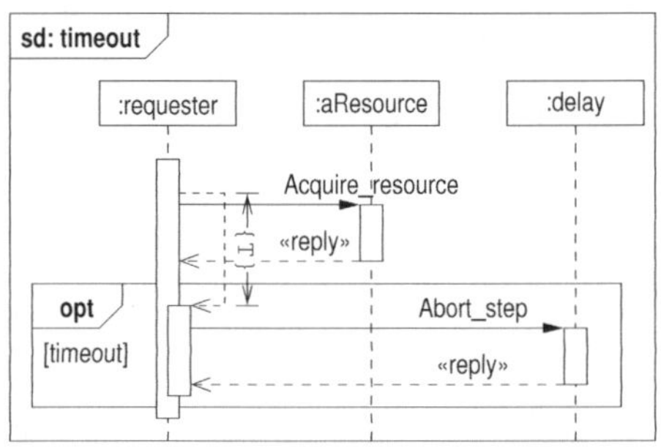

Figure 1: Timeout decision pattern.

The LQN *Timeout* decision pattern was defined in the previous work [11], and combines both timeout and abort decision logic. This generalized timeout decision was implemented in the LQN simulation tool, *LQSIM*. The results produced by LQSIM were verified by the results of the Petri Net solver, GreatSPN [4, 1] using the equivalent Generalized Stochastic Petri Nets (*GSPN*) [12] models. In this paper, LQSIM is used to verified the results of the analytic solution of DPS.

Queueing models are not suitable for modeling exceptions

VALUETOOLS 2016, October 25-28, Taormina, Italy

DOI 10.4108/eai.25-10-2016.2267111

because the likelihood of an exception being raised must be known prior to solving the model. However, exceptions are often raised because of results the performance model produces. For example, excessive response times can lead to timeouts and excessive utilization can lead to lock request failures. One approach to solve this problem in a scalable and timely fashion is through hybrid modeling, where a queueing model is used to solve the bulk of the model, and another model is used to solve the decision, for example the Hybrid Performance Modeling Methodology (HPMM) [20]. However, in general this approach suffers from the need for two or more different models and the need for data interchange between them all.

This paper takes another approach: feed the output of the performance model back as input. This approach is called Dynamic Parameter Substitution (DPS). The advantage of DPS is that iterations between disjoint solvers do not have to be performed. The feasibility of this approach is demonstrated by using the Layered Queueing network eXperiment control language (LQX) [14] to perform the feedback and iteration using a LQN. DPS is developed using LQX to solve a system with a timeout/abort. The results from this model are compared to simulation.

The remainder of the paper is organized as follows. Section 2 describes layered queueing networks, their solution and the LQX language. Section 3 explains how to solving timeout decision using dynamic parameter substitutions and compares the results of DPS to simulation. Section 4 applies the DPS solution to solve a web-base database model (from [20]) with a timeout and abort decision. Finally, Section 5 concludes the paper.

2. LQN MODELS

A layered queueing network is a type of extended queueing network that is particularly suitable for solving performance models of software using remote procedure calls. With this type of software system, clients of servers block awaiting replies to requests. These servers may in turn make requests to other servers. Layering arises by following the call chain from the top-most client all the way down to the lowest level server.

Figure 2 shows an example of a LQN. This model, adapted from [20], represents client web-browsers making requests to a web server, which in turn makes requests to a database. The elements in the model are:

Processors: represented using circles in the figure. Processors are used to consume time in the model. If the processor is a *multi-server*, it is shown using a stacked icon, and the number of copies, n, are shown using a label with brackets '`{n}`'. The output result for a processor is its utilization, U.

Tasks: shown using the large parallelograms in the figure. Tasks are used to model actual tasks running on a processor (e.g. dbWorker), customers to the model (e.g. users), logical resources such as database locks (e.g, dblock), and other physical resources which are not processors such as disks. Tasks may be multi- or infinitely-threaded, in which case they are shown using a stacked icon and labelled accordingly. The primary output result for a task is its throughput, λ.

Entries: shown using small parallelograms within a task.

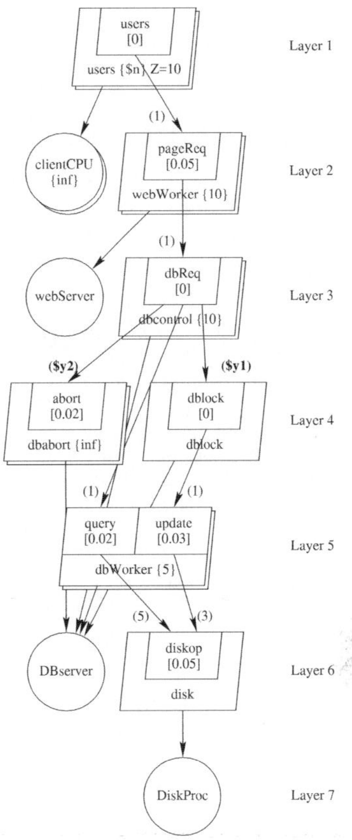

Figure 2: LQN model of a Web Server adapted from Figures 5-15 and 5-24 from [20] for the Abort Pattern.

Entries are used to differentiate the service provided by a task. Entries have *service-time* parameter, s, shown using square brackets '`[s]`' which is consumed on the associated processor. The primary output result for an entry is it's residence time, x, which is the sum of the response times (queuing plus service) to all the entries it calls plus the response time at its processor.

Calls: shown using directed arcs (directed arcs from tasks to processors represent the call for demand on a processor). Calls have a *rate* parameter, y, shown using parenthesis '`(y)`', representing the average number of times the source entry makes a request to its destination entry. The output result for a call is the queuing time, q, at the destination task.

There are many more features of the model which are not described here; refer to [5] for a more complete description of the model. Additional explanations of the basic concepts behind layered queueing can be found in [17, 19].

2.1 Solving a LQN Model

To solve a LQN, the LQNS analytic solver, used here, creates a set of ordinary queueing network "layer submodels", each of which is solved using Mean Value Analysis (MVA) [16]. Other solvers for layered resources that use a similar approach include [5, 10, 13, 15, 17, 19]. The solution process has six steps:

1. Load the model.
2. Construct LQN model objects with parameters.
3. Construct layer submodels by finding all clients making calls to servers in layer $i, i \geq 2$. Note that a task may be used as a *server* in one submodel, but may also be used as a *client* in multiple submodels. Processors are never clients and client tasks representing users are never servers. Figure 3 shows all of the submodels from Figure 2 that involve the task dbcontrol.
4. Initialize layer submodels. Service times, visits and populations for each of the queueing models are initialized based on the input values.
5. Iterate to solve layer submodels to convergence.
6. Write output file.

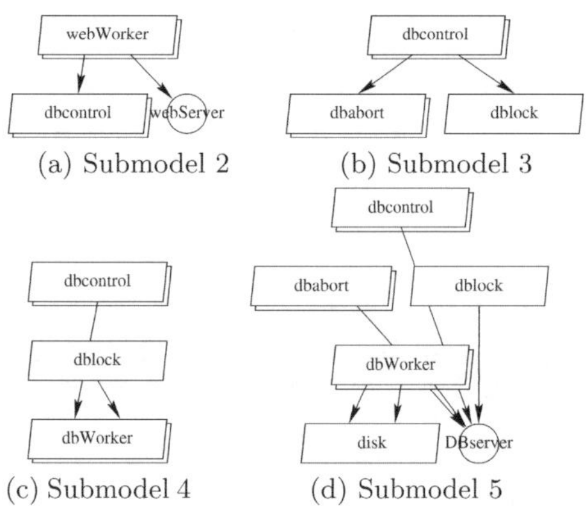

Figure 3: Submodels containing task dbcontrol

2.2 Iterative Solution

LQNS uses four levels of iteration in step 5 to solve a model:

1. The experiment control interpreter, LQX (described in §2.3) calls `solve()`.
2. `Solve()` calls Linearizer [3] over all queueing submodels until convergence.
3. Linearizer calls Bard-Schweitzer at populations $\mathbf{N}$ and with one customer removed from each chain k, $\mathbf{N}-\mathbf{1}_k$, for a submodel.
4. Bard-Schweitzer calls `core()` to find the residence times at the servers until the residence times converge. Response times, w, are found at each server, m, using the function `wait(m)`.

After performing Step 4 above, response times w in a submodel are found from each *client* to its *servers* and are stored in a vector, $\mathbf{W}_i$, indexed by *submodel i*. This vector is then used to set the demands for all of the processors and tasks in the model, regardless of whether the object is acting as a client or a server. When solving submodel i when an object m is acting as a *client*, all but item i in $\mathbf{W}$ are summed to find the service time demand, s:

$$s_{mi} = \sum_{\forall j, j \neq i} W_{mj} \tag{1}$$

This result is the waiting time caused by calls to servers not in the current submodel and is a surrogate delay in the queueing model. When solving submodel i when an object is acting as a *server*, all of the items in $\mathbf{W}$ are totalled:

$$s_m = \sum_{\forall j} W_{mj} \tag{2}$$

After solving submodel i, update $\mathbf{W}$ at index i for all *clients* in the submodel and save the throughput, λ, and utilization, U, for all servers. For example, the waiting time of dbcontrol are set each time queueing submodels 3, 4 and 5 have been solved.

The think time for chain, k, when a task is being used as a *client* is calculated using:

$$Z_m = \frac{(N_k - U_m)}{\lambda_m} \tag{3}$$

where N_k is the population in the chain and U and λ are the utilization and throughput of the task when is was acting as a server in a submodel. For dbcontrol, these values are set after queueing submodel 2 has been solved.

Waiting times propagate up one level while think times propagate down one level for each iteration of Step 2. Step 2 identified above terminates after the root mean square of the differences in the utilizations reaches some small value.

2.3 LQX

Model solution and parameter iteration is controlled using the Layering Queuing eXperiment control language (LQX) [14]. LQX can be written explicitly as part of XML model input (e.g., Listings 1). LQX is high-level, dynamically typed language with a syntax that resembles C. The choice of syntax was made because of pervasiveness of C and it's derivatives; as such it supports many of the language constructs of C. LQX also brings in more modern concepts such as associative arrays and `foreach` loops for iterating over them. LQX supports many common mathematical functions plus functions for generating random variables with various distributions. Finally, it includes I/O operations for reading and writing model data, and for reading LQX programs from external sources.

LQX supports four types: *numeric*, *boolean*, *string* and *object*. Types are automatically inferred. All numeric types are represented internally as double-precision floating point numbers. LQX is strongly typed so mixed type expressions are not permitted without explicit type conversion. The *object* type is used to access objects in the input model and result attributes such as throughput and utilization, namely *processor*, *task*, *activity*, *entry*, *phase*, and *call*.

Input values are set by using \$-variables in the input specification and then writing to these variables using a LQX program. A \$-variable may occur more than once in the input model, so one variable can be used to update multiple parameters simultaneously. There is no support for changing the *structure* of a model through LQX. Rather, separate model files must be created, though they can all share the same LQX program through the use of the LQX import facility.

The LQX function `solve()` is used to solve the model and can be invoked once all of the $-variables have been set. If this function is omitted in an LQX program, `solve()` is invoked implicitly after the program runs.

3. SOLUTION OF DYNAMIC PARAMETER SUBSTITUTION

Dynamic parameter substitution extends the core idea of layered queueing, that is, modifying the parameters of one submodel based on results found from other submodels. Layered queueing typically modifies service and think times of the underlying queueing models. Dynamic parameters extend this concept to allow any input parameter of the underlying queueing network to be modified based on one or more output parameters. For this work, updates to parameters are done using user-defined LQX expressions at the outermost iteration of the solver.

3.1 Dynamic Parameter Substitution

The principle idea behind dynamic parameter substitution is to extend layered queueing networks to handle decisions. The request rates, y, of the execution paths of a decision are set using dynamic parameters, which change as the model is being solved similar to the way the service times are changed over time. A `for` loop is used to call `solve()` repeatedly until the difference in input parameters becomes sufficiently small. This is equivalent to hybrid performance modelling since this approach solves the model to completion each time `solve()` is invoked. However, there is no requirement to solve a model to completion before changing parameters, as this is the essence of layered queueing as described earlier. In [6], all of the inner iterations (Steps 3 and 4 in §2.2) were removed leaving only the outer iteration to execute. For fixed rate and infinite servers, this approach produced the same results as the more expensive technique. Because of this observation, subsequent versions of the solver will move the update process into the inner iterations.

One other necessary step is to find suitable expressions for mapping output parameters such as throughput and utilization to input parameters. These expressions for timeout patterns are found below. Because the DPS solution of timeout decisions is using the DPS solution for abort decision, it is necessary to introduce the DPS solution for abort decision first.

3.2 Abort Decision

The decision on whether to take the success or abort path is based on the probability of finding a customer queued for resource. These probabilities are Pr{success} and Pr{abort} respectively and are used to set the call rates `$y1` and `$y2` in Figure 2. The probability of going to the abort path Pr{abort} is the probability of finding requests in the queue, but not in service, in the success path to dblock, i.e.:

$$\Pr\{\text{abort}\} = \frac{q_{\text{resource}}}{s_{\text{resource}} + q_{\text{resource}}} \tag{4}$$

$$\Pr\{\text{success}\} = 1 - \Pr\{\text{abort}\} \tag{5}$$

where s is the residence time (including requests to lower-level servers) at resource and q_{resource} is the time a request is waiting in the queue but not in service.

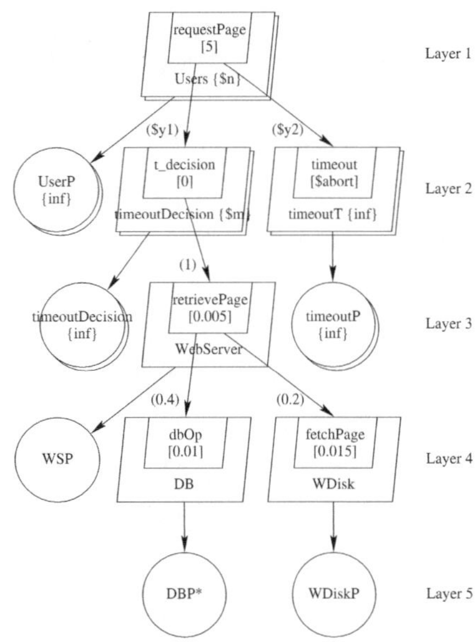

Figure 4: A web server system with timeout.

Increasing the value of `$y2` removes requests that are aborted and also reduces the traffic seen at a server which in turn makes the likelihood of an abort smaller. The next iteration of the solution will then add some traffic back until convergence, then `$y2` reaches the desired value of the abort probability.

3.3 Solving Timeout Decisions

Modeling a timeout directly using feedback may have problems when the timeout probabilities are small. The solution here is to construct an abort decision to solve a timeout decision by adding the auxiliary pseudo task. Figure 4 shows an example of the use of this technique where requests from Users to WebServer can timeout. After adding the auxilliary pseudo task timeoutDecision into this model, the reference task requestPage, the pseudo task timeoutDecision, and the delay task timeoutT form an abort decision. The task timeoutDecision is a pseudo task added to the model to find the response time (queueing plus service) at WebServer to determine whether a request will or will not timeout. The multiplicity of this task, m, is set to

$$m = max\left((m_{\text{WebServer}} + 1), \left\lceil \frac{T_{\text{timeout}}}{x_{\text{WebServer}}} \times m_{\text{WebServer}} \right\rceil\right) \tag{6}$$

where x is the response time at the task WebServer (found using (2)), and $m_{\text{Webserver}}$ is the number of threads of the task WebServer. Each copy of the multiserver timeoutDecision which is busy (i.e., the utilization of the webserver) represents requests which do not time out. Conversely, the queue at timeoutDecision represents requests that do timeout. Note that the multiserver parameter m may change during solution due to delays propagating up to WebServer as the model is solved. m has a minimum value of $(m_{\text{WebServer}} + 1)$, which ensures that some requests queue at the resource.

The second part of the solution is to find the probability

of a timeout, which is used to set **$y1** and **$y2** in Figure 4 where **$y2** is the probability of a timeout, represented using y_2 below. Two other variables are needed, the *upper*-bounds, U, and *lower*-bounds, L, of y_2 which are initialized to 1 and 0 respectively and converge towards each other as the solution progresses.

$$L^{(i+1)} = \max(y_2^{(i)}, L^{(i)}) \quad q_1^{(i)} > 0 \tag{7}$$
$$U^{(i+1)} = \min(y_2^{(i)}, U^{(i)}) \quad q_1^{(i)} = 0 \tag{8}$$

where q_i is the mean queue length at timeoutDecision and i is the iteration number. The probability of a timeout is calculated as the waiting time, q_1, over the residence time at timeoutDecision, x.

$$\Pr\{\text{timeout}\} = \frac{q_1^{(i)}}{q_1^{(i)} + x^{(i)}} \tag{9}$$

Finally, the new value for **$y2** is found using:

$$y_2^{(i+1)} = \begin{cases} \Pr\{\text{timeout}\} & q_1^{(i)} > 0, L \le \Pr\{\text{timeout}\} \le U \\ \frac{L^{(i+1)}+U^{(i)}}{2} & q_1^{(i)} > 0, \Pr\{\text{timeout}\} < L \\ \frac{L^{(i+1)}+U^{(i)}}{2} & q_1^{(i)} > 0, U < \Pr\{\text{timeout}\} \\ \frac{L^{(i)}+U^{(i+1)}}{2} & q_1^{(i)} = 0 \end{cases} \tag{10}$$

The LQX code for solving the models is in Listing 1. Line 18 is used to find m, the number of copies at timeoutDecision, using (6). Lines 20 and 28 are used to find the lower (7) and upper bounds (8) respectively. Finally, lines 23, 25, and 30 are used to find the new value of **$y2** using (10).

The solution for timeout decisions can be easily extended to handle abort decision by setting the dynamic parameter m equal to $m_{\text{Webserver}}$, when $T_{timeout} = 0$ at line 15 in Listing 1.

However, there is a special case needs to be considered. The first condition of this case is the probability of timeout is small, more precisely, when the mean queueing delay at the resource is smaller than $T_{timeout}$. The second condition of this case is the dynamic parameter m is also small, for example, less than five. In this case, $Pr\{timeout\}$ may be very sensitive to the mean response time at the resource at some points. This problem can severely affect the results of timeout probabilities and also may lead to the convergence failure if this problem occurs during solution iterations. The experiments show that small changes upon the response time of a resource server may cause a large difference in the timeout probabilities. For example, the model used in the case study, given $T_{timeout}$ is 0.6 seconds, when the mean response time of the resource (the writer lock) are 0.29 and 0.31 seconds (around 15 customers in the system), the corresponding timeout probabilities are 0.22 and 0.4. The reason is that the value of m is changed from three to two, which results the mean queueing time (q_1) at the decision is increased from 0.2 to 0.4. Consequently, the corresponding timeout probabilities are significantly larger than the simulation results. To address the problem of small timeout probability, the $Pr\{timeout\}$ in (9) is adjusted by a ratio using the queueing time at the resource (q_2), which

Listing 1: LQX program for solving timeout

```
1 lowerbound = 0.001;
2 upperbound = 0.999;
3 T_timeout = 1.0;
4 $abort = T_abort+T_timeout;
5 $m_res = 1;
6 for ($n = 100; $n <= 1000; $n += 100) {
7   $m = $n; i = 1;
8   upper = upperbound; $y1 = upper;
9   lower = lowerbound; $y2 = lower;
10  for (delta = 2; delta > 0.000005 || i <= 2;
       delta = (last_y2-$y2)**2) {
11    last_y2 = $y2;
12    solve();
13    s_succ = phase(entry("retrievepage"),1).
         service_time;
14    w_succ = call(phase(entry("requestPage"),
         1),"t_decision").waiting;
15    if (T_timeout == 0.)
16      $m = $m_res;
17    else
18     $m=max(($m_res+1),ceil(T_timeout/s_succ));
19    if (w_succ > 0.) {
20      lower = max($y2,lower);
21      if (lower <= $y2 && $y2 <= upper) {
22        prob = w_succ/(w_succ+phase(entry(
            "t_decision"),1).service_time);
23        $y2 = ($y2+2.0*prob)/3.0;
24        if ($y2 <= lower || upper <= $y2)
25          $y2 = (upper+lower)/2.0;
26      }
27    } else if (i > 1) {
28      upper = min($y2,upper);
29      if ($y2 > lowerbound)
30        $y2 = (upper+lower)/2.0;
31    }
32    $y1 = 1 - $y2;
33    i += 1;
34  }
35 }
```

is shown in (11).

$$\Pr\{\text{timeout}\} = \frac{q_1^{(i)}}{q_1^{(i)} + x^{(i)}} \times \frac{q_2^{(i)}}{q_1^{(i)} + q_2^{(i)}} \tag{11}$$

The rationale for this adjustment is that when small values of m result in larger values for q_1, they also result in smaller values for q_2. Therefore, the smaller q_2 can stop the increase of $Pr\{timeout\}$. If a model has a larger probability of timeout or a larger value of m, this problem can be eliminated. This fact is demonstrated by the results in the next section, by using the web server model in Figure 4.

3.4 Results

The model shown in Figure 4 is a simple web server model with timeouts that was used to evaluate DPS algorithm in Listing 1. Figures 5a through 5c show the results from solving this model using DPS and from simulation. Simulations were run with confidence intervals of 95%. Simulation results were found using a version of lqsim [7] modified to handle timeouts for requests directly in [11]. These results show that DPS compares favourably to simulation in calculating the server throughput and the probability of a timeout with an average error of under 1%. DPS is less accurate at calculating the waiting time from requestPage to t_decision.

Figure 6 shows the probabilities of timeouts when the

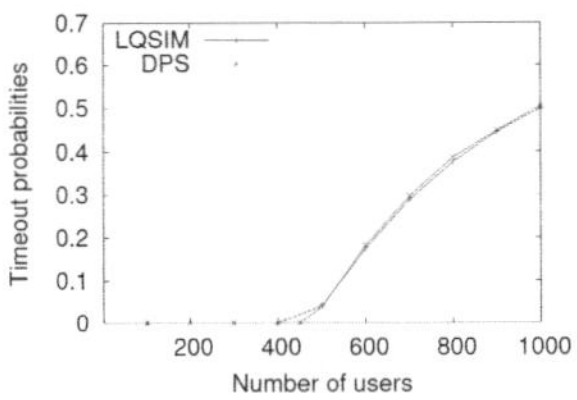

(a) Probability of Timeout.

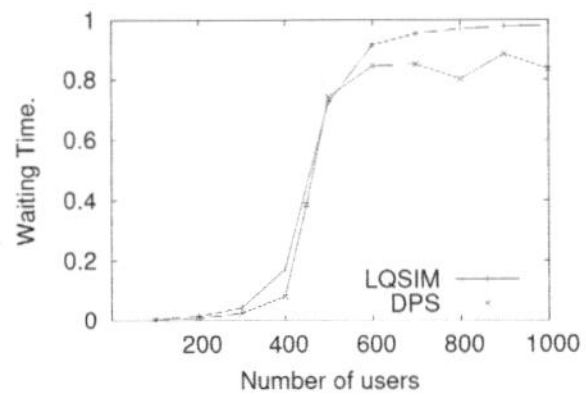

(b) Response Time of web users.

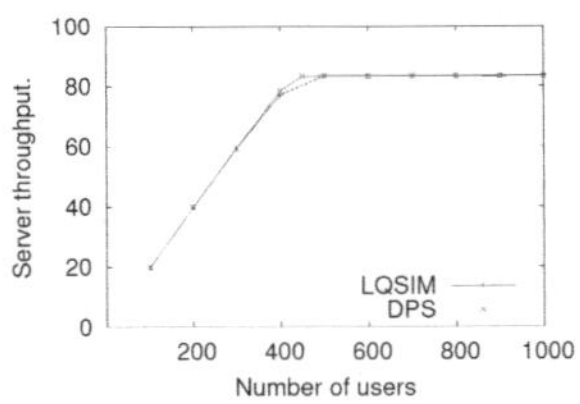

(c) Web server throughput.

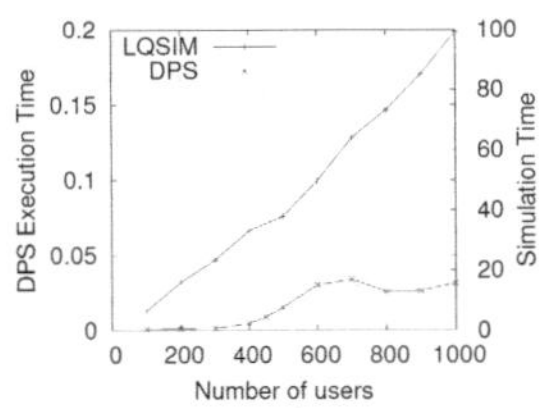

(d) Execution time (Unit:S).

Figure 5: Results from solving the model timeout shown in Figure 4 with lqsim and DPS.

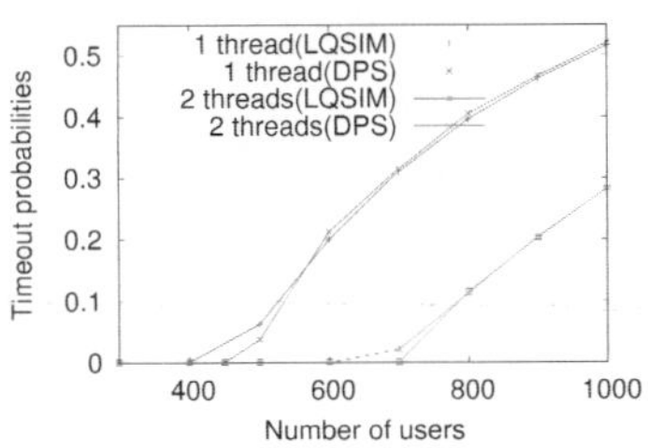

Figure 6: The probabilities of timeouts for the web server model with one thread and two threads resource server.

web server has one and two threads, while $T_{timeout}$ is set to 0.8 second. The results of DPS in both cases are compare favourably to simulation. Lastly, Figure 5d shows the execution time of DPS and simulation time when using a 3GHz Intel Core 2 Duo processor. When the system has 1000 customers, DPS only took 0.025 seconds to solve the model, while the simulations took around 100 seconds on average 95% of the time. Therefore, DPS is significantly efficient comparing to simulation.

4. CASE STUDY

The model used in this case study, shown in Figure 2, was adapted from the model used by Wu [20] to develop a hybrid solution for exception handling in the context of a web application that accesses a database. This model emphasizes the handling of decisions made at the write lock. Update requests from users arrive at dbcontrol, at which point a lock request is made to the underlying database dbWorker. If the lock is available the request follows the call from dbcontrol to dblock. Otherwise, this request will wait for the lock until the specified period expires. This request may acquire the lock or be rejected by routing it to dbabort.

To handle the timeout decision using DPS, the pseudo task dblock was added to this model. The decision on whether to take the success or timeout/abort path is based on the probability of finding a customer queued for this task. These probabilities, namely Pr{success} and Pr{abort}/Pr{timeout}, are used to set the call rates $y1 and $y2 respectively in Figure 2.

4.1 Case 1: Abort Decision

When the timeout threshold $T_{timeout}$ is ZERO, this timeout decision is an abort decision. In this case, the dynamic parameter $\$m$, the multiplicity of the pseudo (timeout) task, is set to one, since the writer lock (dblock) only can have one thread.

Figures 7a through 7e show the results from solving the model using DPS and LQSIM. DPS has average relative errors of less than 4% when compared to the simulation in calculating the lock probability, the holding time for the lock and the "useful" throughput (throughput at entry dblock). Figure 7 also shows the results from solving the model using CSIM and HPMM from [20]. DPS is more accurate when calculating the response time at the web server at high loads when compared with the hybrid approach HPMM.

4.2 Case 2: Timeout Decision

Case 2 uses the database model with a timeout decision shown in Figure 2 where $T_{timeout}$ is set to 0.6 and is an example of the special case discussed in Section 3.3 which occurs when the number of customers is less than 22. Figure 8 shows the results from the model when solved using DPS and LQSIM. The results from DPS are quite accurate in solving the probabilities of timeouts in the special case. However, there is a discontinuity of the probability of lock acquisition in Figure 8a where the calculation of $Pr\{timeout\}$ switches from using (11) to (9) because the mean queueing delays of requests are close to $T_{timeout}$. After this point, the error rates of the probabilities of lock acquisition are less than 8%. The results for the mean lock holding time, the mean response time of web users, and the utilization of the disk (the bottleneck device) are all quite accurate. The error rates of the useful throughput, the throughput of the lock, are same as the error rates of the probabilities of lock acquisition.

Finally, Figures 7f and 8f show the execution time of DPS and simulation for both cases. All the DPS executions are less than 0.8 second, while simulation times are around 30 50 seconds. However, DPS usually requires a more iterations when solving timeout decisions than solving abort decisions.

5. CONCLUSIONS

This paper has shown how the Layered Queueing Experiment Language has been used to implement Dynamic Parameter Substitution to allow the solution of performance models with state-based behaviour, which emphasizes on timeout decisions here. Pure queueing-based solutions to models of this type are not possible because all of the parameters to a queueing network must be known prior to solution. Consequently, state-based solutions, simulation, or combinations of these two techniques with a queueing model have been employed in the past.

Dynamic Parameter substitution takes advantage of the very method used to typically solve a layered queueing network analytically: iterative solution among multiple submodels. With this approach, the results of the solution of a

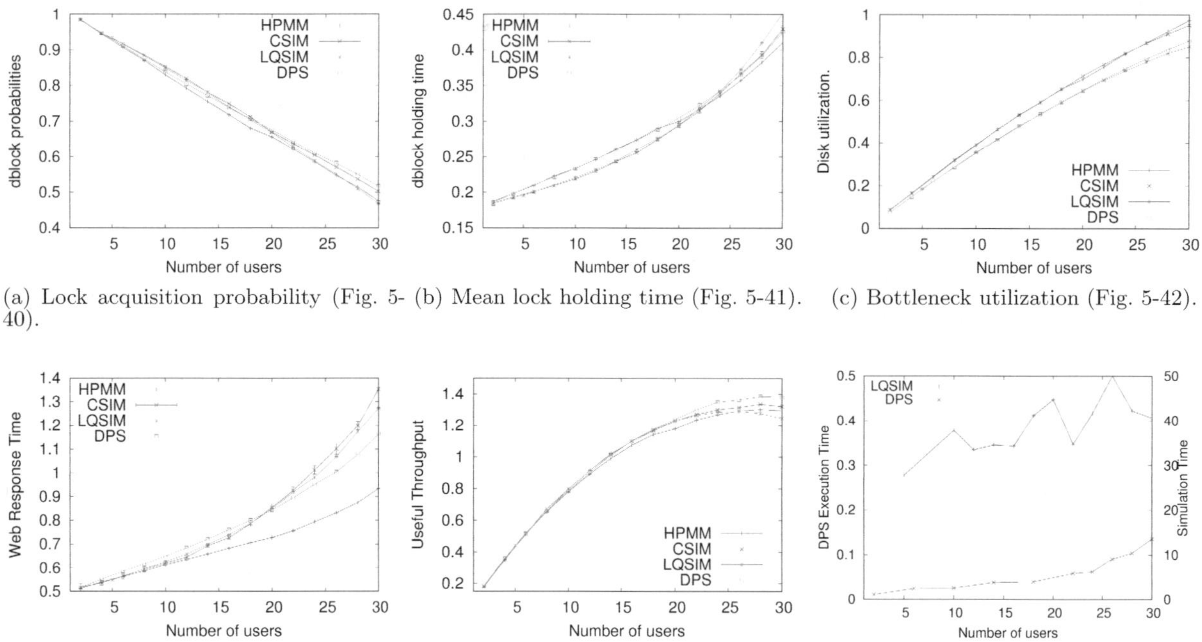

(a) Lock acquisition probability (Fig. 5-40). (b) Mean lock holding time (Fig. 5-41). (c) Bottleneck utilization (Fig. 5-42).

(d) Response time of the Web Server (Fig. 5-43). (e) Useful throughput (Fig. 5-44). (f) Execution time(Unit:S.).

Figure 7: Results from solving the abort model shown in Figure 2 with CSIM, HPMM and DPS. CSIM and HPMM results are from Figures 5-40 through 5-44 of [20].

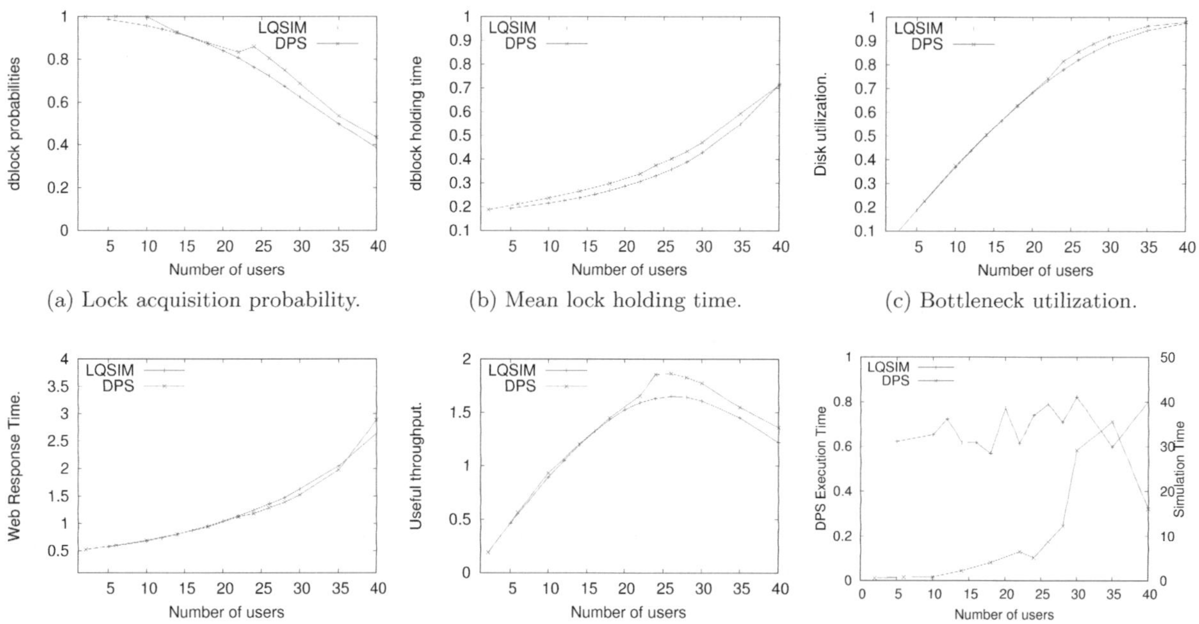

(a) Lock acquisition probability. (b) Mean lock holding time. (c) Bottleneck utilization.

(d) Response time of the Web Server. (e) Useful throughput. (f) Execution time (Unit:S).

Figure 8: Results from solving the timeout decision ($T_{timeout} = 0.6$) model shown in Figure 2.

submodel are used as input to other submodels. Dynamic parameter substitution extends this method to allow arbitrary output to be fed back as input for subsequent iterations of the model. This method is implemented using the LQX language here.

DPS was used to solve LQN models with generalized timeouts, which cover both timeout (on queueing delays) and abort decisions. The novelty of the solution here was the use of a multi-server pseudo task to partition the queue where customers could experience timeouts. Customers that cannot timeout are represented by the copies of the multiserver while customers that will timeout are represented by the queue of the multiserver. This approach was very effective in finding the timeout probabilities and throughput for the system when compared to simulation. With DPS, the average relative error in throughput was less than 8%. DPS has a higher accuracy in solving systems with large number of customers.

The DPS solution is quite efficient. All the execution times of DPS are much less than the simulation time. Since all computation is performed within the context of a single operating system process, no file input/output or process switching is required. This could be of tremendous benefit than the hybrid approach's solution .

The only deficiency of the DPS approach is the requirement to find expressions for feedback. In the future, common decision-based performance scenarios will be integrated into the LQN framework, thus relieving the modeller of this requirement.

Acknowledgement

This research was supported by the Natural Sciences and Engineering Research Council of Canada.

6. REFERENCES

[1] S. Baarir, M. Beccuti, D. Cerotti, M. De Pierro, S. Donatelli, and G. Franceschinis. The GreatSPN tool: Recent enhancements. *SIGMETRICS Perform. Eval. Rev.*, 36(4):4–9, Mar. 2009.

[2] S. Balsamo, A. D. Marco, P. Inverardi, and M. Simeoni. Model-based performance prediction in software development: A survey. *IEEE Trans. Softw. Eng.*, 30(5):295–310, May 2004.

[3] K. M. Chandy and D. Neuse. Linearizer: A heuristic algorithm for queueing network models of computing systems. *Commun. ACM*, 25(2):126–134, Feb. 1982.

[4] G. Chiola, G. Franceschinis, R. Gaeta, and M. Ribaudo. GreatSPN 1.7: GRaphical Editor and analyzer for timed and stochastic Petri nets. *Performance Evaluation*, 24(1):47–68, 1995.

[5] G. Franks, T. Al-Omari, M. Woodside, O. Das, and S. Derisavi. Enhanced modeling and solution of layered queueing networks. *IEEE Trans. Softw. Eng.*, 35(2):148–161, Mar.–Apr. 2009.

[6] G. Franks and L. Li. Efficiency improvements for solving layered queueing networks. In *Proc.* 3rd *WOSP/SIPEW International Conference on Performance Engineering (ICPE '12)*, pages 279–282, Boston, MA, USA, Apr. 22–25 2012.

[7] G. Franks, P. Maly, M. Woodside, D. C. Petriu, and A. Hubbard. *Layered Queueing Network Solver and Simulator User Manual.* Real-time and Distributed Systems Lab, Carleton University, Ottawa. http://www.sce.carleton.ca/rads/lqn/lqn-documentation/.

[8] J. B. Goodenough. Exception handling: Issues and a proposed notation. *Commun. ACM*, 18(12):683–696, Dec. 1975.

[9] R. Jain. *The Art of Computer Systems Performance Analysis: Techniques for Experimental Design, Measurement, Simulation, and Modeling.* John Wiley & Sons, 1991.

[10] P. Kähkipuro. UML based performance modeling framework for object oriented systems. In *UML '99, The Unified Modeling Language, Beyond the Standard*, volume 1723 of *Lecture Notes in Computer Science*, pages 356–371. Springer-Verlag, Berlin, 1999.

[11] L. Li and G. Franks. Modelling decisions in layered queueing networks. July 24–27 2016.

[12] M. A. Marsan, G. Balbo, G. Conte, S. Donatelli, and G. Franceschinis. *Modelling with Generalized Stochastic Petri Nets.* John Wiley & Sons, Inc., New York, NY, USA, 1st edition, 1994.

[13] D. A. Menascé. Two-level iterative queuing modeling of software contention. In *Proc.* 10th *IEEE/ACM International Symposium on Modeling, Analysis and Simulation of Computer and Telecommunication Systems (MASCOTS 2002)*, Fort Worth, TX, Oct. 12–16 2002.

[14] M. Mroz and G. Franks. A performance experiment system supporting fast mapping of system issues. In *Proc.* 4th *International ICST Conference on Performance Evaluation Methodologies and Tools (VALUETOOLS '09)*, Pisa, Italy, Oct. 20–22 2009.

[15] S. Ramesh and H. G. Perros. A multi-layer client-server queueing network model with synchronous and asynchronous messages. In *Proc.* 1st *International Workshop on Software and Performance (WOSP '98)*, pages 107–119, Santa Fe, NM USA, Oct. 12–16 1998.

[16] M. Reiser and S. S. Lavenberg. Mean value analysis of closed multichain queueing networks. *J. ACM*, 27(2):313–322, Apr. 1980.

[17] J. A. Rolia and K. A. Sevcik. The method of layers. *IEEE Trans. Softw. Eng.*, 21(8):689–700, Aug. 1995.

[18] C. U. Smith. Introduction to software performance engineering: Origins and outstanding problems. In M. Bernardo and J. Hillston, editors, *Formal Methods for Performance Evaluation (SFM 2007)*, volume 4486 of *Lecture Notes in Computer Science*, pages 395–428. Springer-Verlag, Berlin, 2007.

[19] C. M. Woodside, J. E. Neilson, D. C. Petriu, and S. Majumdar. The stochastic rendezvous network model for performance of synchronous client-server-like distributed software. *IEEE Trans. Comput.*, 44(8):20–34, Aug. 1995.

[20] P. Wu. *Extending Layered Queueing Network with Hybrid Submodels Representing Exceptions and Decision Making.* PhD thesis, Department of Systems and Computer Engineering, Carleton University, Ottawa, ON, Canada, May 2013.

A Stable Mean Value Analysis Algorithm for Closed Systems with Load-dependent Queues

Lei Zhang
Department of Computing and Software
McMaster University
1280 Main Street West
Hamilton, ON L8S4K1, Canada
zhangl64@mcmaster.ca

Douglas G. Down
Department of Computing and Software
McMaster University
1280 Main Street West
Hamilton, ON L8S4K1, Canada
downd@mcmaster.ca

ABSTRACT

The load-dependent Mean Value Analysis (MVA) algorithm suffers from numerical instability. Different techniques have been adopted to avoid this issue, however, they either have large complexities or restrictive assumptions. In this paper, we introduce a numerically Stable MVA (SMVA) algorithm for product-form networks that allows for load-dependent queues. The SMVA algorithm offers an efficient and accurate approximate solution. We validate SMVA by comparing it to other MVA algorithms in a concrete example, and analyze its errors. We also extend it to a multi-class model.

CCS Concepts

•Mathematics of computing → Queueing theory;

Keywords

Performance evaluation; mean value analysis; numerical stability

1. INTRODUCTION

The Mean Value Analysis (MVA) algorithm for closed queueing networks with product-form steady-state distribution was introduced by Lavenberg and Reiser [7]. It relies on product-form assumptions, which can be violated by common features introduced in modern computer systems, e.g., simultaneous resource possession, locking behaviours, priority scheduling, high service demand variability, and process synchronization (see Chapter 15 in [5]). An approximate solution is to reduce a non-product-form network by using Flow-Equivalent Servers (FES) [3]. An FES is load dependent, whose service rate with n jobs present is equal to the observed throughput of the original network with n jobs (as shown in Figure 1). Then, we can solve the performance model by the load-dependent MVA algorithm [6]. Unfortunately, the load-dependent MVA algorithm suffers from numerical instability issues [6, 7]. The underlying reason is that the computation of state probabilities can yield negative results when the utilization is close to one. Consequently, negative values of mean performance measures (i.e., response times and throughputs) can be produced. Static and dynamic scaling techniques are complex, and Casale and Serazzi [2] show that they do not work in general, as the mean queue length computations are not affected. To the best of our knowledge, the literature is lacking efficient solutions for the numerical instability of MVA.

VALUETOOLS 2016, October 25-28, Taormina, Italy

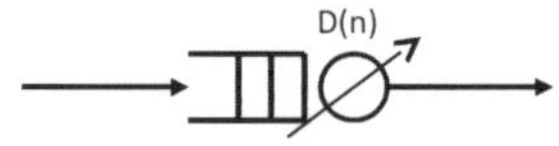

Figure 1: A generic load-dependent queue

To effectively address numerical instability, we propose the Stable MVA (SMVA) algorithm. The main contributions of this paper include: (1) The SMVA algorithm, which is an efficient approximate solution for closed networks with load-dependent queues. (2) An extended multi-class model used to determine class-level mean performance metrics.

2. RELATED WORK

To address numerical issues, Casale [1] introduced the Conditional MVA (CMVA) algorithm, which avoids the computations of the state probabilities, and as a consequence, overcomes the limitation. Although the CMVA algorithm is an exact solution, its time and space complexities grow as $O(MN^2)$, where M is the number of queues, and N is the number of jobs. The time and space complexities for the original MVA algorithm only grow as $O(MN)$.

In the literature, Seidmann's approximation [8] is also widely used to address MVA's numerical issues. However, it is only applicable for multi-server queues in which all servers are load independent. This is a special case of generic load-dependent queues. The basic idea is to replace a queue with m servers by two tandem servers. The first one is a single server queue with service demand D/m, where D is one server's service demand. The second one is a pure delay server with service demand $D \cdot (m-1)/m$. In practice, Seidmann's approximation can yield noticeable errors under intermediate loads, but it has the same time and space complexities as the original MVA algorithm.

3. STABLE MEAN VALUE ANALYSIS

We study a generic load-dependent queue (as shown in

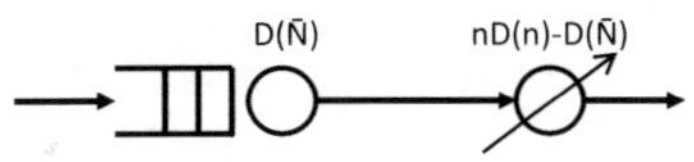

Figure 2: Approximating queues in SMVA

Figure 1) with service demand $D(n)$, where n is the number of jobs in the queue. Here, we assume that the service demand of the load-dependent queue becomes a constant beyond some $\bar{N}$, i.e., there exists a finite $\bar{N}$ such that $D(n) = D(\bar{N})$ for all $n \geq \bar{N}$. This assumption is reasonable for many systems, in particular when $D(n)$ becomes sufficiently close to $D(\bar{N})$.

The SMVA algorithm can be seen as a generalized Seidmann's approximation, replacing the load-dependent queue with two tandem servers (as shown in Figure 2). The first is a load-independent queue with service demand $D^q(n) = D(\bar{N})$. The second is a load-dependent delay centre with service demand

$$D^d(n) = \begin{cases} nD(n) - D(\bar{N}), & \text{if } n < \bar{N} \\ \bar{N} \cdot D(\bar{N}) - D(\bar{N}), & \text{if } n \geq \bar{N}. \end{cases}$$

To make sure the service demands of the delay centre are positive, we assume that $nD(n) \geq D(\bar{N})$, for $n < \bar{N}$. In multi-core systems, it is a common assumption that $D(n)$ decreases as n increases. In other words, we have $D(n) > D(\bar{N})$ when $n < \bar{N}$. Naturally, the assumption of $nD(n) \geq D(\bar{N})$ holds. Although the delay centre is load dependent, there is no need to calculate its state probabilities because it does not have a queue. As a result, the SMVA algorithm is numerically stable.

Algorithm 1 The SMVA algorithm

Input:
$Z, M, N, D_m, \bar{N}_m$
Output:
Q_m, X, R
Condition:
$\forall n, nD_m(n) \geq D_m(\bar{N}_m)$
Initialization:
$Q_m(0) = 0$, for all $m = 1, \ldots, M$
Iteration:
for $m = 1 \rightarrow M$ **do**
  for $n = 1 \rightarrow N$ **do**
    $D^q_m(n) = D_m(\bar{N}_m)$
    $D^d_m(n) = \begin{cases} nD_m(n) - D_m(\bar{N}_m), & \text{if } n < \bar{N}_m \\ \bar{N}_m \cdot D_m(\bar{N}_m) - D_m(\bar{N}_m), & \text{if } n \geq \bar{N}_m \end{cases}$
  end for
end for
for $n = 1 \rightarrow N$ **do**
  for $m = 1 \rightarrow M$ **do**
    $R^q_m(n) = D^q_m(n)[1 + Q_m(n-1)]$
    $R^d_m(n) = D^d_m(n)$
  end for
  $X(n) = n/\{Z + \sum_{m=1}^{M}[R^q_m(n) + R^d_m(n)]\}$
  for $m = 1 \rightarrow M$ **do**
    $Q_m(n) = X(n) \cdot R^q_m(n)$
  end for
end for
$R = \sum_{m=1}^{M}[R^q_m(N) + R^d_m(N)]$

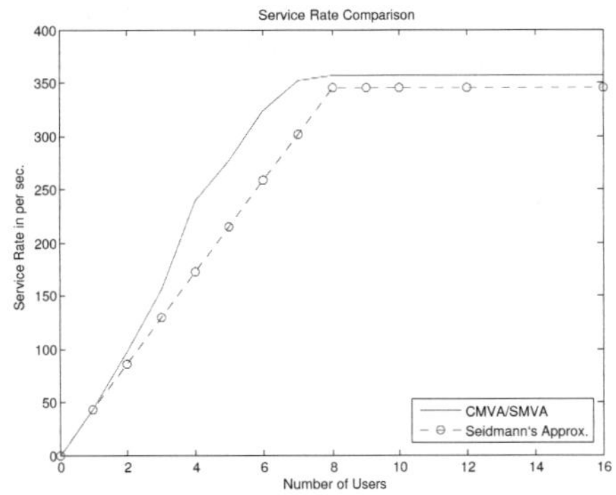

Figure 3: Service rate curves

Under light load, the two tandem servers behave as a server which has service demand $D(n)$. If n jobs are being served and no jobs are waiting in the queue, the time spent by a job in the approximating node is $D(\bar{N}) + nD(n) - D(\bar{N}) = nD(n)$. If there are jobs waiting in the first queue, the time spent by a job in the approximating node is dominated by the time spent at the first queue. The node behaves as a server which has service demand $D(\bar{N})$. As a result, this approximation should perform well for both light and heavy loads. Note that SMVA is identical to Seidmann's approximation when $nD(n) = D(1)$, for $n \leq \bar{N}$.

Algorithm 1 provides the SMVA algorithm. Z is the mean think time. D_m, D^q_m, and D^d_m are the service demands at the mth queue, the queueing resource, and the delay centre, respectively. R, R^q_m, and R^d_m are the response times of the system, the mth queue, and the delay centre, respectively. Finally, X is the system throughput, and Q_m is the mean queue length at the mth queue. The time and space complexities of SMVA are both $O(MN)$. Here, we assume that all queues are load dependent. If the mth queue is load independent, we can simply set $D^q_m = D_m$ and $D^d_m = 0$, and Algorithm 1 is still applicable.

4. EXPERIMENTAL RESULTS

In this section, we compare the results of the CMVA algorithm, Seidmann's approximation, and the SMVA algorithm. We set up a testbed as shown in in Table 1, and employ TPC-W [4] to generate the workload. We aggregate and model the system by an FES. We then obtain service rates (the inverse of service demands) of the FES to parameterize MVA algorithms (as shown in Figure 3). As can be seen in the figure, the service rate curve adopted by Seidmann's approximation can only address the ideal case of a load-dependent server, where $D(n) = D(1)/n$ for $n \leq 8$.

To test the accuracy of SMVA under different loads, we vary the number of users and the mean think times in the system. Both the mean response time and the throughput are compared for the three candidate MVA algorithms. Three sets of results are presented. The results of the first set are presented in Figure 4, where N ranges from 1 to 20, and Z=0. The results of the second set are presented in Figure 5, where N ranges from 1 to 300, and Z=0.7 seconds. The results of the third set are presented in Figure 6, where N ranges from 1 to 1300, and Z=3.5 seconds.

CPU	Memory	Disk	OS	Web Server	Database
Intel i7-2600 quad-core	8 GB	1 TB (7200 RPM)	Ubuntu 12.04.3 LTS	JBoss 3.2.7	MySQL 5.1.70

Table 1: Testbed settings

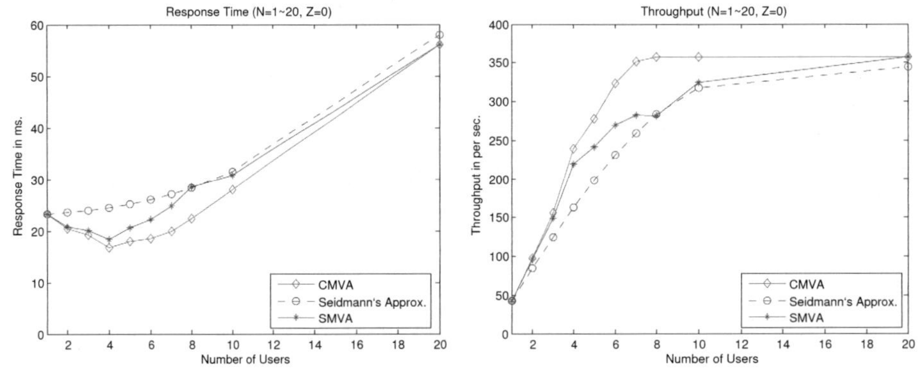

(a) Response time (b) Throughput

Figure 4: Comparison with Z=0

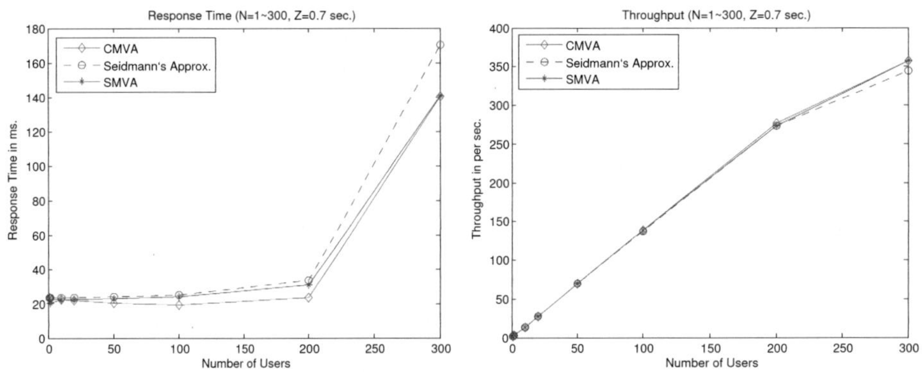

(a) Response time (b) Throughput

Figure 5: Comparison with Z=0.7 seconds

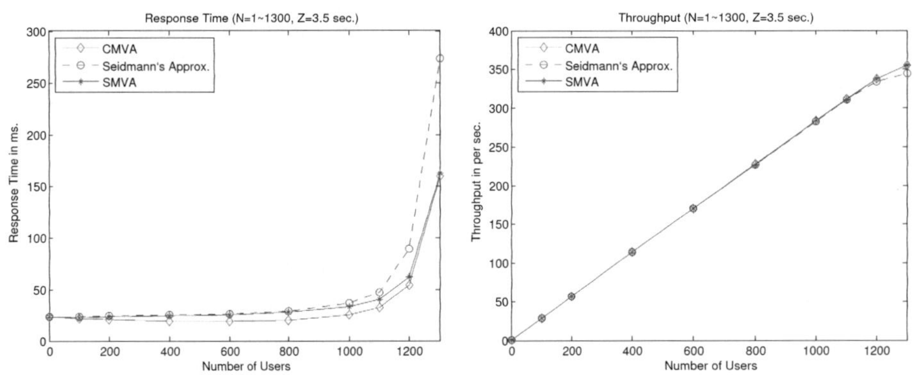

(a) Response time (b) Throughput

Figure 6: Comparison with Z=3.5 seconds

Using CMVA as the benchmark (as it is an exact solution), SMVA works better than Seidmann's approximation in all three cases. However, we also observe some errors for both of the approximate MVA algorithms from those figures, except for Figures 5b and 6b. The reason is that for those figures, the throughput is given by $X(n) = n/[Z + R(n)]$. As Z increases, the error in $R(n)$ has a smaller effect on the accuracy of $X(n)$.

We would like to quantify the errors from SMVA and Seidmann's approximation. In Figure 4, the largest error for the mean response time of SMVA is 27.16%, and the largest error for the throughput of SMVA is −21.36% (negative means underestimate) when $N = 8$. In contrast, the errors for both the mean response time and the throughput of Seidmann's approximation go to the largest when $N = 4$ (46.78% and −31.87%, respectively). We have similar observations from Figures 5 and 6. In Figure 5, the largest error for the mean response time of SMVA is 33.15% when $N = 200$. However, the errors for the throughput are quite small, the largest error is only −1.05% ($N = 200$). In Figure 6, the largest error for the mean response time of SMVA is 35.73% when $N = 800$. The errors for the throughput are negligible. In Figure 6, Seidmann's approximation has its worst case when $N = 1300$, the error for the mean response time is 71.91%.

5. DISCUSSION

Compared to the CMVA algorithm and Seidmann's approximation, the SMVA algorithm has two advantages. First, the time and space complexities of SMVA are a significant improvement over CMVA. Second, the SMVA algorithm is better able to handle cases when the service demands of a load-dependent node do not have a linear relationship.

We have two additional observations about SMVA. Firstly, the SMVA algorithm works as well as the CMVA algorithm for both light and heavy loads. However, the errors of SMVA increase when the system is under intermediate loads (but still performs better than Seidmann's approximation). Secondly, when the mean think time increases with respect to the service demands, the SMVA algorithm might produce less accurate estimates of the mean response times under intermediate load. In contrast, the estimated throughput becomes more accurate.

We conjecture that there are two reasons leading to the more significant error of SMVA under intermediate loads. Firstly, it assumes that all the jobs are being processed at the server when n jobs are in the system. In the load-dependent MVA algorithm, j jobs could be processed with probability $P(j|n)$, where j varies from 1 to n. Secondly, the delay centre can "delay" a job too long, in particular when the time that a job spends at the first queue does not dominate the total time. A good starting point for future research would be to better estimate the service demands of the delay centre.

6. MULTI-CLASS EXTENSION

For completeness, we extend the SMVA algorithm to the case of multi-class closed networks. Consider that there are C classes of transactions, where the job population vector is given by $\vec{N} = (n_1, n_2, \ldots, n_C)$, and the service demand of class c ($1 \le c \le C$) at the mth queueing resource is given by $D^q_{m,c}(n) = D_{m,c}(\bar{N}_m), \forall n$. The service demand at the delay centre becomes

$$D^d_{m,c}(n) = \begin{cases} nD_{m,c}(n) - D_{m,c}(\bar{N}_m), & n < \bar{N}_m \\ (\bar{N}_m - 1)D_{m,c}(\bar{N}_m), & n \ge \bar{N}_m. \end{cases}$$

Then, the multi-class SMVA iterates over all of the classes to compute the mean response times:

$$R^q_{m,c}(\vec{N}) = D^q_{m,c}(n_c)[1 + Q_m(\vec{N} - 1_c)],$$

and $R^d_{m,c}(\vec{N}) = D^d_{m,c}(n_c)$. Here $\vec{N} - 1_c$ is the job population vector with one class c job less in the system. The system throughput of class c is calculated by

$$X_c(\vec{N}) = n_c/\{Z + \sum_{m=1}^{M}[R^q_{m,c}(\vec{N}) + R^d_{m,c}(\vec{N})]\},\ 0 \le n_c \le N_c.$$

The mean queue length at the mth queue is

$$Q_m(\vec{N}) = \sum_{c=1}^{C} X_c(\vec{N}) \cdot R^q_{m,c}(\vec{N}).$$

7. CONCLUSIONS

In this paper, we presented the SMVA algorithm, an efficient approximation to address the numerical instability of the load-dependent MVA algorithm for closed queueing networks. The SMVA algorithm generalizes the applicability of Seidmann's approximation, and achieves better complexities compared to the CMVA algorithm. The SMVA algorithm can be seen as a first step to effectively address the numerical instability of MVA algorithms.

Acknowledgments. The work reported in this paper was supported by the Ontario Research Fund and the Natural Sciences and Engineering Research Council of Canada.

8. REFERENCES

[1] G. Casale. A note on stable flow-equivalent aggregation in closed networks. *Queueing Systems*, 60(3-4):193–202, 2008.

[2] G. Casale and G. Serazzi. Stabilization techniques for load-dependent queueing networks algorithms. In J. A. Barria, editor, *Communication Networks and Computer Systems: A Tribute to Professor Erol Gelenbe*, chapter 8, pages 127–141. Imperial College Press, 2006.

[3] K. M. Chandy, U. Herzog, and L. Woo. Parametric analysis of queuing networks. *IBM Journal of Research and Development*, 19(1):36–42, 1975.

[4] T. Horvath. TPC-W J2EE implementation, 2008. http://www.cs.virginia.edu/~th8k/downloads, last accessed 24 Feburary 2016.

[5] D. A. Menascé, V. A. Almeida, L. W. Dowdy, and L. Dowdy. *Performance by Design: Computer Capacity Planning by Example*. Prentice Hall PTR, 2004.

[6] M. Reiser. Mean-value analysis and convolution method for queue-dependent servers in closed queueing networks. *Performance Evaluation*, 1(1):7–18, 1981.

[7] M. Reiser and S. S. Lavenberg. Mean-value analysis of closed multichain queuing networks. *Journal of the ACM (JACM)*, 27(2):313–322, 1980.

[8] A. Seidmann, J. Paul, and S. Shalev-Oren. Computerized closed queueing network models of flexible manufacturing systems: A comparative evaluation. *Large Scale Systems*, 12:91–107, 1987.

Should I add an Intermittent Server

Raymond A. Marie
IRISA/University Rennes 1
Campus de Beaulieu
35042 Rennes Cedex, France
Raymond.Marie@irisa.fr

ABSTRACT

This paper concerns the situation of a queue with one regular single server and, in order to decrease the mean response time, with a second server i) leaving the back office to join the first server when the number of customers reaches the threshold K, ii) leaving the front office when he has no more customers to serve. This study produces a closed form solution for the steady state probability distribution and for different metrics such as expected response times for customers or expectation of busy periods. Then, for a given value of K, the influence of the intermittent server on the response time is exhibited. The consequences on the primary task of the intermittent server are investigated through metrics such as mean working and pseudo-idle periods. Finally, a determination of an optimal value of the threshold K is proposed.

CCS Concepts

•Mathematics of computing → **Queueing theory;** **•Computing methodologies** → *Simulation evaluation;*

Keywords

Performance Evaluation; Response Time; Markovian model; Intermittent Server.

1. INTRODUCTION

For a course on discrete event simulation, a good example is the one of the supermarket check-out counters where a counter can be activated/deactivated based on the states of the different queues. This argument stays because the queuing model is easy to elaborate and has no (known) analytical solution in its general configuration. This help students to realize all the advantages of a simulation approach. In addition, such a model is easily adaptable to other fields such as those of telecommunication or of data centers. Of course we have to remember that, when possible, an analytical solution must be looked for since its cost is generally lower than the one of the simulation approach.

Although most of the research work in the domain of the M/M/r queue with intermittent servers has been done through the use of simulation, we noted some developments connected to the subject. In 1971, J. Blackburn published a report [1] relative to a M/G/1 queue the server of which is an intermittent server who starts working when the number of customers crosses some threshold. This threshold is the value realizing the optimum of an objective function. A more recent analytical study investigated the case of an airline check-in counters set in an airport [4]. In this study, Parlar et. al elaborated a Markovian model and its transient solution. A major difference with the supermarket check-out system is that the number of customers to be served is known in advance (number of customers who have a reserved seat for a given flight). The problem is to control the number of open check-in counters such that all the customers that will show up before a deadline T will be served on time (such that the plane can take off on time). But most of the literature involving intermittent servers concerns studies where the activations of the servers depend on reliability/availability of the set of servers rather than on the states of the systems.

Another related class of models is the "coupled processor model" where each processor can help the other when it is idle. The two queues have their own arrival processes and service time distributions. Such a class has been the object of intensive analytical works in the past. Close to that is the case where the behaviors of the servers are no more symmetrical and only one processor can, when it becomes idle, give time to the other processor until its own queue reaches a given threshold (see the intensive study of Osogami et al. [3]). Note also the different model known as "the slow server problem" (see [5]) where, depending on the values of the parameters, the use of the slow server may increase the response time.

The present study is different in the sens that the server who gives some part of his time is not idle but works on tasks which are not directly impacting customers (the notion of response time is in some sens meaningless). This study is less general than the one cited above ([3]) but produces a closed form solution for the steady state probability distribution and for different metrics such as expected response times for customers or expectation of busy periods. One objective is to promote a better understanding of the benefits of such a strategy. A second objective is to produce a way to check the simulation software with respect to the case where the number of servers is reduced to two.

The presented application is supposed to come from the banking sector but could come from a more industrial area. The basic situation corresponds to a service counter with one regular single server and, in order to decrease the mean response time, with a second server i) leaving the back office to join the first server when the number of customers reaches the threshold K, ii) leaving the front office when he has no more customers to serve. The aim of this paper is to bring answers to questions such as : for a given value of K, what is the influence of the intermittent server on the response

VALUETOOLS 2016, October 25-28, Taormina, Italy

time? What is the frequency of the interventions of the intermittent server ? What is his mean working time during one stay in the back office ? Respectively, what is his mean working time during one passage in the front office? And finally, what is the cost of such an organization ?

The paper is organized as follows : in Section 2 we present a Markovian model of the investigated system while in the following section we exhibit the steady state probability distribution of the stochastic process and the expression of the mean number of customers (or mean response time) in terms of the different parameters. In Section 4, we conduct the determination of the expectation of the time spent by the second server in one passage in the back office and those of the expectation of one sojourn time at the front office. In the following section we propose a cost function providing an optimal solution as a tool to help a manager in charge of the economical decision. Some conclusions close the paper (Section 6).

2. HYPOTHESES AND MODEL

We consider that the two servers are equivalent and that the service times are independent and identically distributed random variables following an exponential distribution with rate μ. The first server affected to the front office stays available for serving the arriving customers.

When there are $(K-1)$ customers, if the server affected to the back office is not already serving in the front office, then this server leaves the back office at the instant of arrival of a new customer and starts serving it in the front office. Once it is in the front office, the second server stays there until it has no more customers to serve and re-integrates the back office.

We assume the customer arrival process is Poisson with rate λ.

Under these hypotheses, the stochastic process modeling the number of customers in the office is a continuous time Markov chain (CTMC) $\{X(t), t \geq 0\}$ ([2]). Its transition graph is given in Figure 1.

State $(i,0)$ (resp. $(i,1)$) denotes a state with i present customers and where the second server is in the back office (resp. present). State (0) refers to the empty system and, for $i \geq K$, state i designs the system when i customers and the second server are present. Note that the first server is idle in state $(1,1)$. In addition, E_0 (resp. E_1) will denote the subset of states where the second server is in the back office (resp. present) : $E_0 = \{(0), (1,0), ...(K-1,0)\}$, $E_1 = \{(1,1), ...(K-1,1), (K), (K+1), ...\}$.

The steady state probability distribution of this CTMC is determined in the following section.

Note that the case $K=2$ corresponds to a $M/M/2$ queue with a little specificity : once the queue is empty, the first server deals with the new arrival, the second server arriving only when a new arrival finds the first server busy, and going back as soon as there is no more customer to serve in the front office. But from the customer point of view, this specificity does not affect the performance of the queue.

3. STEADY STATE PROBABILITY DISTRIBUTION, MEAN NUMBER OF CUSTOMERS

For any state e, π_e will denote the steady state probability of state e. Defining $\rho = \lambda/2\mu$, note that the steady state probability will exist if $\rho < 1$. Using the Chapmann-Kolmogorov equations (CK eqns) of states $(i,0)$, $i = 2, ..., K-1$, it is not difficult to prove by induction the relation :

$$\pi_{K-i,0} = (\sum_{j=0}^{i-1} \phi^j)\pi_{K-1,0}, \qquad i = 2, ..., K-1 . \tag{1}$$

Use of the cut theorem on the partition $\{E_0, E_1\}$ and of the steady state CK eqn of the state $(1,1)$ gives us

$$\pi_{1,1} = \frac{1}{(1+2\phi)}\pi_{K-1,0} . \tag{2}$$

Then, using using equations (2) and (1) and the CK eqn. for state (0), we can express probability in term of $\pi_{K-1,0}$, for the case $\phi \neq 1$:

$$\pi_{K-1,0} = \pi_0 \frac{(1+2\phi)(1-\phi)}{D_0} , \tag{3}$$

where $D_0 = \phi[(1-\phi) + (1+2\phi)(1-\phi^{K-1})]$. Consider now the CK eqns of states $(i,1)$, $i = 2, ..., K-1$, we can prove by induction that :

$$\pi_{i,1} = \pi_{1,1}\frac{(1+\rho) - 2\rho^i}{(1-\rho)} \qquad i = 2, ..., K , \tag{4}$$

Then, using equations (2) and (3), we express the probability $\pi_K = \pi_{K,1}$ as a function of probability π_0 (for the case where $\phi \neq 1$) :

$$\pi_K = \pi_0 \frac{(1+\rho) - 2\rho^K}{(1-\rho)} \frac{(1-\phi)}{D_0} . \tag{5}$$

Using the cut theorem, it is easy get the equations :

$$\pi_i = \rho^{i-K}\pi_K, \qquad i > K . \tag{6}$$

Thanks to the normalizing equation, it is finally possible to show that the probability π_0 can be written as :

$$\pi_0 = \frac{(1-\rho)(1-\phi)D_0}{D_1} , \tag{7}$$

where

$$\begin{aligned} D_1 &= (1-\rho)\{\phi(1-\phi)^2 + \\ &+(1+2\phi)[(K-1)(1-\phi) - \phi^2(1-\phi^{K-1})]\} + \\ &+(1-\phi)^2[1 + (K-1)(1+\rho)] . \end{aligned}$$

The particular case $\phi = 1$ is easier to deal with and we get at the end :

$$\pi_0 = \frac{2(3K-2)}{3(K(K+3)-2)} .$$

When $K=2$, some of the equations obtained for the general case are no longer valid but it is not difficult to find again the well known result of the $M/M/2$ queue : $\pi_0 = (1-\rho)/(1+\rho)$.

The determination of the mean number of customers is purely technique. For $\phi \neq 1$, it satisfies the following relation :

$$\begin{aligned} E[N] &= \frac{(1-\phi)}{D_1}\Bigg\{(1-\rho)(1+2\phi)\left(\frac{K(K+1)}{2} - \frac{K}{(1-\phi)}\right. \\ &\left. + \frac{\phi(1-\phi^K)}{(1-\phi)^2}\right) + \\ &+(1-\phi)\left((1+\rho)\frac{K(K-1)}{2} + \frac{K+\rho(K-1)}{(1-\rho)}\right)\Bigg\} . \end{aligned}$$

When $K=2$, it is not difficult to find again the well known result of the $M/M/2$ queue : $\mathbb{E}[N] = 2\rho/(1-\rho^2)$.

For a given value of ρ we expect that the expected number of customers is greater than the value given by the $M/M/2$ queue. While, as long as ρ is lower than 0.5, the expected number of customers is lower than the ratio $\frac{2\rho}{1-2\rho}$, which corresponds to the value given by the $M/M/1$ queue with 2ρ as the utilization factor. The plotting of the expectation of the number of customers as a function of ρ, for different values of the integer K, would show that this expectation is increasing with ρ and with K. Note that without the second server, the mean number of customers would tend to infinity when ρ tends to 0.5.

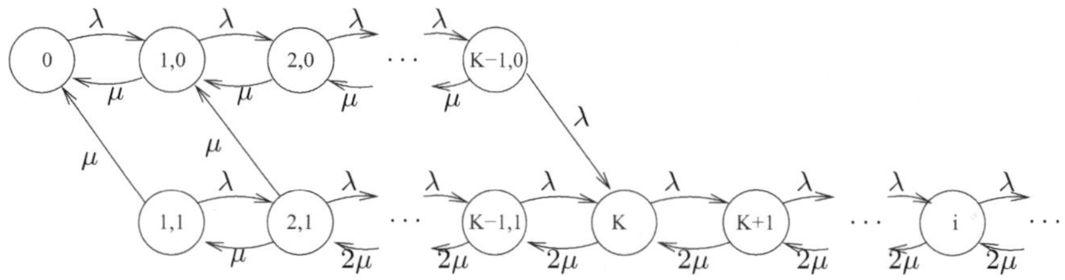

Figure 1: Transition graph of the CTMC.

4. PSEUDO-IDLE AND BUSY PERIODS FOR THE SECOND SERVER

By pseudo-idle period, for the second server, we mean a period of time during which this server is working in the back-office. We are interested by the expectation of such a period because we understand that too short of a period would have a negative effect on the productivity of the server. Such a period corresponds to a sojourn time of the CTMC in the subset E_0 and therefore we need to obtain the expectation of this sojourn time.

4.1 Mean Time of a Passage in the Back Office

First let us determine the probability that a pseudo-idle period starts in state (0) (respectively in state $(1,0)$). Given that the CTMC is in state $(2,1)$, if a service completes before a new arrival, the CTMC joins either state $(1,0)$ if the second server finishes his service first or state $(1,1)$ in the other case. These two events have equal probabilities (0.5 each). If the CTMC joins state $(1,1)$ from state $(2,1)$, this means that the permanent server becomes idle. Then either the second server becomes idle (with probability $\frac{\mu}{\lambda+\mu}$) or the regular server becomes busy again, the CTMC revisiting state $(2,1)$ (with probability $\frac{\lambda}{\lambda+\mu}$).

So, given a service completes when the CTMC is in state $(2,1)$, the CTMC goes to state $(1,0)$ with probability 0.5, goes to state (0) without coming back to state $(2,1)$ with probability $0.5\times\frac{\mu}{\lambda+\mu}$ or comes back to state $(2,1)$ with probability $0.5\times\frac{\lambda}{\lambda+\mu}$. Considering these three eventualities, we see that when the CTMC enters subset E_0, it enters it through state (0) with probability $\frac{0.5(\mu/(\lambda+\mu))}{0.5(1+\mu/(\lambda+\mu))}$ or enters it through state $(1,0)$ with probability $\frac{0.5}{0.5(1+\mu/(\lambda+\mu))}$. These two expressions reducing respectively to $\frac{\phi}{1+2\phi}$ and $\frac{1+\phi}{1+2\phi}$.

Let assume that $X(0)=0$. Let T_A be the sojourn time in the subset $E_0 : T_A = inf\{t|X(t)=K\}$. In order to express the expectation of T_A, we first consider the random variable T_i defined as the time it takes to the CTMC to reach state $(i+1,0)$ given $X(0)=(i,0)$. We also denote the expectation of T_i by α_i. Introducing the discrete random variable I_i such that, for $i\geq 0$, $I_i=1$ (resp. $I_i=0$) if the first transition of the CTMC from state $(i,0)$ is a jump to state $(i+1,0)$ (resp. $(i-1,0)$), we get when conditioning w.r.t. I_i : $\mathbb{E}[T_i|I_i=1]=\frac{1}{\lambda+\mu}$, and $\mathbb{E}[T_i|I_i=0]=\frac{1}{\lambda+\mu}+\alpha_{i-1}+\alpha_i$.

For $i=0$, we have immediately $\mathbb{E}[T_0]=\frac{1}{\lambda}$. Since the departure rate from state $(i,0)$ equals $(\lambda+\mu)$ while the transition rate from state $(i,0)$ to state $(i+1,0)$ equals λ, the probability that the first transition of the CTMC from state $(i,0)$ is a jump to state $(i+1,0)$ is $\mathbb{P}(I_i=1)=\frac{\lambda}{\lambda+\mu}$. Therefore, deconditioning the expectation $\alpha_i=\mathbb{E}[T_i]$ gives us, for $i>0$,

$$\alpha_i=\frac{1}{\lambda+\mu}\frac{\lambda}{\lambda+\mu}+\left(\frac{1}{\lambda+\mu}+\alpha_{i-1}+\alpha_i\right)\frac{\mu}{\lambda+\mu},$$

that reduces to $\alpha_i=\frac{1}{\lambda}(1+\mu\,\alpha_{i-1})$.

Since $\alpha_0=\mathbb{E}[T_0]=\frac{1}{\lambda}$, we can compute successfully $\alpha_0,\alpha_1,\alpha_2,\ldots$.

It is not difficult to prove that $\alpha_i=\frac{1}{\lambda}\sum_{j=0}^{i}\phi^j$.

In addition, $\mathbb{E}[T_A]$ depends on the way the CMTC enters the subset E_0 since $\mathbb{E}[T_A|X(0)=0]=\sum_{j=0}^{K-1}\alpha_j$, while $\mathbb{E}[T_A|X(0)=(1,0)]=\sum_{j=1}^{K-1}\alpha_j$. Therefore, after deconditioning we obtain $\mathbb{E}[T_A]$ that we scale by expressing this time expectation in term of a mean number of service times :

$$\mu\mathbb{E}[T_A]=\frac{\phi}{2(1+\rho)}+\phi\left((K-1)+\sum_{i=1}^{K-1}(K-i)\phi^i\right). \quad (8)$$

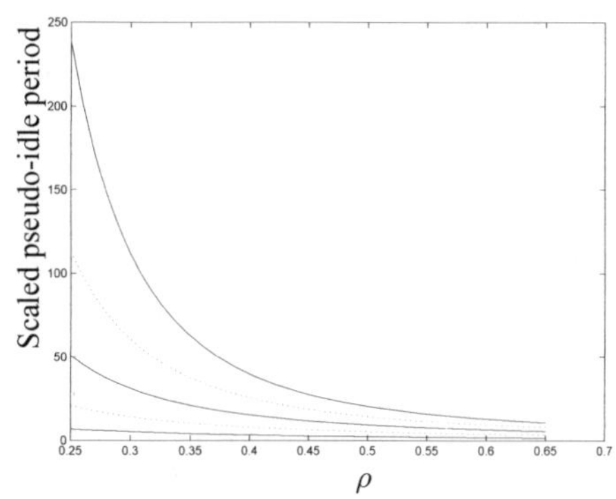

Figure 2: Scaled expectation of the pseudo-idle period of the second server as a function of ρ. For (bottom-up) $K=2,3,4,5$ and 6.

In Figure 2, we have plotted the scaled expectation of the pseudo-idle period of the second server as a function of ρ, for different values of the integer K. We can say that the expectation of the pseudo-idle period of the second server is important when ρ is between 0 and around 0.4, Remember that when $\rho=0.4$, the utilization factor of the single server of the $M/M/1$ queue equals 0.8. As we would expect, this expectation is decreasing with ρ and increasing with K.

Note that if the manager decides to change the rule by switching from K to $(K+1)$, then the scaled expectation will be increased of the quantity $\Delta(\mu\mathbb{E}[T_A])=\mu\mathbb{E}[T_A(K+1)]-\mu\mathbb{E}[T_A(K)]$ corresponding to $\phi\left(\sum_{i=0}^{K}\phi^i\right)$. Even in the case where $\phi=1$ (*i.e.*, $\rho=0.5$), this increase can be shown to correspond to $(K+1)$ mean service times!

4.2 Mean Time of a Passage in the Front Office

Now let $\mathbb{E}[T_P]$ be the expectation of a period spent in the front office by the second server. This server starts such a period with the frequency $\lambda\pi_{K-1,0}$. Using the fact that this frequency must be equal to $(\mathbb{E}[T_A]+\mathbb{E}[T_P])^{-1}$, we can obtain first the expression $\lambda\mathbb{E}[T_P]$ and then the expression of the expectation scaled in term of the mean service time : $\mu\mathbb{E}[T_P] = \frac{1}{2(1-\rho)}\left((K-1) + \frac{1}{(1+\rho)}\right)$. Note that $\mu\mathbb{E}[T_P]$ represents also the expected number of customers served by the intermittent server during a passage in the front office.

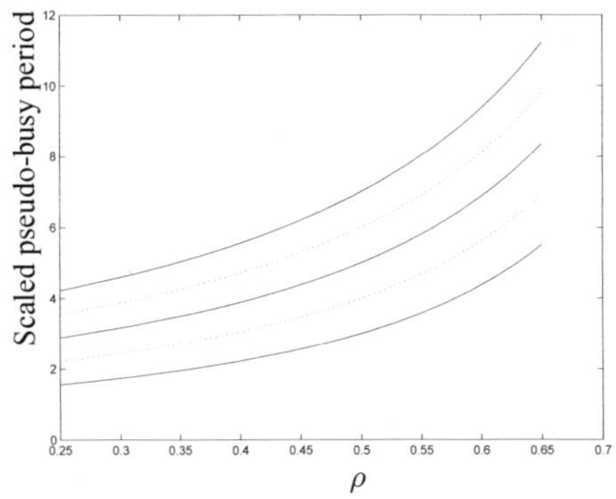

Figure 3: Scaled expectation of the pseudo-busy period of the second server as a function of ρ. For (bottom-up) $K = 2, 3, 4, 5$ and 6.

In Figure 3, we have plotted the scaled expectation of the pseudo-busy period of the second server as a function of ρ, for different values of the integer K. As we would expect, this expectation is increasing with ρ and with K. Moreover, we can say that the expectation of the pseudo-busy period of the second server is relatively small when ρ is between 0 and around 0.4, when we compare it with the one of the pseudo-idle period. From that we understand the interest of introducing the policy of the intermittent server.

5. COST FUNCTION

We have to consider two somewhat different situations. The first one is when the second server is not necessary for the system to be stable (*i.e.,* when ρ is lower than 0.5). The second situation is when the second server is necessary to the system ($\rho \geq 0.5$).

In the first situation, the second server just helps to decrease the mean response time seen by the customers. We have to compare this help with the perturbation of the work done in the back office.

We assume here that there is a fixed penalty c_0 to pay each time the second server has to leave the back office and that the cost per unit of time of this second server is c_1. We also assume that c_2 is the cost per unit of waiting time. Then the function to minimize corresponds to the total variable cost per time unit and is given by :

$$C(K) = c_0(T_A + T_P)^{-1} + c_1 S_1 + c_2\mathbb{E}[N] \,,$$

where $S_1 = \sum_{i=1}^{K-1} \pi_{i,1} + \sum_{i=K}^{\infty} \pi_i$. Note that the sum of probabilities S_1 is also the mean time per time unit spent by the second server in the front office and $\mathbb{E}[N]$ is also the total waiting time per time unit. When the variable K is increased, the first two terms are decreasing (asymptotically to zero) while the term $c_2\mathbb{E}[N]$ is increasing (from $c_2 2\rho/(1-\rho^2)$ when $K = 2$ to the asymptotic value $c_2 2\rho/(1-2\rho)$ when K tends to infinity). In this situation The optimal K may not be finite if the penalty coefficient c_2 is not large enough.

The second situation is different in the sense that K has to be finite in order to have a stable solution. In this case, the intermittent server has to work in the front office a percentage of time S_1 greater than $(\lambda/\mu - 1)$ such that the system has a steady state solution. The maximal feasible value $K_{\max}$ of K is given by $K_{\max} = \max\{K | S_1(K) > \lambda/\mu - 1\}$. Practically, if $K_{\max}$ is large enough (*i.e.,* when $(\lambda/\mu - 1)$ is not close to unity), the cost $c_2\mathbb{E}[N]$ should be large when $K = K_{\max}$ and we may expect the cost function to be convex. However, the convexity of $C(K)$ has not been investigated theoretically. Also, from a practical point of view, the parameter c_2 has again to be not too small with respect to c_0 and c_1 in order to avoid the limit behavior where the second server would come once a year to empty the waiting room. In Figure 4, we have plotted the values of

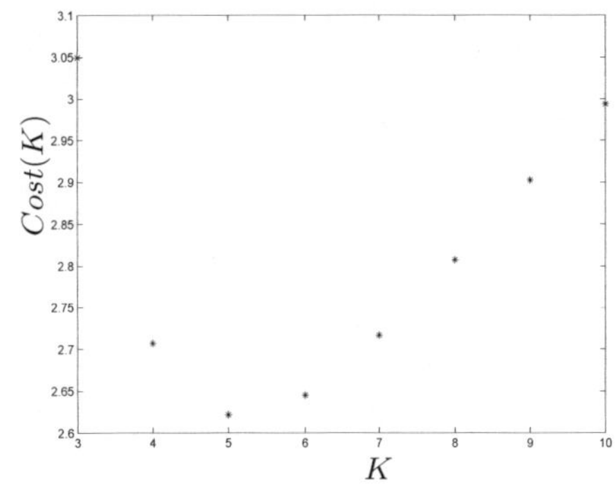

Figure 4: Variable cost function, with $\rho = 0.35$.

$C(K)$ when $\rho = 0.35$ (this means that the single server queue would have a utilization factor of 0.7), for $c_0 = 10$, $c_1 = 5$ and $c_2 = 1.5$. It can be seen that the minimum is achieved with $K = 5$. From Figures (2) and (3), we can check that for this optimal solution the mean pseudo-idle period of the second server is around 70 times the mean service time while the mean pseudo-busy period is close to 4 times the mean service time.

6. CONCLUSIONS

We have shown in this paper the importance of intermittent servers in order to reduce the response times without increasing significantly the idle times of servers. For such situations where a single server would satisfy the stability condition ($\lambda < \mu$), a non trivial result is that the pseudo-idle period of the second server is significantly longer than what would be generally expected by the management and also that the pseudo-busy period stays small ; and so the second server can keep his main activity in the back office.

We can think of applications in architectures for large telecommunication switches where we have "guard" processors to help the congested input queues on demand. Not only these results are interesting by themselves if such a situation occurs in a real situation but also, this study can be used to check simulation models used for a more complex situation.

7. REFERENCES

[1] J. D. Blackburn. Optimal control of queueing systems with intermittent service. Technical report, DTIC Document, 1971.

[2] E. Cinlar. *Introduction to stochastic Processes*. Prentice Hall, New-Jersey, 1975.

[3] T. Osogami, M. Harchol-Balter, and A. Scheller-Wolf. Analysis of cycle stealing with switching times and thresholds. *Performance Evaluation*, 61(4):347–369, 2005.

[4] M. Parlar and M. Sharafali. Dynamic allocation of airline check-in counters: a queueing optimization approach. *Management Science*, 54(8):1410–1424, 2008.

[5] M. Rubinovitch. The slow server problem: a queue with stalling. *Journal of Applied Probability*, 22(4):879–892, 1985.

A Queueing Network Model for Performance Prediction of Apache Cassandra

Salvatore Dipietro
Imperial College London, UK
s.dipietro@imperial.ac.uk

Giuliano Casale
Imperial College London, UK
g.casale@imperial.ac.uk

Giuseppe Serazzi*
Politecnico di Milano, Italy
giuseppe.serazzi@polimi.it

ABSTRACT

NoSQL databases such as Apache Cassandra have attracted large interest in recent years thanks to their high availability, scalability, flexibility and low latency. Still there is limited research work on performance engineering methods for NoSQL databases, which yet are needed since these systems are highly distributed and thus can incur significant cost/performance trade-offs. To address this need, we propose a novel queueing network model for the Cassandra NoSQL database aimed at supporting resource provisioning. The model defines explicitly key configuration parameters of Cassandra such as consistency levels and replication factor, allowing engineers to compare alternative system setups.

Experimental results based on the YCSB benchmark indicate that, with a small amount of training for the estimation of its input parameters, the proposed model achieves good predictive accuracy across different loads and consistency levels. The average performance errors of the model compared to the real results are between 6% and 10%. We also demonstrate the applicability of our model to other NoSQL databases and other possible utilisation of it.

CCS Concepts

•Computing methodologies → Modeling and simulation; •General and reference → *Performance;* **•Information systems →** Database performance evaluation;

Keywords

NoSQL database, Apache Cassandra, queueing network model, simulation

*This paper has been partially supported by the European Union's Horizon 2020 research and innovation programme under grant agreement No. 644869. We would also like to thank XLAB for the support for the ScyllaDB installation and the MIKELANGELO project for cooperation. The data generated in this paper are released under CC-BY license at: https://zenodo.org/record/153836

VALUETOOLS 2016, October 25-28, Taormina, Italy

1. INTRODUCTION

The growing importance of Big Data applications has led in recent years to a rapid growth of interest for NoSQL databases [18]. Compared to traditional databases, NoSQL databases offer simple read and write operations, horizontal scalability and low latency. If tuned for the specific workload at hand, NoSQL databases can provide high availability and reliability guaranteeing leverage on distributed data replication mechanisms.

In spite of their popularity, performance engineering for NoSQL databases is still in its early stages. In particular, NoSQL databases are commonly deployed on cloud platforms where hardware resources are rented, calling for dedicated provisioning methods in order to strike the right trade-off between costs and quality-of-service. Unfortunately, database performance can be challenging to manage in cloud environments, where it can be compromised by several factors, such as network contention and CPU multi-tenancy. For this reason, it is desirable to support engineers with analysis tools to assess risks associated to a target deployment.

Today, service providers tend to over-provision NoSQL databases, wasting resources and increasing the costs for their infrastructure. Finding the optimal configuration, in terms of number of nodes, number of replicas (*Replication Factor*) and data consistency (*Consistency Level*), is thus important and desirable, but still considered a research challenge. Performance prediction based on stochastic models can support sizing activities of this kind by allowing engineers to easily compare alternative system configurations and predict performance and costs before deployment in the cloud.

One of the main challenges in modelling NoSQL databases is to properly account for the replication factors and data consistency levels. The goal of this paper is to develop a model that addresses this need for the Apache Cassandra NoSQL database [19]. Data replication is usually executed asynchronously, reducing response time but achieving a weaker data consistency level than traditional databases [6]. In order to ensure consistency, read requests thus need to hit multiple replicas before the database system can respond to the client. This synchronisation can considerably affect system response time and, for this reason, in this work we focus our attention only on the read requests. Finding the optimal trade off between data consistency, costs and offered performance thus requires a quantitative approach that should assess all of these dimensions.

The proposed model is based on extended queueing networks consisting of fork-join elements, finite capacity regions, and class-switching. Since the model includes several features that are not readily amenable to analytical solution, we focus here on simulation-based assessment. We plan to investigate in the future the applicability of mean-value approximations to our models, such as those used in layered queueing network solvers [12]. Our performance model explicit both replication factor and consistency level, allowing engineers to compare alternative system setups.

We validate the proposed model against experiments based on the YCSB database benchmark [9], under varying consistency levels. Our results indicate that average error for the throughput is lower than 7% and lower than 10% for the response time, increasing prediction robustness compared to existing models.

The rest of the paper is organised as follows. Section 2 summarises related work. Section 3 describes the key features of Apache Cassandra involved in the study. Section 4 introduces the proposed queueing network model, which is subsequently validated in Section 5. We also demonstrate the applicability of our model to another NoSQL database, ScyllaDB, and propose a model-based analysis of Cassandra performance under quorum-based synchronization. Section 6 presents conclusions and future work.

2. RELATED WORK

Database performance modelling has been traditionally focused on relational databases [24]. With the increasing growth in popularity of NoSQL databases over the last ten years, research work in performance evaluation has been increasingly conducted also on these emerging database systems. Prior work has focused on comparing NoSQL systems in terms of read/write performance, scalability and flexibility [6, 22, 2, 17]. To the best of our knowledge only a limited number of works have been conducted on performance modelling of NoSQL databases, and available models specific to Cassandra are few [13, 25]. The models in [13] and [25] use two different modelling techniques due to the difficulty to represent, in the same model, the synchronization and the scheduling of the requests.

Gandini et al. present a high level queueing network model for Cassandra [13]. Each node of the distributed setup is described using two queues: one for the CPU and one for the disk. This model is able to capture throughput and latency for read and write requests. However, compared to our model, it does not take in consideration requests other than those executed locally and there is not synchronization of the tasks between the nodes. Moreover, communication latency is not taken in consideration and there is no representation of the CPU tasks limit that Cassandra has.

Subsequently, [25] presents a model for simulating read requests. The authors use Queueing Petri Nets (QPN) [3] in order to describe synchronization. QPNs are an extension of coloured stochastic Petri nets, particularly useful when the model needs to explicit scheduling at queueing resources. Each node is represented by only CPU processes, described as a timed queue. Compared to the model in [13], the authors limit the number of simultaneously running queries for a node and distinguish between local and remote requests. However, no information about the disk and network latency is considered. In case of records of large size, the disk and network response time can considerably affect performance. The model in [25] is validated by predicting response time and throughput of different Cassandra configurations and appears to be the most accurate among existing performance models. However, for some particular configuration the error between real system and simulation can grow over 40%.

Compared to the previous models, our model is able to capture network and disk latencies, distinguishing the different type of requests (represented in the model as classes) and attributing different CPU demands to each class and to each phase of the query execution. These improvements deliver more accuracy on throughput and response time prediction. In addition, our model is able to represent different data replication factor and simulate the major consistency levels implemented in Cassandra.

Queueing Petri Nets have also been used in [23] to predict and study Cassandra energy consumption. A study on how performance changes in relation to different data model structures has been conducted in [7]. Chebotko et al. present a query-driven data modelling for Cassandra whose results are highly different from the one applied for the traditional databases. The paper also argues about the importance of the modelling consistency levels. The relation between performance and consistency level has been studied in several papers [4, 1, 28]. To achieve higher performance, NoSQL databases prefer eventually consistency instead of strong consistency. For this reason, to achieve strong consistency and meet the consistency levels required by the application without sacrificing the performance, variations of Cassandra database have been developed [8, 14]. Chihoub et al. presents a self-tuning mechanism to change at run-time query consistency levels, taking in consideration system state. Differently, in [14] the Cassandra's node architecture is modified to always achieve strong consistency of the data.

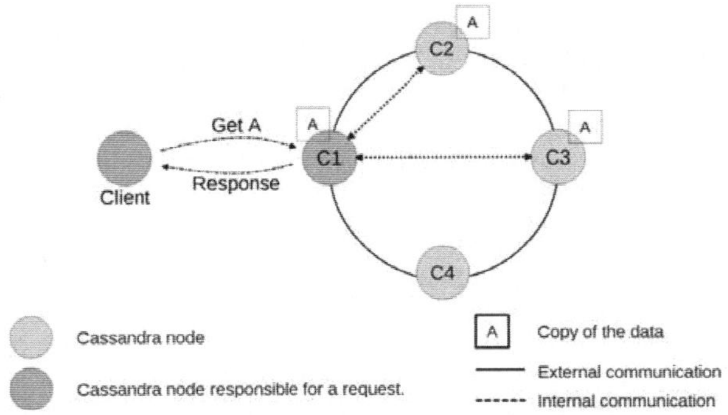

Figure 1: **Cassandra architecture overview.** In this example, Cassandra cluster is composed by 4 nodes with a replication factor of 3. The client is connected to the node c1 and it asks the data 'A' with consistency level ALL.

3. CASSANDRA ARCHITECTURE

Among all NoSQL datastores, Cassandra is one of the most popular and, nowadays, it is used in several Big Data products. Originally developed by Facebook [19], it was released as an open-source Apache project. Strong points are: a completely decentralised architecture without a single point of failure and promising linear scalability, high write performance and tunable consistency levels of the data inside the query.

As shown in Figure 1, a Cassandra cluster is organised as a ring of nodes. Each of these nodes is responsible to store part of the data. To offer an equal data distribution inside the ring, the hash key space is divided by the total number of *tokens* that are set for the database. Based on the number of tokens assigned to a node, a random subset of possible primary hash key values is associated to the node. The node becomes responsible for this subset of data for the entire database. Usually, the number of tokens is the same for each node in the ring. However, if the node characteristics are different inside the ring, the data distribution can take into account these heterogeneities by attributing a different number of tokens to each server. To achieve high availability, Cassandra replicates the data on some other nodes of the ring. The number of replicas is defined by the *Replication Factor* (RF). This implies that, if the cluster is composed by N nodes, each node will store a portion of the key space equal to RF/N.

To avoid network bottlenecks, the architecture allows each node to receive requests directly from the clients. When a client sends a query to a node, the node serves it as *coordinator* and it is responsible for all the necessary operations to complete the query. Depending on the chosen *Consistency Level* (CL), Cassandra shows different behaviours [10]. The CL sets the number of copies that the system has to retrieve and compares before the response is returned to the client. The main CL options are three: ONE, QUORUM and ALL. For the purpose of this paper, we consider CL only for read requests. CL ONE involves the fewest operations and it is the fastest. To reply to the client, only one copy of the data is gathered. Differently, the QUORUM needs $(RF/2) + 1$ versions of the same data. The last option, ALL, requires that all the replicas are gathered to obtain the data, generating the response.

When a node is acting as the coordinator for a request, it performs two activities. First, in the parsing process, the node accepts the client request, locates one or more nodes holding data (according to the CL) and forwards them the requests. Next, in the end process, the node receives all the data from the other nodes, checks the consistency between all the responses and replies to the client. If one of the nodes has an old version of the data, the coordinator sends a query to update it.

Consider now a read request with CL ONE . The data request is sent to one node of the ring. If the data asked is stored in the node, the node performs a local request, fetching the data from the disk and returning it to the client. However, if the data is not stored in the node, the node acts like a *proxy*, asking the data to another node. Before returning the data to the client, the coordinator node checks if the data obtained corresponds to the latest version. Choosing a higher CL, the node needs to act more often as a proxy to ask the data from before to complete the requests. In case of CL ONE or QUORUM, Cassandra selects the node to retrieve data from based on measured node latencies in serving previous requests.

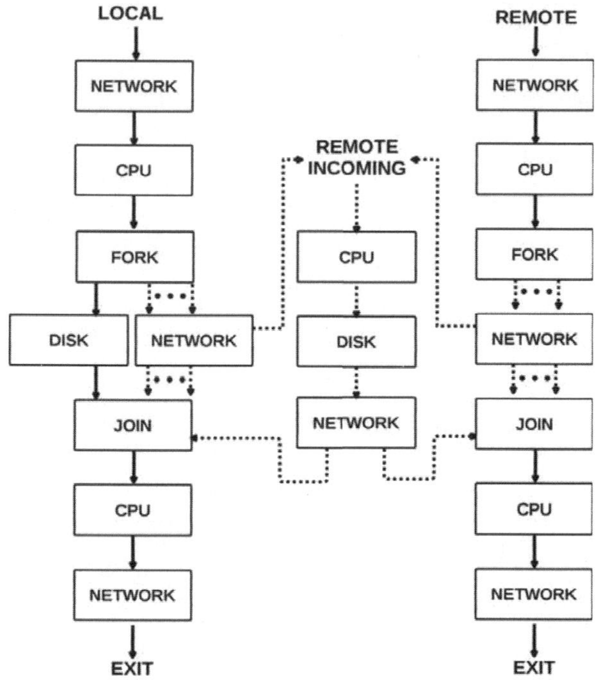

Figure 2: Local, Remote and Remote Incoming requests workflow. The boxes represent the node components used for a single node in our model. The lines represent where the request is forwarded. Continuous lines indicate the connections inside the same node whereas dashed lines represent external node connections.

4. CASSANDRA MODEL

In this section, we present the Cassandra model used to predict database performance. The model is built using queueing network theory [20]. Queuing networks are a classic modelling technique for predicting latencies incurred by jobs that traverse a network of congested resources, each modelled as a queue. To represent and simulate our model, we use the JSIMgraph simulation environment provided with Java Modelling Tool (JMT) [5].

As described in Section 3, each node in Cassandra issues two main types of read requests: read data from the disk (*local request*) or retrieve data from another node (*remote request*). As part of a remote request, if a different node asks the data to the target node, the target node has to provide them (*remote incoming request*). Depending on the type of request that the node needs to process, the request follows different paths through the model. The different workflows are represented in Figure 2.

Figure 3 describes a single Cassandra node (identified as c1). The node is characterized by three queueing stations representing: network (c1_net), CPU (c1_cpu) and disk (c1_disk). For all the queues the scheduling policy used is non-preemptive first-come first-served (FCFS), with the exception of the CPUs for which processor sharing scheduling is used. To model all the functionalities that each node offers, other elements such as class-switches, a fork-join and a finite capacity region have been added to the model. In particular, class-switches are used to change the class of a request inside the model, the fork-join to manage multiple remote requests and finite capacity region to limit the number of simultaneous requests that the system can handle. This limit is static and set by default to 32 requests in the configuration file of each Cassandra node (parameter: concurrent_reads).

In addition, in order to model different types of requests, six different classes are defined in the model (described in Table 1). The number of classes is related to the number of nodes present in the system. In fact, to maintain information about the origin of a request for each read-remote request, a read-remote-*ID* class for each node is created, where *ID* identifies a Cassandra node.

In our model, the initial requests received by the node from the client can be only local or remote and enter in the node via the network queue (c1_net element in Figure 3). Based on the type of request, different paths may be taken. Such paths are presented in the following sections. We also discuss model parametrization and workload characteristics.

4.1 Local Request

Local requests are queries for which the node stores data locally on the disk. In this case it does not need to contact any other node if the CL is ONE. The left column of Figure 2 shows the main steps for this type of request. The read-local request from the network queue goes directly to the CPU queue through the *c1_initial* class-switch. After it has been served, the request goes through the fork and router, reaching the disk. In the case of CL QUORUM or ALL, the fork generates as many remote requests as needed in order to satisfy the CL. When the disk finishes the execution of the request, it reaches the join (*c1_join*) where it waits until all the remote requests come back from all the other nodes. In case of CL ONE, the join fires the request immediately. Afterwards, the request class is changed in read-local-end inside the class-switch *c1_end* and it is forwarded to the CPU to perform the ends operations before it leaves the node through the network queue and the class-switch *exit*.

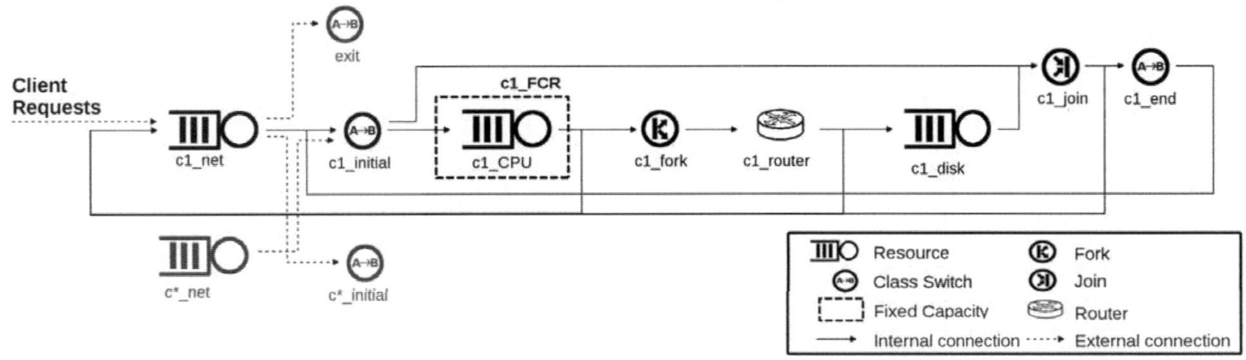

Figure 3: The model representation of a Cassandra node.

#	Class	Description
1	read-local	Local read request
2	read-remote	Remote read request
3	read-remote-*ID*	Remote read request where the *ID* node is acting as proxy
4	read-local-end	Local request that needs to perform the end operations before to return to the client
5	read-remote-end	Remote request that needs to perform the end operations before to return to the client
6	read-remote-return	The returned remote incoming request performed by another node

Table 1: Classes description.

4.2 Remote Incoming Request

Remote Incoming requests (see the central column of Figure 2) are the data that a proxy node retrieves from the target node to complete a query. The data gathering process is defined similarly to local requests. Remote incoming requests enter in the node from the initial class-switch of the node c1. The class request arrived to the node c1 is one of the read-remote-*ID* classes. The request is executed by the CPU. The fork and router forward the request directly to the disk that retrieves the information and sends it to the join. The node network (*c1_net*) takes the request and based on the request class (read-remote-*ID*), forwards it back to the original node (*ID*).

4.3 Remote Request

Remote requests are the requests for which the node does not store the data locally. In this case, the node needs to act as a proxy and issue remote requests towards other nodes to complete it. Requests generated in this scenario are the remote incoming requests received from other nodes. Differently from the local requests, these queries never reach the local disk of the node. After it is served by the network queue, the request reaches the *c1_initial* class-switch in which the request changes class, becoming a read-remote-C1 request, and it continues execution into the CPU. As described in Section 3, this type of requests are characterised by two main CPU operations: parsing and end. When the request hits for the first time the CPU, it executes the parsing phase and after it is sent to the fork. Here, based on the CL applied to the queries, the fork generates as many requests as the CL needs. These requests are forwarded to the router and then redirected to the network queue. Here, the requests are randomly sent to some other nodes of the ring and executed as a remote incoming request by another node.

When the read-remote-C1 requests come back from the remote nodes, they change class in read-remote-return (inside *c1_initial*) and they are forwarded to the join. When all the generated requests come back, the join fires generating a single read-remote-end request that is sent to the CPU via the initial class-switch. Inside the CPU a read-remote-end request is processed to perform the end operations. Finally, the request exits from the node through the network queue (*c1_net*) and is sent back to the client through the *exit* class-switch.

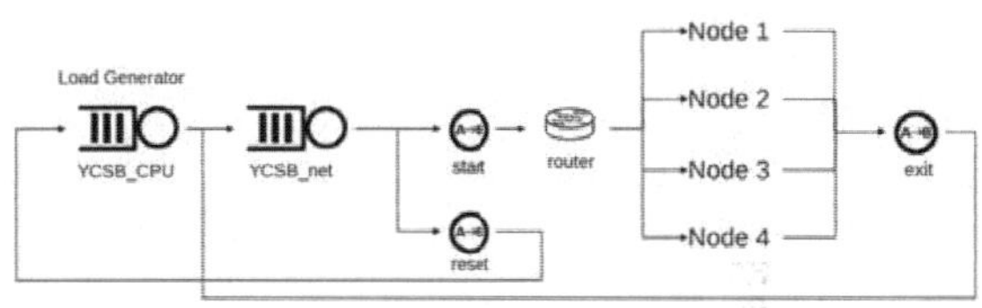

Figure 4: Cassandra model overview at high level of granularity.

4.4 Workload

Another important part of our model is represented by the workload generator. For our experiments, we use the Yahoo! Cloud System Benchmark (YCSB) [9]. The YCSB is a workload generator developed by Yahoo! able to provide different kind of stress-test for various databases. Figure 4 provides an overview of the system, including the YSCB workload generator. In order to approximate better the performance of our model, we have decided to model it with two queues that represents the CPU and the network running the workload generator machine. YCSB CPU queue manages only read-local class requests. The new requests generated by the CPU are sent directly to the *start* class-switch through the network queue. This class-switch changes in read-remote some of the requests, according to the replication factor and CL applied to the system. The proportion of read-remote requests is equal to $(N - RF)/N$. Then, read-local and read-remote requests are forwarded to a router that sends them randomly to the nodes inside the ring.

When the requests have been executed by the node, the network queue of the node sends the response to the *exit* class-switch which

Class	ONE	QUORUM	ALL
read-local	0.8028	0.4078	0.5
read-remote	0.374	0.5712	0.6
read-remote-*ID*	0.6309	0.6423	0.6
read-local-end	0	0.4968	0.5
read-remote-end	0.4994	0.8917	1
read-remote-return	n/a	n/a	n/a

Table 2: CPU demands (in milliseconds) for different classes

Component	Demand value
Network Request	0.01333
Network Data	0.1333
Disk	0.0679
YCSB CPU	0.428

Table 3: Different component demands (in milliseconds).

changes class to read-remote-end. In the end, before being received by the YCSB CPU, the request is sent to the YCSB network and to a class-switch to reset the class in read-local. When the query comes back to YCSB CPU queue, the request is considered completed and a new query is generated by the YCSB workload generator.

4.5 Model Parametrization

To parameterize the model, we need to estimate disk and network capacity and the CPU demands for YCSB and nodes. To gather these information, we set up a Cassandra ring with four nodes and an additional machine for YCSB workload generator. Regarding network latency, two different requests are taken in consideration: query and response. They differ in size of data that they are carrying. We have observed that a normal query size is around 128 bytes. Differently, the response packet is characterized by the size of the data asked. To calculate the network demand, we multiply the packet size with the bandwidth information gathered from the Linux tool iperf [11]. Similarly, we have estimated disk demand using the data size and the Linux tool hdparm [21].

A different approach has been used for the estimation of the time that each class spends inside the CPU (demand). The demand has been calculated using the Complete Information algorithm [26]. To calculate demands, the algorithm requires request timestamps and response times. To gather these information we observed the network traffic exchanged between the nodes and the workload generator (YCSB). Analysing the IP address of different packets, we categorised three types of read requests. For the demand estimation of the different classes we took in consideration the timestamps packets of:

- Local request: the packets arrived from and departed to YCSB IP address.
- Remote incoming request: the packets arrived from and departed to each other node IP address.
- Remote request (parsing phase): from when the packet arrives from YCSB to the last packet departure directed to another node.
- Remote request (end phase): from when the first packet comes back from a node to YCSB response.

In case of local requests with CL QUORUM or ALL, the demand is calculated as a remote request. In the same way, we also estimate CPU demand of YCSB workload generator. The timestamps taken in consideration in this case are, simply, the packets that the server sent to and received from a node. To avoid the simultaneity of multiple requests, all the demand estimation tasks have been taken with a single job in the system. All the demand values estimated are reported in tables 2 and 3.

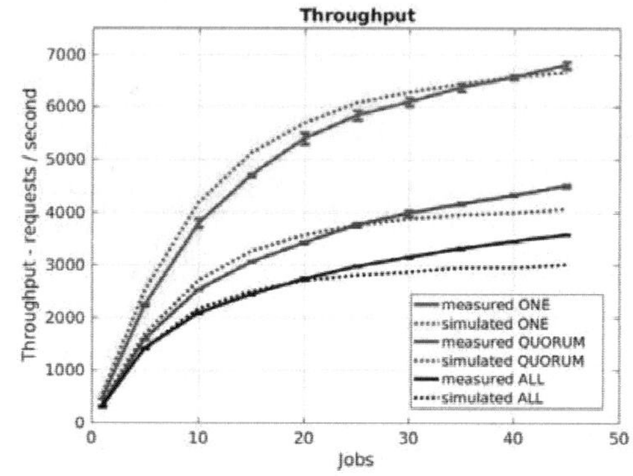

Figure 5: Mean throughput for the Cassandra cluster and our model.

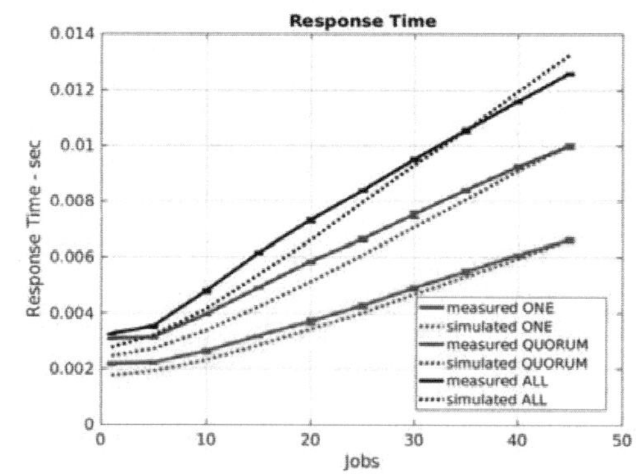

Figure 6: Mean response time for the Cassandra cluster and our model.

5. VALIDATION AND WHAT-IF ANALYSIS

5.1 Experimental Evaluation

To validate our queueing model we set up a Cassandra cluster composed of four nodes with a replication factor of 3. The nodes are installed on a private cloud managed with OpenNebula. The machines used as nodes have 2 CPUs and 4 GBs of memory. Each machine has 2 disks attached: a 20 GBs, where Cassandra commits logs and saved cache files are stored, the second of 100 GBs to store only database data. The operating system is Debian 8 with Sun Java 1.8 and Cassandra version 2.2.4. To avoid interfering with the performance of Cassandra nodes, the workload generator YCSB is installed on a separate virtual machine with 4 CPUs and 4 GBs of memory.

The database is set to equally distribute the key range between all the nodes in the ring. For the workload generator we used the default parameters that come with YCSB. Each row of the database is composed of 10 fields, each filled with 100B of data. The total data size for each record is 1KB, excluding the identification key. The keyspace is filled with 15 million of records. To emulate the

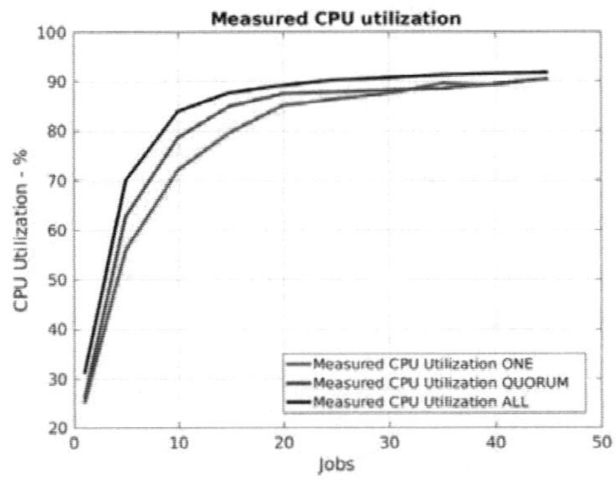

Figure 7: CPU utilisation for a Cassandra node with different Consistency level and clients in the system.

Consistency Level	Average error
ONE	6.79 %
QUORUM	6.41 %
ALL	6.98 %

Table 4: Average throughput relative error with the different consistency levels.

different number of simultaneous clients in the system (also called jobs), the same number of threads are set in YCSB. Each experiment on the real system is repeated three times and it has the duration of 30 minutes, plus 5 minutes of warm-up.

The evaluation compares the throughput and response time of the real system with the results obtained through the simulation of the JMT model. Figure 5 shows the average throughput values recorded by YCSB at the end of the execution of each experiment. The figure also shows the standard deviation values recorded for the same experiment for the data collected from the real system.

Before comparing the result of the two approaches, we can analyse the effects that different CLs have on the real system. Using ONE as CL with 45 jobs in the system, or 45 simultaneous client requests, the system is able to serve around 6800 requests per second. Compared to ONE, the throughput of the system is reduced more than 40% and up to 60% when QUORUM and ALL CL are used. In fact, increasing the CL, the CPU utilisation of each node grows faster like the graph reports in Figure 7. In addition, the response time also changes considerably, increasing linearly the average time that the clients waits for query completion.

Comparing the results obtained from the real system and from our queueing model, it is possible to notice that our model is sensitive to all major changes in the database. As shown in Figure 5, the model is able to approximate with a very small error the throughput of the real system, as the number of jobs and CLs vary. As presented in Table 4, the average throughput relative error is below 7% for all analysed CLs. Using our model, we also estimate the response time of the queries for the same experiments. The results are reported in Figure 6. Even in this case, the model is able to catch with good accuracy the real system performance. The average response time error, as reported in Table 5, is below the 10%.

5.2 Case Study: applicability of our model to other NoSQL databases

As part of our evaluation, we consider the possibility to apply our out-of-the-box model to other NoSQL databases. Due to the similar system architecture and behaviour of the queries execution, we decided to apply the model to ScyllaDB [29].

Consistency Level	Average error
ONE	8.17 %
QUORUM	9.59 %
ALL	7.64 %

Table 5: Average response time relative error with the different consistency levels.

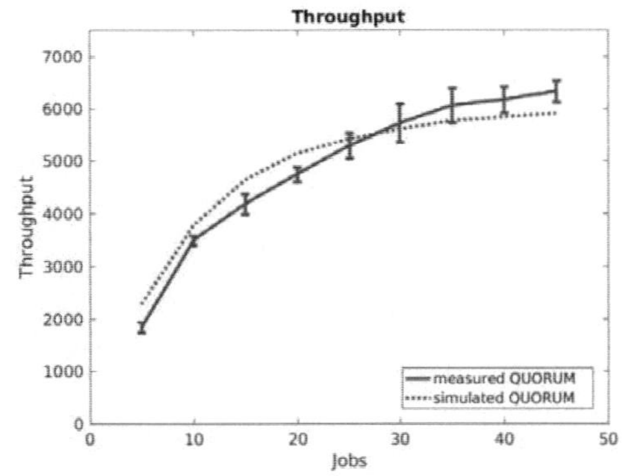

Figure 8: Mean throughput for ScyllaDB cluster and our model.

ScyllaDB is an Apache Cassandra compatible column store database that aims to optimise the performance of each node participating to the database. This increment of performance is obtained using a different programming language (C++) and a complete new software architecture optimised for modern hardware resources. Typically, NoSQL datastores run on a single Java Virtual Machine. To reduce the idle periods generated by the usage of the Garbage Collector, which tend to increase the latency of the system, these applications usually use page cache and complex memory allocation strategies. To avoid these expensive locking mechanisms, ScyllaDB uses an engine for each CPU core of the system, which operates with a low degree of synchronisation. This reflects on the database with a lower usage of the hardware resources and an increment of database performance.

To gather performance data for ScyllaDB, we deploy the same Cassandra configuration used in Section 5.1. The ScyllaDB deployment is composed by four machines, with a replication factor of three and 1KB of data for each record stored. Due to the optimised usage of the recent hardware features, ScyllaDB requires the presence of specific features of the CPU on the VM. For this reason, ScyllaDB VMs are deployed using a different CPU architecture that supports the SSE4.2 CPU flag instructions [16]. To accomplish ScyllaDB requirements, we force the hypervisor to create virtual machines with the Intel Nehalem CPU microarchitecture [15]. The usage of this microarchitecture also brings more benefits to the hardware resources allocated to the VM thanks to a larger bandwidth for the network and disk.

To adapt the model for ScyllaDB, we also need to remove the fixed capacity region set on the CPU because ScyllaDB does not limit the number of simultaneous queries that each node can handle. To parametrize our model, we:

- Estimate the network and disk bandwidth using the Linux tools hdparm and iperf. The two bandwidths have been multi-

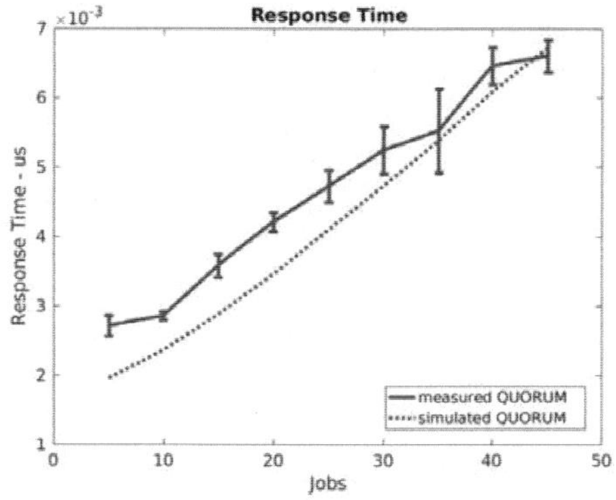

Figure 9: Mean response time for ScyllaDB cluster and our model.

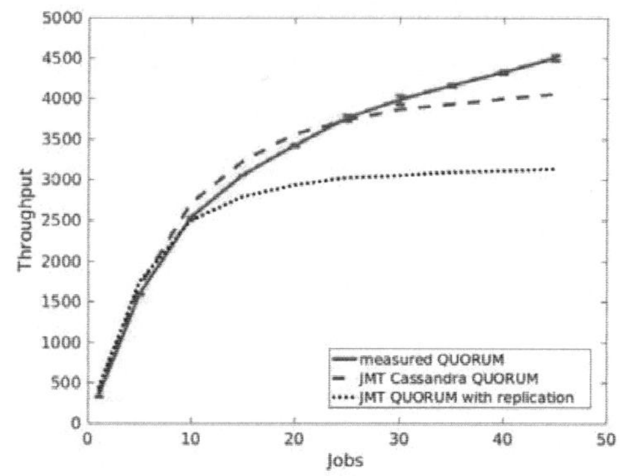

Figure 10: Mean throughput of a Cassandra cluster and the queueing model with Cassandra QUORUM and the real QUORUM.

plied with the average size of the data stored in the database or query network packet size.

- Estimate the YCSB CPU demand analysing the network packet exchanged between the client and a node. We measure the latencies that the client takes to generate a new request when a complete one is received.
- Estimate the node CPU demand for local parsing operations sniffing the network communication of a node. The packets are then analysed to measure the latencies from the instant which a client query arrives to the node to the one in which the node sends the remote incoming request to another machine. This estimation process is the same also for the remote parsing class. These two classes are distinguished by the number of requests that the node generates. The local requests generate one request less than the remote since a copy of the asking data is stored on the local disk of the node.
- Estimate the node CPU demand for local end operations sniffing the network communication of a node. The packets are then analysed to measure the time that a node takes from the instant which the asking data arrives back to the node until when the response to the client is sent. In case of CL ONE the demand for this class is set to zero. The same process is used for the CPU estimation demand of the remote end class.
- Estimate the node CPU demand for remote incoming requests sniffing the network communication of a node. The packets are then analysed to measure the time that a node takes from when a data request comes to the server to when the request is completed and it is sent back to the asking node.

All the CPU demands are calculated with a single job in the system and the collected latencies are processed with the Complete Information algorithm [26] to obtain the final demand for each class. The model is parameterised with the calculated demands for all the classes and, according to the real implementation, the same number of CPU cores are set for each node.

ScyllaDB results, measured and simulated, are shown in the Figures 8 and 9. They represent, respectively, the throughput and the response time of the system. For this case study, only the QUORUM case is taken in consideration. Comparing ScyllaDB with Cassandra QUORUM results, it is possible to observe that ScyllaDB is able to achieve better performance. We observed that, differently from the Cassandra scenario, at high load the workload generator network represents the bottleneck of this set up. The results provided by the simulation tool are close to the measured one and the average relative error is 8% for the throughput and 12.9% for the response time. With this case study, we demonstrate the versatility of our model and the possibility to apply this model to other NoSQL database with minimal adaptations.

5.3 A What-If Scenario: the Impact of Query Replication in Cassandra

We conclude by illustrating an application of the proposed model. Recent research have highlighted the potential advantages of replicating requests in systems in order to consistently achieve low latencies [27]. We here consider a variant of the proposed model to assess the potential impact of query replication on Cassandra.

In the default configuration, when the CL is set to QUORUM, Cassandra generates a fixed number of remote requests. The number of remote requests depends on the RF applied to the database and is equal to $(RF/2)+1$. We now consider a variant of this approach that generates RF requests, but where only the first $(RF/2)+1$ responses needs to be synchronised before completing the query. In this way, the system neither needs to apply any decision on which nodes to send the requests to nor needs to keep track of node performance. Clearly, we expect a trade-off between the enhancement of performance obtained from the higher parallelism and the heightened contention placed on physical resources.

In order to assess this scenario, we have devised an extension of the JMT queueing simulator which allows to synchronise a subset of requests at join nodes. Requests that reach a join after this has completed the synchronization are ignored in the computation of performance metrics. This extension is now integrated in the stable release of JMT version 0.9.3 under the name of *Quorum Join Strategy*. Figure 10 illustrates simulation results. We here compare real Cassandra measurements, with the proposed Cassandra QUORUM mechanism proposed in the previous sections, and the real QUORUM that refers to the replication mechanism. We notice that with a very light load, the throughput under replication is nearly identical to the one without replication. However, at higher loads Cassandra is expected to suffer on average a performance loss compared to the system without replication. This simulation results seem to indicate that increasing replication levels might not be beneficial in a system like Cassandra. While experimental evidence would be needed to corroborate this prediction, this example provides intuition on the ease of performance analysis that comes with the proposed simulation models.

6. CONCLUSION AND FUTURE WORK

In this paper we have proposed a novel queueing network model for the Apache Cassandra database system. Simulation-based analysis shows that our model is able to predict with an error below the 10% the throughput and response time of the system under different consistency levels and number of concurrent requests. The proposed model appears generally more accurate than existing models in the literature that also consider the YCSB benchmark for validation purposes. As part of this paper, we also demonstrate the applicability of our model to another NoSQL database.

As future work, we are planning to evaluate our model with other Cassandra configurations involving a different number of nodes, different data sizes stored in the database and different replication factors. In addition, we are considering to analyse the extended queueing network, possibly LQNs, in order to progress from a simulation model to an analytic evaluation based on mean value analysis algorithms. This would allow computationally-efficient analysis, compatible with usage in nonlinear optimisation programs, which are commonly used for capacity planning under performance and reliability guarantees.

7. REFERENCES

[1] E. Anderson, X. Li, and M. Shah. What consistency does your key-value store actually provide. *Proceedings of the Sixth international conference on Hot topics in system dependability. USENIX Association*, pages 1–16, 2010.

[2] M. Bar-Sinai. Big Data Technology Literature Review. *Proceedings of the twenty-ninth annual ACM symposium on Theory of computing - STOC '97*, 2013(April 2013):654–663, jun 2015.

[3] F. Bause. Queueing Petri Nets-A formalism for the combined qualitative and quantitative analysis of systems. In *Proceedings of 5th International Workshop on Petri Nets and Performance Models*, number class 1, pages 14–23. IEEE Comput. Soc. Press, 1993.

[4] D. Bermbach and S. Tai. Eventual consistency. In *Proceedings of the 6th Workshop on Middleware for Service Oriented Computing - MW4SOC '11*, number May, pages 1–6, New York, New York, USA, 2011. ACM Press.

[5] M. Bertoli, G. Casale, and G. Serazzi. Jmt: performance engineering tools for system modeling. *SIGMETRICS Perform. Eval. Rev.*, 36(4):10–15, 2009.

[6] R. Cattell. Scalable SQL and NoSQL data stores. *ACM SIGMOD Record*, 39(4):12, 2011.

[7] A. Chebotko, A. Kashlev, and S. Lu. A Big Data Modeling Methodology for Apache Cassandra. *2015 IEEE International Congress on Big Data*, pages 238–245, 2015.

[8] H.-e. Chihoub, S. Ibrahim, G. Antoniu, and M. S. Perez. Harmony: Towards Automated Self-Adaptive Consistency in Cloud Storage. In *2012 IEEE International Conference on Cluster Computing*, volume 2012, pages 293–301. IEEE, sep 2012.

[9] B. F. Cooper, A. Silberstein, E. Tam, R. Ramakrishnan, and R. Sears. Benchmarking cloud serving systems with YCSB. In *Proceedings of the 1st ACM symposium on Cloud computing - SoCC '10*, page 143, New York, New York, USA, 2010. ACM Press.

[10] Datastax. Cassandra documentation, jun 2016.

[11] ESnet. Iperf, jun 2016.

[12] G. Franks, T. Al-Omari, M. Woodside, O. Das, and S. Derisavi. Enhanced Modeling and Solution of Layered Queueing Networks. *IEEE Transactions on Software Engineering*, 35(2):148–161, mar 2009.

[13] A. Gandini, M. Gribaudo, W. J. Knottenbelt, R. Osman, and P. Piazzolla. Performance Evaluation of NoSQL Databases. In *Computer Performance Engineering*, pages 16–29. 2014.

[14] P. Garefalakis, P. Papadopoulos, and K. Magoutis. ACaZoo: A Distributed Key-Value Store Based on Replicated LSM-Trees. In *2014 IEEE 33rd International Symposium on Reliable Distributed Systems*, pages 211–220. IEEE, oct 2014.

[15] Intel. Intel next generation microarchitecture (nehalem), jun 2016.

[16] Intel. Intel sse4 programming reference, jun 2016.

[17] S. D. Kuznetsov and A. V. Poskonin. NoSQL data management systems. *Programming and Computer Software*, 40(6):323–332, nov 2014.

[18] A. Labrinidis and H. V. Jagadish. Challenges and opportunities with big data. *Proceedings of the VLDB Endowment*, 5(12):2032–2033, 2012.

[19] A. Lakshman and P. Malik. Cassandra: A Decentralized Structured Storage System. *ACM SIGOPS Operating Systems Review*, 44(2):35, apr 2010.

[20] E. D. Lazowska, J. Zahorjan, G. S. Graham, and K. C. Sevcik. *Quantitative System Performance: Computer System Analysis Using Queueing Network Models*. Prentice-Hall, Inc., Upper Saddle River, NJ, USA, 1984.

[21] M. Lord. hdparm, jun 2016.

[22] J. R. Lourenço, V. Abramova, M. Vieira, B. Cabral, and J. Bernardino. NoSQL Databases: A Software Engineering Perspective. In A. Rocha, A. M. Correia, S. Costanzo, and L. P. Reis, editors, *Advances in Intelligent Systems and Computing*, volume 353 of *Advances in Intelligent Systems and Computing*, pages 741–750. Springer International Publishing, Cham, 2015.

[23] R. Niemann. Towards the Prediction of the Performance and Energy Efficiency of Distributed Data Management Systems. In *Companion Publication for ACM/SPEC on International Conference on Performance Engineering - ICPE '16 Companion*, pages 23–28, New York, New York, USA, 2016. ACM Press.

[24] R. Osman and W. J. Knottenbelt. Database system performance evaluation models: A survey. *Performance Evaluation*, 69(10):471–493, 2012.

[25] R. Osman and P. Piazzolla. Modelling Replication in NoSQL Datastores. In *Quantitative Evaluation of Systems*, pages 194–209. Springer International Publishing, 2014.

[26] J. F. Perez, S. Pacheco-Sanchez, and G. Casale. An Offline Demand Estimation Method for Multi-threaded Applications. In *2013 IEEE 21st International Symposium on Modelling, Analysis and Simulation of Computer and Telecommunication Systems*, pages 21–30. IEEE, aug 2013.

[27] Z. Qiu and J. F. Pérez. Evaluating the effectiveness of replication for tail-tolerance. In *CCGrid*, pages 443–452. IEEE Computer Society, 2015.

[28] H. Wada, A. Fekete, L. Zhao, K. Lee, and A. Liu. Data Consistency Properties and the Trade-offs in Commercial Cloud Storage: the Consumers' Perspective. *Cidr*, pages 134–143, 2011.

[29] XLAB. Scylladb, jul 2016.

Automating the Deployment of Multi-Cloud Applications in Federated Cloud Environments

Alfonso Panarello
DICIEAMA, University of Messina
Messina, Italy
apanarello@unime.it

Uwe Breitenbücher
IAAS, University of Stuttgart
Stuttgart, Germany
breitenbuecher@iaas.uni-stuttgart.de

Frank Leymann
IAAS, University of Stuttgart
Stuttgart, Germany
leymann@iaas.uni-stuttgart.de

Antonio Puliafito
DICIEAMA, University of Messina
Messina, Italy
apuliafito@unime.it

Michael Zimmermann
IAAS, University of Stuttgart
Stuttgart, Germany
zimmermann@iaas.uni-stuttgart.de

ABSTRACT

Cloud federation allows cloud providers to dynamically use resources of other federated providers in order to fulfil the requirements of customer requests. This concept enables the federated cloud providers to use external resources for increasing their profit as they do not have to reject customers in case their own resources are occupied. However, (i) comparing the offers of the federated providers in order to decide which provider to use as well as (ii) adapting the installation scripts of the components to be deployed for the different providers is complex, error-prone, and time consuming. In this paper, we present an approach that enables customers to describe their desired application deployments in the form of a topology model that is independent of any concrete provider. We show how this model can be automatically adapted by a provider participating in a cloud federation to deploy components on different other participants. To ensure the practical feasibility of the approach, we employ the TOSCA standard for describing these models and present a technical system architecture based on existing technologies.

Keywords

Cloud Federation; Federated Multi-Cloud Deployment; Deployment Automation; TOSCA; XMPP

1. INTRODUCTION

The cloud federation concept finds its own roots in the political field and refers to a political organization where several self-governing participants are coordinated by a central government but, at the same time, keeping their independence from it. Adopting this organizational model in the field of IT, we define a cloud federation as a scenario where different clouds, belonging to independent administrative domains, interact with each other in order to share their available resources. Thus, providers participating in such a cloud federation play both roles the *user* and the *Cloud Resource Provider (CRP)* at the same time. In such scenarios, a CRP makes its own unused resources available to other CRPs which need external assets in order to be able to fulfil their users' requests. Cloud federation offers two main benefits to CRPs. First, it allows providers to earn revenue from computing resources that would otherwise be underutilized or unused. Second, cloud federation enables CRPs to virtually expand their offerings making them able to face sudden spikes in demand without having to invest money in new hardware resources. However, the interaction and cooperation among the participating providers is a complex challenge due to (i) different cloud management systems employed by the providers, (ii) proprietary metamodels used for describing application deployments, and (iii) the missing combination of standards to coordinate the available cloud resources and the actual federated application deployment.

In this paper, we propose an automated approach for deploying federated cloud applications across multiple providers based on standards. We introduce an architecture for a *Coordinated Application Deployment System* and show how the deployment of an application consisting of multiple components can be coordinated across multiple providers belonging to the same federation by automatically adapting the deployment model. We validate the practical feasibility of this system based on three technologies: (i) an XMPP server [30], which manages the communication between CRPs, (ii) a pluggable Message Oriented Middleware (MOM), which is XMPP-compliant and able to manage the CRPs' cloud technologies [28][9] and (iii) the TOSCA standard [20], which enables describing deployments in a portable way.

The paper is organized as follows: Section II describes a motivating scenario used throughout this paper and explains fundamentals. Our automated deployment approach and system architecture is presented in the section III. Section IV and V validate the approach by a technical system architecture while Section VI describes related work. Section VII concludes the paper and discusses planned future work.

VALUETOOLS 2016, October 25-28, Taormina, Italy

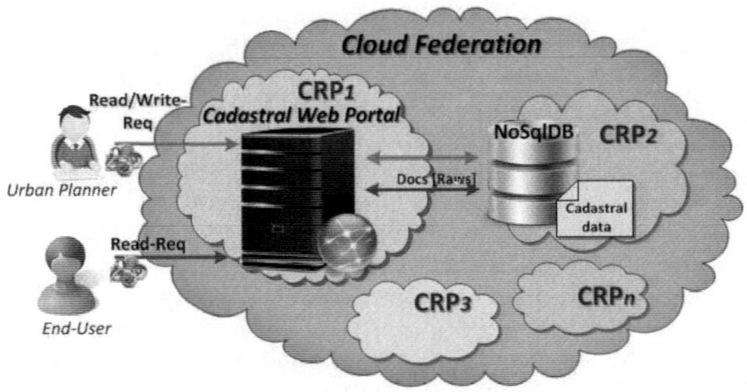

Figure 1: Federated Multi-Cloud Cadastral Web Application

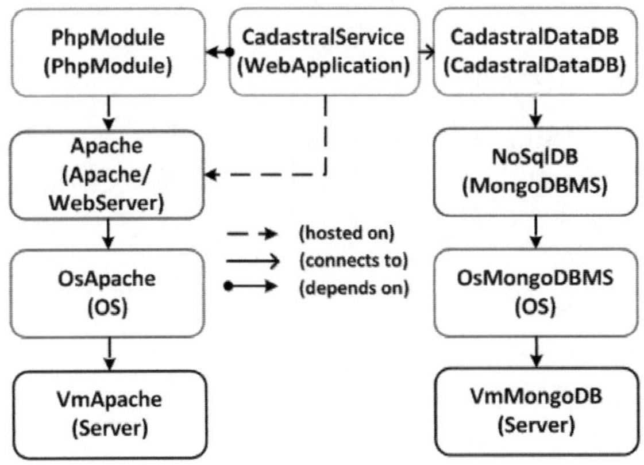

Figure 2: Cadastral Web Application Topology Template

2. MOTIVATION & FUNDAMENTALS

In this section, we introduce a motivating scenario that is used to explain the presented approach. Afterwards, we introduce the TOSCA standard to provide the background required for understanding the concepts of this paper.

2.1 Motivating Scenario

In this subsection, we first describe a motivating scenario that is used to explain the presented concepts. Figure 1 depicts a web application, made available by the public administration, providing "Cadastral Servicies" to citizens. This application enables users to access the cadastral archives containing documents like maps, legal documents, data of real estates' owners, economic rents to calculate the taxes, and so on. The typical users of the system are basically (i) the *end user* and (ii) the *urban planner*. The former assesses the system only in read-mode, while the urban planner has got both read and write permissions. The application consists of two main application blocks: a web portal acting as user interface between the client and the application logic, and a NoSQL-based DB for collecting all the cadastral and user data. The choice to use a NoSQL database is motivated by the kind of data has to be collected: maps, documents, geographic coordinates, and other kind of related meta-data. Our goal is to realize the automated deployment of the application's components across several cloud providers participating in the same federation at runtime, i. e., when a *Public Administration (PA)* asks one CRP to deploy and to set up this an application. The resulting scenario is shown in Fig. 1, where the two mentioned blocks are deployed on two different Cloud Resource Providers, namely CRP_1 and CRP_2 .

In order to be able to automate this kind of deployment, in this paper, we will take advantages of the application modelling and orchestration features provided by the OASIS standard TOSCA. To provide all required background information about TOSCA, we explain the standard in the next Subsection 2.2. However, since TOSCA does not provide cloud federation management capabilities natively, we will exploit two other technologies to manage the federated communications between the involved CRPs: (i) the *XMPP* protocol for message exchanging and (ii) an additional abstraction layer made on top of a Message Oriented Middleware (MOM), which is able to maintain the federation and to drive the underlying piece of middleware of each CRP. These technologies will be deeply discussed in Section 4.

2.2 The TOSCA Standard

The Topology and Orchestration Specification for Cloud Applications (TOSCA) [20, 19, 5] is an official OASIS standard. The main goals of the standard are to describe cloud-applications in an interoperable and portable manner in order to enable automating their deployment and management. TOSCA enables cloud users to model the structure of an application to be deployed using a *topology model.* Applications can be deployed based on these models by a *TOSCA Runtime Environment*, e. g., OpenTOSCA [6]. To automate management functionalities, for example, to scale out an application component, TOSCA employs the concept of *management plans*, which are executable process models, e. g., workflows, implementing a certain management functionality.

Based on these two concepts, TOSCA enables the automated provisioning and management of cloud-applications. TOSCA topology models are modelled in the form of a *topology template* (see Figure 2), which is a directed graph consisting of *node templates* representing the components (e. g., an Apache HTTP Server) and infrastructure resources (e.g. a virtual machine). These nodes are connected through directed edges, called *relationship templates*, which represent the dependencies between the nodes. For example, a relationship template may model that a PHP Web Application is *hosted on* an Apache HTTP Server and needs to be *connected to* a MongoDB database. TOSCA also enables modelling *node types* and *relationship types*, which define the semantics of the node and relationship templates. These type definitions are reusable building blocks specifying properties (e.g. the IP address) and management operations (e.g. "install the component"). These management operations are implemented using so called *implementation artifacts*, which are executable programs such as scripts. The business logic of the nodes themselves are implemented using *deployment artifacts*, which are implementations of the component—for example, a deployment artifact could be an archive containing the PHP files of the application to be deployed.

The standard also specifies the portable and self-contained *Cloud Service ARchive* (CSAR), which enables packaging all the aforementioned management plans, topology models, type definitions, and artifacts. As a result, CSARs can be automatically processed by any standard-compliant TOSCA Runtime Environment to deploy the described application.

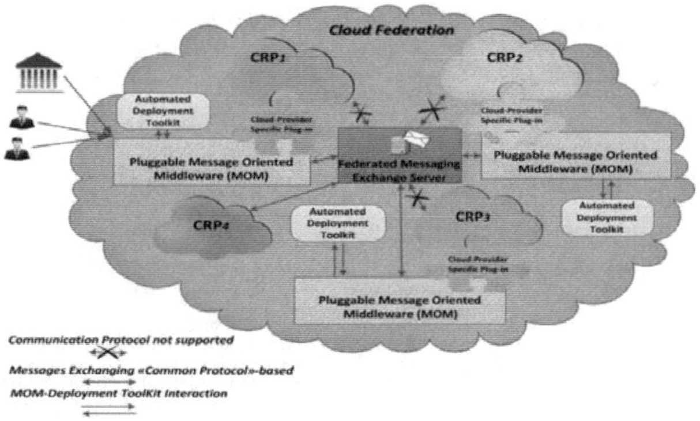

Figure 3: Conceptual Architecture of CADS

3. A CONCEPTUAL ARCHITECTURE FOR FEDERATED CLOUD DEPLOYMENT

In the perspective of deploying multiple application components in a federated cloud environment, this section presents the first contribution of this paper in the form of an approach for coordinating and automating the deployment of components across multiple cloud providers participating in a cloud federation based on a single deployment model. We (i) first describe the conceptual architecture of a *Coordinated Application Deployment System (CADS)* in Section 3.1, followed by concepts for (ii) decision making, and (iii) deployment model completion in Section 3.2 and Section 3.3.

3.1 Overall CADS Architecture

Figure 3 shows a conceptual, high-level architecture of the proposed system. The depicted system aims for managing the multi-component application deployment over multiple federated clouds by splitting the application in different components and placing them on (possibly) different CRPs. The main actors of the system are explained in the following. (i) The *end-user* sends an application deployment request to one CRP participating in the federation where the user has a valid account. This request (a) either refers to an application offered by the provider using an unique application ID or (b) contains a complete deployment model describing the application that shall be deployed, for example, a TOSCA CSAR (see Section 4). In this paper, we focus on the latter scenario. Moreover, (ii) several *CRPs* taking part in the same federation and offering their available resources to end-users and other CRPs represent the second class of actors. (iii) Another actor is introduced by *Message Oriented Middlewares (MOM)* enabling the federation establishment, maintenance, and the communication among the CRPs, for example, to ask for available resources. Each CRP may be connected directly or through such a MOM to a (iv) *Federated Messaging Exchange Server*, which is the central core of the communication mechanism, through which all the messages exchanged by CRPs to coordinate the federated application deployment flow. Each CRP hosts an (vii) *application deployment toolkit*, which is responsible for receiving the deployment requests from the end-user. The toolkit then first decides which components of the received deployment model can be hosted directly by the respective CRP itself and which components shall be hosted on other CRPs of the federation by using the communication mechanism described above. Therefore, the toolkit sends out broadcast requests via the MOM and the exchange server to the federated CRPs that respond with their capabilities, i. e., the resources they are able to offer. After receiving these offers, the toolkit selects the CRPs that fit best for hosting the components and executes the deployment on them.

As shown in Figure 3, we can count four CRPs in the depicted scenario namely CRP_1, CRP_2, CRP_3 and CRP_4. The first three providers do not directly have support for the central communication mechanism, so in order to take part in the federation, they *must* set up and configure the MOM, whereas CRP_4 is natively compliant with that communication mechanism, so it can join the federation without an own MOM. Anyway, in order to handle the runtime application deployment, CRP_4 has to implement its own business intelligence controlling local component deployments requested by a federated provider. In the figure, missing support of the communication mechanism is highlighted by the red-crossed-arrows. The deployment toolkit is the entity in charge to perform the application component deployment.

In a dynamic environment like a cloud federation where CRPs can join and leave whenever they want, each CRP needs to know how many and which CRPs are present within the federation at a given time. For this reason, the communication mechanism is based on the presence concept. In other words, in order to be easily identified and to identify, each available CRP has to provide a software agent that can access to a specific shared location. By exploiting this kind of communication mechanism, CRPs can retrieve (in addition to the presence information) the available resources of the other CRPs participating in the federation.

3.2 Discovery Phase and Decision-Making

According to the previous sections, our goal is to set up an environment which is able to accomplish the automated multi-component application deployment over multiple federated cloud providers. To achieve this goal, we need a software entity that takes as input the desired application deployment model (e. g., a topology model) as well as information about the participating CRPs' resource offerings in order to give as output the deployment choices, namely *where* (on which CRP) the application's components have to be deployed on. However, we are not discussing selection algorithms because this is out of the scope of this paper. Anyway, there are many works in the literature facing this topic in different ways. For example, [10] and [32] propose two similar match-making-based approaches, whereas [17], [24], and [31] propose different mathematical solutions. In this paper, we instead focus on the information retrieval concerning the availability of the CRPs' resources. Because our system adopts a decentralized solution, a CRP, in order to find the other CRPs' resources, needs to broadcast to each of them discovery messages. We call this message broadcasting process and the related response messages *discovery phase*. These information exchanges are performed by the MOMs and the central exchange server that, by means of the presence-based communication mechanism, will query all the other present CRPs retrieving their detailed resource information including the amount of available resources. For the sake of simplicity, we focus on virtual machine resources (VMs), VM types (amount of CPUs, memory, storage), and their price in this paper. However, the presented approach and the following details can be easily applied to other *as a Service* offerings, too, e. g., PaaS offerings. These information about the CRPs will be used as input for the decision-making process. Then, after the system decided on which CRPs the application components shall be deployed, these results are sent to the automated deployment toolkit for the final *deployment phase.* In this phase, the original deployment request or the deployment model sent by the end-user (cf. Section 3.1) gets adapted for the chosen deployment decisions. For example, in case an end-user requested the deployment of an application consisting of several virtual machines described by a topology model, based on the selected CRPs, this model gets automatically adapted by the toolkit in terms of inserting the selected CRP nodes below the virtual machines. In particular, if the topology model depicted in Figure 1 was initially requested by the end-user, the system selects appropriate CRPs for hosting the two servers as virtual machines and inserts the respective nodes that describe these CRPs. Then, the resulting model gets automatically deployed on these CRPs. Based on this adaptation, the application's components get distributed over different cloud providers participating in the federation. This step consists of exploiting the selected CRPs' information to complete the final deployment model and gets explained in the next subsection.

3.3 Deployment Phase and Model Completion

After the CRPs to be employed are selected and which component stack of the application should be deployed to which CRP, the original deployment model needs to be adapted accordingly. There are works, for example the approaches presented by Hirmer et al. [12], for automatically completing incomplete deployment models. However, the available approaches lack support for choosing a specific CRP of a cloud federation based on requirements such as available computing resources or memory — moreover, many available approaches are not based on standards. Therefore, we introduce a software component called *Deployment Model Completion Manager*, which is able to adapt the stacks modelled in a deployment model to specific CRPs. As input, this component gets (i) the deployment model to be adapted as well as (ii) the decisions made by the decision making component described in Section 3.2. Afterwards, for every stack to be deployed, the Deployment Model Completion Manager adds the corresponding infrastructure node defined for the specific selected CRP. This requires a *CRP Registry* containing a list of CRPs and the required information to deploy software on this CRP, for example, information about the employed infrastructure for instantiating new virtual machines, e. g., OpenStack, and the required credentials. Therefore, each CRP maintains such a registry that is based on contracts between the CRPs. Thus, if a new CRP enters the cloud federation, its specific properties need to be added to the registries of participating CRPs, which is typically a manual process based on contracts. Using this information, properties of the infrastructure nodes, for example, credentials and desired ports, which are CRP-specific, are added automatically by the Deployment Model Completion Manager. After this step, the resulting model gets automatically deployed on the modelled CRPs using an appropriate runtime, which accesses the APIs of the involved CRPs to deploy the respective components remotely. In the following section, we explain these steps in detail based on standards.

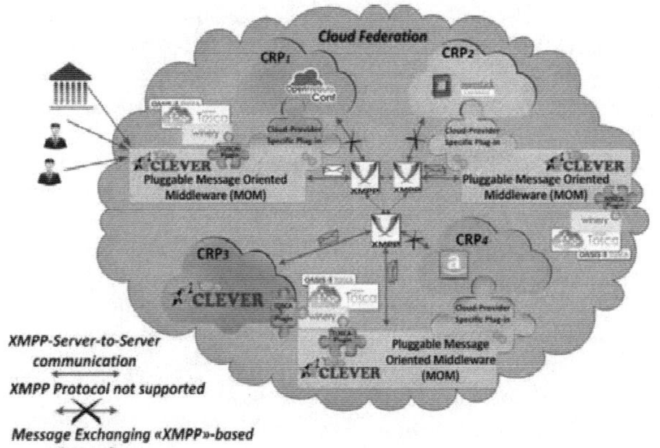

Figure 4: Technical Realization of the CADS Architecture

4. VALIDATION OF THE CADS APPROACH

In this section, we refine the conceptually described CADS approach presented in the previous section based on concrete standards and technologies. In Section 4.1, we first refine the presented CADS architecture and describe in Section 4.2 how the TOSCA standard can be employed to automate deploying application components on different federated providers.

4.1 Standards-based CADS Architecture

Section 3.1 showed an overview of the conceptual CADS architecture. Based on that abstract system presentation, this section presents a validation based on standards and existing technologies. Figure 4 shows a detailed version of the architecture previously seen in Figure 3. Substantially, we replaced the conceptual entities with concrete technologies we identified as best solutions to achieve our goal.

The first refined entity is the end-user asking for the deployment of an application. In this refinement, we focus on the scenario in which the end-user sends a deployment model to be provisioned to a CRP. As we have several CRPs participating in the federation, each of them has its own hardware asset and provides virtualization middleware such as OpenStack. As mentioned earlier, we focus on VMs but the architecture can be easily adapted for other aaS-offerings, too. Another important system's entity is an open source communication protocol exploited by the federated CRPs to exchange all the communication needed to manage the federation. Such a protocol should be based on the presence concept (cf. Section 3.1). In this domain, the *Instant Messaging and Presence Service (IMPS)*[1], the *Session Initiation Protocol (SIP)* and its derivative *SIP for Instant Messaging and Presence Leveraging Extensions (SIMPLE)*[2], as well as the *Extensible Messaging and Presence Protocol (XMPP)* [30] are the most important protocols. We chose XMPP due to its extensible paradigm, its decentralized architecture, its flexibility, and high-level of re-activeness. To exploit the XMPP protocol, there is the need to set up a Jabber/XMPP server (or more) providing basic messaging and XML routing features within the federation. It is possible to have more than one XMPP server, as it can be seen in Figure 4.

[1] http://www.ietf.org/rfc/rfc2778.txt/

[2] https://datatracker.ietf.org/wg/simple/charter/

However, typically not all CRPs are natively XMPP-compliant. Therefore, in order to join the federation, each of them needs to exploit the features of an additional abstraction layer namely a Message Oriented Middleware (MOM) that supports XMPP. Our choice is the *CLoud-Enabled-Virtual-EnviRonment (CLEVER)* [9], which is a secure Message-Oriented Middleware for cloud federation. Our choice is validated by three main reasons: (i) the CLEVER's inherent XMPP-based communication, (ii) its pluggable and (iii) federation management features. These features, therefore, make the CLEVER middleware suitable to manage both the federated communication and the underlying cloud platform. Moreover, in our federated scenario, we can directly have a CLEVER-based CRP (CRP_3 in Figure 4). Once the CLEVER-MOM of a specific CRP receives a deployment application request (including a deployment model), it first analyses the request to figure out how many resources that application needs, and afterwards triggers the "discovery phase". In particular, it sends discovery messages to the other CRPs to retrieve the federated resources' availability and the related information (via response messages). This will take place merely querying the *shared location* on which it is published. More specifically, in an XMPP-based environment, the shared location consists of a specific *XMPP chat-room* where the cloud providers taking part in the federation have to hold a software agent's subscription. The above mentioned messages are XML-based messages. Figure 5 shows a possible structure of these query messages:

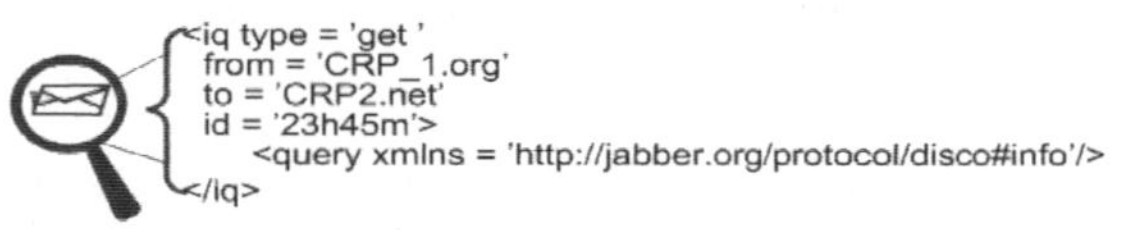

Figure 5: Simplified XMPP Query Message

Figure 6 shows a possible response of a CRP.

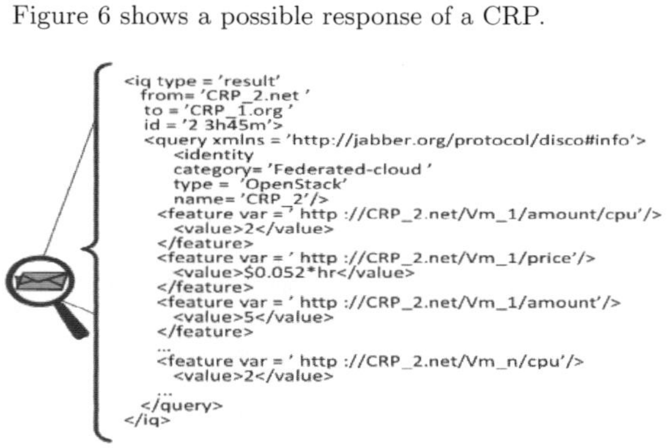

Figure 6: Simplified XMPP Result Message

In order to retrieve information about the CRPs' resource state, the requesting cloud provider sends and XMPP *IQ* stanza of type `get` containing an empty <query/> element qualified by the `http://jabber.org/protocol/disco#info` name-space to all other providers present in the federation room. Each CRP receiving the query message will respond sending an XMPP *IQ* stanza of type `result`, which contains one or more <identity/> elements including static informa-

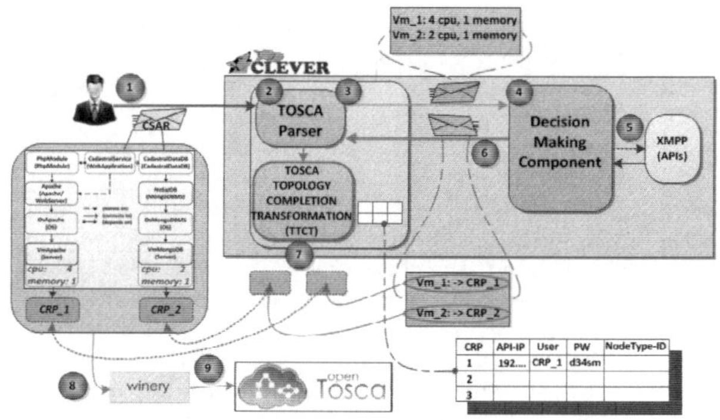

Figure 7: Federated Topology Completion Process

tion and a potentially unbounded number of <feature/> elements describing resource availability information (e. g., number of available VMs at a given moment for a specific type, VMs' properties, VM's price, etc.). This information will be elaborated by the decision-making software component to find out the best deployment solution.

To realize the automated deployment of federated cloud applications, the TOSCA standard is employed. Therefore, a Java-based plugin component is integrated into CLEVER providing a *TOSCA Topology Template Parser* and a *TOSCA Topology Completion Manager (TTCM)*, which implements the concept of the Deployment Model Completion Manager for TOSCA (cf. Section 3.3). The parser is responsible for analysing TOSCA Topology Models requested for deployment by the end-user. Afterwards, CLEVER uses the discovered information to utilize the TTCM for inserting corresponding node and relationship templates for injecting the selected CRPs into the topology template. For automating the actual deployment of the resulting model, a TOSCA Runtime Environment is employed. In our realization, we employ the *OpenTOSCA Runtime Environment* [6][29] as a deployment toolkit, which is a standard-compliant, open-source implementation of a TOSCA Runtime. These two entities work together to accomplish the final topology completion and application deployment. The topology completion process will be discussed in detail in the next subsection.

4.2 TOSCA Topology Completion

In this section, we describe how the Deployment Model Completion Manager can be realized using TOSCA. Figure 7 shows CLEVER's internal components as well as the necessary external tools to achieve the federated application deployment based on TOSCA. The Java-based TOSCA plugin is composed by (i) the TOSCA Topology Parser, (ii) the TOSCA Topology Completion Manager and (iii) the *Decision-Making component.* The process starts (step 1) with the user's deployment request submission. It consists in sending a CSAR containing the incomplete topology template (VMs are modelled but without CRPs). The submitted topology model is the same as the one shown in Figure 2, but now decorated with additional resource requirements. At step 2, the parser gets the CSAR and analyses the topology to figure out how many resources (VMs, CPUs, memory) the application to be deployed needs. At step 3, the parser composes an XML-based message with the above informa-

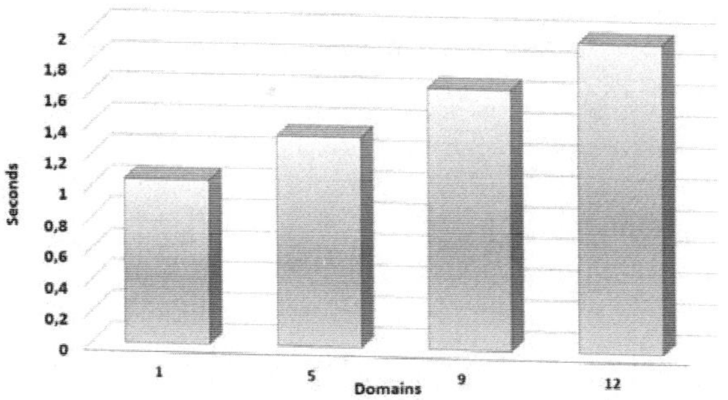

Figure 8: Retrieving Availability Resource Information

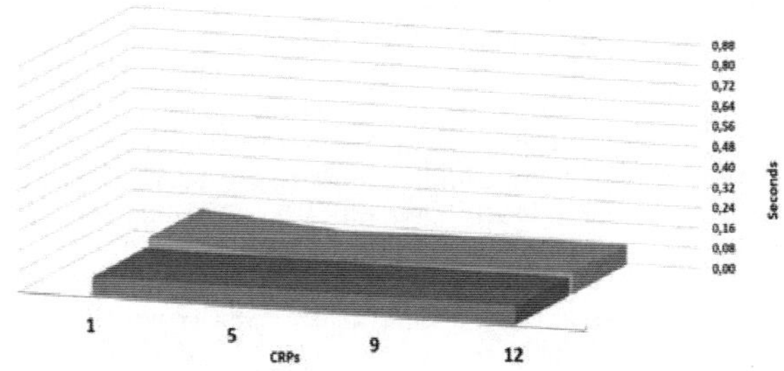

Average Time (s)	0,074			
CRPs	1	5	9	12
Forward Time (s)	0,10745	0,060951299	0,073818345	0,081233154
Conf Interval (98%)(s)	0,00282097	0,00215871	0,001922828	0,002362203

Figure 9: CRP-to-CRP message delivery time

tion and then sends it to the Decision-Making component (step 4). In order to retrieve the federated CRPs' resource offerings, it invokes the XMPP APIs (step 5), thus, triggering the Discovery-Phase. After receiving the federated offerings, the Decision-Making component selects the CRPs which better meet the application components' requirements. Then at step 6, it sends a response XML-message to the parser containing information about the selected CRPs to host the requested VMs. This information is forwarded to the TOSCA Topology Completion Manager, that (step 7) adds the node templates corresponding to the made decision as well as required properties to the incomplete topology model. Therefore, the manager also contains the registry described in Section 3.3, which contains all CRPs involved in the federation and the associated properties as well as the id of the corresponding node template of each CRP. The completed topology template is then sent (step 8) to Winery [16]. Primarily, Winery is a modelling tool supporting the modelling of topologies based on the TOSCA standard. But besides that, Winery also has a repository containing TOSCA related artifacts like implementation artifacts. Therefore, Winery is able to fetch further required artifacts such as the implementation artifacts belonging to the previously added node templates and packages them into a final CSAR. This CSAR now contains a complete topology model and all artifacts required for executing the deployment. Therefore, it can be deployed fully automatically (step 9) using an appropriate standard-compliant TOSCA Runtime Environment.

5. EVALUATION

This Section focuses on several experiments that we carried out on a real test-bed taking in consideration thirteen different CLEVER-based CRPs. With this section, we want to demonstrate that the addition of domains to the federation does not negatively affect the whole application deployment process. We arranged the test-bed considering federation composed of 13 CRPs. Twelve of them act as lender CRPs and only one instead acts as applicant. We assume that the applicant does not have enough resources to fulfil the user's request. These experiments have been conducted with the following hardware configuration: CPU: AMD Opteron 2218 HE Santa Rosa Dual-Core 2.6GHz ; 8GB RAM, running Linux Ubuntu 12.04 x86 64 OS and VirtualBox. Each trial was repeated for 30 times and finally the mean value and confidence intervals were evaluated. Our interest falls on the XMPP-Communication times, specifically we analysed the time to obtain the resource availability from the federated CRPs and the effective time needed to a XMPP-message to go from a CRP to another one. In particular, Figure 8 shows the delay experienced by a CRP when asking for external resources to obtain availability information from all the federated CRPs. We can see how the delay (due to the discovery phase) increases almost linearly when the number of CRPs grows. This behaviour is due to the fact that the discovery algorithm adopts multi-threaded programming. Thus, the software creates a new thread per each CRP that has to be queried. However, such a delay is of only 1 second per each twelve additional CRPs. In fact, Figure 9 shows that the point-to-point message delivery time remains constant, very small, and *negligible* (roughly $74ms$), regardless of the number of CRPs present within the federation. The differences among the obtained values are very small and have an order of magnitude of ms, therefore, they are comparable with network delays. For this reason, it is hard to figure out and argue the trend of the $ForwardTime$. Surely it does not depend on the number of CRPs within the federation.

6. RELATED WORK

This section highlights the main published works concerning the cloud federation, multi-cloud and application deployment topics and approaches similar to ours.

Jung et al. in [14] present an OpenStack-based scheduler able to deploy an application topology over a cluster optimizing the resources utilization of the data center so called *Ostro*. *Ostro*, taking as input the application topology to be deployed and considering the data center's available resources information, gives as output the best VMs placement that better meets the application requirements. This paper anyway does not face the placement across multi cloud providers. In [22], the authors introduce *STRATOS* as a brokering service able to take deployment decisions of cloud application topologies among multiple cloud providers. The STRATOS "Cloud Manager" node receives the application topology description and contacts the *Broker* asking for an instantiation of that topology. Loulloudes et al. [18] and Papaioannou et al. [21] presented two novel frameworks supporting both the TOSCA-based application orchestration. The first one makes easy the cloud application life-cycle management through Simple-Yet-Beautiful Language (SYBL) "*SYBL*" which is a language to specify in detail elasticity monitoring, constraints, and strategies at different cloud application levels. The second architecture system instead aims to capture and store into its internal meta-data repository important application information, such as application descriptions and requirements, cloud providers' characteristics in order to achieve the multi-cloud deployment of complex multi-tier applications. The approach of Antoniades et al. [2] is closely linked to Loulloudes et al. [18] being based on "*CAMF*", too. The main contribution of the paper is to enhance the *TOSCA*-based application description by adding extra user requirements through a novel language called *CARL* (Cloud Application Requirement Language). In [11] Ferry et al. presented their own solution so called *CloudML* (Cloud Modelling Language) which supports matchmaking between deployment requirements and infrastructure descriptions. This solution wants to facilitate the application provisioning, deployment, monitoring, and adaptation in a multi clouds system. CloudML does not support Multi-Cloud provisioning: a single application cannot be spread across multiple providers. In Carrasco et al. [13], Brogi et al. [8], and [4] the authors presented a TOSCA-CAMP-based approach for managing and deploying applications over different and independent cloud providers. The works couple TOSCA's and CAMP's features and their respective approaches to exploit the benefits of both standards. Specifically, in Brogi et al. [8], the authors present *SeaClouds* and implemented an extension of TOSCA by defining a new element "*location*" into the node template enriching it with information about the target providers where each component has to be deployed. SeaClouds works on top technologies such as *DeltaCLoud*, *CAMP* and TOSCA adding for the latter the support to the applications over multiple clouds. Anyway, they do not focus specifically on the federation. In fact the authors do not give information regarding the maintenance of the federated environment and the communication technologies between the involved CRPs. Also Pham et al. [23] introduced a prototype of a novel framework for the multi-tier application deployment over multiple clouds. The different approach against Brogi et al.[8] is the use of a DSL-language for describing the application topology. Each component description also provides the dependencies between that component and the others. Trummer et al. [27] tackled the challenge of cost optimization. Their idea is very similar to that of Brogi et al. [8]. The input of the presented mathematical algorithm is an application template described as a graph where each node is a component of the application. Also in this scenario, the cloud providers are independent and they do not stipulate any federated agreement. In *Uni4Cloud* [26], the authors present a *OVF*- and *OCCI*-based framework enabling the automated multi-tier application deployment on multiple clouds. It is able to translate a High-Level Application Model in an OVF package (.ova extension). The framework plays only the role of a broker, which able to talk with several providers thanks to the OCCI APIs. Ardagna et al. [3] presented *MODAClouds*, which is a framework enabling the design and execution of applications over multiple clouds. MODAClouds performs a gradual transformation of a high-level application model into a final cloud provider-specific model enabling the installation and orchestration of the application on the selected clouds. Juve et al. [15] faces the topic of automating application deployment over a single or multi cloud infrastructure. Especially, the authors present their system called *Wrangler*, which is able to deploy and orchestrate VMs in an automated way. The system's central component is the "Coordinator" which receives the users' application deployment requests (a XML application descriptor) and makes decisions regarding the application deployment across multiple clouds. In Wrangler, a prior step to prepare the VMs is installing the wrangler agent and configuring it to connect to the coordinator node. In Rochwerger et al. [1], the authors present the *Reservoir* architecture ([25]). This architecture creates a dedicated virtual environment (VEE) where each application component can be executed. These VEEs can be placed in the VEE hosts within a single Reservoir site or on different sites. One of the main *Reservoir* elements is the *Service Manifest*, which contains information about the structure of the application components such as master image references, resource requirements of a single instance (CPUs, memory size, etc.) and more. The Service Manifest extends the OVF standard.The Reservoir project is considered the ancestor of our presented work. The paper Bresnahan et al. [7] presents an interesting tool called "*Cloudinit.d*" for automating the virtual machine (VM) creation and maintaining processes (launching,configuring, monitoring, and repairing operations), the contextualization, and the coordination of service deployment. Cloudinit.d tool takes as input an *.ini* configuration file. This file contains the service description: the (IaaS provider) location where it will be run, the VM information, and the file system path (within the VM) of the *scripts* that need to be executed in order to install and configure the required software to start-up the service. However, enabling the VMs contextualization, using simple scripts could not be a good way in complex scenarios with multiple VMs and different kinds of operating systems.

7. CONCLUSION

In this paper, we tackled the challenge of a *multi-component application deployment over multiple federated cloud providers* by presenting a deployment system architecture. We described and designed the architectural solution highlighting the peculiarities of the selected technologies to achieve the desired goal. Moreover, the paper analyses the XMPP communication delay to demonstrate that it does not negatively affect the overall application deployment process. In future work, we are going to test the performances of such a cross-cloud federation deployments to evaluate not only the XMPP communication time but all its components' behaviour. In this scope, we will consider, for example, realistic and more complex multi-component applications and a federated environments characterized by hundreds of clouds that can dynamically take part and leave the federation in order to test the system's scalability.

8. REFERENCES

[1] B. R. andothers. The reservoir model and architecture for open federated cloud computing. *IBM Journal of Research and Development*, July 2009.

[2] D. Antoniades et al. Enabling Cloud Application Portability. In *Proceedings of the 8th International Conference on Utility and Cloud Computing (UCC)*, pages 354–360. IEEE, Dec. 2015.

[3] D. Ardagna et al. MODAClouds: A model-driven approach for the design and execution of applications on multiple clouds. In *Proceedings of the 4th International Workshop on Modeling in Software Engineering (MISE)*, pages 50–56. IEEE, June 2012.

[4] G. Baryannis et al. Lifecycle management of service-based applications on multi-clouds. In *Proceedings of the 2013 international workshop on Multi-cloud applications and federated clouds - MultiCloud 13*, pages 13–20. ACM), 2013.

[5] T. Binz, U. Breitenbücher, O. Kopp, and F. Leymann. *TOSCA: Portable Automated Deployment and Management of Cloud Applications*, pages 527–549. Advanced Web Services. Springer, Jan. 2014.

[6] T. Binz et al. OpenTOSCA - A Runtime for TOSCA-based Cloud Applications. In *Proceedings of the 11th International Conference on Service-Oriented Computing (ICSOC 2013)*. Springer, Dec. 2013.

[7] J. Bresnahan et al. Managing appliance launches in infrastructure clouds. In *Proceedings of the 2011 TeraGrid Conference on Extreme Digital Discovery*. ACM, 2011.

[8] A. Brogi, A. Ibrahim, J. Soldani, J. Carrasco, J. Cubo, E. Pimentel, and F. D'Andria. SeaClouds. *SIGSOFT Softw. Eng. Notes*, pages 1–4, Feb. 2014.

[9] A. Celesti, M. Fazio, and M. Villari. SE CLEVER: A secure message oriented Middleware for Cloud federation. In *Symposium on Computers and Communications (ISCC)*. IEEE, July 2013.

[10] A. Celesti, F. Tusa, M. Villari, and A. Puliafito. How to Enhance Cloud Architectures to Enable Cross-Federation. In *Proceedings of the 3rd International Conference on Cloud Computing*, pages 337–345. IEEE, July 2010.

[11] N. Ferry, A. Rossini, F. Chauvel, B. Morin, and A. Solberg. Towards Model-Driven Provisioning, Deployment, Monitoring, and Adaptation of Multi-cloud Systems. In *Proceedings of the 6th International Conference on Cloud Computing*, pages 887–894. IEEE, June 2013.

[12] P. Hirmer, U. Breitenbücher, T. Binz, and F. Leymann. Automatic Topology Completion of TOSCA-based Cloud Applications. In *Proceedings des CloudCycle14 Workshops auf der 44. Jahrestagung der Gesellschaft für Informatik e.V. (GI)*, pages 247–258. GI, 2014.

[13] C. Jose, C. Javier, and P. Ernesto. Towards a Flexible Deployment of Multi-cloud Applications Based on TOSCA and CAMP. In *Communications in Computer and Information Science*. Springer, 2015.

[14] G. Jung, M. Hiltunen, K. Joshi, R. Panta, and R. Schlichting. Ostro: Scalable Placement Optimization of Complex Application Topologies in Large-Scale Data Centers. In *Proceedings of the 35th International Conference on Distributed Computing Systems*, pages 143–152. IEEE, June 2015.

[15] G. Juve and E. Deelman. Automating Application Deployment in Infrastructure Clouds. In *Proceedings of the 3rd International Conference on Cloud Computing Technology and Science*, pages 658–665. IEEE, 2011.

[16] O. Kopp, T. Binz, U. Breitenbücher, and F. Leymann. Winery – A Modeling Tool for TOSCA-based Cloud Applications. In *Proceedings of the 11th International Conference on Service-Oriented Computing (ICSOC 2013)*, pages 700–704. Springer, Dec. 2013.

[17] C.-Y. Liu, K.-C. Huang, Y.-H. Lee, and K.-C. Lai. Efficient Resource Allocation Mechanism for Federated Clouds. *International Journal of Grid and High Performance Computing*, pages 74–87, Oct. 2015.

[18] N. Loulloudes et al. Enabling Interoperable Cloud Application Management through an Open Source Ecosystem. *IEEE Internet Computing*, pages 54–59, May 2015.

[19] OASIS. *Topology and Orchestration Specification for Cloud Applications (TOSCA) Primer Version 1.0*, 2013.

[20] OASIS. Topology and Orchestration Specification for Cloud Applications Version 1.0, 2013.

[21] A. Papaioannou and K. Magoutis. An Architecture for Evaluating Distributed Application Deployments in Multi-clouds. In *Proceedings of the 5th International Conference on Cloud Computing Technology and Science*, pages 547–554. IEEE, Dec. 2013.

[22] P. Pawluk, B. Simmons, M. Smit, M. Litoiu, and S. Mankovski. Introducing STRATOS: A Cloud Broker Service. In *Proceedings of the 5th International Conference on Cloud Computing*, pages 891–898. IEEE, June 2012.

[23] L. M. Pham, A. Tchana, D. Donsez, V. Zurczak, P.-Y. Gibello, and N. de Palma. An adaptable framework to deploy complex applications onto multi-cloud platforms. In *Proceedings of the International Conference on Computing & Communication Technologies*, pages 169–174. IEEE, Jan. 2015.

[24] S. Rebai, M. Hadji, and D. Zeghlache. Improving profit through cloud federation. In *Proceedings of the 12th Annual IEEE Consumer Communications and Networking Conference (CCNC)*. IEEE, Jan. 2015.

[25] B. Rochwerger et al. Reservoir - When One Cloud Is Not Enough. *Computer*, pages 44–51, Mar. 2011.

[26] A. Sampaio and N. Mendonça. Uni4Cloud. In *Proceeding of the 2nd international workshop on Software engineering for cloud computing - SECLOUD '11*, pages 15–21. Association for Computing Machinery (ACM), 2011.

[27] I. Trummer, F. Leymann, R. Mietzner, and W. Binder. Cost-Optimal Outsourcing of Applications into the Clouds. In *Proceedings of the Second International Conference on Cloud Computing Technology and Science*, pages 135–142. IEEE, Nov. 2010.

[28] F. Tusa, M. Paone, and M. Villari. CLEVER. In *Theory and Practice*, pages 219–241. IGI Global, 2012.

[29] University of Stuttgart – Institute of Architecture of Application Systems. OpenTOSCA – Open Source TOSCA Ecosystem, 2016. http://www.iaas.uni-stuttgart.de/OpenTOSCA/indexE.php.

[30] XSF. Extensible Messaging and Presence Protocol (XMPP): Core. Internet RFC 3920, October 2004.

[31] W. Yao and L. Lu. A Selection Algorithm of Service Providers for Optimized Data Placement in Multi-Cloud Storage Environment. In *Communications in Computer and Information Science*. Springer, 2015.

[32] K.-H. Yeh. An Efficient Resource Allocation Framework for Cloud Federations. *Information Technology And Control*, pages 64–76, Mar. 2015.

Semantic SPARQL queries: a novel federation model and implementation towards Enterprise Data Governance

Mirco Casoni, Stefano Monti, Francesco Sprotetto
Imola Informatica s.p.a.
Via Selice, 66/a
40026 Imola, (BO), Italy
{mcasoni, smonti, fsprotetti}@imolinfo.it

Antonio Corradi, Luca Foschini
DISI – University of Bologna
Viale del Risorgimento, 2
40136 Bologna, Italy
{antonio.corradi, luca.foschini}@unibo.it

Riccardo Venanzi
Department of Engineering – University of Ferrara
Via Saragat, 1
44122 Ferrara, Italy
riccardo.venanzi@unife.it
riccardo.venanzi@unibo.it

ABSTRACT
Data Governance and Federation in large complex organizations pose non-trivial challenges due to the integration of heterogeneous, distributed data sources. Semantic Web, and its de-facto standard query language – SPARQL – have proven to be key in defining and searching semantic over any sort of content on the Web, thus easily letting information clients discover hidden relationships among very heterogeneous data. However, current SPARQL support Data Federation is fairly limited, making it impractical for real-world scenarios. Our work proposes an open and autonomous platform for Data Federation that overcomes traditional SPARQL limitations and opens up unprecedented opportunities for Data Governance in large organizations.

CCS Concepts
- **Information systems for semantic web description languages**

Keywords
Enterprise Data Governance; Federation; Semantic Web.

1. INTRODUCTION
The governance of large distributed organizations poses non trivial challenges in discovering, aggregating, and managing data in heterogeneous forms and from different and distributed sources, both within and outside the organization boundaries. That produces governance models where data integration and organization knowledge is typically limited and with no flexibility. A typical example would be the case of the integration of Enterprice Resource Planning (ERP) systems data with both traditional Custom Relationship Management (CRM)/marketing analysis and with novel social media analysis systems to proactively influence enterprise production and operations, e.g., supply chain and stock management tuning as well as workforce optimization.

Semantic web principles, methodologies, and techniques have l ong ago proven to be crucial in modeling and managing complex relationships between entities/data and to support interoperability, reasoning and inference/automation in coarse-grained, semi-structured, and heterogeneous data environments: in this field, the SPARQL protocol (based on the Resource Description Framework – RDF – specification [1]) has become the de-facto standard to extract and manipulate information from distributed data sources on the web [2, 3].

However, traditional Semantic Web methodologies and techniques typically exhibit severe limitations in large heterogeneous scenarios where multiple distributed data sources have to be integrated. In those cases, Semantic approaches would require complete *a priori* knowledge of all data sources and their network distribution and topology.

That limitation becomes particularly crucial in Enterprise IT/Data Governance scenarios where a complete, durable, and a priori data source knowledge is often unrealistic and infeasible. A typical example would be one where multiple public and private academic institutions are willing to integrate to optimize their geographic and demographic coverage (e.g., to avoid geographic course overlap from different academia). Such synergic education offering would require a continuous data integration flow from both education (e.g., currently available courses and teaching areas) and administrative departments (e.g., students distribution, cost and revenue distribution per area and department), with demographic data from municipalities (e.g. Open Data about citizen distribution per geographic area and age).

Both municipalities and academic institutions will likely feature their own, very different and constrained data sources, information systems and data gathering and management processes, so making them converge to single, uniform and standardized data sources, systems, and processes would be simply unrealistic. Similarly, both academic institutions and municipalities should be left free to change/evolve their own IT infrastructures/systems and processes, and still guarantee data interoperability and integration.

Despite the aforementioned limitations in terms of distributed data source knowledge, we strongly believe that flexibility and extensibility of Semantic approaches are particularly suitable for IT/Data Governance scenarios such as the ones described above. This paper proposes a novel, semantic-based approach to overcome organization governance complexity and to mitigate/hide heterogeneity and distribution of data sources: our work describes a reference architecture model that relies on a federation of SPARQL endpoints, as well as a full implementation on top of an existing, enterprise-grade largely adopted Semantic framework, and real use-case scenarios to prove the viability of our proposal.

Our approach goes further than traditional governance models (where data harvesting and integration are expensive, difficult, and often limited to specific domains/areas), and fosters a much

VALUETOOLS 2016, October 25-28, Taormina, Italy

broader-scoped, horizontal, and continuous integration of data: our federated approach promotes a higher level of data normalization and integration which proposes a more proactive governance model where data analysis may be used not only to lead retrospective analysis, but also to proactively support upcoming strategic decisions. We are going to use the above integration example as a fil rouge throughout the paper.

Section 2 describes related work in the area of both Data Governance and Semantic approaches and Section 3 defines the conceptual model of our solution. Section 4 and 5 provide relevant insights in both design choices and implementation details of our work, and Section 6 describes some empirical evaluations to prove the feasibility of our approach. Finally, Section 7 includes conclusions and future work we are planning to carry on this topic.

2. RELATED WORK

Information systems have long become valuable assets for companies. IT and Data Governance are key disciplines that drive methodologies and techniques for managing such crucial IT assets.

IT Governance has become one of the most relevant decision-making processes, and supports the dynamic adaptation to ever-changing business/market needs and goal achievement. In particular, it deals with Strategic Alignment, Delivering Value, Risk Management, Resource Management, and Performance Measurement [4, 5]. Data Governance strategies involve the convergence of multiple functionalities such as Data Quality, Data Management, Risk Management, and Policies definition and enforcement [6, 7].

The importance of Data Governance relies on its ability to understand how data flows across an organization, which are the constraints that must be considered, which is the regulatory landscape, who is responsible for the data and who can use the data themselves. Once these issues have been clearly shaped, Data Governance aims at defining rules on the data model and the data itself.

In the synergic academic offering example we depicted in Section 1, a Data Governance initiative in such a distributed ecosystem would for instance:

- identify data sources among academia/municipalities information systems;
- identify data responsibility and ownership: e.g., information about current students involved in courses may come from both education and administrative departments, and deciding which one should be considered master in case of disputes is key;
- identify private, non-shareable data and enforce data privacy: e.g., personal students information such as age, gender and personal contact information should be provided only as aggregate data;
- guarantee a minimum set of data to be provided by each data source (e.g., each academic institution should at least provide student distribution per age and geographic site).

Data federation – the ability to seamlessly and transparently integrate data stored at different places - plays a crucial role in Data Governance. Data federation is usually seen as a specialization of Data integration systems, where data storage abandons the idea of single centralized physical endpoints, and leverage fully integrated, fully distributed models.

In the above example, Data federation guarantees transparent data interoperability and integration no matter the actual information system technology and vendor (e.g., depending on the specific academic institution, student distribution may reside on databases of different vendors, on legacy CSV files, as well as proprietary ERP systems data formats).

Semantic Web has long ago emerged as the transformation of the World Wide Web in an environment where contents (HTML pages, binary files, images/media content, and so on) are enriched with metadata that specify the semantic context of any content itself. Metadata languages and formats (such as RDF and OWL) are primarily conceived to easily express information about content, and automatically perform semantic data query (e.g., via search engines), interpretation, and, more generally, to automatic aggregation and reasoning. Semantic Web advances interaction between computers and humans one step further, and allows humans to leverage a more autonomous and intelligent machine support in the execution of the generic tasks.

A key element of the Semantic Web is W3C SPARQL, which is a query language for Resource Description Framework (RDF), and has long set itself as the *de facto* standard to perform semantic queries on content exposed on the Web. RDF describes the concepts and relationships about them through the introduction of *triples* (subject-predicate-object); *triples* that have some elements in common become parts of a knowledge graph. SPARQL helps navigating such knowledge graphs and searching for sub-graphs corresponding to user requests.

Semantic Web and SPARQL query language form a promising platform to support Data Governance and federation needs, and allow building a connected network of information [8].

However, federation of semantic data and navigation via SPARQL queries is still at an early stage and requires users to explicitly express the distributed nodes upon which to perform semantic queries and subsequent result aggregations, therefore negating the intrinsic benefits of adopting a semantic approach to distributed data aggregation and reasoning [9, 10].

3. THE SPARQL FEDERATION MODEL

Data Federation is crucial in letting organizations easily and effectively shaping and supporting information flow across organization branches.

Our work aims at defining a viable and effective model and implementation to adopt Semantic Web methodologies and the SPARQL implementation to overcome typical issues such as heterogeneity and distribution of data sources.

Key principles in defining our solution are

- *Openness*: data federation and integration in large organizations typically means integrating data sources from heterogeneous (both custom and third party) systems; avoiding vendor lock-in and preserving openness and portability is key in defining a sustainable, long-term data federation strategy for any organization;
- *Lightweightness*: the proposed solution should pose from a limited up to no overhead on running systems, so as to minimize the impact of Data Federation on large organizations with complex, highly distributed data sources;
- *Autonomy and ease of use*: the proposed solution should be able to cope with uncertainty, and to autonomously discover relationships among federated data even in case of partial a priori data model and network knowledge.

Semantic Web standards and the SPARQL query language have long proven to be the key in enabling open, autonomous, machine-driven content matching and reasoning knowledge management infrastructures.

However, SPARQL support for data federation – via the SERVICE construct (e.g. distributed data source integration and query) – is still at an early stage and it is still poorly suitable for large, real-world scenarios.

Current SPARQL data federation limitations mainly relate to the fact that designing federated queries requires complete, a priori knowledge of data models and actual data across all data sources involved; this clearly becomes a relevant constraint in large complex scenarios where data sources are heterogeneous and can change frequently and at different paces from each other. The only way to overcome that limit is to find new mechanisms capable of dynamic behavior for a suitable adaptation to any scenario change, very likely to occur in large environments with many actors.

4. ARCHITECTURE

This section highlights three main architectural alternative we have evaluated to realize a fully scalable and extensible SPARQL endpoint federation. We have also defined several qualitative Key Performance Indicators (KPIs) to help us to organize and compare benefits and shortcomings of these alternatives, and to ultimately facilitate the choice of the proposed solution. Any proposed solutions are checked against those KPIs to compare their properties and ease the choice.

4.1 KPIs

Ease of development. Our SPARQL federation should require limited development efforts, no matter the specific Semantic framework implementation.

Integration. Our SPARQL federation solution should easily integrate with other framework features, with little or no additional effort.

Maintenance. Our SPARQL federation solution should be conceived so as to limit development effort in case of bug fixing or feature adaptation activities.

Evolution. Our solution should be easily extensible in order to cope with new requirements.

4.2 Alternatives

Endpoint extension. This solution extends the internal logic of a SPARQL endpoint, from the classic logic to the execution of the query for extracting data to a model for the interception of the query, the query rewriting through the wired application logic, by inserting the statement required to query all the nodes in the federation, and finally performing on the various endpoints, returning the result in accordance with the provisions of the specific SERVICE clause SPARQL 1.1.

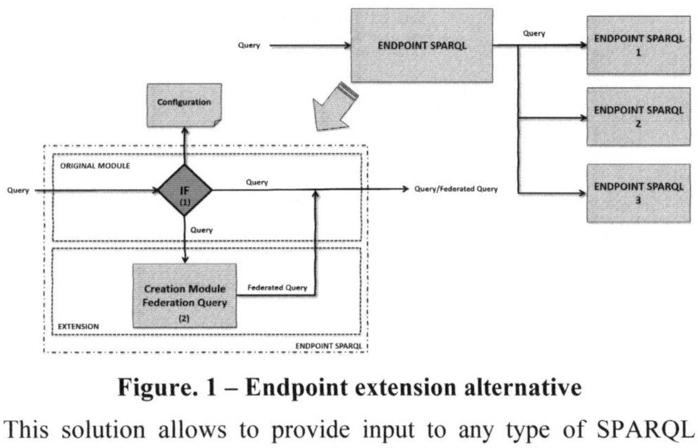

Figure. 1 – Endpoint extension alternative

This solution allows to provide input to any type of SPARQL query, with the only constraint of not being able to use the SERVICE clause, both because this is used as the main construct for the manipulation, either because it would make the handling and the high complexity of final query.

This aspect is important as it does not allow the use of all the constructs that conform to the standard SPARQL 1.1, giving the value added to the product that more to the solution.

Another aspect to consider is the difficulty in handling the query itself, which could lead to not-trivial query implementation and poor performance. In fact approach is extremely platform-dependent from both a technical point of view (need to modify existing SPARQL endpoint source code), and a management one (modifying source code from other vendors and distributing it may pose legal and organizational challenges in terms of distribution process and code ownership), therefore achieving a low score on each KPI.

Plugin. Some Semantic platforms and SPARQL implementations typically allow developers to extend platform features via plugin modules. Data federation may be realized as *a dedicated plugin that transparently handles data federation across nodes*, and overcomes current SPARQL limitations.

This approach poses non-trivial technology issues:

- plugin implementation strictly depends on the actual semantic platform, therefore allowing to federate only nodes that rely on the same semantic platform
- only a subset of currently available, production-grade semantic platforms support a plugin model.

These limitations adversely impact all KPIs, thus making this option viable only for controlled environments where the semantic platform is shared across the federation and supports a plugin model.

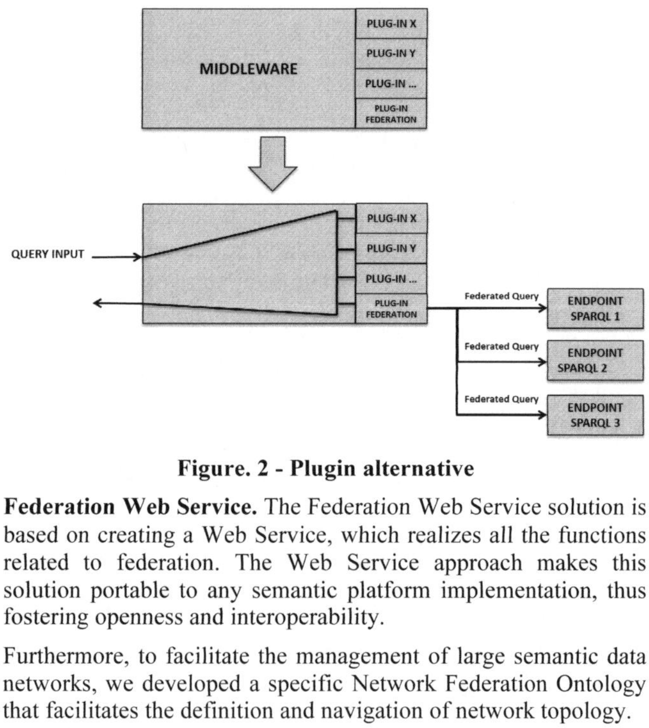

Figure. 2 - Plugin alternative

Federation Web Service. The Federation Web Service solution is based on creating a Web Service, which realizes all the functions related to federation. The Web Service approach makes this solution portable to any semantic platform implementation, thus fostering openness and interoperability.

Furthermore, to facilitate the management of large semantic data networks, we developed a specific Network Federation Ontology that facilitates the definition and navigation of network topology.

The Federation Web Service relies on such a ontology to transparently determine which nodes and endpoints should be involved, thus facilitating the definition of federated semantic queries.

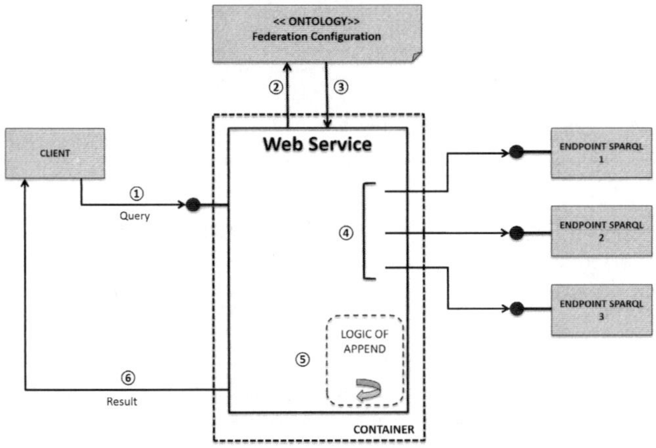

Figure. 3 – Federation Web Service alternative

The logical flow of the Federation Web Service is as follows:

- Federation resolution: thanks to the Federation Ontology, the Federation Web Service determines the actual endpoints involved in the federation;
- Query execution: the Federation Web Service performs queries on all individual nodes involved in the federated query;
- Result aggregation: the Federation Web Service aggregates the results obtained from single nodes and returns them to the caller. The aggregation techniques can be managed through the typical constructs of the SPARQL language, such as the UNION clause.

4.3 KPI evaluation and choice

Table 1. Alternatives comparison

	Endpoint extension	Plugin development	Federation WS
Ease of dev.	LOW - Platform-dependent	LOW - Platform-dependent	HIGH
Integration	LOW - requires distributing a new version of the endpoint	LOW - Platform-dependent	HIGH – no vendor lock-in
Maintenance	LOW - Platform-dependent	LOW - Platform-dependent	HIGH
Evolution	LOW - Platform-dependent	LOW - Platform-dependent	HIGH – no vendor lock-in

Openness and portability of the Federation Web Service model grant this solution high KPI values, from both a development (ease) and management (integration, maintenance, evolution) point of view.

Our architectural choice therefore relies on the definition and implementation of a Federation Web Service.

5. IMPLEMENTATION DETAILS

This section highlights some relevant implementation details related to the selection of the Semantic middleware for our proposal (and related evaluation KPIs) and Federation Web Service implementation.

5.1 Middleware selection

The first step in realizing our SPARQL federation model relates to the selection of a Semantic middleware platform on top of which to built our solution.

We evaluated four main, widely-diffused Semantic middleware solutions, again on the base of a set of relevant qualitative KPIs.

Apache JENA [11]. Apache JENA is one of the most widespread, open-source semantic middleware on the market today. It is supported by the Apache community and is written entirely in Java programming language. JENA does not natively support SPARQL and SPARQL endpoints, though specific external libraries exist that provide both features (namely, the ARQ package [12] and the Joseki extension).

Sesame [13]. Sesame is an open source, Java-based RDF storage that natively supports SPARQL and exposes REST services to facilitate integration with external systems and services.

Allegrograph [14]. Allegrograph is an open source, Java-based RDF storage that natively supports SPARQL and exposes REST services to facilitate integration with external systems and services. SPARQL is the default query language in Allegrograph, and a implementation of the TWINQL [15] specification is also available; this specification provides relevant query optimization features.

Openlink Virtuoso [16]. Virtuoso is a multi-model data storage solution that combines traditional RDBMS storage features, with advanced Semantic storage, reasoning support (e.g., RDF), and an extensive set of integration features (e.g., REST/WebServices integration). SPARQL support is native in Virtuoso.

5.1.1 KPIs

KPIs provided in the following are qualitative evaluation criteria relevant for any middleware choice. Our scoring attribution is based on the Capability Maturity Model Integration framework (CMMI), that provides a common reference model to assess the maturity of a system with respect to a given evaluation aspect [17].

Each KPI is evaluated against a set of values between 0 (no feature/characteristic support) to 5 (full, enterprise-grade feature/characteristic support).

Federation support. This KPI relates to the maturity of federation features provided by the candidate framework, and is the most relevant KPI in our evaluation model (i.e., highest weight).

Jena, Virtuoso, and Allegrograph provide no support for federation besides the limited SPARQL SERVICE directive, hence scoring an evaluation of 0 (no support) for this KPI. Sesame, instead, supports some sort of data sources federation, but data model sharing is still at an early stage, hence scoring an evaluation of 1.

Community support. This KPI relates to the maturity of the community involved in the development and maintenance of the candidate framework. Typical community support features relate to bug tracking and resolution processes, documentation, wiki, online support, etc, and are crucial for long-term manageability and stability of the platform. Allegrograph has virtually no active community and provides only a static documentation of the platform, hence scoring a lowest result. Jena and Sesame provide a fairly active community that involves bug tracking/resolution, and product roadmap definition. Virtuoso features the most active community and provides bug tracking and resolution, product roadmap definition and direct on-call (chat) support.

Commercial support. Besides community support, commercial support is generally required in enterprise-grade software solutions to guarantee long-term stability. Commercial support typically provides highly skilled, special-purpose consulting resources as well as the ability to provide specific developments/extension and integrations.

Jena has no commercial support, Allegrograph and Sesame provide some level of consulting support, and Virtuoso provides the most comprehensive commercial ecosystem that offers also specific developments by need.

SPARQL Endpoint support. This KPI describes the availability of SPARQL endpoint APIs within the candidate middleware.

Virtuoso provides full endpoint exposition and support, whereas other candidates have only limited functionalities.

Java support. This KPI relates to product compatibility with the Java programming language. This KPI is particularly relevant due to the widespread adoption of Java (and its enterprise counterpart JEE) in developing large enterprise applications.

Jena implementation is fully based on the Java programming language, and exposes fully workable Java APIs; on the contrary Virtuoso is entirely written in C# and has limited API support for Java.

Market adoption. This KPI describes the availability skilled professional resources on the candidate framework. This KPI is especially relevant to guarantee manageability and evolvability of our solution. Virtuoso and Jena are leaders in terms of market adoption, hence featuring a larger market workforce share.

Product maturity. This KPI defines the overall maturity of the product, specifically in terms release process: products with frequent and long-term planned release schedules and roadmaps tend to be more reliable from a business point of view.

5.1.2 Middleware choice

This section synthesizes KPIs as described above, for each candidate middleware. Our evaluation is based on a weighted sum of KPIs, where the weight distribution reflects KPI relevance in our vision: federation support and market adoption are particularly crucial in our evaluation.

Table 2 details both KPI weight distribution (values ranging from 0 to 1) and scores for each KPI and middleware platform.

Aggregate results are obtained as a weighted sum of all KPIs: despite its poor Java support and lack of native federation support, Openlink Virtuoso is the Semantic platform that best fits our business needs and provides a stable and reliable option.

Table 2. Semantic middleware comparison

	Weight	Jena	Allegrograph	**Virtuoso**	Sesame
Federation support	0,3	0	0	**0**	1
Community	0,1	4	2	**5**	4
Commercial support	0,1	0	2	**5**	3
SPARQL endpoint support	0,1	1	2	**5**	1
Java prog. language	0,1	4	2	**1**	3
Market adoption	0,2	3	1	**3**	1
Product maturity	0,1	3	2	**4**	2
	1	1,8	1,2	**2,6**	1,8

5.2 Federation web service implementation

The implementation of federation consists of two main aspects: the Federation Ontology, and the Federation Web Service that together can grant the full support needed in our project.

5.2.1 Federation Ontology

Enterprise contexts stress the need to manage large amounts of data that show properties such as heterogeneity and distribution of the data model. However, aggregation of heterogeneous data is crucial for business processes such as Decision Making, Data Quality, and Data Management. This aggregation supports the concept of federation, which provides a federative pact on which to build the federation itself.

The implementation has gone in this direction, defining a uniform data model and to be shared between all members of the federation, in order to eliminate the problems described above.

The proposed ontology is composed by three main elements:

- the concept of federation
- the concept of the federation member
- the *member_of* relationship that represents the relationship between the member of the federation and the federation itself.

The ontology described above enables the management of the federation independently of semantic platform and can be deployed and queried to any SPARQL endpoint.

From an implementation standpoint, we realized our ontology according to the RDF schema modeling.

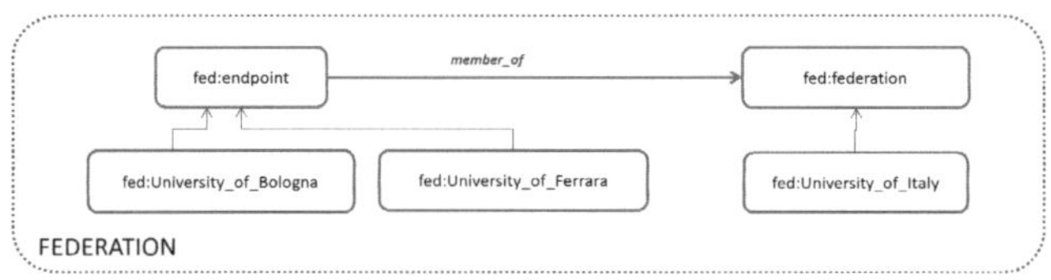

Fig. 4 – Federation Ontology

Figure 4 describes an implementation of our ontology that maps Italian academic institutions: *fed:University_of_Italy* represents a federation of universities, and *fed:University_of_Bologna* and *fed:University_of_Ferrara* are endpoint members of the *fed:University_of_Italy* federation.

5.2.2 Federation Web Service

The Federation Web Service manages semantic data query and aggregation via the steps described in the following.

1. Clients can query the Web Service with a standard SPARQL query, and express a specific federation (in our examples, we modeled disparate data sets from Italian universities)
2. The Web Service inspects the federation to determine which endpoints should be queried
3. The Web Service performs the semantic query on each such node

4. The Web Service aggregates results from the above queries and returns them back to the caller

Result aggregation is a particularly crucial task, and our Federated Web Services support three main strategies:

- APPEND strategy: results coming from different endpoints are simply stacked on top of each other, and sent back to the client once all replies are received; this strategy is implemented via the APPEND operator and does not handle result triple duplications;
- INTERSECTION strategy: this approach returns all the triples that are common to each involved endpoint;
- UNION strategy: results from endpoints are combined into a set of unique triples, hence performing duplicate detection and removal.

The Federation Web Service clearly decouples the query definition, execution, and aggregation from the definition and management of the data set distribution. Even though our solution may conceptually handle highly distributed data sets, some management concerns may arise:

- endpoint time-out: how to handle alive nodes that fail to reply to queries in a given amount of time (e.g., due to temporary network issues); ignore/retry strategies should be carefully planned to reach a viable balance between result completeness (e.g. retrying queries in order to overcome the temporary network outage), and total response time;
- endpoint unavailability: endpoints may become unavailable for larger amounts of time, e.g. due to severe server/system failures. .

6. EVALUATION

In this section we describe some Semantic platform benchmarks, as well as a specific use case of our SPARQL federation model.

6.1 Semantic platforms benchmarking

In order to prove the feasibility of our approach, we provide some useful insights about semantic platform performance under heavy load.

These quantitative analyses justify both Virtuoso adoption as the Semantic middleware/platform of our choice with respect to other contenders, and shed some light on absolute performance of Virtuoso under load.

Dataset load time. Loading large amounts of data becomes crucial in complex distributed scenarios where each node may contribute with a set of millions of records, thus limiting the overall performance of the whole system. The table below shows a load time comparison for datasets ranging from 1M to 100M entries, the times in the table are expressed according the dd-hh-mm-ss format.

Table 3. Semantic middleware performance – dataset load time

	1M	25M	100M
Sesame	00:02:59	12:17:05	3:06:27:25
Virtuoso	**00:00:34**	**00:17:15**	**1:03:53**
Allegrograph	00:00:52	00:36:49	00:48:30
Jena TDB	00:49	00:16:53	01:34:14

Query execution. Querying large amounts of data becomes crucial in complex distributed scenarios where each node may contribute with a set of millions of records, thus limiting the overall performance of the whole system. The table below shows a load time comparison for datasets ranging from 1M to 100M entries (Query per hour).

Table 4. Semantic middleware performance – query execution/single client

Single client	1M	25M	100M
Sesame	18094	1343	254
Virtuoso	**17424**	**12972**	**4407**
Allegrograph	4075	493	656
Jena TDB	4450	353	81

Table 5. Semantic middleware performance – query execution/multiple clients

Multi client	1M	25M	100M
Sesame	19057	18295	16517
Virtuoso	**28985**	**32668**	**33339**
Allegrograph	5861	7453	7888
Jena TDB	6752	8453	8664

The Semantic middleware we adopted for our reference implementation – Virtuoso – clearly outperforms its contenders both in terms of initial dataset load time, and in terms of query efficiency.

These numbers also clearly evidence how Virtuoso may scale linearly and handle extremely high workloads both in terms of initial dataset load, and in terms of single/parallel query executions, thus proving itself as a viable, production-grade option for large real data federation scenarios.

6.2 Use case

Our SPARQL Federation model allowed us to realize the complex integration scenario described in Section 1.

We realized a proof of concept Federated Education Portal that provides a synergic academic offering that federates education and administrative data sources from Italian academic institutions together with citizenship distribution data sources from Italian municipalities in order to realize a more integrated education offering.

A traditional Semantic approach allows to decouple actual data sources and their implementations, hence allowing to reuse the same SPARQL query over any academic and municipality data source, no matter the real data source implementation (would it be an ERP system backed by a traditional RDBMS, or a legacy mainframe system).

However, a SPARQL-only approach for our Federated Education Portal would require to:

- have a priori knowledge of all municipalities and universities involved in the overall integrated offering;
- explicitly/manually perform the same SPARQL query on academic data sources to retrieve students distribution;
- explicitly/manually perform the same SPARQL query on municipality data sources to retrieve citizen distribution;

- explicitly map and combine both semantic result sets into a cohesive data set that highlights gaps in actual course offering with respect to real citizen distribution.

This process is obviously largely inefficient and poorly extensible: our Federated Education Portal should be extended any time new data sources get added, in order to query new endpoints and combine results with old ones.

Our approach leverages the following elements:

- A Federation Ontology implementation that maps Italian municipalities and relevant information about citizen geographic distribution;
- A Federation Ontology implementation that maps Italian academic institutions and relevant information about courses and student distribution;
- Students and Citizens are linked via the semantic notion of person (via the *foaf:Person* ontology);
- a set of Virtuoso instances as the default Semantic middleware;
- a set of SPARQL endpoints, for both municipalities and universities, on top of Virtuoso Semantic middleware
- an instance of our Federation Web Service.

In this scenario

- our Federated Education Portal performs a single query to retrieve geographic distribution of both persons involved in academic courses (students), and persons (citizens) from municipalities;
- the Federation Web Service identifies all involved academic and municipality data sources and transparently query each one of them;
- the Federation Web Service takes care of combining results (e.g., via an INTERSECTION strategy).

Our approach dramatically facilitated the realization of the Federated Education Portal:

- no a priori data source knowledge should be hard-coded into the Federated Education Portal, hence resulting in a more open and flexible solution
- a single query can be executed both on academia and on municipality endpoints, hence facilitating the development efforts of the overall solution.

7. CONCLUSIONS

Discovery, aggregation, and manipulation of distributed, diverse sets of data have become key in supporting core Enterprise processes. Semantic approaches have been proven valid to infer relationships and dependencies from heterogeneous sets of information pieces, however the current de facto standard query language SPARQL falls short when performing truly federated data navigation, with no exact knowledge of data distribution.

This work proposes a lightweight Federation Ontology and a Federation Web Service to map information sources across organizations, so as to address current SPARQL limitations in terms of a priori network knowledge.

Our Federated Web Service represents a portable, non vendor-specific solution that relies on the Federation Ontology to infer network endpoints upon with to perform queries. The Federated Web Service then aggregates results via different composition strategies.

We adopted our Federation Web Service and Ontology to realize a Federated Education Portal that integrates data sets from both academic institutions and municipalities: our Federation Web Service and Ontology allowed us to dramatically ease the development of the portal itself. The system have been adopted by some of the involved organization as a reference for their internal projects.

We are currently investigating and testing strategies to overcome current limitations in terms of endpoint time-outs and unavailability.

8. REFERENCES

[1] W3C Recommendation: *Semantic Web*. W3C, 2015 http://www.w3.org/2001/sw/

[2] W3C Recommendation: *OWL Web Ontology Languange*. W3C, 2004, http://www.w3.org/TR/owl-ref/

[3] W3C Recommendation: "SPARQL 1.1 Federated Query", W3C, 2013, http://www.w3.org/TR/2013/REC-sparql11-federated-query-20130321/

[4] D. Carstoiu; A. S. Cernian; V. Sgarciu; A. Olteanu, *The architecture of a distributed enterprise information management system based on Semantic Web*. 2010, Automation Quality and Testing Robotics (AQTR), 2010 IEEE International Conference on

[5] L. Janahi, M. Griffiths, H. Al-Ammal. *A conceptual model for IT Governance: A case study research, Computer Vision and Image Analysis Applications*. (ICCVIA), 2015 International Conference on, Jan. 2015

[6] P. P. Tallon. *Corporate Governance of Big Data: Perspectives on Value, Risk, and Cost*. IEEE Computer, Jun. 2013

[7] T. Priebe, S. Markus. *Business information modeling: A methodology for data-intensive projects, data science and big data governance*. Big Data (Big Data), 2015 IEEE International Conference on

[8] G. Antunes, J. Borbinha, A. Caetano. *An Application of Semantic Techniques to the Analysis of Enterprise Architecture Models*. 2016, 49th Hawaii International Conference on System Sciences (HICSS)

[9] N. A. Rakhmawati, M. Hausenblas. *On the Impact of Data Distribution in Federated SPARQL Queries*. 2012, Semantic Computing (ICSC), 2012 IEEE Sixth International Conference on

[10] A. Zimmermann; M. Pretz; G. Zimmermann; D. G. Firesmith; I. Petrov. *Towards Service-Oriented Enterprise Architectures for Big Data Applications in the Cloud*. 2013, 17th IEEE International Enterprise Distributed Object Computing Conference Workshops

[11] APACHE Jena, https://jena.apache.org/

[12] APACHE Jena ARQ, https://jena.apache.org/documentation/query/

[13] Sesame, http://rdf4j.org/

[14] Allegrograph, http://franz.com/agraph/allegrograph/

[15] TwinQL extension, http://www.cliki.net/twinql

[16] Openlink Virtuoso, http://virtuoso.openlinksw.com/

[17] CMMI Model, http://cmmiinstitute.com/

Towards an Ontology development for automated applications in Smart City environment of SmartME Project

Nidhi Kushwaha
Indian Institute of Information Technology, Allahabad
India
+91-9792881438
kkush6887@gmail.com

O P Vyas
International Institute of Information Technology, Naya Raipur
India
+91-9425501450
dropvyas@gmail.com

Carlo Puliafito
Dipartimento di Ingegneria Elettrica Elettronica e Informatica,
University of Catania, Italy
+39-3463315554
carlopulia@gmail.com

Ranjana Vyas
Indian Institute of Information Technology, Allahabad
India
+91-8677955160
ranjana@iiita.ac.in

ABSTRACT
Cities are becoming everyday smarter, with an increasing multitude of electronic nodes distributed throughout the territory. These range from rather simple ones, such as sensors/actuators, but also smartphones, to more complex ones, such as data centers and workstations. Citizens may have a central role in consuming, but also producing the data. The consequence of all this is that the amount of data collected is enormous and these data need to be properly processed in order to make the most of them. Unfortunately, there are several challenges in data processing, but exploiting the Semantic Web technologies and linking data among them is the right way to face them. This paper introduces the SmartME project developed by the University of Messina, Italy, and discusses the technologies and approached that cat be utilized to properly manage the collected data. In this paper, we are working towards the incorporation of semantic layer with the SmartME project of University of Messina. In this, our contribution is to built logic for maintaining sensors and their collected information query them in more meaningful way for getting accurate results. Also, we have presented a way of modifying a previously developed Ontology, SSN and customized it for our purpose. Other than manual entry of a new sensor, which mitigates the burden of manual entry. To build up this logic, we have exploited Jena API of Semantic Web in Java.

Keywords
Linked Open Sensor Data, Semantic Web; Sensor; IoT; Protégé; SmartME; Smart City.

VALUETOOLS 2016, October 25-28, Taormina, Italy

1. EMERGENCE OF LINKED OPEN DATA
Linked Open Data provides an opportunity to harness the background data for the use of various applications such as Data Integration, Publishing, Information Retrieval, Data Miming and Feature Generation. It can be explored for the use of smart device due to its universal format and ease of data publishing and availability. These smart devices may be able to help their users to control HVAC (Heating, Ventilating, and Air Conditioning), window lighting control and so on. Already today, smartphone applications, such as CenceMe, exist that infer the activity of the person wearing phone, from sensor data and publish this on the Web [1]. Linked Open Sensor Data, which was produced by Kno.e.sis in 2011 (https://datahub.io/dataset/knoesis-linked-sensor-data), enable sensor data to be openly accessible on the Linked Open Data (LOD) Cloud. It contains expressive description of ~20000 weather stations in the United States, with more than 18,000 links to GeoNames places. Data are in the format of RDF descriptions of hurricane and blizzard observations in the United State. The data set includes observations within the entire United States during the time periods that several major storms were active including Hurricane Katrina, like Bill Bertha, Wilma, Charley, Gustav and a major blizzard in Nevada in 2002. These observation are generated by weather stations described in the MesoWest/Kno.e.sis Sensor Description Dataset introduced [2]. Currently, this dataset contains around one billion triples. On average, there are about five sensors per weather station measuring phenomena such as temperature, visibility, precipitation, pressure, wind speed, humidity, etc. In addition to location attributes such as latitude, longitude, and elevation, there are also links to locations in Geonames that are near each weather station. This sensors description dataset is now part of the Linked Open Data. This key work published the data in openly available knowledge base and also introduces the vocabulary of sensor network. This vocabulary was further exploited by many researches in recent years [3][4].

2. MOTIVATION & RELATED WORK

The cities in future will have billions of heterogeneous devices ranging from tiny communicating objects (e.g. actuators, sensor, tags), able to interact with the surrounding environments and remote system, to high-end nodes (e.g. data centers, workstations) capable of complex operations and to process a huge amount of information. They are also capable of delivering Intelligence on the go. The smartphone penetration in the urban population may be leveraged for its integration into the Smart City Technology framework as this will facilitate active and enabling the decision makers to feel "The pulse of your city in palm of your hand". In this futuristic scenario, citizen in Smart City are constantly connected with whatever surrounds them and they are formidable information consumers; their role is not limited to this though. In a study including Smart Bikes Project, it was highlighted by Nathalie and Herve et al [5] that citizens roaming around the city may be considered as mobile probes. It is proposed in their study that if properly instrumented, bikes going across the cities can constitute a dedicated crowd-sensing platform, monitoring the urban environment where and when it is most relevant. The useful data generation is this project was subjected to appropriate analytics for decision support purposes and suggests that smart phones can also be combined with the wireless sensing.

The wealth of data being generated by data sources needs to be appropriately processed using Data Mining techniques and Machine Learning approached. The complexity of a Smart City data analysis manifests due to a variety of issues as described in next subsection.

2.1 Challenges & Issues

1. The first challenging problem is that devices are not interoperable at any level with each other since most of the time technologies differ from one to another. For instance, in contemporary IoT (Internet of Things) applications multiple competing application level protocols such as CoAP (Constrained Application Protocol) (http://coap.technology/), MQTT (Message Queue Telemetry Transport) (http://mqtt.org/) and XMPP (Extensible Messaging and Presence Protocol) (http://xmpp.org/) are becoming popular. Each protocol possesses unique characteristics and messaging architecture helpful for different types of IoT (Internet of Things) applications. However, a smart IoT application architecture should be independent of messaging protocol standards, while also providing integration and translation between various popular messaging protocols. Thus, connecting and publishing the real time sensor data to LOD is a challenge;
2. Connecting sensors to the Internet and storing the data into Resource Description Framework (RDF). At the data level, devices do not use common terms or vocabulary to describe interoperable IoT data;
3. The current use of IoT is targeted to a single domain and most of the times the number of sensors are duplicated unnecessarily. For instance, temperature sensors in a building are primarily used for a Heating, Ventilating, and Air conditioning (HVAC) application; however, values produced by temperature sensors could be used in other applications, such as fire detection. The primary advantage of using common sensors in various applications is that it can reduce development, maintenance and deployment costs and promote device reusability. For this, automatic annotation of the new sensor which enters into an already deployed sensor network would play a significant role;
4. Mapping sensor's raw output into high level states. To achieve this requirement, a smart IoT system has to provide high level knowledge that can map sensors to real world entities and sensor's raw output to high level states;
5. Integrating the prediction model with SPARQL or exploiting periodic patterns from past state. For example, how to predict the probability of the heavy rainfall in June, 2017 will be approximately 0.8;
6. Multiple Data sources generate Structured, Semi-Structured and Un-structured Data;
7. Analysis and interpretation of cross thematic data (Urban Transport, Energy, Water etc);
8. The need for real-time processing of data streams for proactive information delivery and risks analysis.
9. To utilize LOD with semantic annotations for data analysis.

2.2 Research Possibilities

We can use the already built vocabulary of Linked Open Sensor Data. Furthermore, the newly entered sensor can be automatically annotated by matching the similarities of collected data on one side and location of the already deployed sensors on the other. Besides, Linked Open Sensor Data provides historical data regarding previous events that would help to predict future information. Smart IoT systems need to interconnect data produced by various sensors to understand the meaning of data in order to automatically take decisions or to provide suggestions. Thus, dealing with the interoperability of heterogeneous data is required. Data is stored in different files (e.g., CSV, Excel) and structured with different models (e.g., Ontology, schemas). To deal with heterogeneous data, Semantic Web technologies bring several benefits as they:

1. Unify data;
2. Link IoT data to external knowledge bases;
3. Explicitly add metadata (i.e. semantic enrichment/enhancement);
4. Deduce new knowledge.

Semantic Web technologies enable the interconnection with knowledge graphs. By interconnecting IoT data with such graphs (datasets and Ontologies used to structure the datasets), IoT systems are becoming smarter. A knowledge graphs that is widely available and useful is "Linked Open Data" (LOD). Major internet companies such as Facebook and Google are building private knowledge graphs based on Schema.org (agreement on common schemas to structure data) that is widely adopted by search engines, in addition to components of LOD such as DBpedia, Wikipedia and/or Wikidata. Knowledge graphs are built to get access to the information requested more easily and in an automatic way. Companies have chosen to use different representations for semantic data, which include unlabeled and labeled graphs, W3C ratified Semantic Web languages such as RDF and RDFS to explicitly describe the data, and OWL, a language to describe Ontologies/vocabularies [6]. Sensor's information can be collected on Web pages and parsed using Web crawler and converted into RDF version using Jena Semantic Web parser and converter [7]. Thus, we explore the IoT applications using Semantic Web technologies to semantically annotate sensor data, deduce new knowledge and combine IoT applicative domains.

3. REPRESENTING IoT ENTITIES AND THEIR ENVIRONMENT

In this paper we refer to the SmartME project of the University of Messina, Italy, according to which "smart cities may be regarded as complex ecosystems composed of heterogeneous interconnected things providing sensing and actuating facilities", and we tried to give it our contribution. In the scenario depicted above, new services and applications can be envisioned like traffic monitoring, energy management, e-health, disaster management, etc. Though, to develop these applications, a powerful proliferation of mobile and IoT devices, including sensors/actuators, wearable, smart appliances and cyber physical system is needed. In the SmartME project, a data oriented approach is used, in which heterogeneous IoT devices send data to the Cloud and applications are built on top of standard Cloud facilities. Open source technologies and standards are involved in the SmartME project. Stack4Things[1], an OpenStack-based framework, has been developed by the University of Messina in order to "manage sensing and actuation resources, remotely controlling nodes as well as virtualizing their functions and creating network overlays among them. Thus, the aim is not that of using Cloud Computing simply to manage data, but to shift to Sensing-and-Actuation-as-a-Service (SAaaS) perspective in which to provide developers or final users with actual or virtualized sensing and actuation resources" [8]. Web Application Messaging Protocol (WAMP) has been used as an open standard WebSocket subprotocol for Publish/Subscribe and RPC communication patterns. At the edge of the system, the IoT nodes are Arduino YUN-like boards. Furthermore, for building IoT applications, Node.js has been used, as it is open source, lightweight and efficient. Data collected by the nodes are open and users can visualize them through Comprehensive Knowledge Archive Network (CKAN), open source data portal software. CKAN is built with Python on the backend and Javascript on the frontend and its database engine is PostgreSQL. It also offers a powerful API that allows third-part applications and services to be built around it [9]. Raw data captured by sensor networks in the SmartME project are required to be stored, thus a network level integration between that system and sensors is needed. To annotate raw data, explicit mappings are needed for a particular application: for example, a rain fall greater than 250mm in 24 hours means heavy rain fall. Besides, fusing the output of multiple sensors for meaningful information generation is also a challenging task to deal with. For the task of storing these raw data in a more meaningful way, their conversion will be done using the RDF (Resource Description Framework) and sensor networks vocabularies (SSN). This annotation provides the machine readability of the sensor data. For suitability and ease of access, the data will be stored inside a Cloud environment. To make this data open and available to all for future extensions, we have also proposed data to be published on LOD Cloud by following standards/rules of data publishing on LOD [9]. Among the possible applications, collected data can be utilized for event predictions (e.g. catastrophes). For this purpose, we will exploit some past as well as current data. These data are then analyzed for finding patterns in them, thus to help the municipality take the necessary actions as soon as possible. In the SmartME project, there are about six types of sensors (temperature, visibility, precipitation, pressure, wind speed and humidity), as shown in Figure 1. These sensors generate data and store them in Cloud environment, making them openly viewable by anyone. But, due to the lack of semantics, these sensors are not uniquely identified and queried, thus the information is of little interest for human beings. Our basic aim in this paper is to provide a semantic layer below the user interface.

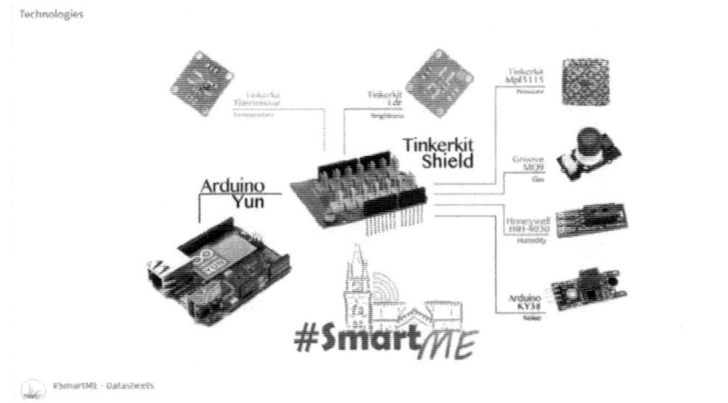

Figure 1. Sensor used in SmartME project

4. QUERYING WITH SPARQL FOR RETRIVAL

We have used the Protégé tool for modifying SSN Ontology which was previously developed by Kno.e.sis in 2011. Figure 2 shows the annotation (in Protégé) of all types of sensors present in SmartME, while Figure 3 shows a graphical view of a temperature sensor instance (Sendor_HMP50). A modification has been carried out in SSN Ontology, which made it suitable for specific queries as the ones shown in Figures 4-8. Before SPARQL querying, SSN Ontology has been modified using the Protégé tool as the Temperature sensor hierarchy shown in the Figure 3. Our modified Ontology is capable to answer various different and important questions that are needed to develop a suitable IoT environment. These questions can be triggered any time, and their output can be combined to present many fruitful results. For example: *Sensor_Temp1* is an instance of temperature sensor, located near *Location_01* and its measured minimum & maximum temperature is 8.7 & 19.67 Celsius, during day hours.

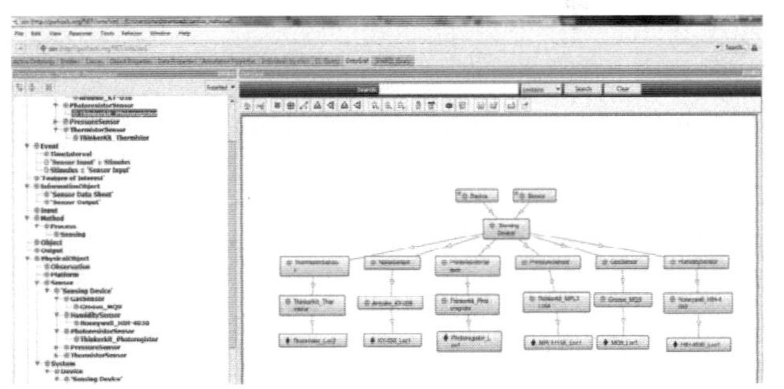

Figure 2. Annotate the type of sensors in protégé tool

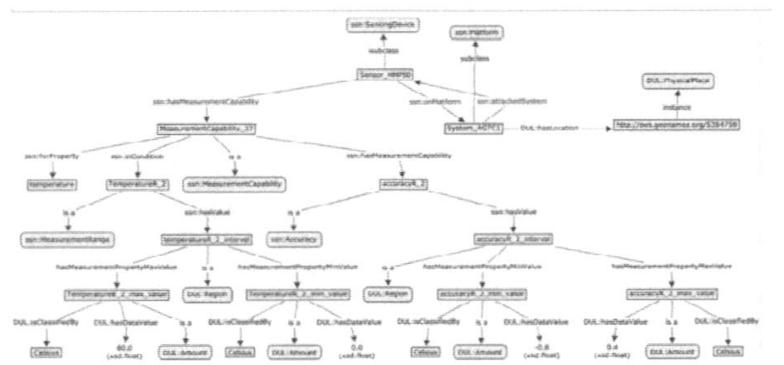

Figure 3. Graphical view of a temperature sensor instance

Q1: What type of sensor have been used

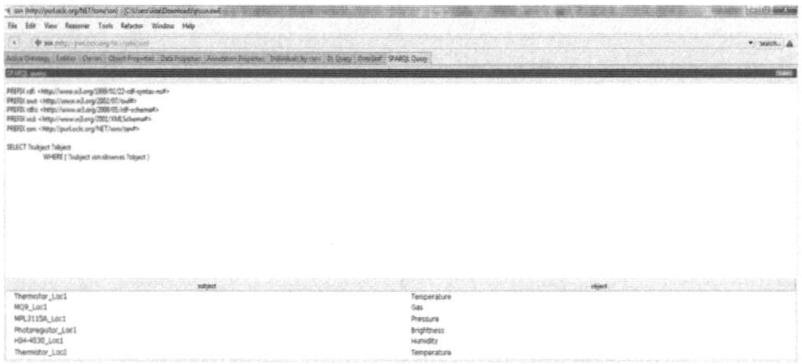

Figure 4. SPARQL query for different types of sensors

Q2: What is the type of specific sensor?

Figure 5. SPARQL query for displaying the type of a sensor instance

Q3: What is the location of the sensor?

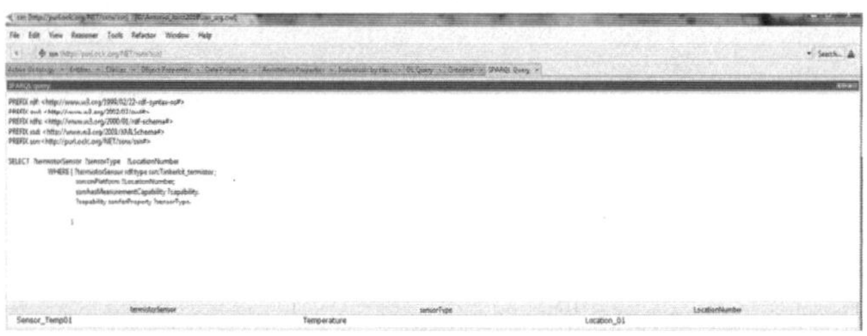

Figure 6. SPARQL query for displaying the location of a sensor instance

5. CONCLUDING REMARKS

Today, when we think about Smart Cities, we think about several applications such as traffic monitoring, energy management, e-health, disaster management, etc. For fast uptake of IoT devices, the key issues like semantic interoperability and cloud technologies have been taken into account in this project. Our main aim was to integrate a semantic layer with the SmartME project of the University of Messina for the betterment of several IoT applications. To do so, we have considered previously developed sensor Ontology, SSN, and according to the requirements of the SmartME project, we have customized this Ontology with Protégé tool. Furthermore, to check the applicability of the modified SSN ontology, we have fire various SPARQL queries on it.

Q4: What are the maximum and minimum temperatures measured by that sensor and when were they measured?

Figure 7. SPARQL query for displaying max. & min. temperature captured by a sensor instance

Q5: What is the unit of measured temperature?

Figure 8. SPARQL query knowing the unit of temperature captured by a sensor instance

6. REFERENCES

[1] Pfisterer, D., Römer, K., Bimschas, D., Kleine, O., Mietz, R., Truong, C., Hasemann, H., Kröller, A., Pagel, M.,Hauswirth, M. and Karnstedt, M., 2011. SPITFIRE: toward a semantic web of things. *IEEE Communications Magazine,* 49, 40-48.

[2] Compton et. al. 2011. The SSN Ontology of the Semantic Sensor Networks Incubator Gr., *J. of Web Sem.*, 17, 25-32..

[3] Barnaghi, P. et al. 2012. Semantics for the Internet of Things: early progress and back to the future. *International J. on Semantic Web and Information Systems (IJSWIS)* 8, 1-21.

[4] Ploennigs, J., Schumann, A. and Lecue. F. 2014. Extending Semantic Sensor Networks for Automatically Tackling Smart Building Problems. *Frontiers in Artificial Intelligence and Applications*, 1211-1212.

[5] Mitton, N., Rivano, H. 2015. On the use of city bikes to make the city even smarter. *In Proceedings of SMARTCOMP workshop on Sensors and Smart Cities*, China. 3-8.

[6] Gyrard, A., Patel, P., Sheth, A. and Serrano, M. 2016. Building the Web of Knowledge with Smart IoT Applications, Kno.e.sis Central Technical Report.

[7] https://jena.apache.org/documentation/io/

[8] Giacobbe, M., Puliafito, C., Scarpa, M. 2016. The Big Bucket: An IoT Cloud Solution For Smart Waste Management in Smart Cities, In Proceedings of the 4th Int. W. on Cloud for IoT, Austria.

[9] https://www.w3.org/TR/ld-bp

Quantitative evaluation of Cloud-based network virtualization mechanisms for IoT

Giovanni Merlino
Università degli Studi di Messina, Italy
gmerlino@unime.it

Francesco Longo
Università degli Studi di Messina, Italy
flongo@unime.it

Salvatore Distefano
Università degli Studi di Messina, Italy
sdistefano@unime.it
Kazan Federal University, Russia
sdistefano@kpfu.ru

Dario Bruneo
Università degli Studi di Messina, Italy
flongo@unime.it

Antonio Puliafito
Università degli Studi di Messina, Italy
apuliafito@unime.it

ABSTRACT

Integration of the Internet of Things (IoT) with the Cloud may lead to a range of different architectures and solutions. Our efforts in this domain are mainly geared towards making IoT systems available as service-oriented infrastructure. Under Infrastructure-as-a-Service (IaaS) scenarios, network virtualization is a core building block of any solution, even more so for IoT-focused Cloud providers. Enabling mechanisms are required to support virtualization of the networking facilities for IoT resources that are managed by the Cloud. This work describes an approach to network virtualization based on popular off-the-shelf tools and protocols in place of application-specific logic, acting as a blueprint in the design of the Stack4Things architecture, an OpenStack-derived framework to provide IaaS-like services from a pool of IoT devices. We quantitatively evaluate the underlying mechanisms demonstrating that the proposed approach exhibits mostly comparable performance with respect to standard technologies for virtual private networks, or at least good enough for the kind of underlying hardware, e.g., smart boards, whilst still representing a more flexible solution.

Keywords

IoT; Cloud; OpenStack; network virtualization; VPN; reverse tunneling; performance evaluation

1. INTRODUCTION

In a typical Infrastructure-as-a-Service (IaaS) Cloud, users are able to create and bring up virtual machines (VMs), access the instances through ssh, VNC, or Web-based virtual console as well as to instantiate even topologically complex virtual networks among a set of VMs. Any solution meant to take advantage of IoT resources available outside the datacenter, if those are to be provided according to IaaS principles, would need to implement at least similar facilities.

In a heavily distributed ecosystem, such as IoT-related scenarios, many requirements diverge significantly in comparison to typical IaaS Cloud environments, such as the presence of nodes installed behind firewalls and/or NATs (especially when IPv6 deployments are not an option) or, more in general, the necessity to deal with any restricted environment with denied-by-default (institutional or corporate) security policies. Such constraints call for more powerful mechanisms to enable core functionalities for virtual infrastructure management, i.e., remote access to board-hosted resources and instantiation of virtual networks.

Any network virtualization [2],[5] mechanism for IoT infrastructure thus requires at least some form of reconfiguration capabilities for board-side networking facilities as well. Yet, in contrast to typically datacenter-oriented IaaS, the physical environment (cabling and media access setup, logical topologies and hierarchies, role allocation for equipment) in IoT scenarios is not always under control of the designer of the infrastructure, which may as well be opportunistically assembled, e.g., volunteer-contributed.

This paper describes a rationale and some mechanisms to enable such functionalities when dealing with the unique requirements and challenges dictated by IoT environments, e.g., embedded boards and other constrained devices. In particular, network virtualization is addressed here to provide suitable facilities on top of Cloud-managed IoT resources in a technology agnostic fashion, still taking into account the limitations of smart devices, while at the same time suitable to be mapped onto an IaaS-focused solution, as investigated in [3] in terms of a device-centric approach for sensor-hosting nodes.

VALUETOOLS 2016, October 25-28, Taormina, Italy

2. STACK4THINGS

In our infrastructure-oriented approach we envisioned a *virtualization* layer for boards, able to provide access to I/O pins, such as GPIO, as a Service through RESTful interfaces, and to send (predefined or custom) commands to the environment running on the board. Here, we propose our implementation of such an approach, namely the Stack4Things [7] framework, from now on referred to as S4T, designed by extending the relevant OpenStack subsystems to smoothly integrate and leverage as much existing functionalities as possible.

In terms of hardware options with regard to boards, we confine the discussion on purpose to relatively smart embedded devices, such as modern Raspberry PI or Arduino-based hybrid systems, hosting either kind of (low power) microprocessor (MPU) and/or micro-controller (MCU) units. Such kind of boards is suited to host a minimal Linux distro, e.g., OpenWRT, able then to host a number of tools and runtime environments, such as Node.js or Python, where the *S4T lightning-rod*, the node-side component of the S4T architecture, runs on the MPU and interacts with the OS tools and services of the board, and with sensing and actuation resources through I/O pins. It represents the point of contact with the Cloud infrastructure. This is ensured by a WAMP and WebSocket-based communication between the S4T lightning-rod and its Cloud counterpart, namely the *S4T IoTronic service*, which is characterized by the standard architecture of an OpenStack service.

The main goals of IoTronic lie in extending the OpenStack architecture towards the management of sensing and actuation resources, i.e., to be an implementation of the SAaaS paradigm. However, in this work we focus on the mechanisms providing network virtualization facilities as described in the following section.

3. NETWORK VIRTUALIZATION FOR IOT

Our approach to network virtualization is based on enabling mechanisms in terms of custom layering and board-side tunneling facilities, to be coupled with the corresponding Cloud-side adaptations.

3.1 Tunneling and layering model

As remote infrastructure, boards are possibly going to be available over very restrictive, IPv4-only deployments. The only assumption that can (for all purposes, always) be considered true is outgoing Web traffic being permitted, i.e., board-initiated communication over standard HTTP/HTTPS ports. We thus resorted to an HTTP-borne mechanism for bidirectional connectivity and reachability of internal services, namely WS. WebSockets [4] as channels between a browser and a server are considered standard facilities for bidirectional communication and in particular server-pushed messaging. One of the main advantages of WS is that it is network agnostic, by just piggybacking communication onto standard HTTP interactions. This is of benefit for those environments which block Web-unrelated traffic using firewalls. Less explored is the creation of generic TCP tunnels over WS, a way to get client-initiated connectivity to any server-side local (or remote) service.

In early work [9] we devised a design and implementation of a novel *reverse* tunneling technique, as a way to provide server-initiated, e.g., Cloud-triggered, connectivity to any board-hosted service, or any other node on a contributed resource network, e.g., a WSN. In particular the latter may enable typical IoT scenarios, e.g., Machine-to-Machine (M2M) interactions, by supporting these patterns in a device-centric [3] fashion. This way, a gateway acting not only as a proxy for access to data gathered from mostly passive resources, but also as a relay to activate remoting toward nodes in a masqueraded network is available, thus allowing to explore options beyond protocols such as Traversal Using Relays around NAT (TURN) [8].

3.2 Server-less mesh implementation

Thank to the availability of an always-on WAMP control channel, the above mentioned scenario can also be reproduced in a fully peer-to-peer fashion. In such a case, one board, out of the set of IoT devices that need to be connected over a certain virtual network, is selected by the Cloud to act as a central node in a star topology, according to a ranking for suitability in taking that role, on the basis of current availability of on-board resources and load. An ad-hoc variation of the TCP *hole punching* [13] technique, in which the Cloud would preliminarily act as the required third party in the phase of connection establishment, is exploited to allow all the other devices belonging to the virtual network to connect to the chosen central node by establishing WebSocket-based reverse tunnels. On top of such a peer-based WebSocket-based infrastructure, the virtual network is built, in a star topology. Once the virtual network is formed, network communication is fully peer-to-peer and does not require any further action from the Cloud until the (virtual) network needs to be torn down. Moreover, other topologies may be enabled as well, such as a full-mesh at layer 2 among all the boards selected to be interconnected over a Cloud-initiated virtual network.

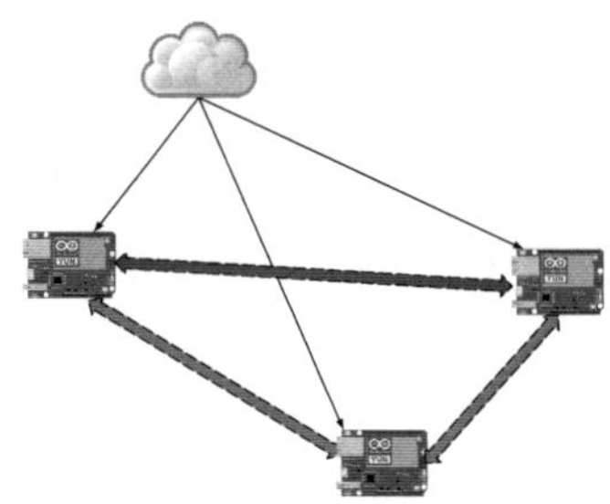

Figure 1: Cloud-enabled server-less star and mesh topologies.

In Figure 1 a simple 3-node network (plus the Cloud) is depicted, where the thick double-sided blue arrows correspond to the star topology, when the node in the middle of the figure is chosen as the center of the star, whilst a similar arrow in red stands for the missing link among peers to establish a full mesh. The thin single-sided black arrow represents both (transient) WS-based connection establishment, and just steady command streams afterwards, having the Cloud at that point already hole-punched the nodes and subsequently torn down its tunnels to those.

In that case the topology would be a tree over the set of bridges exposed by the boards, dynamically instantiated by means of, e.g., a protocol for automatic configuration of bridges belonging to the Spanning Tree family. In this case the virtual network would not feature any single point of failure, nor have a node be the bottleneck for all the generated traffic inside the network itself. On the other hand, this configuration requires a longer setup phase, due to the establishment of an higher number of tunnels, $n(n-1)/2$, in proportion to the number of nodes n, compared to the star topology, $n-1$, and more importantly a slightly higher baseline in terms of requirements, as each node would host a virtual bridge, not just the central node.

4. A USE CASE

In order to test and validate the proposed solution, we developed experiments on a smart city environment. #SmartME [1] is a crowdfounding project that aims at collecting a number of field-deployed networks of sensors and actuators in Messina into a federated Smart City infrastructure, provided as-a-service [10], actually an instance of a so-called Software-Defined City [11]. Thanks to such an infrastructure, it will be possible to collect data and information to build services for citizens, who may take part in this network through the involvement of smartphones and other mobile devices by which it will be possible to interact with objects and may even themselves turn into data producers.

4.1 Description

For our network virtualization approach, #SmartME represents an interesting testbed and case study, thanks to a development, deployment and testing platform integrated with networks of sensors, actuators or other smart devices already deployed to the district area, and to this day employed exclusively for specific application domains and a limited number of purposes.

The virtual networking subsystem has been put to test in this context by exploiting the #SmartME testbed, considering two main scenarios, one based on clients (e.g., boards) behind residential xDSL gateways, e.g., at home, and another one based on clients belonging to the (Fast) Ethernet-switched network of the university campus, respectively.

The first one is thus about connectivity scenarios over a Wide-Area Network, whereas the second one over a LAN, respectively.

4.2 Quantitave evaluation

Here we provide an evaluation focusing on specific key performance indices, namely latency and throughput.

Table 1 and Table 2 report on the set of experiments that have been conducted. The experiments are based on the *iperf3* [14] tool for measuring throughput and the ubiquitous *ping* tool to gauge latency, the latter by means of ICMP echo requests to obtain Round-Trip Time values as estimation of delay. In both cases, the test setup consists in having a server ready, and generating traffic over TCP (iperf) or ICMP requests (ping) from the client, which collects partial and final statistics. Values in the table are averages computed over a number of 1000 samples, where each chunk of 10 samples represent a single run for the tool. We did not include variance values because they are negligible.

The first column indicates the kind of technology employed and under which topology: in particular, *direct* refers to tests between two hosts directly connected, over WAN or LAN, respectively. The *vpn-p2p* abbreviation refers to an OpenVPN server to which an OpenVPN client is connected, under the same roles as the two aforementioned hosts. Same happens for *s4t-p2p*, in this case with two hosts controlled by the S4T Cloud which, by first hole-punching through in the setup phase, connects one to the other directly over a WebSocket tunnel in combination with SOCAT. In the *vpn-srv* and *s4t-srv* cases, the OpenVPN server and the S4T Cloud, respectively, enable two clients to act as the two hosts, connected over a bridge which resides on the server (or the Cloud).

For the sake of comparing under the most relevant conditions, OpenVPN has been tested in TCP mode, and various parameters (e.g., MTU of the TUN interfaces, MSS for both iperf and the TCP tunnels) had already been tuned for S4T in the implementation phases, as also discussed below. As latencies are absolutely aligned in the various scenarios, or at least very predictable (e.g., natural increase for multi-hop setups, such as server-based OpenVPN or S4T Cloud-based virtual network for two clients), we will focus the discussion on the more interesting and insightful values obtained for the throughput metric, albeit it is actually latency that may be considered the most relevant metric for the use case under consideration, as it is key for near real-time (e.g., multimedia) applications, and the most reliable metric in general for embedded systems, considering that throughput is naturally more susceptible to other factors, e.g., high CPU load or RAM usage, differences in the media interface, etc.

iPerf3 works by repeatedly sending an array of *len* bytes for *time* seconds, where *len* by default is 128KB for TCP, and the default for *time* is 10 seconds. Even if not reported in the table, retransmissions, equal to about 500 in case of SOCAT-based TUN-over-TCP, i.e., where the *s4t-p2p* scenario is stripped of the WS tunnel, in a 10-second period, ramp up to almost 5000 for the same time interval when also piping over WS, i.e., the full end-to-end *s4t-p2p*, thus roughly increasing retransmissions ten-fold. Throughput thus decreases correspondingly to about a tenth, from almost 90Mbps to about 10Mbps to be precise.

This degradation in the performance with regard to throughput derives from a limited CWND (Congestion Window) on average, less than 10KBytes, compared to 2-3M under ideal conditions, i.e., corresponding to about 90Mbps throughput as seen in the table. The problem then lies in a relatively high number of retransmissions, leading to a comparatively small congestion window. Some workarounds exist, either to lower retransmissions in this scenario, such as disabling Nagle's algorithm, or to make TCP more aggressively reactive to retransmissions, ramping up speed more quickly, such as switching to a different congestion control policy, in particular *Scalable* [6], both of which have been applied during testing.

Otherwise, it is intrinsic to how TCP works (i.e., the streaming model) the inability to fully control how TUN-inbound datagrams are encapsulated and delivered as payload in the data stream. This means that there are bound to be packet losses (and thus retransmissions) due, for instance, to the splicing of two (IP) datagrams as payload of a single (TCP) segment. When that happens, the payload cannot be passed without errors to the (outbound) TUN on the other side of the tunnel, which expects the delivery of single (whole) datagrams, and either rejects or truncates what it gets due to mismatches between the MTU and the size of such segments

In this sense, the presence of a tunnel based on WebSockets exacerbates the behaviour by introducing a further chance to introduce randomness in the delivery by virtue of TCP-level decapsulation and subsequent re-encapsulation, the latter as a result of the TCP channel established over WebSockets. This as a result of trading off raw performance, at the price of high application-level complexity and an (internal) ad-hoc architecture, as is the case for OpenVPN, with the simplicity and flexibility of off-the-shelf tools act-

Table 1: Throughput and latency measurements: xDSL.

Topology/Technology	iperf: *throughput [Mbps]*	ping: *latency (RTT) [ms]*
direct	0.993	85.2
vpn-p2p	0.964	88.95
vpn-srv	0.811	136.8
s4t-p2p	0.405	83.38
s4t-srv	0.335	123.6

Table 2: Throughput and latency measurements: campus network.

Topology/Technology	iperf: *throughput [Mbps]*	ping: *latency (RTT) [ms]*
direct	92.5	0.23
vpn-p2p	88.02	0.725
vpn-srv	81.75	1.501
s4t-p2p	10.65	1.813
s4t-srv	4.017	3.579

ing as separate subsystems and taking care of different facets of the communication model, in line with the UNIX philosophy of using one (good) tool for each job.

Fortunately results are still absolutely decent, and ensure the viability of such a solution for embedded systems where the throughput of any modular solution, when fully in userspace, is typically lower anyway, since it may be capped by the CPU maxing out, as is the case for the Node.js-based reverse tunneling, possibly due to the current limitations of the V8 engine under MIPS.

When considering the case of WAN-level connectivity, e.g., featuring significantly lower bandwidth and naturally higher delay, it may be noticed that throughput for the S4T-based setups degrades less sharply, only down to about 50%, as can be seen in Table 1. Moreover, there is room for improvement considering that, compared to plain TCP sockets, WebSockets support delimiting payloads according to a specific *message*-oriented semantics for delivery, a facility which may indeed be exploited in this very sense.

5. CONCLUSIONS

Our opinion is that a novel approach is required for IoT and Cloud integration, and models and mechanisms which are agnostic to field deployments and topologies are essential to IoT infrastructure management and service provisioning.

Our approach to Cloud-enabled virtual networking for IoT tries to provide a blueprint for a combined solution, where VPN-like behavior, albeit the most easily advertised functionality and the one most easily picked up for a comparison, is actually just one out of many features. Other useful ones include always-on centralized control by means of WS-based command streams, bypassing restrictive firewall policies by piggybacking onto HTTP, relaying traffic through the Cloud for NAT traversal, Cloud-initiated hole punching to support server-less star and tree topologies for peer-to-peer networks, or even exposing internal services through reverse tunneling.

Moreover, functional requirements aside, performance has been shown to be mostly comparable and in all cases absolutely acceptable considering inherent limitations of the hardware platforms under consideration.

In terms of performance, the aforementioned considerations about the results will be the starting point for further improvements to the design, in particular resorting to facilities such as the WebSockets message-based semantics to partly overcome limitations intrinsic to the communication model, or even modifying some of the system-level tools, e.g., SOCAT, by employing low-overhead simple bytestream-oriented protocols on top of TCP, such as SLIP [12], to mark packet boundaries within the (TCP) payload.

6. REFERENCES

[1] D. Bruneo, S. Distefano, F. Longo, and G. Merlino. An IoT testbed for the Software Defined City vision: The #SmartMe project. In *2016 IEEE International Conference on Smart Computing (SMARTCOMP)*, pages 1–6, May 2016.

[2] N. M. K. Chowdhury and R. Boutaba. A survey of network virtualization. *Computer Networks*, 54(5):862 – 876, 2010.

[3] S. Distefano, G. Merlino, and A. Puliafito. Device-centric Sensing: an alternative to data-centric approaches. *IEEE Systems Journal*, 2015.

[4] I. Fette and A. Melnikov. The WebSocket protocol. RFC 6455.

[5] A. Fischer, J. Botero, M. Till Beck, H. de Meer, and X. Hesselbach. Virtual network embedding: a survey. *Communications Surveys Tutorials, IEEE*, 15(4):1888–1906, Fourth 2013.

[6] T. Kelly. Scalable TCP: improving performance in highspeed Wide Area Networks. *SIGCOMM Comput. Commun. Rev.*, 33(2):83–91, Apr. 2003.

[7] F. Longo, D. Bruneo, S. Distefano, G. Merlino, and A. Puliafito. Stack4Things: a Sensing-and-Actuation-as-a-Service framework for IoT and Cloud integration. *Annals of Telecommunications*, pages 1–18, 2016.

[8] R. Mahy, P. Matthews, and J. Rosenberg. Traversal Using Relays around Nat (turn): Relay extensions to Session Traversal Utilities for Nat (stun). RFC 5766.

[9] G. Merlino, D. Bruneo, S. Distefano, F. Longo, and A. Puliafito. Enabling mechanisms for Cloud-based network virtualization in IoT. pages 268–273, 2015.

[10] G. Merlino, D. Bruneo, S. Distefano, F. Longo, and A. Puliafito. Stack4Things: Integrating IoT with OpenStack in a Smart City context. 2015.

[11] G. Merlino, D. Bruneo, F. Longo, A. Puliafito, and S. Distefano. Software Defined Cities: a novel paradigm for Smart Cities through IoT clouds. pages 909–916, 2015.

[12] J. Romkey. Nonstandard for transmission of IP datagrams over serial lines: SLIP. STD 47, RFC Editor.

[13] P. Srisuresh, B. Ford, and D. Kegel. State of Peer-to-Peer (P2P) communication across Network Address Translators (NATs). RFC 5128.

[14] A. Tirumala, F. Qin, J. Dugan, J. Ferguson, and K. Gibbs. iPerf: the TCP/UDP bandwidth measurement tool. *http://software.es.net/iperf/*, 2005.

Performance Prediction for Burstable Cloud Resources*

Daniel J. Dubois, Giuliano Casale
Imperial College London, Department of Computing, London, United Kingdom
{daniel.dubois, g.casale}@imperial.ac.uk

ABSTRACT

We propose ForeBurst, an open source tool for performance prediction for complex cloud-based applications. ForeBurst leverages queueing network models for predicting performance metrics such as resource utilizations, request response times, and credit usage in burstable resources, such as the Amazon EC2 T-family instances.

CCS Concepts

•Computing methodologies → Simulation evaluation; •Software and its engineering → Software performance;

Keywords

Burstable cloud; performance prediction; cloud simulator.

1. INTRODUCTION

Cloud computing success derives from the possibility for organizations to provision computing resources over the Internet and pay only for the ones actually used. The most common pricing models are: *(i) on-demand* resources with fixed price and fixed performance; *(ii) spot* resources in which the prices fluctuate; *(iii) preemtible* resources that do not have a guaranteed availability; and finally *(iv) burstable* resources, in which the resource performance changes based on utilization history.

One of the main problems cloud users face is the minimization of the costs for provisioning the computational requirements while still fulfilling their performance needs. Current research efforts are tackling this problem by providing means to predict the performance of a cloud application from a model of the application itself, which may be, for example, in the form of an annotated UML model or a queueing network (QN) model. Most existing works focus on static on-demand resources only [3, 5], while more recent ones also consider additional types of pricing models, such as spot and preemptible pricing models [2, 1]. For what concerns the burstable resources, some works that study their behavior already exist [7], but an usable tool to predict the performance from the application model in this situation is currently missing.

The purpose of this paper is to propose ForeBurst, a performance prediction tool, which supports the analysis of burstable cloud resources. In Section 2 we describe the system model, the prediction problem, and the solution. Section 3 describes the tool and shows some results. Finally, Section 4 concludes the paper.

2. MODEL, PROBLEM, AND SOLUTION

The Model. We consider cloud applications modeled as a queueing network (QN), which is a model that can be automatically derived from other commonly used models such as annotated UML diagrams [5]. In particular, we consider closed multi-class and multi-queue QN models with exponentially distributed services times. Each queue represents a cloud resource running an application component (e.g., a DB server). The *service rate* μ of each queue, defined as the average number of jobs that can be processed per time unit, is assumed scaled proportionally to the speed of the cloud resource in which the application component is deployed.

The Problem. The main problem we want to address is the prediction of performance information, such as – for example – the utilization, the response time distribution, etc. This problem has already been solved by several existing tools (e.g., [4]) under the assumption that μ is constant, which unfortunately is not true for application components deployed on burstable resources. In such resources the μ of every queue can change over time depending on the jobs processed in the past. A real implementation of a burstable cloud resource is the Amazon EC2 T2.micro resource. This resource encodes past history in the form of a number credits k that increases when the resource utilization is under a certain threshold, and decreases when the utilization is over such threshold. Low credits result in a slower resource (lower μ), while high credits result in a faster resource (higher μ).

The Solution. We have solved this problem in the specific case of the T2.micro resources. However, the same method can be used for other types of burstable resources as well. In our approach we had first to measure through experiments how μ varies with respect to the number of credits, thus obtaining a $\mu(k)$ function that is not currently given by the cloud providers. Second, we had to determine the period in which the actual μ is updated as the number of k varies: in the case of the T2.micro resources, updates happen every 5 minutes. Since μ is periodically constant for each queue, we can solve the QN until the next μ is expected to change. To solve the QN we used LINE [4], which, thanks to the fact that it solves the QN using a system of ODEs, it is able to predict the evolution of the QN after a customized period of time. This result can then be used to estimate the utilization and therefore any change in k and μ. At

*Daniel J. Dubois has been partially funded by the People Programme (Marie Curie Actions) SPANDO FP7 project (FP7-629982). Giuliano Casale has been supported by the European Unions Horizon 2020 research and innovation programme under grant agreement No. 644869 (DICE). The data generated in this paper are available at: http://dx.doi.org/10.5281/zenodo.49068.

VALUETOOLS 2016, October 25-28, Taormina, Italy

this point we can solve again the QN using the final ODEs state of the previous evaluation as starting state for the new evaluation, but with the new updated service rate. Finally, by iterating this process it is eventually possible to predict the future performance with no limitations.

3. THE TOOL

We have developed ForeBurst as a MATLAB module downloadable from [6]. It uses LINE [4] as its backend QN solver, and expands its functionality with the possibility to mark some queues as burstable. Each burstable queue requires the specification of the initial number of credits, the maximum credits, how credits are accrued or deducted based on previous utilization (amount and periodicity), the service rate function $\mu(k)$, and the utilization discount value L. L is a factor that reduces the utilization measured by the cloud provider with respect to the real utilization. All the parameters are given by the cloud provider, except for $\mu(k)$ and L, which – in the case of Amazon EC2 – had to be measured from experiments in the real system.

Fig. 1 shows some plots of the prediction data produced by ForeBurst in the case of a system of 100 jobs and two queues: a Web server and a DB server, both deployed on Amazon EC2 T2.micro instances with 30 initial credits. The Web server can process 1000 jobs/s at full credits, while the DB server can process 500 jobs/s. By looking at the evolution of the available credits for 7200 seconds, we can see that the DB server depletes its starting credits, while the Web server eventually accrues new credits. The reason is that the DB server loses its credits first because of the high utilization. Once the service rate of the DB server is scaled down, most jobs are stuck in its queue, thus leaving the web server severely underutilized with few jobs to process.

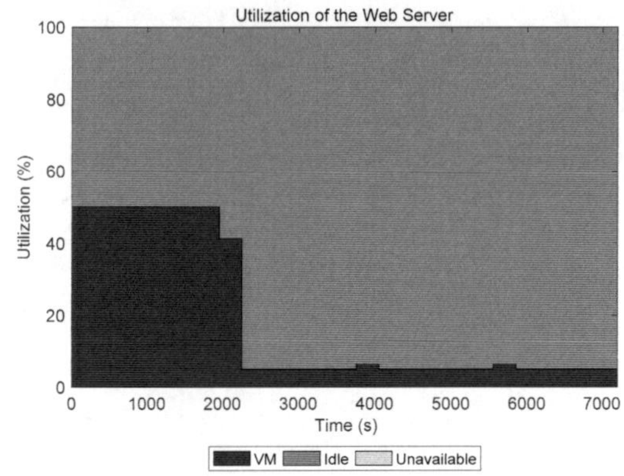

(a) Web Server Utilization.

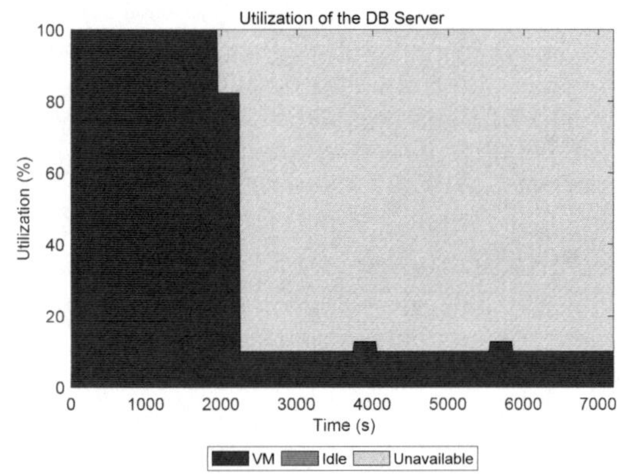

(b) DB Server Utilization.

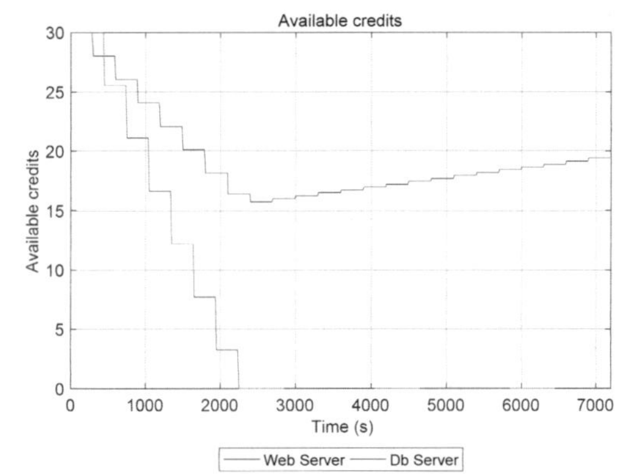

(c) Credit balance.

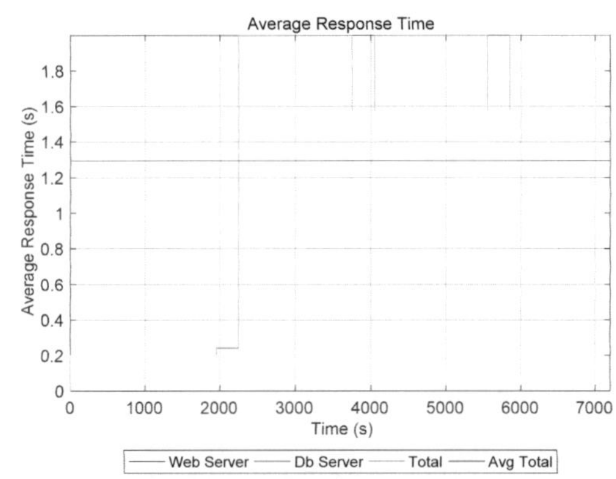

(d) Average Response Time.

Figure 1: Results produced by the ForeBurst tool.

4. CONCLUSIONS

In this paper we have presented ForeBurst as a tool for predicting the performance of cloud applications deployed on burstable cloud resources, whose performance can change based on past utilization. The tool can be downloaded from [6]. We envision that this tool will make possible to study and better understand the performance–cost tradeoff that this type of resources actually offers. In the future we plan to integrate ForeBurst in an optimization framework so that the decision whether to use a certain type of resources or not can be automated.

5. REFERENCES

[1] D. J. Dubois and G. Casale. OptiSpot: minimizing application deployment cost using spot cloud resources. *Cluster Comp.*, 2016.

[2] D. J. Dubois, C. Trubiani, and G. Casale. Autonomic Provisioning and Application Mapping on Spot Cloud Resources. In *IEEE CLOUD '16*, 2016.

[3] D. Franceschelli, D. Ardagna, M. Ciavotta, and E. Di Nitto. SPACE4CLOUD: A Tool for System Performance and Cost Evaluation of Cloud Systems. In *MultiCloud '13*, pages 27–34, 2013.

[4] Line solver http://line-solver.sourceforge.net.

[5] J. F. Perez and G. Casale. Assessing SLA Compliance from Palladio Component Models. In *MICAS '13*, pages 409–416, 2013.

[6] SPANDO EU Project. Software download: http://www.spando.org/software.

[7] J. Wen, L. Lu, G. Casale, and E. Smirni. Less can be more: Micro-managing vms in amazon ec2. In *IEEE CLOUD '15*, pages 317–324, 2015.

Modeling and shaping the lifetime of target detection sensor networks

Lorenzo Donatiello
Computer Science and Engineering Department
University of Bologna
Bologna, Italy
lorenzo.donatiello@unibo.it

Gustavo Marfia
Department for Life Quality Studies
University of Bologna
Bologna, Italy
gustavo.marfia@unibo.it

ABSTRACT

In this work we model the lifetime of a clustered sensor network deployed for target detection. We assume sensors are randomly dropped on a bidimensional field in order to detect target traversals occuring stochastically. Once a target enters the sensing area of a sensor, the sensor transmits such information to a cluster head, in charge of receiving and retransmitting the messages received from the sensors deployed on the field. The contribution of this work is threefold. We first identify the sensing nodes whose behavior is key to model the duration of sensing operations. We then proceed, providing a heuristic estimation of the traffic received by the cluster head to quantify its energy requirements, resorting to specific lifetime definitions. We finally evaluate the relationship between our probabilistic and heuristic models and the time until when the network fulfills its purpose, i.e., it remains capable of detecting and reporting the traversal of any target to a sink, as obtained by simulation.

Keywords

Surveillance sensor network; lifetime definition; stochastic analysis.

1. INTRODUCTION

It is difficult to delimit the fields of application of sensor networks, as they have reached any type of context and site (e.g., body, underwater, vehicular, Internet of Things, etc.) [1,5,16,17]. Among the many challenges these networks pose, finding ways of characterizing and increasing their lifetime amounts to one of the main ones [2]: as nodes deplete their energy and shutdown, the sensing power a network degrades, until no longer capable of fulfilling its scope.

Lifetime analysis is challenging, as no unique and widely accepted definition exists which well adapts to all possible application scenarios. In a context where the monitored variable is the surface temperature of a field, for example, an acceptable metric may amount to the lifetime of the longest lasting sensor, when all deployed sensors are expected to provide sample values which are very close to each other, no matter where positioned. In a single barrier coverage situation, instead, the time of death of the first sensor may coincide with the lifetime of the network, as beyond such time the network may no longer be capable of guaranteeing the detection of a target crossing an area of interest. In this work we adopt a perspective which is close to this second example, as we study the key variables which influence most the efficacy and duration of a surveillance system composed by a number of sensors randomly dropped to monitor the traversal of a given bidimensional area.

In particular, the surveillance system amounts to a clustered sensor network whose scope is to detect and report specific type of events: the traversals of targets across an area of interest (e.g., herds of animals crossing a canyon, soldiers moving through a minecamp, etc.). As a target enters, moves across the area and reaches its exit, it enters the sensing region of different sensors. All those sensors that detect the presence of the target transmit a message to a cluster head, in charge of receiving and retransmitting the messages received by all sensors to a sink. In such scenario, our aim is to individuate and model the nodes whose lifetime matches the lifetime of the surveillance system, as determined by the following definition [9]: *the lifetime of a surveillance system is assumed to be represented by the lifetime(s) of its most critical traversal path(s), the path(s) that will first be available to a target for an undetected traversal.*

To proceed with such analysis, we assume a sufficient number of nodes are initially deployed to guarantee the detection of a target at any inner point within the area of interest. In addition, we assume the availability of prior: (a) target arrival and mobility models and, (b) an energy consumption model per target detection and message transmission/reception. We then probabilistically model and analyze two classes of key sensing nodes: (a) the node(s) which exhibit the highest probability of dying first, and, (b) a specific subset (which subset, will become clear in Section 4) of the node(s), located on the path(s) which traverse the node(s) determined at the previous point, with the highest probability of dying last. Resorting to such models, we provide an approximation of the probabilistic distribution function of a surveillance system lifetime as provided by the aforementioned definition. Finally, such results are also utilized to heuristically estimate the amount of energy required by the cluster head, in order to guarantee the forwarding of any messages received during the active phase of the surveillance

VALUETOOLS 2016, October 25-28, Taormina, Italy

system.

The remainder of this paper is structured as follows. Section 2 provides an overview of the state-of-the-art, from a point of view of the stochastic analysis of sensor network lifetime. In Section 3 we delineate the system scenario of interest, whereas in Section 4 we provide our models. An evaluation of our model is provided in Section 5, whereas Section 6 concludes this work.

2. RELATED WORK

Studies evaluating the lifetime model of wireless sensor networks may be found in a plethora of scientific contributions [6, 14, 15, 19, 21, 23]. However, only a few have analyzed the node and network lifetimes in a pure probabilistic way [4, 7, 18, 20]. In the following, we provide an overview of three of such works.

[18] presents a lifetime analysis of a randomly deployed clustered network, where a cluster head collects data from the nodes within its cluster, performing data aggregation and compression, finally relaying such data to a sink. The main characteristics of this model are: (a) an approximation for the complementary cumulative distribution function of cluster lifetime is found for event-driven networks, (b) two sensing modes are considered, one where an event is only reported by the closest node and a second by all nodes, (c) the stochastic nature of the network lifetime follows from the randomness of the sensors deployment, the amount of energy required to transmit a data packet at different distances, the events' appearance time and location, and, (d) the sensor network lifetime is assumed active as long as β out of N sensors are still alive [19].

Also [20] proposes a stochastic analysis of the energy consumption in a random network environment providing: (a) a cross-layer Markov process based framework to characterize the energy consumption distribution during a given period of time, (b) where energy consumption is shown converge to a Normal distribution, if the time period is large enough, and, (c) with the consequent computation of node lifetime and network lifetime distributions. In addition, authors assume that event arrivals are independent and identically distributed at all nodes and in correspondence of an arrival an equal amount of data is transmitted.

The contribution presented in [7] assumes an event may not always be detected by a sensor network, modeling the probability of detecting an event adopting an exponential negative decay law dependent on the distance from the interested node [11]. In addition, a node is represented as a network entity which can transmit a maximum number of packets, not considering the fact that energy resources are spent also while in idle mode.

This main differences between our work and [7,18,20] are: (a) two different lifetime definition are considered, which well adapt to the specific scenario of interest, (b) events are not modeled as instantaneous and punctiform, an event is here also characterized by the path followed by a target when traversing the monitored area, and, (c) when a target traverses the monitored area, only those sensors whose sensing range cover the path are involved in the detection and reporting of the event.

3. SYSTEM MODEL

We consider a bidimensional field A of arbitrary shape, where N sensors are randomly dropped to monitor the traversals of targets which may appear at random times. The N dropped nodes are supposed to be sufficient to cover every single point in A and to report the detection of a target to a fixed cluster head. The cluster head is also equipped with a limited amount of energy, which may be more than the one provided to single sensors. The following summarizes the system assumptions made to formulate our analysis.

A sensor node, in general, consumes energy for sensing, receiving, transmitting, data processing, sleeping and also during the idle mode when no data sensing, processing or exchange happens. Such model is here simplified, considering the following modes of operation as the ones necessary to determine the lifetime of a node for the scenario of interest: sensing, transmitting and idle. The idle state does not correspond to the sleep one, as a sensing node is capable of detecting an event during idle mode. We also assume that the energy consumed while active, monitoring for the occurrence of events, is much lower than the energy spent during sensing and transmitting phases. A similar model is also adopted for the cluster head, with the difference that the cluster head is solely devoted to receive and retransmit messages to a sink node. Hence, during reception and transmissions, we assume the cluster head consumes an amount of energy which is much higher than the amount of energy spent during idle mode, when scanning the channel for the reception of any transmission. Now, instead of energy, we will directly deal with the corresponding lifetime quantities. Instead of considering the total energy of a given node i, we will refer to its maximum lifetime, $l_{max,i}$, here defined as the lifetime of node i while permanently staying in idle mode. For what concerns detection and transmission phases (or receival and retransmission at the cluster head), we assume i consumes a constant amount of lifetime equal to $l_{eh,i}$. As in previous works, events are assumed arriving to the monitored area according to a Poisson process. The Poisson distribution has been widely used in the literature to model events whose time/place of occurrence are random and independent from each other [3]. Also, in vehicle interarrival in highway scenarios, the Poisson distribution has been found an interesting model [13]. Unlike previous approaches, events do not popup at given points in space, but are detected by sensors as targets move along random trajectories within the area under observation. The shape of the monitored area may be random, depending on the application needs and on how the sensors spread when dropped. Our assumption is that it may always be possible to individuate an entry and an exit to the area. Different approaches may, then, be utilized to represent mobility within the area. A successful approach, adopted in literature, amounts to n-th order Markov Chains, $MC(n)$, where the probability of reaching a given state depends upon the n previously visited ones [12].

As anticipated, we consider a scenario where a sensor network organizes itself into clusters. With the adoption of a clustering scheme, nodes self-organize themselves into hierarchical layers. We assume three layers: (a) a bottom layer composed of sensing nodes in charge of detecting targets entering their sensing region and transmitting such information to the cluster head, (b) an intermediate one, made of a cluster head which receives and retransmits messages and, (c) a top one where a sink node collects all the information received by the cluster head. Assuming such type of organization, a time division multiple access (TDMA) scheme may be employed at the MAC layer, where the cluster head takes care of coordinating the time scheduling among the nodes. TDMA well fits our scenario of interest, as it is a common choice, at the MAC layer, for clustered WSNs [22]. Finally, such assumption also ensures the avoidance of collisions, allowing the modeling of intra-cluster transmissions as ideal.

4. LIFETIME MODEL

As anticipated, we consider two classes of sensing nodes to compute the lifetime of the surveillance system. The first class is very simple to identify: these are the node(s) that die first (exhaust their energy first) [8]. The second class, instead, is individuated as the subset of the node(s), which lying along the paths that contain the node(s) which are expected to die first, will die last [10]. Which subset we are referring to will become clear by the end of this Section.

Before proceeding, however, let us remind that in this paper we assume a generic sensing node i is equipped with an initial lifetime $l_{max,i}$, the time node i would live in case it was always idle. A sensing node i which, hence, utilizes part of its energy resources to detect targets and transmit messages, lives for an interval of time which is lower than $l_{max,i}$. Lifetime l_i may hence be written as: $l_i = l_{max,i} - l_{EH,i}$, where $l_{EH,i}$ amounts to the lifetime reserved and available for sensing and message transmission activities. We also assume all sensing nodes in the network are equipped with the same amount of energy at the beginning and that the amount of energy spent in correspondence of a sensing/message transmission activity is constant and equal for all nodes.

Now, the lifetime of a sensing node depends on how often it is involved in sensing/message transmission operations, i.e., on its probability of activation. The probability of activation, in turn, depends on the position of the sensing node within A and on the mobility model of targets. This means that depending on its position, but also on its sensing reach, a sensing node may be more often, or less, activated.

The individuation of the node that will die first, among all sensing nodes, can be performed individuating the position(s) with the highest activation probability, i.e., the highest probability of detecting a target: in fact, the sensors located in such position(s) will most probably exhaust their energy before any other.

The position(s) of the node(s) that will die first can also be put to good use to determine the sensor network lifetime according to the second approach of interest. In fact, with the individuation of the node(s) that will, with the highest chance, exhaust their energy first, it is also possible to individuate the path(s) that will, most probably, exhaust the energy of the monitoring sensors first, and their lifetime, as follows. Say, for example, only one position with the maximum activation probability value may be found in a specific area A. Denote such point as (x_M, y_M), with a corresponding activation probability equal to $p(x_M, y_M)$. Next, among all possible paths that traverse (x_M, y_M), individuate the path(s) characterized by the highest probability to be used to traverse the critical area (for simplicity, from now on we assume only one of such paths exist and indicate it as T). Such condition implies T is the path with the highest probability of exhausting its energy resources first, becoming viable for a target seeking an undetected traversal. Please note that the lifetime of T, and hence of the sensor network, may be analyzed modeling the behavior of the node exhibiting the lowest probability of activation: the lifetime of such node(s) amounts to the second lifetime metric considered in this work. Clearly, resorting to such probability metrics concerning the critical path one can establish several other heuristics which may result useful to compute stochastic bounds of the variable of interest.

To visualize how the location of the two nodes of interest may be individuated, consider Figure 1. In particular, Subfigure 1b represents the activation probability values of a 1 x 1 square, where targets can enter from any point on the $y = 0$ segment, traverse the area walking along a straight line, exiting from any point on the $y = 1$ segment. According to Subfigure 1b, the node that is expected to die first, i.e., the one with the highest probability of activation, falls exactly at the center of the area. Now, the position of the second node of interest can be found as follows: of all paths which start at some point on the $y = 0$ segment and end on the $y = 1$ one, take the one exhibiting the maximum value of all the minimum activation probabilities. Following such rule, we find such path as the one crossing the area along the $x = 0.5$ segment (the activation probabilities along the $x = 0.5$ segment are plotted in Subfigure 1a). Finally, referring again to Subfigure 1b, we conclude saying that the first lifetime of interest may be computed modeling the behavior of a node located in $(0.5, 0.5)$ (the location with highest activation probability), whereas second lifetime metric can be obtained analyzing the node(s) located in $(0.5, 0)$ and $(0.5, 1)$. In fact, when the sensor(s) located in $(0.5, 0)$ and $(0.5, 1)$ exhaust their energy, it is probabilistically plausible that the path connecting $(0.5, 0)$ to $(0.5, 1)$ will result free of active sensing devices. This is the most critical path in such scenario.

Before concluding, please note that the cluster head amounts to an important bottleneck for the flow of information from the field of sensing nodes to the sink. Because of this, we will show how it is possible to put to good use the lifetime definitions provided in this Section to compute the amount of energy required by the cluster head. In the following we show how it is possible to obtain: (a) a stochastic model for sensing nodes lifetime according to the two aforementioned definitions, and, (b) a heuristic function which may be used to define the energy requirements of a cluster head. To do this, we first show how it may be possible to compute the activation probability of a node within a cluster and the move on to model the probability of activating a given number of nodes in correspondence of a traversal.

4.1 Node activation probability

From now on, for the sake of simplicity, we consider a situation where A is a square, of size X^2, with N sensor nodes located inside. N is big enough to guarantee that each point (x, y) in A is covered by at least one sensor, assuming each sensor can detect, according to a boolean model, a target moving within a radius r.

We want to compute the probability a generic node i, located in (x_i, y_i), is activated every time a target traverses A. Such probability may be computed searching, first of all, for the probability that i is activated when a single target traverses A. When a target traverses A, all the sensors that are within a distance of r units are activated, hence if i lies in a stripe determined by such quantity, i is activated. To

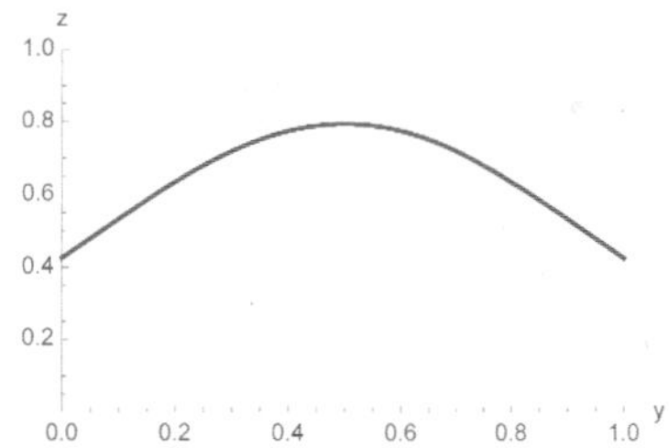

(a) Trajectory, among those crossing (x_{max}, y_{max}), which exhibits the maximum among the minimum probability of activation.

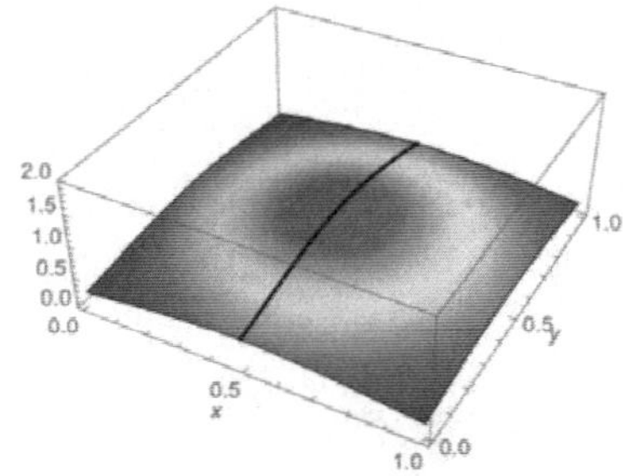

(b) Probability of activation field along with the trajectory that traverses (x_{max}, y_{max}) and exhibits the maximum among the minimum activation probabilities.

Figure 1: Activation probability example.

find such probability hence, it is necessary to compute the probability that a random segment, describing the traversal of a target, falls within distance r from i.

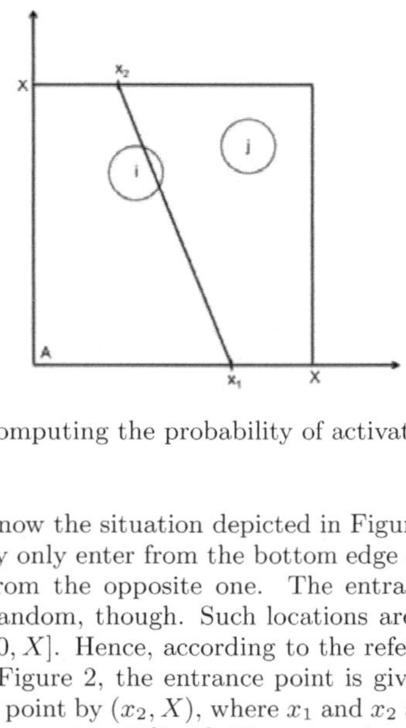

Figure 2: Computing the probability of activation of sensor i.

Consider now the situation depicted in Figure 2. Assume a target may only enter from the bottom edge of the square and leave from the opposite one. The entrance and exit points are random, though. Such locations are chosen uniformely in $[0, X]$. Hence, according to the reference system adopted in Figure 2, the entrance point is given by $(x_1, 0)$ and the exit point by (x_2, X), where x_1 and x_2 are i.i.d. uniform random variables $U[0, X]$. The event that i is activated amounts to the event that a possible trajectory T intersects the sensing area of i. Such event is here indicated as $T \cap i$ and its probability is given by:

$$P(T \cap i) = \int_T P(T \cap i|T) \times P(T), \tag{1}$$

where $P(T \cap i|T)$ amounts to the probability of intersection, for a given trajectory T, and $P(T)$ to the probability of a given trajectory T. Let us start considering the problem of determining $P(T)$. Its value can be easily found considering the fact that $P(T) = P(x_1 \wedge x_2)$. Reminding that x_1 and x_2 are i.i.d. uniform random variables $U[0, X]$, we have that $P(T) = 1/X^2$. For what concerns $P(T \cap i|T)$, we have that:

$$P(T \cap i|T) = \begin{cases} 1 & \text{if the sensing area of } i \text{ and } T \text{ intersect,} \\ 0 & \text{otherwise.} \end{cases} \tag{2}$$

Now, it is possible to determine whether T and the sensing area of i intersect, for example, computing the distance between i's coordinates, (x_i, y_i) and trajectory T. Hence, may be written as $P(T \cap i|T) = \mathbb{1}_{\{d((x_i, y_i), T) \leq r\}}$. Equation 1 may hence be rewritten as:

$$P(T \cap i) = \frac{1}{X^2} \times \int_0^X \int_0^X \mathbb{1}_{\{d((x_i, y_i), T) \leq r\}} dx_1 dx_2. \tag{3}$$

4.2 Number of detections per traversal

Computing the cluster head lifetime entails finding the number of events it will be handling. This quantity, in turn, depends on the number of targets traversing A and on the number of sensor nodes that are activated in correspondence of each single traversal. We here start computing the probability a given number of sensing nodes are activated in correspondence of a single traversal. Such function may be computed observing that, in correspondence of a traversal, all the nodes that fall within distance r will be activated. In essence, it is possible to approximate the area where all activated sensing nodes fall as a rectangle of dimensions $2 \times r$ by x, where $X \leq x \leq \sqrt{2} \times X$. With such assumption, we determine the probability a given number of sensing nodes falls in a rectangle of dimensions $2 \times r \times x$, given x. Such probability can be obtained resorting to a Binomial distribution, as our initial assumption is that nodes are dropped in a uniform way in A:

$$P(N' = n|x) = \binom{N}{n} \times \left(\frac{2 \times r \times x}{X^2}\right)^n \times \left(1 - \frac{2 \times r \times x}{X^2}\right)^{N-n}. \tag{4}$$

Now, Equation 4 may be put to good use the compute the probability of activating resorting to the law of total probability:

$$P(N' = n) = \int_X^{\sqrt{2}X} P(N' = n|x) \times P(x) dx, \tag{5}$$

with $P(x)$ the probability a target traverses A walking along a path of length x. It is possible to show geometrically that $P(x) = 2 \times x \times (X - \sqrt{x^2 - X^2})/X^2)$, from which we obtain:

$$P(N'=n)=\int_X^{\sqrt{2}X}\binom{N}{n}\times\left(\frac{2\times r\times x}{X^2}\right)^n\times$$
$$\times\left(1-\frac{2\times r\times x}{X^2}\right)^{N-n}\times\frac{2\times x\times(X-\sqrt{x^2-X^2})}{X^2}dx, \tag{6}$$

Equation that is here put to good use to compute a heuristic function which may return a significant value of the cluster head lifetime and consequent energy requirements.

4.3 Event lifetime consumption model

In this Subsection we proceed first providing a model which may be put to good use to compute the probability distribution function of the lifetime of any node in the cluster and then move on to provide the heuristic function which is utilized to estimate the energy requirements of the cluster head. Clearly, the proposed consumption model may be subject to modifications depending on the particular application scenario. The same may be said for the heuristic proposed to compute the energy required by the cluster head.

4.3.1 Sensing node lifetime

Assuming targets arrive in A according to a Poisson model with intensity γ, each single sensor i keeps seeing Poisson traffic with intensity $\gamma_i = p_i \times \gamma$, where p_i is obtained as in Equation 3.

Assuming a constant amount of lifetime $l_{eh,i}$ is lost at node i every time a target crosses its range, the problem amounts to a simple budgetary problem: an equal amount of energy is subtracted from the initial lifetime $l_{EH,i} = l_{max,i} - l_i$ available per each message detection and transmission procedure.

The probability of spending less than $l_{EH,i}$ units of lifetime assuming Z events are detected and handled is:

$$P(Z\times l_{eh,i} < l_{EH,i}|Z)=\begin{cases}1 & \text{if } Z < l_{EH,i}/l_{eh,i},\\ 0 & \text{if } Z \geq l_{EH,i}/l_{eh,i}.\end{cases} \tag{7}$$

Using an alternative notation, $P(Z \times l_{eh,i} < l_{EH,i}|Z)$ amounts to the unit step function $u(l_{EH,i}/l_{eh,i} - Z)$. Taking now into account all possible arrivals, resorting to the total probability theorem, we can write:

$$F(l_{EH,i},l_i)=\sum_{Z=0}^{\infty}F(l_{EH,i},l_i|Z)\times e^{-\gamma_i l_i}\frac{(\gamma_i l_i)^Z}{Z!}=$$
$$=e^{-\gamma_i l_i}\times\sum_{Z=0}^{\lfloor\frac{l_{EH,i}}{l_{eh,i}}\rfloor}\frac{(\gamma_i l_i)^Z}{Z!}. \tag{8}$$

Equation 8, computed for $F(l_{max,i} - l_i, l_i)$, returns the probability of spending less than the amount of available lifetime for event handling, when the lifetime of node i is l_i. In other words, it provides us with the probability of i lasting at least l_i units of time.

4.3.2 Cluster head lifetime heuristic function

The lifetime $l_{EH,CH}$ spent by the cluster head for event handling may be obtained as the sum of all detections made by the cluster multiplied by the amount of energy spent per each relay operation. If Z traversals occur, the amount of battery lifetime required at the cluster head to manage all can be written as $l_{EH,CH} = l_{eh,CH} \times \sum_{i=1}^{Z} n_i$, where n_i amounts to the number of nodes activated in correspondence of the i-th traversal and $l_{eh,CH}$ the constant amount of lifetime spent at the cluster head in correspondence of an event handling.

This said, the heuristic function that is proposed in this work to assess the amount of battery lifetime $\tilde{l}_{EH,CH}$ required by the cluster head for event handling is:

$$\tilde{l}_{EH,CH} = Z^{90\%} \times n^{90\%} \times l_{eh,CH}, \tag{9}$$

where $Z^{90\%}$ amounts to the 90-percentile of random variable representing the number of arrivals in A during the given mission time and $n^{90\%}$ the 90-percentile of the number of activations per traversal. In Section 5 we verify how the value of $l_{max,CH} - \tilde{l}_{EH,CH}$ relates to the cluster head lifetime value l_{CH} obtained by simulation.

5. EVALUATION

We here validate ours models resorting to simulation results, produced with a custom simulator developed in Mathematica. We consider a square area A with $X = 6$ units. The situation is the one presented in Subsection 4.1: intruders have an equal probability of entering at any point of only one edge of square A and of exiting from any point of on the edge opposite to the entrance (no targets can enter from the remaining two edges). Parameter values are $N = 100$, $l_{max,i} = 100$, $l_{eh,i} = 5$, $\gamma = 1$ and $r = 0.5$ for all sensing nodes i.

In Figure 3 we plot all alive and dead nodes observed in 100 simulations within A, considering intermediate time steps before 80 units of time. As expected, the nodes that first stop operating are those closer to the center of the square. At time $t = 60$ the detection system is no longer reliable (Figure 3c).

5.1 Sensing nodes lifetime

At this point we proceed computing the lifetime probability of two virtual nodes, one located in $(3, 0)$ and one in $(3, 3)$. In fact, in A, only one activation probability maximum exists, located at the center of the square ($p(3, 3) = 0.33$). Given the uniform condition on the entrance and exit edges, infinite trajectories T may be found, all crossing $(3, 3)$. All of them exhibit the minimum activation probability on the entrance and exit edges, which is the same for all. We hence consider, as second point of interest, $(3, 0)$. Equation 8 is plotted for $l_{max,i} = 100$, $l_{eh,i} = 5$, $\gamma = 1$ (hence $\gamma_{(3,0)} = 0.17$ and $\gamma_{(3,3)} = 0.33$), as a function of l_i in Figures 4a and 4b for positions $(3, 0)$ and $(3, 3)$, respectively. As l_i approaches the value of $l_{max,i}$ the probability of being capable of handling incoming events goes to zero. Please note both Figures 4a and 4b represent complementary cumulative distribution functions, as a function of l_i, as $l_{EH,i} = l_{max,i} - l_i$.

5.2 Cluster head energy requirements

To quantify the energy requirements of the cluster head, we first analyze the number of detections that occur in correspondence of one traversal resorting to Equation 6 and to our simulator. Figures 5a, 5b and 5c, in particular, show the empirical probability of being detected by a given number of

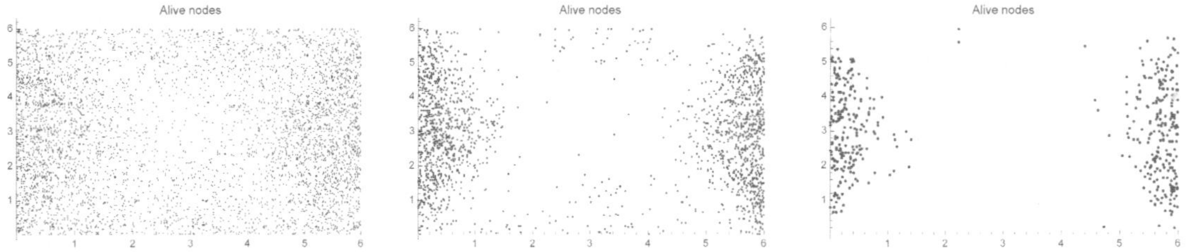

(a) Alive nodes, time = 20, mission time = 80. (b) Alive nodes, time = 40, mission time = 80. (c) Alive nodes, time = 60, mission time = 80.

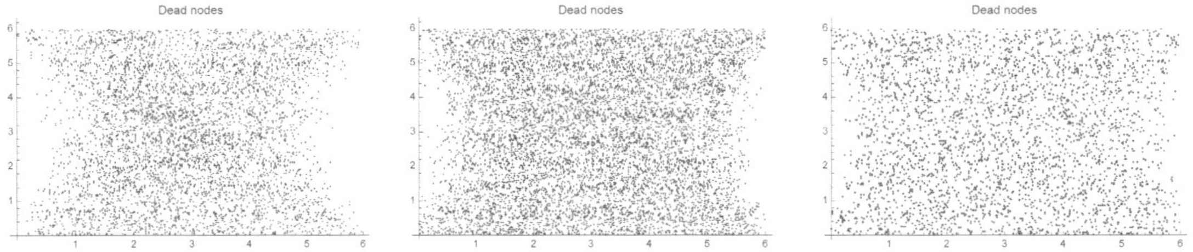

(d) Dead nodes, time = 20, mission time = 80. (e) Dead nodes, time = 40, mission time = 80. (f) Dead nodes, time = 60, mission time = 80.

Figure 3: Spatial distribution of alive and dead nodes as a function time, before the end of mission time.

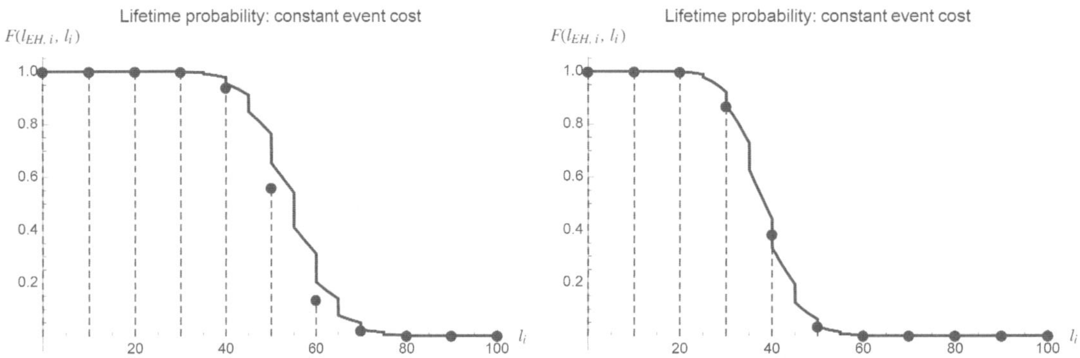

(a) Node located in $(3, 0)$. (b) Node located in $(3, 3)$.

Figure 4: Computing the lifetime of a sensor network: model (continuous line) vs simulation (dots).

nodes in corrispondence of a traversal: as the mission time increases, more nodes deplete their battery resources and the probability of not being detected by any sensing node increases. In Figure 5d we, instead, show that our model perfectly matches simulation results, in the case where sensing nodes are equipped with an infinite amount of energy.

We now assume battery lifetime the cluster head consumes in correspondence of an event is set to $l_{eh,CH} = 10$. The 10-percentile of lifetime of nodes located in $(3, 0)$ and $(3, 3)$ is instead obtained utilizing Equation 8: $l^{10\%}_{(3,0)} = 45$, whereas $l^{10\%}_{(3,3)} = 30$. Such values amount to two possible hypothetical mission times which we will assume from now on. Resorting to our heuristic function reported in Equation 9, for mission times 30 and 45, $\tilde{l}_{EH,CH}$ results equal to 8,418 and 12,233, respectively. We now aim at understanding how well such heuristic function works, utilizing fraction of such values as initial battery lifetime in 1,000 simulation runs for each row reported Tables 1 and 2, where $l^{10\%}_{CH}$ amount to the lifetime of the cluster head obtained as the 10-percentile of the 1,000 simulation results. Tables 1 and 2 report $l^{10\%}_{CH}$ values as higher fractions of the computed battery lifetime are employed. For mission time 30, 80% of the battery lifetime given by our heuristic is sufficient to probabilistically guarantee that in the 90% of cases the cluster head will also last at least 30 units of time. Something similar happens also when the mission time is equal to 45, thus confirming the fact that the heuristic rule provided in Equation 8 tends to return amounts of battery lifetime that are larger than those that are really necessary.

5.3 System lifetime: models vs. simulation

Our analysis, to this point, tells us that with an initial maximum battery lifetime $l_{max,i} = 100$ we may obtain a lifetime of 30 units of time, when taking as a reference node $(3, 3)$ and equipping the cluster head with an initial battery lifetime greater than $l_{max,CH} = 6,764$. If, instead, we take as a reference the sensing node located in $(3, 0)$, such lifetime grows to 45 units of time, when equipping the

CH battery lifetime used in simulation (% of $\tilde{l}_{max,CH}$)	10-percentile of CH lifetime $l_{CH}^{10\%}$ obtained running 1,000 simulations
5,081 (60%)	22
5,923 (70%)	26
6,764 (80%)	30

Table 1: Cluster head 10-percentile lifetime obtained from 1,000 simulations for mission time = 30 as a function of different fractions of the initial battery lifetime value ($\tilde{l}_{max,CH} = l_{CH} + \tilde{l}_{EH,CH} = 30 + 8,418 = 8,448$).

CH battery lifetime used in simulation (% of $\tilde{l}_{max,CH}$)	10-percentile of CH lifetime $l_{CH}^{10\%}$ obtained running 1,000 simulations
6,161 (50%)	28
7,385 (60%)	37
8,608 (70%)	45

Table 2: Cluster head 10-percentile lifetime obtained from 1,000 simulations for mission time = 45, as a function of different fractions of the initial battery lifetime ($\tilde{l}_{max,CH} = l_{CH} + \tilde{l}_{EH,CH} = 45 + 12,233 = 12,278$).

cluster head of a battery lifetime that is at least equal to $l_{max,CH} = 8,608$. The two different reference nodes return remarkably different lifetime values and cluster head battery lifetime requirements, thus of paramount importance is to understand which, of the considered nodes, may be considered a reliable indicator of the sensor system lifetime. To this aim, we designed a test that builds upon the results plotted in Figure 3. In essence, in our simulations, after an event is handled, we check whether a potential undetected path, i.e., an open path, has become available. However, to limit its computation time, we limit our search to all the feasible paths containing $(3,3)$. When fixing the mission time to 30 units of time, we find that no open path becomes available. When the mission time amounts to 45, instead, we obtain a 10-percentile of 41.5 units of time (i.e., in the 90% of cases an open path will become available after 41.5) and a minimum value of 28.6. The statistical values of interest are plotted in Figure 6 for different mission times. Note that for mission times 45, 50 and 60 the maximum values amount to 45, 50, and 60 respectively, as simulations are interrupted at such times. Beyond mission time 60, instead, an undetected path opens up always before the completion of mission time. In this Figure, we may also observe that the median and 10-percentile values (49.2 and 37.7, respectively) grow up to 50, falling beyond this value. As the mission time increases, less lifetime resources are available for target detection and message transmission. For what, instead, concerns our original question, which sensing node appears as the best sensing system lifetime indicator, we observe that no open path becomes available when the mission time equals 30, whereas in the 90% of cases a path opens after 41.5 units of time when the mission time amounts to 45. To be thorough, we find that in the 82% of cases an open path open at or after 45 units of time. In essence, the lifetime value obtained observing node $(3,3)$ appears too low and conservative, whereas the lifetime value obtained observing $(3,0)$ is slightly optimistic.

6. CONCLUSION

In this work we modeled the lifetime of a clustered sensor network deployed for target detection. Compared to other approches, we here considered the influence that the target mobility model has on the duration of surveillance operations. The validity of the adopted approach has been proven confronting our models with our simulation results.

7. REFERENCES

[1] I. Akyildiz, Y. Sankarasubramaniam, and E. Cayirci. A survey on sensor networks. *IEEE Communications Magazine*, 40(8):102–114, aug 2002.

[2] G. Anastasi, M. Conti, M. Di Francesco, and A. Passarella. Energy conservation in wireless sensor networks: A survey. *Ad Hoc Networks*, 7(3):537–568, may 2009.

[3] J. Aylor. System lifetime optimization for heterogeneous sensor networks with a hub-spoke technology. *IEEE Transactions on Mobile Computing*, 3(3):286–294, jul 2004.

[4] D. Bruneo, S. Distefano, F. Longo, A. Puliafito, and M. Scarpa. Evaluating wireless sensor node longevity through Markovian techniques. *Computer Networks*, 56(2):521–532, 2012.

[5] I. Butun, S. D. Morgera, and R. Sankar. A Survey of Intrusion Detection Systems in Wireless Sensor Networks. *IEEE Communications Surveys & Tutorials*, 16(1):266–282, 2014.

[6] M. Cardei, M. Thai, Y. Yingshu Li, and W. Weili Wu. Energy-efficient target coverage in wireless sensor networks. In *Proceedings IEEE 24th Annual Joint Conference of the IEEE Computer and Communications Societies.*, volume 3, pages 1976–1984. IEEE, 2005.

[7] A. Chakraborty, R. R. Rout, A. Chakrabarti, and S. K. Ghosh. On Network Lifetime Expectancy With Realistic Sensing and Traffic Generation Model in Wireless Sensor Networks. *IEEE Sensors Journal*, 13(7):2771–2779, jul 2013.

[8] I. Dietrich and F. Dressler. On the lifetime of wireless sensor networks. *ACM Transactions on Sensor Networks*, 5(1):1–39, 2009.

[9] L. Donatiello and G. Marfia. Leveraging on Mobility Models for Sensor Network Lifetime Modeling. In *Proceedings of the 14th ACM International Symposium on Mobility Management and Wireless Access - MobiWac '16*, pages 155–162, New York, New York, USA, 2016. ACM Press.

[10] L. Donatiello and G. Marfia. Leveraging on mobility models for sensor network lifetime modeling. In *Submitted for publication*, 2016.

[11] A. Elfes. Occupancy Grids: A Stochastic Spatial Representation for Active Robot Perception. mar 2013.

[12] S. Gambs, M.-O. Killijian, and M. N. del Prado Cortez. Next place prediction using mobility Markov chains. In *Proceedings of the First Workshop on Measurement, Privacy, and Mobility - MPM '12*, pages 1–6, New York, New York, USA, 2012. ACM Press.

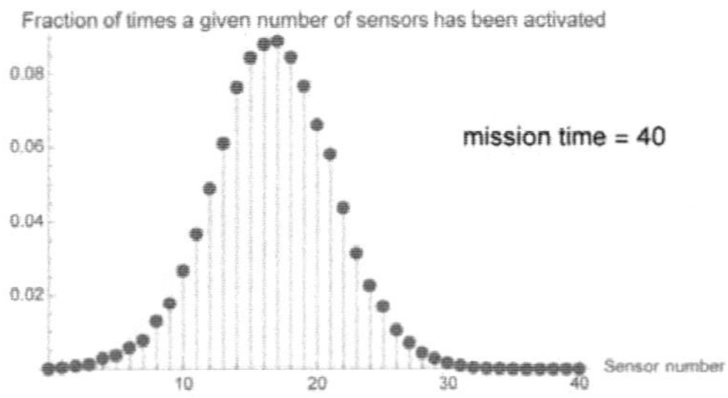

(a) Mission time = 40.

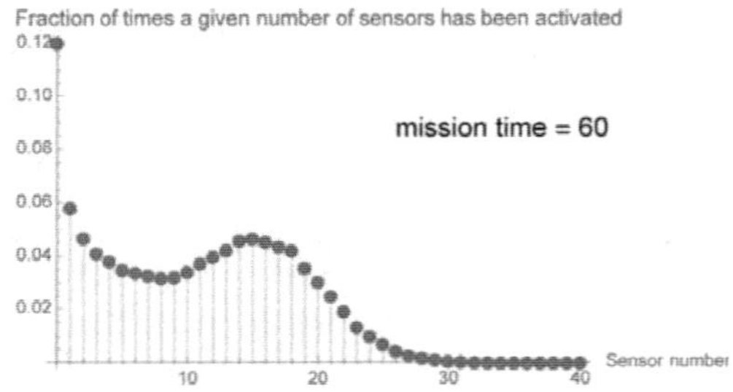

(b) Mission time = 60.

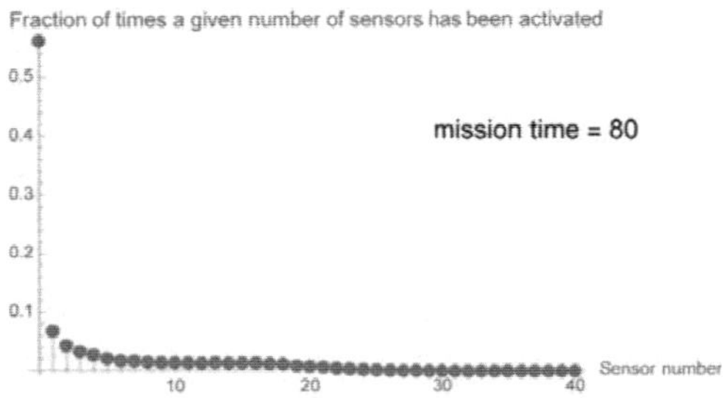

(c) Mission time = 80.

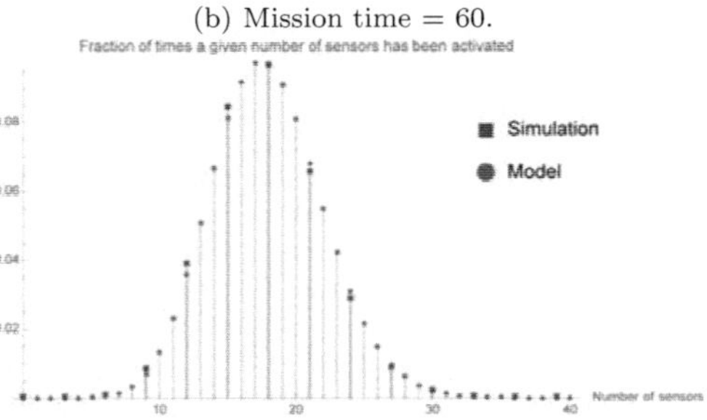

(d) Number of detections probability during an ideal traversal (all nodes always on): model vs simulation comparison.

Figure 5: Number of detections per traversal probability when sensor nodes stop working as they deplete their batteries (Figures 5a, 5b and 5c). Ideal situation, when nodes never die Figure 5d.

[13] D. L. Gerlough. THE USE OF THE POISSON DISTRIBUTION IN HIGHWAY TRAFFIC. 1955.

[14] D. Jung, T. Teixeira, and A. Savvides. Sensor node lifetime analysis. *ACM Transactions on Sensor Networks*, 5(1):1–33, feb 2009.

[15] S. Kumar, A. Arora, and T. Lai. On the lifetime analysis of always-on wireless sensor network applications. In *IEEE International Conference on Mobile Adhoc and Sensor Systems Conference, 2005.*, pages 186–188. IEEE, 2005.

[16] B. Latré, B. Braem, I. Moerman, C. Blondia, and P. Demeester. A survey on wireless body area networks. *Wireless Networks*, 17(1):1–18, nov 2010.

[17] L. Mainetti, L. Patrono, and A. Vilei. Evolution of wireless sensor networks towards the Internet of Things: A survey. In *Software, Telecommunications and Computer Networks (SoftCOM), 2011 19th International Conference on*, pages 1–6. IEEE, 2011.

[18] M. Noori and M. Ardakani. Lifetime Analysis of Random Event-Driven Clustered Wireless Sensor Networks. *IEEE Transactions on Mobile Computing*, 10(10):1448–1458, oct 2011.

[19] D. Tian and N. D. Georganas. A coverage-preserving node scheduling scheme for large wireless sensor networks. In *Proceedings of the 1st ACM international workshop on Wireless sensor networks and applications - WSNA '02*, page 32, New York, New York, USA, 2002. ACM Press.

[20] Y. Wang, M. C. Vuran, and S. Goddard. Stochastic Analysis of Energy Consumption in Wireless Sensor Networks. In *2010 7th Annual IEEE Communications Society Conference on Sensor, Mesh and Ad Hoc Communications and Networks (SECON)*, pages 1–9. IEEE, jun 2010.

[21] K. Wu, Y. Gao, F. Li, and Y. Xiao. Lightweight Deployment-Aware Scheduling for Wireless Sensor Networks. *Mobile Networks and Applications*, 10(6):837–852, dec 2005.

[22] O. Younis, M. Krunz, and S. Ramasubramanian. Node clustering in wireless sensor networks: recent developments and deployment challenges. *IEEE Network*, 20(3):20–25, may 2006.

[23] H. Zhang and J. Hou. On deriving the upper bound of α-lifetime for large sensor networks. In *Proceedings of the 5th ACM international symposium on Mobile ad hoc networking and computing - MobiHoc '04*, page 121, New York, New York, USA, may 2004. ACM Press.

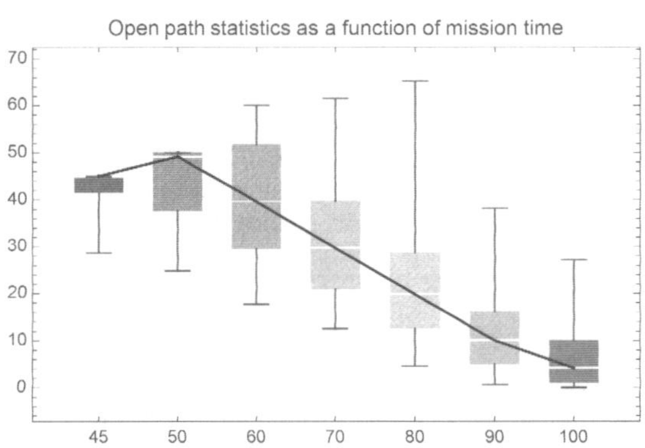

Figure 6: Maximum, 90-percentile, median, 10-percentile and minimum value obtained for the open path variable from 1,000 simulations in correspondence of different mission time values.

Resiliency Quantification for Large Scale Systems: An IaaS Cloud Use Case

Rahul Ghosh
Xerox Research Center, India
rahul.ghosh@xerox.com

Francesco Longo
Università degli Studi di Messina, Italy
flongo@unime.it

Vijay K. Naik
IBM T. J. Watson Research Center, USA
vkn@us.ibm.com

Andrew J. Rindos
IBM, USA
rindos@us.ibm.com

Kishor S. Trivedi
Duke University, USA
ktrivedi@duke.edu

ABSTRACT

We quantify the resiliency of large scale systems upon *changes* encountered beyond the normal system behavior. General steps for resiliency quantification are shown and resiliency metrics are defined to quantify the effects of changes. The proposed approach is illustrated through an Infrastructure-as-a-Service (IaaS) Cloud use case. Specifically, we assess the impact of changes in demand and available capacity on the Cloud resiliency using interacting state-space based sub-models. Since resiliency quantification involves understanding the transient behavior of the system, fixed-point variables evolve with time leading to non-homogenous Markov chains. In this paper, we present an algorithm for resiliency analysis when dealing with such non-homogenous sub-models. A comparison is shown with our past research, where we quantified the resiliency of IaaS Cloud performance using a one level monolithic model. Numerical results show that the approach proposed in this paper can scale for a real sized Cloud without significantly compromising the accuracy.

Keywords

Cloud, resiliency, interacting sub-models, non-homogeneous Markov chains.

1. INTRODUCTION

Large enterprise systems are difficult to manage due to their scale and complexity. Although such systems are carefully designed, they may still fail to deliver expected services due to failures or unexpected variations in the load. For business critical systems, such deviations from normal behavior may cause violation of service level agreements (SLA). Hence, during the design stage of such systems, a notion of built-in *resiliency* is necessary.

However, quantifying the system resiliency is difficult because of two key reasons: (1) lack of consensus on the definition of resiliency and (2) lack of systematic approaches for quantifying resiliency measures. The term resiliency is used in different fields and several definitions are present. Many researchers interpret resiliency as a synonym for fault-tolerance. However, the effect of fault tolerance can be captured by traditional dependability measures, such as reliability, availability, maintainability, and safety [4, 1]. De-Bardeleben *et al.* [3] defined resiliency of a high end computing system as the ability to keep applications running and maintain an acceptable level of service when facing transient, intermittent, and permanent faults. However, the quantification of the effects of failures/repairs on a system is covered under the umbrella of dependability, joint analysis of contention/queuing and failures/repairs is known as performability [9], and the effect of failures/repairs on individual tasks is covered under the umbrella of task completion time analysis [2, 12]. Impact of (large scale) failures (e.g., natural disasters), intrusions, or attacks on systems/services and subsequent transient behavior is quantified by survivability analysis [10, 14, 17]. Sterbenz *et al.* [16] defined resiliency as the combination of trustworthiness (dependability, security, and performability) and tolerance (survivability, disruption tolerance, and traffic tolerance).

Our work about resiliency starts from the definition of Sterbenz *et al.* and is inspired from Laprie's [13] and Simoncini's [15] work in which resiliency is defined as the persistence of service delivery that can justifiably be trusted when facing *changes* - usually not encountered under normal operating conditions. Note that dynamic redundancy features in traditional fault tolerance with detection followed by reconfiguration are already included in classic dependability measures. The *changes* we are referring to here are beyond the envelope of system configurations already considered during the design stage and thus beyond fault tolerance. We also emphasize that survivability quantification only deals with *changes* due to (large scale) failures, intrusions, or attacks. The notion of resiliency is broader than survivability as the *changes* encountered by the system can be unexpected variations in the workload, faultload, or system capacity.

This paper presents a general approach for resiliency quantification of large scale systems through analytic models. The approach is illustrated by an Infrastructure-as-a-Service (IaaS) Cloud use case. IaaS Cloud provides computational resources in the form of virtual machine (VM) instances deployed in the provider's data center. Resiliency is a key

VALUETOOLS 2016, October 25-28, Taormina, Italy

feature in a Cloud environment in order to maintain quality of service offerings and to respect SLAs established with Cloud users. Our contributions are summarized below:

(1) We develop a general resiliency quantification approach for large scale systems using state-space based analytic models. Several resiliency metrics are defined to quantify resiliency for a variety of measures of interest. In contrast to the traditional view of synonymizing resiliency with dependability, we show *how resiliency can be quantified even with respect to performance measures.* Nevertheless, the resiliency analysis approach proposed in this paper can also be applied to other dependability attributes, e.g., reliability, availability, and performability.

(2) Steady state performance of a large scale system is quantified using interacting sub-models where interdependencies are resolved by fixed-point iterations [8, 7]. Resiliency quantification involves understanding the transient behavior of the system. Transient analysis of interacting sub-models coupled with fixed-point iterations becomes non-trivial as the values of fixed-point variables change with time – leading to non-homogenous Markov sub-models. This paper presents an algorithm for the resiliency quantification when dealing with such non-homogenous, interacting Markov sub-models. To the best of our knowledge, ours is the first attempt to perform transient analysis of state-space based fixed-point iterative sub-models.

(3) Considering an IaaS Cloud use case, we quantify resiliency of two performance measures: job rejection rate and provisioning response delay (a function of the mean number of jobs under provision). Using resiliency metrics, we quantify the effects of sudden changes in client demand, i.e., job arrival rate and in system capacity, i.e., the number of available physical machines (PMs). We compute the values of resiliency metrics for ten different cases that capture the effects of sudden changes in demand and capacity.

(4) A comparison of the proposed resiliency quantification approach is shown with our past research [5] in which we quantified resiliency of an IaaS Cloud using a one level monolithic performance model. Such monolithic model becomes intractable as the size of the Cloud increases. Thus, resiliency quantification shown in our past research is restricted to toy examples while the approach developed in this paper extends our previous results to real sized Clouds. We show the scalability and accuracy of the new resiliency quantification approach by comparing it to the approach shown in [5]. Numerical results show that our new approach can quickly provide model solutions for large scale IaaS Cloud without significantly compromising the accuracy.

The paper is organized as follows. Our idea of resiliency quantification along with the definitions of resiliency metrics is presented in Section 2. Section 3 describes the IaaS Cloud system taken as a use case and formulates the problem. The proposed resiliency quantification approach is shown in Section 4. Numerical results are shown in Section 5 and concluding remarks are made in Section 6.

2. PROPOSED RESILIENCY QUANTIFICATION APPROACH

In this section, we outline the general steps of the approach for the resiliency quantification of a system via analytic models we propose. Moreover, we report formal definitions for our resiliency metrics.

Resiliency quantification. The general steps in our resiliency quantification approach are:

(1) Construct a stochastic analytic model of a given system to find measures of interest. With respect to such measures, the model can be a performance, availability, or performability model of the system.

(2) Determine the system measures of interest under normal conditions from the model developed in step (1). In this step, we compute the steady state value of the measures of interest without any application of changes.

(3) Apply changes to the system. Changes can be classified into two broad categories: (a) non-structural changes and (b) structural changes. Non-structural changes can be enforced by increasing (or decreasing) the values of input parameters of the model. Examples of such changes are variation of arrival rates or hardware/software failure rates. In a state-space model, structural changes can be enforced by adding (or removing) states and/or transitions. Examples of structural changes can be addition or removal of system components.

(4) Analyze the transient behavior of the system model to compute the measures of interest after applying the changes. Initial probabilities for this transient analysis are obtained from the steady state probabilities as computed from the normal behavior of the system model in step (2). After the changes are applied, transient response of the performance, reliability, availability, and performability measures quantifies the resiliency of the system.

Resiliency Metrics. Closely following the survivability definitions in [17], we define resiliency metrics to quantify the resiliency of a system when changes are enforced. Let $M_{ss}^{(bc)}$ and $M_{ss}^{(ac)}$ denote the steady state values of the measures (for which resiliency is computed) before and after the application of change, respectively. The following four metrics are defined:

(1) Settling Time (t_{set})**.** This is defined as the elapsed duration from the time when the change is applied to the system, until the measure of interest reaches and stays within $M_{ss}^{(ac)} \pm \delta\%$ of $|M_{ss}^{(bc)} - M_{ss}^{(ac)}|$.

(2) Peak Overshoot (PO) **or Undershoot** (PU)**.** Let $M_{peak}^{(ac)}$ be the maximum deviation of the measure from its steady state value after change is applied. Peak overshoot/undershoot (in percentage) is defined as:

$$PO(\%) = \frac{|M_{peak}^{(ac)} - M_{ss}^{(ac)}|}{M_{ss}^{(ac)}} \times 100 \qquad (1)$$

(3) Peak Time (t_{peak})**.** It is defined as the elapsed duration from the time when the change is applied to the system until the measure of interest reaches the maximum deviation $M_{peak}^{(ac)}$.

(4) γ-Percentile Time ($t_{percentile}$)**.** It is defined for two cases: (1) when $M_{ss}^{(bc)} \geq M_{ss}^{(ac)}$, it is the elapsed duration from the time when the change is applied to the system until the output measure reaches $M_{ss}^{(ac)} + (100-\gamma)\%$ of $|M_{ss}^{(bc)} - M_{ss}^{(ac)}|$ for the first time, and (2) when $M_{ss}^{(bc)} \leq M_{ss}^{(ac)}$, it is the elapsed duration from the time when the change is applied to the system until the output measure reaches $M_{ss}^{(ac)} - (100-\gamma)\%$ of $|M_{ss}^{(bc)} - M_{ss}^{(ac)}|$ for the first time. $(100-\gamma)$ is always greater than δ as used in settling time definition.

We illustrate the proposed approach via resiliency quantification of an IaaS Cloud.

3. CASE STUDY FOR IAAS CLOUD PERFORMANCE

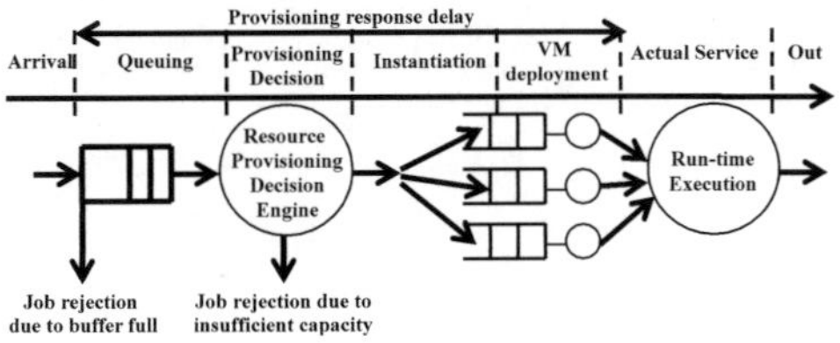

Figure 1: Provisioning and servicing steps in IaaS Cloud.

System Description. In an IaaS Cloud, when a request is processed, a pre-built image is used to deploy one or more VM instances or a pre-deployed VM is customized and made available to the requester. VMs are deployed on PMs each of which may be shared by multiple VMs. The deployed VMs are provisioned with request specific CPU, RAM, and disk capacity. In this paper, we show the analysis for an IaaS Cloud where the PMs are grouped into three pools: hot (running), warm (turned on, but not ready) and cold (turned off). A pre-instantiated VM can be readily provisioned and brought to ready state on a running PM (hot PM) with minimum provisioning delay. Instantiating a VM from an image and deploying it on a warm PM needs additional provisioning time. PMs in the cold pool are turned-off when not in use and deploying a VM on such a PM requires additional startup delays. Thus, organization of PMs in multiple pools helps to minimize power and cooling costs without incurring into high startup delays for all VMs. We assume that all PMs in a pool are identical and all requests are homogeneous, where each request is for one VM. Shown in Fig. 1 is the life-cycle of a request as it moves through the system. Submitted user requests enter a first-come, first-served (FCFS) queue. The request at the head of the queue is processed by a Resource Provisioning Decision Engine (RPDE) as follows. The request is provisioned on a hot PM if a pre-instantiated but unassigned VM exists. If no hot PM is available, a PM from the warm pool is used for provisioning the requested VM. If all warm PMs are busy, a PM from the cold pool is used. If no PM is available, the request is rejected (service unavailable). When a running job exits, the capacity used by that VM is released and becomes available for provisioning the next job.

Problem Statement. Performance of the above described IaaS Cloud can be quantified using scalable interacting sub-models that capture different phases in the life-cycle of a request. If all the inter-event times are assumed to be exponentially distributed, the sub-models are homogeneous continuous time Markov chains (CTMC). However, during transient analysis, the generator matrices of interacting sub-models evolve with time thus leading to non-homogeneous CTMCs. This paper describes an algorithm for resiliency quantification when dealing with non-homogeneous, interacting sub-models. We quantify the resiliency of IaaS Cloud for two performance measures - (i) job rejection rate (ρ_{reject}) and (ii) mean number of jobs in RPDE ($E[N_{RPDE}]$). Resiliency metrics are computed to quantify the effects on the system due to changes in job arrival rate and system capacity. Finally, the scalability and accuracy of the proposed resiliency quantification approach are compared with the resiliency quantification approach for a monolithic model of the system.

4. RESILIENCY QUANTIFICATION FOR A SCALABLE CLOUD PERFORMANCE MODEL

In this section, we briefly describe the interacting sub-models approach for performance quantification of IaaS Cloud followed by an algorithm for resiliency quantification using such sub-models. The detailed performance model can be found in [8]. Final solution of the overall model is obtained by fixed-point iteration over individual sub-models.

4.1 An interacting sub-models approach

Resource provisioning decision engine (RPDE) sub-model. Fig. 2 shows RPDE sub-model. States of the sub-

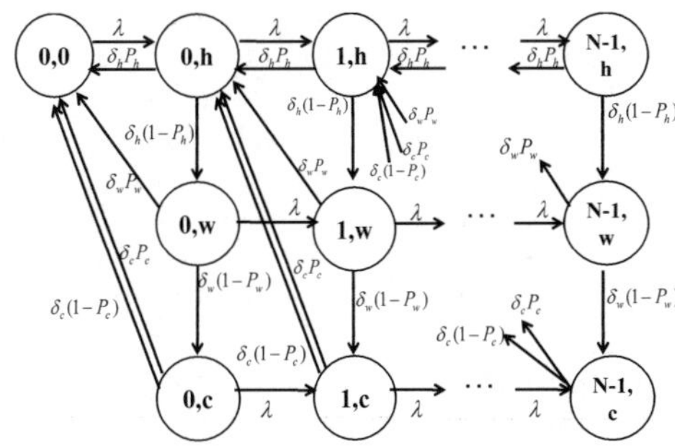

Figure 2: CTMC sub-model for RPDE.

model in Fig. 2 are indexed by (q, x), where q denotes the number of jobs in the RPDE queue and $x \in \{h, w, c\}$ denotes the pool in which the RPDE is searching for available PMs. Input parameters for this sub-model are: (i) job arrival rate (λ), (ii) mean search delays to find a PM from hot/warm/cold pool that can be used for resource provisioning ($1/\delta_h$, $1/\delta_w$ and $1/\delta_c$, respectively), (iii) probabilities that a hot/warm/cold PM can accept a job for resource provisioning (P_h, P_w and P_c, respectively) and (iv) maximum number of jobs in RPDE (N). Among all the input parameters, P_h, P_w, and P_c are computed as outputs from the VM provisioning sub-models described later. From the RPDE sub-model, using Markov reward approach [18], we compute job rejection probability due to buffer full (P_{block}), rejection probability due to insufficient capacity (P_{drop}), their sum: $P_{reject} = P_{block} + P_{drop}$, and mean number of jobs in RPDE ($E[N_{RPDE}]$). Then, multiplying by arrival rate, we can compute job rejection rate due to buffer full (ρ_{block}), rejection rate due to insufficient capacity ρ_{drop}, and their sum: $\rho_{reject} = \rho_{block} + \rho_{drop}$.

VM provisioning sub-models. VM provisioning sub-

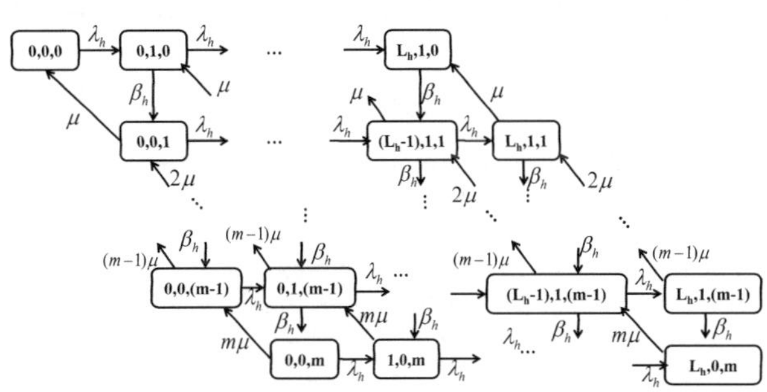

Figure 3: VM provisioning sub-model for a hot PM.

models capture the provisioning and deployment of requested

VMs to accepted jobs. For each hot, warm, and cold PM, we have one CTMC which keeps track of the number of running VMs. VM provisioning sub-model of a pool is the union of individual provisioning sub-models of each PM in that pool.

Fig. 3 shows VM provisioning sub-model for a hot PM. Conceptually, the overall hot pool is modeled by a set of independent hot PM sub-models. Note that only one PM sub-model needs to be solved. States of the sub-model in Fig. 3 are indexed by (i, j, k), where i denotes the number of jobs in the PM buffer, j denotes the number of VMs currently being provisioned, k denotes the number of running VMs. Input parameters for a hot PM CTMC are: (i) effective job arrival rate to each hot PM (λ_h), (ii) rate at which VM instantiation, provisioning, and configuration occurs (β_h), (iii) job service rate (μ), (iv) buffer size of hot PM (L_h), and (v) maximum number of VMs that can be deployed on a PM (m). Assuming a total of n_h PMs in the hot pool, λ_h is given by $\lambda(1 - P_{block})/n_h$. Observe that P_{block} is computed from RPDE sub-model. Output of the hot pool sub-model is the steady state probability P_h that at least one PM in the hot pool can accept a job for provisioning.

CTMC for a warm PM [8] is similar to the hot PM sub-model, with few differences: (i) Effective arrival rate to each warm PM is λ_w. (ii) When no VM is running or being provisioned, warm PM is turned on but not ready for use. Upon a job arrival in this state, the warm PM requires some additional startup time to make it ready for use. Rate at which warm PM is made ready for use is γ_w. (iii) Rate of VM instantiation, provisioning, and configuration for first VM is β_w while for subsequent VMs rate is β_h. Buffer size of each warm PM is L_w. Assuming a total of n_w PMs in the warm pool, λ_w is given by $\lambda(1-P_{block})(1-P_h)/n_w$. Output of the warm pool sub-model is the steady state probability P_w that at least one PM in the warm pool can accept a job for provisioning.

CTMC for a cold PM is similar to the warm PM sub-model and cold pool sub-model is the set of n_c independent cold PM sub-models. Main differences between a warm and a cold PM sub-model are: (i) effective arrival rate (λ_c), (ii) rate at which startup is executed (γ_c), (iii) initial VM provisioning rate (β_c) and buffer size (L_c). λ_c is given by $\lambda(1 - P_{block})(1 - P_h)(1 - P_w)/n_c$. Output of the cold pool sub-model is the steady state probability P_c that at least one PM in the cold pool can accept a job for provisioning. Probabilities P_h, P_w, and P_c as obtained from hot, warm, and cold pool sub-models, respectively, are used in RPDE sub-model as input parameters.

4.2 Resiliency quantification using interacting sub-models

As described in Section 2, resiliency quantification requires analyzing transient behavior of a system after a change is applied. However, in interacting sub-models approach, generator matrices of sub-models evolve with time, leading to sub-models that are non-homogeneous continuous time Markov chains (NHCTMC) [18]. We explain this phenomenon with an example. During transient analysis of interacting sub-models, P_{block}, obtained as an output measure from RPDE sub-model, is used in VM provisioning sub-models as an input parameter to compute P_h, P_w, and P_c. Since the transient value of P_{block} changes with time, values of job-arrival rates in hot, warm, and cold sub-models, as derived from P_{block}, also change with time. As a result, the

Algorithm 1 Resiliency quantification using interacting sub-models

Input: (i) hot, warm, cold and RPDE sub-models, (ii) ω_1 and ω_2: values of an input parameter before and after the change respectively, (iii) $[0, T]$: length of the time interval for transient analysis, (iv) Δ: length of the sub-intervals.

Output: Values of performance measures at the end of each sub-interval.

```
1: declare H, H', H'', W, W', W'', C, C', C'', R, R', R'': vector of probability;
2: declare P_h, P'_h, P''_h, P_w, P'_w, P''_w, P_c, P'_c, P''_c, P_block, P'_block, P''_block, P'''_block: probability;
3: declare ε_f: upper bound on error;
4: declare stop: boolean;
5: declare t: time instant;
6: t ← 0;
7: {H', W', C', R', P_h, P_w, P_c, P_block} ← fp_steady(ω_1);
8: output the values of performance measures at steady state;
9: {H, W, C, R} ← map(H', W', C', R');
10: stop ← false;
11: do:
12:     t ← t + Δ;
13:     P'_block ← P_block; P'_h ← P_h; P'_w ← P_w; P'_c ← P_c;
14:     do:
15:         P'''_block ← P_block;
16:         {H'', P''_h} ← hot_transient(H, P_block, ω_2, Δ);
17:         P_h ← (P''_h + P'_h)/2;
18:         {W'', P''_w} ← warm_transient(W, P_block, P_h, ω_2, Δ);
19:         P_w ← (P''_w + P'_w)/2;
20:         {C'', P''_c} ← cold_transient(C, P_block, P_h, P_w, ω_2, Δ);
21:         P_c ← (P''_c + P'_c)/2;
22:         {R'', P''_block} ← rpde_transient(R, P_h, P_w, P_c, ω_2, Δ);
23:         P_block ← min(P_block, P''_block) + |P''_block − P_block|/2;
24:         P_block ← (P_block + P'_block)/2;
25:     while |P_block − P'''_block| < ε_f
26:     repeat steps 15-24 to update: H'', W'', C'', R'', P_h, P_w, P_c, P_block, at t
27:     H ← H''; W ← W''; C ← C''; R ← R'';
28:     output the values of performance measures at time t;
29:     if t ≥ T:
30:         stop ← true;
31: while stop is false
```

generator matrices of hot, warm, and cold sub-models become time-dependent. The transient values of P_h, P_w, and P_c are used to compute transition rates in the RPDE sub-model. This leads to a time-dependent generator matrix of RPDE sub-model. To solve this problem, we use an approach inspired from piece-wise constant approximation method [18]. We divide the time interval for transient analysis into small sub-intervals and we assume that the values of NHCTMC transition rates are constant within these sub-intervals. Fixed-point iteration among the sub-models is carried out for each sub-interval and outputs from one sub-interval are transferred as inputs to the next sub-interval. In order to automate such operations, in the next section we propose an algorithm for resiliency quantification using interacting sub-models.

Resiliency quantification algorithm for large scale IaaS Cloud. Algorithm 1 presents the pseudocode for resiliency quantification using interacting sub-models approach. Input parameters to this algorithm are: (i) hot, warm, cold, and RPDE sub-models, (ii) values of an input parameter before and after the change (ω_1 and ω_2 respectively), (iii) length of the time interval ($[0, T]$) for transient analysis, and (iv) length of the sub-intervals (Δ) used in the piece-wise constant approximation method. In this paper, for IaaS Cloud resiliency quantification, parameters ω_1 and ω_2 represent values of job arrival rate or number of PMs per pool. At the end of each sub-interval, output measures from Algorithm 1 are the values of performance measures.

To understand the system behavior before the change is applied, we solve the sub-models iteratively for steady state analysis, using the function *fp_steady(.)*. From steady state analysis, we obtain: (i) state probability vectors of the hot, warm, cold, and RPDE sub-models, (ii) steady state values of fixed-point variables, and (iii) steady state values of performance measures.

Before the transient analysis, it is necessary to map the state spaces of the sub-models before the change into the state spaces of the sub-models after the change. This is performed by function *map(.)*. A mapping is one-to-one if non-structural change is applied to a sub-model (i.e., if the state space of the sub-model before and after the change is exactly same). Otherwise, one-to-many or many-to-one mapping is performed (i.e., if the state space of the sub-model is modified after the change).

Next, the sub-models are solved for transient analysis. In Algorithm 1, outer loop (step 11 to step 31) runs until we finish the transient analysis for all sub-intervals. The inner loop (step 14 to step 25) represents the fixed-point iteration within each sub-interval. For transient analysis in the first sub-interval, initial state probability vectors ($\mathbf{H}, \mathbf{W}, \mathbf{C}$, and $\mathbf{R}$) and fixed point variables (P_h, P_w, P_c, and P_{block}) are obtained from the steady state analysis. For subsequent sub-intervals, values of $\mathbf{H}, \mathbf{W}, \mathbf{C}, \mathbf{R}, P_h, P_w, P_c$, and P_{block} are obtained from transient analysis in previous sub-intervals. However, an average is computed between the current value of each fixed-point variable and the value obtained from previous sub-interval. Such averaging process reduces the errors introduced due to non-homogeneous behavior of the system. Before starting the fixed-point iteration within a sub-interval, we store the values of fixed point variables (P'_h, P'_w, P'_c, and P'_{block}) obtained from previous sub-intervals. It can be shown that fixed-point variables P_h, P_w, and P_c can be expressed as a function of P_{block}. So, we check the values of P_{block} in successive iterations to determine the condition for convergence in fixed-point iteration. Fixed point iteration for a sub-interval starts by calling the function *hot_transient(.)* to obtain the transient solution of the hot sub-model. Observe that we use ω_2 to enforce the change in the system behavior. Outputs of *hot_transient(.)* are the transient state probability vector of the hot sub-model ($\mathbf{H}''$) and the transient probability that the job can be accepted in the hot pool (P''_h). P_h is updated by taking an average of its current value (P''_h) and the value obtained from the previous sub-interval (P'_h). Function *warm_transient(.)* uses this updated P_h as an input parameter and solves the warm sub-model for transient solution. Outputs of *warm_transient(.)* are the transient state probability vector of the warm sub-model ($\mathbf{W}''$) and the transient probability that job can be accepted in the warm pool (P''_w). P_w is updated by taking average of P''_w and P'_w. Function *cold_transient(.)* uses updated values of P_h and P_w to solve the cold sub-model for transient solution. Outputs of *cold_transient(.)* are the transient state probability vector of the cold sub-model ($\mathbf{C}''$) and the transient probability that the job can be accepted in the cold pool (P''_c). P_c is updated by taking average of P''_c and P'_c. Function *rpde_transient(.)* uses updated values of P_h, P_w, and P_c to solve the RPDE sub-model for transient solution. Outputs of *rpde_transient(.)* are the transient state probability vector of the RPDE sub-model ($\mathbf{R}''$) and P''_{block}. Value of P_{block} is updated twice: (i) for improving the rate of convergence in successive fixed-point iteration (step 23 in Algorithm 1) and (ii) for reducing the errors due to non-homogenous behavior of the system (step 24 in Algorithm 1). After the fixed-point iteration in a sub-interval finishes, we update the values of initial state probability vectors ($\mathbf{H}, \mathbf{W}, \mathbf{C}$, and $\mathbf{R}$) as well as the fixed-point variables (P_h, P_w, P_c, and P_{block}). We use these updated values in the next sub-interval. Observe that within a sub-interval, fixed-point variables (used as input parameters to the sub-models) are updated in each iteration while the initial state probability vectors used to obtain the transient solutions of the sub-models remain unchanged.

5. NUMERICAL RESULTS

Case	Description
case-I	Increase in λ, 100 PMs in each pool
case-II	Increase in λ, 1000 PMs in each pool
case-III	Decrease in λ, 100 PMs in each pool
case-IV	Decrease in λ, 1000 PMs in each pool
case-V	Removal of 900 PMs from hot, 750 PMs from warm and cold pool each
case-VI	Removal of 850 PMs from hot and warm each, 700 PMs from cold pool
case-VII	Removal of 800 PMs from each pool
case-VIII	Addition of 150 PMs to hot pool
case-IX	Addition of 75 PMs to hot and warm pool each
case-X	Addition of 50 PMs to each pool

Table 1: Description of the considered cases.

In this section, we discuss key results for large scale IaaS Cloud resiliency quantification using scalable interacting sub-models. Subsequently, model solution time and accuracy of our proposed resiliency algorithm for interacting sub-models are compared with the monolithic model shown in [5].

5.1 Resiliency quantification for large scale IaaS Cloud

We use SHARPE [19] software package to solve interacting sub-models and quantify the IaaS Cloud resiliency of the performance measures. Using Python scripts, we automate the generation of SHARPE input files and implement the following tasks: (i) mapping the state space of the sub-models before the change into the state space of the sub-models after the change, (ii) transferring the initial probability vectors and fixed-point variables from current sub-interval to the next sub-interval. We quantified large scale IaaS Cloud resiliency upon two types of changes: change in job-arrival rate and change in the number of PMs. In Table 1, we define ten cases that we have analyzed and we numerically compare the corresponding resiliency metrics (with $\gamma = 90$ and $\delta = 0.1$) in Table 2.

Effect of changing job-arrival rate (λ). Fig. 4(a) shows the transient effects of changing the job arrival rate (λ) on job rejection rate. We analyze the resiliency of two Cloud configurations with 100 PMs and 1000 PMs in each pool. For both configurations, maximum 2 VMs can run simultaneously on a PM. At time instance $t = 0$, arrival rate is increased from 1000 to 1300 jobs/hr. In case-I and case-II, settling times are $t_{set}^{(I)}$ and $t_{set}^{(II)}$ respectively. At $t = 1.5$ hr,

Cases	Resiliency metrics for job rejection rate				Resiliency metrics for mean number of jobs in RPDE			
	t_{set}	$PO(\%)$	t_{peak}	$t_{percentile}$	t_{set}	$PO(\%)$	t_{peak}	$t_{percentile}$
case-I	0.47	1.45	0.13	0.06	0.35	0.16	0.13	0.05
case-II	0.52	-	-	0.21	0.48	-	-	0.16
case-III	0.55	1.1	0.29	0.06	0.78	0.27	0.32	0.13
case-IV	0.28	-	-	0.07	0.36	-	-	0.13
case-V	0.87	-	-	0.37	0.75	-	-	0.29
case-VI	1.22	-	-	0.61	1.17	-	-	0.56
case-VII	1.73	-	-	0.90	1.75	-	-	0.88
case-VIII	0.78	-	-	0.15	0.89	-	-	0.20
case-IX	0.98	-	-	0.21	1.05	-	-	0.26
case-X	0.91	-	-	0.22	0.97	-	-	0.27

Table 2: Comparison of resiliency metrics for the different cases described in Table 1.

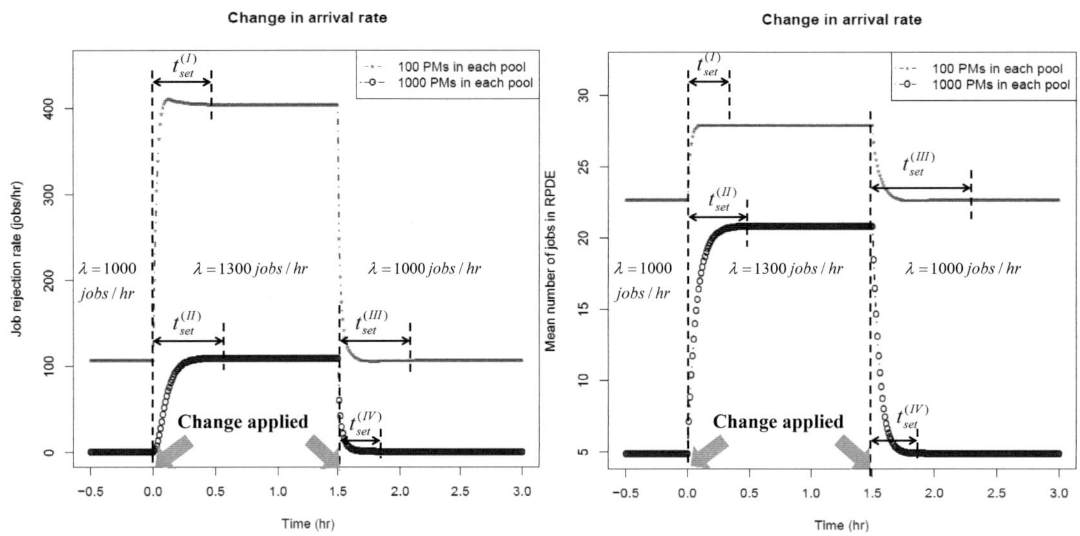

(a) (b)

Figure 4: Effect of changing job arrival rate (a) job rejection rate and (b) mean number of jobs in the RPDE.

job arrival rate is reduced to initial value, i.e., 1000 jobs/hr. When the change is removed, settling times are $t_{set}^{(III)}$ and $t_{set}^{(IV)}$ respectively.

(#PMs in each pool, maximum # VMs per PM)	Monolithic model	Interacting sub-models
(1, 1)	912	27
(1, 2)	4, 655	35
(1, 4)	20, 691	47
(1, 8)	116, 603	71
(1, 16)	768, 075	119
(1, 32)	5, 543, 915	215
(1, 38)	9, 848, 061	251
(1, 39)	Memory overflow	257
(2, 1)	43, 776	27
(3, 1)	2, 101, 248	27
(4, 1)	Memory overflow	27
(500, 64)	–	407

Table 3: Comparison of model states.

In Fig. 4(b), similar transient effects are shown for the mean number of jobs in RPDE (a measure of congestion in the Cloud).

Effect of changing system capacity. Next, we quantify the resiliency of IaaS Cloud due to addition or removal of PMs. Fig. 5(a) shows the transient effects of removing PMs on the job rejection rate. We start with a scenario where 1000 PMs are equally distributed in each pool (as denoted by (1000, 1000, 1000)). At $t = 0$, we remove total 2400 PMs in three different ways: (i) 900 PMs are removed from hot pool and 750 PMs are removed from warm and cold pool each (denoted by (100, 250, 250)), (ii) 850 PMs are removed from hot and warm pool each and 700 PMs are removed from cold pool (denoted by (150, 150, 300)), and (iii) 800 PMs are removed from each pool (denoted by (200, 200, 200)). After the removal of the PMs, rejection rate increases and finally reaches a steady state. Settling time is maximum when 800 PMs are removed from each pool, i.e., the Cloud configuration is changed from (1000, 1000, 1000) to (200, 200, 200). Although, observe that the job rejection rate is maximum when the Cloud configuration is changed from (1000, 1000, 1000) to (100, 250, 250). Similar effects on the mean number of jobs in RPDE are shown in Fig. 5(b).

(#PMs in each pool, maximum # VMs per PM)	Monolithic model	Interacting sub-models
(1, 1)	0.124	0.066
(1, 2)	0.196	0.074
(1, 4)	0.556	0.088
(1, 8)	2.998	0.141
(1, 16)	79.563	0.208
(1, 32)	188.174	0.346
(1, 38)	293.672	0.399
(1, 39)	Memory overflow	0.406
(2, 1)	2.024	0.063
(3, 1)	166.704	0.062
(4, 1)	Memory overflow	0.060
(500, 64)	–	0.055

Table 4: Comparison of model solution times in seconds.

Fig. 6(a) shows the transient effects of adding new PMs

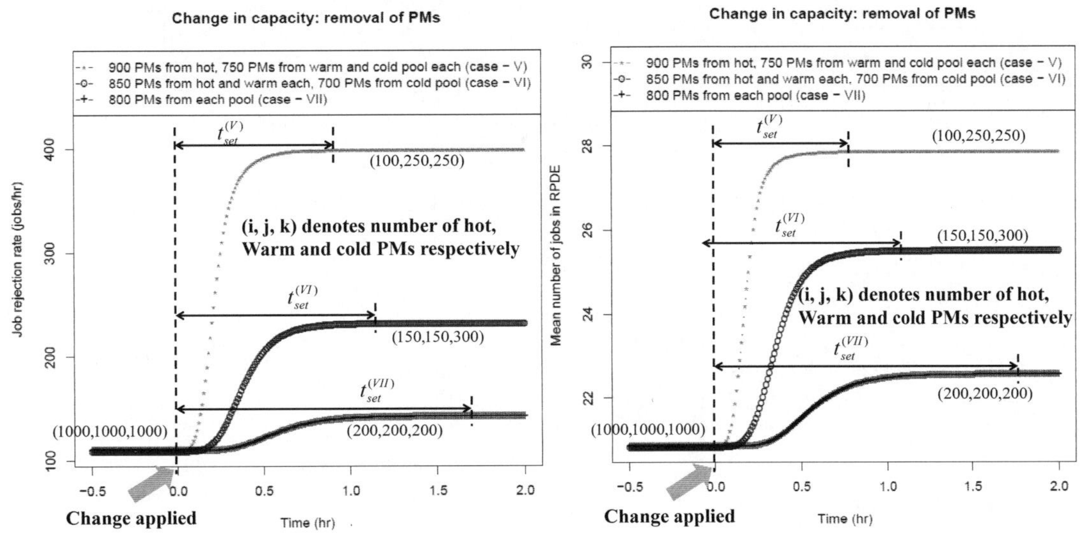

(a) (b)

Figure 5: Effect of removing PMs on (a) job rejection rate and (b) mean number of jobs in the RPDE.

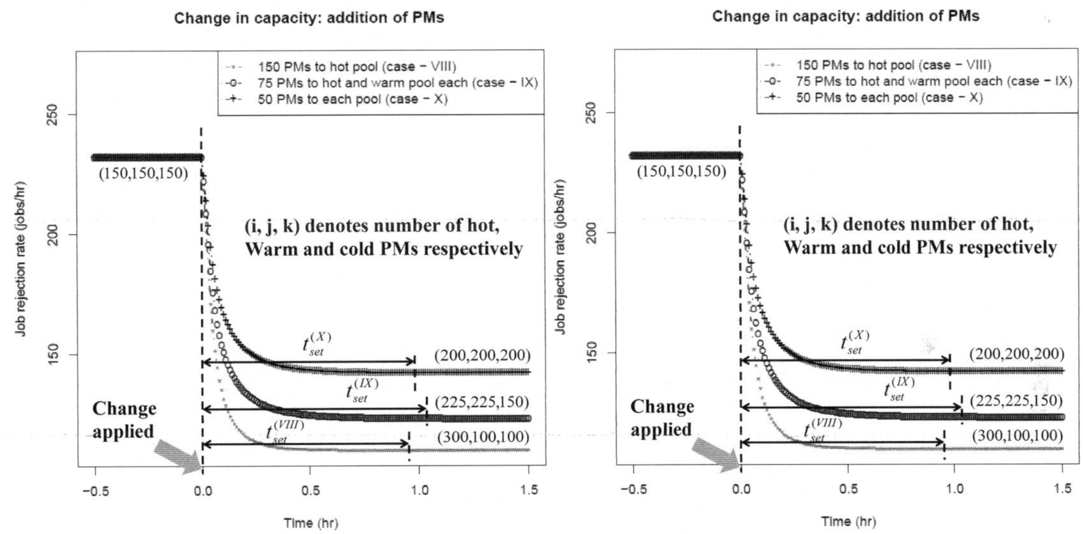

(a) (b)

Figure 6: Effect of adding PMs on (a) job rejection rate and (b) mean number of jobs in the RPDE.

on job rejection rate. We start with a scenario where 150 PMs are equally distributed in each pool (as denoted by $(150, 150, 150)$). At $t = 0$, we add total 150 PMs in three different ways: (i) 150 PMs are added to hot pool (denoted by $(300, 150, 150)$), (ii) 75 PMs are added to hot and warm pool each (denoted by $(225, 225, 150)$), and (iii) 50 PMs are added to each pool (denoted by $(200, 200, 200)$). After the addition of the PMs, rejection rate decreases and finally reaches a steady state. Among the three changes, settling time is minimum when PMs are added only to the hot pool. Similar effects on the mean number of jobs in RPDE are shown in Fig. 6(b).

5.2 Comparison of scalability with monolithic model.

We use Stochastic Petri Net Package (SPNP) [11] for resiliency quantification using the monolithic model. SPNP allows to easily map the state space of the model before the change into the state space of the model after the change and to compute the initial probability vectors in a straightforward manner. Both the interacting sub-models and the monolithic model were solved using a desktop PC with Intel Core 2 Duo processor (E8400, 3.0 GHz) and 4 GB memory. In Table 3, we report the state space for both the monolithic model and interacting sub-models. Monolithic model runs into a memory overflow problem when the number of PMs in each pool increases beyond 3 and the number of VMs per PM increases beyond 38. We observe that the state space size of the monolithic model increases quickly and becomes too large to construct the reachability graph even for small

Algorithms	**Resiliency metrics for job rejection rate**				**Resiliency metrics for mean number of jobs in RPDE**			
	t_{set}	$PO(\%)$	t_{peak}	$t_{percentile}$	t_{set}	$PO(\%)$	t_{peak}	$t_{percentile}$
Interactive sub-models	0.12	$1.52e-04$	0.20	0.04	0.10	$0.21e-04$	0.18	0.04
Monolithic model	0.10	$0.85e-04$	0.21	0.04	0.11	$0.24e-04$	0.23	0.04

Table 5: Comparison of resiliency metrics between the two algorithm when arrival rate is increased.

number of PMs. However, with interacting sub-models approach, the state space increases at a slower rate as the maximum number of VMs per PM is increased and remains constant with increasing number PMs. A comparison of solution times is shown in Table 4. Solution time for monolithic model increases almost exponentially with the increase in model size. Solution time for interacting sub-models remains almost constant with the increase in model size. Clearly, interacting sub-models approach facilitates fast quantification of large scale IaaS Cloud resiliency.

5.3 Comparison of accuracy

Using 2 PMs per pool and 1 VM per PM, we compare the accuracy of resiliency quantification using monolithic model and interacting sub-models approach. We quantify the resiliency of two performance measures: job rejection rate and mean number of jobs in RPDE respectively, when subjected to a change in arrival rate (λ). At $t = 0$, we change the job arrival rate from 350 jobs/hr to 400 jobs/hr. In Table 5, we observe that the resiliency metrics are comparable in both the approaches. There are two sources of errors in interacting sub-models based resiliency quantification approach. They are: (i) errors due to decomposition of the monolithic model and (ii) errors due to non-homogeneous behavior of the system during transient phase. In this paper, we only focus on resiliency metrics that capture the errors in the transient analysis. Analysis of errors due to model decomposition, is shown in [6].

6. CONCLUSIONS AND FUTURE WORK

In this paper, we quantify the resiliency of IaaS Cloud upon changes in job arrival rate and system capacity. To the best of our knowledge, ours is perhaps the first work that quantifies resiliency of large IaaS Cloud using a scalable and fast analytic approach. Resiliency metrics described in this paper can be used to quantify the transient behavior of a IaaS Cloud under sudden changes and can help during design stage of the IaaS Cloud. In fact, using the resiliency metrics, different configurations and design alternatives (faster provisioning vs. slower provisioning, different distributions of PMs in pools) can be evaluated that can meet provider specific service goals. Although, the resiliency approach described in this paper is built around performance models, proposed approach is general and can be applied to any state-space based model.

7. REFERENCES

[1] D. Bruneo, S. Distefano, F. Longo, A. Puliafito, and M. Scarpa. Reliability assessment of wireless sensor nodes with non-linear battery discharge. 2010.

[2] P. F. Chimento and K. S. Trivedi. The completion time of programs on processors subject to failure and repair. *IEEE Trans. on Computers*, 42(10):1184–1194, 1993.

[3] N. DeBardeleben et al. *High-End Computing Resilience: Analysis of Issues Facing the HEC Community and Path-Forward for Research and Development.* 2010.

[4] S. Distefano, F. Longo, and M. Scarpa. Symbolic representation techniques in dynamic reliability evaluation. pages 45–53, 2010.

[5] R. Ghosh, F. Longo, V. K. Naik, and K. S. Trivedi. Quantifying resiliency of IaaS cloud. In *RACOS Workshop*, 2010.

[6] R. Ghosh, F. Longo, V. K. Naik, and K. S. Trivedi. Modeling and performance analysis of large scale iaas clouds. *Elsevier Future Generation Computer Systems*, 29(5):1216–1234, 2013.

[7] R. Ghosh, F. Longo, R. Xia, V. Naik, and K. Trivedi. Stochastic model driven capacity planning for an infrastructure-as-a-service cloud. *IEEE Transactions on Services Computing*, 7(4):667–680, 2014.

[8] R. Ghosh, K. S. Trivedi, V. K. Naik, and D. S. Kim. Performability analysis for Infrastructure-as-a-Service cloud: An interacting stochastic models approach. In *PRDC*, 2010.

[9] B. Haverkort, R. Marie, G. Rubino, and K. S. Trivedi (eds.). *Performability Modeling Tools and Techniques.* Wiley, 2001.

[10] P. Heegard and K. S. Trivedi. Network survivability modeling. *Computer Networks*, 53(8):1215–1234, 2009.

[11] C. Hirel, B. Tuffin, and K. S. Trivedi. SPNP: stochastic petri nets. version 6. In *Lecture Notes in Computer Science*, 2000.

[12] V. G. Kulkarni et al. The completion time of a job on multimode systems. *Adv. Appl. Prob.*, 19(4):932–954, 1987.

[13] J. C. Laprie. From dependability to resilience. In *DSN*, 2008.

[14] Y. Liu and K. S. Trivedi. Survivability quantification: The analytical modeling approach. *Intl. Journal of Performability Eng.*, 2(1):29–44, 2006.

[15] L. Simoncini. Resilient computing: An engineering discipline. In *IPDPS*, 2009.

[16] J. P. Sterbenz et al. Resilience and survivability in communication networks: Strategies, principles, and survey of disciplines. *Elsevier Computer Networks*, 54(8):1245 – 1265, June 2010.

[17] T1A1.2 Working Group on Network Survivability Performance. Enhanced Network Survivability Performance. Technical Report T1.TR.68-2001, February 2001.

[18] K. S. Trivedi. *Probability and Statistics with Reliability, Queuing and Computer Science Applications.* Wiley, 2001.

[19] K. S. Trivedi and R. Sahner. Sharpe at the age of twenty two. *SIGMETRICS Perform. Eval. Rev.*, 36(4):52–57, Mar. 2009.

Vulnerability Evaluation of Distributed Reputation Management Systems

Vincenzo Agate
vincenzo.agate@unipa.it

Alessandra De Paola
alessandra.depaola@unipa.it

Giuseppe Lo Re
giuseppe.lore@unipa.it

Marco Morana
marco.morana@unipa.it

Università degli Studi di Palermo
Viale delle Scienze, Ed.6, Palermo, Italy

ABSTRACT

In distributed environments, Reputation Management Systems (RMSs) aim to estimate agents' trustworthiness by exploiting different sources of information. The distributed nature of these systems makes them vulnerable to several types of security attacks, and the response provided by a specific RMS depends on various factors, such as the algorithms adopted for estimating the reputation values and the communication protocols used to enable the cooperation among agents. This work examines the most important security attacks against RMSs and proposes a set of metrics for a quantitative evaluation of the RMS vulnerabilities. A parallel simulation framework is used to automatically give a vulnerability score to a RMS according to the computed metrics. Experiments performed on a case-study RMS show the effectiveness of the metrics we defined, and the convenience of using a simulation environment to support the design of a secure RMS.

CCS Concepts

•**Security and privacy** → **Distributed systems security;** •**Computing methodologies** → *Simulation tools;*

Keywords

Distributed Reputation Management; Security Attacks; Evaluation Metrics

1. INTRODUCTION

Several distributed services, such as peer-to-peer applications [19], Service Oriented Architectures [16, 5], and e-Commerce frameworks [9], rely on Reputation Management Systems (RMSs) in order to estimate the behavior of unknown agents.

VALUETOOLS 2016, October 25-28, Taormina, Italy

The role of RMSs is particularly relevant if the benefit perceived by the agents that constitute the distributed system depends on the cooperativeness of other agents, so that a non-cooperative behavior may cause a detriment for the whole community.

In a distributed RMS, a central authority is missing and a common value of reputation is produced by all the agents according to several sources of information, such as their direct experience or information provided by other agents. Such systems allow to avoid the presence of a single point of failure, that can represent also a performance bottleneck, and provide a well scalable solution.

Nevertheless, the distributed nature of such systems makes them vulnerable to several types of security attacks, performed by isolated or colluding malicious agents that aim to obtain an advantage over other agents, or to abuse system resources. The response provided by a specific RMS to an attack depends on various factors, such as the algorithms adopted to estimate the reputation values and the communication protocols used to enable the cooperation among agents.

In this work we propose a set of metrics for evaluating the vulnerability of a RMS to different attacks, so as to understand the effect of different design choices on the RMS's performance. Moreover, a parallel simulation framework has been designed to allow researchers to easily specify the behavior of their RMS, to simply test its responses in different scenarios, and to obtain the corresponding vulnerability indices.

The remainder of the paper is organized as follows: related work is reported in Section 2. The RMS features and components in uencing its response under attack are presented in Section 3. Section 4 describes the four security attacks considered here, whilst Section 5 illustrates the proposed vulnerability metrics. The simulation framework is presented in Section 6, and the experimental results are shown and discusses in Section 7. Finally, conclusions follow in Section 8.

2. RELATED WORK

Several reputation management models for distributed systems have been proposed in the literature. The authors of [25] analyzed the main components of trust systems in the context of multi-agent systems, identifying a *trust evalua-*

tion phase, which assesses the reliability of the agents involved in the interactions, and a *trust-aware decision making* phase that uses reputation values to select the agents to interact with. Moreover, the authors classified trust evaluation methods in four classes, depending on the fact that they are based on: (i) past direct interactions, (ii) opinions and testimonies from other agents, (iii) knowledge about social relationships among agents, and (iv) certificates provided by third-party authorities. RMSs for distributed systems, where a central authority is missing, belong to the second class, according to which each agent relies on a distributed protocol to obtain opinions from other agents, and merges them with its past experience in order to compute the reputation of a given agent.

In recent years, a great attention has been devoted to identify and analyze the security attacks against RMSs, which exhibit many vulnerabilities due to their intrinsic distributed nature. To the best of our knowledge, works addressing this topic miss the definition of quantitative vulnerability metric for RMSs, and a tangible experimental evaluation that can drive researchers to select the best design approach according to the desired behavior.

Authors of [13] describe five attacks against RMSs, partially referenced in Section 4, and outline the defense techniques adopted by some RMSs presented in literature. A similar analysis, focusing only on *feedback-based reputation systems*, is proposed in [21].

Some testbeds and simulators have been proposed for assessing the performances of a RMS. ART (*Agent Reputation and trust*) [10], a popular simulation testbed in the field of multi-agent systems, allows to apply several evaluation metrics, and to define competitions in which different strategies can be combined and compared with respect to the utility obtained by each agent at the end of the simulation. TREET [15] limits the evaluation of RMSs in a marketplace scenario. This framework allows to measure the resistance of the RMS to some attacks, but does not consider other typical attacks, which are instead addressed in our work. In [4] the RMSs are modeled as a sequence of transformations on a graph that represents transactions and trust among agents. Even thought this tool allows to evaluate the effects of some relevant attacks, it does not simulate agent interactions making not possible to perform large-scale simulations in which agents may modify their behavior. The solutions discussed so far do not allow for large-scale simulations of the behavior of a RMS under security attacks.

In this work we extend the parallel simulation framework described in [2] and [1], in order to support researchers to evaluate the behavior of a RMS through large-scale simulations of different security attacks, and to obtain the corresponding vulnerability indices. Our framework, presented in Section 6, allows to specify the behavior of a RMS and to neglect the low-level details necessary to run the simulation, making it possible to focus only on the high-level response of the RMS under attack.

3. RMS ARCHITECTURE

As highlighted in [13], RMSs have a common structure and their differences depend on the algorithmic specification of their constituting components. Two steps can be identified: (i) a formulation and calculation phase during which agents collect and manage information in order to obtain a value for the adopted reputation metric, and (ii) a dissemination phase, when agents cooperate to compute the complete reputation values.

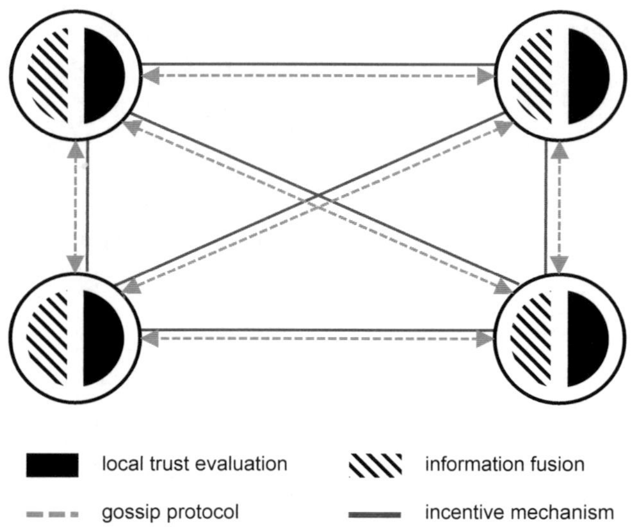

Figure 1: The components of a distributed RMS. Each agent privately performs the local trust evaluation and the information fusion algorithms; the gossip protocol and the incentive mechanism regulate the interactions with other agents.

We move step forward by considering four main components, as shown in Figure 1. Such higher level of detail allows to deeply analyze how different attacks exploit system vulnerabilities. The first component is the *local trust evaluation* which uses information from past direct interactions with other agents in order to provide an initial and partial estimation of their reputations. By considering only this component, each agent would have a very limited view of other agents behavior, and would not be able to predict the actions of unknown agents. For such reason, distributed RMSs comprise other two components that allow agents to cooperate obtaining a more precise estimation of the reputation of their neighbors, namely a *gossip protocol* which propagates information among different agents, and an *information fusion* mechanism which allows each agent to merge the direct experience with information obtained through the gossip protocol. RMSs which aim not only to detect antisocial behaviors, but also to discourage them, comprise also an *incentive mechanism* which uses reputation values to reward honest agents and to limit malicious ones.

4. SECURITY ATTACKS ON RMSS

The distributed nature of RMSs makes them vulnerable to several types of security attacks, as described in [13, 21].

We consider the worst case of attackers that are insiders, i.e., authorized users of the system that can take part to all phases of the reputation evaluation. Moreover, we assume that an attacker can get multiple identities and that it can also cooperate with other malicious agents. A classification of security attacks can be made on the basis of their goals: *self-promoting*, *slandering*, *whitewashing*, and *traitor* attacks. The classification presented in [13] includes also the *denial of service* attack, that is not considered here since it is more frequent in a centralized system, where malicious agents may overwhelm the central server, thus hindering the reputation evaluation tasks.

4.1 Self-promoting

In a *self-promoting* attack [17], a malicious agent aims to increment its own reputation value, generally in order to hide an antisocial behavior, or to achieve an unjustified advantage over its competitors, e.g., in an e-commerce scenario. This type of attack requires an orchestrated plan involving several malicious agents, since, generally, reputation management systems do not allow an agent to disseminate reputation information about himself. In order to analyze the resistance of a RMS to a self-promoting attack, it is irrelevant whether it is conducted by distinct malicious agents or by multiple identities of a single malicious agent.

The classical way to perform the self-promoting attack is to introduce false positive information into the system through the gossip protocol. The RMS component capable of resisting to such attack is the *information fusion* mechanism, which determines the balance between gossiped information and direct experiences, and that can also assign different weights to information obtained, e.g., on the basis of the reputation of gossiper agents.

4.2 Slandering

The *slandering* attack [3] aims to decrease the reputation of some \victim" agents. Such attack may be performed by a single malicious agent, but in a large-scale system, an isolated intervention would have a limited effect. For this reason, slandering attacks are generally performed by a group of colluding agents. Also in this case, it is not relevant whether such malicious group is composed by distinct agents or by duplicated identities. Such an attack is typical of e-commerce systems, where the attacker aims to sabotage a competitor in order to obtain an indirect economic profit. The slandering attack is performed by introducing false negative information through the gossip protocol, and, similarly as the self-promoting attack, the *information fusion* mechanism is the main component that can let the system resist through an opportune balancing of gossiped information.

4.3 Whitewashing

The *whitewashing* attack [8] is performed by a malicious agent that wants to avoid the consequences of its bad past behavior. The malicious agent leaves the system and rejoins it with a new identity obtaining the default reputation value assigned to new users. The main vulnerability exploited by this type of attack is that a new agent receives a default reputation value comparable with the long-term reputation of a honest agent. RMSs that adopt such initial value have an optimistic approach and rely on negative feedbacks in order to discover a malicious behavior. A greater resistance is expected by RMSs that impose a low initial reputation value and use positive feedbacks to rise the reputation value. Moreover, a whitewashing attack can be reinforced by a combined self-promoting attack to extend its effect.

4.4 Traitor

In such type of attack, a *traitor* agent [19], with a bad reputation, acts honestly for a limited portion of time in order to increase its reputation. Once such goal is achieved, the traitor begins to abuse system resources again, and maintains an antisocial behavior until its reputation became too low; from this point the loop repeats, by alternating good and bad behaviors. A traitor attack is convenient in RMSs where the default reputation value is low, and thus a whitewashing attack does not produce an immediate benefit for the attacker, that has to behave honestly for a given time period before being able to obtain system resources. RMSs more vulnerable to such type of attack are those which weight the past history more than the recent experience.

5. SECURITY METRICS

The evaluation of a RMS requires new metrics to be defined while respecting some overall principles, partially inspired by the guidelines proposed in [20] and adopted in [22] to define some security metrics for distributed systems:

P1. the metrics should be assigned by measuring specific, unambiguous facts rather than abstract rules;

P2. the security of the RMS should be evaluated by considering all the observed vulnerabilities;

P3. the metrics should be intuitive;

P4. the metrics should be computed in an efficient way.

According to these principles, we propose to use a set of intuitive metrics (P3) that allow to measure the effort required to perform a specific attack (P1), and to evaluate and how long an attacker is able to exploit system resources:

m1) Time-to-compromise: the time necessary to reach the goal of an attack aimed to alter the reputation of some agents, i.e., the number of time steps required for the attack to succeed;

m2) Exploitation-time: the time a malicious agent is able to exploit the system resources before its behavior is detected;

m3) Collusion-complexity: the number of agents involved in cooperative attacks.

Following P2, we adopted distinct metrics for each attack so as to separately evaluate the robustness of RMSs against different threats. Each of the selected metrics is then mapped to a set of qualitative ratings that provide a textual representation of the numeric scores S, where $0 \leq S \leq 10$. The qualitative severity rating scale we used is that defined by the Common Vulnerability Scoring System (CVSS) [6], a well-established standard for classifying the severity of security vulnerabilities. In particular, the simulation framework rates the significance of each vulnerability as *none* (if $S < 0.1$), *low* ($0.1 \leq S < 4.0$), *medium* ($4.0 \leq S < 7.0$), *high* ($7.0 \leq S < 9.0$), *critical* ($9.0 \leq S \leq 10.0$). At the end of this analysis, the final user is notified of the vulnerabilities marked as *high* or *critical*.

The last principle, P4, is satisfied by guaranteeing that all the metrics are computed by the simulator quickly and automatically.

In order to determine whether a specific attack has achieved his goal, we also need to define the following success conditions (defined for a RMS in which reputation values are included in $[0, 1]$):

- **Self-promoting (SP)** is successfully completed if the long-term reputation of the non-cooperative, malicious agent, computed by one of its trustworthy neighbors, is greater than 0.5.
- **Slandering (S)** is successfully completed if the long-term reputation of the victim, computed by one of its trustworthy neighbors, is lower than 0.5.
- **Whitewashing (W)** is achieved within a temporal window T, if, in such window, the reputation of the non-cooperative, malicious agent, computed by one of its trustworthy neighbors, is greater than 0.5.
- **Traitor (T)** is achieved if the reputation of the malicious agent, computed by one of its trustworthy neighbors, is always greater than 0.5.

The long-term reputation is the reputation value observed after T_{max} time steps, given that at each time step an interaction between at least two agents occurs. The value of T_{max} has been set to 500 time steps by empirically analyzing the point when many state-of-the-art RMSs converge to a stable reputation values in a network composed by 100 agents and where each agent has 6 neighbors on average. The time T_{max} is also used both to scale *time-to-compromise* and *exploitation-time*, and to determine an intermediate threshold, $T_{th} = T_{max}/2$, needed to compute the *collusion-complexity*.

According to these definitions, being N the number of simulation time steps required to complete an attack, the time-to-compromise TTC is computed as:

$$TTC = N/T_{max}, \quad (1)$$

where $TTC = 1$ if the attack has failed.

When considering slandering or self-promoting attacks, the time-to-compromise also depends on the percentage of malicious agents that interact with the observer. For this reason different TTC values are computed while varying this percentage from 10-100 in 10% increments, and the average TTC is actually considered.

The *collusion-complexity*, CC, is defined as the percentage of corrupted agents needed for completing the attack within a time T_{th}.

Thus, the vulnerabilities of a RMS to slandering and self-promoting attacks can be expressed as:

$$V_S = [1 - TTC(slandering)] \times [1 - CC(slandering)].$$
$$V_{SP} = [1 - TTC(self\text{-}prom)] \times [1 - CC(self\text{-}prom)]. \quad (2)$$

The temporal metric that allows to evaluate whitewashing and traitor attacks is quite different from TTC.

In whitewashing attacks we can state that a malicious agent is maintaining his fraudulent behavior as long as his reputation is greater than a threshold $R_{th} = 0.5$. Thus, assuming that N time steps are required for the reputation to go under R_{th}, the *exploitation-time*, and consequently the vulnerability index, can be defined as:

$$V_W = ET(whitewashing) = N/T_{max}, \quad (3)$$

For traitor attacks, the *exploitation-time* is the time a malicious agent can act in a non-cooperative way before its reputation goes under a threshold $R_{th} = 0.5$ This condition is usually reached by alternating right and bad behavior for a certain number of time steps, N_{good} and N_{bad} respectively. Thus, the *exploitation-time* for traitor attacks, and consequently the vulnerability index, can be defined as:

$$V_T = ET(traitor) = N_{good}/(N_{good} + N_{bad}). \quad (4)$$

In order to obtain vulnerability scores in [0, 10] while having significant values in the whole range, a gamma correction, with $\gamma = 0.5$, and a scale factor $K = 10$, is applied:

$$V^* = K \times V^{\gamma}. \quad (5)$$

According to the previous definitions, the overall vulnerability of a RMS is given by a vector containing the list of the detected vulnerabilities V^* and the number of those marked as *high* or *critical*:

$$RMS\_vulnerability =$$
$$= \{V^*, num\_of\_V^*_{high\&critical}\} =$$
$$= \{[V^*_{SP}, V^*_S, V^*_W, V^*_T], num\_of\_V^*_{high\&critical}\}.$$

The extended simulation framework we describe in next Section not only allows to analyze the effects of different security attacks on the target RMS, but also makes a clear assessment of the RMS robustness by providing the user with an overall score computed on the basis of different vulnerability metrics.

6. PARALLEL SIMULATOR

To support the evaluation of the above described RMS, we propose here an extension of the simulation framework preliminarily described in [2] and [1], which aims to make easier the assessment of new reputation management strategies in different scenarios. The simulation is based on the synchronous time-discrete model proposed in [18] to describe synchronous distributed algorithms.

In order to separate low-level functionalities from the routines that describe the RMS's behavior, the software architecture of the simulator consists of two different logic layers.

The *reputation layer* is made of nodes connected to each other according to a customizable network topology provided by the user. This is the topmost layer, thus at this level of abstraction all the interactions between the agents occur in a totally distributed way, i.e., without the coordination of any central authority. The simulation environment is totally customizable by means of a set of of high-level configuration utilities that allow the user to specify the number of agents involved in the simulation, set the behavior and the cooperativeness degree of each agent, create ad-hoc network topologies, and specify the parameters of the reputation management strategy.

The level below is named *simulation layer*. Here, each agent is mapped to a distinct software process and the simulation proceeds in rounds according to a synchronous model, i.e., at each round all processes act simultaneously. At each iteration a process performs the operations requested to the corresponding agent: generate and send resource requests to the neighbors, evaluate incoming requests, determine a proper response, send resource responses, use local trust evaluation to update the current view of the reputation network, send updated reputation values by means of the gossip protocol, and update the information fusion mechanism. The set of processes running at the simulation layer also includes a leading process, that is responsible for coordinating the simulation by creating new processes or changing the behavior of those that already exist.

Since each process can run on a distinct remote host, the framework utilizes the Message Passing Interface (MPI) to enable communication among different distributed processes.

In order to evaluate the TTC index for slandering and self-promoting attacks, the framework performs different simulations by varying the percentage of malicious agents that interact with the neutral node, i.e., the observer, used for measuring the reputation of the victim (for slandering) or of the promoted agent (for self-promoting). For each run, the framework stores the reputation trend of the involved agents, and the time step when the goal of the attack is achieved. The final value of the TTC metric is obtained by averaging all these time steps.

The evaluation of the CC index for slandering and self-promoting attacks requires to identify the smallest percentage of colluding agents needed to reach the goal of the attack goal within T_{th} time steps. For this purpose, it is possible to exploit the same simulation runs performed to evaluate the TTC index, so as to identify the percentage interval within which the goal is achieved. A further run is performed by selecting an intermediate percentage value inside such interval, in order to obtain the CC index with a 5% granularity.

For the whitewashing attack, the ET is simply obtained by analyzing the reputation trend of the malicious agent, observed by a neutral node, and by identifying the time step in which its reputation goes under the R_{th} value. This value is the normalized with respect to T_{max}.

In order to evaluate the ET metric for the traitor attack, different simulations are performed while varying with step of 5% the fraction of time during which the traitor acts non-cooperatively. The ET index is the greatest fraction which guarantees that the reputation of the attacker never goes under the R_{th} during the whole simulation.

7. EXPERIMENTAL EVALUATION

7.1 Case Study: the RMS

In order to evaluate the effect of the security attacks on RMSs designed according to different approaches, we adopted as case-study a RMS that explicitly manages, through tunable parameters, the relationship between past and recent experiences, and between direct experience and gossiped information.

This RMS includes the four components described in Section 3 and is inspired by [14] and [7]. The *local trust evaluation mechanism*, as in [14], requires that each agent i stores the number of satisfactory, $sat(i,j)$, and unsatisfactory, $unsat(i,j)$, transactions occurred with other agents j in the network, during the last time interval. The percentage of satisfied requests in such time interval is considered the *local trust*, lt_{ij}, which is defined according to the following equation:

$$lt_{ij} = \frac{sat(i,j)}{sat(i,j) + unsat(i,j)}. \qquad (6)$$

The local trust value in uences the reputation that i holds about j, weighted by a factor $\alpha \in [0,1]$:

$$lr_{ij}(t) = \alpha * lt_{ij} + (1-\alpha) * r_{ij}(t-1), \qquad (7)$$

where lr_{ij} indicates the *local reputation*, that is the past reputation r_{ij} updated according to the last local experience.

The *gossip protocol* simply states that each agent sends its reputation values, r_{ij}, to all its neighbors, thus, each agent knows the opinion of all its one-hop neighbors about the reputation of its two-hop neighborhood.

The *information fusion* phase is inspired to [7], where each agent merges only information coming from reliable agents, i.e., those whose reputation is beyond a given threshold τ. Merged information is weighted with the reputation of the gossiper agents, and the resulting reputation value r_{ij} is obtained by linearly combining this weighted mean with the local reputation:

$$r_{ij}(t) = (1-\beta) * lr_{ij}(t) + \beta * \frac{\sum_{k\in K} r_{ik}(t-1) * r_{kj}(t-1)}{\sum_{k\in K} r_{ik}(t-1)}, \qquad (8)$$

where β is a coefficient in $[0,1]$ and K is the set of reliable agents:

$$K = \{k : r_{ik}(t-1) \geq \tau\}. \qquad (9)$$

The adoption of a weighted sum between the local reputation and the average values reported by other agents is a common solution in the literature [23, 24].

Finally, our RMS implements a simple *incentive mechanism* that allows an agent to obtain resources with a probability proportional to its reputation [5].

7.2 Experimental Results

In this section we provide a set of experiments aimed to understand which factors mostly in uence the performance of a RMS under attack. Moreover, we show as such results may be concisely represented through the proposed vulnerability metrics.

The RMS which represents the base line for our evaluations, is characterized by the following parameters: the α factor, which weights the local trust to produce the local reputation, is $\alpha = 0.1$; the β factor, which weights the gossiped information to produce the final reputation, is $\beta = 0.1$; the default reputation value assigned to new users is $rep_{ij}(t_0) = 0.9$; the reputation threshold used to select reliable gossiper agents during the *information fusion* mechanism is $\tau = 0.4$; finally, the time interval considered for collecting data about the direct experience, needed to evaluate the local trust, consists of 30 time steps.

Such baseline parameters have been selected so as to obtain a RMS with a fair behavior and in which each attack (i) can be performed successfully and (ii) can be detected in a reasonable time. It is worth to specify that our goal is not to propose a specific RMS, but rather to show the potential of the proposed simulator for analyzing the security response of any RMS, and providing a score which depends on different vulnerability metrics.

The following experimental results have been obtained by simulating a network composed of 100 nodes, where each node has 6 neighbors on average, randomly selected ensuring that the network is not partitioned in isolated clusters.

As described in Section 4, slandering attacks are performed by a set of malicious agents that disseminate false negative feedbacks about a victim. In order to understand how the consequences of slandering attacks can be dependent on the gossip protocol used to propagate the reputation values through the reputation network, different simulations were run while varying the value of β (see equation 8) that weights direct and gossiped information. For ex-

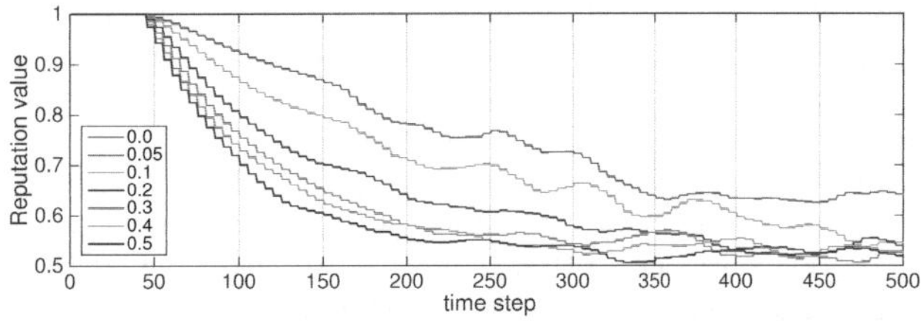

Figure 2: Slandering attack: reputation values of the victim agent as observed by neutral agents while varying the weight β of direct and gossiped information, when 50% of the agents interacting with the neutral agents are malicious.

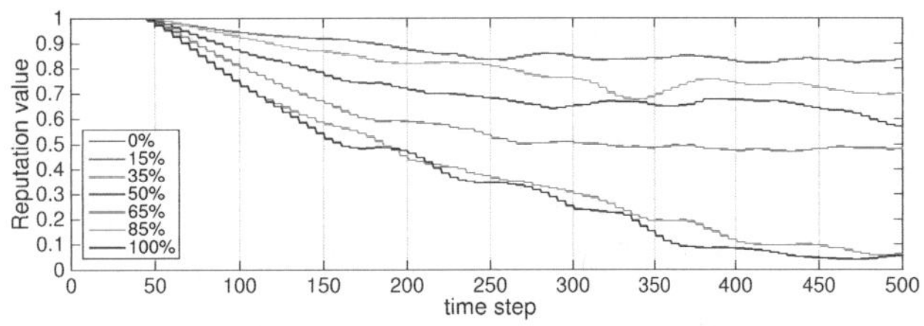

Figure 3: Slandering attack: reputation values of the victim agent as observed by neutral agents while varying the percentage of attacking agents.

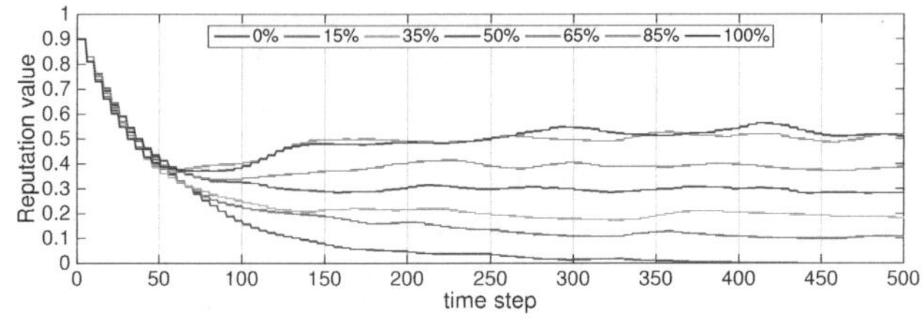

Figure 4: Self-promoting attack: reputation values of the selfish agent as observed by a trustworthy agent while varying the percentage of malicious agents supporting the attack.

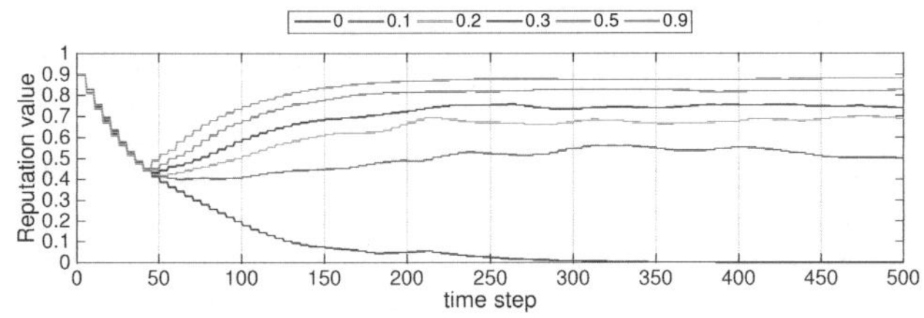

Figure 5: Self-promoting attack: reputation values of the selfish agent as observed by a trustworthy agent while varying the weight β of gossiped information.

ample, β = 0.2 means that during the information fusion phase, the information from the gossiper agents is scaled by a factor 0.2, whilst the local reputation is weighted with a factor 0.8. Fig. 2 shows that the more is the importance of the gossiped reputation, the more is the effectiveness of the slandering attack.

Obviously, we expected that also the number of attacking agents affects the reputation of the victim. Such hypothesis was confirmed by a set of experiments performed while varying the percentage of malicious agents, from 0 to 100. Fig. 3 shows the reputation of the victim as observed by neutral agents. As expected, the greater is the number of attacking agents, the more effective is the attack. However, even though the 65% of the agents in the network are malicious, the reputation of the victim decrease of only 0.5. As more agents are involved, the reputation of the victim continues to lower, approaching zero when the 85% of the agents are malicious.

Such a behavior is summarized by the slandering vulnerability index. As already said, the $TTC(slandering)$ is the average number of time steps required to put the reputation of the victim agent under R_{th} = 0.5, normalized with respect to T_{max} = 500, whilst $CC(slandering)$ is the percentage of colluding agents needed to complete the attack within T_{th} = 250 time steps.

Figure 3 shows that these conditions are satisfied when at least the 65% of the agents interact with the neutral observer. The resulting value for the slandering vulnerability metrics are the following:

$$TTC(slandering) = 0.71$$
$$CC(slandering) = 0.65$$
$$V_S^* = 3.18$$

The self-promoting attack exploits the same vulnerabilities exploited by the slandering attack, but with the goal of increasing the reputation of a non-coperative agent by means of false information provided by a set of colluding agents. Some experiments were conducted to understand how the reputation of this non-cooperative agent is perceived by a trustworthy agent that interacts directly with it. Fig. 4 shows that even though the behavior of the selfish agent remains unchanged during the simulation, its reputation increases the more malicious agent are involved in the attack. It is worth noting that, since the direct experience is negative, even if the malicious agents provide positive information, the low value of the local trust prevents the reputation value from rising over 0.5. Obviously, if gossiped information weight more than direct experience, such protection misses. Fig. 5 addresses this circumstance and describes a set of experiments where a trustworthy observer is surrounded only by dishonest agents which cooperate in order to promote the reputation of a malicious agent.

The experimental results show that our baseline RMS has a greater resistance to self-promoting attacks than to slandering attacks. Such feature is concisely represented by the self-promoting vulnerability metrics:

$$TTC(self-promoting) = 0.79$$
$$CC(self-promoting) = 0.85$$
$$V_{SP}^* = 1.78$$

The evaluation of the impact of the whitewashing attack, in a system that does not pose restriction on the creation of new accounts, corresponds to analyze how the reputation of a new user varies according to its behavior. The benefit of performing such attack depends on the default reputation value assigned to new users. Fig. 6 shows how the reputation of a new non-cooperative, malicious, agent that joins the network after 70 time steps varies according to the

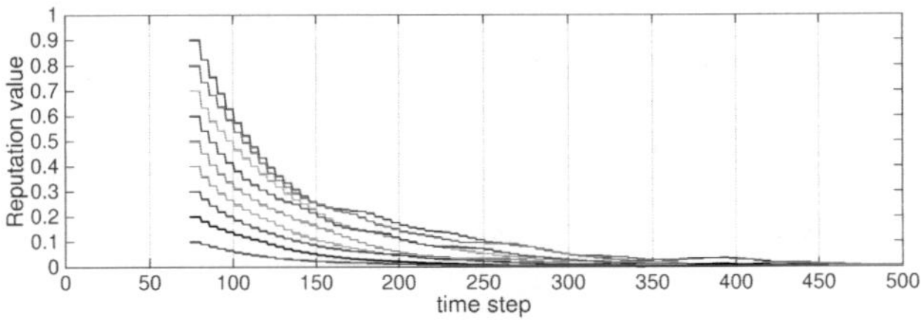

Figure 6: Whitewashing attack: reputation values of a non-cooperative agent that joins the network after 70 time steps, while varying the initial reputation value assigned by the RMS.

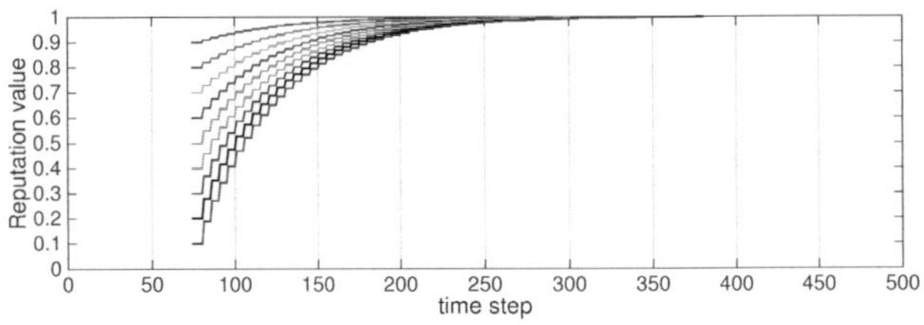

Figure 7: Whitewashing attack: reputation values of a trustworthy agent that joins the network after 70 time steps, while varying the initial reputation value assigned by the RMS.

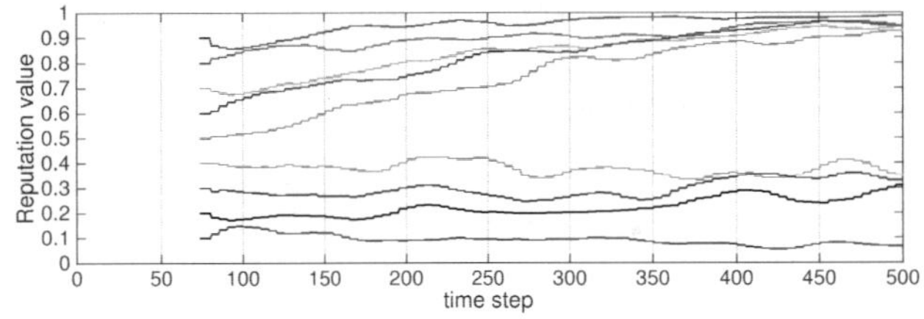

Figure 8: Whitewashing attack: reputation values of a trustworthy agent that joins the network after 70 time steps, while varying the initial reputation value assigned by the RMS, with an automatic *incentive mechanism* enabled.

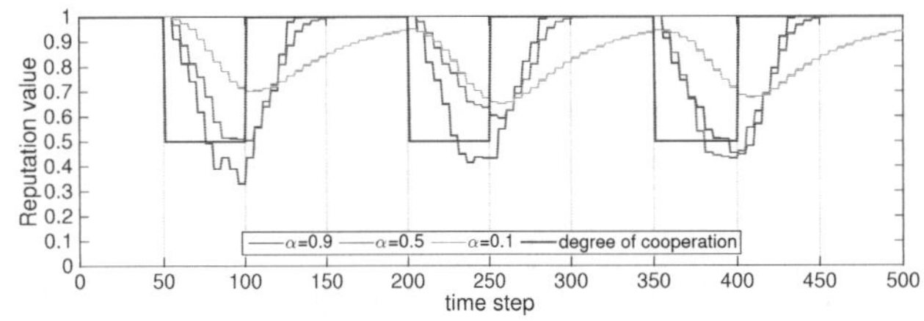

Figure 9: Traitor attack: reputation values of a traitor agent which alternates honest and non-cooperative behaviors, while varying the α factor that weights the recent experience to build the local reputation.

default reputation value. With the baseline settings the dishonest behavior is always discovered, but varying the default reputation value changes the time interval during which the malicious agent is able to abuse the community resources. For such reason, the main defense technique is to assign a low reputation value to new agents that join the system; the weakness of this solution is that a low initial reputation is also assigned to new trustworthy agents, that, consequently, experience a slow start phase, as shown by Fig. 7.

Moreover, a low default reputation value may be very disadvantageous if an *incentive mechanism* is automatically executed in order to provide each agent with a percentage of resources proportional to its reputation. Indeed, if a new user is evaluated with a low reputation, the other agents will give him few resources. As a consequence, its opinion of other agents will decrease, and it will give them few resources, thus confirming its bad reputation. In other words, if the *incentive mechanism* is blindly performed, new honest users are not able to improve their initial reputation, as shown in Fig. 8. It is worth noting that during the experiments described by Fig. 7, honest agents always satisfy the received requests, i.e., they do not apply the *incentive mechanism*.

With the baseline settings, which adopts 0.9 as initial reputation value, the corresponding vulnerability metrics have the following values:

$$ET(whitewashing) = 0.054$$
$$V^*_W = 2.32$$

In order to evaluate the impact of the traitor attack, we performed some experiments where a malicious agent alternates cooperative and partially cooperative behavior (i.e., only 50% of received requests are satisfied). The honest behavior is maintained for a longer time interval in order to guarantee that the reputation value increases enough. As expected, Fig. 9 shows that RMSs with higher values of α, i.e., the weight of recent experience, detect earlier a change in agent behavior.

Moreover, experimental results show that the percentage of time during which the traitor can behave non-cooperatively without being detected is 20%, against a percentage of 35% for a partially cooperative behavior. The resulting vulnerability index is then:

$$ET(traitor) = 0.25$$
$$V^*_T = 5.00$$

In conclusion, the baseline RMS does not exhibit high or critical vulnerabilities, whilst a medium vulnerability to traitor attack is detected. These characteristics are summarized by the following vulnerability indexes:

$$\begin{aligned} &RMS\_vulnerability = \\ &= \{V^*, num\_of\_V^*_{high\&critical}\} = \\ &= \{[V^*_{SP}, V^*_S, V^*_W, V^*_T], num\_of\_V^*_{high\&critical}\} = \\ &= \{[1.78, 3.18, 2.32, 5.00], 0\}. \end{aligned}$$

8. CONCLUSIONS AND FUTURE WORK

In this work we presented a set of vulnerability metrics to quantitatively evaluate the behavior of a Reputation Management System under attack. These metrics allow to compare the effects of different design choices on the overall security of the RMS. We used a parallel simulation framework for automatically compute the vulnerability indexes associated to four state-of-the-art attacks. This tool allowed us to test the security of a case study RMS while varying the behavior of its inner components, namely local trust, gossiped information and information fusion, and some general characteristics, such as the default reputation values assigned to new agents.

Results showed that the impact the different attacks have on the RMS deeply depends on the choices made since its design. For example, in order to overcome a slandering attack a RMS should rely more on the direct experience than gossiped information, whilst is recommended to give more importance to the direct and recent experience when dealing with traitor attacks.

As future work, we plan to experimentally analyze the security of some of the most popular distributed RMSs, and to consider possible attacks to the system architecture. In particular, masquerading attacks could allow malicious agents to pretend to be loyal agents, so as to diffuse false feedbacks through the gossip protocol. Moreover, we are considering to extend our analysis to RMSs operating within large-scale social networks [11, 12].

9. REFERENCES

[1] V. Agate, A. De Paola, S. Gaglio, G. Lo Re, and M. Morana. A framework for parallel assessment of reputation management systems. In *Proceedings of the International Conference on Computer Systems and Technologies (CompSysTech)*, june 2016.

[2] V. Agate, A. De Paola, G. Lo Re, and M. Morana. A simulation framework for evaluating distributed reputation management systems. In *Proc. of the 13th Int. Conf. on Distributed Computing and Artificial Intelligence (DCAI'16)*, pages 1{8, 2016.

[3] S. Ba and P. A. Pavlou. Evidence of the effect of trust building technology in electronic markets: Price premiums and buyer behavior. *MIS quarterly*, pages 243{268, 2002.

[4] P. Chandrasekaran and B. Esfandiari. Toward a testbed for evaluating computational trust models: experiments and analysis. *J. of Trust Management*, 2(1):1{27, 2015.

[5] C. Crapanzano, F. Milazzo, A. De Paola, and G. Lo Re. Reputation management for distributed service-oriented architectures. In *Proc. of the 2010 Fourth IEEE Int. Conf. on Self-Adaptive and Self-Organizing Systems Workshop (SASOW)*, pages 160{165, 2010.

[6] CVSS. Common vulnerability scoring system v3.0. https://www.first.org/cvss, 2015.

[7] A. De Paola and A. Tamburo. Reputation Management in Distributed Systems. In *Proc. of the 3rd Int. Symp. on Communications, Control and Signal Processing (ISCCSP)*, pages 666{670, 2008.

[8] M. Feldman, C. Papadimitriou, J. Chuang, and I. Stoica. Free-riding and whitewashing in peer-to-peer systems. In *Proc. of the ACM SIGCOMM workshop on Practice and theory of incentives in networked systems*, pages 228{236. ACM, 2004.

[9] P. Fouliras. A novel reputation-based model for e-commerce. *Operational research*, 13(1):113{138, 2013.

[10] K. K. Fullam, T. B. Klos, G. Muller, J. Sabater, A. Schlosser, Z. Topol, K. S. Barber, J. S. Rosenschein, L. Vercouter, and M. Voss. A specification of the agent reputation and trust (ART) testbed: experimentation and competition for trust in agent societies. In *Proc. of the 4th Int. joint Conf. on Autonomous agents and multiagent systems*, pages 512{518, 2005.

[11] S. Gaglio, G. Lo Re, and M. Morana. Real-time detection of Twitter social events from the user's perspective. In *Proc. of the 2015 IEEE Int. Conf. on Communications (ICC)*, pages 1207{1212, 2015.

[12] S. Gaglio, G. Lo Re, and M. Morana. A framework for real-time Twitter data analysis. *Computer Communications*, 73, Part B:236 { 242, 2016.

[13] K. Hoffman, D. Zage, and C. Nita-Rotaru. A survey of attack and defense techniques for reputation systems. *ACM Computing Surveys (CSUR)*, 42(1):1, 2009.

[14] S. D. Kamvar, M. T. Schlosser, and H. Garcia-Molina. The Eigentrust algorithm for reputation management in P2P networks. In *Proc. of the 12th Int. Conf. on World Wide Web*, pages 640{651, 2003.

[15] R. Kerr and R. Cohen. Smart cheaters do prosper: defeating trust and reputation systems. In *Proc. of the 8th Int. Conf. on Autonomous Agents and Multiagent Systems-Volume 2*, pages 993{1000, 2009.

[16] J. Lee, J. Zhang, Z. Huang, and K.-J. Lin. Context-based reputation management for service composition and reconfiguration. In *Proc. of the IEEE 14th Int. Conf. on Commerce and Enterprise Computing (CEC)*, pages 57{61, 2012.

[17] Q. Lian, Z. Zhang, M. Yang, B. Y. Zhao, Y. Dai, and X. Li. An empirical study of collusion behavior in the maze p2p file-sharing system. In *Proc. of the 27th Int. Conf. on Distributed Computing Systems (ICDCS'07)*, pages 56{56. IEEE , 2007.

[18] N. A. Lynch. *Distributed algorithms*. Morgan Kaufmann, 1996.

[19] S. Marti and H. Garcia-Molina. Taxonomy of trust: Categorizing p2p reputation systems. *Computer Networks*, 50(4):472{484, 2006.

[20] M. K. Reiter and S. G. Stubblebine. Authentication metric analysis and design. *ACM Trans. Inf. Syst. Secur.*, 2(2):138{158, May 1999.

[21] Y. Sun and Y. Liu. Security of online reputation systems: The evolution of attacks and defenses. *IEEE Signal Processing Mag.*, 29(2):87{97, 2012.

[22] L. Wang, A. Singhal, and S. Jajodia. Toward measuring network security using attack graphs. In *Proceedings of the 2007 ACM Workshop on Quality of Protection*, QoP '07, pages 49{54, New York, NY, USA, 2007. ACM.

[23] J. Weng, Z. Shen, C. Miao, A. Goh, and C. Leung. Credibility: How agents can handle unfair third-party testimonies in computational trust models. *IEEE Trans. on Knowledge and Data Engineering*, 22(9):1286{1298, 2010.

[24] H. Yu, S. Liu, A. Kot, C. Miao, and C. Leung. Dynamic witness selection for trustworthy distributed cooperative sensing in cognitive radio networks. In *Proc. of the 2011 IEEE 13th Int. Conf. on Communication Technology (ICCT)*, pages 1{6, 2011.

[25] H. Yu, Z. Shen, C. Leung, C. Miao, and V. R. Lesser. A survey of multi-agent trust management systems. *Access, IEEE*, 1:35{50, 2013.

Fluid Petri Nets for the Performance Evaluation of MapReduce Applications

Eugenio Gianniti
Politecnico di Milano
Dipartimento di Elettronica, Informazione e Bioingegneria
Via Golgi 42 20133 Milano, Italy
eugenio.gianniti@polimi.it

Alessandro Maria Rizzi
Politecnico di Milano
Dipartimento di Elettronica, Informazione e Bioingegneria
Via Golgi 42 20133 Milano, Italy
alessandromaria.rizzi@polimi.it

Enrico Barbierato
Politecnico di Milano
Dipartimento di Elettronica, Informazione e Bioingegneria
via Ponzio 34/5 20133 Milano, Italy
enrico.barbierato@polimi.it

Marco Gribaudo
Politecnico di Milano
Dipartimento di Elettronica, Informazione e Bioingegneria
via Ponzio 34/5 20133 Milano, Italy
marco.gribaudo@polimi.it

Danilo Ardagna
Politecnico di Milano
Dipartimento di Elettronica, Informazione e Bioingegneria
Via Golgi 42 20133 Milano, Italy
danilo.ardagna@polimi.it

ABSTRACT

Big Data applications allow to successfully analyze large amounts of data not necessarily structured, though at the same time they present new challenges. For example, predicting the performance of frameworks such as Hadoop can be a costly task, hence the necessity to provide models that can be a valuable support for designers and developers. This paper provides a new contribution in studying a novel modeling approach based on fluid Petri nets to predict MapReduce jobs execution time.

The experiments we performed at CINECA, the Italian supercomputing center, have shown that the achieved accuracy is within 16% of the actual measurements on average.

Keywords

Map Reduce, Hadoop, fluid Petri nets

1. INTRODUCTION

The implementation of Big Data applications is steadily growing today [12]. According to recent analysis, the Big Data market reached \$16.9 billion in 2015 with a compound annual growth rate of 39.4%, about seven times the one of the overall ICT market [1].

From the technological perspective, MapReduce is capable of analyzing very efficiently large amounts of unstructured data, i.e., it is a viable solution to support both the variety and volume requirements of Big Data analyses [14].

VALUETOOLS 2016, October 25-28, Taormina, Italy

MapReduce has been adopted in multiple application domains, e.g., machine learning, graph processing, and data mining [25]. Its open source implementation, Hadoop 2.x, recently introduced a wide set of performance enhancements (e.g., SSD support, caching, and I/O barriers mitigation). IDC estimates that Hadoop touched half of the world data last year [13], supporting both traditional batch and interactive data analysis applications [23].

In this context, one of the main challenges [17, 24] is that the execution time of a MapReduce job is generally unknown in advance. Because of this, predicting the execution time of Hadoop jobs is usually done empirically through experimentation, requiring a costly setup [10]. In alternative, it is possible to develop models for predicting performance. Models may be used to support design-time decisions during the initial development and deployment of Big Data applications or at run-time to trigger system reconfiguration. For example, design-time models can help to determine the appropriate size of a cluster or to predict the budget required to run Hadoop in public Clouds (a trending scenario, since by 2020 nearly 40% of Big Data analyses will be supported by public Clouds [1]). Models can also be kept alive at run-time and lead the dynamic adjustment of the system configuration [3, 22], for instance to cope with workload fluctuations or to reduce energy costs.

While in early Hadoop versions CPU *slots* and other resources were separated between mapper and reducers using a static approach, in Hadoop 2.x containers are distributed among ready tasks in a dynamic fashion. On the one hand, this allows a better cluster utilization, on the other hand modeling the performance is not a task of negligible difficulty.

The originality of this paper consists of a new modeling technique concerning the dynamic assignment of the available cluster resources. We assume that the cluster is governed by the Capacity Scheduler, which partitions the available resources among multiple customers through queues, each queue being regulated by a FIFO policy.

This work proposes a fluid Petri Nets model to estimate

MapReduce jobs execution time, combining real experimentation and model-based evaluation and exploring different properties of the MapReduce process to unveil the characteristics of the YARN Capacity Scheduler that have the highest influence in its performance and therefore should be represented in the models used for a model-based performance evaluation.

The accuracy of the model is evaluated on real systems by performing experiments based on the TPC-DS industry benchmark for business intelligence data warehouse applications. The Italian supercomputing center, CINECA, has been considered as target deployment.

Results and experiments performed on real systems have shown that the achieved accuracy is within 16% of the actual measurements on average. With respect to previous literature, to the best of our knowledge this article is one of the first contributions able to study the performance of Hadoop-2.x-based clusters, where the dynamic allocation of resources between map and reduce stages makes the performance analysis much more challenging.

This paper is organized as follows. Section 2 compares this work with other proposals available in the literature; Section 3 presents our novel proposals for Hadoop modeling, via fluid Petri Nets. Next, Section 4 reports some experimental results to validate and study the properties of our models. Finally, Section 5 draws the conclusions, providing the lines for future work.

2. RELATED WORK

The literature provides a large number of performance studies for Hadoop 1.x, since the framework has been widely adopted in the ICT industry, often supporting core business activities. Two main approaches have been explored: i) simulation-based models implement the single constituents of Hadoop and of the job, replaying in a simulated environment the steps and delays of the real system; ii) analytical models, on the other hand, define a mathematical representation of those constituents, avoiding the costs of running multiple simulations. Both approaches make use of information such as input dataset size, cluster resources, and Hadoop specific parameters. The computational effort and the time spent in running simulation-based models make them hardly fit for the purposes of runtime cluster management: thus, we hereby consider only analytical models, according to the focus of our paper.

The authors of [24] propose the ARIA framework for estimating the makespan of jobs in MapReduce clusters. This approach relies on information extracted from the logs of previous executions of similar jobs. Adopting scheduling techniques, the authors prove lower and upper bounds on makespans. From these results, they derive formulae for performance prediction. They obtain both a conservative estimate, suitable for hard deadlines, and an alternative that does not offer guarantees of meeting deadlines, but boasts a relative error below 10% in the validation against measured timings.

Another performance model estimating the execution time by considering the single costs of the various phases of a MapReduce job is described in [18]. In this work, the authors go down to the very low level elements that determine the cost of single job phases, writing a 37-parameter model that provides execution times within 10% of those measured in a real cluster. Even with such an accurate model, the validation considers just single job executions.

In queueing network (QN) literature, the fork/join paradigm (see [21] and [4]) is used to denote the modeling of the concurrent execution of many tasks within higher level jobs. Specifically, this approach operates through two steps: i) jobs are spawned at a fork node in multiple tasks, then ii) they are submitted to queueing stations that, in turn, model the available servers.

Once all the tasks have been served, they can synchronize at a join node. It has to be noted that when a fork-join network has more than two queues, a closed-form solution is not possible. That said, it is possible to mitigate the issue by using a special kind of structure, as shown in [16] which considers the Markov Chain underlying the QN representing the possible states of the system. Unfortunately, as noted in [9, 19], the state space grows exponentially when the tasks number corresponds to realistic MapReduce jobs—in the order of thousands—thus making the above approaches unsuitable.

An interesting alternative in the shape of approximation methods is introduced in [20], which proposes a method based on exponentially distributed service times, though it is not applicable to Hadoop deployments. Indeed, as per preliminary experiments conducted in this work, it is safe to assume that phase type (or in some cases Erlang) can approximate the general distributions of mapper and reducer times, while assuming an exponential distribution led to around 50–60% relative error on the prediction of the overall job execution time. To this concern, see also [16], where an approximate mean value analysis technique is proposed, by using an iterative hierarchical approach.

Other approaches prefer adopting a MapReduce modeling based on Petri nets (PNs). For example, in [8] the authors use a stochastic PN, applying Mean Field Analysis to calculate average metrics and estimate the performance of a Big Data architecture based on Hadoop.

In order to capture the performance of Hive queries, Generalized Stochastic Petri Nets together with other formalisms (i.e., process algebras or Markov chains) are used to create multi-formalism models in [5]. Specifically, the authors show how performance can depend on some configuration parameters.

In [2], the authors propose colored PNs to determine the feasibility of a distributed file system project. After designing a deployment of HDFS (using a set of spare resources in a cluster of workstations in order to provide a sufficiently available distributed file system), the system availability is assessed by exploiting PNs.

Though earlier methods exploited static resource allocation (at different levels of detail) to model Hadoop 1.0 clusters, the fluid Petri Net models used here can capture the dynamic assignment of YARN resource containers (for example, by using the model presented in [7]) and are capable of estimating performance of Hadoop 2.x jobs very efficiently.

3. FLUID MODELS

Very often modelers are bound to face several problems when trying to provide a description of a physical system by using a formalism. Typically, these problems are more evident in techniques using discrete states, since the analysis produces a state space explosion, with an exponential growth in the number of states following the complexity of the model. Different alternatives to mitigate this problem have been proposed. Specifically, *hybrid* techniques involving a continuous and discrete part have proved to reduce significantly the severity of the issue. Continuous variables can be exploited in different scenarios: for example, they can be used to represent the rising temperature in a closed room or the water leaking out of a full bucket.

In literature, fluid models have been presented in different ways for what concerns the realization of the continuous aspect. Among the different flavors, in [11], the authors refer to i) Fluid Stochastic Petri Nets (FSPNs), ii) Reward and iii) Fluid models. FSPNs add to Stochastic Petri Nets introducing the ability to handle continuous parts. In reward models, the idea consists in using a Markov chain and associating a Reward rate, a positive weight whose value depends on the time spent in a particular state.

Fluid models can be used to successfully study the MapReduce framework and even more sophisticate ones, such as Spark [26], including paradigms like concurrent programming. In [7], the authors consider a scenario to analyze the energy-related performance metrics by using a broad Markov chain, taking into account different configuration parameters and finally focusing on the solution process that is run in parallel on all the available cores. The completion times are taken as a benchmark. It is noted that all the observed cases show a ladder-like shape, denoting the level of parallelism considered.

In the following, Section 3.1 describes the FSPN used, while Section 3.2 describes how to generate an approximation of the average execution time of jobs with deterministic execution time.

3.1 FSPN Model for a MapReduce Job

In order to formalize the fluid model proposed in this paper, we will describe it using the FSPN shown in Figure 1 (the purpose of this FSPN model is just to specify the underlying fluid model without enumerating its states).

In this formalization, single circles represent *discrete places*, which can hold an integer number of tokens; single boxes represent *timed transitions* that can fire after an exponential amount of time; bars represent *immediate transitions*, which fire as soon as they are enabled; thin lines define *standard arcs* that move tokens among places and enable the connected transitions; and thin lines with circular ends define *inhibitor arcs*, which prevent the corresponding transitions from firing whenever the input place is marked. Double circles represent *fluid places*, that can hold a continuous amount of fluid; double boxes identify *fluid transitions*, that continuously pump fluid in and out of continuous places; double arrows represents *fluid arcs* that can remove fluid from their input places; and thick arrows represents *set arcs*, that immediately insert a given amount of fluid in their destination place when their input transition fires.

The discrete amount of tokens is moved across the discrete arcs as usual. With regard to the fluid places, they include a level denoted by a continuous variable, which flows according to an instantaneous rate. The discrete FSPN component regulates the fluid flow through the continuous part, while the conditions enabling a transition depend on the discrete component only.

The model considers N users (corresponding to the marking of place `Users`) that can submit jobs to the system after a think time Z. The submission of jobs from a user is modeled by the firing of transition `Think` characterized by the infinite server semantic. According to the YARN Capacity Scheduler, we consider that only one job at a time can be executed by the system: this is obtained via place `Available`, which holds a token whenever the infrastructure is ready to run a new job, thus enabling the corresponding `Start` transition. Both the map and reduce phases are modeled by a similar sub-network. Place `Ready` holds a token whenever the phase is ready to start, and its beginning is modeled by the firing of immediate transition `Start`. This transition inserts (using its output set arc) the number of tasks (either map or reduce) that need to be executed in the corresponding phase in fluid place `Queue`. The execution of the jobs is modeled by the time-dependent fluid transition `Exec`, which is connected to place `Queue` with an output arc. Transitions `Exec` have a special time-dependent semantic that will be described in the following paragraphs: for this reason it is represented with a small clock drawn at its side. Whenever the queue is empty, the next phase can start or the job can end thanks to the firing of transition `End`.

Following [6], the fluid evolution is defined as a function $\phi : \mathbb{R}^2 \rightarrow \mathbb{R}$, which defines how the fluid level of the corresponding place changes with time. In particular, $\phi(x,t)$ represents the fluid level reached by a place at time t, if it starts at level x at time $t = 0$. This semantic is represented graphically by drawing a fluid arc that connects a fluid place (`Queue` in Figure 1) to a time-dependent fluid transition (`Exec` in Figure 1). In the model, two functions $\phi_M(x,t)$ and $\phi_R(x,t)$ are associated respectively to the map and reduce phases. These functions regulate the evolution of the fluid in the corresponding places, so that the fluid level x represents the average remaining number of tasks that still need to be executed in a phase. In the following, the representation of function $\phi(x,t)$ to model the average execution time of jobs with deterministic task duration is provided. This is an initial approximation, which is acceptable within the scope of this paper.

3.2 Deterministic Task Execution Time

Task duration distributions can be generally regarded as phase-type or Erlang, parameterized according to the observed coefficient of variation (CV). The CV ranges between 0 and 1, whence the two limiting cases of deterministic and exponential distribution, respectively. In this paper we adopt the low CV approximation with deterministic task execution times, in accordance with the observed distributions.

Let us suppose that our MapReduce jobs are executed by C containers. Let us also assume that a phase is composed of N tasks, and that each task requires a deterministic time T to be executed. Figure 2 represents the evolution of the number of remaining tasks as function of time, which in our fluid model corresponds to the fluid evolution function $\phi(N,t)$. At time $t = 0$, C out of N tasks are immediately assigned to the C containers. Since their duration is deterministic, all the C tasks will end at the same time T, leaving just $N - C$ tasks left to be executed in the system. Then the next batch of C tasks will start, and it will end at $2T$, leaving in the system $N - 2C$ jobs. Function $\phi(x,t)$ can then be defined as follows:

$$\phi(x,t) = \max\left(0, x - \left\lfloor \frac{t}{T} \right\rfloor C\right) \tag{1}$$

In this scenario, the time $\tau(N,C,T)$ required to run N

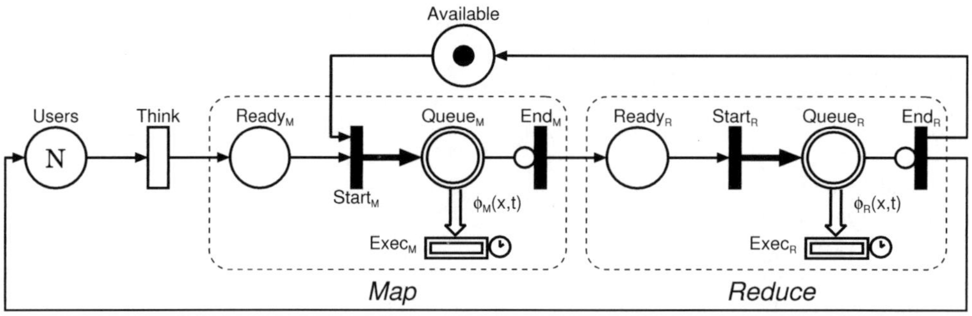

Figure 1: FSPN representation of the fluid model underlying a MapReduce job.

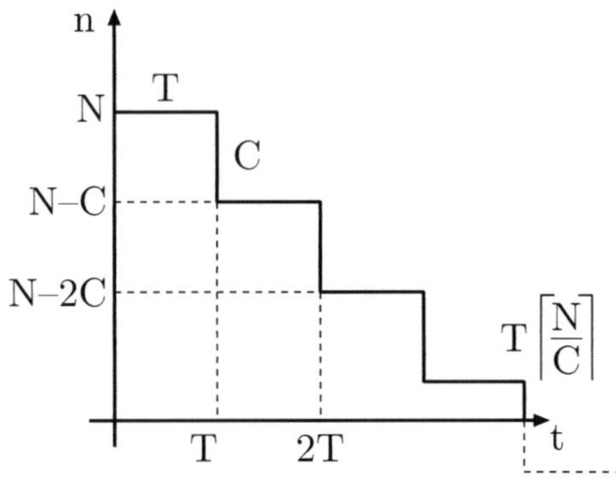

Figure 2: Fluid evolution: Deterministic task execution time

tasks with deterministic running time T on C containers can be computed as:

$$\tau(N, C, T) = T\left\lceil \frac{N}{C} \right\rceil \tag{2}$$

4. EXPERIMENTS

In this section, we describe the results of the experiments we conducted to validate our approach. All these experiments have been performed at CINECA, the Italian supercomputing center. The experiments consist of a set of Hive queries taken from the TPC-DS benchmark suite and run on a dedicated Hadoop cluster. The rest of the section is organized as follows: Section 4.1 thoroughly describes how the experiments have been executed; Section 4.2 presents the obtained results by applying the fluid models.

4.1 Experimental Settings

The models presented in the previous sections have been validated with an experimental campaign on CINECA, the Italian supercomputing center.

PICO[1], the Big Data cluster available at CINECA, is composed of 74 nodes, each of them boasting two Intel Xeon 10-core 2670 v2@2.5GHz, with 128 GB RAM per node. Out of this 74 nodes, up to 66 are available for computation. In our experiments on PICO, we used several configurations ranging from 40 to 120 cores and set up the scheduler to provide one container per core.

[1]http://www.hpc.cineca.it/hardware/pico

```
select avg(ws_quantity),
       avg(ws_ext_sales_price),
       avg(ws_ext_wholesale_cost),
       sum(ws_ext_wholesale_cost)
from web_sales
where (web_sales.ws_sales_price
       between 100.00 and 150.00)
  or (web_sales.ws_net_profit
      between 100 and 200)
group by ws_web_page_sk
limit 100;
```

(a) R1

```
select inv_item_sk, inv_warehouse_sk
from inventory
where inv_quantity_on_hand > 10
group by inv_item_sk, inv_warehouse_sk
having sum(inv_quantity_on_hand) > 20
limit 100;
```

(b) R2

```
select avg(ss_quantity),
       avg(ss_net_profit)
from store_sales
where ss_quantity > 10
  and ss_net_profit > 0
group by ss_store_sk
having avg(ss_quantity) > 20
limit 100;
```

(c) R3

```
select cs_item_sk, avg(cs_quantity) as aq
from catalog_sales
where cs_quantity > 2
group by cs_item_sk;
```

(d) R4

```
select inv_warehouse_sk,
       sum(inv_quantity_on_hand)
from inventory
group by inv_warehouse_sk
having sum(inv_quantity_on_hand) > 5
limit 100;
```

(e) R5

Figure 3: Interactive queries

The cluster is shared among different users, hence resources are managed by the Portable Batch System (PBS). PBS Professional allows for submitting jobs and checking their progress, configuring at a fine-grained level the computational requirements: for all submissions it is possible to request a number of nodes and to define how many CPUs and what amount of memory are needed on each of them. Since the cluster is shared among different users, the performance of single jobs depends on the overall system load, even though PBS tries to split the resources. Due to this, it is possible to have large variations in performance according to the total usage of the cluster. In particular, storage is not handled directly by PBS, thus leading to an even greater impact on performance.

We tried to mitigate this variability first of all by requesting entire nodes of the cluster for the execution of our experiments. In such a way, we could be sure that nobody else could run other jobs on the same nodes, thus interfering with the performance measurement.

An ephemeral Hadoop cluster has been created at the beginning of each experiment on the allocated nodes. The PICO cluster provides the myHadoop tool for setting up a Hadoop 2.5.1 cluster, upon which we used Hive 1.2.1. HDFS is kept locally on the selected nodes, in order to experience lower variability than the one observed using the centralized storage.

In spite of these settings, still the experiments showed high variability, in particular with a few runs characterized by extremely high execution time. To further reduce this variability, in our analyses we discarded runs with an anomalous execution time, taking out all the experiments that lie more than three standard deviations away from the average computed for the same configuration.

The dataset used for testing has been generated using the TPC-DS benchmark[2] data generator, creating at a scale factor ranging from 250 GB to 1 TB several files directly used as external tables by Hive. We chose the TPC-DS benchmark as it is the industry standard for benchmarking data warehouses. Further, we performed experiments on five Hive queries, dubbed R1–5 and shown in Figure 3. These are *ad hoc* queries[3] that Hive runs as a single MapReduce job. The profiling phase has been conducted by extracting average task durations from at least twenty runs of each query. The numbers of map and reduce tasks varied, respectively, in the ranges $[2, 1560]$ and $[2, 1009]$. The discussed parameters are shown in Table 1. In the table we report the scale factor d, the number of tasks of each phase, respectively n^{M} and n^{R} for mappers and reducers, and the average task durations, respectively $\bar{t}^{\mathrm{M}}$ and $\bar{t}^{\mathrm{R}}$.

Table 1: Fitted parameters

Query	d [GB]	n^{M}	$\bar{t}^{\mathrm{M}}$ [ms]	n^{M}	$\bar{t}^{\mathrm{R}}$ [ms]
R1	250	144	25970	151	2346
R1	500	287	32159	300	1958
R1	750	434	34244	455	1996
R1	1000	591	40534	619	3063
R2	250	4	57326	4	8785
R2	500	2	42202	2	6582
R2	750	3	48869	3	7500
R2	1000	65	1082274	68	13086
R3	250	381	28659	400	2369
R3	500	757	37018	793	2570
R3	750	1148	42348	1009	2785
R3	1000	1560	41961	1009	3048
R4	250	288	25087	302	2958
R4	500	573	41007	601	2961
R4	750	868	43902	910	3259
R4	1000	1183	42615	1009	8667
R5	250	4	13456	4	1424
R5	500	2	11774	2	1499
R5	750	3	12682	3	1462
R5	1000	64	19557	68	1610

4.2 Experimental Results

In this section we present and discuss the results obtained with the previously described fluid techniques. First of all, we studied the empirical cumulative distribution functions (CDFs) of task durations on different nodes, in order to identify the cases in which performance was strongly affected by exogenous interference. We then considered the accuracy that can be reached assuming deterministic task execution time.

4.2.1 *Performance by Node*

Figures 4, 5, 6 and 7 show the empirical CDFs derived from the measurements. Figures 4 and 5 refer to subsequent phases of the same experimental run, namely, query R3 running on the six-node, 120-container cluster deployment over the 500 GB dataset. Accordingly, Figures 6 and 7 show query R2 on the two-node, 40-container cluster over the same dataset.

As a general trend well represented in Figures 5 and 7, reducers tend to behave quite regularly. Most likely, possible variabilities spread across the shuffle stage that overlaps with the map phase, hence end up being hardly noticeable in each reducer task duration.

On the other hand, mappers suffer a stronger impact from external interference. In the reported graphics we have examples of both good and problematic performance. Figure 4 shows how all but one node have a very similar behavior. Further, the only different node is not significantly distant from the others, hence probably the low variability is imputable to the physiological effects of data locality. Instead, Figure 6 reports that the two involved nodes have a strongly diverse performance, with a twofold difference in task durations. In this case, since we are dealing with a small interactive query, any exogenous interference may cause a strong impact on the overall response time, thus making prediction harder.

4.2.2 *Accuracy*

Table 2 reports the results of the accuracy assessment for the proposed method. In particular, we consider the fluid evolution function discussed in Section 3.2. For several experiments we report the involved query, the total number of containers available in the cluster (c), the scale factor for the dataset generator (d), the average measured (t) and predicted (τ) execution time, and the relative error (ε). The latter is defined as:

$$\varepsilon \triangleq \frac{\tau - t}{t} \tag{3}$$

[2]http://www.tpc.org/tpcds/

[3]https://github.com/deib-polimi/Hive-Experiment-Runner

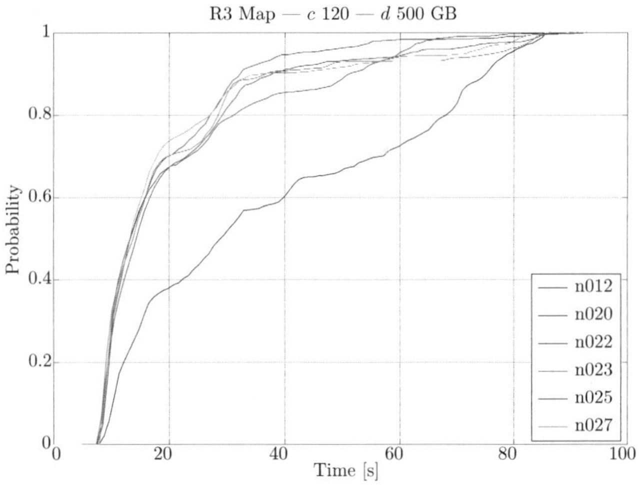

Figure 4: R3 map, 120 containers, 500 GB dataset

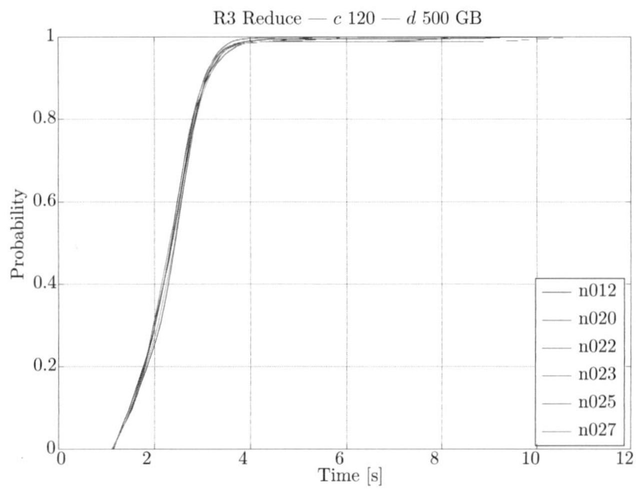

Figure 5: R3 reduce, 120 containers, 500 GB dataset

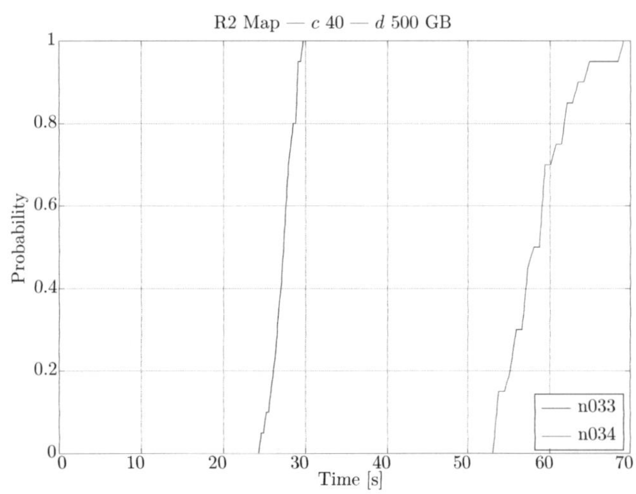

Figure 6: R2 map, 40 containers, 500 GB dataset

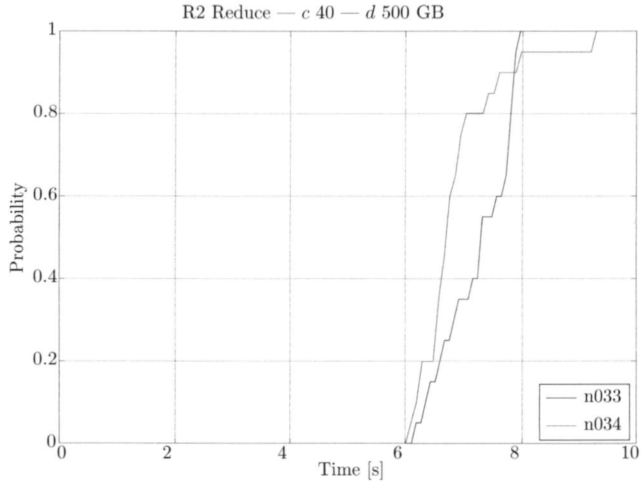

Figure 7: R2 reduce, 40 containers, 500 GB dataset

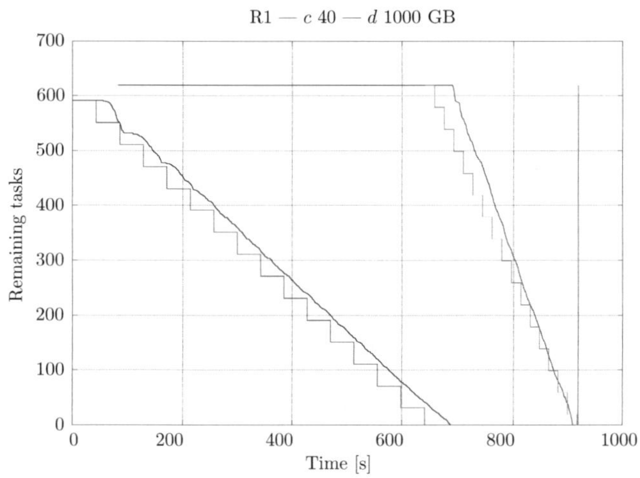

Figure 8: Query R1, 40 containers, 1 TB dataset

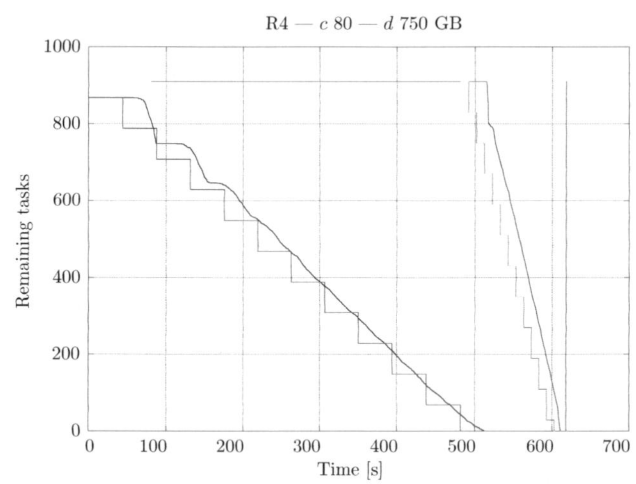

Figure 9: Query R4, 80 containers, 750 GB dataset

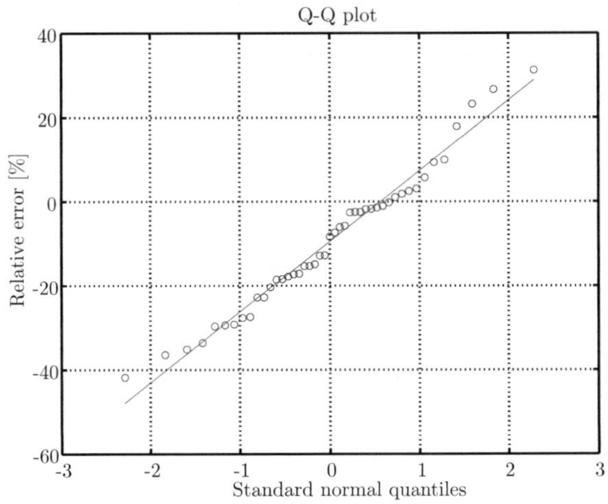

Figure 10: Q-Q plot of the errors

The average accuracy achieved with the approximate formula is 15.33%, perfectly in line with the expectations in the performance prediction field [15], where a 30% accuracy on response times is reasonable. The Q-Q plot in Figure 10 shows that the errors follow a Gaussian distribution, as expected. Only a handful of experiments show a relatively high error, peaking at 41.79% in absolute value. Nonetheless, the standard error of the mean is 1.75%. The largest relative errors tend to appear either in the experiments involving R2 and R5, small queries both in terms of number of tasks and of overall duration, or in those run at 120 containers. This behavior suggests that the relative abundance of resources might amplify the effects of variability, whilst the basic assumption of the deterministic approximation for the fluid evolution is that the CV is null.

Moreover, you can see how the approximate formula (2) compares to the measured data for a couple of experiments in Figures 8 and 9. The blue lines represent the average completion times of each task in the map phase, analogously the red lines for the reduce phase. Notice that the latter begins when the first reducer container was allocated: all the overlapping time spent shuffling has not been considered to improve prediction accuracy. The stair-shaped green and cyan lines are the approximate fluid function in the limiting case of deterministic task duration, respectively for the map and reduce phase. In the end, the purple vertical line shows the average measured response time of the whole query.

5. CONCLUSIONS

In this paper we proposed fluid Petri Nets able to model the execution of MapReduce jobs running in Hadoop 2.x clusters governed by the Capacity Scheduler. Preliminary experimental results have shown that the average percentage error that can be achieved is around 16%, making the approach suitable for design-time capacity planning or run-time cluster management. Future work will consider the extension of the approach to cope with jobs described as directed acyclic graphs, characteristic of Apache Tez or Spark. Moreover, the framework will be integrated within an optimization tool for run-time cluster management.

Table 2: Accuracy with the approximate formula

Query	c	d [GB]	t [ms]	τ [ms]	ε [%]
R1	40	250	122084	106528	−12.74
R2	40	250	83364	69119	−17.09
R3	40	250	525374	530780	1.03
R1	40	500	383265	390264	1.83
R2	40	500	86864	57697	−33.58
R3	40	500	1033004	1006209	−2.59
R1	40	750	603006	592265	−1.78
R2	40	750	81292	58983	−27.44
R3	40	750	1534601	1512636	−1.43
R1	40	1000	918454	916637	−0.20
R2	40	1000	3774111	4953744	31.26
R1	60	250	80316	82314	2.49
R2	60	250	84551	68916	−18.49
R3	60	250	275684	228130	−17.25
R4	60	250	219243	201000	−8.32
R5	60	250	25924	16827	−35.09
R1	60	1000	556680	547176	−1.71
R2	60	1000	2009929	2546188	26.68
R3	60	1000	1374024	1295475	−5.72
R4	60	1000	1374244	1502290	9.32
R5	60	1000	48839	60180	23.22
R1	80	250	82531	67386	−18.35
R3	80	250	197388	138850	−29.66
R4	80	250	164811	131252	−20.36
R1	80	500	143139	103568	−27.65
R3	80	500	526760	494960	−6.04
R4	80	500	410376	423152	3.11
R1	80	750	268821	228888	−14.85
R3	80	750	791314	783088	−1.04
R4	80	750	618045	602829	−2.46
R1	80	1000	439052	406720	−7.36
R3	80	1000	1019973	994976	−2.45
R4	80	1000	960985	1015617	5.69
R1	120	250	46215	50790	9.90
R3	120	250	143650	101708	−29.20
R4	120	250	97829	82851	−15.31
R1	120	500	91809	80058	−12.80
R3	120	500	303843	214438	−29.42
R4	120	500	275407	226472	−17.77
R1	120	750	199234	115968	−41.79
R3	120	750	661214	510431	−22.80
R4	120	750	507861	430320	−15.27
R1	120	1000	349425	222165	−36.42
R3	120	1000	838708	647536	−22.79
R4	120	1000	2837286	3344833	17.89

Acknowledgments

The results of this paper have been partially funded by EUBra-BIGSEA (grant agreement no. 690116), a Research and Innovation Action (RIA) funded by the European Commission under the Cooperation Programme, Horizon 2020 and the Ministério de Ciência, Tecnologia e Inovação (MCTI), RNP/Brazil (grant GA0000000650/04).

Eugenio Gianniti is also partially supported by the DICE H2020 research project (grant agreement no. 644869).

6. REFERENCES

[1] The digital universe in 2020. http://idcdocserv.com/1414.

[2] L. Aguilera-Mendoza and M. T. Llorente-Quesada. Modeling and simulation of Hadoop Distributed File System in a cluster of workstations. In A. Cuzzocrea and S. Maabout, editors, *Model and Data Engineering*, volume 8216 of *Lecture Notes in Computer Science*, pages 1–12. Springer Berlin Heidelberg, 2013.

[3] D. Ardagna, C. Ghezzi, and R. Mirandola. Rethinking the use of models in software architecture. In *QoSA 2008*, pages 1–27. Springer Berlin Heidelberg, Oct. 2008.

[4] S. Balsamo, P. G. Harrison, and A. Marin. Methodological construction of product-form stochastic petri nets for performance evaluation. *Journal of Systems and Software*, 85(7):1520–1539, 2012.

[5] E. Barbierato, M. Gribaudo, and M. Iacono. Modeling Apache Hive based applications in Big Data architectures. In *Proceedings of the 7th International Conference on Performance Evaluation Methodologies and Tools*, ValueTools '13, pages 30–38. ICST, 2013.

[6] E. Barbierato, M. Gribaudo, and M. Iacono. Modeling hybrid systems in SIMTHESys. In *Proceedings of the 8th International Workshop on Practical Applications of Stochastic Modelling*. to appear, 2016.

[7] E. Barbierato, M. Gribaudo, and D. Manini. *Fluid Approximation of Pool Depletion Systems*, pages 60–75. Springer International Publishing, Cham, 2016.

[8] A. Castiglione, M. Gribaudo, M. Iacono, and F. Palmieri. Exploiting mean field analysis to model performances of Big Data architectures. *Future Generation Computer Systems*, 37:203–211, 2014.

[9] W. W. Chu, C.-M. Sit, and K. K. Leung. Task response time for real-time distributed systems with resource contentions. *IEEE Trans. Softw. Eng.*, 17(10):1076–1092, Oct. 1991.

[10] G. P. Gibilisco, M. Li, L. Zhang, and D. Ardagna. Stage aware performance modeling of DAG based in memory analytic platforms. In *Cloud*, 2016.

[11] M. Gribaudo and M. Telek. *Fluid Models in Performance Analysis*, pages 271–317. Springer Berlin Heidelberg, Berlin, Heidelberg, 2007.

[12] H. V. Jagadish, J. Gehrke, A. Labrinidis, Y. Papakonstantinou, J. M. Patel, R. Ramakrishnan, and C. Shahabi. Big Data and its technical challenges. *Commun. ACM*, 57(7):86–94, July 2014.

[13] K. Kambatla, G. Kollias, V. Kumar, and A. Grama. Trends in Big Data analytics. *Journal of Parallel and Distributed Computing*, 74(7):2561–2573, 2014.

[14] D. Laney. 3D data management: Controlling data volume, velocity, and variety. Technical report, META Group, 2012.

[15] E. D. Lazowska, J. Zahorjan, G. S. Graham, and K. C. Sevcik. *Quantitative System Performance*. Prentice-Hall, 1984.

[16] D.-R. Liang and S. K. Tripathi. On performance prediction of parallel computations with precedent constraints. *IEEE Trans. Parallel Distrib. Syst.*, 11(5):491–508, May 2000.

[17] M. Lin, L. Zhang, A. Wierman, and J. Tan. Joint optimization of overlapping phases in MapReduce. *SIGMETRICS Performance Evaluation Review*, 41(3):16–18, 2013.

[18] X. Lin, Z. Meng, C. Xu, and M. Wang. A practical performance model for Hadoop MapReduce. In *International Conference on Cluster Computing Workshops*. IEEE, 2012.

[19] V. W. Mak and S. F. Lundstrom. Predicting performance of parallel computations. *IEEE Trans. Parallel Distrib. Syst.*, 1(3):257–270, July 1990.

[20] R. D. Nelson and A. N. Tantawi. Approximate analysis of fork/join synchronization in parallel queues. *IEEE Trans. Computers*, 37(6):739–743, 1988.

[21] R. Osman and P. G. Harrison. Approximating closed fork-join queueing networks using product-form stochastic petri-nets. *J. Syst. Softw.*, 110(C):264–278, Dec. 2015.

[22] J. Polo, Y. Becerra, D. Carrera, M. Steinder, I. Whalley, J. Torres, and E. Ayguadé. Deadline-based MapReduce workload management. *IEEE Trans. Network and Service Management*, 10(2):231–244, 2013.

[23] C. Shanklin. Benchmarking Apache Hive 13 for enterprise Hadoop. https://hadoop.apache.org/docs/r2.4.1/hadoop-yarn/hadoop-yarn-site/CapacityScheduler.html.

[24] A. Verma, L. Cherkasova, and R. H. Campbell. ARIA: Automatic resource inference and allocation for MapReduce environments. In *ICAC '11*, June 2011.

[25] E. Vianna, G. Comarela, T. Pontes, J. M. Almeida, V. A. F. Almeida, K. Wilkinson, H. A. Kuno, and U. Dayal. Analytical performance models for MapReduce workloads. *International Journal of Parallel Programming*, 41(4):495–525, 2013.

[26] M. Zaharia, M. Chowdhury, M. J. Franklin, S. Shenker, and I. Stoica. Spark: Cluster computing with working sets. In *Proceedings of the 2Nd USENIX Conference on Hot Topics in Cloud Computing*, HotCloud'10, pages 10–10, Berkeley, CA, USA, 2010. USENIX Association.

A Correlation-based Methodology to Infer Communication Patterns between Cloud Virtual Machines

Claudia Canali
Department of Engineering "Enzo Ferrari"
University of Modena and Reggio Emilia
Via P. Vivarelli 10
41125, Modena, Italy
claudia.canali@unimore.it

Riccardo Lancellotti
Department of Engineering "Enzo Ferrari"
University of Modena and Reggio Emilia
Via P. Vivarelli 10
41125, Modena, Italy
riccardo.lancellotti@unimore.it

ABSTRACT

The VMs allocation over the servers of a cloud data center is becoming a critical task to guarantee energy savings and high performance. Only recently network-aware techniques for VMs allocation have been proposed. However, a network-aware placement requires the knowledge of data transfer patterns between VMs, so that VMs exchanging significant amount of information can be placed on low cost communication paths (e.g. on the same server). The knowledge of this information is not easy to obtain unless a specialized monitoring function is deployed over the data center infrastructure. In this paper, we propose a correlation-based methodology that aims to infer communication patterns starting from the network traffic time series of each VM without relaying on a special purpose monitoring. Our study focuses on the case where a data center hosts a multi-tier application deployed using horizontal replication. This typical case of application deployment makes particularly challenging the identification of VMs communications because the traffic patterns are similar in every VM belonging to the same application tier. In the evaluation of the proposed methodology, we compare different correlation indexes and we consider different time granularities for the monitoring of network traffic. Our study demonstrates the feasibility of the proposed approach, that can identify which VMs are interacting among themselves even in the challenging scenario considered in our experiments.

1. INTRODUCTION

The problem of energy-efficient VMs allocation in cloud data centers is becoming a popular research field. Most research studies merely consider VMs allocation as a way to reduce the number of active servers [2, 5, 3], while more recent proposals also take into account the energy related to the data transfered between VMs, attempting to locate on the same server the VMs that tend to exchange more data among themselves [4, 8]. However, the adoption of a network-aware VMs allocation strategy requires the knowledge about the communication patterns between VMs; unfortunately, it is not possible to obtain a data transfer matrix between the VMs unless a specialized monitoringinfrastructure is developed and deployed over the cloud data center, as in [6, 9]. On the other hand, the most popular monitoring services in industry[1] and literature [1] just limit their output to the inbound/outbound aggregate traffic of each VM, without a per-source/per-destination breakdown.

In order to address this issue, we propose a different approach explicitly aiming to identify pairs of VMs communicating among themselves by identifying co-occurring similarities in the communications patterns of different VMs. Our approach is explicitly focused on the identification of communicating VMs in the case where multi-tier applications are horizontally replicated over a cloud infrastructure. In this scenario, each VM typically hosts a different software tier of the application, and a request dispatcher distributes the workload over each vertical stack composed by the multiple application tiers. It is important to note that the presence of a load-balancing request dispatcher leads to very similar utilization and communication patterns in the VMs corresponding to the same tier of the application. This similarity represents one of the most challenging aspects for the problem of inferring the communication patterns among different VMs.

In this paper we introduce a methodology that exploits correlation to identify groups of VMs that communicate among themselves, starting from the time series of the global network utilization of each VM. Furthermore, we compare different indexes to measure the level of correlation among VMs network utilization time series and evaluate the capability of the proposed methodology to identify communicating VMs. Our experiments, based on the deployment of a benchmark over a cloud infrastructure, show that the analysis of the correlation among VMs network utilization time series is a promising way to identify VMs that exchange large amount of data among themselves.

The remainder of this paper is organized as follows. Section 2 models the problem and outlines the proposed methodology. Section 3 describes the experimental results used to validate our proposal. Finally, Section 4 concludes the paper with some final remarks and outlines open research problems.

2. METHODOLOGY

Our reference scenario is a cloud data center hosting multi-tier applications, where the tiers of an application are organized in vertical stacks, which are horizontally replicated as in Figure 1.

Let us consider a set $\mathcal{N}$ of VMs. We define $P_{j_1}^{out}$ as the time series describing the output packet rate of VM $j_1 \in \mathcal{N}$. In a similar way, we can define $P_{j_2}^{in}$ as the time series of input packet rate for a generic VM j_2. We denote as τ the time interval between samples. Starting from these time series, we aim to infer which VMs communicate among themselves by considering the correlation in

[1]https://aws.amazon.com/cloudwatch/

VALUETOOLS 2016, October 25-28, Taormina, Italy

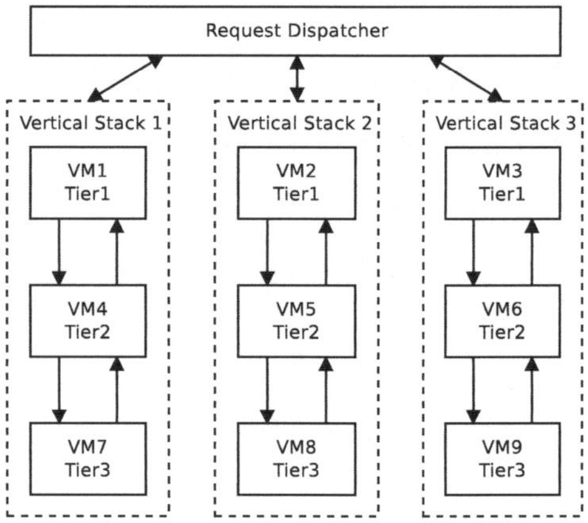

Figure 1: Multi-tier application deployed over a cloud data center

their network activity. The proposed methodology is based on the following steps: 1) Interpolation and synchronization of the traces; 2) Computation of a correlation matrix; 3) Identification of group of interacting VMs.

2.1 Traces interpolation and synchronization

The cloud monitor that collects information about the VMs network utilization is based on the prototype described in [1]. The data collector produces a sequence of tuples in the form `<timestamp, pkt_in, pkt_out>`, where the last two values contain the number of packets received and transmitted since the last data sampling. However, the agents monitoring each VM are not explicitly synchronized. As a result, traces collected from different VMs may be not synchronized.

Preliminary tests with artificially generated traces demonstrate the detrimental effect of not synchronizing traces before applying the correlation analysis of network traffic patterns belonging to different VMs. For this reason, we introduce in our system a trace synchronization step: to achieve this result we rely on data interpolation. Our approach can be summarized as follows:

- we remove samples at the beginning from each time series such that each time series starts in the time interval $[t_0, t_0+\tau]$ and we make sure that each time series contains T samples;
- we compute a synchronization time t_0^* that is the average of the starting times of each trace; from this time we have the interpolated time series timestamps that we define as $t_0^*, t_0^* + \tau, \ldots, t_0^* + i\tau, \ldots, t_0^* + T\tau$;
- for each time series P_{j1}^{out}, we define a synchronized time series P_{j1}^{*out} using cubic interpolation. In our prototype the implementation of the cubic interpolation is provided by the python *Pandas*[2] framework. A similar procedure is carried out also for the time series of inbound packets P_{j2}^{in}.

As a simplified notation, in the following of the paper we will use $P_{j1}^{*out}(i)$ and $P_{j2}^{*in}(i)$ for the i-th sample of a synchronized time series.

2.2 Correlation matrix

Starting from the synchronized time series we can compute the correlation matrix $\mathbf{C}$ between input and output packet rates of each pair of VMs. Specifically, we define the generic element c_{j_i,j_2} of the matrix as:

$$c_{j_i,j_2} = \mathrm{Cor}(P_{j1}^{*out}, P_{j2}^{*in}) \quad (1)$$

where j_1 and j_2 are two generic VMs and $\mathrm{Cor}(\cdot)$ is a function that computes the correlation among two different time series. In literature multiple functions have been proposed to measure the correlation between data series. In our analysis we consider two different alternatives, that are the Pearson and the Spearman correlation functions [7]. The first is the most widely used solution to compare time series, while the second emerged in preliminary results as one of the most interesting alternatives in terms of ability to discriminate groups of time series characterized by similar long-term trends, as is the case of our experiments.

We recall that the Pearson correlation index ρ is defined as:

$$\rho(P_{j1}^{*out}, P_{j2}^{*in}) = \frac{E[(P_{j1}^{*out} - \mu(P_{j1}^{*out}))(P_{j2}^{in} - \mu(P_{j2}^{*in}))]}{\sigma(P_{j1}^{*out})\sigma(P_{j2}^{*in})} \quad (2)$$

where $\mu(\cdot)$ is the mean value of a time series, $\sigma(\cdot)$ is the standard deviation, and $E[\cdot]$ is a shorthand for the average function (in equation 2 the average is used to compute the covariance of the two time series).

The Spearman correlation index ρ_s corresponds to the correlation between two time series where the original values have been substituted by their ranks in the time series:

$$\rho_s(P_{j1}^{*out}, P_{j2}^{*in}) = 1 - \frac{6\sum_{i=0}^{T} r(P_{j1}^{*out}(i)) - r(P_{j2}^{*in}(i))}{T(T^2-1)} \quad (3)$$

where T is the number of samples in the time series and $r(\cdot)$ is the rank of a sample among the other samples of the same time series. Switching from the values to the ranks in a time series increases significantly the capacity of this function to discriminate the small fluctuations in the packet rate that may place apart two time series with the same long-term behavior. This is a promising solution to cope with the characteristics of our scenario, where we assume to have a similar workload on every element of the replicated vertical stacks of the considered application.

2.3 Identification of interacting VMs

The final step of our proposal is the definition of groups of VMs; this step exploits the correlation matrix as an input to identify the groups of communicating VMs, that are VMs belonging to the same vertical stack. To this aim, we use a threshold to filter out *correlated* and *uncorrelated* time series of network resource utilization. Basically, we consider as correlated every couple of time series with a correlation value higher or equal than a defined threshold, while if the correlation value is lower than the threshold we assume the corresponding time series to be uncorrelated.

After applying the threshold, VMs belonging to the same vertical stack can be identified looking for the connected components in the correlation matrix.

3. EXPERIMENTAL RESULTS

3.1 Experimental setup

We test our infrastructure using an experimental setup where multiple copies of the TPC-W benchmark[3] are executed in parallel over a cloud data center hosted by the Amazon EC2 infrastructure[4]. The monitoring is based on the architecture described

[2]http://pandas.pydata.org/

[3]www.tpc.org/tpcw/

[4]https://aws.amazon.com/ec2/

in [1]. Our traces refer to a TPC-W run with 12 VMs divided into 4 vertical stacks for a period of 12 hours, with samples collected by default every 30 seconds (but we present also experiments with traces where data collection has a granularity of 1 and 2 minutes).

As metrics for the comparison of the different correlation functions, we consider the classic measures of classification problems, that are *precision*, *recall*, and *accuracy*. *Precision* is defined as the fraction of identified couples of VMs that are actually communicating, while *recall* is the fraction of commucating couples of VMs that are correctly identified. In terms of true/false positives/negatives, we can define $Precision = \frac{TP}{TP+FP}$, $Recall = \frac{TP}{TP+FN}$, and $Accuracy = \frac{TP+TN}{TP+TN+FP+FN}$.

3.2 Comparison of correlation functions

We first present the correlation matrices computed over every couple of time series (including correlation between couples of input and couples of output packet rate time series) using both Pearson and Spearman correlation indexes.

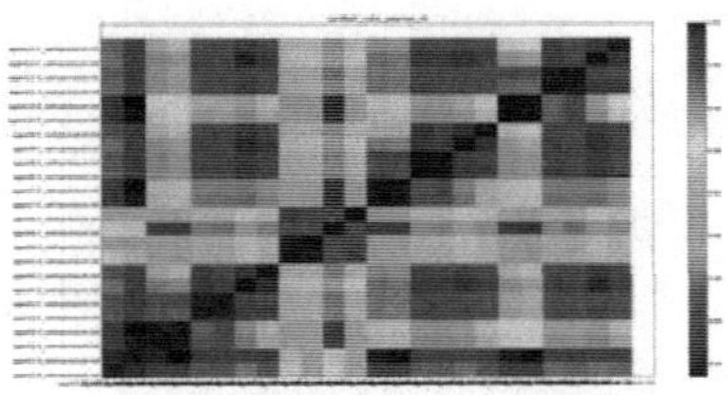

(a) Pearson correlation index

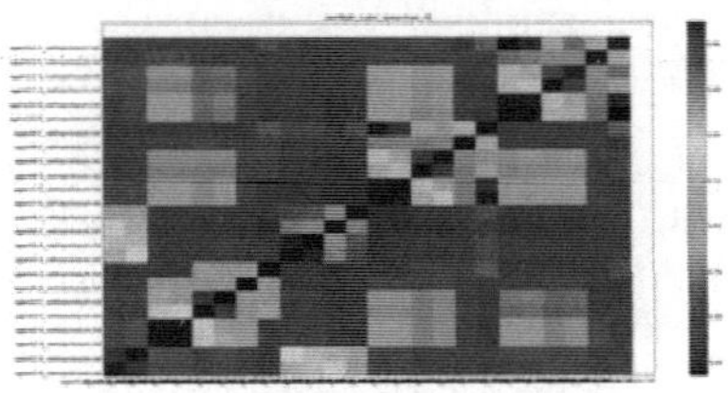

(b) Spearman correlation index

Figure 2: Heatmap of the correlation matrices

Figure 2 represents the two correlation matrices represented as heat maps. The structure of the vertical stacks should appear as four square blocks of correlated VMs on the main diagonal of the matrix. A qualitative analysis of these two figures provides some interesting insights: we observe clearly that the Pearson correlation index (Figure 2a) tends to return higher values (as testified by the general predominance of reddish colors). Particularly critical is the presence of red-orange shades far from the main diagonal, that suggest high correlation also between VMs belonging to different vertical stacks. On the other hand, the Spearman correlation index (Figure 2b) provides clearer distinction between groups of VMs in the same vertical stack (the red areas close to the diagonal) and VMs belonging to different stacks, suggesting a better capacity to distinguish communicating from not interacting VMs.

We now consider the sensitivity of the VMs classification to the threshold value: Figure 3 shows precision, recall and accuracy values as a function of the threshold. From the results, we have a confirmation of the better performance of the Spearman correlation index. Even if both correlation functions show similar traits, such as the precision increasing and the recall decreasing with the

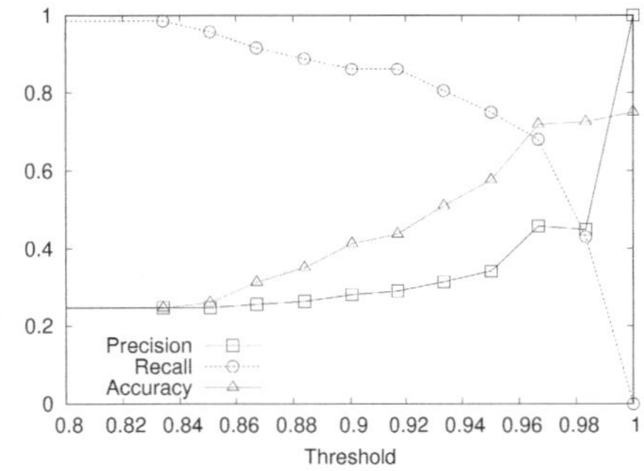

(a) Pearson correlation index

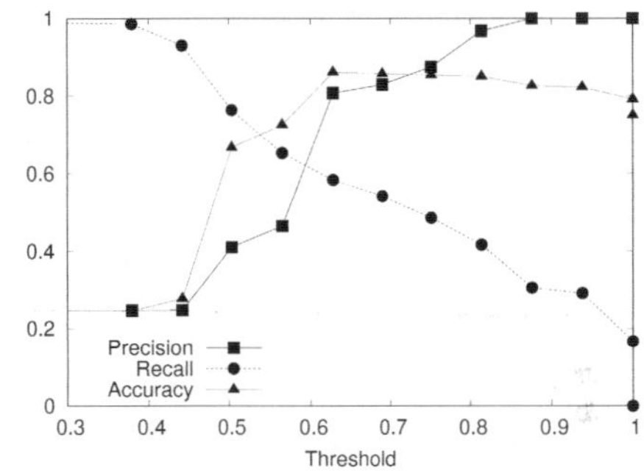

(b) Spearman correlation index

Figure 3: Precision, Recall, and Accuracy

threshold values, Figure 3a shows that the Pearson correlation index tends to have very high values for every couple of time series (we restrict our analysis in the range [0.8–1] to better observe the impact of the threshold choice). Even worse, the Pearson index determines a low precision in the identification of correlated traces, that increases only when the threshold is very close to 1; the accuracy describes effectively this behavior, reaching the highest values just on the rightmost part of the figure. On the other hand, if we consider the Spearman correlation index (Figure 3b), we observe that the sensitivity to the threshold value is less evident, with an high precision achieved even for low threshold values (in the order of 0.6) and with an accuracy that remains rather high for threshold values in the range [0.6–1].

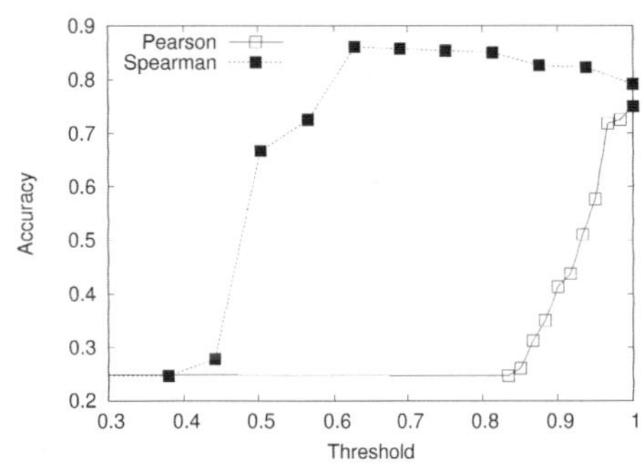

Figure 4: Accuracy comparison

Figure 4 summarizes this comparison showing the accuracy for

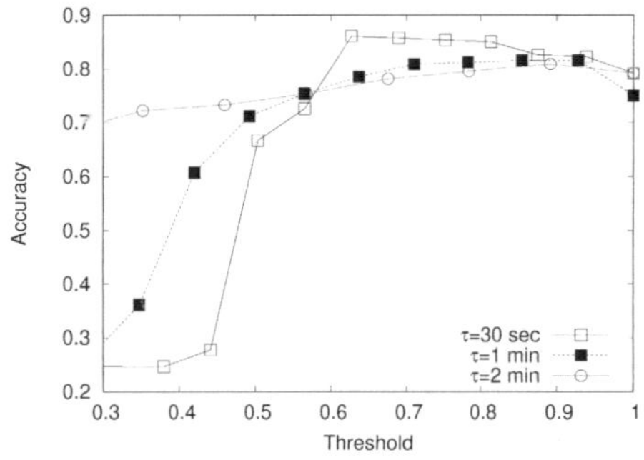

Figure 5: Sensitivity to sampling period τ

both correlation indexes as a function of the threshold value. It is clear that the Spearman correlation index provides a twofold advantage. First, it achieves better performance than the Pearson index, with higher accuracy values for every threshold. Second, it provides more stable performance with a range of threshold values returning an accuracy higher than 0.8 that spans from 0.6 to 1, while the best values for the Person function are limited in a tiny range from 0.96 to 1 (ten times smaller than the alternative).

3.3 Comparison of time sampling intervals

As a final analysis, we evaluate how the data sampling granularity affects the quality of the classification of correlated and non-correlated time series. To this aim, Figure 5 compares the accuracy achieved by the classification based on the Spearman correlation index as the sampling period τ of the network utilization ranges from 30 seconds to 2 minutes. We observe that, even with this small change in the sampling granularity, the impact on the classification accuracy is very significant. Specifically, we observe two main effects of a coarse-grained data collection. First, the sensitivity of the Spearman correlation to the threshold value is further reduced if we consider a large sampling period. This higher robustness is effect of the smoothed time series: basically, we work with a time series where only the most evident fluctuations are taken into account. This means that the low-frequency and highly evident fluctuations, that are the only way to distinguish two vertical stacks, are easier to identify even over a wider range of threshold values, thus explaining the observed stability with respect to different theshold values. Second, if we consider the threshold range related to the higher accuracy ([0.6-0.9]), we observe that the accuracy tends to decrease as the sampling interval increases. This effect is rather intuitive, because by increasing the sampling period, we obtain a smoother time series of network resource utilization. This effect still captures the main effects of correlation, but high frequency fluctuations that allow us to distinguish two vertical stacks are lost, with a consequent reduction of the classification accuracy.

4. CONCLUSIONS AND FUTURE WORK

In this paper we analyzed the problem of identifying groups of VMs in a cloud infrastructure that exchange information without having access to a detailed model of the data transfer among them. In particular, we focus on the case of horizontally replicated vertical stacks, where each VM in a vertical stack corresponds to a tier of an application. We pointed out that this case is very common and challenging in a cloud scenario where scalability is achieved though replication.

We described a methodology to identify communicating VMs that is based on the analysis of correlation between the time series of network traffic of each VMs. We compare different correlation indexes to identify the most suitable alternative. Our experiments show that the use of ranking-based techniques (as in the Spearman correlation index) clearly outperforms traditional correlation metrics, such as the Person index. A further qualifying point of our analysis is to demonstrate that fine-grained data collection is essential to achieve high accuracy in the identification of communicating VMs.

This paper is just a preliminary study addressing the issue of inferring VMs communication patterns in a cloud data center. Further research directions are related to the investigation of a more detailed methodology (including clustering techniques to identify the groups of connected VMs) and the evaluation of our methodology over a wider experimental setup, including different applications, a higher number of VMs involved, and a real workload.

Acknowledgement

The authors acknowledge the support of the University of Modena and Reggio Emilia through the project *SAMMClouds: Secure and Adaptive Management of Multi-Clouds*. The authors also thank Davide Ferrari for his help in conducting the experiments.

5. REFERENCES

[1] M. Andreolini, M. Colajanni, and M. Pietri. A scalable architecture for real-time monitoring of large information systems. In *Proc. IEEE Symposium on Network Cloud Computing and Applications*, London, UK, Dec. 2012.

[2] A. Beloglazov, J. Abawajy, and R. Buyya. Energy-aware resource allocation heuristics for efficient management of data centers for cloud computing. *Future generation computer systems*, 28(5):755–768, 2012.

[3] C. Canali and R. Lancellotti. Exploiting Classes of Virtual Machines for Scalable IaaS Cloud Management. In *Proc. of the 4th Symposium on Network Cloud Computing and Applications (NCCA)*, Jun. 2015.

[4] A. Marotta and S. Avallone. A Simulated Annealing Based Approach for Power Efficient Virtual Machines Consolidation. In *Proc. of 8th International Conference on Cloud Computing (CLOUD)*. IEEE, 2015.

[5] C. Mastroianni, M. Meo, and G. Papuzzo. Probabilistic Consolidation of Virtual Machines in Self-Organizing Cloud Data Centers. *IEEE Transactions on Cloud Computing*, 1(2):215–228, 2013.

[6] X. Meng, V. Pappas, and L. Zhang. Improving the Scalability of Data Center Networks with Traffic-aware Virtual Machine Placement. In *Proc. of the 29th Conference on Information Communications (INFOCOM)*, San Diego, California, USA, Mar. 2010.

[7] L. Myers and M. J. Sirois. *Spearman Correlation Coefficients, Differences between*. John Wiley & Sons, Ltd, 2014.

[8] M. Shojafar, C. Canali, R. Lancellotti, and E. Baccarelli. Minimizing computing-plus-communication energy consumptions in virtualized networked data centers. In *Proc. of The 21st IEEE Symposium on Computers and Communications (ISCC 2016)*. IEEE, 2016.

[9] J. Sonnek, J. Greensky, R. Reutiman, and A. Chandra. Starling: Minimizing Communication Overhead in Virtualized Computing Platforms Using Decentralized Affinity-Aware Migration. In *Proc. of 39th International Conference on Parallel Processing (ICPP)*, San Diego, CA, Sept 2010.

Extending Queuing Networks to Assess Mobile CrowdSensing Application Performance

Riccardo Pinciroli
DEIB, Politecnico di Milano
Via Ponzio 34/5, 20133 Milano, Italy.
riccardo.pinciroli@polimi.it

Salvatore Distefano
Università di Messina
Contrada di Dio, S. Agata, 98166 Messina, Italy.
Kazan Federal University
35 Kremlyovskaya street, 420008 Kazan, Russia.
sdistefano@{unime.it, kpfu.ru}

ABSTRACT

The widespread and pervasive adoption of smart devices is boosting Internet of Things and contribution-based paradigms. In particular, Mobile Crowdsensing (MCS), due to its big potential of sharing and collecting large population of contributors-devices, is acquiring interest. Devices such as smartphones and smart boards are equipped with different sensors and actuators able to probe data about the physical environment. In a typical MCS scenario, data produced by sensors are sent to the remote server, where they are collected and processed by the applications. To exploit the MCS paradigm in large-scale business contexts the quality of service of MCS applications must be monitored and guaranteed. Therefore, techniques and tools able to represent and evaluate MCS system quality attributes such as performance and energy consumption are required. However, modeling MCS system is quite challenging since not only the number of users but also the number of contributors may vary. In this paper, we propose to adopt queuing networks, a well-known formalism able to deal with large number of requests, to address this issue. In particular we introduce and implement a new policy allowing the number of server to be variable. The proposed model is then adopted in the evaluation of an example, providing interesting insights on contribution, provisioning and usage impacts in terms of some performance and energy consumption metrics.

Keywords

Mobile Crowdsensing; queuing networks; performance; energy consumption.

1. INTRODUCTION

Mobile CrowdSensing (MCS) is a quite new paradigm lying at the intersection of Internet of things (IoT) and volunteer-/crowd-based computing [9]. Its success, confirmed by more and more applications adopting the MCS paradigm [4, 7, 17], is due to the capability of gathering and managing a large population of nodes, mainly providing sensing functionalities, while dealing with scalability issues. Consequently, both academic and business communities are investing resources and efforts to both develop appropriate middleware mechanisms [18, 21] and investigate on a potential commercial exploitation for MCS.

This calls for a refactoring of MCS, rethinking main concepts and ideas of this paradigm to enlarge its scope towards business contexts where quality of service (QoS) requirements are specified through a service level agreement (SLA). Tools supporting design and operation of MCS services, such as those related to QoS modeling and evaluation, monitoring, prediction and enforcement are therefore strongly required. The main challenge to deal with in QoS modeling and evaluation is related to the *churning* management. Contributors may join and leave the system randomly and unpredictably, at their needs and wills, entering or exiting the region of interest, according to their device battery life.

This poses an interesting challenge to the QoS/performance community: how to deal with a system where not only end-users, jobs or requests, but also contributors, nodes or servers may vary in time? A proper MCS system model has to adopt stochastic processes to properly represent arrival and service processes. Furthermore, appropriate memory management mechanisms should be implemented, since the stochastic quantities characterizing these processes are usually generally distributed. In MCS systems, service requests are usually split in simple tasks to be performed by contributor nodes. Due to the churning, these tasks could be interrupted before termination, and thus rescheduled. Some MCS services implement checkpointing policies to limit the impact of this phenomenon on QoS and performance. This way, after rescheduling the task restarts from the last checkpoint condition, thus requiring adequate mechanisms for dealing with memory issues in modeling and evaluation.

Existing solutions partially address these issues, mainly through state space based models [6, 5, 12, 11] and simulation [16]. An open problem in literature is related to complexity, in particular for state space based models where state space may *"explode"*. Some of them allow to represent contribution dynamics and churning, mainly neglecting the memory problem, except [6]. None of them take into account checkpointing policies and related issues.

Thus, the main contribution of this paper is to provide a technique addressing all such issues altogether. It is based on

VALUETOOLS 2016, October 25-28, Taormina, Italy

queueing networks (QNs), able to deal with open and closed workloads, also taking into account queueing phenomena. To cope with contribution dynamics, a new policy allowing variable number of servers is introduced and a specific model is defined for MCS system. Checkpointing strategies and related memory mechanisms are implemented, thus providing a framework for the assessment of actual MCS services that could be applied in real applications. Furthermore, to the best of our knowledge, this is the first attempt in evaluating energy consumption metrics, providing information from three different perspectives, i.e., contributors, service provider and end users.

This paper is therefore organized as follows. Section 2 describes the MCS scenario also providing an overview of related work. The QN model is then detailed in Section 3, while Section 4 presents the results obtained by evaluating an MCS example. Finally, conlusions and future work are discussed in Section 5.

2. PROBLEM OVERVIEW AND RELATED WORK

2.1 Scenario

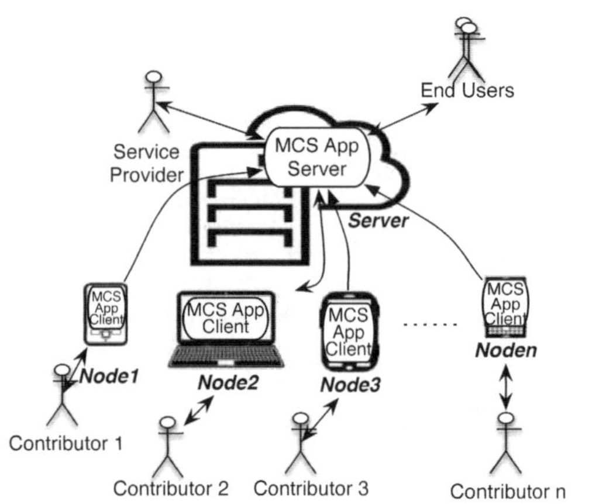

Figure 1: MCS application scenario.

MCS [9] is a kind of volunteer computing paradigm where contributors share their sensors and data, usually provided by their personal devices (smartphones, tablets, PDAs, laptops, etc.), with specific applications gathering and aggregating all the collected data for further processing. In this scenario, depicted in Figure 1, three different stakeholders can be identified:

- *contributors* are the owners of the devices shared to build up the sensing infrastructure environment;
- the *service provider* manages the whole system and service by gathering, managing and processing data and results from contributors;
- *end users* use the MCS application to access the services and the information it provides.

An MCS application, from a high level perspective, is composed of two main phases implemented by the elements showed in Figure 1. Firstly, through the MCS application client deployed on each involved node (usually after it has been explicitly downloaded and installed by the contributor on the device), data are produced, (pre-)processed and sent to the server. Then, MCS application server collects, aggregates, further processes (if required) and stores the data, providing the information and results to the end users.

Each node can elaborate zero, one or more *tasks* whose results are collected for further processing by the application server. The application client can also be intelligent and predict the leave of a contributor (e.g., in case of low battery). In that case, it sends partially processed data, (i.e., a checkpoint) to restart future elaboration on other available nodes.

The MCS paradigm is already adopted in several tools such as OpenStreetmap [10], Waze [20], Nericell [17], as an effective solution for problems related to mobility [22, 7, 4], traffic monitoring [20, 17], public safety [1], smart cities [2] environment and pollution monitoring [22], emergency and crowd management [15], to mention but a few. But most of the potential of MCS is still untapped due to the limits of contribution approach, often unreliable and unpredictable, implying high uncertainty in the service fruition. Indeed, in MCS applications, contributors join and leave the system randomly, often without even completing their assigned tasks. Thus, focusing on the MCS pattern rather than on a specific application, we have to skip the application functional properties while investigating the behaviour of the overall MCS system and its impact on the MCS application. Indeed, the overall MCS system infrastructure is not able to change the behavior of the application from inside, i.e., to modify the application functionalities and functional properties, while could strongly affect the non functional properties of the application. In other words, to properly evaluate the suitability of the MCS pattern/paradigm we have to investigate how it influences the MCS application behavior and, since it cannot affect the application functionalities, proper metrics to assess the impact are those related to non functional properties. For example, reliability, availability and performance of an MCS applications strongly depends on the number of available contributors.

In particular, several metrics of interest can be identified from the different perspectives in Table 1. A contributor is mainly interested in knowing the impact of contribution on his/her device or node, in terms of computing resource utilization (CPU, memory, storage) and battery charge. Instead, service provider is mainly interested in managing the resources, i.e., maximizing their utilization and reducing power consumption, while reducing the time for processing a task and increasing the system throughput. This also affects the response time for processing a request, which is the main metric of interest for the end users.

A model or a modeling technique can provide a valid support to the design, deployment and assessment of the MCS applications. However, several aspects must be taken into account to properly represent an MCS system. Among them, one of the most challenging is the fluctuation of the number of contributors, that strongly impacts on the MCS underlying infrastructure and on the non functional properties of the application. An MCS system representation should take into consideration also the contribution dynamics, in order to stochastically characterize both arrival (join) and departure (leave) time of the contributors

Perspective *Metric*	*Contributor*	*Service Provider*	*End User*
Resource Utilization	Node	Server	-
Energy Consumption	Battery	Server	-
Response Time	-	Task	Service
Throughput	-	Task	

Table 1: MCS system metrics of interests

by specific probability distributions. Stochastic characterization by proper distribution is also needed for service time of both the nodes (clients) and the servers, and for arrival rate of the jobs. In general such distributions are not always Markovian, since their stochastic behaviors not necessarily observes the memoryless property of exponential distribution. Furthermore, the model has also to deal with the complexity of an MCS system, for example, taking into account queueing effects as well as checkpointing policies.

2.2 Related work

Several approaches to the MCS challenges can be found in literature, since it is an umbrella term enclosing different paradigms such as opportunistic, participatory and social sensing [9]. Modeling techniques are required to understand the MCS application behaviours when this application operate under different scenarios. As an example, simulation is proposed for the evaluation of MCS system performance in [5], while Karaliopoulos et al. [13] use stochastic model to face the problem of user mobility, selecting users for crowdsensing campaign through an optimization problem. Stochastic models are also used to investigate how to maximize utility [12] and profit [11] in MCS applications. In both cases, Lyapunov optimization is used to find the best solution for the considered problem. Liu et al. [14] adopt a continuous time Markov chain (CTMC) to study the data collected by sensing vehicles, focusing on the spatial distribution of the vehicles. In [6] and [16] MCS applications are modeled to analyze their QoS. In particular, the authors adopt an extended version of Stochastic Petri net formalism to consider the elements that can affect the performance of an MCS system (i.e., contributors and workload fluctuations). In [16] they also propose an MCS as-a-Service paradigm to address actual business challenges. The main problem of all such techniques lies on complexity. State space based models have intrinsic limitations in dealing with such an issue due to the well know state space explosion problem. Also simulation time could be significantly affected by the MCS system complexity, even if in a less critical way than state space models.

In this paper we recur to queueing theory to model MCS user and contributor arrival processes, since it allows to represent complex systems with both open and closed workloads. The only problem is that the contributors have to be considered as servers in the corresponding queueing network (QN) model, thus implying to introduce a new multiserver policy able to cope with contributor-server fluctuations. Furthermore, in order to provide quantitative results from different perspectives (contributors, service provider and end users), we also have to evaluate energy related metrics on nodes and servers. Conti et al. [5] identify this aspect as one of the key challenges to motivate participants in contributing. Indeed, since the battery capacity of these devices is often very limited, MCS applications should have a low impact on the battery depletion, letting users be almost unaware of their contributions to MCS.

3. A QUEUING NETWORK MODEL

Based on the scenario of Figure 1, two different layers have been identified for the proposed QN model: the contribution and the processing subsystems (Figure 2). Contributors are modeled in the contribution QN, whereas end user's requests are represented by jobs in the processing QN. These two networks are strictly related to model the stochastic behaviour of the MCS system. In fact, when a contributor joins the contribution QN, a server in the processing network is turned on and can serve incoming requests. The server is turned off when the contributor associated with that server leaves the contribution QN. Note that a server is related to a specific contributor until it leaves the system. Once a contributor leaves the contribution QN, the server in the processing network may be turned on by another contributor. In other words, at most only one active contributor at time can be associated with a server, while any contributor can be associated with a server when it is idle. The two sub-networks are detailed in next Sections.

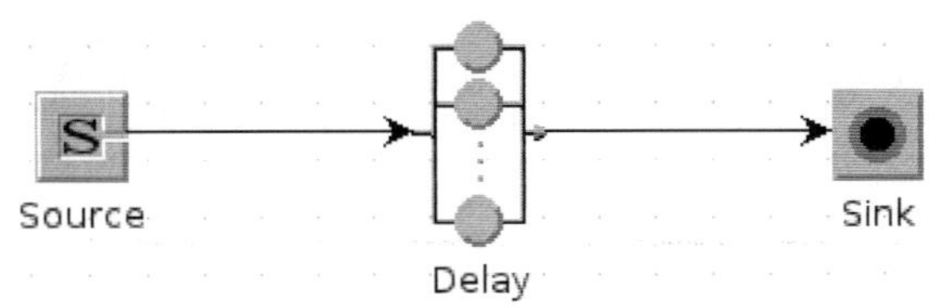

(a)

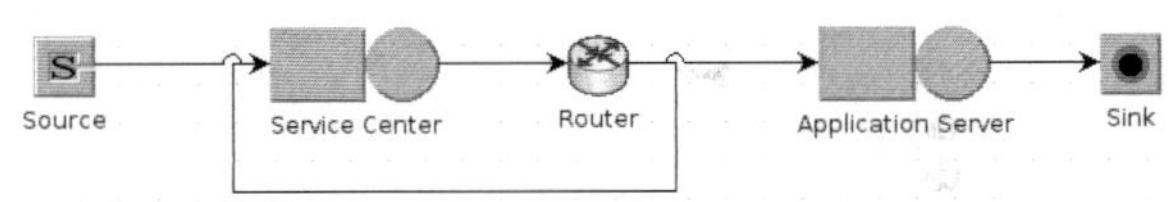

(b)

Figure 2: The MCS application model with the contribution (a) and processing (b) queueing networks.

3.1 The contribution QN

The contribution QN represents contribution dynamics. Contributors join and leave the MCS system randomly, spending in the system their contribution time. The contribution QN is shown in Figure 2(a).

Every job in the `Delay` station (i.e., a $G/G/\infty$ queue) models a contributor that is sharing its resources. The arrival rate to `Delay` and the time a job spends in it may be characterized by any general distribution. They represent the arrivals of the contributors in the system and their contribution times (i.e., the time they are available to serve the end user's requests), respectively. As discussed above, the `Delay` station of this network is connected to the `Service Center` one in the processing QN. The number of servers in the processing QN is equal to the number of jobs in the `Delay` station of contribution QN.

3.2 The processing QN

The processing QN represents the requests incoming from MCS end users, which are served by the contributors' nodes. Figure 2(b) shows the corresponding QN. An end user request is decomposed into n task requests which are served by contributor nodes. The task request arrival process is characterized by a general distribution and does not depend on the contribution QN. It is modeled by the `Source` station. Also the service time of the `Application Server` station does not depend on the contribution QN and is generally distributed (i.e., a $G/G/1$ queue). This station models the commit of a request once it has been completed. On the other hand, the `Service Center` station depends on the contribution QN. It is a $G/G/x$ queue, with generally distributed arrival and service times and variable number of servers $x \in [0, \infty)$. It is important to remark that, the number of servers x follows the number of contributors that are in the system and therefore is variable depending on the contribution dynamics.

A task request is served by only one server at a time, but it may be served by different servers till it is completely processed. Indeed, a request exits from the `Service Center` whether it has been fully served or the i-th server that is serving the task is turned off, meaning that the contributor related to that server leaves the system. In the former case, the completed task request is sent to the `Application Server` by the `Router` and it leaves the system after the end-user request is processed by the server, i.e., once n task requests are processed. In the latter case, when the task request is not completed, it is sent by the `Router` back to the `Service Center`, waiting to be fully processed by a free server.

Priority policies may be applied to the `Service Center` in order to prioritize dropped requests, since the number of available servers may be lower than the number of requests that need to be served. This way, a task request that has been interrupted can be rescheduled for processing with a higher priority. Indeed only x requests can be served at the same time by the `Service Center`.

3.3 Measurements

Once the model has been specified, we have to discuss how to evaluate its performance. Referring to Table 1, an end user is interested in the average *Push time*, the time needed by the system to process an end user request, i.e. the processing of n task requests and their further elaboration by the application server. It can be specified as:

$$PushTime = \frac{\sum_{i=0}^{\lfloor C_T/n \rfloor} CompletionTime_i}{\lfloor C_T/n \rfloor} \quad (1)$$

where C_T is the number of completed task requests, n is the number of committed requests that the system collects before returning some results and $CompletionTime_i$ is the time at which the i-th set of n requests have been committed.

The service provider may be interested in the average system response time R_P and the throughput X_P. The former is computed observing each task request and evaluating how long it spends in the system. The latter as $X_P = C_T/T$, where T is the observation time.

Finally, a contributor is interested in knowing the impact of contribution on his/her devices, quantified by the utilization U_C and the battery energy consumed by the MCS app during contribution. To this purpose, we evaluate U_C of each node as:

$$U_C = \frac{\sum_{i=0}^{x_{max}} ActivityTime_i}{\sum_{i=0}^{x_{max}} OnTime_i} \quad (2)$$

where $ActivityTime_i$ is the time spent by the server i in the `Service Center` serving a request, $OnTime_i$ is the total time that server i is available for the MCS application, either busy to serve a task request or idle, waiting for a task request to serve, and x_{max} is the maximum number of server in the `Service Center`. Assuming that the device is mainly used for computations, we evaluate the power consumption P_C of each node as shown in [8]:

$$P_C(U_C) = P_C^{idle} + (P_C^{busy} - P_C^{idle})U_C \quad (3)$$

where P_C^{idle} is the power consumption when the device is idle, P_C^{busy} is the power consumption of the device when it is fully utilized and U_C is the utilization of the device as obtained by eq. (2). Once the power consumption has been computed, the average energy consumption E_C is derived as:

$$E_C = P_C \cdot S_C \quad (4)$$

where S_C is the contributor service time, i.e., the overall time the contributor spends in the system. We estimate the percentage of battery depleted by the contributor for the contribution to the MCS system as:

$$Battery\ consumption = \frac{E_C}{W_C} \quad (5)$$

where W_C is the battery capacity of the node.

4. A NUMERICAL EXAMPLE

In order to explain the proposed technique and the model thus obtained, in this Section we discuss an example on an MCS system, taking parameters from existing literature when available.

4.1 Description

In the MCS system described above, end users submit requests to the MCS application. Each request is split in n simpler tasks, that are performed by the contributor nodes. Once the n tasks have been processed, the provider application server gathers the results and provides the overall elaboration outcomes to the end users. As discussed in Section 2.1, memory strategies may be taken into account in task request processing, since these may be often interrupted and therefore rescheduled for processing. We therefore evaluate an MCS system with and without memory strategies. In the former case, a checkpoint strategy lets the system keep memory of the task requests processing. In the latter case, the computation of the task requests restarts from scratch every time they are served by a new contributor.

The parameters used in the experiments have been taken from literature when possible. The contributor and request arrivals are exponentially distributed, as well as the service time of the `Delay` and the `Application Server` stations. The service time of each server in the `Service Center` station is characterized by an Erlang distribution with 3 stages, similarly to [6]. The average service time of `Application Server` S_{AS} and `Delay` S_{Contr} is always the same for all the experiments, i.e. 10 seconds and 30 minutes, respectively. The inter-arrival time of the two networks (i.e., A_{Contr} and

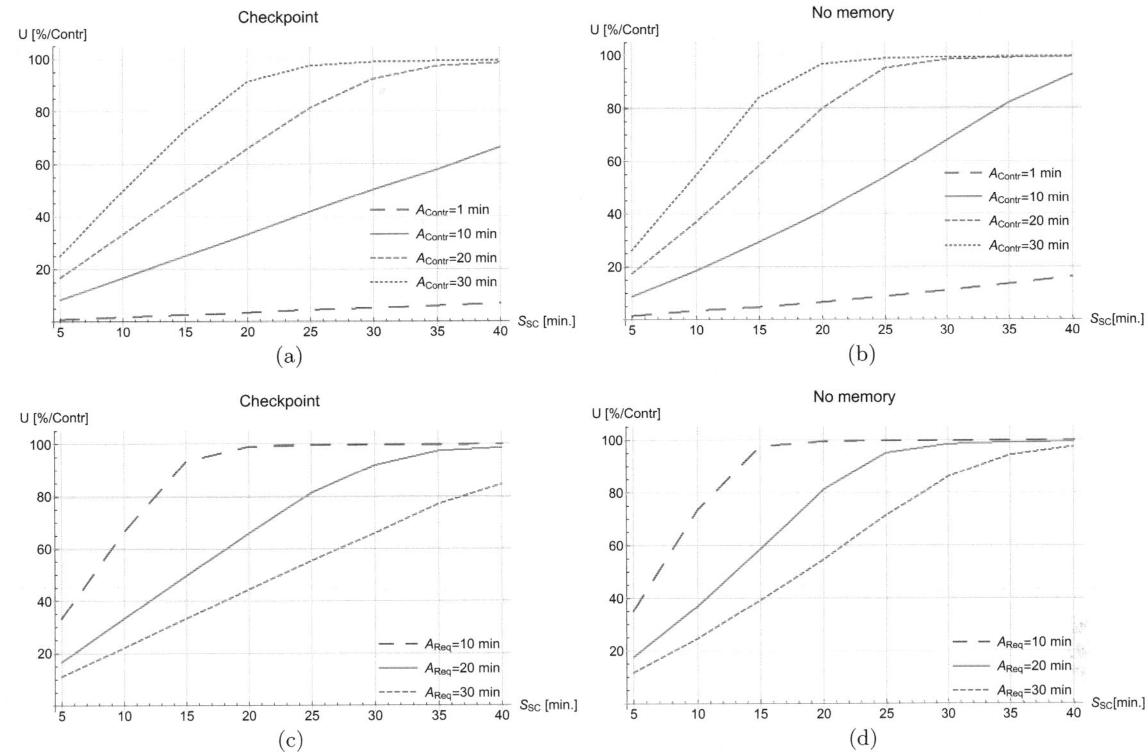

Figure 3: Average utilization per contributor as a function of service time with fixed request inter-arrival time and either checkpoint (a) or without checkpoint (b), and with fixed contributors inter-arrival time and either checkpoint (c) or without checkpoint (d).

A_{Req} for contribution and processing QN, respectively) and the average service time of server in the `Service Center` S_{SC} have different values in each experiment. More specifically: $A_{Contr} = \{1, 10, 20, 30\}$ minutes; $A_{Req} = \{10, 20, 30\}$ minutes; $S_{SC} = \{5, 10, 15, 20, 25, 30, 35, 40\}$ minutes. When the system is analyzed varying A_{Contr} (or A_{Req}), the parameter A_{Req} (or A_{Contr}) is set to 20 minutes. Each experiment is evaluated for all the values that S_{SC} can assume. Notice that, a more complex request is associated with a larger value of S_{SC}. The system is always observed for 100 hours. The strategy used in the `Service Center` to select the next request to be processed is a FIFO with priority. The priority of a request increases every time the request is sent from the server back to the queue. The job with the largest priority is the first to be served. If two or more jobs have identical priority value, FIFO strategy is adopted. The number of requests that must be committed before the system returns some results to end user is $n = 10$.

In all the experiments, the idle and the maximum power consumptions and the battery capacity for all the devices are $P_C^{idle} = 0.268W$, $P_C^{busy} = 1W$ and $W_C = 7.77$ Watthour [3], respectively.

4.2 Evaluation

All the experiments have been performed through discrete event simulation using OMNeT++ [19]. It is an extensible, modular, component-based C++ simulation library and framework used to build network simulators. We patched version 4.6 in order to study the model described in Section 3. In particular, we implemented the relation between the contribution and the processing queueing networks and edited the `Job` implementation in order to consider different memory strategies as described in Section 4.1. The results obtained are discussed in the following Sections from the different stakeholder perspectives identified for the MCS system. Each simulation performed 500 runs and all the measurements have been computed with 99% confidence intervals.

4.2.1 Contributors

Contributors are mainly interested in quantifying the impact of the contribution on their resources, mainly evaluated by the utilization and the battery consumption of their nodes. We analyze these quantities through the measurements specified by eq. (2-5). Results are shown in Figure 3, where the average utilization per contributor as a function of the average service time of `Service Center` is plotted. In Figures 3(a) and 3(b) different inter-arrival time of the contributors are considered whit requests arrival time of 20 minutes, comparing the two strategies (i.e., checkpoint and no memory, respectively). As expected, the smaller the contribution inter-arrival time, the lower the node utilization since the total number of contributors (i.e., $N_C = S_C/A_C$) increases when the inter-arrival time A_C decreases, being the average contribution time constant, i.e., $S_C = 30$ minutes. Furthermore, if checkpoint memory strategy is used,

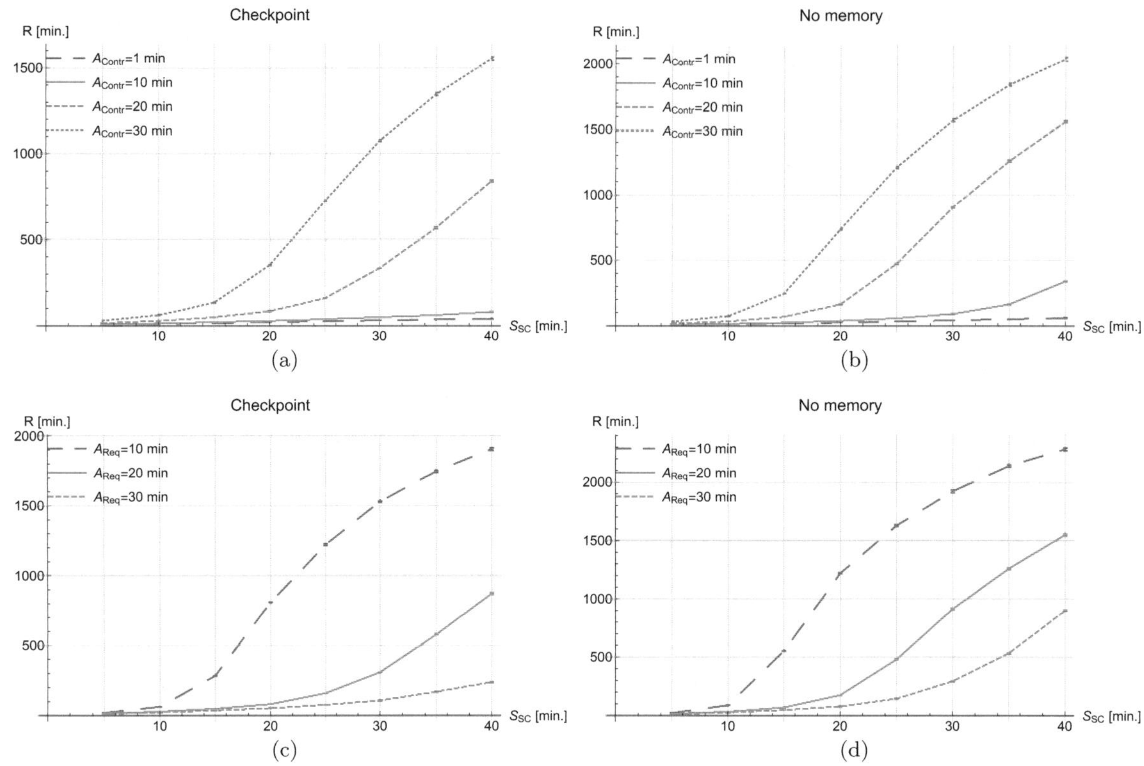

Figure 4: Average system response time for task requests, as a function of service time with fixed request inter-arrival time and either checkpoint (a) or without checkpoint (b), and with fixed contributors inter-arrival time and either checkpoint (c) or without checkpoint (d).

the utilization of each device is lower than the service without memory, since contributors have to perform a greater amount of work when no checkpoint is adopted. In Figures 3(c) and 3(d) the inter-arrival time of contributors is set to 20 minutes, whereas arrival time of the requests varies. Also in this case the contributors utilization is larger when requests are served with no memory. A larger utilization is also observed when the inter-arrival time of the requests is smaller. Indeed, in that case a greater amount of requests is in the system.

The utilization analysis is useful to study the energy consumption. The power absorption – by which energy consumption is derived – is computed through eq. (3) that is linear with respect to utilization. For this reason, energy consumption curves have the same trend of utilization ones and have not been plotted for the sake of space. However, considering the parameters given in Section 4, the battery depletion for a 30 minutes contribution is never greater than 7%, when $U = 100\%$.

4.2.2 Service provider

The MCS service provider is interested in several metrics that allow to monitor the MCS system. Utilization is an important measure also for the service provider. In this case, it is used to see when the system saturates (i.e., utilization of each contributor is 100%). When it happens, the performance of the system degrades and the requested QoS cannot be satisfied, driving to SLA violations.

System response time is plotted in Figure 4 against service time. Also in this case, different memory strategies have been considered. In Figures 4(a) and 4(b) arrival time of the requests is set to 20 minutes and the one of the contributors varies. In the former the checkpoint memory strategy is used, in the latter no memory strategies are adopted. It can be observed that the smaller is the number of contributors in the system – and consequently the greater is their utilization – the larger is the system response time. This performance index strongly depends on how many contributors are in the system. Indeed, if there are enough contributors, the task requests are served without interruption and they are completed as soon as possible. Instead, when the number of the contributors is too low, each task request may spend several time waiting to be served. This behaviour is worse when no memory about the work done by previous contributors is kept, since a task request must be processed from the beginning every time it enters `Service Center`.

Figures 4(c) and 4(d) show the system response time for the requests when contributors arrival time is 20 minutes and inter-arrival time of requests changes. As in the previous case, similar consideration can be drawn. In particular, the higher the requests arrival time (i.e., the larger is the number of requests concurrently in the system) the higher their response time.

The provider may be also interested in the system throughput, since it is often constrained by SLAs. For the sake of space, system throughput graphs are not shown. A larger number of contributors (i.e., smaller value of contributors arrival time) lets the system provide the largest throughput also when complex requests are in the system. When the requests inter-arrival time is larger, the throughput has its maximum value when the activity is simple, whereas it decreases when the job to be completed is harder. Also in this case the checkpoint memory policy is better than the no memory strategy.

4.2.3 End user

The push time is the time elapsed from the submission of the end user's request, until the system provides the results. In our example, the system processes $n = 10$ task requests before returning a value. The push time is plotted in Figure 5 against service time, comparing checkpoint and no memory strategies, for different values of either contributors or requests inter-arrival time. In Figures 5(a) and 5(b) the contributors arrival time varies. The minimum push time value is 200 minutes for each value of A_C, with request inter-arrival time of 20 minutes. The push time increases if either the requests are too complex to solve (i.e., for larger service time values) or the number of available contributors is lower (i.e., for larger A_C values).

Different behavior is observed when A_T changes and A_C is set. In this case, each curve has its own minimum, since different values for requests inter-arrival time are considered. It is worth notice that the larger the number of requests in the system, the earlier the push time starts increasing. Indeed, requests with the same complexity can easily affect the system performance when several other requests are already in the system. In both the considered cases, checkpoint strategy provides the best results.

5. CONCLUSIONS AND FUTURE WORK

MCS applications is attracting more and more interest as a new research field in IoT. In this paper, they are analyzed through queuing network models. In particular, we focused on the QoS of the MCS system, and we analyzed several performance metrics that may be of interest for the different stakeholders (i.e., contributors, system provider and end users). System provider can implement some memory strategies in order to improve performance and optimize battery life. Energy consumption is an important performance metric, since it may stimulate contributors to join the MCS system. Indeed, if energy consumption is too high only few contributors may join the system, affecting all the other performance indices. Through simulation on an MCS system taken as example, it has been shown that a checkpoint strategy lets the system work with better performance.

This paper is only a first step toward a new model for the MCS applications. Even if the results here presented show the importance of this model, we still need to validate it against either real system or a detailed simulation of the MCS services. Another interesting development could be on considering different quality properties and metrics altogether. To this purpose, an optimization problem should be specified, to identify the best configuration for the MCS system. Moreover, it may be of interest to consider different memory strategies and different classes of requests and contributors. In the former case, several policies can be evaluated and compared to the checkpointing one. In the latter case a more detailed model of an MCS system can be provided. For the same reason, also different priority strategies for choosing the request to be processed should be further investigated. Finally, it could also be interesting to study a single server version of `Service Center` as proposed in [6], comparing the results thus obtained against the latter ones.

6. REFERENCES

[1] E. Aubry, T. Silverston, A. Lahmadi, and O. Festor. Crowdout: A mobile crowdsourcing service for road safety in digital cities. In *Pervasive Computing and Communications Workshops (PERCOM Workshops), 2014 IEEE International Conference on*, pages 86–91, March 2014.

[2] G. Cardone, L. Foschini, P. Bellavista, A. Corradi, C. Borcea, M. Talasila, and R. Curtmola. Fostering participaction in smart cities: a geo-social crowdsensing platform. *Communications Magazine, IEEE*, 51(6):112–119, June 2013.

[3] A. Carroll and G. Heiser. An analysis of power consumption in a smartphone. In *USENIX annual technical conference*, volume 14. Boston, MA, 2010.

[4] Y. Chon, N. D. Lane, F. Li, H. Cha, and F. Zhao. Automatically characterizing places with opportunistic crowdsensing using smartphones. In *Proceedings of the 2012 ACM Conference on Ubiquitous Computing*, pages 481–490. ACM, 2012.

[5] M. Conti, C. Boldrini, S. S. Kanhere, E. Mingozzi, E. Pagani, P. M. Ruiz, and M. Younis. From manet to people-centric networking: milestones and open research challenges. *Computer Communications*, 71:1–21, 2015.

[6] S. Distefano, F. Longo, and M. Scarpa. Qos assessment of mobile crowdsensing services. *Journal of Grid computing*, 14, 2016.

[7] S. B. Eisenman, E. Miluzzo, N. D. Lane, R. A. Peterson, G.-S. Ahn, and A. T. Campbell. Bikenet: A mobile sensing system for cyclist experience mapping. *ACM Transactions on Sensor Networks (TOSN)*, 6(1):6, 2009.

[8] X. Fan, W.-D. Weber, and L. A. Barroso. Power provisioning for a warehouse-sized computer. In *ACM SIGARCH Computer Architecture News*, volume 35, pages 13–23. ACM, 2007.

[9] R. K. Ganti, F. Ye, and H. Lei. Mobile crowdsensing: current state and future challenges. *Communications Magazine, IEEE*, 49(11):32–39, 2011.

[10] M. Haklay and P. Weber. Openstreetmap: User-generated street maps. *Pervasive Computing, IEEE*, 7(4):12–18, Oct 2008.

[11] Y. Han and Y. Zhu. Profit-maximizing stochastic control for mobile crowd sensing platforms. In *2014 IEEE 11th International Conference on Mobile Ad Hoc and Sensor Systems*, pages 145–153. IEEE, 2014.

[12] Y. Han, Y. Zhu, and J. Yu. Utility-maximizing data collection in crowd sensing: An optimal scheduling approach. In *Sensing, Communication, and Networking (SECON), 2015 12th Annual IEEE International Conference on*, pages 345–353. IEEE, 2015.

[13] M. Karaliopoulos, O. Telelis, and I. Koutsopoulos. User recruitment for mobile crowdsensing over opportunistic networks. In *2015 IEEE Conference on*

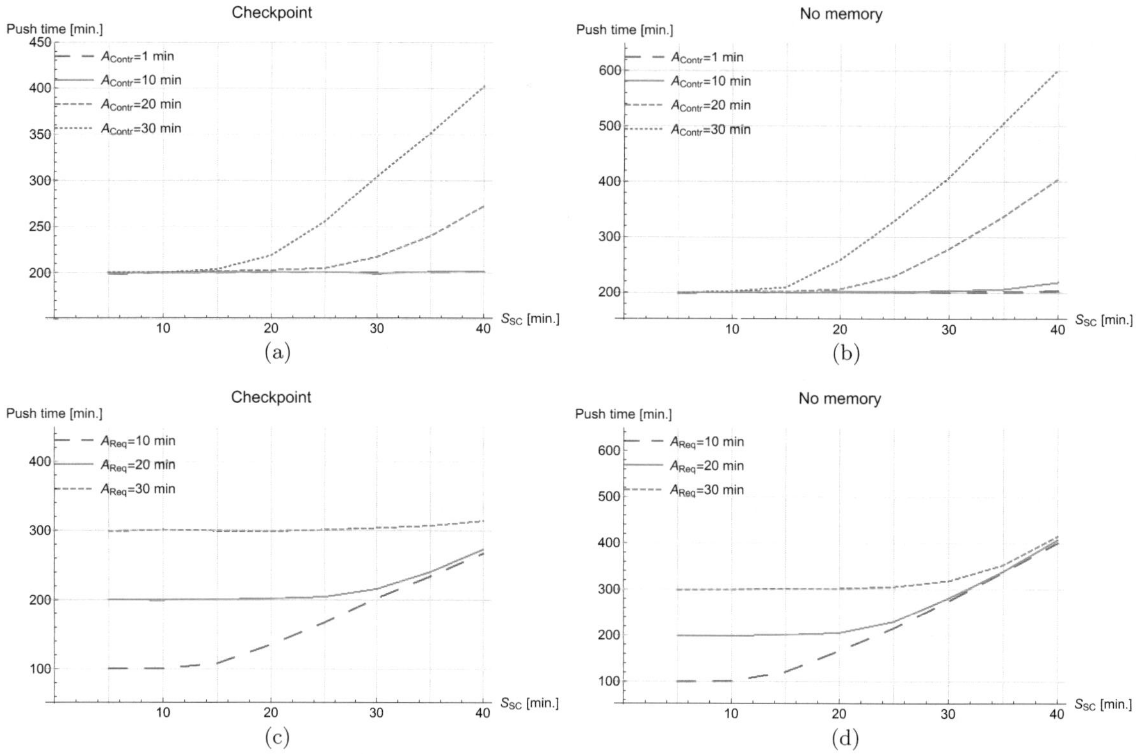

Figure 5: Average push time, as a function of service time with fixed request inter-arrival time and either checkpoint (a) or without checkpoint (b), and with fixed contributors inter-arrival time and either checkpoint (c) or without checkpoint (d).

Computer Communications (INFOCOM), pages 2254–2262. IEEE, 2015.

[14] Y. Liu, J. Niu, and X. Liu. Comprehensive tempo-spatial data collection in crowd sensing using a heterogeneous sensing vehicle selection method. *Personal and Ubiquitous Computing*, 20(3):397–411, 2016.

[15] T. Ludwig, C. Reuter, T. Siebigteroth, and V. Pipek. Crowdmonitor: Mobile crowd sensing for assessing physical and digital activities of citizens during emergencies. In *Proceedings of the 33rd Annual ACM Conference on Human Factors in Computing Systems*, CHI '15, pages 4083–4092, New York, NY, USA, 2015. ACM.

[16] G. Merlino, S. Arkoulis, S. Distefano, C. Papagianni, A. Puliafito, and S. Papavassiliou. Mobile crowdsensing as a service: a platform for applications on top of sensing clouds. *Future Generation Computer Systems*, 56:623–639, 2016.

[17] P. Mohan, V. N. Padmanabhan, and R. Ramjee. Nericell: rich monitoring of road and traffic conditions using mobile smartphones. In *Proceedings of the 6th ACM conference on Embedded network sensor systems*, pages 323–336. ACM, 2008.

[18] M.-R. Ra, B. Liu, T. F. La Porta, and R. Govindan. Medusa: A programming framework for crowd-sensing applications. In *Proceedings of the 10th international conference on Mobile systems, applications, and services*, pages 337–350. ACM, 2012.

[19] A. Varga and R. Hornig. An overview of the omnet++ simulation environment. In *Proceedings of the 1st international conference on Simulation tools and techniques for communications, networks and systems & workshops*, page 60. ICST (Institute for Computer Sciences, Social-Informatics and Telecommunications Engineering), 2008.

[20] Waze Mobile. Waze website, 2006.

[21] Y. Xiao, P. Simoens, P. Pillai, K. Ha, and M. Satyanarayanan. Lowering the barriers to large-scale mobile crowdsensing. In *Proceedings of the 14th Workshop on Mobile Computing Systems and Applications*, page 9. ACM, 2013.

[22] X. Yu, W. Zhang, L. Zhang, V. O. Li, J. Yuan, and I. You. Understanding urban dynamics based on pervasive sensing: An experimental study on traffic density and air pollution. *Mathematical and Computer Modelling*, 58(5âĂŞ6):1328 – 1339, 2013. The Measurement of Undesirable Outputs: Models Development and Empirical Analyses and Advances in mobile, ubiquitous and cognitive computing.

Joint Operator Replication and Placement Optimization for Distributed Streaming Applications

Valeria Cardellini
cardellini@ing.uniroma2.it

Vincenzo Grassi
vincenzo.grassi@uniroma2.it

Francesco Lo Presti
lopresti@info.uniroma2.it

Matteo Nardelli
nardelli@ing.uniroma2.it

Department of Civil Engineering and Computer Science Engineering
University of Rome Tor Vergata, Italy

ABSTRACT

In the last few years, several processing approaches have emerged to deal with Big Data. Exploiting on-the-fly computation, Data Stream Processing (DSP) applications can process unbounded streams of data to extract valuable information in a near real-time fashion. To keep up with the high volume of daily produced data, the operators that compose a DSP application can be replicated and placed on multiple, possibly distributed, computing nodes, so to process the incoming data flow in parallel.

In this paper, we present Optimal DSP Replication and Placement (ODRP), a unified general formulation of the operator replication and placement problem that takes into account the heterogeneity of application requirements and infrastructural resources. A key feature of ODRP is the joint optimization of the operators replication and their placement. We evaluate the proposed model through a set of numerical experiments that demonstrates its flexibility and the benefits that derive from the joint optimization.

CCS Concepts

•Software and its engineering → Distributed systems organizing principles;

Keywords

Data stream processing, Operator placement, Replication, QoS

1. INTRODUCTION

Today we have access to a huge amount of data from which we would like to extract valuable information, e.g., analysis of customers sentiment from social network data, prediction of health problems from wearable devices, optimization of the transportation system in response to social events. The volume and velocity of daily produced data have fostered the development of new processing approaches that rely on the usage of multiple computing machines. Nowadays, two opposite approaches are commonly adopted: batch processing and stream processing. The former stores all the data, usually on a distributed file system, and then operates on them on the basis of different programming models, among which the well-known MapReduce [4]. The latter processes all the data on-the-fly, i.e., without storing them, so it can produce results in a near real-time fashion. Therefore, Data Stream Processing (DSP) applications are widely used to process unbounded streams of data and timely extract valuable information. We focus on this kind of applications.

DSP applications can be represented relying on a directed acyclic graph (DAG), with data sources, operators, and final consumers as vertices, and streams as edges. Each *operator* can be seen as a black-box processing element that continuously receives incoming streams, applies a transformation, and generates new outgoing streams. In the Big Data era, DSP applications should deal with a great amount of incoming load, so there is the need of scaling their execution on multiple computing nodes, because a single machine cannot provide enough processing power. To this end, these applications usually exploit *data parallelism*, which consists in increasing or decreasing the number of parallel instances for the operators, so that each instance can process a subset of the incoming data flow in parallel (e.g., [7, 10]). Moreover, since data sources can be geographically distributed, the execution of DSP applications can also take advantage of the ever increasing presence of distributed Cloud and Fog computing resources,which can improve the system scalability and reduce latency by moving the computation towards the network edge, closer to data sources. Nevertheless, the use of such distributed infrastructure poses new challenges, that include network and system heterogeneity, geographic distribution as well as non-negligible network latencies [14].

In this paper, we address the problem of determining the degree of replication of the DSP operators and their placement over a set of distributed computing nodes. Building on our previous work [2], we present Optimal DSP Replication and Placement (**ODRP**). Differently from most works in literature [5, 11, 12, 15], **ODRP** provides a unified formulation of the replication and placement problem, which allows us to jointly optimize the placement and replication of the DSP application's operators, while maximizing the Quality of Service (QoS) attributes of the application.

VALUETOOLS 2016, October 25-28, Taormina, Italy

Beside computing the optimal placement and degree of parallelism of the operators, ODRP provides a benchmark against which other centralized and decentralized placement and replication algorithms can be evaluated.

The rest of this paper is organized as follows. We review related work in Section 2; in Section 3 we describe the system model and the problem under investigation and formulate ODRP as an Integer Linear Programming (ILP) problem in Section 4. We evaluate the flexibility and the benefits of ODRP through numerical experiments in Section 5 and conclude with Section 6.

2. RELATED WORK

Most works in literature consider DSP operator placement and operator replication as independent and orthogonal decisions, where the operator placement is first carried out without determining the optimal number of replicas for each operator. Then, in response to some performance deterioration, the operators to be replicated and their new replication degree are identified. This two-stage approach requires to reschedule the DSP application in order to take the new application configuration into account and may incur in a significant overhead. In this paper, we propose a *single-stage* approach to determine both the placement and the parallelism degree of the operators in a DSP application.

The DSP placement problem has been widely investigated in literature under different modeling assumptions and optimization goals, e.g., [2, 5, 15]. In [2] we proposed a general formulation of the optimal DSP placement which takes into account the heterogeneity of computing and networking resources and which encompasses the different solutions proposed in the literature. In this paper, we extend that formulation in such a way to determine the optimal number of replicas for each operator contextually to their placement on the underlying computing and networking resources.

Since the placement problem is NP-hard, several heuristics have been proposed, e.g. [1, 13, 16]. They aim at minimizing a diversity of utility functions, such as the DSP application end-to-end latency, the inter-node traffic, and the network usage. Our problem formulation can be adjusted to take into account these different utility functions.

A consistent number of research works have focused on scaling the amount of operator replicas in response to changes observed in some monitored performance metric. Some works, e.g., [3, 9], exploit threshold-based policies based on the utilization of either the system nodes or the operator instances. Other works, e.g., [7, 11, 12], use more complex policies to determine the scaling decisions. Lohrmann et al. [11] propose a strategy that enforces latency constraints by relying on a predictive latency model based on queueing theory. Mencagli [12] presents a game-theoretic approach where the control logic is distributed on each operator.

An important issue related to operator replication regards the stateful operators, that require state migration to preserve the application integrity [7]. The approach we propose in this paper jointly places and replicates operators, thus saving the overhead and latency penalty incurred by stateful operator migrations in case of disjointed replication and placement decisions.

The works most closely related to ours have been presented by Heinze et al. [8, 10]. They propose a model to estimate the latency spike created by a set of operator movements and use it to define an operator placement algorithm based on a bin packing heuristic that minimizes the latency violations and focuses only on the placement of the newly added operators. We present an optimal problem formulation that targets the initial placement decision and can be used to benchmark existing heuristics.

So far, we have considered the replication of operators, that is a kind of scale out/in at the DSP application level and thus changes the processing graph topology; a different kind of replication exploited in literature occurs at the level of the computing resources assigned to each DSP operator [6].

Storm, Spark Streaming, and Flink, which are the most popular open-source DSP frameworks, use directed graphs to model DSP applications and therefore our problem formulation can be integrated into their scheduler; however, they require to manually tune the amount of replicas for each operator. We postpone to future work the development into Storm of the proposed approach, for whom we will exploit our previous prototypes presented in [2, 3].

Table 1: Main notation adopted in the paper.

Symbol	Description
G_{dsp}	Graph representing the DSP application
V_{dsp}	Set of vertices (operators) of G_{dsp}
E_{dsp}	Set of edges (streams) of G_{dsp}
C_i	Cost of deploying operator $i \in V_{dsp}$
R_i	Latency of $i \in V_{dsp}$ on a reference processor
Res_i	Resources required to execute $i \in V_{dsp}$
$\lambda_{(i,j)}$	Average tuple rate exchanged on $(i,j) \in E_{dsp}$
$b_{(i,j)}$	Avg. number of byte per tuple on $(i,j) \in E_{dsp}$
G_{res}	Graph representing computing and network resources
V_{res}	Set of vertices (computing nodes) of G_{res}
E_{res}	Set of edges (logical links) of G_{res}
A_u	Availability of node $u \in V_{res}$
Res_u	Amount of resources available on $u \in V_{res}$
S_u	Processing speed-up of $u \in V_{res}$
$A_{(u,v)}$	Availability of $(u,v) \in E_{res}$
$C_{(u,v)}$	Transmission cost per data on $(u,v) \in E_{res}$
$d_{(u,v)}$	Network delay on $(u,v) \in E_{res}$
$V_{res}^i \subseteq V_{res}$	Subset of nodes where $i \in V_{dsp}$ can be placed
$\mathcal{X} \sqsubset X$	Multiset of elements in X
$x_{i,\mathcal{U}}$	Placement of $i \in V_{dsp}$ on nodes in $\mathcal{U} \sqsubset V_{res}^i$
$y_{(i,j),(\mathcal{U},\mathcal{V})}$	Placement of $(i,j) \in E_{dsp}$ on the network paths from nodes in $\mathcal{U} \sqsubset V_{res}^i$ to nodes in $\mathcal{V} \sqsubset V_{res}^j$
z_u	Activation variable for $u \in V_{res}$
$z_{(u,v)}$	Activation variable for $(u,v) \in E_{res}$

3. SYSTEM MODEL AND PROBLEM STATEMENT

In this section we present the DSP application and resource model and define the operator replication and placement problem. For the sake of clarity, in Table 1 we summarize the notation used throughout the paper.

3.1 Abstract DSP Model

A DSP application can be represented at different levels of abstraction. The DSP *abstract model* defines the streams and their characteristics, along with the type, role and granularity of the stream processing elements. At this level, the DSP application can be regarded as a network of operators connected by streams. An operator is a self-contained processing element that carries out a specific operation (e.g., filtering, aggregation, merging) or something more complex (e.g., POS-tagging), whereas a stream is an unbounded sequence of data (e.g., packet, tuple, file chunk).

A DSP abstract model can be represented as a labeled directed acyclic graph (DAG) $G_{dsp} = (V_{dsp}, E_{dsp})$, where the nodes in V_{dsp} represent the application operators as well as the data stream sources (i.e., nodes without incoming links) and sinks (i.e., nodes without outgoing links), and the links in E_{dsp} represent the streams, i.e., data flows, between nodes. Due to the difficulties of formalizing the non-functional attributes of an abstract operator, we characterize the operator with the non-functional attributes of a reference implementation on a reference architecture: Res_i, the amount of resources required for its execution; R_i, the operator latency (which accounts for the waiting time on the input queues as well as the execution time of a unit of data); C_i, the cost of deploying an instance of the operator. We characterize the stream exchanged from operator i to j, $(i, j) \in E_{dsp}$, with its average tuple rate $\lambda_{(i,j)}$ and average number of bytes per tuple $b_{(i,j)}$. To model load-dependent latency, we assume that the latency is function of λ_i, the operator input tuple rate, $R_i = R_i(\lambda_i)$, where $\lambda_i = \sum_{j \in V_{dsp}} \lambda_{(j,i)}$; without loss of generality, we also assume that R_i is an increasing function in λ_i. In this paper, we assume that Res_i is a scalar value, but our placement model can be easily extended to consider Res_i as a vector of required resources.

3.2 Resource Model

Computing and network resources can be represented as a labeled fully connected directed graph $G_{res} = (V_{res}, E_{res})$, where the set of nodes V_{res} represents the distributed computing resources, and the set of links E_{res} represents the *logical connectivity* between nodes. Observe that, at this level, links represent the logical links across the networks corresponding to the network paths between nodes (as determined by the network operator routing strategies). Each node $u \in V_{res}$ is characterized by Res_u, the amount of resources available at node u; S_u, the processing speed-up on a reference processor; and A_u, its availability, i.e., the probability that u is up and running. Each link $(u, v) \in E_{res}$, with $u, v \in V_{res}$ is characterized by: $d_{(u,v)}$, the network delay between node u and v; $A_{(u,v)}$, the link availability, i.e., the probability that the link between u and v is active; and, $C_{(u,v)}$, the cost per unit of data transmitted along the network path between u and v. This model considers also edges of the type (u, u); they capture network connectivity between operators placed in the same node u, and are considered as perfect links, i.e., always active with no network delay. We assume that the considered QoS attributes can be obtained by means of either active/passive measurements or with some network support (e.g., SDN).

3.3 Operator Replication and Placement

The DSP replication and placement problem consists in determining, for each operator $i \in V_{dsp}$, the number of replicas and where to deploy them on the computing nodes in V_{res}. Operators do not necessarily need to be mapped to a single node. In general, in order to improve performance, multiple instances of the same DSP operator can be instantiated over different computing nodes. The premise is that by partitioning the streams over multiple processing elements, we reduce the load of each processing element which in turn yields lower operator (and overall application) latency. Figure 1 represents a simple instance of the problem. Observe that a DSP operator cannot be usually placed on every node in V_{res}, because of physical (i.e., *pinned* operator) or other motivations (e.g., security, privacy). This observation allows us to consider for each operator $i \in V_{dsp}$ a subset of candidate resources $V^i_{res} \subseteq V_{res}$ where it can be deployed. For example, if sources and sinks ($I \subset V_{dsp}$) are external applications, their placement is fixed, that is $\forall i \in I, |V^i_{res}| = 1$.

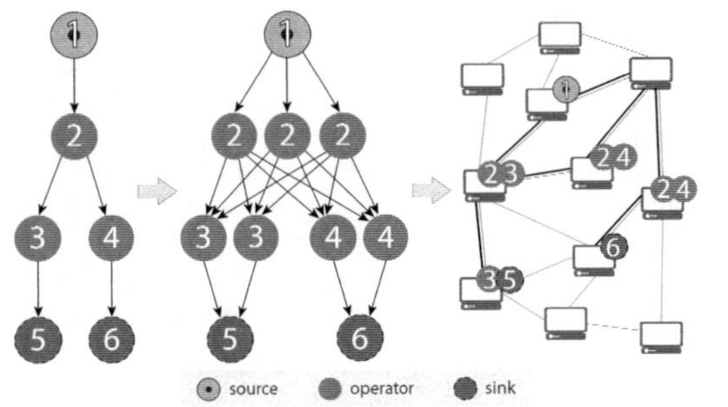

Figure 1: Replication of the application operators and their placement on the computing resources

The operator placement can be represented by a function *map* which maps an operator $i \in V_{dsp}$ to a multiset of computing nodes in V^i_{res}. We recur to multisets because a deployment can place multiple replicas of the same operator on the same computing node. For instance, $map(i) = \{u, u, v\}$, $i \in V_{dsp}$, $u, v \in V^i_{res}$, indicates that operator i deployment consists of 3 replicas, two of which on node u and one on node v. A multiset $\mathcal{X}$ over a set X, which we denote as $\mathcal{X} \sqsubset X$, is defined as a mapping $\mathcal{X} : X \to \mathbb{N}$ where for $x \in X$, $\mathcal{X}(x)$ denotes the multiplicity of x in $\mathcal{X}$. $x \in \mathcal{X}$ if and only if $\mathcal{X}(x) \geq 1$. The cardinality of a multiset $\mathcal{X}$, denoted $|\mathcal{X}|$, is defined by the number of elements in $\mathcal{X}$, that is $|\mathcal{X}| = \sum_{x \in \mathcal{X}} \mathcal{X}(x)$. Hereafter, without lack of generality, we will assume that in a deployment each operator $i \in V_{dsp}$ can be replicated at most k_i times.

We also find convenient to define the power multiset $\mathcal{P}(X)$ of a set X as the set of all multisets with elements taken from X and the subset $\mathcal{P}(X; k) \subset \mathcal{P}(X)$ of the multiset over X with cardinality no greater of k, that is $\mathcal{P}(X; k) = \{\mathcal{X} \in \mathcal{P}(X) | \sum_{x \in \mathcal{X}} \mathcal{X}(x) \leq k\}$.

4. OPTIMAL REPLICATION AND PLACEMENT MODEL

In this section we present our model for the ODRP problem. As the optimal solution depends on non-functional attributes, we first derive the expression for the different QoS metrics of interest and then present the ODRP formulation.

4.1 ODRP Variables

We model the ODRP problem with binary variables $x_{i,\mathcal{U}}$, $i \in V_{dsp}$ and $\mathcal{U} \sqsubset V^i_{res}$: $x_{i,\mathcal{U}} = 1$ if and only if the operator $map(i) = \mathcal{U}$, that is, i is replicated in $|\mathcal{U}|$ instances with exactly $\mathcal{U}(u)$ copies deployed in u, with $u \in \mathcal{U}$.

We also find convenient to consider binary variables associated to links, namely $y_{(i,j),(\mathcal{U},\mathcal{V})}$, $(i, j) \in E_{dsp}$, $\mathcal{U} \sqsubset V^i_{res}$, $\mathcal{V} \sqsubset V^j_{res}$, which denotes whether the data stream flowing from operator i to operator j traverses the network paths from nodes in $\mathcal{U}$ to nodes in $\mathcal{V}$. By definition, we have $y_{(i,j),(\mathcal{U},\mathcal{V})} = x_{i,\mathcal{U}} \wedge x_{j,\mathcal{V}}$.

Finally, we also consider the variables z_u, $u \in V_{res}$ which denote whether at least an operator is deployed on node u and the variables $z_{(u,v)}$, $(u,v) \in E_{res}$ which denote whether a stream (or a portion of it) traverses the network path (u,v). By definition, we have $z_u = \vee_{i \in V_{dsp}, \mathcal{U} \in \mathcal{P}(V^i_{res};k_i)} x_{i,\mathcal{U}}$ and $z_{(u,v)} = \vee_{(i,j) \in E_{dsp}, \mathcal{U} \in \mathcal{P}(V^i_{res};k_i), \mathcal{V} \in \mathcal{P}(V^j_{res};k_j)} y_{(i,j),(\mathcal{U},\mathcal{V})}$.

For short, in the following we denote by $\boldsymbol{x}$ and $\boldsymbol{y}$ the placement vectors for nodes and edges, respectively, where $\boldsymbol{x} = \langle x_{i,\mathcal{U}} \rangle$, $\forall i \in V_{dsp}$, $\forall \mathcal{U} \in \mathcal{P}(V^i_{res};k_i)$, and $\boldsymbol{y} = \langle y_{(i,j),(\mathcal{U},\mathcal{V})} \rangle$, $\forall x_{i,\mathcal{U}}, x_{j,\mathcal{V}} \in \boldsymbol{x}$. Similarly, we denote by $\boldsymbol{z_V}$ and $\boldsymbol{z_E}$ the vectors $\boldsymbol{z_V} = \langle z_u \rangle$, $\forall u \in V_{res}$, and $\boldsymbol{z_E} = \langle z_{(u,v)} \rangle$, $\forall (u,v) \in E_{res}$.

4.2 Qos Metrics

4.2.1 Operator QoS Metrics

Let us first consider an operator in isolation. For each $i \in V_{dsp}$, the QoS of the operator deployment depends on the deployment $\mathcal{U}$. Let $R_{i,\mathcal{U}}$, $C_{i,\mathcal{U}}$, and $A_{i,\mathcal{U}}$ denote the maximum latency, the cost, and the availability of the deployment $\mathcal{U}$, respectively. We readily have:

$$R_{i,\mathcal{U}} = \max_{u \in \mathcal{U}} \frac{R_i(\frac{\lambda_i}{|\mathcal{U}|})}{S_u} \quad (1)$$

$$C_{i,\mathcal{U}} = \sum_{u \in \mathcal{U}} \mathcal{U}(u) C_i Res_i \quad (2)$$

$$A_{i,\mathcal{U}} = \prod_{u \in \mathcal{U}} A_u \quad (3)$$

under the assumption that the traffic is equally split among the different operator replicas.

4.2.2 Stream QoS Attributes

We now turn our attention to the QoS attributes related to a stream. For a stream (i,j), the QoS depends on the upstream and downstream operators' deployments $\mathcal{U}$ and $\mathcal{V}$. Let $d_{(i,j),(\mathcal{U},\mathcal{V})}$, $C_{(i,j),(\mathcal{U},\mathcal{V})}$, and $A_{(i,j),(\mathcal{U},\mathcal{V})}$ denote the maximum latency, the cost, and the availability of the deployments $\mathcal{U}$ and $\mathcal{V}$, respectively. We readily have:

$$d_{(i,j),(\mathcal{U},\mathcal{V})} = d_{(\mathcal{U},\mathcal{V})} = \max_{u \in \mathcal{U}, v \in \mathcal{V}} d_{(u,v)} \quad (4)$$

$$C_{(i,j),(\mathcal{U},\mathcal{V})} = \sum_{u \in \mathcal{U}, v \in \mathcal{V}} \lambda_{(i,j),(\mathcal{U},\mathcal{V})} C_{u,v} \quad (5)$$

$$A_{i,(\mathcal{U},\mathcal{V})} = \prod_{u \in \mathcal{U}, v \in \mathcal{V}} A_{(u,v)} \quad (6)$$

where

$$\lambda_{(i,j),(\mathcal{U},\mathcal{V})} = \frac{\lambda_{(i,j)}}{|\mathcal{U}||\mathcal{V}|} \quad u \in \mathcal{U}, v \in \mathcal{V} \quad (7)$$

is the amount of stream (i,j) traffic exchanged between two operator replicas under the deployments $\mathcal{U}$ and $\mathcal{V}$.

4.2.3 DSP Application QoS Metrics

We consider both user-oriented and system-oriented QoS metrics, such as application response time and availability for the former, and network related metrics for the latter.

Response Time: For a DSP application, with data flowing from several sources to several destinations, there is no unique definition of response time. In the following, we consider as response time R the worst end-to-end delay from a source to a sink. Given this definition, we have that:

$$R = \max_{p \in \pi_{G_{dsp}}} R_p \quad (8)$$

being R_p the delay along path p and $\pi_{G_{dsp}}$ the set of all source-sink paths in G_{dsp}. Given a placement vector $\boldsymbol{x}$ (and resulting $\boldsymbol{y}$) and a path $p = (i_1, i_2, \ldots, i_{n_p})$, we have $R = R(\boldsymbol{x}, \boldsymbol{y}) = \max_{p \in \pi_{G_{dsp}}} R_p(\boldsymbol{x}, \boldsymbol{y})$ with $R_p(\boldsymbol{x}, \boldsymbol{y})$ defined as:

$$R_p(\boldsymbol{x}, \boldsymbol{y}) = \sum_{k=1}^{n_p} R_{i_k}(\boldsymbol{x}) + \sum_{k=1}^{n_p - 1} D_{(i_k, i_{k+1})}(\boldsymbol{y}) \quad (9)$$

where

$$R_i(\boldsymbol{x}) = \sum_{\mathcal{U} \in \mathcal{P}(V^i_{res};k_i)} R_{i,\mathcal{U}} x_{i,\mathcal{U}} \quad (10)$$

$$D_{(i,j)}(\boldsymbol{y}) = \sum_{\substack{\mathcal{U} \in \mathcal{P}(V^i_{res};k_i) \\ \mathcal{V} \in \mathcal{P}(V^j_{res};k_j)}} d_{(\mathcal{U},\mathcal{V})} y_{(i,j),(\mathcal{U},\mathcal{V})} \quad (11)$$

denote respectively the execution time of operator i when deployed over the multiset $\mathcal{U}$ and the worst case network delay for transferring data from i to j when the two operators are mapped over $\mathcal{U}$ and $\mathcal{V}$, respectively.

Cost: We define the cost C of the DSP application as the monetary cost of all the computing resources and paths involved in the processing and transmission of the application data streams. We have:

$$C(\boldsymbol{x}, \boldsymbol{y}) = \sum_{i \in V_{dsp}} C_i(\boldsymbol{x}) + \sum_{(i,j) \in E_{dsp}} C_{(i,j)}(\boldsymbol{y}) \quad (12)$$

where

$$C_i(\boldsymbol{x}) = \sum_{\mathcal{U} \in \mathcal{P}(V^i_{res};k_i)} C_{i,\mathcal{U}} x_{i,\mathcal{U}} \quad (13)$$

$$C_{(i,j)}(\boldsymbol{y}) = \sum_{\substack{\mathcal{U} \in \mathcal{P}(V^i_{res};k_i) \\ \mathcal{V} \in \mathcal{P}(V^j_{res};k_j)}} C_{(i,j),(\mathcal{U},\mathcal{V})} y_{(i,j),(\mathcal{U},\mathcal{V})} \quad (14)$$

Availability: We define the application availability A as the availability of all the nodes and paths involved in the processing and transmission of the application data streams. For the sake of simplicity, we assume the availability of the different components to be independent. We acknowledge that independence does not hold true in general and that a more detailed model is needed to capture the dependency relationship among logical components sharing physical nodes and networks links; we postpone it to future work. With the independence assumption, we readily have:

$$A(\boldsymbol{z_V}, \boldsymbol{z_E}) = \prod_{u \in V_{res}: z_u = 1} A_u z_u \cdot \prod_{(u,v) \in E_{res}: z_{(u,v)} = 1} A_{(u,v)} z_{(u,v)} \quad (15)$$

To obtain a linear expression, we consider the logarithm of the availability, obtaining:

$$\log A(\boldsymbol{z_V}, \boldsymbol{z_E}) = \sum_{u \in V_{res}} a_u z_u + \sum_{(u,v) \in E_{res}} a_{(u,v)} z_{(u,v)} \quad (16)$$

where $a_u = \log A_u$ and $a_{(u,v)} = \log A_{(u,v)}$. It is worth observing that in (16) we can take the summation over all $u \in V_{res}$ and $(u,v) \in E_{res}$ since the terms not appearing in (15) are those corresponding to $z_u = 0$ or $z_{(u,v)} = 0$, which do not affect the summation in (16).

Network Related QoS Metrics: In the DSP literature, several alternative network-aware metrics have been defined, including the inter-node traffic T [1], the network usage N [16], and an approximation of the elastic energy EE [13]. Let $Z(\boldsymbol{y})$, $Z = T|N|EE$, denote the QoS attribute of the DSP application under the placement policy $\boldsymbol{y}$, we have:

$$Z(\boldsymbol{y}) = \sum_{(i,j)\in E_{dsp}} Z_{(i,j)}(\boldsymbol{y}) \tag{17}$$

where $Z_{(i,j)}(\boldsymbol{y})$ is defined as follows.

The *inter-node traffic* T is the overall amount of data exchanged per time unit between operators placed on different nodes. Therefore, using the placement policy $\boldsymbol{y}$, the stream $(i, j) \in E_{dsp}$ generates an inter-node traffic equals to:

$$T_{(i,j)}(\boldsymbol{y}) = \sum_{\substack{u\in\mathcal{U}, v\in\mathcal{V}, u\neq v\\ \mathcal{U}\in\mathcal{P}(V^i_{res};k_i)\\ \mathcal{V}\in\mathcal{P}(V^j_{res};k_j)}} b_{(i,j)}\lambda_{(i,j),(\mathcal{U},\mathcal{V})}y_{(i,j),(\mathcal{U},\mathcal{V})} \tag{18}$$

The *network usage* N is the amount of data that traverses the network at a given time; therefore, the stream $(i, j) \in E_{dsp}$ imposes a load expressed by:

$$N_{(i,j)}(\boldsymbol{y}) = \sum_{\substack{u\in\mathcal{U}, v\in\mathcal{V}, u\neq v\\ \mathcal{U}\in\mathcal{P}(V^i_{res};k_i)\\ \mathcal{V}\in\mathcal{P}(V^j_{res};k_j)}} b_{(i,j)}\lambda_{(i,j),(\mathcal{U},\mathcal{V})}d_{(u,v)}y_{(i,j),(\mathcal{U},\mathcal{V})} \tag{19}$$

where $d_{(u,v)}$ is the network delay among nodes $u, v \in V_{res}$, with $u \neq v$.

In their paper [13], Pietzuch et al. indirectly minimize the network usage through the minimization of the elastic energy, which results from the equivalent system of springs that represents the application. Basically, their solution minimizes the amount of data that traverses each link weighted by the latency of the link itself. Hence, the stream $(i, j) \in E_{dsp}$ contributes to the elastic energy of the system with:

$$EE_{(i,j)}(\boldsymbol{y}) = \sum_{\substack{u\in\mathcal{U}, v\in\mathcal{V}, u\neq v\\ \mathcal{U}\in\mathcal{P}(V^i_{res};k_i)\\ \mathcal{V}\in\mathcal{P}(V^j_{res};k_j)}} b_{(i,j)}\lambda_{(i,j),(\mathcal{U},\mathcal{V})}d^2_{(u,v)}y_{(i,j),(\mathcal{U},\mathcal{V})} \tag{20}$$

Observe that, in all cases, $Z(\boldsymbol{y})$ is a linear function of $\boldsymbol{y}$.

4.3 ODRP Formulation

Depending on the usage scenario, a DSP replication and placement strategy could be aimed at optimizing different, possibly conflicting, QoS attributes. To this end, we use the Simple Additive Weighting (SAW) technique [17] to define the utility function $F(\boldsymbol{x}, \boldsymbol{y}, \boldsymbol{z_V}, \boldsymbol{z_E})$ as a weighted sum of the normalized QoS attributes of the application, as follows:

$$F(\boldsymbol{x}, \boldsymbol{y}, \boldsymbol{z_V}, \boldsymbol{z_E}) = w_r\frac{R_{\max} - R(\boldsymbol{x}, \boldsymbol{y})}{R_{\max} - R_{\min}} + w_a\frac{\log A(\boldsymbol{z_V}, \boldsymbol{z_E}) - \log A_{\min}}{\log A_{\max} - \log A_{\min}} + w_c\frac{C_{\max} - C(\boldsymbol{x}, \boldsymbol{y})}{C_{\max} - C_{\min}} + w_z\frac{Z_{\max} - Z(\boldsymbol{x}, \boldsymbol{y})}{Z_{\max} - Z_{\min}} \tag{21}$$

where w_r, w_a, w_c, $w_z \geq 0$, $w_r + w_a + w_c + w_z = 1$, are weights associated to the different QoS attributes. $R_{\max}$ ($R_{\min}$), $A_{\max}$ ($A_{\min}$), $C_{\max}$ ($C_{\min}$), and $Z_{\max}$ ($Z_{\min}$) denote, respectively, the maximum (minimum) value for the overall expected response time, availability, cost and network related metric. Observe that after normalization, each metric ranges in the interval $[0, 1]$.

We formulate the ODRP problem as an Integer Linear Programming (ILP) model as follows:

$$\max_{\boldsymbol{x},\boldsymbol{y},r} F'(\boldsymbol{x}, \boldsymbol{y}, \boldsymbol{z_V}, \boldsymbol{z_E}, r)$$

subject to:

$$r \geq \sum_{\substack{k=1,\dots,n_p\\ \mathcal{U}\in\mathcal{P}(V^i_{res};k_i)}} R_{i,\mathcal{U}}x_{i,\mathcal{U}} + \sum_{\substack{k=1,\dots,n_p=1\\ \mathcal{U}\in\mathcal{P}(V^i_{res};k_i)\\ \mathcal{V}\in\mathcal{P}(V^j_{res};k_j)}} d_{(\mathcal{U},\mathcal{V})}y_{(i,j),(\mathcal{U},\mathcal{V})} \quad \forall p \in \pi_G \tag{22}$$

$$Res_u \geq \sum_{\substack{i\in V_{dsp}\\ \mathcal{U}\in\mathcal{P}(V^i_{res})}} \mathcal{U}(u)Res_i x_{i,\mathcal{U}} \quad \forall u \in V_{res} \tag{23}$$

$$z_u \geq \frac{\sum_{\substack{i\in V_{dsp}\\ \mathcal{U}\in\mathcal{P}(V^i_{res};k_i)}} x_{i,\mathcal{U}}}{M} \quad u \in V_{res} \tag{24}$$

$$z_{(u,v)} \geq \frac{\sum_{\substack{(i,j)\in E_{dsp}\\ \mathcal{U}\in\mathcal{P}(V^i_{res};k_i)\\ \mathcal{V}\in\mathcal{P}(V^j_{res};k_j)}} y_{(i,j),(\mathcal{U},\mathcal{V})}}{N} \quad (u,v) \in E_{res} \tag{25}$$

$$\sum_{\mathcal{U}\in\mathcal{P}(V^i_{res};k_i)} x_{i,\mathcal{U}} = 1 \quad \forall i \in V_{dsp} \tag{26}$$

$$x_{i,\mathcal{U}} = \sum_{\mathcal{V}\in\mathcal{P}(V^j_{res};k_j)} y_{(i,j),(\mathcal{U},\mathcal{V})} \quad \forall (i,j)\in E_{dsp}, \mathcal{U}\in\mathcal{P}(V^i_{res};k_i) \tag{27}$$

$$x_{j,\mathcal{V}} = \sum_{\mathcal{U}\in\mathcal{P}(V^i_{res};k_u)} y_{(i,j),(\mathcal{U},\mathcal{V})} \quad \forall (i,j)\in E_{dsp}, \mathcal{V}\in\mathcal{P}(V^j_{res};k_j) \tag{28}$$

$$x_{i,\mathcal{U}} \in \{0,1\} \quad \forall i\in V_{dsp}, \mathcal{U}\in\mathcal{P}(V^i_{res};k_i) \tag{29}$$

$$y_{(i,j),(\mathcal{U},\mathcal{V})} \in \{0,1\} \quad \forall (i,j)\in E_{dsp}, \mathcal{U}\in\mathcal{P}(V^i_{res};k_i), \mathcal{V}\in\mathcal{P}(V^j_{res};k_j) \tag{30}$$

$$z_u \in \{0,1\} \quad \forall u \in V_{res} \tag{31}$$

$$z_{(u,v)} \in \{0,1\} \quad \forall (u,v) \in E_{res} \tag{32}$$

In the problem formulation we use the objective function $F'(\boldsymbol{x}, \boldsymbol{y}, \boldsymbol{z_V}, \boldsymbol{z_E}, r)$ that is obtained from $F(\boldsymbol{x}, \boldsymbol{y}, \boldsymbol{z_V}, \boldsymbol{z_E})$ by replacing $R(\boldsymbol{x}, \boldsymbol{y})$ with the auxiliary variable r, which represents the application response time in the optimization problem, in order to obtain a linear objective function. Observe that, indeed, while F is nonlinear in $\boldsymbol{x}$, $\boldsymbol{y}$ since $R(\boldsymbol{x}, \boldsymbol{y}) = \max_{p\in\pi_{G_{dsp}}} R_p(\boldsymbol{x}, \boldsymbol{y})$ is a nonlinear term, F' is linear in r as well as in $\boldsymbol{x}$ and $\boldsymbol{y}$. Equation (22) follows from (8)–(11). Since r must be larger or equal than the response time of any path and, at the optimum, r is minimized, $r = \max_{p\in\pi_{G_{dsp}}} R_p(\boldsymbol{x}, \boldsymbol{y}) = R(\boldsymbol{x}, \boldsymbol{y})$. The constraint (23) limits the placement of operators on a node $u \in V_{res}$ ac-

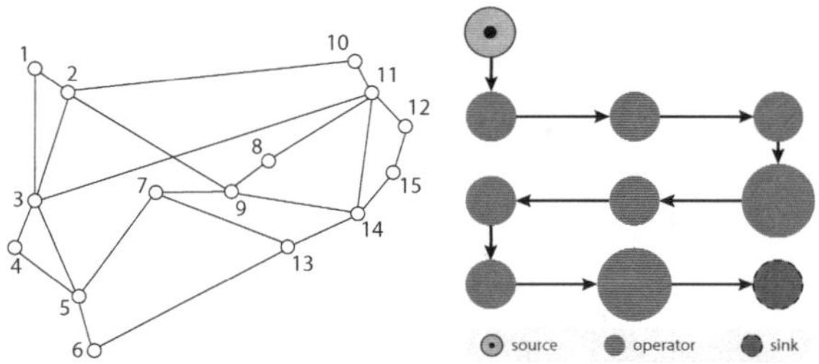

(a) Subset of ANSNET nodes (b) Reference application

Figure 2: Reference infrastructure and DSP application

cording to its available resources. Constraints (24) and (25) are the activation constraints for the variable z_u and $z_{(u,v)}$, respectively, with M and N large constants. Equation (26) guarantees that each operator $i \in V_{dsp}$ is placed on one and only one node $u \in V_{res}^i$. Finally, constraints (27)–(28) model the logical **AND** between the placement variables, that is, $y_{(i,j),(u,v)} = x_{i,u} \wedge x_{j,v}$.

THEOREM 1. *The ODRP problem is an NP-hard problem.*

PROOF. It is sufficient to observe that the Optimal DSP Replication and Placement problem is a generalization of the Optimal DSP Placement problem we presented in [2], which has been shown to be NP-hard. □

5. EXPERIMENTAL RESULTS

We evaluate the ODRP model through a set of numerical experiments that aim at demonstrating the flexibility of the formulation and the benefits that derive from the joint optimization of operators placement and replication. We analyze in Section 5.2 how the ODRP formulation allows us to consider the optimization of several QoS metrics, such as response time, cost, availability, and inter-node traffic. Then, in Section 5.3 we show the impact of replication when the DSP application is subject to an increasing load.

5.1 Experimental Setup

The ODRP model allows us to define the operators placement and replication by optimizing different QoS attributes, whose importance depends on the utilization scenario.

We solve the ILP problem using CPLEX© (version 12.6.2) on an Amazon EC2 virtual machine (c4.xlarge with 4 vCPU and 7.5 GB RAM). In the experiments, G_{res} models a portion of ANSNET, a geographically distributed network where 15 computing nodes are interconnected with non-negligible network delays. Within this network, we assume that a logical link $(u, v) \in E_{res}$ between any two computing resources $u, v \in V_{res}$ always exists; each logic link results by the underlying physical network paths, which are represented in Figure 2a, and a shortest-path routing strategy.

As reference application, we consider the topology represented in Figure 2b, which is made of a sequence of 10 operators, where the first and last one are respectively the source and sink. If not otherwise specified, the application includes two CPU-intensive operators, represented with a bigger shape, which require twice of the computing resources Res_i and have a service time five times longer than the other operators. We summarize the application and infrastructure configuration parameters in Table 2.

Table 2: Parameters of the experimental setup

Processing and network resources

Parameter	Value	Parameter	Value
$\|V_{res}\|$	15	$A_{(u,v)}$	100 %
A_u	Uniform in [97, 99.99999] %	$C_{(u,v)}$	0.02
Res_u	5	avg $d_{(u,v)}$	32 ms
S_u	1.0		

Application

Parameter	Value	Parameter	Value
$\|V_{dsp}\|$	10	Res_i	1
C_i	1	μ_i	0.02 ms^{-1}
$R_i(\lambda_i/\|\mathcal{U}\|)$	$\frac{1}{\mu_i - \lambda_i/\|\mathcal{U}\|}$ ms	$b_{(i,j)}$	1500 B/tuple
λ_i	14 tuples/s		

Normalization factors for the ODRP utility function

Parameter	Value	Parameter	Value
$R_{\min}$	1230 ms	$R_{\max}$	2810 ms
$A_{\min}$	85 %	$A_{\max}$	98.8 %
$C_{\min}$	11.0	$C_{\max}$	25.0
$Z_{\min}$	8.0 KB/s	$Z_{\max}$	40.0 KB/s

We rely on ODRP to define the optimal placement and replication of each operator but the source and sink, which are placed a-priori. In the experiments, we assume that each operator can be replicated at most twice (i.e., $k_i = 2$, $\forall i$), while the source and sink are not replicated. In the ODRP model, we obtain the response time R_i of the operator i subject to the incoming load $\lambda_i/|\mathcal{U}|$ by modeling the underlying computing node as an M/M/1 queue.

5.2 Joint Optimization of Operator Placement and Replication

This first experiment evaluates the effect on QoS metrics of different optimization objectives. We first compute the replication and placement solution by optimizing a single QoS metric. For example, to optimize the response time we set the weights as $w_r = 1$, $w_a = w_c = w_z = 0$. Then, we optimize the multi-objective function by uniformly weighting each metrics contribution (i.e., $w_r = w_a = w_c = w_z = 0.25$); we report in Table 2 the normalization factors used in Equation (21). Since the position of data source and sink affects the optimal solution, we execute a run for each configuration that results by pinning these components on every pair of distinct nodes. Figure 3 presents the results in term of the different QoS metrics. For each optimization objective, a boxplot represents the performance distribution that results from the different locations of data source and sink. Each boxplot reports the minimum value, the 5th percentile, the median, the 95th percentile, and the maximum value.

When ODRP optimizes the response time R, the solution achieves the minimum achievable response time, as shown in Figure 3a, but also requires that all the operators are replicated, as shown in Figure 3d. Since the cost of running a configuration is directly proportional to the total number of operator instances, this is also the most expensive solution. We can also observe from Figure 3b that the inter-node traffic is indirectly minimized, because transmitting data over the network rather than locally introduces network delays that penalize the response time.

When ODRP optimizes the cost C, the placement solution tries to use less computing resources as possible, therefore no operator is replicated as shown in Figure 3d. This strategy penalizes the response time which almost doubles

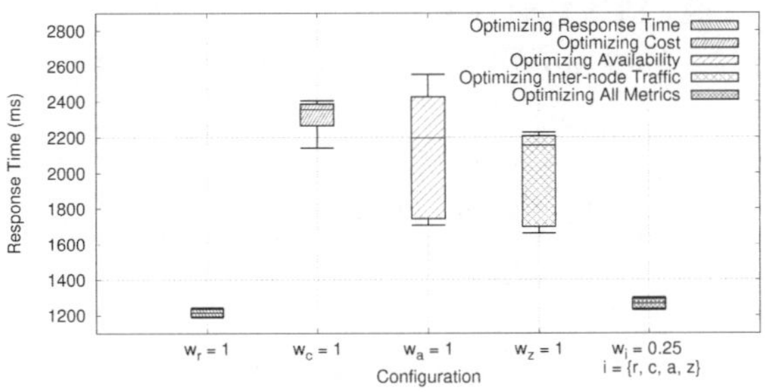

(a) Application response time

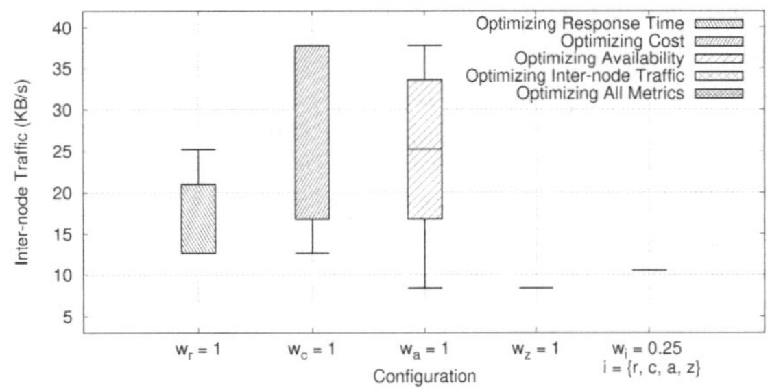

(b) Inter-node traffic

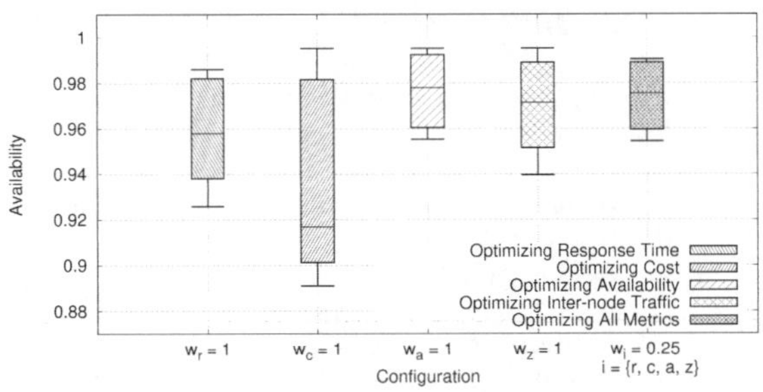

(c) Application availability

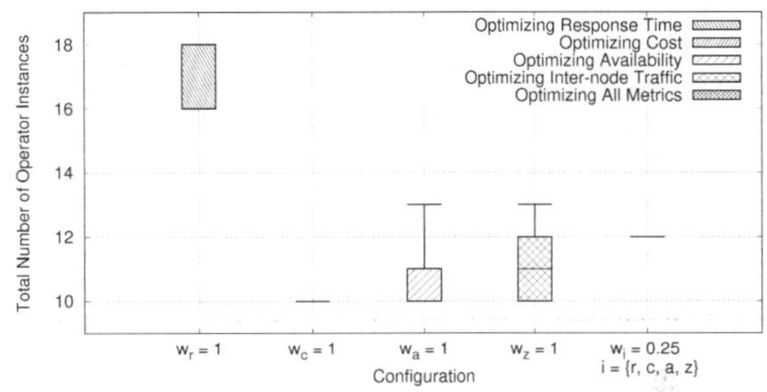

(d) Total number of operator instances

Figure 3: Impact of different optimization objectives on the QoS metrics

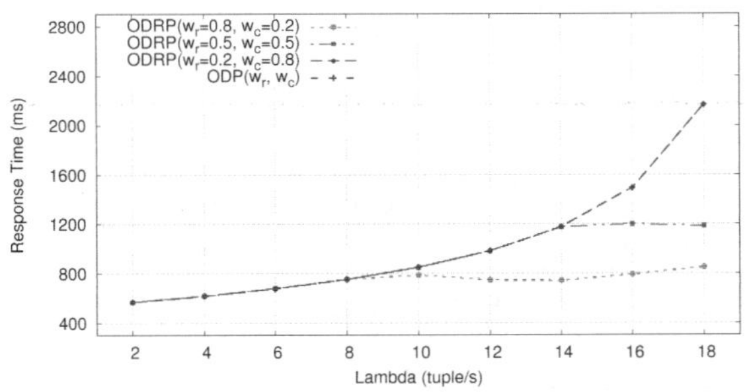

(a) Response time

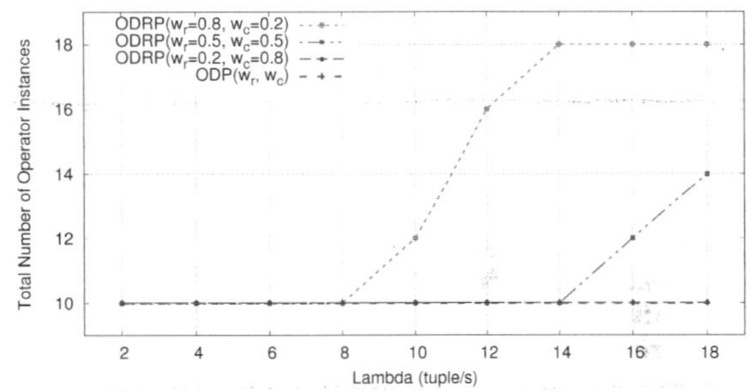

(b) Total number of operator instances

Figure 4: Impact of replication on the application performance

with respect to the minimum value, as shown in Figure 3a. Nothing can be concluded about the application availability (Figure 3c) and inter-node traffic (Figure 3b): since these metrics are not optimized, there is a set of equally optimal solutions that differ each other only in the operator placement on the same set of computing resources.

At a first sight, the results obtained when ODRP optimizes the application availability seem to be unexpected, because, as shown in Figure 3c, the application availability is not maximized. However, this behavior can be easily explained recalling that the data source and sink are placed a-priori on each pair of computing nodes, so their availability drives the overall application availability. In some cases ODRP increases the number of operator instances to improve the application availability: from Figure 3d, we can see that the maximum number of instances in this configuration is 13, i.e., 3 operators are replicated with degree 2.

When ODRP optimizes the inter-node traffic, the solution tries to co-locate the operator instances on the least number of nodes, so to reduce the amount of data transmitted over the network (see Figure 3b). An interesting behavior is highlighted by Figure 3d: sometimes ODRP takes advantage of replication in order to reduce the amount of data transmitted on the network; this behavior is analytically explained by Equation (7).

When ODRP optimizes all the considered QoS metrics, the resulting placement and replication solution has a response time (Figure 3a) and an inter-node traffic (Figure 3b) which are very close to the values achievable when optimizing a single-objective function. The total number of operator instances is always equal to 12, as shown in Figure 3d, therefore only two operators are replicated. Recalling the topology of our application, we can readily identify that these two replicated operators are the application bottlenecks.

5.3 Impact of Replication

In the last experiment we want to investigate the replication benefits when the application is subject to an increasing traffic load. Differently from the previous experiment, now each operator emits only 95 % of the incoming data; in this way, every operator imposes a different load which decreases from the source to the sink. We compare the performance achieved by ODRP with ODP, which optimizes only the operator placement [2]. Note that ODP is a special case of ODRP where $k_i = 1, \forall i \in V_{dsp}$. Both the models are solved with the following configurations of weights: $(w_r = 0.8, w_c = 0.2)$, $(w_r = 0.5, w_c = 0.5)$, and $(w_r = 0.2, w_c = 0.8)$. The other weights are set to 0. In Figure 4 we indicate with "ODP(w_r, w_c)" the curves obtained by ODP under the different weight configurations, which overlap one another. Note also that "ODP(w_r, w_c)" overlaps with "ODRP$(w_r = 0.2, w_c = 0.8)$".

During the experiment, the incoming load increases from 2 to 18 tuples/s, therefore the bottleneck operator imposes a load on the underlying computing node that ranges from 10% to 90% of its capacity. Although ODP cannot replicate the operators, it can find the optimal placement that minimizes the response time. As shown in Figure 4a, when the system becomes overloaded, i.e., after 14 tuples/s, the response time grows quickly, up to become 4 times higher than the case of medium load. A similar result is obtained when ODRP is configured with $(w_r = 0.2, w_c = 0.8)$: being the application cost much more important than the response time, ODRP tries not to replicate the operators. The opposite result is achieved when ODRP is configured with $(w_r = 0.8, w_c = 0.2)$, because replication is exploited to reduce the application response time. Figure 4b shows the number of operator instances. We can observe that, when the incoming load exceeds 8 tuples/s, ODRP with $(w_r = 0.8, w_c = 0.2)$ starts replicating the bottleneck operators one by one up to 18 instances, i.e., when every operator is replicated. As shown in Figure 4a, this strategy is beneficial for the response time, which does not increase more than 1.5 times with respect to the case of lightly loaded system.

6. CONCLUSIONS

In this paper, we presented ODRP, an ILP formulation that jointly optimizes the replication and placement of DSP applications. ODRP is a general and flexible model that can take into account the heterogeneity of computing and networking resources and can be conveniently configured to optimize different QoS metrics, whose importance depends on the application scenario. The experimental evaluation has validated the proposed model and has shown the benefits of a joint optimization of the operators placement and their replication on the application performance.

As future work, we plan to develop efficient heuristics to deal with large problem instances for the initial application replication and placement. Moreover, we plan to extend our model in order to support on-line reconfigurations, where the operator deployment needs to be adapted at run-time to properly handle input streams or execution environments with continuously changing properties.

7. ACKNOWLEDGMENTS

This publication is supported by COST Action ACROSS (IC1304).

8. REFERENCES

[1] L. Aniello, R. Baldoni, and L. Querzoni. Adaptive online scheduling in Storm. In *Proc. of ACM DEBS '13*, pages 207–218, 2013.

[2] V. Cardellini, V. Grassi, F. Lo Presti, and M. Nardelli. Optimal operator placement for distributed stream processing applications. In *Proc. of ACM DEBS '16*, pages 69–80, 2016.

[3] V. Cardellini, M. Nardelli, and D. Luzi. Elastic stateful stream processing in Storm. In *Proc. of HPCS '16*, pages 583–590. IEEE, 2016.

[4] J. Dean and S. Ghemawat. MapReduce: Simplified data processing on large clusters. In *Proc. of OSDI '04*. USENIX Association, 2004.

[5] R. Eidenbenz and T. Locher. Task allocation for distributed stream processing. In *Proc. of IEEE INFOCOM '16*, 2016.

[6] T. Z. J. Fu, J. Ding, R. T. B. Ma, M. Winslett, et al. DRS: Dynamic resource scheduling for real-time analytics over fast streams. In *Proc. of IEEE ICDCS 2015*, pages 411–420, 2015.

[7] B. Gedik, S. Schneider, M. Hirzel, and K.-L. Wu. Elastic scaling for data stream processing. *IEEE Trans. Parallel Distrib. Syst.*, 25(6):1447–1463, 2014.

[8] T. Heinze, Z. Jerzak, G. Hackenbroich, and C. Fetzer. Latency-aware elastic scaling for distributed data stream processing systems. In *Proc. of ACM DEBS '14*, pages 13–22, 2014.

[9] T. Heinze, V. Pappalardo, Z. Jerzak, and C. Fetzer. Auto-scaling techniques for elastic data stream processing. In *Proc. of IEEE ICDEW '14*, pages 296–302, 2014.

[10] T. Heinze, L. Roediger, A. Meister, Y. Ji, et al. Online parameter optimization for elastic data stream processing. In *Proc. of ACM SoCC '15*, pages 276–287, 2015.

[11] B. Lohrmann, P. Janacik, and O. Kao. Elastic stream processing with latency guarantees. In *Proc. of IEEE ICDCS '15*, pages 399–410, 2015.

[12] G. Mencagli. A game-theoretic approach for elastic distributed data stream processing. *ACM Trans. on Autonomous and Adaptive Systems*, 11(2), 2016.

[13] P. Pietzuch, J. Ledlie, J. Shneidman, M. Roussopoulos, et al. Network-aware operator placement for stream-processing systems. In *Proc. of IEEE ICDE '06*, 2006.

[14] W. Shi, J. Cao, Q. Zhang, Y. Li, and L. Xu. Edge computing: Vision and challenges. *IEEE Internet of Things J.*, 3(5):637–646, Oct. 2016.

[15] C. Thoma, A. Labrinidis, and A. Lee. Automated operator placement in distributed data stream management systems subject to user constraints. In *Proc. of IEEE ICDEW '14*, pages 310–316, 2014.

[16] J. Xu, Z. Chen, J. Tang, and S. Su. T-Storm: traffic-aware online scheduling in Storm. In *Proc. of IEEE ICDCS '14*, pages 535–544, 2014.

[17] K. P. Yoon and C.-L. Hwang. *Multiple Attribute Decision Making: an Introduction.* Sage Pubns, 1995.

A Latency-Aware Reward Model Based Greedy Heuristic for the Virtual Network Embedding Problem

Francesco Bianchi
Department of Civil Engineering and
Computer Science Engineering
University of Rome "Tor Vergata", Italy
f.bianchi@ing.uniroma2.it

Francesco Lo Presti
Department of Civil Engineering and
Computer Science Engineering
University of Rome "Tor Vergata", Italy
lopresti@info.uniroma2.it

ABSTRACT

The increasing use of virtualization (e.g., in Cloud Computing, Software Defined Networks), demands to Infrastructure Providers (InPs) to optimize the placement of the virtual network requests (VNRs) into a substrate network. In addition to that, they need to cope with QoS, in particular for the rising number of time critical applications (e.g., healthcare, VoIP). Granting resource optimization along with QoS compliance, are two competing goals. In this work, we propose a two-stage virtual network embedding (VNE) algorithm, which maps first virtual nodes to substrate nodes based on a suitable latency-aware ranking algorithm and then maps links along the shortest paths, in terms of latencies. The central component of our approach is a new node ranking algorithm, MCRR-LA, based on Markov Reward Processes, which associates a metric that accounts for and well captures the amount of local resources combined with latency values available in the vicinity of a certain node. The metric is complemented with a Breadth-First search. We widely evaluated our algorithm through simulation. Our experiments point out that our algorithm is able to reduce the average path delay while granting good resource performances in terms of lower VNR blocking rate and higher revenues. We compared our algorithm with a previous two-stage approach obtaining good results useful to underline the strengths of the novel approach.

Keywords

Cloud computing; delay; latency; Markov chain; Markov reward process (MRP); network virtualization; node ranking; quality of service (QoS); random walk; topology-aware; virtual network embedding (VNE)

1. INTRODUCTION

The base for the future Internet is characterized by the Infrastructure as a Service (IaaS) service model [11], producing a decoupling of the ISP (Internet Service Provider) into two novel players: the Infrastructure Provider (InP) and the Service Provider (SP). The InPs (e.g., Cloud providers), who own and manage the infrastructure, rent out parts of the network resources to the SPs (e.g., Cloud users), who in turn meet the end-users demands, making virtual networks (VNs) and providing end-to-end services [10, 11]. In this very adaptive multi-layer architecture, the InPs have the challenging task to manage the substrate network efficiently in order to maximize the number of mapped virtual network requests (VNRs) along with the revenue. In practice, the InPs have to determine, on-line, a subset of physical nodes and links with sufficient resources to host each VNR composed by a set of virtual nodes and links with a certain amount of resource attributes, e.g., computational capacity, link bandwidth.

This problem is referred to as Virtual Network Embedding (VNE) which is a well known NP-complete problem [1, 22]. In order to support on-line operations, many heuristics have been proposed in the literature (e.g., [24, 17, 22, 9, 8, 23, 20, 16]) under different settings and assumptions.

In this paper, we study the VNE embedding problem under maximum latency QoS constraints. Our goal is to determine a set of node and link resources in a substrate network which minimize the end-to-end latency between pair of nodes. This is motivated by the growing number of multimedia and other delay-sensitive applications (Cisco envisioned that about 90% of Internet traffic is related to delay-sensitive applications [14]).

Building on our prior work on VNE embedding [6], we present a new algorithm, called MCRR-LA (Markov Chain with Rewards Ranking-Latency Aware), for the VNE problem subjected to QoS constraints (e.g., latency). The approach is inspired by [13, 8, 23] which devised so called *coordinated* two-stage VNE algorithms: in the first stage the algorithm embeds virtual nodes into physical (also called substrate) nodes; then, in the second stage, the algorithm embeds the logical links into physical paths between the nodes. To this end, they adopt a suitable metric which captures the availability of resources, in a node neighborhood. The mapping is then performed adopting a simple greedy strategy, by ranking the virtual and physical nodes utilizing the proposed metric. These works draw inspiration from the PageRank algorithm [7] which is extensively employed to rank web pages, and the contrived metrics imitate the PageRank concept by associating to nodes a metric which represents their relative "importance" in terms of resources.

Following the two-stage approach idea, we propose a novel latency-aware metric for a two-stage coordinated VNE al-

VALUETOOLS 2016, October 25-28, Taormina, Italy

gorithm: MCRR-LA. Differently from earlier methods, our ranking metric relies on the accumulated reward of a suitable Markov Chain. The intuition is that the accumulated reward, with each node reward being function of the amount of the node resources, penalized proportionally according to the delay over the physical links, should well capture the amount of resources available in a node area and the overall QoS (in term of latency). In this way, this combined metric is useful also to detect low-latency network areas. In the first phase, both virtual and substrate nodes are ranked based on the latency-aware metric. Then, substrate nodes are rearranged in a new list which holds in the first positions those nodes which not only have more resources but that also are closer to the highest ranked substrate node. Subsequently, virtual nodes are mapped, in a greedy manner, the highest ranked virtual node to the first substrate node in the list, the second highest virtual node to the second substrate node, etc.. In the second phase the algorithm embeds each virtual link onto a physical path, using the shortest path between each pair of originally connected nodes. We have evaluated our algorithm through simulation. Our results show that our solution is able to greatly reduce the average path delay of the embedded VNRs almost preserving good performances regarding blocking probability and revenue.

The rest of the paper is organized as follows. In section 3 we formalize the VNE problem. The new ranking algorithm (MCRR-LA), based on Markov Reward Processes, and the VNE algorithm are presented in section 4. In section 5 we evaluate MCRR-LA through simulation. Section 6 concludes the paper.

2. RELATED WORK

The VNE is a well known widely investigated problem which has been studied under different assumptions. Since the VNE problem is NP-complete [1, 22] most solutions focus on efficient heuristics (e.g., [24, 17, 22, 9, 8, 23, 20, 16]).

Among the others, many algorithms work in two successive stages for the node and for the link mapping. Lately, a new class of two-stage VNE algorithms has been proposed, named coordinated algorithms (e.g.: CO-VNE [13]). The principal feature of this new category of algorithms (e.g., [13, 8, 23]) is that the information concerning the links, required for the second stage (i.e., link mapping), is also considered in the first one (i.e., node mapping). In particular, these solutions take into account the topology, by associating to each node a metric which represents the resources of the node and of those of its neighbours, combined in one metric. The embedding is then executed via an easy greedy approach, by ranking the virtual and substrate nodes according to this metric and mapping the highly ranked virtual nodes onto the matching highly ranked substrate ones. Noticeably, the majority of these works drew inspiration from the PageRank algorithm [7]. The PageRank algorithm relies on the assumption that the importance of a web page is function of the importance of the web pages that link to it: the higher the number of incoming links and the importance of the web pages that link to it, the more important the web page is. By interpreting the web surfing as a Random Walk, it turns out that the importance of a web page corresponds to the stationary probability of a Markov Chain induced by the web links themselves, where the pages represent the Markov Chain states and the links the transitions between states. Following the same approach, the aforementioned VNE algorithms associate to each node a metric which captures the relative "importance" of a node in terms of resources, which accounts for the local resources and those of the connected links and the nearby nodes. As for the PageRank algorithm, this metric can be computed as a stationary probability of a suitable Markov Chain.

As explained in the introduction, while we consider a similar approach, we follow a totally different direction in determining the ranking metrics and adopt the cumulated reward of a suitable Markov Chain rather than the node stationary probability.

Many QoS objectives have been taken into account in solving the VNE problem: energy efficiency [18], survivability and resiliency [19], etc. [11]. Nevertheless, just a few researchers studied the latency-aware VNE. Chowdhury et al. [9] consider a requested location constraint (e.g., using geographic coordinates) for every virtual node and a maximum distance threshold indicating how far from the demanded location can be placed each node. They solve an optimization problem using mixed integer programming. This type of approach deals indirectly with delay.

Similar to our approach, Behrouznia et al. in a recent work [4] propose a two-stage QoS-aware algorithm, where the key feature is the adapted computation of quality of the physical paths, introduced in [21]. The objective metrics are both cost-effectiveness and QoS. In the first phase, the algorithm sorts the substrate nodes according to the metric of the node's available resources (available computational capacity of the node multiplied by the outgoing available bandwidth). In the second phase, in order to map each virtual link, the algorithm finds the K shortest paths between each couple of involved mapped virtual nodes (through K-Shortest-Paths algorithm). Then it computes the quality of the links making up the paths that comply with the requested bandwidth and QoS constraints of the relative virtual link. The virtual link is then mapped on the highest quality path. Differently, we calculate instead a topology-aware metric for both the request and substrate network. For the substrate network the metric is also delay-aware and is supplemented by a mechanism to shorten the physical paths.

3. VNE: PROBLEM DESCRIPTION

3.1 Substrate Network

We model the substrate network as an undirected graph, weighted on both nodes and edges, $G^s = (N^s, E^s, C^s, B^s, L^s)$, where N^s is the set of substrate nodes, E^s is the set of substrate links, C^s is the set of available CPU capacity associated with each node[1], B^s is the set of available bandwidth associated with each link and L^s is the set of the network delay associated to each link. We denote the set of substrate paths, without cycles, with P^s. Figure 1 reports an example of substrate network where the numbers inside the rectangles denote the available node CPU capacities, those near the edges the link available bandwidth, and the numbers inside green hexagons the link latency.

3.2 Virtual Network Request

[1]We only consider the computational capacity as node resource metric. The algorithm can be extended in case of multiple resources, *e.g.*, memory, I/O bandwidth

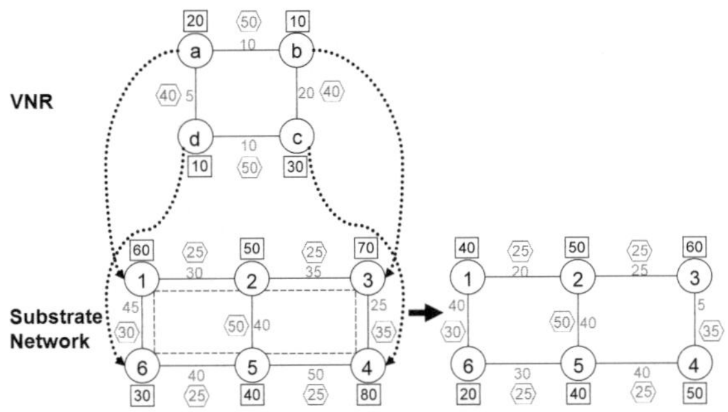

Figure 1: A VNR, the substrate network and a feasible mapping of the VNR with the deriving updated substrate network. Numbers inside rectangles near the nodes (circles), those near the edges (solid lines) and those inside green hexagons, represent the computational capacity, the link bandwidth and the link latency, respectively. Dotted lines and dashed lines show the node mapping and the consequent link mapping, respectively.

Table 1: Notations

Notations	Meaning
G^s	Substrate network
N^s	Set of substrate nodes
E^s	Set of substrate links
C^s	Set of available CPU capacities
B^s	Set of available bandwidth capacities
L^s	Set of latencies
P^s	Set of substrate paths without cycles
G^v	Virtual network request
N^v	Set of virtual nodes
E^v	Set of virtual links
C^v	Set of CPU requests
B^v	Set of bandwidth requests
L^v	Set of latency constraints
t_a	Arrival time of the VNR
t_d	Lifetime of the VNR

We also model a virtual network request as an undirected graph, weighted on both nodes and edges, $G^v = (N^v, E^v, C^v, B^v, L^v)$, where N^v is the set of virtual nodes, E^v is the set of virtual links, C^v is the set of requested CPU capacity associated with each node, B^v is the set of requested bandwidth associated with each link and L^v is the set of the network delay constraints associated to each link. We will also write $VNR(t_a, t_d)$ to denote a VNR with arrival time t_a and lifetime t_d. Figure 1 shows a VNR made up of four nodes and four links with the same notation of the substrate network about the requested capacities and latencies. The set of notations is reported in Table 1.

3.3 Virtual Network Mapping

Virtual network mapping $M : G^v \rightarrow G^s$ is the embedding of a VNR, G^v, in the physical network G^s. In particular, the set of virtual nodes is embedded into a subset of substrate nodes and the set of virtual links is embedded into a subset of substrate links, namely a subset of the substrate paths P^s. This procedure is made up of two phases: node mapping and link mapping.

The node mapping phase provides a mapping function from a virtual node to a substrate one, $M_{node} : N^v \rightarrow N^s$, such that: $\forall n^v, m^v \in N^v$

$$M_{node}(n^v) = n^s \in N^s, \tag{1}$$

subject to:

- $M_{node}(n^v) = M_{node}(m^v)$ if and only if $m^v = n^v$;
- $C^v(n^v) \leq C^s(M_{node}(n^v))$.

Each virtual node is mapped to a distinct physical node provided that the latter has at least the same quantity of available resources. In Figure 1 the resulting node mapping for the VNR is $\{a \rightarrow 1, b \rightarrow 3, c \rightarrow 4, d \rightarrow 6\}$, graphically represented with dotted lines.

The link mapping provides a mapping function of a virtual link to a substrate path, with no cycles, consisting of one or more links, $M_{link} : E^v \rightarrow P^s$, such that: $\forall e^v = (m^v n^v) \in E^v$

$$M_{link}(m^v n^v) = p^s(M_{node}(m^v), M_{node}(n^v)) \in P^s(M_{node}(m^v), M_{node}(n^v)),$$

subject to:

- $B^v(e^v) \leq \min_{e^s \in p^s(M_{link}(e^v))} B^s(e^s)$;
- $L^v(e^v) \geq \sum_{e^s \in p^s(M_{link}(e^v))} L^s(e^s)$.

Each substrate link in the path, must possess at least the same quantity of resources of the virtual link. Furthermore, the overall latency of each physical path must comply with the requested virtual link's latency constraint. In Figure 1 the resulting link mapping for the VNR is $\{(ab) \rightarrow (12, 23), (bc) \rightarrow (34), (cd) \rightarrow (45, 56), (da) \rightarrow (61)\}$, denoted by dashed lines.

3.4 Objective

The goal of the InP is to maximize the revenue, while optimizing resource utilization. The SP, instead, wants to pay just the agreed resource costs. Following previous approaches [22, 24, 9, 23, 13], we define the revenue $R(G^v, t_a, t_d)$ for the InP for accepting a VNR with lifetime t_d, at time t_a, as:

$$R(G^v, t_a, t_d) = \begin{cases} R_0(G^v, t_a, t_d) \cdot t_d, & \text{if accepted} \\ 0, & \text{otherwise} \end{cases}, \tag{2}$$

where $R_0(G^v, t_a, t_d)$ represents the revenue per time unit for $VNR(t_a, t_d)$ that can be defined as:

$$R_0(G^v, t_a, t_d) = \alpha_c \sum_{n^v \in N^v} C^v(n^v) + \alpha_b \sum_{e^v \in E^v} B^v(e^v), \tag{3}$$

where α_c is the unit price for the computational resources and α_b is the unit price for the bandwidth resources.

Generally, as highlighted in other works [22, 9, 8], the main objective for the InP is to maximize the long term time-average revenue:

$$R_{tot} = \lim_{T \rightarrow \infty} \frac{\sum_{i=1}^{N_T} R(G^{v,(i)}, t_a^{(i)}, t_d^{(i)})}{T}, \tag{4}$$

where N_T is the number of requests arrived within time T, and $R(G^{v,(i)}, t_a^{(i)}, t_d^{(i)})$ is the revenue gained from the i-th VNR with arrival time $t_a^{(i)}$ and lifetime $t_d^{(i)}$.

An additional important index, which has an impact on the former one, is the blocking ratio, namely the blocking probability:

$$BR = \lim_{T \to \infty} \frac{\sum_{j=1}^{NREJ_T} VNR_{rej}^{(j)}(t_a^{(j)}, t_d^{(j)})}{\sum_{i=1}^{N_T} VNR^{(i)}(t_a^{(i)}, t_d^{(i)})}, \quad (5)$$

where $NREJ_T$ is the total number of rejected VNRs within time T and $VNR_{rej}^{(j)}(t_a^{(j)}, t_d^{(j)})$ is the j-th rejected VNR.

Furthermore, as suggested in [2], we make use of the average path delay of each accepted VNR as a key metric which meaning is how well a VNR performs after it has been mapped into the physical network.

4. MARKOV CHAIN REWARDS BASED LATENCY AWARE NODE RANKING ALGORITHM

Following previous works in the literature [8, 23, 13], our VNE algorithm is made up of two distinct, sequential stages, namely, the node mapping stage and the link mapping stage: when a VNR arrives, first of all virtual nodes are mapped to physical nodes with adequate resources following a greedy strategy which also takes into account the link latency; then, in the link mapping stage, virtual links are mapped to substrate paths with sufficient link capacity, following a shortest-path (in terms of latency values) based link mapping.

In section 4.1, we first present our approach to latency aware node ranking, MCRR-LA, based on Markov Chains with rewards model [12], which captures the amount of resources (computational capacity, network bandwidth) available in a node and its surrounding area coupled with the network latency between nodes. Then, in Section 4.2 we describe the node and link mapping algorithms in detail.

4.1 MCRR-LA Node Ranking Metric

As noticed in [13], a ranking metric for the VNE problem should account for both local and neighboring nodes resources. By intuition, the higher the amount of resources in terms of computing and network capacity in a node neighborhood, the more likely a virtual network can be embedded in that portion of the physical network. We are going to add to the above mentioned criteria a penalization proportional with respect to the level of latency.

First of all, we introduce the concept of latency-aware node resources. Without loss of generality, we follow an approach similar to the one proposed by Zhang et al. in [23][2] and formulate the amount of available resources $CBL(n)$ of a node n by the product of the available CPU resource and the sum of the bandwidth resources, each multiplied by the normalized link latency as follows:

$$CBL(n) = C^s(n) \cdot \sum_{m \in N(n)} \left[B^s((n,m)) \cdot \left(1 - \left(\frac{L^s((n,m)) - min\_lat}{max\_lat - min\_lat} \right) \right) \right], \quad (6)$$

[2]The ranking metric can be similarly defined using alternative resource metrics, *e.g.*, [13].

where $N(n)$ is the set of neighbors of node n. In (6), $L^s((n,m))$ is the latency over the physical link between nodes n and m, and $[min\_lat, max\_lat]$ is the range of latency values in the network. The latency in CBL is thus normalized in the interval $[0,1]$, with 1 corresponding to links with minimum latency and 0 to links with maximum latency. The node resources are then normalized as follows:

$$Res(n) = \frac{CBL(n)}{\sum_{m \in N^s} CBL(m)}. \quad (7)$$

We define the MCRR-LA ranking metric $V_\gamma(n)$ of node n, recursively, as a weighted sum of the local resources and the neighbouring nodes metric as follows

$$V_\gamma(n) = (1-\gamma)Res(n) + \gamma \sum_{m \in N(n)} \frac{Res(m)}{\sum_{h \in N(n)} Res(h)} V_\gamma(m), \quad (8)$$

with $\gamma \in [0,1)$ the relative weight of the neighbours metric. In (8), each neighbour contributes to the sum in proportion to its amount of resources with respect to the other adjacent nodes (represented by the factor $\frac{Res(m)}{\sum_{h \in N(n)} Res(h)}$). To rewrite (8) in a compact form, let $\mathbf{P}$ a $|N| \times |N|$ matrix defined as follows:

$$P(n,m) = \begin{cases} \frac{Res(m)}{\sum_{h \in N(n)} Res(h)} & \text{if } (n,m) \in E^s \\ 0 & \text{otherwise} \end{cases}, \quad (9)$$

By construction, P is a stochastic matrix with all rows summing to 1. We can now conveniently rewrite (8) as:

$$V_\gamma(n) = (1-\gamma)Res(n) + \gamma \cdot \sum_{n' \in N} P(n,n')V_\gamma(n'), \quad (10)$$

or in matrix form

$$\mathbf{V}_\gamma = (1-\gamma)\mathbf{Res} + \gamma \mathbf{P} \mathbf{V}_\gamma, \quad (11)$$

where $\mathbf{Res} = (Res(1), Res(2), \ldots, Res(|N|))^T$, and $\mathbf{V}_\gamma = (V_\gamma(1), V_\gamma(2), \ldots, V_\gamma(|N|))^T$.

The recursive equations (11) have an elegant physical interpretation. Indeed, (11) can be regarded as the Bellman equations [5] of the discounted cumulative reward, with discount factor γ, of the Markov Chain with transition probability matrix $\mathbf{P}$ over the set of nodes N, and rewards vector $\mathbf{Rew} = (Rew(1), Rew(2), \ldots, Rew(|N|))$, with $Rew(n) = (1-\gamma)Res(n)$, $n \in N$. In other words, the ranking metric of node n, $V_\gamma(n)$, is the expected discounted accumulated reward of a Markov Chain with transition probability $\mathbf{P}$, that is

$$V_\gamma(n) = \lim_{k \to \infty} \mathbb{E}_{\mathbf{P}} \left[\sum_{i=0}^{k} \gamma^i Rew(n_i) \right], \quad (12)$$

where $n_0, n_1, n_2, \ldots$, denotes a sample path with initial state $n_0 = n$.

$\mathbf{V}_\gamma$ can be calculated as the unique solution of Eq.(11). By observing that since $\mathbf{P}$ is stochastic, $(\mathbf{I} - \gamma\mathbf{P})$, $0 \leq \gamma < 1$, is invertible, and we readily obtain

$$\mathbf{V}_\gamma = (\mathbf{I} - \gamma\mathbf{P})^{-1}(1-\gamma)\mathbf{Res}. \quad (13)$$

From the above definition, it is clear that the higher the node ranking $V_\gamma(n)$ of a node, the higher resource in the node and its neighborhood. In addition, if we consider nodes with same resource state in their respective areas, we will experience lower $V_\gamma(n)$ values for the nodes with low latency neighbourhood, since higher latency values affect more negatively the (accumulated) rewards. The discount factor γ is a measure of the size of the neighborhood taken into account to determine the node metric: $\gamma = 0$ only the local resources are taken into account, while as γ increases, larger and larger portion of the graph close to a node is accounted for in the metric. It is worth noting that while metric $V_\gamma(n)$ has been so far implicitly applied only to the substrate network nodes, it can be applied to the virtual network nodes too. In this latter case, though, instead of the amount of available resources, $V_\gamma(n)$ represents the amount of resources *required* by a virtual node and its neighboring nodes. This demand-availability relationship suggests that as a heuristic we can simply map virtual nodes with higher ranking metric to physical nodes with higher ranking.

4.2 Full Mapping Algorithm

As we mentioned before, our approach to solve the VNE problem consists of a coordinated two-stage algorithm. In the first phase, namely nodes mapping (Algorithm 1), we first order them in non increasing order according to the MCRR-LA metric (line 12-13). Then, using the physical node with the highest metric value (line 14) as root node, we determine a subset of nodes using a Breadth-First search (BFS) (lines 17-23). The starting maximum search hop-distance is obtained dividing the number of virtual nodes by the average degree of the substrate nodes (line 16). In this BFS search, only the nodes with computing capacity greater than or equal to the minimum computing capacity required by the VNR nodes are considered. Unless the BFS finds at least the sufficient number of physical nodes to host the requested nodes, the search is extended by increasing the searching distance by one unit (line 20-21). Next, two lists are created, both sorted according to the MCRR-LA metric (line 24-26): the first, containing the substrate nodes selected by the BFS search; the second, with the rest of the substrate nodes. The two lists are then concatenated. We then proceed to the node mapping itself (lines 28-36): using a simple greedy approach, following the order determined by the MCRR-LA metric, the virtual nodes are mapped to the first physical node in the above list which has adequate resources to host them, provided that each physical node can just host one virtual node. If all virtual nodes are successfully embedded, the VNE mapping continues with the second phase, otherwise, the mapping procedure aborts and the VNR is blocked.

In the second phase (Algorithm 2), the algorithm computes the shortest path (Dijkstra algorithm), in terms of latency, between each pair of substrate nodes. For the sake of efficiency, the substrate links without enough bandwidth are cut before executing the calculation of the shortest paths (lines 6-10). If it is impossible to find a path between two physical nodes, meeting both bandwidth and latency constraints demanded by the currently processed virtual link, the heuristic is unable to determine a suitable assignment and the VNR is refused (lines 14-22).

Remark The second stage simply determines the shortest path among nodes, thus selecting the minimum latency path among them, irrespectively of the number of hops among nodes. In order to minimize resource consumption, the algorithm should also minimize the number of hops. We achieve this goal implicitly by using the BFS algorithm. Indeed, using the BFS search in the first stage we determine as best candidates for node mapping not only the nodes with higher resources in their vicinity, but also the nodes which are closer in terms of network hops (using the best node - the root - as reference node).

Algorithm 1 *NodeMapping*

Input : VNR $G^v(N^v, E^v, C^v, B^v, L^v)$, Substrate net $G^s(N^s, E^s, C^s, B^s, L^s)$, nodes rank vector for VNR V_γ^v, nodes rank vector for substrate net V_γ^s ;
Output: Mapping of nodes M_{node};

1: data initialization;
2: $M_{node} \leftarrow \mathbf{0}$;
3: $counter \leftarrow 0$;
4: $nodes\_mapping\_success \leftarrow false$;
5: $root\_node \leftarrow \mathbf{0}$;
6: $search\_dist \leftarrow 0$;
7: $average\_degree \leftarrow 0$;
8: # set of selected neighbour nodes of the root node
9: $SN \leftarrow \mathbf{0}$;
10: $UN \leftarrow \mathbf{0}$; # set of unselected nodes
11: $SUN \leftarrow \mathbf{0}$; # set of selected + unselected nodes
12: $V_{\gamma sort}^v \leftarrow sort(V_\gamma^v)$; # according to MCRR-LA
13: $V_{\gamma sort}^s \leftarrow sort(V_\gamma^s)$; #
14: $root\_node \leftarrow find\_root\_node(N^s, V_{\gamma sort}^s)$;
15: $average\_degree \leftarrow compute\_average\_degree(G^s)$;
16: $search\_dist \leftarrow \left\lfloor \frac{|N^v|}{average\_degree} \right\rfloor$;
17: **while** $|SN| < |N^v|$ **do**
18:     # CPU of selected nodes is $\geq \min_{n^v \in N^v} C^v(n^v)$
19:     $SN \leftarrow BFS(G^s, root\_node, search\_dist)$;
20:     **if** $|SN| < |N^v|$ **then**
21:         $search\_dist = search\_dist + 1$;
22:     **end if**
23: **end while**
24: $SN_{sort} \leftarrow sort(SN, V_{\gamma sort}^s)$; # accor. to $V_{\gamma sort}^s$
25: $UN \leftarrow N^s \setminus SN$;
26: $UN_{sort} \leftarrow sort(UN, V_{\gamma sort}^s)$; # accor. to $V_{\gamma sort}^s$
27: $SUN \leftarrow SN_{sort} + UN_{sort}$;
28: **for all** *nodes* n^v *ordered according* $V_{\gamma sort}^v$ **do**
29:     **for all** *unused nodes* $n^s \in SUN$ **do**
30:         **if** $C^v(n^v) \leq C^s(n^s)$ **then**
31:             $counter = counter + 1$;
32:             $M_{node}(n^v) = n^s$; # map n^v to n^s
33:             **break**;
34:         **end if**
35:     **end for**
36: **end for**
37: # if all the virtual nodes are successfully mapped
38: **if** $counter = |N^v|$ **then**
39:     $nodes\_mapping\_success \leftarrow true$;
40:     update the CPU capacities C^s;
41: **else**
42:     mark the VNR as rejected;
43: **end if**

5. EXPERIMENTAL EVALUATION

We have evaluated our ranking algorithm through numerical evaluation. We have written a VNE simulator which im-

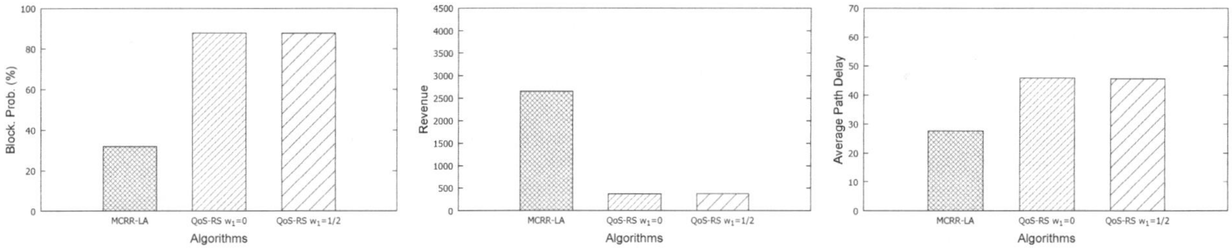

(a) Blocking Probability (b) Revenue (c) Average Path Delay

Figure 2: MCRR-LA vs QoS-RS: requested basic latency bounds · $\delta = 1.5$.

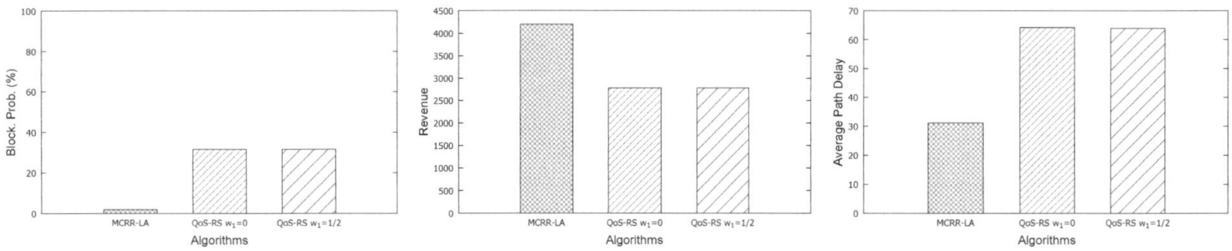

(a) Blocking Probability (b) Revenue (c) Average Path Delay

Figure 3: MCRR-LA vs QoS-RS: requested basic latency bounds · $\delta = 3$.

plements the proposed MCRR-LA algorithm and, for comparison, the algorithm proposed in [4][3], hereafter referred to as QoS-RS (QoS-Resource Selection) for brevity. We report the results based on a 32 node substrate network with 58 links (ANSNET [15], slightly modified as in [23]).

We assume that the VNR arrival process complies with a Poisson process with rate $\lambda = 5$. VNR lifetime is exponentially distributed with average lifetime T_{VNR} equal to 12 time units, corresponding to a medium load scenario. Every VNR is a random graph with a number of nodes uniformly distributed in $\{4, \ldots, 10\}$ with varying link connectivity rate in the different experiments. The VNR CPU, bandwidth requirements are randomly drawn node per node and link by link in the sets $\{4, \ldots, 8\}$ and $\{2, \ldots, 5\}$, respectively. The substrate network physical resources in terms of CPU and bandwidth are normalized and all equal to the nominal value of 100. The substrate network links latency are proportional to the geographical distance between nodes. The basic VNR latency requirements over the links are randomly generated in the interval between the average and the maximum latency value of the substrate network links times a multiplicative factor δ.

For the following results, every simulation experiment was 5000 time units long and was repeated 10 times. For the sake of clarity, we do not report the confidence interval which were in general not considerable.

In the experiments we compare MCRR-LA with QoS-RS using VNRs randomly generated with link connectivity rate of $\frac{ln(|N^v|)}{|N^v|-1}$ (to ensure that each node has $O(ln(|N^v|))$ incident edges). We tested the two algorithms under different ranges of latency VNR demands. Following [6], for MCRR-LA we adopt a value of $\gamma = 0.98$ (the discount factor of the Markov Reward Model). In the implementation of the QoS-RS algorithm, we do not consider the node location constraint and the links packet loss constraint which have no counterpart in our proposed solution (we plan to include such constraints in our future work). The K-Shortest-Paths algorithm used by QoS-RS is set with $K = 4$. In order to compute the quality of the physical paths, QoS-RS contemplates the use of weights (summing to 1), as in [21], to balance the importance of the bandwidth (w_1) and delay (w_2) attributes. Since our tests showed that the performance is not considerably affected by the different combination of the weights and since MCRR-LA aims to reduce the latency when it comes to compute the shortest paths, we plot the results of just two combinations: $w_1 = 0.5, w_2 = 0.5$ and $w_1 = 0.0, w_2 = 1.0$.

In Figures 2(a)–(c) we plot the VNR blocking probability, the average revenue and the average path delay of the algorithms, assuming the VNR latency bounds with a multiplicative factor $\delta = 1.5$ (that is, each VNR link latency requirement is randomly drawn in the interval $[1.5 \cdot average\_lat, 1.5 \cdot max\_lat]$, where $average\_lat$ and max_lat are the average and maximum substrate network link latency, respectively). From the figure, we can observe that MCRR-LA considerably outperforms QoS-RS in terms of lower blocking probability, higher revenue and lower average path delay. From the simulations, the lower blocking probability (also reflected in terms of higher revenue) is due to a more uniform use of the substrate network resources (both nodes and links) by MCRR-LA. Also MCRR-LA allows to reduce significantly the average path delay of the mapped VNRs compared to QoS-RS. Similar, albeit less pronounced differences can be observed with VNR latency bounds with a multiplicative factor $\delta = 3$ (corresponding to less stringent VNR links delay bounds) as shown in Figures 3(a)–(c).

Algorithm 2 *LinksMapping*

Input : VNR $G^v(N^v, E^v, C^v, B^v, L^v)$, Substrate net $G^s(N^s, E^s, C^s, B^s, L^s)$, mapping of nodes M_{node};
Output: Mapping of links M_{link};

$M_{link} \leftarrow \mathbf{0}$;
links_mapping_success $\leftarrow$ *true*;
for all *virtual links* $e^v = (m^v n^v) \in E^v$ **do**
  $G^s_{clone} \leftarrow G^s$;   # clone the substrate network
  # pre-cut links in G^s_{clone} without enough bandwidth
  for all *physical links* $e^s \in E^s_{clone}$ **do**
    if $B^s(e^s) < B^v(e^v)$ **then**
      cut link $e^s = (m^s n^s) \in E^s_{clone}$;
    end if
  end for
  compute a shortest path, $p^s(M_{node}(m^v), M_{node}(n^v))$, between the two nodes $M_{node}(m^v)$ and $M_{node}(n^v)$ in G^s_{clone}, in terms of latency;
  # if a shortest path, in terms of latency, was found
  # and it meets the requested latency constraint
  if $|p^s(M_{node}(m^v), M_{node}(n^v))| \neq 0$ **and** $p^s(M_{node}(m^v), M_{node}(n^v)).tot\_lat \leq L^v(e^v)$ **then**
    # mapping
    $M_{link}(m^v n^v) \leftarrow p^s(M_{node}(m^v), M_{node}(n^v))$;
    update the bandwidth B^s of involved links in G^s;
  else
    links_mapping_success $\leftarrow$ *false*;
    mark the VNR as rejected;
    break;
  end if
end for
if *links_mapping_success* $=$ *false* **then**
  undo the CPU and bandwidth updates to G^s;
end if

The better performance of MCRR-LA can be ascribed to the use of latency aware metric in determining the node ranking which gives preference during the node mapping phase not only to the node with more resources (computational capacity and link bandwidth) but also with low latency. Indeed, despite the fact that QoS-RS uses a method to determine the quality of the paths during the link mapping, the nodes mapping phase is first carried out without considering latency. These results stress the importance of including link related QoS metric in the node mapping phase of two-stage mapping algorithms.

6. CONCLUSIONS

In this paper, we have presented a new approach to the Virtual Network Embedding problem based on Markov Reward Processes, the aim of which is to achieve a good trade-off between resource utilization and QoS (e.g., latency). The main idea is to calculate the embedding potential of each node, that is aggregate resources in their respective neighborhood in terms of accumulated reward of a suitable random walk with the node as initial state. For both physical and virtual nodes, this value is penalized proportionally by the latency over the links. Based on this new metric, we proposed a two-stage VNE algorithm which ranks virtual nodes according to the previously computed latency aware metric, and physical nodes according to the previously computed latency aware metric combined with a Breadth-First search on the highly ranked node. Subsequently, the algorithm carries out the node mapping accordingly and finally performs the link mapping utilizing the shortest path in terms of latency. Experimental outcomes show that our algorithm is able to reduce the average path delay of the embedded VNRs compared to alternative approaches. As future work, we plan to improve the algorithm acting both on nodes and links mapping stages, to execute more experiments in realistic setting, and to extend MCRR-LA to account for additional VNR QoS requirements, including network resiliency.

7. REFERENCES

[1] D. G. Andersen. Theoretical approaches to node assignment. Unpublished Manuscript, Dec. 2002.

[2] M. T. Beck and C. Linnhoff-Popien. On delay-aware embedding of virtual networks. In *The sixth international conference on advances in future internet, AFIN*, 2014.

[3] S. Behrouznia. A qos-based resource selection approach for virtual networks. Master's thesis, Concordia University, April 2015.

[4] S. Behrouznia, R. Dssouli, and M. El Barachi. A qos-based resource selection approach for virtual networks. In *International Conference on Computer and Information Science and Technology, 2015. CIST'15.*, May 2015.

[5] R. Bellman. *Dynamic Programming*. Princeton University Press, Princeton, NJ, USA, 1 edition, 1957.

[6] F. Bianchi and F. Lo Presti. A markov reward model based greedy heuristic for the virtual network embedding problem. In *Modeling, Analysis and Simulation of Computer and Telecommunication Systems (MASCOTS), 2016 IEEE 24th International Symposium on*, 2016.

[7] S. Brin and L. Page. The anatomy of a large-scale hypertextual web search engine. *Comput. Netw. ISDN Syst.*, 30(1-7):107–117, Apr. 1998.

[8] X. Cheng, S. Su, Z. Zhang, H. Wang, F. Yang, Y. Luo, and J. Wang. Virtual network embedding through topology-aware node ranking. *SIGCOMM Comput. Commun. Rev.*, 41(2):38–47, Apr. 2011.

[9] N. Chowdhury, M. Rahman, and R. Boutaba. Virtual network embedding with coordinated node and link mapping. In *INFOCOM 2009, IEEE*, pages 783–791, April 2009.

[10] N. Feamster, L. Gao, and J. Rexford. How to Lease the Internet in Your Spare Time. *SIGCOMM Comput. Commun. Rev.*, 37(1):61–64, Jan. 2007.

[11] A. Fischer, J. Botero, M. Till Beck, H. de Meer, and X. Hesselbach. Virtual network embedding: A survey. *Communications Surveys Tutorials, IEEE*, 15(4):1888–1906, Fourth 2013.

[12] R. G. Gallager. *Stochastic processes: theory for applications.* Cambridge University Press, Cambridge, 2013.

[13] L. Gong, Y. Wen, Z. Zhu, and T. Lee. Toward profit-seeking virtual network embedding algorithm via global resource capacity. In *INFOCOM, 2014 Proceedings IEEE*, pages 1–9, April 2014.

[14] K. Ivaturi and T. Wolf. Mapping of delay-sensitive virtual networks. In *Computing, Networking and Communications (ICNC), 2014 International Conference on*, pages 341–347, Feb 2014.

[15] Z. Li and J. J. Garcia-Luna-Aceves. Finding multi-constrained feasible paths by using depth-first search. *Wirel. Netw.*, 13(3):323–334, June 2007.

[16] J. Lischka and H. Karl. A virtual network mapping algorithm based on subgraph isomorphism detection. In *Proceedings of the 1st ACM Workshop on Virtualized Infrastructure Systems and Architectures*, VISA '09, pages 81–88, New York, NY, USA, 2009. ACM.

[17] J. Lu and J. Turner. Efficient Mapping of Virtual Networks onto a Shared Substrate. Technical Report 2006-35, Washington University in St. Louis, 2006.

[18] L. Nonde, T. E. H. El-Gorashi, and J. M. H. Elmirghani. Energy efficient virtual network embedding for cloud networks. *Journal of Lightwave Technology*, 33(9):1828–1849, May 2015.

[19] M. R. Rahman and R. Boutaba. Svne: Survivable virtual network embedding algorithms for network virtualization. *IEEE Transactions on Network and Service Management*, 10(2):105–118, June 2013.

[20] A. Razzaq and M. Rathore. An approach towards resource efficient virtual network embedding. In *Evolving Internet (INTERNET), 2010 Second International Conference on*, pages 68–73, Sept 2010.

[21] J. Shamsi and M. Brockmeyer. Qosmap: Qos aware mapping of virtual networks for resiliency and efficiency. In *2007 IEEE Globecom Workshops*, pages 1–6, Nov 2007.

[22] M. Yu, Y. Yi, J. Rexford, and M. Chiang. Rethinking virtual network embedding: Substrate support for path splitting and migration. *SIGCOMM Comput. Commun. Rev.*, 38(2):17–29, Mar. 2008.

[23] S. Zhang, Z. Qian, J. Wu, and S. Lu. An opportunistic resource sharing and topology-aware mapping framework for virtual networks. In *INFOCOM, 2012 Proceedings IEEE*, pages 2408–2416, March 2012.

[24] Y. Zhu and M. Ammar. Algorithms for assigning substrate network resources to virtual network components. In *INFOCOM 2006. 25th IEEE International Conference on Computer Communications. Proceedings*, pages 1–12, April 2006.

Dealing with indetermination in biochemical networks

Niccolò Totis
University of Turin, Computer Science Department
Corso Svizzera 185
Turin, Italy
ntotis@di.unito.it

Marco Beccuti
University of Turin, Computer Science Department
Corso Svizzera 185
Turin, Italy
beccuti@di.unito.it

Francesca Cordero
University of Turin, Computer Science Department
Corso Svizzera 185
Turin, Italy
fcordero@di.unito.it

Laura Follia
University of Turin, Molecular Biotechnology and Health Sciences Department
Via Santena 5
Turin, Italy
laura.follia@unito.it

Chiara Riganti
University of Turin, Oncology Department
Via Santena 5/bis
Turin, Italy
chiara.riganti@unito.it

Francesco Novelli
University of Turin, Molecular Biotechnology and Health Sciences Department
Via Santena 5
Turin, Italy
franco.novelli@unito.it

ABSTRACT

A main aspect in computational modelling of biological systems is the determination of model structure and model parameters. Due to economical and technical reasons, only part of these details are well characterized, while the rest are unknown. To deal with this difficulty, many reverse engineering and parameter estimation methods have been proposed in the literature, however these methods often need an amount of experimental data not always available.

In this paper we propose an alternative approach, which overcomes model indetermination solving an Optimization Problem (OP) with an objective function that, similarly to Flux Balance Analysis, is derived from an empirical biological knowledge and does not require large amounts of data. The system behaviour is described by a set of Ordinary Differential Equations (ODE). Model indetermination is resolved selecting time-varying coefficients that maximize/minimize the objective function at each ODE integration step. Moreover, to facilitate the modelling phase we provide a graphical formalism, based on Petri Nets, which can be used to derive the corresponding ODEs and OP. Finally, the approach is illustrated on a case study focused on cancer metabolism.

CCS Concepts

•**Computing methodologies** → **Modeling methodologies;** *Uncertainty quantification;* •**Applied computing** → Systems biology; •**Software and its engineering** → Petri nets

VALUETOOLS 2016, October 25-28, Taormina, Italy

Keywords

indetermination, Ordinary Differential Equation, optimization problems, Petri net.

1. INTRODUCTION

The inherent complexity of biological systems makes the study of their dynamics and behaviours a difficult issue. Within this context, computational modelling can help biologists/clinicians to identify which molecules and interactions have a crucial role on the global behaviour of the system. Many modelling approaches have been proposed in the literature. An appropriate choice among them depends on the specific biological question being addressed and on the available data. An extensive review of the most successful modelling approaches used for metabolic, and more in general for any biochemical network, is reported in [4], where the authors divide these approaches into three classes (i.e. *interaction-based*, *constraint-based* and *mechanism-based* approaches) depending on the used level of abstraction. For instance, *interaction-based* approaches do not consider any quantitative aspect, so that they allow only a topological analysis of the system. Instead, *constraint-based* approaches rely on the assumption of steady state and typically exploit Flux Balance Analysis (FBA) and its extensions [17] to study the system at equilibrium. *Mechanism-based* approaches describe interactions with high level of detail and are the most likely candidates to provide a complete understanding of biochemical dynamics.

In order to build a mechanism-based the modeller has to specify all its characteristics, like, for instance, the structure of the system, the mechanism of the events that produce changes in variables and the mathematical expressions used to represent them, with all their parameters defined. This considerable amount of preliminary information requires the modeller to acquire an extensive knowledge of the biological phenomena and to formulate all the assumptions on which the model relies. In this article we will focus on a particular type of biochemical systems, namely metabolic systems, and on modelling these systems with Ordinary Differential Equations (ODEs). Due to economical and technical reasons, the complete information needed to build the set of

ODEs is rarely available, causing the modeller to face situations of indetermination. In this study we will consider in particular those metabolic models in which part of the reactions are fully characterized while the rest are not. Two groups of reactions are thus defined: determined reactions, having well characterized structure, mathematical expression and parametrization, and undetermined reactions, described just by their stoichiometry.
Issues of indetermination have been already deeply studied in literature and solutions have been proposed at different levels, depending on the type of missing information. Techniques of reverse engineering (RE) and Parameter Estimation (PE), for instance, overcome this indetermination by means of available experimental data and optimization algorithms [4, 14, 8].
In this article we propose an alternative approach to deal with situations in which insufficient experimental data hamper the application of PE and RE methods. To overcome the lack of information concerning undetermined reactions we chose to exploit an empirical biological knowledge that helps us formulate some modelling assumptions and define an optimization problem (OP).
Since the direct definition of the ODEs and of the OP may be difficult and may require advanced modelling skills, we facilitate this process providing a high level graphical formalism based on Petri Nets (PNs). The paper is organized as follows. Section 2 gives a general outlook on other methods currently used for similar purposes, while Section 3 provides the necessary background on PNs and OPs. In Section 4 our approach is introduced: a formal definition of our PN extension and how to automatically translate a model described through such a high level formalism into the underlying ODE system and OP are provided. In Section 5 some experimental results are shown, and our method is compared to others present in literature. In Section 6 we conclude presenting some future works.

2. STATE OF THE ART

As mentioned in the introduction, situations of inadequate biochemical characterization are traditionally managed with **Reverse Engineering** (RE) or **Parameter Estimation** (PE) computational techniques. When the topology of the network is not known, several techniques of RE can be used. Besides topology, the parametrization of the model represents at present the main area of lacking information. The parameters required for a kinetic model include both the kinetic parameters and the initial conditions. Many parameters have been experimentally calculated with biochemical assays, and have been reported in literature, but many others are still unavailable. As some authors have pointed out, if we consider the parametrization of the mathematical expressions of enzyme activity: "for the foreseeable future, full availability of *true* rate equations for all enzymes is certainly an illusion" [3]. To cope with this situation, many PE techniques have proposed different approaches that aim to automatically infer model parameters from experimental data. In general, the inputs of PE methods include network topology, initial conditions and discrete-time time series of some biochemical species present in the model. When parameters and network topology are unknown, PE has to be embedded in the solution of a Reverse Engineering problem [4]. Instead, if parameters and initial conditions are unavailable, a joint state-kinetic constants estimation (see,e.g., [12]) has to be performed. PE performs a global optimization of a fitness function which evaluates the distance between the simulated solution and the experimental data points. Several alternative optimization algorithms can be found in literature, each adopting a specific approach to escape from local minima and to limit the computational complexity. The difficulty of PE lies in the availability of experimental data, which in many real cases are very scarce. In this paper we present an approach that can be used in situations where both part of the network structure and part of the parametrization are unknown, representing an alternative to a PE embedded in a RE process. Differently from these techniques, our method tries to escape a strict dependency from experimental data using an OP that relies on biological empirical knowledge. This OP exploits an objective function that is conceived to represent a specific biological behaviour or phenotype, as it will be discussed in Section 5.

The use of an objective function with a biological meaning has already been incorporated in **Flux Balance Analysis** and **Cybernetic Modelling** (CM). In most FBA studies the objective function describes an objective that we believe is physiologically relevant for the cell, like the maximisation of biomass. This is used to predict a physiological behaviour of the cell. The idea that a system, like a cell, seeks a biological objective is justified acknowledging the apparent goal-directedness of nature. Other computational approaches, like cybernetic modelling [21], have taken advantage of this concept, which has been formally defined with the word teleonomy. A teleonomic view of nature indeed considers that the genetic programs of all living organisms has been shaped by evolution in a way that highly performing phenotypes have been selected [21]. Both FBA and cybernetic modelling have proved that this perspective can be used in different ways to simulate real biological behaviours. However, referring to the modelling categories defined in the introduction, FBA pertains to the group of *constraint-based* models, which are able to offer only a representation of the system at steady state. In FBA, the assumption is that the period in which the concentrations of biochemical species fluctuate can be neglected, while primary relevance is attributed to the condition in which the system is at equilibrium, i.e. when concentrations do not change in time any more. A further improvement of FBA is represented by **dynamic Flux Balance Analysis** (dFBA), proposed by Mahadevan and coworkers [19]. Here the extracellular space is modelled dynamically while inside the cell the steady-state assumption holds. In dFBA an ODE system is built to describe all extracellular events while the distribution of intracellular fluxes is calculated via a static optimization algorithm (SOA) or a dynamic optimization algorithm (DOA). For reasons of similarity with our approach we will focus specifically on the SOA algorithm, in which a biological objective function, like cellular growth rate or biomass, is maximized at each integration step of the ODEs. It is worth highlighting that dFBA always considers the intracellular system at steady state, so it neglects all the dynamic fluctuations of internal metabolites. In the field of mechanism based models, the CM [21] closely follows the teleonomic perspective, producing a long history of progressive refinements of their technique. Besides teleonomy, the CM approach also assumes that (i) the topology of the network is completely known, that (ii)metabolic enzymes are regulated at the gene expression level or via allosteric mechanisms, that (iii) some economic principles govern the way the cell implements these regulations, meaning that the cell, as if it were a rational investor, enhances those reactions that assure the highest yield in terms of the objective function. Finally CM assumes that (iv) accurate mathematical expressions with a complete list of kinetic parameters are available. These assumptions limit the good predictions of cybernetic models only to situations in which all parameters are available or where sufficient experimental data allow PE methods to be employed.

3. BACKGROUND

In this section we first introduce a brief overview of the (Stochastic) PN (SPN) formalism highlighting how it is possible to derive from an SPN model an ODE system that can be used to study the system's behaviour. Subsequently, we will re-call the basis of the OPs and their solution techniques which will be used in the sequel of this paper.

Stochastic Petri Nets. PN and their extensions are graphical modelling formalisms which are becoming quite popular to build models of biological systems. The reason of this appeal is their capabilities of representing in a simple and intuitive manner many important features of these systems and thus of constructing models that are easy to understand also by non-mathematicians and non-computer scientists. PNs are bipartite directed graphs with two types of nodes called *places* and *transitions*. The *places*, graphically represented as circles, correspond to the system variables (e.g. enzymes and compounds), while the transitions, graphically represented as rectangles, encode the events (e.g. interactions among biochemical entities) which cause the system evolution. Arcs connecting places to transitions (and vice versa) express the relations between states and event occurrences. Places can contain tokens, graphically represented as black dots, that in the context of systems biology, often describe the number of molecules of the corresponding entities. An example of a PN model is shown in Fig. 1 which describes glycolysis in human red blood cells.

The state of a PN, called *marking*, is defined as the number of tokens in each place. An example of marking for the PN in Fig. 1 is showed in the third column of the Table in Fig. 2 . The system evolution is given by the occurrence of enabled transitions, where a transition is enabled if each input place contains a number of tokens greater or equal than a given threshold defined by the multiplicity of the corresponding input arc. A transition occurrence, called *firing*, removes a fixed number of tokens from its input places and adds a fixed number of tokens to its output places. The multiplicities of the input/output arcs determine the number of tokens involved by transition firings. The set of all the markings, that a net can reach through transition firings from an initial marking, is called the *Reachability Set* (RS). Instead, the behaviour of the net is encoded by means of the *Reachability Graph* (RG), a directed graph whose nodes are the markings of the RS and whose arcs are tagged with the labels of the transitions that cause the corresponding marking changes.

Temporal specifications must be introduced to model and study the temporal dynamics of a PN. Several timed extensions have been proposed in the literature [18]. In this paper we focus on Stochastic PN (SPN) [15], in which exponentially distributed random delays (interpreted as durations of certain activities) are associated with transition firings. Thanks to this assumption the temporal behaviour of the system can be modelled with a random process governed by the so-called Chapman-Kolmogorov differential equations [5]. These equations correspond to the Master Chemical Equations [6] that are used to describe the behaviour of biological systems, thus making this formalism quite attractive for these types of applications. Specifically, the underlying stochastic process corresponds to a Continuous Time Markov Chain (CTMC) that can be represented as a graph isomorphic to the RG of the net. Formally an SPN can be defined as follows:

DEFINITION 1. *A stochastic Petri net system is a tuple*

$$\mathcal{N} = (P, T, I, O, \mathbf{m}_0, \lambda)$$

where:

- $P = \{p_i\}_{1 \le i \le n_p}$ *is a finite and non empty set of* places *of cardinality* n_p*;*
- $T = \{t_i\}_{1 \le i \le n_t}$ *is a finite, non empty set of* transitions *with cardinality* n_t *and such that* $P \cap T = \emptyset$*. All these transitions are Timed transitions which fire with a random delay characterized by a negative exponential probability distribution;*
- $I, O : P \times T \to \mathbb{N}$ *are the* input*,* output *functions that define the arcs of the net and that specify their multiplicities;*
- $\mathbf{m}_0 : P \to \mathbb{N}$ *is a multiset on* P *representing the* initial marking*; the notation* $m_0(p_i)$ *specifies the initial marking of the place* p_i*;*
- $\lambda : T \to \mathbb{R}$ *gives the* firing intensities *of the transitions.*

The values assumed by the functions I and O can be collected in $n_p \times n_t$ matrices (which we still call I and O) and whose entries are $I(p_i, t_j)$ and $O(p_i, t_j)$, respectively. By $I(t)$ we denote the column of I corresponding to transition t (the same holds for O). The set of input places of transition t (i.e. the preset of t), denoted $^\bullet t$, and the set of output places of t (i.e. postset of t), denoted $t^\bullet$, are defined as follows: $^\bullet t = \{p \in P \mid I(p,t) \neq 0\}$, and $t^\bullet = \{p \in P \mid O(p,t) \neq 0\}$.

From SPN to ODE. It often happens that, in case of very complex models, the underlying CTMC can not be derived or/and solved due to the well-known state space explosion problem. To cope with this difficulty, whenever the stochasticity of the modelled system can be neglected (e.g. due to huge number of molecules), the so-called deterministic approach can be exploited, assuming that the behavior of entities contained in a place of the net is described with an Ordinary Differential Equation (ODE) and that the whole model is specified with a system of ODEs, one for each place of the net. In the literature, different laws (e.g. Michaelis-Menten, Hill-equation, etc.) have been proposed to encode each reaction of the biological system into an ODE. Here we focus on the Mass Action (MA) law [20][1] in which the ODEs describing the model have the following form:

$$\frac{dx_{p_i}(\nu)}{d\nu} = \sum_{j:O(p_i,t_j)\neq 0} O(p_i,t_j)\lambda(t_j) \prod_{h:I(p_h,t_j)\neq 0} x_{p_h}(\nu)^{I(p_h,t_j)} - \sum_{j:I(p_i,t_j)\neq 0} I(p_i,t_j)\lambda(t_j) \prod_{h:I(p_h,t_j)\neq 0} x_{p_h}(\nu)^{I(p_h,t_j)} \quad (1)$$

[1]Observe that this choice does not affect the generality of our approach that can be applied independently of the assumed law.

where $x_{p_i}(\nu)$ represents the amount of the entity in place p_i at time ν assuming that $x_{p_i}(0)$ is defined through the initial marking of the net so that $x_{p_i}(0) = m_0(p_i)$.

For instance, considering the PN model in Fig.1 the behavior of place GLC is described by the following ODE equation assuming the MA law:

$$\frac{dx_{GLC}(\nu)}{d\nu} = +\lambda(K_{F_1}) \cdot x_{HK} \cdot x_{GLC} \cdot x_{ATP} \quad (2)$$
$$-\lambda(K_{R_1}) \cdot x_{HK} \cdot x_{G6P} \cdot x_{ADP}$$

Optimization problem. In Mathematics, Computer Science, and Operations Research, optimization or mathematical programming consists of minimizing (or maximizing) a function by systematically choosing the values of its variables from a set of feasible possibilities properly exploiting analytical or numerical methods. In Systems Biology optimization is not a new concept since it has been already proposed to reconstruct gene regulatory networks, transcriptional regulatory networks, protein interaction networks, conditional specific sub-networks, and active pathways [10], and to perform FBA. Formally an optimization problem with inequality constrains can be defined as follows:

$$\begin{aligned} \underset{\mathbf{y}}{\text{minimize}} \quad & \mathcal{F}_{opt}(\mathbf{y}) \\ \text{subject to} \quad & \mathcal{G}_i(\mathbf{y}) \geq b_i, \quad 1 \leq i \leq l \\ & \mathcal{L}_i(\mathbf{y}) \leq c_j, \quad 1 \leq j \leq m \end{aligned}$$

where the vector $\mathbf{y} = (y_1, \ldots, y_n)$ is the *variable vector*, the function $\mathcal{F}_{opt} : \mathbb{R}^n \to \mathbb{R}$ is the *objective function*, the functions $\mathcal{G}_i(\mathbf{y}) : \mathbb{R}^n \to \mathbb{R}$ and $\mathcal{L}_i(\mathbf{y}) : \mathbb{R}^n \to \mathbb{R}$ are *inequality constraint functions*, and the constants $b_1, \ldots, b_l, c_1, \ldots, c_m$ are the *bounds* for the constraints. A vector $\mathbf{y}^\bullet$, called *optimal*, is the solution of the OP if, among all vectors that satisfy the constraints, it is that which yields the smallest (largest) value of the optimization function: $\forall \mathbf{z}$ s.t. $\mathcal{G}_1(\mathbf{z}) \geq b_1, \ldots, \mathcal{L}_1(\mathbf{z}) \leq c_m$ we have that $\mathcal{F}_{opt}(\mathbf{z}) \geq \mathcal{F}_{opt}(\mathbf{y}^\bullet)$.

We recall that an OP is called a *linear program* if the objective and constraint functions are linear and *non-linear* otherwise. As shown in the next sections of this paper, we will focus on non-linear programs in which constraints can be non-linear as well. To solve this type of OPs, several algorithms have been proposed in the literature, and the reader can find a complete survey of these methods in [11].

4. OUR APPROACH

Before describing our approach in details, we introduce the biological considerations which motivated our proposal.

First, in our method we assume that both the topology and the kinetic parameters of the network are specified with different level of detail, depending on the biochemical event we are observing. Since in biochemical systems events are generally represented as biochemical reactions, we decide to divide all the reactions into two classes: *determined* reactions and *undetermined* reactions.

We assume that for determined reactions the mechanism of their biochemical interaction has been properly analysed, so that they can be clearly characterized and modelled.

Instead, regarding undetermined reactions, we assume that in this part of the network the topology is only partially known, so that while all the reagents, all the products and some modifiers are specified, we do not exclude that other modifiers could be present.

For instance, this assumption can be motivated by many studies that showed how many cells of different organisms own different isoforms of the same enzyme and that every isoform has a specific affinity for a group of molecular regulators [16]. Thus, in a specific cell, the resulting kinetic behaviour of a reaction is a direct consequence of the proportion at which these isoforms are present [16] [2]. In some situations this proportion may hardly be defined, and, even if it is known, the list of modifiers for secondary isoforms is not always clear.

Moreover, for specific conditions, like cancer, cells may present genetic mutations and quantitative alterations or isoform swithces that change the affinity between enzymes and their regulators, thus affecting the overall enzymatic dynamics. Assuming the molecular interactions of an enzyme are unclear necessarily implies that its activity is not expressible with a precise mathematical formulation.

Finally, as anticipated in Section 2, we assume that an objective function with a biological meaning can be profitably used to formulate an OP and to reproduce an actual biological behaviour. From our point of view, this biological objective can be interpreted in different ways. For instance, it can be related to its definition in FBA or CM and formulated similarly. In FBA, according to the teleonomic perspective, the objective function describes an objective that we believe is physiologically relevant for the cell, like the maximisation of biomass. This is used to predict a physiological behaviour of the cell. Inspired by other successful applications of FBA, also in our approach the objective function can express a non-physiological goal of the cell, like the maximisation of ATP production, and used to identify some property of the network, or, it may be used to impose an engineering (e.g. maximisation of the production of a particular amminoacid) or therapeutic (e.g. minimisation of some reaction fluxes vital for cancer cells) objective to a metabolic system. More in general, the objective function is intended to represent any relevant biological behaviour that has been experimentally measured or that has to be achieved. Our approach thus tries to investigate if and how this specific biological phenotype can be reproduced in a biochemical system where the topology and the parametrization are just partially known.

In details we propose a method that exploits iterative optimizations: at each simulation step, an objective function with the aforementioned biological meaning allows us to estimate the activities of undetermined reactions, and thus to obtain a complete description of system behaviour.

To facilitate the construction of the model we propose a new graphical formalism based on PN, which allows to automatically translate the model into its mathematical representation, consisting of the ODEs system and the Optimization Problem (OP).

According to this we decide to present our approach firstly introducing this new graphical formalism, and then providing its automatic translation into a ODE system in which indeterminate transitions are tackled through an OP. For this purpose we use the model of Fig.1 as a "running example" that we comment in the rest of the paper to discuss the features of this new modelling formalism.

SPN with Indetermination. The formal definition of a new PN extension called Stochastic Petri Net with Indetermination (SPNI) is the following:

Definition 2. *A stochastic Petri net with indetermination is a tuple*

$$\mathcal{N} = (P, T, I, O, \mathbf{m}_0, \lambda_n, \Lambda_u, \mathcal{F}_{opt}^{\mathcal{N}})$$

where:

- *P, I, O,* $\mathbf{m}_0$ *are defined as in the SPN formalism;*
- $T = T_n \cup T_u$ *is a finite, non empty set of timed transitions with* $T_n \cap T_u = \emptyset$*.* T_n *is the set of the determined transitions, while* T_u *is the set of undetermined transitions.*
- $\lambda_n : T_n \to \mathbb{R}$ *gives the firing intensity of* T_n *transitions.*
- $\Lambda_u : T_u \to \mathbb{R}^2$ *gives the range of variation of the flux of* T_u *transitions.*
- $\mathcal{F}_{opt}^{\mathcal{N}} : T \times P \to \mathbb{R}$ *is an objective function whose terms are represented by place markings and transition firing intensities.*

We use the notation $\Lambda_u^L(t)$ (resp. $\Lambda_u^H(t)$) to denote the lower (resp. higher) bound values of the *firing intensity* interval associated with a $t \in T_u$; $\Lambda_u(t)$ then represents a possible firing intensity of the (undetermined) transition t compatible with its specified lower and higher bounds. For instance in the gray boxes of Fig.1 are represented the transitions affected by a level of indetermination(i.e. K_{f1}, K_{r1}, K_{f3}, K_{r3}, K_{f12}, k_{r12}).

From SPNI to ODE and OP.
Due to the indetermination associated with the T_u transitions, it is not possible to directly use Eq. 1 to represent the deterministic behavior of an SPNI model. We can however re-write Eq. 1 as follows:

$$\frac{dx_{p_i}(\nu)}{d\nu} = \sum_{j:O(p_i,t_j)\neq 0} O(p_i,t_j)\mathcal{M}_{t_j}(\nu) \prod_{h:I(p_h,t_j)\neq 0} x_{p_h}(\nu)^{I(p_h,t_j)} - \sum_{j:I(p_i,t_j)\neq 0} I(p_i,t_j)\mathcal{M}_{t_j}(\nu) \prod_{h:I(p_h,t_j)\neq 0} x_{p_h}(\nu)^{I(p_h,t_j)} \quad (3)$$

where $\mathcal{M}$ is a function defined in the following way:

$$\mathcal{M}_t(\nu) = \begin{cases} \lambda_n(t) & if\ t \in T_n \\ y_t(\nu) & otherwise \end{cases} \quad (4)$$

The parameter $y_t(\nu)$ encodes the indetermination associated with the undetermined transition t at time ν and must be properly estimated to solve the ODE system.

As we already pointed out, the undetermined transitions are part of the model either because their exact specification is not relevant with respect to the goals of the analysis carried on with the SPNI or because they are too difficult to identify in a precise manner. Independently of the context of the modelling experiment, it is usually the case that we want to minimize (or maximize) certain measures defined on the portion of the state of the system that is not directly affected by undetermined transitions. These measures, that may assume complex definitions, become the optimization functions that we use to study these models. To cope with this problem we thus propose to proceed in two steps where we first reduce the indetermination of the model solving an optimisation problem in which the firing intensity of T_u transitions are estimated according to a user-defined objective function. Subsequently, we use these estimated values in the ODE system which thus becomes properly defined and ready to be solved.

Given an SPNI model, the corresponding OP, whose solution will be used to estimate the firing intensity values of the T_u transitions, is derived using the following definition.

Definition 3. *The OP derived by the SPNI is a tuple*

$$\mathcal{O} = (\mathbf{y}_\nu, \mathcal{F}_{opt}, \mathcal{G}, \mathcal{L})$$

where:

- $\mathbf{y}_\nu$ *represents the optimizing values of undetermined transitions at time* ν*, i.e.* $\forall t \in T_u \Rightarrow y_t(\nu) \in \mathbf{y}_\nu$*;*
- $\mathcal{F}_{opt} = \mathcal{F}_{opt}^{\mathcal{N}}$*;*
- $\mathcal{G}$ *is defined by*

$$\forall t \in T_u \Rightarrow y_t(\nu) \prod_{h:I(p_h,t)\neq 0} x_{p_h}(\nu)^{I(p_h,t)} \geq \Lambda_u^L(t)$$

- $\mathcal{L}$ *is defined by*

$$\forall t \in T_u \Rightarrow y_t(\nu) \prod_{h:I(p_h,t_j)\neq 0} x_{p_h}(\nu)^{I(p_h,t_j)} \leq \Lambda_u^U(t)$$

For instance, considering the SPNI in Fig. 1 the vector $\mathbf{y}(\nu)$ has size six and represents the optimal values of the firing rates of transitions K_{f1}, K_{r1}, K_{f3}, K_{r3}, K_{f12}, and K_{r12}. An example of objective function could be the maximization of the Lactate (LAC) as described in our case study in Section 5. Moreover in our example $\mathcal{G}(K_{f1})$ is $y_{K_{f1}} \cdot x_{HK} \cdot x_{G6P} \cdot x_{ADP} \geq 8.0E^5$ and $\mathcal{L}(K_{f1})$ is $y_{K_{f1}} \cdot x_{HK} \cdot x_{G6P} \cdot x_{ADP} \leq 9.0E^4$ with limit values chosen as explained in Section 5

How to compute the model behavior. The numerical integration of Eq. 3 provides the behavior of the model $\mathbf{x}(\nu+\tau)$ at time $\nu+\tau$, in terms of the behavior $\mathbf{x}(\nu)$ computed at time ν and of a set of parameters deriving from the structure of the SPNI (I, and O), the firing intensities of the definite transitions of the net (λ_n) and of the firing intensities of the undetermined transitions estimated at time ν and collectively represented as $y(\nu)$. The values of $\mathbf{x}(\nu+\tau)$ are thus the results of the evaluation of a function whose input parameters are represented by a tuple $B(\nu) = (B, B_u(\nu))$ where $B = (I, O, \lambda_n)$ and $B_u(\nu) = (\mathbf{x}(\nu), \mathbf{y}(\nu))$ [2]. The integration step s identifies the time points $\nu_i = i * \tau$ where the evaluation of the model behavior is of interest.

Role of the estimation phase of our method is that of finding a set $\mathbf{y}(\nu)$ that, being compatible with the constraints of the SPNI model (Λ_u), minimizes the objective function at time $\nu+s$. The optimization phase identifies a number K of initial conditions, that we denote with $B_u^{[k]}(\nu), k = 1, ..., K$, consisting of the behavior of the model computed at time ν and of K random points within the space of firing intensities of the undetermined transitions identified by the constraints Λ. From each of these configurations the method numerically integrates the system of ODEs up to time $\nu+s$ to derive $\mathbf{y}(\nu)$. Letting $B^{[k]}(\nu) = \left(B, B_u^{[k]}(\nu)\right)$, with $B_u^{[k]}(\nu) = (\mathbf{x}(\nu), \mathbf{y}^{[k]}(\nu))$, the solutions obtained from the integration of the ODEs with parameters $B^{[k]}(\nu), k = 0, 1, ..., K$ and up to time $\nu+s$ are compared to identify the choice of $B^{[k]}(\nu)$ which provides the best evaluation of the objective function, thus identifying $\mathbf{y}^{[k]}(\nu+s) = \mathbf{y}(\nu)$. Crucial in this optimization step is that the numerical integration of the ODEs is performed with a method capable of identifying an integration step h small enough to allow a precise solution of the

[2]In the sequel of the paper we will indifferently use $\mathbf{y}_t(\nu)$ or $\Lambda_u(t, \nu)$ to represent the undetermined parameters of our models as provided by the optimization problem at time ν.

Algorithm 1 Algorithm to solve ODE system with Indetermination

1: **function** SolveODEI($ODEI, \mathcal{G}, \mathcal{L}, \mathcal{F}_{opt}, \tau, FinalTime$)
2: $\quad \nu = 0.0$;
3: $\quad$ *ODEI.Init(Value)*;
4: $\quad$ **while** ($\nu \leq FinalTime$) **do**
5: $\qquad$ **print**(*time, Value*);
6: $\qquad$ $Rate_{T_u}$=*SolveOpt*($Value, ODEI, \nu + \tau, \mathcal{G}, \mathcal{L}, \mathcal{F}_{opt}$);
7: $\qquad$ *Value=ODEI.SolverODE*($Value, \nu + \tau, Rate_{T_u}$);
8: $\qquad \nu \mathrel{+}= \tau$;
9: $\quad$ **end while**
10: **end function**

ODEs during these "tentative" evaluations that are used to select the firing intensities of the undetermined transitions.

In general, this whole method is repeated for each time point ν_i starting from $\nu_0 = 0$. However, solving the OP for each value of ν_i can be excessively costly and we can thus reduce this computational effort by identifying a time interval ρ that is a multiple of τ and that determines the time points where the optimization is requested. By doing so, if we set $\rho = m \cdot \tau$, we assume that for $m - 1$ intermediate evaluation steps the values of $\mathbf{\Lambda}_u(\nu)$ (i.e. $\mathbf{y}(\nu)$) remain constant and an approximation is introduced.

Having discussed how to derive from an SPNI model (i) an ODE system with indetermination (see Eq.3), and (ii) an OP (see Def.3), we can devise an algorithm which combines them to derive the model behavior.

The pseudo-code of this algorithm is shown in Alg. 1. It takes as input the ODE system with indetermination (i.e. *ODEI*), the OP (i.e. described by functions $\mathcal{G}$, $\mathcal{L}$ and $\mathcal{F}_{opt}$), the step size used for the optimization schema (i.e. τ), and the final time (i.e. *FinalTime*). The output of the algorithm is represented by the values generated for each system entity at different time points (i.e. ν_i). In details, the method *Init()* at line 3 initializes the vector *Value* encoding the initial values assumed for all the entities of the model. Then, the code from line 6 to line 8 is repeated until the time horizon is not reached. In each iteration the function *print()* is called to print the current values of the system entities. Subsequently, the function *SolveOpt()* solves the optimisation and returns an estimated value for each T_u transition. It takes in input the current values of the entities (i.e. *Value*), the final time in which the objective function will be evaluated (i.e. $\nu + \tau$), the ODE system (i.e. *ODE*), and a set of functions encoding the OP (i.e. $\mathcal{G}, \mathcal{L}$ and $\mathcal{F}_{opt}$). The functions $\mathcal{G}$ and $\mathcal{L}$ are used by the optimization solver to test if a new vector $\mathbf{y}$, randomly generated according to the parameter constrains, is a feasible solution. Indeed the functions $\mathcal{G}$ and $\mathcal{L}$ verify if $\mathbf{y}$ satisfies the inequality constraints. The function $\mathcal{F}_{opt}$ is instead called by the optimization solver to compute the value of the objective function associated with a feasible vector $\mathbf{y}$. This function, takes as input the vector $\mathbf{y}$, the current values of the entities (i.e. *Value*), the ODE system (i.e. *ODE*), and the final time in which the objective function must be evaluated (i.e. $\nu + \tau$). First it computes the quantities values at $\nu + \tau$ assuming the missing rates to be equal to $\mathbf{y}$. Then, the computed values are used to evaluate the objective function, whose derived value is returned. When the optimization step is terminated returning the rate estimations, the ODE system with indetermination (i.e. *ODEI*) can be solved (i.e. method *SolveODE()*), and the vector *Value* is updated with the new computed values.

5. EXPERIMENTAL RESULTS AND DISCUSSION

In this section we report a case study to illustrate how our approach can be used to investigate the metabolic behaviour of cancer cells. The model represents the glycolytic pathway in a generic human cell. It is inspired by the model presented in [9], which describes glycolysis in human red blood cells. In physiological conditions glycolysis leads to a consumption of Glucose (GLC) and a progressive production of Pyruvate (PYR) and energy, in the form of Adenosine Triphosphate (ATP). Then, in the presence of oxygen, PYR is metabolised by other pathways to generate the majority of the energy consumed by the cell. In absence of oxygen, PYR is converted to LAC without further energetic yields. Differently form normal cells, cancer cells exhibit an enhancement of glycolysis and production of LAC even in the presence of oxygen, Warburg Effect [7]. This phenomenon inspired the experiment discussed below. The model is characterized by fourteen metabolic reactions, the related equations are reported in the first column of the Table in Fig. 2, and it can be graphically described by the SPN model in Fig. 1 where place names are chosen to recall the corresponding biological compounds.

Our implementation. The experiments have been performed using a prototype implementation of the proposed method integrated in the *GreatSPN* framework [1]. With this extension, *GreatSPN* allows the generation of an ODE system with/without indetermination from an SPNI model, and then the *R environment* is used to compute its solutions. In particular the *deSolve* library is used to solve the ODE system, while *GenSA* library to solve the OP.

As already pointed out, in cancer cells the metabolism is characterised by the Warburg Effect [7]. Moreover, it has been recently shown that cancer cells preferentially rely on specific isoforms of their metabolic enzymes. In particular, it seems that isoforms of **Hexokinase** (HK), **Phosphofructokinase** (PFK) and **Pyruvate Kinase** (PK) may have an eminent role in the deregulation of cancer metabolism [13]. Despite these discoveries, it is still complicated to characterize the *in vivo* kinetics of these isoforms. Conditioned by these constraints, we chose to set the reactions involving HK, PFK and PK as undetermined transitions, i.e deficient of a complete list of regulators, of its mathematical expression and its parametrization. Our approach is here used as an attempt to acquire a deeper understanding of these metabolic dynamics. The idea is to use an objective function that encodes the Warburg Effect in every type of cancer at every possible tumour stage. For this reason the firing intensities K_{f_1}, K_{r_1}, K_{f_3}, K_{r_3}, $K_{f_{12}}$ and $K_{r_{12}}$ were allowed to vary in a wide range that agrees with biological knowledge. This was formalized as the maximization of LAC production at every integration step.

Fig. 3 shows the evolution of LAC over time. The black line represents the results of the model of a normal cell, where all parameters are well characterized. Blue triangles show the time evolution of LAC when uncertainty is applied. It can be noticed that this objective function is able to drive the system to accelerate LAC production. Even if the difference might not seem large enough to represent the Warburg Effect, we point out that these diagrams show the behaviour of our model for a very short time interval. Fig. 4 shows the

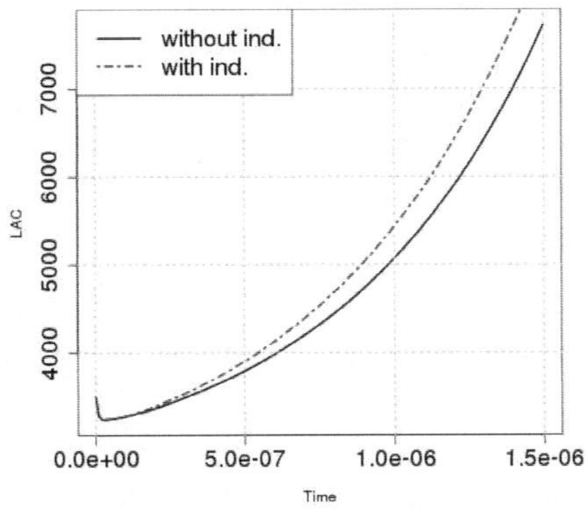

Figure 3: Behaviours of place *LAC*

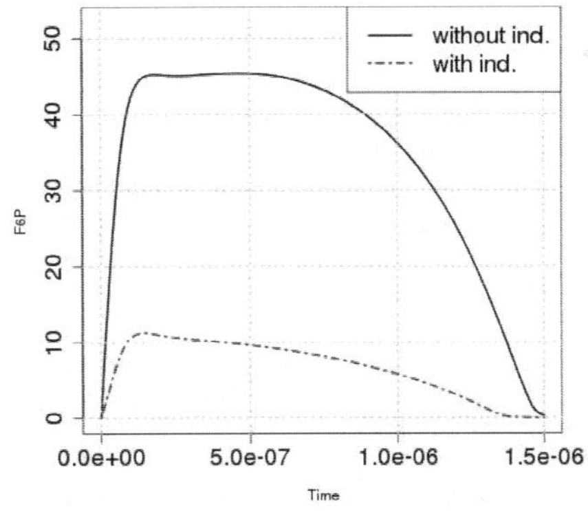

Figure 4: Behaviours of place *F6P*

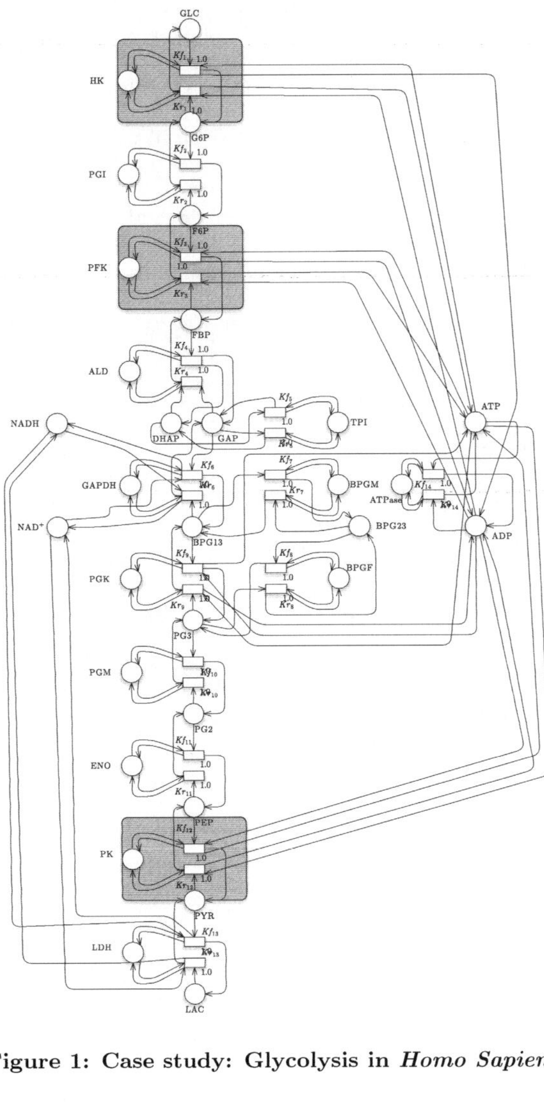

Figure 1: Case study: Glycolysis in *Homo Sapiens*.

Reactions	Rate Equations	Initial Marking
$HK+GLC+ATP \underset{Kr1}{\overset{Kf1}{\rightleftarrows}} HK+G6P+ADP$	$Kf_1 = 6.48E+05, Kr_1 = 4.9E+03$	$GLC_0 = 5E+03, HK_0 = 4$
$PGI+G6P+ATP \underset{Kr2}{\overset{Kf2}{\rightleftarrows}} PGI+F6P$	$Kf_2 = 1.15E+03, Kr_2 = 2,68E+03$	$G6P_0 = 0, PGI_0 = 8E+03$
$PFK+F6P+ATP \underset{Kr3}{\overset{Kf3}{\rightleftarrows}} PFK+FBP+ADP$	$Kf_3 = 1E+09, Kr_3 = 8.47E+04$	$F6P_0 = 0, PFK_0 = 10$
$ALD+FBP \underset{Kr4}{\overset{Kf4}{\rightleftarrows}} ALD+DHAP+GAP$	$Kf_4 = 1.46E+02, Kr_4 = 1.18E+00$	$FBP_0 = 0, ALD_0 = 2E+04, DHAP_0 = 0$
$TPI+GAP \underset{Kr5}{\overset{Kf5}{\rightleftarrows}} TPI+DHAP$	$Kf_5 = 7.93E+00, Kr_5 = 4.53E-01$	$TPI_0 = 2E+06, GAP_0 = 0$
$GAPDH+GAP+NAD^+ \underset{Kr6}{\overset{Kf6}{\rightleftarrows}} GAPDH+BPG13+NADH$	$Kf_6 = 1.42E+05, Kr_6 = 5.28E+06$	$GAPDH_0 = 4E+02, NAD_0^+ = 1E+04, NADH_0 = 0$
$BPGM+BPG13 \underset{Kr7}{\overset{Kf7}{\rightleftarrows}} BPGM+BPG23$	$Kf_7 = 1E+08, Kr_7 = 1E+05$	$BPGM_0 = 5, BPG13_0 = 0$
$BPGF+BPG23 \underset{Kr8}{\overset{Kf8}{\rightleftarrows}} BPGF+PG3$	$Kf_8 = 6.84E+02, Kr_8 = 1E-09$	$BPGF_0 = 1E+02, BPG23_0 = 0$
$PGK+BPG13+ADP \underset{Kr9}{\overset{Kf9}{\rightleftarrows}} PGK+PG3+ATP$	$Kf_9 = 2.61E+04, Kr_9 = 1.45E+01$	$PGK_0 = 1E+02$
$PGM+PG3 \underset{Kr10}{\overset{Kf10}{\rightleftarrows}} PGM+PG2$	$Kf_{10} = 5.38E+01, Kr_{10} = 7.92E+00$	$PGM_0 = 9E+05, PG3_0 = 0$
$ENO+PG2 \underset{Kr11}{\overset{Kf11}{\rightleftarrows}} ENO+PEP$	$Kf_{11} = 5.82E+02, Kr_{11} = 3.44E+02$	$ENO_0 = 1E+05, PG2_0 = 0$
$PK+PEP+ADP \underset{Kr12}{\overset{Kf12}{\rightleftarrows}} PK+PYR+ATP$	$Kf_{12} = 5.17E+02, Kr_{12} = 5.17E-01$	$PEP_0 = 0, PK_0 = 9E+03,$
$LDH+PYR+NADH \underset{Kr13}{\overset{Kf13}{\rightleftarrows}} LDH+LAC+NAD^+$	$Kf_{13} = 1.04E+03, Kr_{13} = 2.34E+00$	$PYR_0 = 1E+02, LDH_0 = 4E+02, LAC_0 = 3.5E+03$
$ATPase+ATP \underset{Kr14}{\overset{Kf14}{\rightleftarrows}} ATPase+ADP$	$Kf_{14} = 9.74E-01, Kr_{14} = 9.74E-04$	$ATPase_0 = 1E+02, ATP_0 = 7E+02, ADP_0 = 5E+02$

Figure 2: Table: Reactions, Equations and Initial marking of glycolysis in *Homo Sapiens*.

rapid accumulation of Fructose 6-Phosphate (F6P) in the normal cell model compared to a more balanced production-consumption dynamics in the cancer model. F6P, a high glycolitic intermediate, increases as a direct consequence of GLC degradation and is later processed by PFK. It is then significant to see which parameters the optimizer independently chooses to tune in order to maximize its objective function. While parameter values of HK and PK did not vary markedly if compared to the normal cell model (data not shown), the highest difference regarded PFK. Many articles as [16] have demonstrated that PFK kinetics is highly non-linear and depends on many allosteric interactions. Our results seem to reinforce the Mulukutla's thesis [16] that the regulation of PFK activity has a crucial impact on the glycolitic flux and may be relevant to explain metabolic alterations in cancer.

Discussion. It is important to observe that our approach differently by dFBA and CM allows us to define objective functions that may mimic the behaviours experimentally observed, as the LAC maximisation. Moreover, our proposed approach does not assume the steady state of the intracellular metabolites as in dFBA, and it does not require a full understanding of model kinetics as in CM. Finally, unlike PE it is not limited by the lack of experimental data, as normally happens in cancer cell scenarios.

6. CONCLUSIONS

In this work we proposed a new approach to deal with the biochemical models with lacking kinetic information. As discussed in Section 5 it may be useful for different applications, although additional experiments will provide a further validation and will show its actual relevance. For the future we intend to apply our approach to study different networks, either in microorganisms, in single human cells or in population of cells. Because the performances of our approach are highly dependent on the optimization algorithms we plan to test different algorithms comparing their performance in terms of memory saving and execution time. Great efforts will be also spent to investigate which available biological data can be effectively used to adapt the model to the specific situation under study. Transcriptomics, proteomics and metabolomics profiles, as well as reaction fluxes and thermodynamic information are all possible candidates. These data will provide a fundamental support to define the initial conditions of the model and to set the constraints for the optimization. Finally, we will investigate the possibility of extending our approach to grab stochastic behaviours, so that the model will be approximated by a system of stochastic differential equations.

7. ADDITIONAL AUTHORS

Gianfranco Balbo (University of Turin, Computer Science Department, Corso Svizzera 185 Turin Italy, email: *balbo@di.unito.it*)

8. REFERENCES

[1] J. Babar, M. Beccuti, S. Donatelli, and A. S. Miner. Greatspn enhanced with decision diagram data structures. In *Proceedings of 31st Int. Conf. of Applications and Theory of Petri Nets*, pages 308–317. IEEE Computer Society, June 2010.

[2] B. D. Bennett, E. H. Kimball, M. Gao, R. Osterhout, S. J. V. Dien, and J. D. Rabinowit. Absolute metabolite concentrations and implied enzyme active site occupancy in escherichia coli. *Nature Chemical Biology*, 5(8):593–599, 2009.

[3] S. Bulik, S. Grimbs, C. Huthmacher, J. Selbig, and H. G. HolzhÃijtter. Kinetic hybrid models composed of mechanistic and simplified enzymatic rate laws - a promising method for speeding up the kinetic modelling of complex metabolic networks. *FEBS Journal*, 276(2):410–424, 2009.

[4] P. Cazzaniga, C. Daminani, D. Besozzi, R. Colombo, M. Nobile, D. Gaglio, D. Pescini, S. Molinari, G. Mauri, L. Alberghina, and M. Vanoni. Computational strategies for a system-level understanding of metabolism. *Metabolites*, 4:1034–1087, 2014.

[5] W. Feller. *An Introduction to Probability Theory*, volume 1. Wiley, New York, NY, 1968.

[6] D. T. Gillespie. A rigorous derivation of the chemical master equation. *Physica A: Statistical Mechanics and its Applications*, 188(1-3):404–425, 1992.

[7] M. V. Heiden. Targeting cancer metabolism: a therapeutic window opens. *Nature Reviews. Drug discovery*, 10(9):671–684, 2011.

[8] D. M. Hendrickx, M. M. W. B. Hendriks, P. H. C. Eilers, A. K. Smilde, and H. C. J. Hoefsloot. Reverse engineering of metabolic networks, a critical assessment. *Molecular BioSystems*, 7:511–520, 2011.

[9] N. Jamshidi and B. O. Palsson. Mass action stoichiometric simulation models: Incorporating kinetics and regulatoin into stoichiometric models. *Biophysical Journal*, 98(2):175185, 2010.

[10] R.-S. W. L. Chen and X.-S. Zhang. *Biomolecular Networks: Methods and Applications in Systems Biology*. Wiley, New York, NY, 2009.

[11] K. Lange. *Optimization*. Springer, New York, NY, second edition, 2013.

[12] X. Liu and M. Niranjan. State and parameter estimation of the heat shock response system using kalman and particle filters. *Bioinformatics*, 28(11):1501–1507, 2012.

[13] U. E. Martinez-Outschoorn, M. Peiris-PagÃl's, R. G. Pestell, F. Sotgia, and M. P. Lisanti. Cancer metabolism: a therapeutic perspective. *Nature Reviews Clinical Oncology*, May 2016.

[14] C. G. Moles, P. Mendes, and J. R. Banga. Parameter estimation in biochemical pathways: A comparison of global optimization methods. *Genome Research*, 13(11):2467–2474, 2003.

[15] M. K. Molloy. Performance analysis using stochastic petri nets. *IEEE Transactions on Computers*, 31(9):913–917, 1982.

[16] B. C. Mulukutla, A. Yongky, P. Daoutidis, and W.-S. Hu. Bistability in glycolysis pathway as a physiological switch in energy metabolism. *PLoS ONE*, 9(6):1–12, June 2014.

[17] J. D. Orth, I. Thiele, and B. Ã. Palsson. What is flux balance analysis? *Nature biotechnology*, 28:245–248, March 2010.

[18] L. Popova-Zeugmann. *Time and Petri nets*. Springer, Heidelberg, GE, 2013.

[19] M. Radhakrishnan, J. S. Edwards, and F. J. Doyle. Dynamic flux balance analysis of diauxic growth in escherichia coli. *Biophysical Journal 83.3 (2002)*, 83(3):1331–1340, 2002.

[20] E. O. Voit. *Computational analysis of biochemical systems : a practical guide for biochemists and molecular biologists*. Cambridge University Press, Cambridge, New York, 2000.

[21] J. D. Young. Learning from the steersman: A natural history of cybernetic models. *Industrial & Engineering Chemistry Research*, 54(42):10162–10169, 2015.

Autonomic Orchestration of Containers: Problem Definition and Research Challenges

Emiliano Casalicchio
Blekinge Institute of Technology
Karlskrona, Sweden
Emiliano.Casalicchio@bth.se

ABSTRACT

Today, a new technology is going to change the way cloud platforms are designed and managed. This technology is called container. A container is a software environment where to install an application or application component and all the library dependencies, the binaries, and a basic configuration needed to run the application. The container technology promises to solve many cloud application issues, for example the application portability problem and the virtual machine performance overhead problem. The cloud industry is adopting the container technology both for internal usage and as commercial offering. However, we are far away from the maturity stage and there are still many research challenges to be solved. One of them is container orchestration, that make it possible to define how to select, deploy, monitor, and dynamically control the configuration of multi-container packaged applications in the cloud. This paper presents the problem of autonomic container orchestration, analyze the state of the art solutions and discuss open challenges.

CCS Concepts

• **Computing methodologies~Self-organization** • **Computer systems organization~Cloud computing** • *Information systems~Computing platforms* • *Applied computing~Service-oriented architectures* • Theory of computation~Distributed computing models

Keywords

Container; Docker; Cloud Computing; Autonomic Computing; Service Orchestration.

1. INTRODUCTION

Operating system and application virtualization, also known as *container* (or *Docker container* or simply *Docker* [1]), became popular since 2013 with the launch of the Docker open source project (docker.com) and with the growing interest of PaaS providers [2] and Internet service providers [3]. A container is a software environment where one can install an application or application component (the so called microservice) and all the library dependencies, the binaries, and a basic configuration needed to run the application. Containers provide a higher level of abstraction for the process lifecycle management, with the ability not only to start/stop but also to upgrade and release a new version of a containerized service in a seamless way. IBM researcher *"believe that the new cloud operating environment will be built using containers as a foundation. No virtual machines..."*[4].

Containers became so popular because they potentially may solve many cloud application issues, for example: the *"dependency hell" problem*, typical of complex distributed applications. Containers give the possibility to separate components, wrapping up the application with all its dependencies in a self-contained piece of software, that can be executed on any platform that supports the container technology. The *application portability problem*; a microservice can be executed on any platform supporting container and moreover the Docker container management framework is compliant with the cloud portability frameworks TOSCA [5][6]. The *performance overhead problem*; containers are lightweight and introduce lower overhead compared to VMs. The literature shows that the overhead introduced by containers, compared to bare-metal installations, is around 10% while hardware virtualization (classical VMs) introduce an overhead of the 40% [7]; moreover, launching and shouting down a container requires 1-2 seconds rather than minutes. Besides, the concept of microservices and the portability feature of containers make it possible to satisfy typical constraints imposed by the legislation and the regulation e.g., the data sovereignty and the vendor-lock-in.

For all those reasons, and more, the cloud industry adopted the container technology both for internal usage [8] and for offering container-based services and container development platforms [2]. Examples are Google container engine [8], Amazon ECS [9], Alauda (alauda.io), Seastar (seastar.io), Tutum (tutum.com), Azure Container Service (azure.microsoft.com). Containers are also the state of the art solution adopted to deploy large scale applications, for example big data applications requiring high elasticity in managing a very large amount of concurrent components (e.g. [10][11]).

Despite that wide interest in containers, we are far away from the maturity stage and there are still many challenges to be solved, for example: the need for reducing networking overheads compared to hypervisors; the need for secure resource sharing and isolation to enable multi-tenancy; the need for improving container monitoring capabilities; the need for improving container resource management at run time (e.g. vertical scaling of a container is not possible) and the need for improving orchestration policies and adaptation models adding autonomic capabilities.

This work defines and discusses the problem of container orchestration with a focus on autonomic mechanisms. The paper is organized as in what follow. Section 2 defines container orchestration. Section 3 discusses the related work. The research problem of autonomic container orchestration is formulated in Section 4. Research challenges and final remarks are presented in Section 5.

VALUETOOLS 2016, October 25-28, Taormina, Italy

2. CONTAINER ORCHESTRATION

Orchestration is intended as the set of operations that cloud providers and application owners undertake (either manually or automatically) for selecting, deploying, monitoring, and dynamically controlling the configuration of resources to guarantee a certain level of quality of service [6]. In the same way, *container orchestration allows cloud and application providers to define how to select, to deploy, to monitor, and to dynamically control the configuration of multi-container packaged applications in the cloud.*

Container orchestration is not only concerned with the initial deployment of multi-container applications, but it also includes the management at runtime, for example: scaling a multi-container application as a single entity; controlling multi-tenant container-based applications; composing containers in high available software architectures; optimizing the networking of the application, e.g. executing computation near the data.

Because the highly dynamic and complex environment in which containers are operated, the orchestration actions must be automatically adapted at run time, without human intervention, and that entails autonomic orchestration mechanisms.

Today, the container orchestration frameworks are at their infancy and do not include any autonomic feature [12]. Cloudify (getcloudify.org) and Kubernetes (kubernetes.io) are the main TOSCA compliant implementations allowing orchestration of Docker containers. However, how to execute and orchestrate container in a distributed environment without leveraging on hypervisors is still an open issue. Docker Swarm requires a static setup of the cluster nodes. Core OS (coreos.com) is a first step toward in this direction, but it is a young solution, and again it is effected by the standardization problem. The auto-scaling policy implemented in Kubernetes is a simple threshold based algorithms that only uses CPU usage metrics. The scheduling and load distribution policy implemented in Swarm is rather naïve.

To realize autonomic container orchestration many research problems must be addressed, among them: resource management at run time, synchronization between design and execution environments, monitoring, performance profiling and characterization, performance modeling, definition of optimization models for orchestration and adaptation.

3. RELATED WORK

Autonomic orchestration of Docker containers could leverage more than ten years of research results in the field of autonomic computing [15], autonomic service oriented systems [16], autonomic cloud computing [17][18].

A recent survey on service level management in the cloud [17] found that: the monitor-analysis-plan-execute (MAPE) architecture style [14] is predominant in autonomic cloud systems; and, heuristics (e.g. [19][13]), and optimization policies (e.g. [20][13][21]) are the most commonly used techniques for resource allocation. In [18] the authors review literature on autonomic QoS-aware resource management in cloud computing since 2009. Both from [17] and [18] it results that mainly researchers consider time, availability, cost (in general), energy consumption, as main constraints or objective of the adaptation. A few works contemplate security, but no-one considers constraints imposed by legal rules [22][23], e.g. sovereignty of data.

The idea of container dates back to 1992 [24] and matured over the years with the introduction of Linux namespace [25] and the LXC project (linuxcontainers.org), a solution designed to execute full operating system images in containers. From operating system virtualization the idea has moved to application container [1]. The experiments in [7] show that Docker performs as bare-metal systems and outperforms KVM in most of the cases but that it is weak for I/O and network intensive workloads. In [26] the authors shown that for specific memory configuration Docker is capable to perform slightly better than VMs while executing scientific workloads.

The adoption of container technologies calls for new autonomic management solutions. An early study on container management is presented in [27]. Here the authors compare a VM-based and Elastic Application Container based resource management with regards to their feasibility and resource-efficiency. The results show that the container-based solution outperforms the VM-based approach in terms of feasibility and resource-efficiency. Today, there are technologies that specifically support container orchestration but the level of automation is very naïve. CoreOS integrates an orchestrator, called fleet, that supports live container migration from one host to another and the possibility to modify at runtime the environment of running containers. Google Kubernetes adopts a mixed approach to the virtualization that allows to scale both the computing resources available to containers and the number containers available to applications. In that way, application can rapidly scale up and down according to their needs. In [12] the authors analyze the state of the art and challenges in container orchestration pointing out the high fragmentation of technologies, lack of standard image format and immaturity of monitoring systems. C-Port [28] is the first example of orchestrator that make it possible to deploy and manage container across multiple clouds. The authors plan to address the issues of resource discovery and coordination, container scheduling and placement, and dynamic adaptation. However, the research is at an early stage. In term of orchestration policy, they developed a constraint-programming model that can be used for dynamic resource discovery and selection. The constraints that they considered are availability, cost, performance, security, or power consumption.

4. RESEARCH PROBLEM

The orchestration of container is a broad research topic because it covers the whole life-cycle management. In this work we focuses on the elastic properties of container management over distributed datacenters and in multitenant environments. We concentrate our attention on **why**, **when**, **where** and **how** to deploy, to launch, to run, to migrate and to shut down container. All those actions are defined in what is called an **orchestration** or **adaptation policy**. **Why** orchestration action should occur is determined by specific events such as an increase in the workload intensity or volume, the arrival of a new tenant, change of SLA, node failures, critical node load/health state, and so on. Figure 1 shows our approach to autonomic container orchestration. It is based on the classical MAPE-K cycle [14].

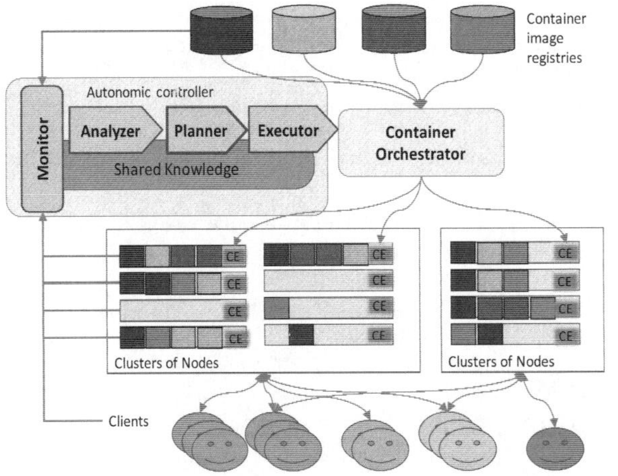

Figure 2 The container orchestration approach

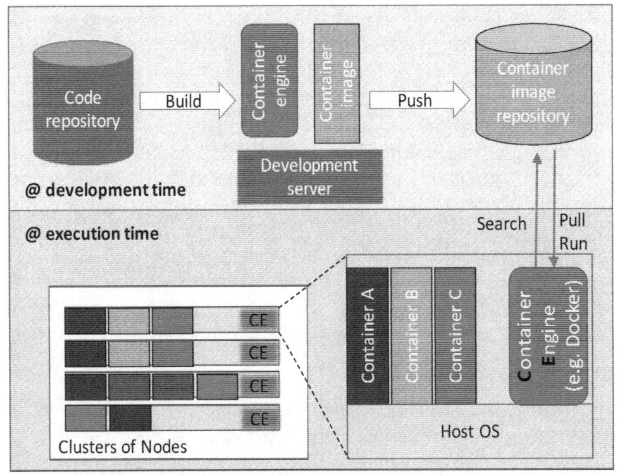

Figure 1 Container life cycle

Containers are stored in repositories called Container Image Registries. The orchestrator decides also **when** to adapt the system (e.g. to start the execution of a container) and **where** the adaptation will take place (e.g. on what computing node containers will run). Computing nodes are grouped in clusters that can be part of the same datacenter or can be geographically distributed. Each computing node in a cluster can run one or more containers, and the execution of containers is managed by the container engine (CE) on the node (see Figure 2). The orchestrator communicates with the container engine of each node to coordinate the execution of the containers. The decisions taken by the orchestrator are based on the system and environment state information collected by the Monitor component and analyzed by the Analyzer component (see Figure 1). The Planner component executes the orchestration policy to find the appropriate system configuration, that is, it solves a system model, or it runs an heuristic algorithm. Typically, the adaptation policy finds the optimal or sub-optimal system configuration that maximizes the provider utility and that satisfies non-functional and functional constraints. The Executor component implements the adaptation plan properly interacting with the Container Orchestrator component (e.g., Kubernetes). **How** the container is deployed and executed is another open issue. In the problem description we envisioned a centralized approach to orchestration. However, also decentralized solutions, i.e. choreography, apply and must be carefully investigated.

5. RESEARCH CHALLENGES

As pointed out in the previous sections, state of the art mechanisms for container orchestration should be enhanced introducing models and algorithms for runtime self-adaptation. Among the many research challenges, an urgent answer is required for the followings.

Monitoring, profiling and characterization. Monitoring of containers includes monitoring of the containerized environment (i.e., of the application) and monitoring of the container engine/platform. Monitoring techniques and tools used for the operating system and application levels do not allow to catch a wide range of QoS metrics and health state metrics for containers. Moreover, there is no a commonly agreed definition of QoS metrics for container based systems. Docker offers the `docker stat` command that returns CPU and memory utilization for each running container. More detailed CPU, memory and network statistics can be accessed through the `/containers/(id)/stats` API (docs.docker.com).

In a recent work [29], the authors the authors modify Docker and Docker Swarm in order to monitor the I/O capacity and utilization of the containers with the goal of controlling the QoS level of a Docker cluster.

Also performance characterization studies are limited, an example is [7]. Profiling and characterization of the performance of containers and container orchestration technologies is fundamental for the definition of performance models and autonomic orchestration policies.

Performance models. Validated performance models and energy consumption models of container-based systems are inexistent. Performance models are widely used in autonomic computing as representation of the system that must be adapted and as a tool to determine the reconfiguration actions needed to maintain the desired level of service. An alternative approach is the use of machine learning techniques to determine the more appropriate reconfiguration action (e.g. reinforcement learning [30]).

Adaptation models for container orchestration. As already pointed out, the container orchestration policies used until now are very simple and no autonomic mechanisms are used. This is also consequence of the lack of performance characterization and performance models. What the industry need is the definition of a framework for QoS-aware, energy-aware and legislation-aware optimal adaptation for container orchestration. This framework should allow to define system models, QoS, energy and legal constraints, to find optimal adaptation policies for container orchestration at run time.

That models, to be effective, must account for real systems limitations such as: the impossibility to change the resource assigned to a container at run time (that makes impossible vertical scaling) and the practical difficulty to synchronize the design and execution environment [31]. For example, if the execution environment is modified at run time for orchestration needs, that will impact the existing system architecture design, that must be synchronized. Off course, with the time, advancements in resource management and synchronization will overcome these limitation, and new adaptation policies can be designed.

To conclude, the way toward the next generation of cloud computing platforms is based on application virtualization rather than on hardware virtualization; and it requires a strong contribution from the research community not only focused on the above discussed orchestration problem but also on different area, for example: improving networking management to reduce overheads compared to hypervisors networking; enhancing, secure resource sharing and isolation to enable multi-tenancy; refining application design methodologies to find the right balance between the micro-service fragmentation and performances.

6. ACKNOWLEDGMENTS

This work is funded by the research project "Scalable resource-efficient systems for big data analytics" financed by the Knowledge Foundation (grant: 20140032) in Sweden.

7. REFERENCES

[1] D. Merkel. (2014). Docker: lightweight Linux containers for consistent development and deployment. *Linux J.* 2014,

[2] R. Dua, A. R. Raja, D. Kakadia, (2014) Virtualization vs containerization to support PaaS, in: Proc. of 2014 IEEE Int'l Conf. on Cloud Engineering, IC2E'14, 2014, pp. 610 - 614.

[3] S. Natarajan, A. Ghanwani, D. Krishnaswamy, R. Krishnan, P. Willis and A. Chaudhary: An Analysis of Container-based Platforms for NFV. IETF draft, Apr. 2016.

[4] IBM Container Cloud Operating System project, http://researcher.watson.ibm.com/researcher/view_group.php?id=6302

[5] OASIS, (2013) Topology and orchestration specification for cloud applications, Tech. Rep. Ver.1.0, OASIS Standard

[6] B. D. Martino, G. Cretella, A. Esposito, (2015) Advances in applications portability and services interoperability among multiple clouds, IEEE Cloud Computing 2 (2) (2015) 22-28.

[7] W. Felter, A. Ferreira, R. Rajamony, J. Rubio, (2014) An Updated Performance Comparison of Virtual Machines and Linux Containers, IBM Research Report, RC25482 (AUS1407-001) July 21, 2014

[8] B. Burns, B. Grant, D. Oppenheimer, E. Brewer, and J. Wilkes. (2016). Borg, Omega, and Kubernetes. *Queue* 14, 1, pages 10 (January 2016), 24 pages.

[9] W. Vogels, Under the Hood of Amazon EC2 Container Service, 20 July 2015, http://www.allthingsdistributed.com/

[10] W. Gerlach, et al.. (2014). Skyport: container-based execution environment management for multi-cloud scientific workflows. IEEE DataCloud '14. IEEE Press, Piscataway, NJ, USA, 25-32.

[11] DT-T. Nguyen et al. (2016). An Index Scheme for Similarity Search on Cloud Computing using MapReduce over Docker Container. In *ACM* IMCOM '16. ACM, New York, NY, USA, Article 60 , 6 pages.

[12] A. Tosatto, P. Ruiu, A. Attanasio,(2015) Container-based orchestration in cloud: State of the art and challenges, in: Proc. of 9th Int'l Conf. on Complex, Intelligent, and Software Intensive Systems, CISIS '15, 2015, pp. 70-75.

[13] E. Casalicchio, D.A.Menasce, A. Aldhalaan (2013), Autonomic resource provisioning in cloud systems with availability goals, ACM Conference on Autonomic Computing CAC'13, August 5–9, 2013, Miami, FL, USA

[14] J. O. Kephart, D. M. Chess, (2003) The vision of autonomic computing, in Computer, vol. 36, no. 1, pp. 41-50, Jan 2003.

[15] M. C. Huebscher and J. A. McCann. (2008). A survey of autonomic computing—degrees, models, and applications. *ACM Comput. Surv.* 40, 3, 7 (August 2008).

[16] A. L. Lemos, F. Daniel, and B. Benatallah. (2015). Web Service Composition: A Survey of Techniques and Tools. *ACM Comput. Surv.* 48, 3, Article 33 (December 2015).

[17] F. Faniyi and R. Bahsoon. (2015). A Systematic Review of Service Level Management in the Cloud. *ACM Comput. Surv.* 48, 3, Article 43 (December 2015), 27 pages.

[18] S. Singh and I. Chana. (2015). QoS-Aware Autonomic Resource Management in Cloud Computing: A Systematic Review. ACM Comput. Surv. 48, 3, Article 42 (December 2015), 46 pages

[19] A. Beloglazov, J. Abawajy, and R. Buyya. (2012). Energy-aware resource allocation heuristics for efficient management of data centers for cloud computing. Future Generation Comput. Syst. 28, 5 (2012), 755–768.

[20] D. Ardagna, B. Panicucci, M. Trubian, and L. Zhang. (2012). Energy-aware autonomic resource allocation in multitier virtualized environments. IEEE Trans. Services Comput. 5, 1 (2012),

[21] M. Maggio et al. (2012). Comparison of decision-making strategies for self- optimization in autonomic computing systems. ACM Trans. Auton. Adapt. Syst. 7, 4 (2012) 1–32.

[22] E. Casalicchio, M. Palmirani (2015) A Cloud Service Broker with Legal-Rule Compliance Checking and Quality Assurance Capabilities, Procedia Computer Science, Elsevier

[23] B. D. Martino, G. Cretella, A. Esposito (2015) Towards a legislation-aware cloud computing framework, Procedia Computer Science (2015)

[24] R. Pike, D. Presotto, K. Thompson, H. Trickey, P. Winterbottom, (1993) The use of name spaces in plan 9, SIGOPS Oper. Syst. Rev. 27 (2) (1993) 72-76.

[25] E. W. Biederman, Multiple instances of the global Linux namespaces, in: 2006 Ottawa Linux Symposium, 2006.

[26] T. Adufu, J. Choi and Y. Kim (2015) Is container-based technology a winner for high performance scientific applications?, *Network Operations and Management Symposium, 17th Asia-Pacific*, Busan, 2015, pp. 507-510.

[27] S. He, et al. (2012) Elastic Application Container: A Lightweight Approach for Cloud Resource Provisioning, *IEEE 26th Int. Conf. on Advanced Information Networking and Applications*, Fukuoka, 2012

[28] M. Abdelbaky et al., (2015) Docker Containers across Multiple Clouds and Data Centers, *2015 IEEE/ACM 8th Int. Conf. on Utility and Cloud Computing*, Limassol, 2015.

[29] S. McDaniel, S. Herbein and M. Taufer, (2015) A Two-Tiered Approach to I/O Quality of Service in Docker Containers *2015 IEEE Int. Conf. on Cluster Computing*.

[30] A. Pelaez, A. Quiroz and M. Parashar, "Dynamic Adaptation of Policies Using Machine Learning," *2016 16th IEEE/ACM International Symposium on Cluster, Cloud and Grid Computing (CCGrid)*, Cartagena, Colombia, 2016,

[31] F. Paraiso, S. Challita, Y. Al-Dhuraibi, P. Merle. Model-Driven Management of Docker Containers. 9th IEEE International Conference on Cloud Computing (CLOUD), Jun 2016, San Francisco, United Stat

Performability Evaluation of Software Defined Networking Infrastructures

Mario Di Mauro
University of Salerno
Via Giovanni Paolo II, 132,
I-84084, Fisciano (SA), Italy
mdimauro@unisa.it

Maurizio Longo
University of Salerno
Via Giovanni Paolo II, 132,
I-84084, Fisciano (SA), Italy
longo@unisa.it

Fabio Postiglione
University of Salerno
Via Giovanni Paolo II, 132,
I-84084, Fisciano (SA), Italy
fpostiglione@unisa.it

ABSTRACT

An innovative model in traffic engineering, named Software Defined Networking (SDN), has been recently proposed to simplify network management and control by means of programmability concepts. This emerging strategy addresses the recent network challenges by decoupling the packet forwarding features, namely the data plane, from the decision system, namely the control plane, via OpenFlow, a specific standardized protocol. The controller element of an SDN infrastructure represents the core entity in charge of managing the whole service logic and, being this module failure-prone, its performance and its availability are crucial issues for an accurate plan of an SDN-based network. The approaches considering both performance and availability assessment in data and telecommunication networks are frequently referred to as the performability evaluations. Thus, a performability evaluation is presented in this work to the aim of selecting the most convenient redundancy scheme of the SDN controller, where the controller has been modeled by a finite number of virtual operator instances serving different network zones. By assuming that the SDN controlling unit is described by a Continuous-Time Markov Chain with a vector state, the availability in long runs of the SDN controller in parallel redundancy configuration is computed by an approach based on the Universal Generating Function tailored for the vector case, and the minimal cost redundant configuration for the SDN controller is found out.

Keywords

Software Defined Networking, Performability Evaluation, Multivariate Universal Generating Function.

1. INTRODUCTION

Recently, a ground-breaking networking model named Software Defined Networking (SDN) has been proposed in order to decouple control protocols from network forwarding mechanisms and thus to simplify network management and to reinforce the provisioning and configuration of telecommunication services. This separation addresses a new vision of the network concepts where the switches are now assuming the basic role of packet forwarding devices containing the flow tables, a set of rules imposed by a central element called controller acting as depository of the network intelligence. In the SDN environment, a crucial role is played by OpenFlow [14], a novel protocol aiming to enable the communication between the control entity, named the *SDN controller*, and the devices (*switches* in the SDN jargon) at the data level.

Such a new vision, where control and forwarding entities are strongly decoupled, allows for an extensive set of flexible network solutions. A logically centralized controller in fact provides a unified programmable interface for software and higher level applications deployment, by offering an abstraction level similar to the Operating System (OS) where, *mutatis mutandis*, the controller acts as the OS kernel [1].

In this paper, the authors address a performance evaluation model in an SDN environment, with focus on the Controller designed as an appliance hosting some (virtual) operator instances that manage a set of network devices through the OpenFlow protocol when random failures occur.

An overview about the performance evaluation methods for multi-state systems and the availability issues and models is offered in [12, 13], whereas an application in the context of innovative network and telecommunication scenarios has been presented in [8, 9].

This paper is organized as follows: in Section 2, an overview of the SDN paradigm by describing the main features of the proposed infrastructure is offered. Section 3 provides a vector performance model of the controller in the presence of random failures. Section 4 introduces the Multivariate Universal Generating Function (MUGF) concept, expressly designed for a multivariate environment, aiming to finding out the minimal cost SDN configuration in terms of redundant elements. Section 5 provides an evaluation of an exemplary SDN scenario by applying the proposed MUGF approach and by using realistic telecommunication data. Finally, Section 6 concludes the paper.

2. AN OVERVIEW OF THE SOFTWARE DEFINED NETWORKING APPROACH

The SDN paradigm has been systematized starting from two seminal works: the SANE Ethene project [4], and the Routing Control Platform [3]. Basically, the SDN architecture includes a set of network entities with switching functionalities, managed and supervised by a critical entity

VALUETOOLS 2016, October 25-28, Taormina, Italy

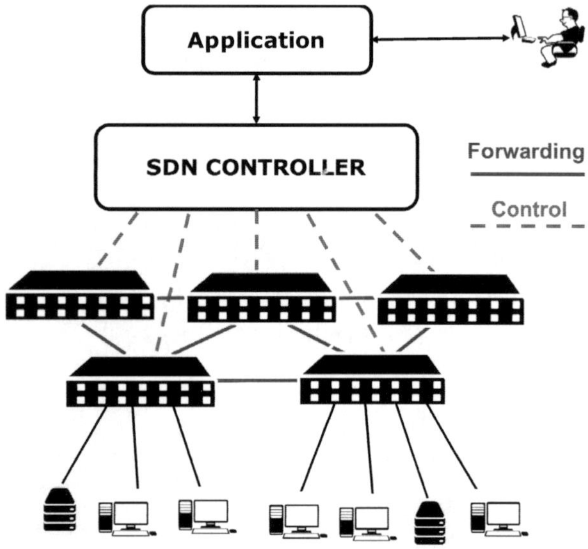

Figure 1: An SDN architecture, Forwarding (red solid lines) and Control (green dashed lines) planes.

named *Controller* through the OpenFlow protocol. The key idea of the SDN approach relies on a network view based on some centralized control agents devoted to elaborate routing service logic, such as access control agent, routing agent, and traffic management agent, and light-weighted network appliances (i.e. switches, firewalls, routers) designated to communicate with the Controller and execute commands.

2.1 OpenFlow

The OpenFlow protocol, proposed and maintained by Open Networking Forum (ONF), describes a set of specifications that represent a standard communication interface between data and control layers on a OpenFlow capable device.

Such a protocol allows the communication between controller and SDN devices (usually named switches) by implementing some messages and interoperability formats. In particular, the standard proposes three types of messages: *Asynchronous*, *Controller-to-Switch* and *Symmetric*, with various sub-types. *Asynchronous* messages are sent by switches to warn the SDN controller about critical events (node failures, network issues etc.). *Controller-to-Switch* messages come from SDN controller and are exploited to govern or audit the state of a single switch. *Symmetric* messages are sent by switches or controller and do not need to be triggered by specific events. Ultimately, OpenFlow defines the behaviour that SDN switches should have when solicited by the controller element; it is based on TCP and, if required, it supports Transport Layer Security (TLS) as an asymmetrical encryption standard.

A sketch of an SDN architecture is depicted in Figure 1, where Forwarding (or Data) and Control Planes are marked by continuous red lines and dashed green lines, respectively. The OpenFlow protocol acts through che control messages exchanged between the SDN controller and the SDN devices. On top of the controller lies an application layer offering the possibility to extremely customize the control logic on behalf of dedicated dashboards and command line interfaces.

Specific Application Program Interfaces (APIs) allow to deploy some functionalities on board the SDN devices such as: abstraction layers, communication interfaces to guarantee an interaction with the controller, and packet-processing engines [6]. When dealing with physical elements, the latter feature is embodied in the hardware design logic while in case of virtual appliances it is deployed as a software-based agent. The abstraction layer is in charge of managing the flow tables that, after a packet inspection operation, instruct the SDN device to perform specific actions including packet forwarding, packet dropping and so forth. A representation of a flow table is offered in Figure 2, where two elements emerge: *match fields* devoted to packet comparison and *actions* denoting the operations to perform on packets.

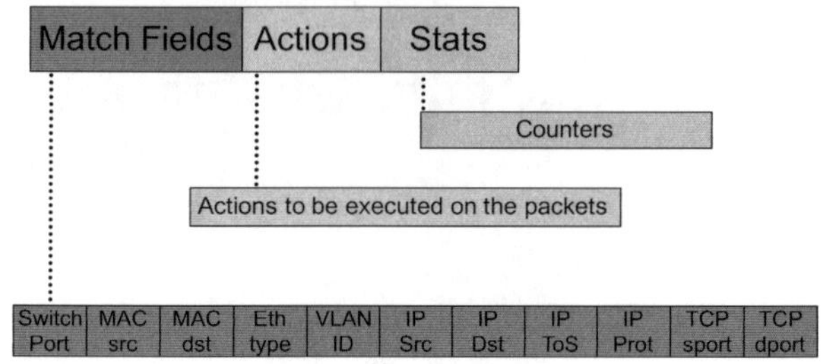

Figure 2: Example of OpenFlow table with a specific flow entry.

2.2 The core element of the architecture: SDN Controller

As before said, the controller is responsible for remotely managing the switch rules playing the same role of a router that, on behalf of specific routing algorithms, is in charge of programming and filling (or deleting) the forwarding tables. More in details, once the controller loads a specific flow table in an SDN switch, the latter is able to fastly manage every packet flow that results in an exact match. On the contrary, when a table entry is missed, the following sequence is activated:

1. The first un-matched packet of the flow is sent from the switch to the controller;
2. The forwarding path for the flow is computed by the controller;
3. The controller sends the appropriate forwarding entries to the device by filling the corresponding flow table;
4. All ensuing packets that belong to the pertaining flow are forwarded with no further intervention of the control plane.

OpenFlow is able to support three different configuration schemes of connection between controller and switches: *Master*, *Slave*, and *Equal*. These operating modes can be appropriately combined in order to build certain redundant configurations to satisfy high availability constraints and/or implement load balancing schemes. Master and Equal schemes allow the SDN controller to actively instruct the switch. The main differences is that only one controller can play the Master role, while multiple (eventually synchronized) SDN controllers can be configured in Equal mode. In Slave mode, SDN controller can just collect data for statistics but no changes in switches configurations are permitted.

2.3 Related Works

An interesting work focused on a complete refactoring of network management functionalities in a distributed environment appears in [7]. More in details, a novel architecture is proposed in which the decision logic and the protocols governing the interactions among network elements are completely separated. Moreover, main challenges of the SDN paradigm are identified:

- *Security.* The centralized SDN controller should be adequately protected being the most sensitive element of the entire architecture.
- *Scale.* SDN controller is in charge of managing the whole topological infrastructure of the network and the computation of best routes, resulting in a scalability problem that has to be necessarily considered.
- *Latency.* The presence of SDN controller entails that some (eventually critical) decisions will be affected by non negligible round-trip delay.
- *High availability.* Some redundancy policies have to be taken into account with regard to the SDN controller, so to avoid a single-point-of-failure issue.

A wireless-based SDN infrastructure has been pointed in [2], where the authors discuss about the Control and Provisioning of Wireless Access Points (CAPWAP), a protocol that exploits a generic encapsulation method, making it independent of a specific radio technology. On behalf of such a protocol, control frames are delivered to a central network element responsible for MAC layer control in a way similar to the mechanisms operated by the OpenFlow protocol when it delivers to the controller messages about new incoming flows.

In [16], the authors propose *HyperFlow*, a logically centralized and physically distributed SDN-based control plane. The decision making logic is transferred via *HyperFlow*, to individual controllers thus minimizing the response time from the control plane.

Still based on a distributed architecture, the framework *DIFANE*, presented in [20], introduces a dedicated routing protocol aimed at fostering the switch interactions with no need of controller supervision.

Another branch of works, concerns the reliability evaluation of SDN infrastructures by taking into account the controller placement issue. Accordingly, in [10], the authors introduce some placement algorithms based on a novel reliability metric (expected percentage of CPL - control path loss) and find out that the simulated annealing algorithm provides an almost optimal solution. More specifically, the problem of placing k controllers among $|V|$ locations is faced; the proposed algorithm first produces a list of the possible locations, say L, increasingly ranked according to switches fault probabilities, and then picks one location at time from the first $w|V|$ $(0 < w \leq 1)$ in L, indicated as entrant locations for hosting controllers.

A further track, instead, concerns the interaction between SDN infrastructures and the virtualization concepts introduced by recent NFV paradigm. In line with this latter perspective is the Google SDN Wireless Area Network project, described in [11]. The key idea behind such project relates with setting up a WAN network connecting multiple data centers with significant bandwidth requirements governed by an SDN-based infrastructure.

Again, a module named *FlowVisor* that acts as an hypervisor in a virtualized environment, is introduced in [15]. Basically, such a module plays the role of a transparent proxy between OpenFlow switches and multiple OpenFlow controllers.

Furthermore, the authors in [19] propose an analytical performance model of OpenFlow networks based on queueing theory. In particular, they model the packet forwarding mechanism of SDN switches and the packet-in message processing of the SDN controller as the queueing systems MX/M/1 and M/G/1, respectively. A queueing model of the whole SDN networks in terms of packet forwarding performance is then presented by solving its closed-form expression.

3. SDN CONTROLLER PERFORMABILITY EVALUATION

By considering benefits and advantages a virtualized SDN-based solution can offer (as discussed in a recent work of the same authors [5]), we consider an architecture where a single SDN controller hosts and manages a number of virtual software instances as depicted in Figure 3. Each software instance S acts for the Master controller related to a specific provider; it is named Virtual Provider Instance (VPI) in the SDN jargon and is in charge of managing a bunch of OpenFlow-enabled devices. In the following, we use S_i *in lieu* of VPI i. Such an approach provides a lot of benefits in terms of managing in a ductile way the whole network infrastructure that can be effectively rearranged according to the quality of service requirements of the providers, after negotiating opportune Service Level Agreements (SLAs). On the contrary, the principal flaw concerns the possibility that the SDN controller might become a unique point-of-failure so that some redundancy procedures have to be established.

We model an SDN controller as formed by:

- a *core part*, comprising every kind of hardware equipment (e.g. power supply, blades, processors, memories etc.) and generic software (e.g. hypervisor, operating system etc.);
- a *software part*, corresponding to the VPIs, able to handle a given number of sessions providing instructions to the switches.

It is worth noting that the proposed SDN controller model is generic, but it can be adapted to describe peculiar implementations. Starting from it, we build a performance model for the controller based on the number of coexisting OpenFlow sessions that each (virtual) operator is able to control. Firstly, we suppose that a single SDN controller is able to govern k VPIs and every VPI is in charge of managing n OpenFlow concurrent sessions. We assume also that: *i)* the main elements (VPIs and core) are modelled as a two-state system (up/down), *ii)* VPI i and core failures are statistically independent Homogeneous Poisson processes (HPPs), characterized by independent and exponentially-distributed inter failure arrivals and constant hazard rates λ_i and λ_c, respectively, *iii)* repair times are independent and exponentially-distributed with rates μ_s and μ_c, respectively.

By conveying in each state the information on the VPIs working conditions (up/down), the model of the considered

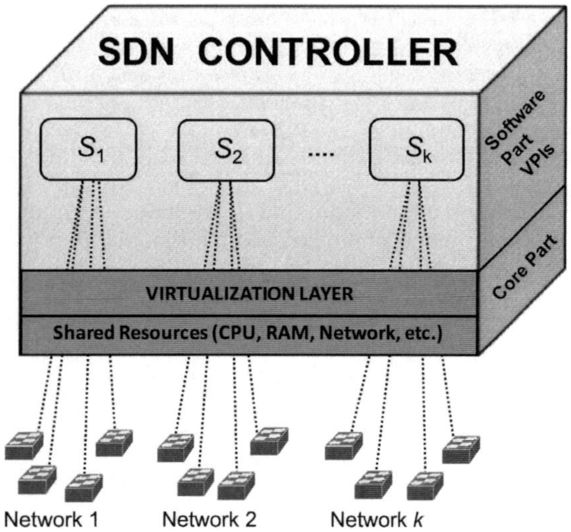

Figure 3: A set of k VPIs supervised by an SDN Controller.

Table 1: Correspondence map between states, VPIs condition and performance triples.

State number	VPIs condition	Performance
7	(S_1, S_2, S_3)	(n, n, n)
6	$(S_1, S_2, \overline{S_3})$	$(n, n, 0)$
5	$(S_1, \overline{S_2}, S_3)$	$(n, 0, n)$
4	$(\overline{S_1}, S_2, S_3)$	$(0, n, n)$
3	$(S_1, \overline{S_2}, \overline{S_3})$	$(n, 0, 0)$
2	$(\overline{S_1}, S_2, \overline{S_3})$	$(0, n, 0)$
1	$(\overline{S_1}, \overline{S_2}, S_3)$	$(0, 0, n)$
0	$(\overline{S_1}, \overline{S_2}, \overline{S_3})$	$(0, 0, 0)$
-1 (core fault)	$(\overline{S_1}, \overline{S_2}, \overline{S_3})$	$(0, 0, 0)$

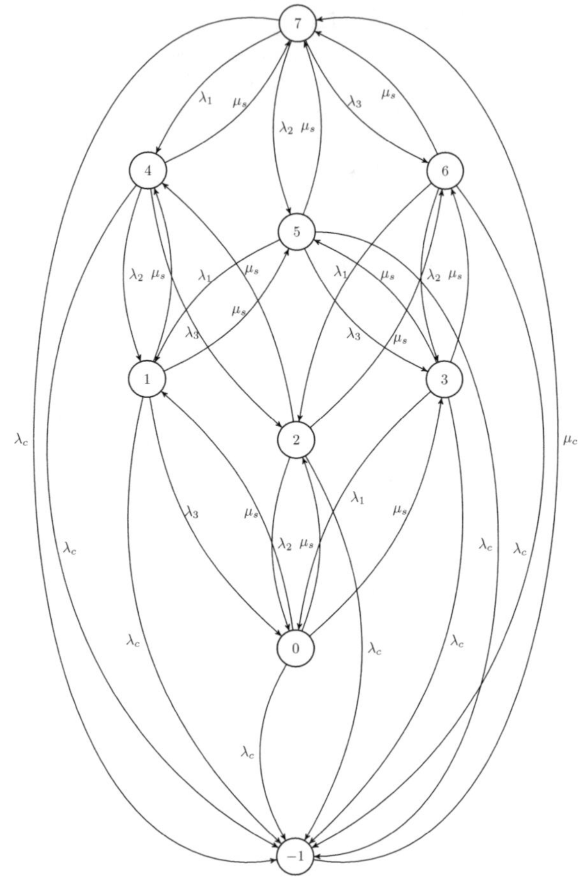

Figure 4: CTMC representing an SDN controller supervising 3 VPIs.

controller results in a multi-state Continuous-Time Markov Chain (CTMC) where:

- $2^k + 1$ represents the total number of states. Table 1 contains information about the mapping among states and VPIs condition/performance for the case $k = 3$, namely from the state -1 to the state $2^k - 1 = 7$. S_i and $\overline{S_i}$ indicate up and down conditions (see second column), whereas the corresponding serving capacity is indicated by n or 0 (see third column), respectively.

- state -1 takes into account the not-working condition of the core component (*core fault*) implying that no VPI can be up, and corresponding to the k-tuple $(\overline{S_1}, \ldots, \overline{S_k})$. From this state, only one transition towards a completely repaired controller is presumed.

A exemplary CTMC model of an SDN controller with $k = 3$ VPIs is shown in Figure 4, where the state probabilities $p_j(t)$, $j = -1, 0, 1, .., 7$ are derived by solving the system (1), with the initial conditions $p_7(0) = 1$ and $p_i(0) = 0$, $\forall i = -1, 0, ..., 6$, representing a fully working system at the starting time $t = 0$.

$$\begin{cases} \frac{dp_7(t)}{dt} = \mu_s[p_4(t) + p_5(t) + p_6(t)] + \mu_c p_{-1}(t) + \\ \quad -(\lambda_1 + \lambda_2 + \lambda_3 + \lambda_c)p_7(t) \\ \frac{dp_6(t)}{dt} = \mu_s[p_2(t) + p_3(t)] + \lambda_3 p_7(t) + \\ \quad -(\lambda_1 + \lambda_2 + \lambda_c + \mu_s)p_6(t) \\ \frac{dp_5(t)}{dt} = \mu_s[p_1(t) + p_3(t)] + \lambda_2 p_7(t) + \\ \quad -(\lambda_1 + \lambda_3 + \lambda_c + \mu_s)p_5(t) \\ \frac{dp_4(t)}{dt} = \mu_s[p_1(t) + p_2(t)] + \lambda_1 p_7(t) + \\ \quad -(\lambda_2 + \lambda_3 + \lambda_c + \mu_s)p_4(t) \\ \frac{dp_3(t)}{dt} = \mu_s p_0(t) + \lambda_3 p_5(t) + \lambda_2 p_6(t) + \\ \quad -(\lambda_1 + \lambda_c + 2\mu_s)p_3(t) \\ \frac{dp_2(t)}{dt} = \mu_s p_0(t) + \lambda_3 p_4(t) + \lambda_1 p_6(t) + \\ \quad -(\lambda_2 + \lambda_c + 2\mu_s)p_2(t) \\ \frac{dp_1(t)}{dt} = \mu_s p_0(t) + \lambda_2 p_4(t) + \lambda_1 p_5(t) + \\ \quad -(\lambda_3 + \lambda_c + 2\mu_s)p_3(t) \\ \frac{dp_0(t)}{dt} = -(\lambda_c + 3\mu_s)p_0(t) + \\ \quad +\lambda_3 p_1(t) + \lambda_2 p_2(t) + \lambda_1 p_3(t) \\ \frac{dp_{-1}(t)}{dt} = -\mu_c p_{-1}(t) + \lambda_c \sum_{i=0}^{7} p_{(i)}(t) \end{cases} \quad (1)$$

It is worth noting that the performance levels pertaining to states of the proposed model of the SDN controller are described by a vector enclosing the number of coexisting sessions that each VPI is able to handle (see Table 1).

Since some redundancy is needed for the SDN controller in real-case applications, the vectors of node r are in the set

$$\mathbf{g}^{(r)} = \{\mathbf{g}_{-1}^{(r)}, \mathbf{g}_0^{(r)}, ..., \mathbf{g}_{2^k-1}^{(r)}\}, \tag{2}$$

where the k-dimensional vector $\mathbf{g}_j^{(r)} = \left(g_{1,j}^{(r)}, ..., g_{k,j}^{(r)}\right)$ contains the serving capacities $g_{i,j}^{(r)}$ offered by VPI i, $\forall i = 1, \ldots, k$, when SDN controller node r is in the state $j = -1, 0, ..., 2^k - 1$. Accordingly, the vector stochastic process $\mathbf{G}^{(r)}(t) \in \mathbf{g}^{(r)}$ describes the performance level of node r, $\forall t \geq 0$, whose probability $p_j^{(r)}(t) = \Pr\{\mathbf{G}^{(r)}(t) = \mathbf{g}_j^{(r)}\}$ is derived by solving the system (1).

Therefore, the steady-state probabilities of the CTMC describing controller node r are:

$$p_j^{(r)} = \lim_{t \longrightarrow \infty} \Pr\{\mathbf{G}^{(r)}(t) = \mathbf{g}_j^{(r)}\}, \tag{3}$$

that can be computed by (1), with all the derivatives equal to 0 and $p_j^{(r)}(t)$ replaced by $p_j^{(r)}$, along with the condition:

$$\sum_{j=-1}^{2^k-1} p_j^{(r)} = 1. \tag{4}$$

4. MULTIVARIATE UNIVERSAL GENERATING FUNCTION FOR AVAILABILITY EVALUATION

We start by considering the SDN controller as fully working when a needed *demand* (a minimal performance level for a correct service delivery) is met, thus a demand vector $\mathbf{W}(t) = (W_1(t), ..., W_k(t))$ is advanced.

In many realistic deployments, for instance in order to satisfy SLAs, a certain redundancy level for the SDN controller has to be planned. In our work, we consider a Master-Slave scheme, where replicas of a single controller (composed by core and VPIs) are allowed: in such scenario, all VPIs associated to each domain are aligned and have all the information about the flows traversing the switches they control. Thus, it becomes irrelevant which is the specific VPI replica to have managed a certain flow entry.

Besides, the SDN controller is modeled as a network node having h parallel units without *flow dispersion* [12], and the stochastic process accounting for the performance level (coexisting OpenFlow sessions) provided to network i is the maximum performance level offered by all the VPIs replicas responsible of managing network domain i, viz.

$$G_i(t) = \max_{r=1,\ldots,h} G_i^{(r)}(t), \tag{5}$$

where $G_i^{(r)}(t)$ represents the element i of the vector random process $\mathbf{G}^{(r)}(t)$.

For long runs ($t \to \infty$), the values of random processes $G_i(t)$, for $i = 1, ..., k$, can be expressed by a random vector $\mathbf{G} = (G_1, ..., G_k)$ characterized by a multivariate probability function $p_{\mathbf{G}}(\cdot)$, represented by the steady-state distribution pertaining to the CTMC describing the dynamic behavior of the parallel redundancy configuration of the SDN controller.

Conforming to [12], the controller *instantaneous availability* $A_{SDN}(t)$ represents the probability that, at $t > 0$, the controller is in one of the possible states characterized by a performance level not less than demand $W_i(t)$ for each network domain $i = 1, ..., k$, namely,

$$A_{SDN}(t) = \Pr\{G_i(t) - W_i(t) \geq 0, \forall i = 1, ..., k\}. \tag{6}$$

As $t \to \infty$, the initial state of the SDN controller has no sensible effect on its availability. If we consider one and the same constant demand level $W_i(t) = w, i = 1, ..., k$, the *steady-state availability* $A_{SDN}(w)$ of the controller is expressed by:

$$A_{SDN}(w) = \sum_{j=1}^{m} p_{\mathbf{G}}\left(\mathbf{g}_j^{SDN}\right) \cdot \mathbf{1}\left(g_{i,j}^{SDN} \geq w, \forall i = 1, ..., k\right), \tag{7}$$

where $\mathbf{g}_j^{SDN}$ identifies the state j of the controller with parallel units, whose overall model is a CTMC composed by m states, and where $\mathbf{1}(\mathcal{A}) = 1$ when the condition $\mathcal{A}$ is true, 0 otherwise.

In order to perform the availability evaluation of the SDN controller in a parallel redundancy configuration, we exploit the Universal Generating Function (UGF) methodology that appeared for the first time in [17].

The UGF can be considered a kind of hierarchical approach that avoids to solve the overall CTMC model describing the performance of the whole system under analysis, whose solution is typically unfeasible due to the high dimension of the state space. The UGF allows to combine the performance distribution of the subsystems (much simpler to be solved) composing the complex series-parallel system, by means of some suitable operators for both parallel and series configurations of subsystems. Further details are available in [12].

A (discrete) random variable Y admits the following UGF representation:

$$u(z) = \sum_{i=1}^{A} \alpha_i z^{y_i}, \tag{8}$$

where $\alpha_i = \Pr\{Y = y_i\}$ and Y has A values y_i. The UGF of a random variable represents the performance levels of a system with multiple states thus allowing availability evaluation. In addition, the UGF of a complex system can be proficiently calculated by applying series and parallel operators to the UGF functions of the subsystems, according to their logical connections.

In this work we propose an extension of classical UGF to a multivariate case to manage performance vectors $\mathbf{G}$ and $\mathbf{G}^{(r)}$. Such an extension is called *Multivariate* UGF (MUGF) and is defined for a vector $\mathbf{G}$, having k dimensions and values in $\{\mathbf{g}_1, ..., \mathbf{g}_m\}$, by the following expression:

$$u(\mathbf{z}) = \sum_{j=1}^{m} p_{\mathbf{G}}(\mathbf{g}_j) \prod_{i=1}^{k} z_i^{g_{i,j}}, \tag{9}$$

where $p_{\mathbf{G}}(\cdot)$ is the multivariate probability function of $\mathbf{G}$, and $\mathbf{z} = (z_1, ..., z_k)$.

Denoting by h the number of parallel units (without flow dispersion) that constitute the controller with performance levels (in terms of concurrent OpenFlow sessions) governed by (5), it is possible to express the MUGF of the SDN controller via the π operator defined as follows:

$$\begin{aligned} u_{SDN}(\mathbf{z}) &= \sum_r p_r \prod_{i=1}^{k} z_i^{g_{i,r}^{SDN}} \\ &= \pi\left(u_1(\mathbf{z}), \ldots, u_h(\mathbf{z})\right) \\ &= \sum_{j_1=-1}^{2^k-1} \cdots \sum_{j_h=-1}^{2^k-1} \prod_{r=1}^{h} p_{j_r}^{(r)} \prod_{i=1}^{k} z_i^{\max_{r=1,\ldots,h} g_{i,j_r}^{(r)}}, \end{aligned} \tag{10}$$

where the steady-state probabilities $p_{j_r}^{(r)}$ are derived by (3), being related to the performance levels vector $\mathbf{g}_{j_r}^{(r)}$ in (2). The SDN controller steady-state availability is obtained by (7), by using p_r and $g_{i,r}^{SDN}$ derived from the MUGF (10).

The final objective is to compute the minimal number of SDN controller units h^* in parallel redundancy configuration so that a given steady-state availability level A_0 is reached, that is provided by:

$$h^* = \arg\min_{h\in\mathbb{N}} \left(A_{SDN}(w,h) \geq A_0\right). \tag{11}$$

The problem in (11) is a simple version of "redundancy optimization problem" [18].

5. A NUMERICAL EXPERIMENT

In the present section, we provide a numerical example of the proposed methodological approach. We assume one and the same serving capacity of $n = 5000$ sessions per time unit (stu) for all the three VPIs ($k = 3$). We assume also the same SLAs for every Service Provider, so the same number of coexisting sessions are to be handled by the SDN controller for each VPI, and we require a pretty high service level to consider available a VPI: we choose $w = 4800$ stu.

To the aim of accounting for a plausible differentiation in terms of capabilities allocated for every single service operator, we consider diverse failure rates for every VPI in our model. On the other hand, we consider the same value μ_s by guessing common repair actions for all software instances and then for all VPI. Thus, the following failure and repair rates are adopted: $\lambda_1 = 3.858 \times 10^{-7}$ s^{-1} (equivalent to 1 fault per month for S_1), $\lambda_2 = 7.716 \times 10^{-7}$ s^{-1} (equivalent to 2 fault per month for S_2), $\lambda_3 = 1.157 \times 10^{-6}$ s^{-1} (equivalent to 3 fault per month for S_3), and $\mu_s = 1.388 \times 10^{-4}$ s^{-1} (equivalent to a mean repair time of 2 hours for every VPI).

According to the SDN controller model presented in Figure 3, we recall that all the VPI software instances run on the top of a core part (virtualization layer, operating system and shared hardware resources). The core part failure rate is assumed to be $\lambda_c = 1.268 \times 10^{-7}$ s^{-1} (equivalent to 4 core faults per year), while the rate of the repair activity on a failed core part is $\mu_c = 3.472 \times 10^{-5}$ s^{-1} (equivalent to a mean repair time of 8 hours). This activity is supposed to completely restore the node functionalities by eventually reactivating also VPI instances in down conditions, as modeled in Figure 4 and remarked in Section 3.

In Table 2, all the parameters values adopted in the numerical experiment are listed. It is worth noting that all the selected values, although arbitrarily chosen, are in keeping with the experience of system engineers.

By solving (1) with all the derivatives equal to 0 and by using the condition (4), the steady-state probabilities $p_j^{(r)}$ in (3) are computed for a single node r, whose 3-dimensional performance vectors $\mathbf{g}_j^{(r)}$ are reported in Table 1, for each state $j = -1, 0, \ldots, 7$. Subsequently, the MUGF of the vector performance distribution of node r is derived after (9).

Table 2: Parameters values in the numerical experiment

Parameter	Value
k	3
n	5000 stu
λ_1	3.858×10^{-7} s^{-1}
λ_2	7.716×10^{-7} s^{-1}
λ_3	1.157×10^{-6} s^{-1}
μ_s	1.388×10^{-4} s^{-1}
λ_c	1.268×10^{-7} s^{-1}
μ_c	3.472×10^{-5} s^{-1}
w	4800 stu
A_0	0.999999

The redundancy optimization problem (11) is solved by implementing the MUGF π operator in (10) and by computing the steady-state availability (7) directly from the MUGF of the system composed by the nodes connected in parallel. Given $A_0 = 0.999999$, the "six 9s" availability condition (increasingly desirable in telecommunication systems) of the SDN controller is reached (and even exceeded) with at least $h^* = 4$ parallel elements; indeed, the steady-state availability of this redundant configuration of the SDN controller is:

$$A_{SDN}(w, h^*)\Big|_{\substack{w=4800\\ h^*=4}} = p_7 = 0.999999971.$$

Table 3 reports the complete list of the performance vectors and the corresponding steady-state probabilities for an SDN controller in the same redundant configuration.

The numerical experiment has been performed by a Mathematica routine implementing the MUGF approach. The execution time of the said routine, running on a notebook based on an Intel Core i7-4960 HQ CPU@2.6GHz, is about 0.0327 s, which shows that the proposed MUGF approach is very fast to apply.

In order to evaluate and appreciate the differences in terms of availability by varying the number h of redundant elements, we refer to Figure 5 where, for sake of simplicity, we consider the steady-state unavailability of the system $1 - A_{SDN}(w, h)$. The horizontal dashed line in the aforementioned figure represents the required steady-state unavailability $1 - A_0 = 10^{-6}$. It is worth noting that in case of $h = 3$ redundant elements, the resulting A_{SDN} value amounts to 0.999997403 that is considered by now not fully compliant

Table 3: Performance vectors and steady-state probabilities of an SDN controller composed by 4 parallel units

Probability	Performance vectors
1.755×10^{-10}	$(0, 0, 0)$
8.903×10^{-12}	$(5000, 0, 0)$
4.410×10^{-12}	$(0, 5000, 0)$
1.964×10^{-8}	$(5000, 5000, 0)$
2.931×10^{-12}	$(0, 0, 5000)$
6.789×10^{-9}	$(5000, 0, 5000)$
1.491×10^{-9}	$(0, 5000, 5000)$
0.999999971	$(5000, 5000, 5000)$

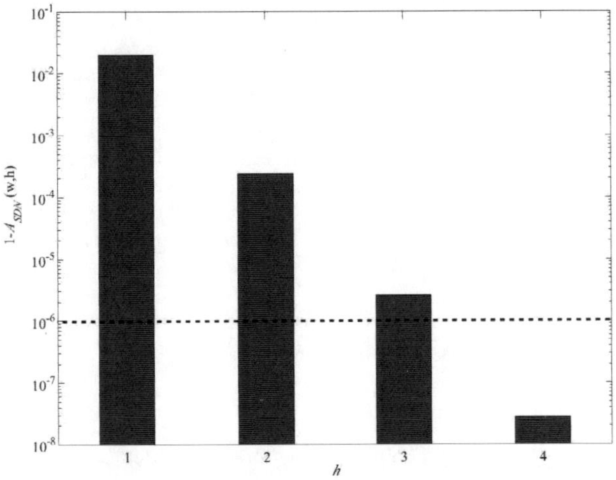

Figure 5: Unavailability $1 - A_{SDN}(w, h)$ of the SDN controller architecture for $h = 1, 2, 3, 4$ parallel elements. The horizontal dashed line represents the required steady-state unavailability $1 - A_0 = 10^{-6}$ of the SDN controller architecture.

with the modern standard requirements of very high availability. Besides, some changes in the values of the repair rates μ_c and μ_s does not weaken the "six 9s" availability condition, as shown in Figures 6 and 7, respectively.

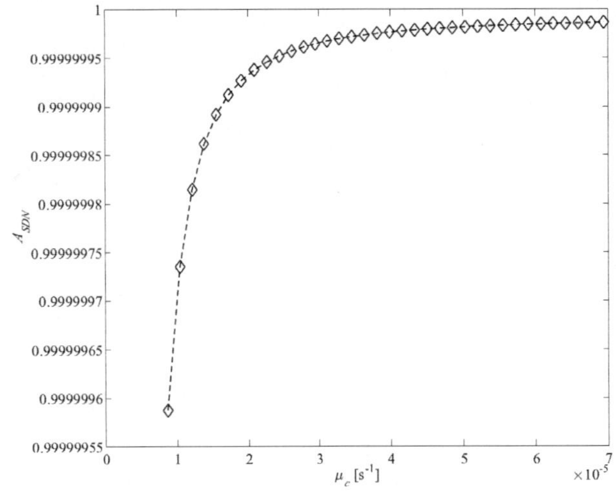

Figure 6: Influence of core repair rate on an SDN controller composed by 4 parallel units.

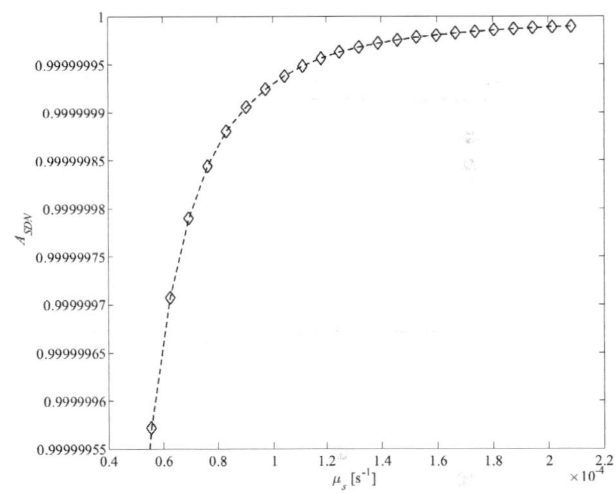

Figure 7: Influence of software instances (VPIs) repair rate on an SDN controller composed by 4 parallel units.

6. CONCLUSIONS

In an SDN environment, the network control and forwarding functions are decoupled, and the network intelligence is centralized and managed by the controller, the most critical element on the entire SDN infrastructure. Being the controller a failure-prone network element, we propose a performability analysis aiming to obtain the so called "six 9s" availability condition, increasingly required by the telecommunication world. In our modeling, some virtualized software instances (representing different virtual telecom operators) are managed by the SDN controller. Such instances, referred to as VPIs, are supposed to manage a set of SDN switches via OpenFlow protocol. Therefore, the number of coexistent OpenFlow sessions has been selected as performance metric and the minimal cost redundant configuration of the SDN controller was found. The performability analysis of the controller has been faced by the Multivariate UGF, a novel extension of UGF introduced to deal with performance vectors. Such an approach results advantageous in a multi-operator environment where different VPIs can share the same information. In a future work, the authors will try to consider a more challenging environment that accounts for Network Function Virtualization (NFV) paradigm and its interaction with the considered SDN infrastructure.

7. REFERENCES

[1] S. Ali, V. Sivaraman, A. Radford, and S. Jha. A survey of securing networks using software defined networking. *IEEE Transactions on Reliability*, 64(3):1086–1097, 2015.

[2] C. Bernardos, A. De La Oliva, P. Serrano, A. Banchs, L. Contreras, H. Jin, and J. Ziga. An architecture for software defined wireless networking. *IEEE Wireless Communications*, 21(3):52–61, 2014.

[3] M. Caesar, D. Caldwell, N. Feamster, J. Rexford, A. Shaikh, and J. van der Merwe. Design and implementation of a routing control platform. In *Proceedings of 2nd Symposium on Networked Systems Design & Implementation - Volume 2*, pages 15–28, 2005.

[4] M. Casado, T. Garfinkel, A. Akella, M. J. Freedman, D. Boneh, N. McKeown, and S. Shenker. Sane: A protection architecture for enterprise networks. In *Proceedings of 15th Conference on USENIX Security Symposium - Volume 15*, 2006.

[5] M. Di Mauro, F. Postiglione, and M. Longo. Reliability analysis of the controller architecture in Software Defined Networks. *Safety and Reliability of Complex Engineered Systems: ESREL2015*, pages 1503–1510, 2015.

[6] P. Goransson and C. Black. *Software Defined Networks: A Comprehensive Approach.* Morgan Kaufmann, Burlington, 2014.

[7] A. Greenberg, G. Hjalmtysson, D. Maltz, A. Myers, J. Rexford, G. Xie, H. Yan, J. Zhan, and H. Zhang. A clean slate 4d approach to network control and management. *Computer Communication Review*, 35(5):41–54, 2005.

[8] M. Guida, M. Longo, and F. Postiglione. Reliability analysis of next generation mobile networks. In Briš, G. Soares, and Martorell, editors, *Reliability, Risk and Safety, three volume set:Theory and Applications*, volume 3, pages 1999–2006. Taylor & Francis Group, London, 2010.

[9] M. Guida, M. Longo, F. Postiglione, K. Trivedi, and X. Yin. Semi-Markov models for performance evaluation of failure-prone IP multimedia subsystem core networks. *Proceedings of the Institution of Mechanical Engineers, Part O: Journal of Risk and Reliability*, 227(3):290–301, 2013.

[10] Y. Hu, W. Wendong, X. Gong, X. Que, and C. Shiduan. Reliability-aware controller placement for software-defined networks. In *Proceedings of IFIP/IEEE International Symposium on Integrated Network Management (IM 2013)*, pages 672–675, 2013.

[11] S. Jain, A. Kumar, S. Mandal, J. Ong, L. Poutievski, A. Singh, S. Venkata, J. Wanderer, J. Zhou, M. Zhu, J. Zolla, U. Hölzle, S. Stuart, and A. Vahdat. B4: Experience with a globally-deployed Software Defined Wan. *ACM SIGCOMM Comput. Commun. Rev.*, 43(4):3–14, 2013.

[12] G. Levitin and A. Lisnianski. *Multi-state system reliability: assessment, optimization and applications.* World Scientific, Singapore, 2003.

[13] Y. Liu and K. S. Trivedi. Survivability quantification: The analytical modeling approach. *International Journal on Performability Engineering*, 2(1):29–44, 2006.

[14] N. McKeown, T. Anderson, H. Balakrishnan, G. Parulkar, L. Peterson, J. Rexford, S. Shenker, and J. Turner. Openflow: Enabling innovation in campus networks. *Computer Commununication Review*, 38(2):69–74, 2008.

[15] R. Sherwood, G. Gibb, K.-K. Yap, G. Appenzeller, M. Casado, N. McKeown, and G. Parulkar. FlowVisor: A Network Virtualization Layer. Technical report, Deutsche Telekom Inc. R&D Lab, Stanford, Nicira Networks, 2009.

[16] A. Tootoonchian and Y. Ganjali. Hyperflow: A distributed control plane for OpenFlow. In *Proceedings of Internet Network Management Conf. on Research on Enterprise Networking*, pages 3–3, 2010.

[17] I. A. Ushakov. A universal generating function. *Soviet Journal of Computing System Science*, 24(5):37–49, 1986.

[18] I. A. Ushakov. Optimal standby problems and a universal generating function. *Soviet Journal of Computing System Science*, 25(4):79–82, 1987.

[19] B. Xiong, K. Yang, J. Zhao, W. Li, and K. Li. Performance evaluation of openflow-based software-defined networks based on queueing model. *Computer Networks*, 102:172–185, 2016.

[20] M. Yu, J. Rexford, M. J. Freedman, and J. Wang. Scalable flow-based networking with difane. *Computer Commununication Review*, 41(4):351–362, 2010.

AUTHOR INDEX

AUTHOR INDEX